Felicity Meakins and Patrick McConvell
A Grammar of Gurindji

Mouton Grammar Library

Edited by
Georg Bossong
Bernard Comrie
Patience L. Epps
Irina Nikolaeva

Volume 91

Felicity Meakins and Patrick McConvell

A Grammar of Gurindji

As spoken by Violet Wadrill, Ronnie Wavehill, Dandy Danbayarri, Biddy Wavehill, Topsy Dodd Ngarnjal, Long Johnny Kijngayarri, Banjo Ryan, Pincher Nyurrmiari and Blanche Bulngari

The Gurindji knowledge in this book is the intellectual property of Gurindji people. This knowledge should only be used with the written consent of the intellectual property owners and with proper attribution.

ISBN 978-3-11-127594-9
e-ISBN (PDF) 978-3-11-074688-4
e-ISBN (EPUB) 978-3-11-074694-5
ISSN 0933-7636

Library of Congress Control Number: 2021935856

Bibliographic information published by the Deutsche Nationalbibliothek
The Deutsche Nationalbibliothek lists this publication in the Deutsche Nationalbibliografie; detailed bibliographic data are available on the Internet at http://dnb.dnb.de.

This volume is text- and page-identical with the hardback published in 2021.

Typesetting: Integra Software Services Pvt. Ltd.
Printing and binding: CPI books GmbH, Leck

www.degruyter.com

Kajijirri-wu marlurluka-wu
'For the women and men who came before'

Preface

This grammar is based on the original sketch grammar produced by Patrick McConvell in 1996. We have expanded this sketch significantly based on the Gurindji corpus which now contains 75 hours of recordings collected since the 1970s. The original recordings were made by Patrick McConvell with Johnny Kijngayarri, Nugget Jinpal, Blanche Bulngari, Tommy Ngaliwin and Jimmy Manngayarri in the 1970s. In the 1980s, Helen and Norm McNair then worked with Dandy Danbayarri, Blanche Bulngari, Pincher Nyurrmiari and Horace Walman. Erika Charola contributed a significant narrative collection from work with Ronnie Wavehill Wirrpnga, Dandy Danbayarri, Ida Malyik, Violet Wadrill, Molly Tupngali and Biddy Wavehill Yamawurr in the 1990s. Felicity Meakins continued the work with Violet Wadrill, Topsy Dodd Ngarnjal, Biddy Wavehill Yamawurr, Banjo Ryan, Kitty Mintawurr, Teresa Yibwoin and Connie Ngarrmaya in the 2000s. The nature of the corpus is described in detail in 'Recording Metadata' section, and the history of its collection is detailed in individual sections in §1.5.

The corpus has been utilised in many forms. It is the basis of the *Gurindji to English Dictionary* (Meakins et al., 2013) and two significant text collections *Yijarni: True Stories from Gurindji Country* and *Mayarni-kari Yurrk: More Stories from Gurindji Country* (Charola & Meakins, 2016b, 2016c), and smaller books including *Kawarla: How to Make a Coolamon* (Wadrill, Wavehill, & Meakins, 2015) and *Karu: Growing up Gurindji* (Wadrill, Wavehill, Dodd, & Meakins, 2019). Many church and school picture books were also produced by Helen and Norm McNair. An ethnobiology of Bilinarra, Gurindji and Malngin was compiled with Gurindji elders and ethnobiologist Glenn Wightman (Hector et al., 2012). This ethnobiology provided the basis of a set of four posters on fish, birds, bush medicines and foods which were created with the Murnkurrumurnkurru ranger group. Finally, a series of procedural videos about bush medicines and foods was produced by Felicity Meakins with Violet Wadrill, Topsy Dodd Ngarnjal and Biddy Wavehill Yamawurr. A second set of 15 short sign language videos and 4 posters were produced by Jenny Green, Cassandra Algy and Felicity Meakins.

If you are reading the epub, just click on the symbol next to the example to hear the sound file, if you are reading the ebook (pdf) or the hard copy, the sound files can be accessed at https://www.degruyter.com/document/isbn/9783110746884/html. The password is Gurindji1966.

https://doi.org/10.1515/9783110746884-202

Acknowledgements

Our first and foremost thanks goes to the Gurindji knowledge custodians who showed patience working with us over the years as we captured the nuances of their language. We extend our particular thanks to Johnny Kijngayarri, Nugget Jinpal, Blanche Bulngari, Pincher Nyurrmiari and Jimmy Manngayarri (Patrick); and Violet Wadrill, Topsy Dodd Ngarnjal and Biddy Wavehill Yamawurr (Felicity). We are also extremely grateful to Helen McNair, Norm McNair, Erika Charola and Lauren Campbell; and the Gurindji families they worked with who generously shared their recordings. We particularly acknowledge the families of Dandy Danbayarri, Blanche Bulngari, Pincher Nyurrmiari and Ronnie Wavehill Wirrpnga who have since passed away. We hope that this grammar is just one way that their knowledge will be passed onto the next generation.

In another and better world, these elders would have been the professors at universities. Some elders were remarkable orators and philosophers, particularly Ronnie Wavehill, Dandy Danbayarri, Pincher Nyurrmiari, Jimmy Manngayarri, Blanche Bulngari and Banjo Ryan. Others were teachers and linguists in their own right, in particular Violet Wadrill and Ronnie Wavehill. To your families: it was an extraordinary privilege and honour working with your old people and we only hope that we have done justice to their exceptional minds. This grammar is simply our interpretation of your language, but the Gurindji language remains yours and the community's intellectual achievement.

This grammar has also benefited from many conversations over the years with other linguists working on Australian languages. This community has developed over the years as an incredibly generous and welcoming place for conversations. Particular thanks to our Ngumpin-Yapa colleagues: Erika Charola, Caroline Jones, Mary Laughren, David Nash, Carmel O'Shannessy, Jane Simpson and Tasaku Tsunoda; and the most recent group of Ngumpin-Yapa-ists emerging from the University of Queensland over the last 10 years: Jackie van den Bos, Mitch Browne, Vivien Dunn, Tom Ennever, Amanda Hamilton-Hollaway, David Osgarby, Bodean Sloan and Sasha Wilmoth. More broadly many thanks to Brett Baker, Joe Blythe, Samantha Disbray, Nick Evans, Alice Gaby, Jenny Green, Mark Harvey, Harold Koch, John Mansfield, Bill McGregor, Ilana Mushin, Rachel Nordlinger, Rob Pensalfini, Erich Round, Nick Thieberger, Ruth Singer, Eva Schultze-Berndt, Myf Turpin and Jean-Christophe Verstraete.

We are also grateful to a number of organisations and funding bodies. Patrick McConvell's work has been largely supported by the Australian Institute of Aboriginal and Torres Strait Islander Studies (AIATSIS). Erika Charola, Felicity Meakins and Lauren Campbell's work was supported by Diwurruwurru-jaru Aboriginal Corporation (DAC) or Katherine Regional Aboriginal Language Centre, which was instrumental in supporting the documentation, maintenance and revitalisation of Aboriginal languages in the Katherine region from 1991 to 2009. Its closure in 2009 left a

https://doi.org/10.1515/9783110746884-203

significant gap in language services at a critical time for these languages. Patrick McConvell, Erika Charola and Felicity Meakins' subsequent work was supported by a DOBES grant (*Jaminjungan and Eastern Ngumpin Documentation* project 2007–2010, C.I. Eva Schultze-Berndt) which was administered by the University of Manchester (UK). Felicity Meakins' work was also supported by an ELDP grant (*The Documentation of Gurindji Kriol, an Australian Mixed Language* 2008–2011, IPF0134, C.I. Meakins) which was also administered by the University of Manchester (UK) and the Australian Research Council grant (*Something old, something new: Indigenous languages since colonisation*, 2018–2022, FT170100042, C.I. Meakins). Additional support has come from Penny Smith at Karungkarni Arts. The establishment of Karungkarni Arts in 2010 has seen a renaissance of Gurindji artistic and cultural expression which we have been privileged to be a part of.

Thanks to Brenda Thornley for her beautiful cartography work through the grammar. Thanks also to the people who shared their photographs: Brenda L Croft, Jennifer Green, Darrell Lewis, Glenn Wightman and Penny Smith. Many thanks to Charles Darwin University Library, National Library of Australia, NAA, South Australia Museum, Berndt Museum, Minoru Hokari's family and Brian Manning's family for permission to use the archive photos in Chapter One. Many thanks to Bernard Comrie for his close reading and comments on the manuscript as editor. Finally, an enormous thanks to Paul Williams who undertook much of the grunt work for the grammar with the energy and enthusiasm required to speed this project to completion. Paul formatted example sentences, extracted sound clips for these sentences (with a sharp ear!), created the appendices and index, and copyedited the manuscript.

Contents

List of figures

https://doi.org/10.1515/9783110746884-205

List of tables

https://doi.org/10.1515/9783110746884-206

List of abbreviations

ABL	ablative
ABS	absolutive
ACC	accusative
ADJ	adjectival
ADMON	admonitive
AGAIN	again
AGENT	agentive
ALL	allative
ALLE	allegedly
ALMOST	almost
ALONE	alone
AMONG	among
AND	and
ASSOC	associative
AUG	augmented
AVERS	aversive
AXIS	axis
BEL	belonging
BETTER	better
BIT	a little bit
BUT	but
CAT	catalyst
CAUS	because
COM	comitative
CORRECT	correct
CV	coverbaliser
DAT	dative
DOWN	down
DU	dual
DUB	dubitative
DWELL	dweller
DYAD	kinship pairing
EDGE	edge
EP	epenthetic
ERG	ergative
ETC	etc
EXC	exclusive
EXCESS	excess
FACT	factitive
FIRST	initiator
FOC	focus
GROUP	group
HITH	hither
HORT	hortative
IMM	immediate
IMP	imperative
IMPF	imperfective
LATE	deceased
LIKE	resemble
LOC	locative
MAYBE	maybe
MIN	minimal
MOT	motivative
NEG	negative
NMLZ	nominaliser
NOM	nominative
NS	non-subject
OBL	oblique
ONLY	restrictive
OTHER	(an)other
OWNER	owner
PAUC	paucal
PERF	perfect
PERL	perlative
PL	plural
POT	potential
PRIV	privative
PROP	proprietive
PROPER	properly
PRS	present
PST	past
PURP	purposive
Q	question
REALLY	intensifier
REDUP	reduplication
REL	relativiser
RR	reflexive/reciprocal
S	subject
SEASON	season
SEQ	sequential
SIDE	side
SITE	place
SOURCE	source
SUBSECT	skin name
SUPERL	superlative
TERM	terminative
THITH	thither
TIME	time period
TOGETHER	together
TOP	topic
TOY	toy
TR	transitive
TURN	turn
UA	unit augmented

https://doi.org/10.1515/9783110746884-207

INC	inclusive	UP	up
INF	infinitive	WELL	well
IO	indirect object	1	first person
JUST	just	2	second person
LACK	lacking	3	third person

Conventions used in transcription and glossing

-	morpheme break
=	clitic boundary
.	separates categories encoded by a portmanteau morpheme
>	acting on
...	follow-on utterance

Conventions used to indicate source of data

Most of the Gurindji examples are accompanied by a reference containing certain information shown schematically below:

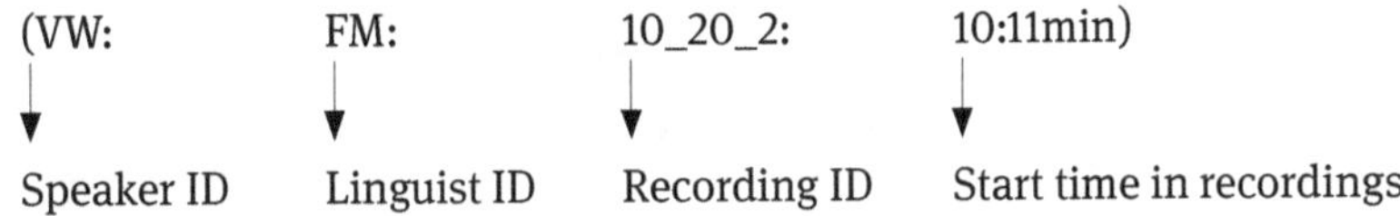

Often the recording ID contains information about the year the recording was made e.g. FM10_20_2 was recorded in 2010. Note that many of the sentences from Patrick McConvell's work do not have an archive reference. These sentences came from the original sketch grammar and are unable to be matched with an original recording.

Speaker ID:

BB	Blanche Bulngari
BR	Banjo Ryan
BW	Biddy Wavehill
CE	Cecelia Edwards
CN	Connie Ngarrmaya
DB	Doris Butler
DD	Dandy Danbayarri
DW	Doris Warnmal
EO	Ena Oscar
IM	Ida Malyik
JK	Johnny Kijngayarri
KM	Kitty Mintawurr
PN	Pincher Nyurrmiari
PP	Peanut Pontiari
RW	Ronnie Wavehill
SM	Smiler Major
SO	Sarah Oscar

https://doi.org/10.1515/9783110746884-208

TD	Topsy Dodd Ngarnjal
TN	Tommy Ngaliwin
VW	Violet Wadrill

Linguist ID (see §1.2.1):

EC	Erika Charola
FM	Felicity Meakins
KH	Ken Hale
LC	Lauren Campbell
MCCONVELL	Patrick McConvell
MCNAIR	Helen and Norm McNair

Metadata for recordings

The examples in this grammar come from a number of sources which are described below. Metadata is not given for individual recordings because the information is too extensive. Where recordings have been lodged with AIATSIS, The Language Archive or the Endangered Language Archive, the information about each recording is publicly available.

HALE_K06 recordings

This is a subset of the larger Ken Hale corpus which contains extensive and comprehensive elicitation of languages across northern and central Australia. In the case of Gurindji, it is a set of 120 pages of fieldnotes (a neatly written set of fieldnotes derived from a larger less legible set) and two hours of accompanying recordings made with Smiler Major at Wave Hill Station in 1959. They are lodged with AIATSIS as MS864(1) and HALE_K06-004553-004455. We are grateful to David Nash for copying the notes for us.

MCCONVELL_P02 and _P04 recordings

These recordings were made at Daguragu in May 1974 by Patrick McConvell with Johnny Kijngayarri, Nugget Jinpal, Blanche Bulngari, Tommy Ngaliwin and Jimmy Manngayarri. They constitute around 17.5 hours of elicitation, narratives, conversations and procedural texts. They were transcribed, glossed and translated by hand originally and have since been typed up and sound-linked in CLAN through a UQ Summer Research Program. The full audio recordings and handwritten transcripts are archived with AIATSIS. They are archived under MCCONVELL_P02 and MCCONVELL_P04, but we use the original tape numbers.

MCNAIR recordings

This set of 6.5 hours of recordings were made from 1977–1981 by Helen and Norm McNair through the Summer Institute of Linguistics (now AuSIL) at Kalkaringi. Most of the recordings were made with Dandy Danbayarri, Blanche Bulngari and Pincher Nyurrmiari, with some additional recordings made with Clancy Pangkarna, Horace Walman, Doris Butler and Lily Punayi. The recordings are mostly narratives. They were transcribed (typed), translated and glossed at the time. Meakins since had the subcorpus keyed in and sound linked in CLAN by UQ Summer Research scholars including Elizabeth Hall, Jackie van den Bos and Vivien Dunn.

https://doi.org/10.1515/9783110746884-209

EC recordings

This set of 8.5 hours of recordings were made by Erika Charola from 1997–1999 through Diwurruwurru-jaru Aboriginal Corporation (Katherine Regional Aboriginal Language Centre) at Kalkaringi. Most of the recordings were made with Ronnie Wavehill Wirrpnga and Dandy Danbayarri, with additional recordings made with Ida Malyik Nampin, Violet Wadrill, Molly Tupngali Nawurla and Biddy Wavehill Yamawurr. Most of the recordings consist of Dreaming stories and oral history accounts of the Victoria River District region.

FM recordings

This is a set of 42.5 hours of audio and video recordings which were made by Felicity Meakins between 2007–2018 through a number of grants including a DoBeS and ELDP grant and three Australian Research Council fellowships. Most of the recordings were made with Violet Wadrill, Biddy Wavehill Yamawurr and Topsy Dodd. Additional recordings were made with Banjo Ryan, Kitty Mintawurr, Sarah Oscar, Ena Oscar, Theresa Yibwoin, Connie Ngarrmaya, Marie Japan and Ronnie Wavehill. The recordings were transcribed and translated in CLAN. They consist of procedural texts, for example bush medicine and food collection and preparation, example sentence elicitation for the dictionary and narratives about Dreamings and history.

1 The language and its speakers

1.1 Introduction

Gurindji is a Pama-Nyungan language of the southern Victoria River District of the Northern Territory (Australia), spoken in the twin communities of Kalkaringi and Daguragu,[1] which are in the heart of Gurindji country. It is a member of the Ngumpin branch of the Ngumpin-Yapa subgroup (Bowern & Atkinson, 2012; McConvell & Laughren, 2004). Ngumpin-Yapa languages are found across north-western Australia, from Fitzroy Crossing in the west, where Walmajarri and Juwaliny are spoken, all of the way east to Elliott, where Mudburra is spoken. The northern-most Ngumpin-Yapa language is Ngarinyman, centred around the Aboriginal communities of Yarralin, Amanbidji and Bulla. Warlpiri, the best known of this language family, is spoken as far south as Yuendumu and Nyirrpi. Figure 1 gives the location of Gurindji and other Ngumpin-Yapa languages in relation to Jarragan and Mirndi languages (non-Pama-Nyungan) (Meakins, Ennever, Osgarby, Browne, & Hamilton-Hollaway, 2021).

Ngumpin languages are further divided into the Western branch, consisting of Walmajarri and Juwaliny (Hudson, 1977; Richards, 1979), Ngardi (Cataldi, 2011; Ennever, 2021), Jaru and its dialects Nyininy (Tsunoda, 1981) and Kartangarurru (also called Pirlingarna) (McConvell, 1976); and the Eastern Ngumpin branch, made up of Gurindji (Meakins et al., 2013) and its dialects Malngin (Ise, 1998), Wanyjirra (Senge, 2015); Bilinarra (Meakins, 2013; Meakins & Nordlinger, 2014), Ngarinyman and Wurlayi (which are dialects) (Jones, Schultze-Berndt, Dennis, et al., 2019); and Karrangpurru (also called Karranga) and Mudburra (Green et al., 2019; Osgarby, 2018b). The Yapa languages are Warlpiri (Hale, 1982; Laughren & Hoogenraad, 1996; Legate, 2002; Nash, 1986; Simpson, 1991; Swartz, 2012) and Warlmanpa (Browne, 2021; Nash, 1981). Figure 2 shows the Ngumpin-Yapa family tree.

Sadly, Gurindji is now a highly endangered language, with few elderly first language speakers and no child language learners. Nonetheless many aspects of Gurindji are being maintained through mixing practices. The most common language practice of older and middle-aged Gurindji people is code-switching between Gurindji and Kriol. This code-switching has melded into a mixed language referred to as Gurindji Kriol. This is the main language spoken by Gurindji people under the age of 45 at Kalkaringi and Daguragu. It is also spoken further north by Bilinarra and Ngarinyman people at Nitjpurru and Yarralin (McConvell, 2008; McConvell & Meakins, 2005; Meakins, 2011b, 2012). Although the primary focus of this book is traditional Gurindji, the position of Gurindji within community linguistic practices is discussed further in §1.7.3.

1 Throughout the grammar we generally only refer to Kalkaringi for simplicity, but the reader should understand this to mean 'Kalkaringi and Daguragu'. Note though that Daguragu was chosen by the 'strike mob' as the headquarters of the Gurindji in the 1960s and 1970s.

https://doi.org/10.1515/9783110746884-001

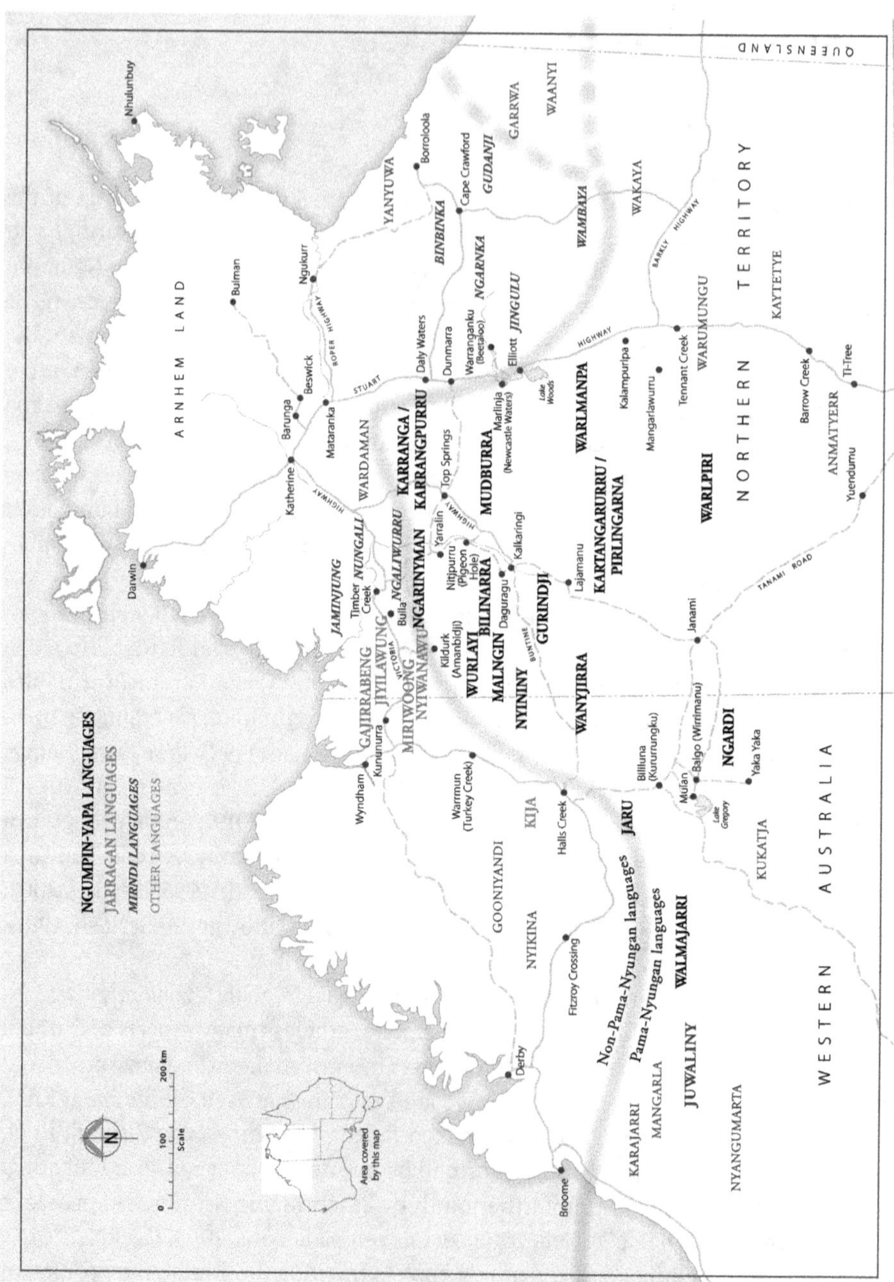

Figure 1: Location of Ngumpin-Yapa languages and their neighbours (Map: Brenda Thornley 2017) (Meakins et al., forthcoming).

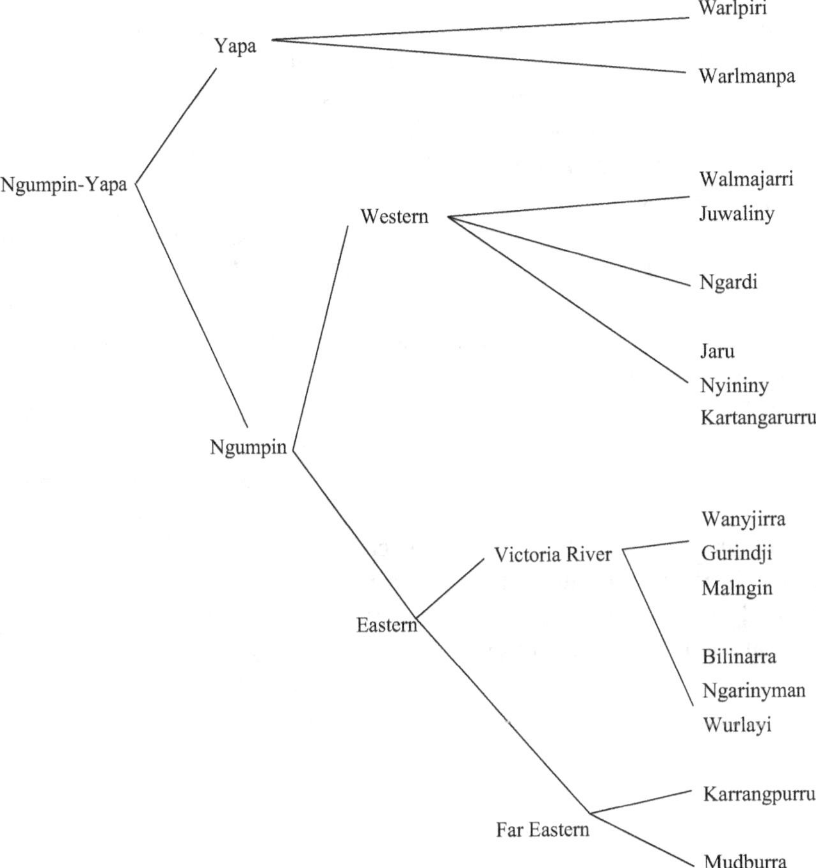

Figure 2: Internal structure of Ngumpin-Yapa (adapted from McConvell, 2009a).

Gurindji is the best documented of the Ngumpin languages. Most of the materials on which this grammatical description is based were collected by Patrick McConvell with Johnny Kijngayarri, Nugget Jinpal, Blanche Bulngari and Jimmy Manngayarri in the 1970s (§1.5.8); Helen and Norm McNair with Dandy Danbayarri, Blanche Bulngari, Pincher Nyurrmiari and Horace Walman in the 1980s (§1.5.9); Erika Charola with Ronnie Wavehill Wirrpnga, Dandy Danbayarri, Ida Malyik, Violet Wadrill, Molly Tupngali and Biddy Wavehill Yamawurr in the 1990s (§1.5.10); and Felicity Meakins with Violet Wadrill, Topsy Dodd Ngarnjal, Biddy Wavehill Yamawurr, Kitty Mintawurr, Banjo Ryan and Connie Ngarrmaya in the 2000s (§1.5.11). Together they constitute 75 hours of transcribed and translated audio-visual recordings. McConvell's corpus is housed in AIATSIS in Canberra. Charola's and part of Meakins' corpora were collected as a part of a DoBeS project and are held through the Language Archive, which is a digital archive hosted at the MPI (Nijmegen).[2] Another part of Meakins' corpus was created as a part of an ELDP project and is deposited with ELAR at SOAS (London).[3] A full corpus is currently under development to be hosted by PARADISEC. The nature of the corpus is described in detail in 'Recording Metadata' section, and the history of their collection is detailed in individual sections in §1.5.

The corpus also forms the basis of the *Gurindji to English Dictionary* (Meakins et al., 2013) and two significant text collections *Yijarni: True Stories from Gurindji Country* and *Mayarni-kari Yurrk: More Stories from Gurindji Country* (Charola & Meakins, 2016b, 2016c), and smaller books including *Kawarla: How to Make a Coolamon* (Wadrill et al., 2015) and *Karu: Growing up Gurindji* (Wadrill et al., 2019). Many church and school picture books were also produced by Helen and Norm McNair. The church books are held at Kalkaringi Baptist Church and the school books are available digitally through the Living Archive of Aboriginal Languages (LAAL).[4] A comprehensive ethnobiology of Gurindji (and Bilinarra and Malngin) was compiled with ethnobiologist Glenn Wightman (Hector et al., 2012). This ethnobiology provided the basis of a set of four posters on fish,[5] birds,[6] bush medicines[7] and foods[8] which were created with the local Gurindji ranger group. Finally, a series of procedural videos about bush medicines and foods was produced by Felicity Meakins with Violet Wadrill, Topsy Dodd Ngarnjal and Biddy Wavehill Yamawurr. A second set of 15 short sign language videos and 4 posters[9] were produced by Jenny Green, Felicity Meakins and Cassandra Algy. All videos were broadcast by ICTV between 2018–2019 and are available through the Gurindji Portal of ICTV *inLanguage*.[10]

1.2 The language

Gurindji is a fairly typical Pama-Nyungan language. The phoneme inventory contains five places of articulation for stops which all have corresponding nasals (bilabial, apico-alveolar, retroflex, palatal and velar); three laterals (apico-alveolar, retroflex and palatal); two rhotics (a trill/flap and a retroflex continuant) and three vowels (/a/, /i/ and /u/). Among the stops, voicing is not phonemically distinctive and no interdental distinction is made. More phonetic work is required to fully describe

2 https://archive.mpi.nl/tla/islandora/object/tla%3A1839_00_0000_0000_0004_DF7A_E
3 https://elar.soas.ac.uk/Collection/MPI171874
4 https://livingarchive.cdu.edu.au
5 http://batchelorpress.com/node/331
6 http://batchelorpress.com/node/280
7 http://batchelorpress.com/node/364
8 http://batchelorpress.com/node/377
9 http://batchelorpress.com/node/373
10 https://ictv.com.au/languages/gurindji

the stop series, which is beyond this grammar. For example, the retroflex stops and nasals are quite difficult to distinguish from apico-alveolars compared with Warlpiri. In addition, the /j/ stop is more like an affricate phonetically (Ennever, Meakins, & Round, 2017). The Gurindji vowel phoneme inventory consists of three vowels, each contrastive for length. The length contrast also has a somewhat marginal status, derived from elided consonants, e.g. uwu → uu; iyi → ii. One striking morpho-phonological process found in Gurindji is the nasal cluster dissimilation (NCD) rule (McConvell, 1988b) (also known as nasal coda denasalisation/deletion) which has been noted for its resistance to straightforward treatments in auto-segmental theory (cf. Evans, 1995a, p. 734).

Most words are disyllabic or longer. There are some monosyllabic coverbs, most of which can be attributed to old borrowings from Wardaman, Jarragan and Mirndi languages (McConvell, 2009a), see §7.2.1). Words begin with a consonant or a glide (there are no words with initial /rr/ or /ly/) (§2.2.3) and may end with any phoneme except for a glide. This is fairly unusual for words in Pama-Nyungan languages which are generally vowel-final (§2.2.4). Clusters of two consonants are found medially and, in some coverbs, word-finally (§2.2.5.1). Clusters of three consonants are found only across morpheme boundaries (§2.2.5.2).

Gurindji has nine distinct parts of speech: nominals (including nouns, adjectives, demonstratives, free pronouns, ignoratives), bound pronouns (cross-referencing enclitics which agree with argument, obliques and some adjunct NPs in person, number and case), inflecting verbs, coverbs, adverbs, clitics, complementisers, particles and interjections. These parts of speech are quite standard for Ngumpin-Yapa languages (Meakins et al., forthcoming) and are described in §3.

Gurindji is morphologically agglutinative and suffixing, exhibiting a mix of dependent-marking and head-marking (cf. Nichols, 1992) and therefore a dual system of argument-marking. Nominals are marked according to an ergative-absolutive alignment pattern while pronominal clitics follow a nominative-accusative system and free pronouns follow neither system. Consequently, Ngumpin-Yapa languages are often termed split-ergative languages, however they may be analysed as having a single tripartite case system that distinguishes the three core case categories: ergative, nominative and accusative, which map onto the A, S and O arguments respectively (cf. Goddard, 1982). An accusative marking pattern in the bound pronoun paradigm then is the result of syncretism between the ergative and nominative case forms, and an ergative pattern in the nominal system arises from syncretism between the nominative and accusative case forms. Other case markers found are the dative, comitative, locative, allative, purposive, ablative, source, perlative, terminative and motivative. The motivative case is not found in other Ngumpin-Yapa languages and is only used rarely in Gurindji (§4.3). Two adnominal cases, the proprietive and privative are also in evidence, and the dative is also used adnominally (§4.6).

Nominals in Gurindji generally do not distinguish number, which is expressed instead by obligatory cross-referencing bound pronouns (§6.2), and optional numerals

(§4.4.1) or reduplication either in the nominals themselves (§4.4.9) or coverbs (§7.2.4.4). Kinship nouns include a highly complex paradigm of tri-relational kinship terms, this is not the first language to have been observed with such a system (see Hansen, 1974 for Pintupi; see Mervyn Meggitt, 1962 for Warlpiri; see O'Grady & Mooney, 1973 for Nyangumarta), but the first to have a comprehensive description (McConvell, 1982a), and which is now described for other Australian languages (Garde, 2013). Directional nominals encode three absolute systems: 'up/down', 'upstream/downstream' and 'north/south/east/west'. The use of both river drainage and cardinals is unusual for a Ngumpin-Yapa language, only in evidence in Gurindji, Bilinarra and Ngarinyman, but like most Australian languages, Gurindji does not have a relative left/right system for expressing spatial relations (Meakins, 2011c) (§5.2). Also like all Ngumpin-Yapa languages, there is also no gender, noun class or classifier system in Gurindji, nor are there any examples of 'generic-specific' constructions found in some Australian languages (e.g. Blake, 1987). NPs in Gurindji also do not specify definiteness (although sometimes the demonstrative *nyila* 'that' is used for this purpose).

Free and bound pronouns distinguish person (1st, 2nd and 3rd) and three numbers (minimal, unit augmented and augmented). 1st person non-minimal pronouns also make an inclusive/exclusive distinction (§6.1 and §5.2). There is no gender distinction made among 3rd person pronouns. The use of the minimal-augmented system is unusual for a Pama-Nyungan language, but is maybe the result of contact with the Mirndi languages, Jaminjung and Ngaliwurru, since Bilinarra has a similar distinction (Meakins & Nordlinger, 2014, p. 226 onwards). Bound pronouns in Gurindji mostly attach to a catalyst as they do in many other Ngumpin languages, however the catalyst does not encode any TAM distinctions, which is unusual for a Ngumpin-Yapa language. The position of attachment is determined by complex discourse principles, which are discussed in §6.2.6.

Like many Pama-Nyungan and non-Pama-Nyungan languages in northern Australia (e.g. McGregor, 2002; Schultze-Berndt, 2000), the Gurindji verb complex consists of two elements – the inflecting verb (§7.1) and the coverb (§7.2). Inflecting verbs belong to a closed class of verbs which are grammatically obligatory in the verb complex (except in some circumstances, for instance commands where coverbs can occur solo). 34 inflecting verbs have been documented for Gurindji, which is relatively small in Ngumpin-Yapa terms, but normal for the Ngumpin languages in the Victoria River District. For example, Warlpiri has around 120 inflecting verbs but another Victoria River District language, Bilinarra contains only 23 (Meakins et al., forthcoming). Inflecting verbs encode basic meanings such as motion and transfer (*go, fall, take, give, get*), manipulation (*put, throw*), impact (*hit, strike, bite, pierce*), perception (*hear, see*), as well as other general meanings, for example *cook, talk* and a copular *be*. Inflecting verbs can occur as the sole verbal predicate or can combine with a coverb to form a complex predicate. In the latter case, the main contribution of the inflecting verb to the verb complex is in TAM information, and the bulk of the semantics is provided by the coverb. There are five conjugation classes for Gurindji inflecting verbs, with only two irregular verbs in evidence (*karrinyana* 'to be, sit' and *waninyana* 'fall') (§7.1).

Coverbs are an open class and are uninflected (except for iterative marking and some other mostly lexicalised suffixes). They carry the semantic weight of the complex verb, expressing information about posture, direction of gaze, manner of motion, speech, cooking, change of state, and so forth. Unlike the inflecting verbs, coverbs are an optional element of the verb complex. Coverbs can also be found as the sole predicate in imperative clauses and reduced subordinate clauses. Phonologically, they demonstrate some rather exceptional phonotactics for Pama-Nyungan languages (§7.2.1).

Word order in Gurindji is grammatically free, and largely determined by information structure, with discourse prominent constituents presented in first and second position (see Meakins & Nordlinger, 2014 for a discussion of this for Bilinarra; Simpson, 2007; Simpson & Mushin, 2008; Swartz, 1988 for Warlpiri). Gurindji is also typical of many non-configurational languages in Australia, such as Warlpiri, Bilinarra and Wambaya (Jelinek, 1984; Meakins & Nordlinger, 2014; Nordlinger, 1998a; Simpson, 1991), in that nominals are commonly omitted and arguments are cross-referenced by pronominal clitics. There are no conjunctions in Gurindji, so simple sentences are often just placed in apposition (§9.1). There are also a number of possibilities for subordinate clauses, both finite (§9.2) and non-finite (§9.3).

1.3 Language name

Because the Gurindji are famous, their name is found in many books and in the press, with the spelling 'Gurindji'. This is also the spelling used by the Kalkaringi community, where many Gurindji live, and in official sources. Consequently, this spelling has been used in this grammar, although it is not in accordance with the practical orthography generally used for the language, including in this grammar, which would spell the name 'Kuurrinyji'. The language and the group of people both share this name. The name Gurindji (Kuurrinyji) is probably an ethnonym which derives from the Wardaman word *korrong* 'south' with a suffix *–ji* (McConvell, 2002b), although Gurindji people are not aware of this potential etymology and offer no explanation of the language name themselves.

The original referent of the name 'Gurindji' in times before and around first European contact was a dialect group who lived around the headwaters of the Victoria River (see Figure 3). In later years, the term 'Gurindji' was applied by local Aboriginal people more broadly and loosely to a group of closely related dialects, spoken across a wider area of the southern Victoria River District. Today it is used even more broadly to include Malngin, Wanyjirra, Bilinarra and Western Mudburra people who often identify themselves first to outsiders as 'Gurindji' before specifying their affiliation. The creation of this broader cultural block is likely the result of the convergence of different tribal groups on Wave Hill Station in the early to mid-1900s and then the Gurindji Walk Off in 1966 which further united Aboriginal people in the lower Victoria River District.[11]

1.4 Gurindji country

Before colonisation and the establishment of Aboriginal communities, Gurindji people lived in close proximity to other groups such as the Bilinarra, Malngin and Mudburra. The Bilinarra lived just north of Mangurlu (Seale Yard) and Lartajarni[12] and their country stretches upstream and north. The Mudburra lived along stretches of the Camfield River called Japuwuny and Yilyilyimarri and their country stretches from Jinparrak (old Wave Hill Station) through Cattle Creek to Marlinja (Newcastle Waters). Malngin country begins at Jirrngawu (Bamboo Springs, an excision from Waterloo Station) in the west and ends at Lurlunginyi[13] (the head of G.B. Creek) in the east. The Ord River (running through Mistake Creek Station) marks the western boundary of this territory. West of Ord Creek is Gija country. North of Midnight Yard is Bilinarra country and west of Nigger Creek[14] is Nungali and Miriwoong (Wurlayinypurru people). A similar span of territory is also described in Ise (1998, p. 6). These places are shown in Figure 3.

There were also different groups of Gurindji people who mostly lived close to the major rivers. The Jiyiljurrung lived in the Seale Gorge area. The Yilyilyimawu lived on the upper reaches of the Victoria River from Nguma (Four Mile which is at the junction of the Victoria River and Wattie Creek) to Murnturluk (Catfish). From Murnturluk south to Lajamanu and beyond[15] lived the Kartangarurru (Pirlingarna)[16] or 'Hill People'. These locations are shown in the map in Figure 3.

11 Note that this is more the view of Meakins and not of McConvell.

12 Black Gin Yard is the non-Indigenous name given to this site. We only mention it in this footnote because the name 'Lartajarni' is not known to most younger generations of Gurindji people who use the name 'Black Gin Yard' themselves. Most younger Gurindji people do use the name *lartaj* 'rough-tailed goanna' which the name derives from. Sadly, non-Indigenous names such as this one exist right across Australia. We are aware that continuing to use them only perpetuates racist ideologies.

13 This place name consists of *lurlu* (sit) + *-nginyi* (source) and translates as either 'after sitting' or 'as a result of sitting'.

14 There is no Gurindji name for the creek, only place names along it, hence our use of such an offensive term. Again, it must be noted that English names such as this are prevalent across the country and we understand that the continued use of these names is upsetting to Indigenous people.

15 Lajamanu, although now a largely Warlpiri community with some Kartangarurru descendants, is located on Gurindji country. 'Lajaman' is the Gurindji name of the place and 'Lajamanu' is the Warlpiri word. The Warlpiri claim the word consists of *laja* + *manu* 'shoulder' + 'do' i.e. 'carry on shoulder' but this is probably just folk etymology (David Nash, per. comm.).

16 The name Pirlingarna is transparently derived from *pirli* 'stone, hill' and *-ngarna* 'associative'.

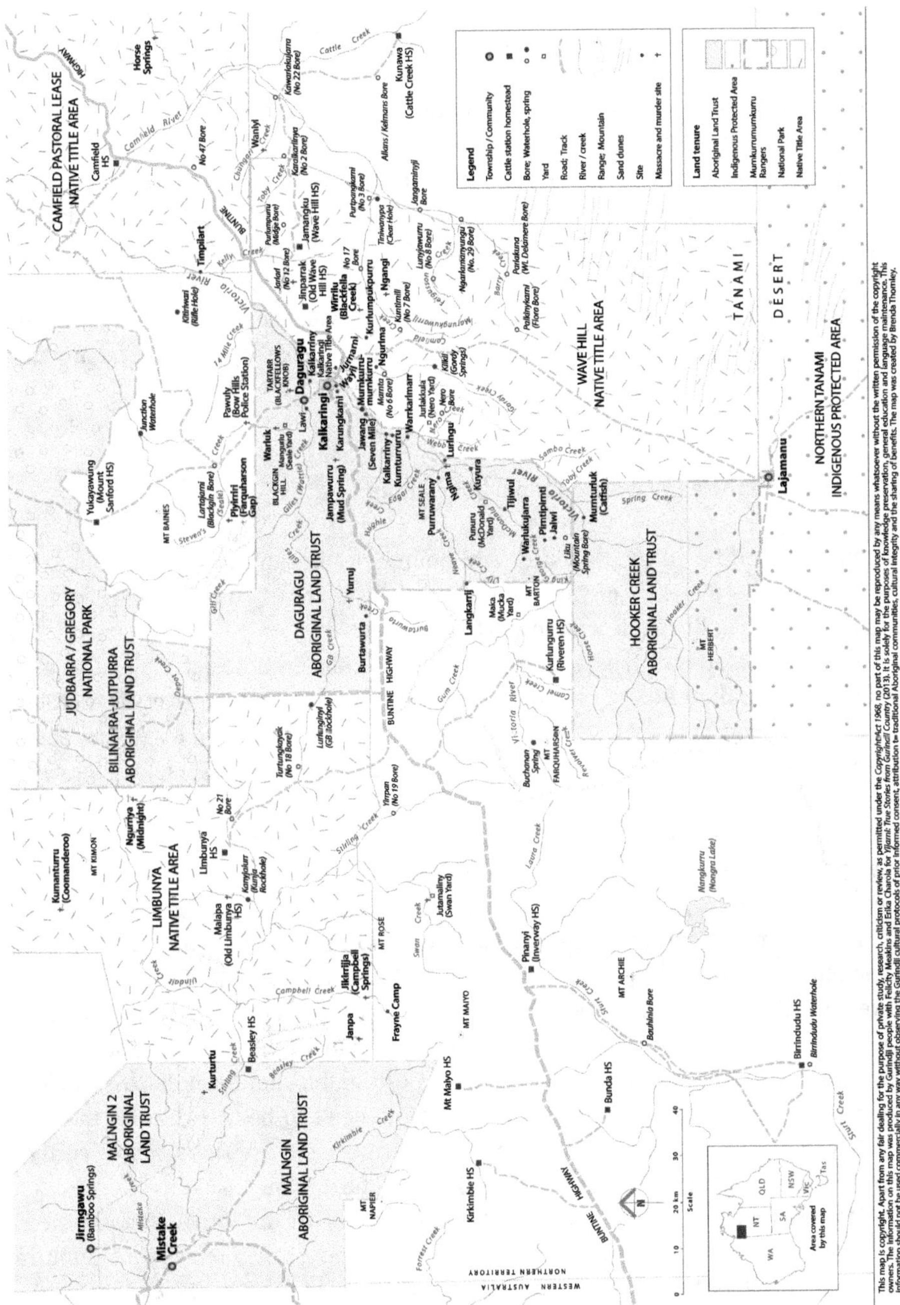

Figure 3: Map of Gurindji country and beyond including many important place names (Map: Brenda Thornley) (Note this map deliberately does not delineate tribal boundaries and should not be used as a legal document).

Note that the map in Figure 3 does not show even a fraction of the names Gurindji people give to their country. Names for places along the Victoria River are provided in the *Gurindji to English Dictionary* (Meakins et al., 2013, pp. 580–592), along with other densely named creeks and regions. Most of the Victoria River names were documented by Meakins with Ronnie Wavehill who had an encyclopaedic memory of local places and their names. Other place names are scattered throughout the dictionary and are largely derived from Land Claim mapping work undertaken by McConvell in the 1980s and checked by Meakins with current Gurindji elders. McConvell worked with many elders in the 1980s to create a certainly exhaustive map of the region. This map is held by the Central Land Council, but we are not able to access it or reproduce it here for legal reasons.

1.4.1 Notes on the early work on tribal boundaries

Mapping Gurindji country, its places and boundaries began in the late 1800s. This section provides the work of various anthropologists, mostly for historical interest, and to draw Gurindji people's attention to these sources.

Robert H. Mathews (see also §1.5 and §1.8.4), an ethnologist who published widely on Australian Aboriginal culture, did not visit the Victoria River District, but did publish short accounts of some aspects of social organisation of groups based on information from correspondents obtained around 1899–1901. This includes some details communicated by Mr. N. H. Stretch at Sturt Creek station[17] based on information supplied by an Aboriginal stockman whose home country was said to be the 'Jeelowng' territory at the mouth of the Victoria River (Mathews, 1900, p. 497; also spelled 'Geelowng'; 1901, p. 70).

In the same article and elsewhere Mathews (1901, p. 72) refers to a 'Chee-al' tribe as among those of the upper Victoria River, and distinct from the 'Jeelowng' on the lower Victoria. The former (Chee-al) is likely to be a version of the term Jiyil (Willshire's 'Jael', see §1.5). The source of Mathews' information about the 'Chee-al' and what, if anything, he had been told about their exact position has not been discovered. The 'Chee-al' subsection terms (§1.8.1) are said by Mathews to be the same as those of the Bilyanurra (Bilinarra) and Kwaranjee (Kuwarrinji) and are the same as current Gurindji and Mudburra forms. These are discussed further in §1.8.4.

Mathews includes the 'Koorangie' as another tribe of the upper Victoria River, which most probably refers to the Gurindji. Similar names also refer to a Mudburra dialect group 'Kuwarrinji', also known as 'Kuwarrangu' (cf. Rob Pensalfini, 2003, pp. 6–7). Both names Gurindji (Kuurrinyji) and Kuwarrinyji (as well the names Karranga and Karrangpurru) have the same origin in a word for 'south' in Wardaman

17 Copies of letters from Stretch 1900 can be found in Mathews' papers at AIATSIS.

(§1.3), which explains their similarity (McConvell, 2002b, 2006b) (see also §1.3). Elsewhere Mathews (1901, p. 72) refers to the 'Kwaranjee' as lying between the 'Chingalee' (Jingili) and the Victoria River District, which is more compatible with the position of the Western Mudburra dialect.

Michael Terry visited Wave Hill Station in August 1924 shortly after the flood which wiped out the original Wave Hill Station (§1.5.1, see Figure 4). In Terry's work, the locations of the tribal groups are very much the same as the present generations report. Gurindji ('Cooringi') is situated across Malyalyimalyalyi and Lipanangku[18] (Terry, 1926, pp. 193–194). This site is located less than 2km from Kalkaringi. Terry names this area as being central to the 'Corindji' area. 'Mootburra' (Mudburra) is located east of 'Cooringi' and south of 'Bilinurra' (Bilinarra) – 'Bilinurra' is (correctly) given as "near Mount Sandford [sic]". These locations of neighbouring groups in relation to Gurindji are in fact more accurate than the mistaken positions in Stanner and Tindale.

Figure 4: The 1924 flood waters at the highest point reached. (Photo: Vestey collection, courtesy of Charles Darwin University Library).

Stanner (1934, p. 48) provided the following characterisation of the extent of Gurindji country and the sketch map, given in Figure 5 (see also §1.5.3 for more details of Stanner's visit to Wave Hill).

> Ko:wo:rindji country from Barry Knob in the north-west and Longreach in the north to Mountain Creek [Liku] and Catfish [Murnturluk] in the south.

18 Note that the original pronunciation of Lipanangku was Lipananyku.

This does not do justice to the southern extent of Gurindji country, which is to the south of the upper Victoria River, but is otherwise rather accurate and clearly includes within it what is now the Kalkaringi block. He also notes that the "(o)ld Station at Wave Hill is Ko:wo:rindji" (Malyalyimalyalyi/Lipanangku). Since this location is only about 2km north-east of Kalkaringi and there is no mention of a boundary between them this confirms that Kalkaringi is unambiguously Gurindji. There is no mention of a Jiyiljurrung subgroup of Gurindji, indicating that 'Gurindji' has been the name of the society as a whole for at least 70 years. The eastern cross on the map in Figure 5 in Koworindji country near its border probably represents the old station at Wave Hill very close to the present-day Kalkaringi. It is shown as being very close to the western boundary of Mudburra, which is correct according to local understanding in the 1980s and today (5–10km). The more westerly cross is unnamed, but in comparison with other sketch maps by Stanner, makes it seem likely that it represents the important Flying-fox sites in the middle of Wattie Creek (*Kuyanpululu* etc).

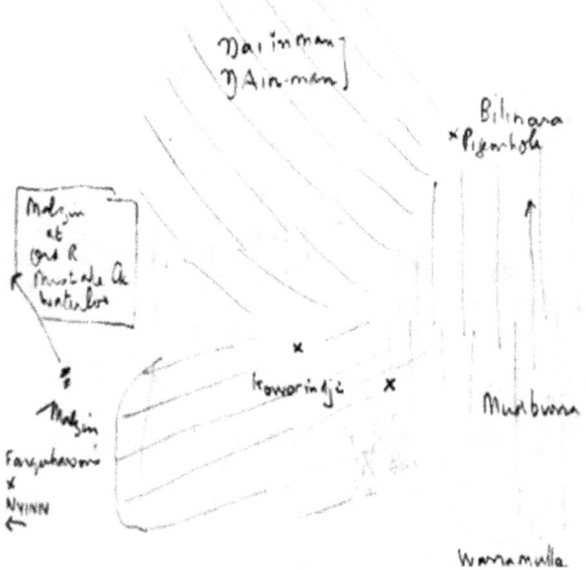

Figure 5: Stanner's sketch map of Gurindji country (Stanner, 1934, p. 30).

Birdsell (1952–54, p. 1107ff; 1974) locates the Gurindji (Korindji) territory as follows:

> On headwaters of Victoria River south from Munjan (Mount Sanford Station) and Tjalwa or Longreach Waterhole, extending westward to G.B. Rockhole (n.n. ['Loma]) and east to Bullock Creek and Camfield River; at Wave Hill. On Cattle Creek in the southeast they meet the Mutpura. They do not go east into the parallel sandhill country. Their southern boundary lies near Hooker Creek (n.n. ['O:lajai]). Mackay (1959 MS) maps the name Manu, otherwise identified with the Wandjira, as in Korindji tribal area. In the Karaman [Murrinh-patha] language ['kori] = west-the

present tribal name may therefore once have meant 'westerners'; no other has been suggested. Co-ordinates: 130°40'E x 17°40'S Area: 8,400 sq. m. (21,800 sq. km) References: Mathews, 1900 (Gr. 6575); Berndt, 1944 MS, 1965; Tindale, 1953 MS; Meggitt, 1955. Alternative Names: Guirindji, Gurindji, Garundji, Koorangie.

This is more accurate than his location of Jiyil (Tjial), but the territory goes too far north and well into Bilinarra country at Mount Sanford and Longreach Waterhole (this is related to the serious mispositioning of Bilinarra territory by Tindale); and too far east into Mudburra country, which in reality starts far west of Cattle Creek, around Jinparrak, the second Wave Hill station site. Tindale's suggestion about the origin of the ethnonym Kuurrinyji is probably on the right track, but it is actually derived from a word for 'southerners', from the point of view of Wardaman, a language to the north (McConvell 2002a) (see also §1.3). The section of his tribal map of the Victoria River District is reproduced in Figure 6 below.

The Tindale map, which draws on Birdsell's work shows Kalkaringi very much in the heart of the northern part of Gurindji territory. In fact, it is in the north-eastern corner of Gurindji territory. This distortion on the Tindale map is caused by the overextension of Gurindji territory to the east at the expense of Mudburra, and its overextension in the north-east. The positioning of the northern neighbours Bilinarra and Ngarinyman is incorrect: in fact, Bilinarra is the immediate northern neighbour and Ngarinyman north of Bilinarra. The western neighbours are also misplaced due largely to Birdsell or Tindale's confusion over Tjial, particularly Tjial [a hybrid of Jiyil and Jiyiljawung] and Ngaliwuru [Ngaliwurru].

From his fieldnotes it is clear that Birdsell did not spend much time at Wave Hill talking to people about country and culture, and took no genealogies, nor did he visit Bilinarra or Ngarinyman people. Most of his work was at Inverway Station to the west. His colleague, Tindale, seems to have relied largely on older sources for the map, which may explain the distortions (see also §1.5.4 for more details about Birdsell's visit to Inverway and Wave Hill and the misattribution of Birdsell's work to Tindale).

The southern and western boundaries of Gurindji on the Tindale map are approximately correct. However, in the south-east, the whole of the Camfield River catchment is actually Mudburra and is not part of Gurindji country. The northern part of the area marked Warlpiri is actually Kartangarurru a language group omitted by Tindale.

The description of Gurindji territory that accompanies the 1974 map is as follows (place names in square brackets provide the orthographic standard):

(T)he head waters of the Victoria River from south of *Indidi* (Catfish Waterhole [Yintiti]) and O:lajan (Hooker Creek Well [Wurlayin]; to Munjan (Mount Sanford Station) and Tjalwa (Longreach Waterhole [Jalwa]) in the north and from Loma (GB Rockhole) [Luma] in the west nearly to Bullock Creek and specifically to near to Putpungani (Bilyanarri Hill [Putpungkarni]) and Birida (Biri Hill [*birirda* – Mudburra for 'leg' (R. Green et al., 2019, p. 91)] Koroka the junction below Birida is a boundary marker. On the east at Cattle Creek and at Camfield River they meet the Mutpure . . . (Tindale, 1974, pp. 228–229)

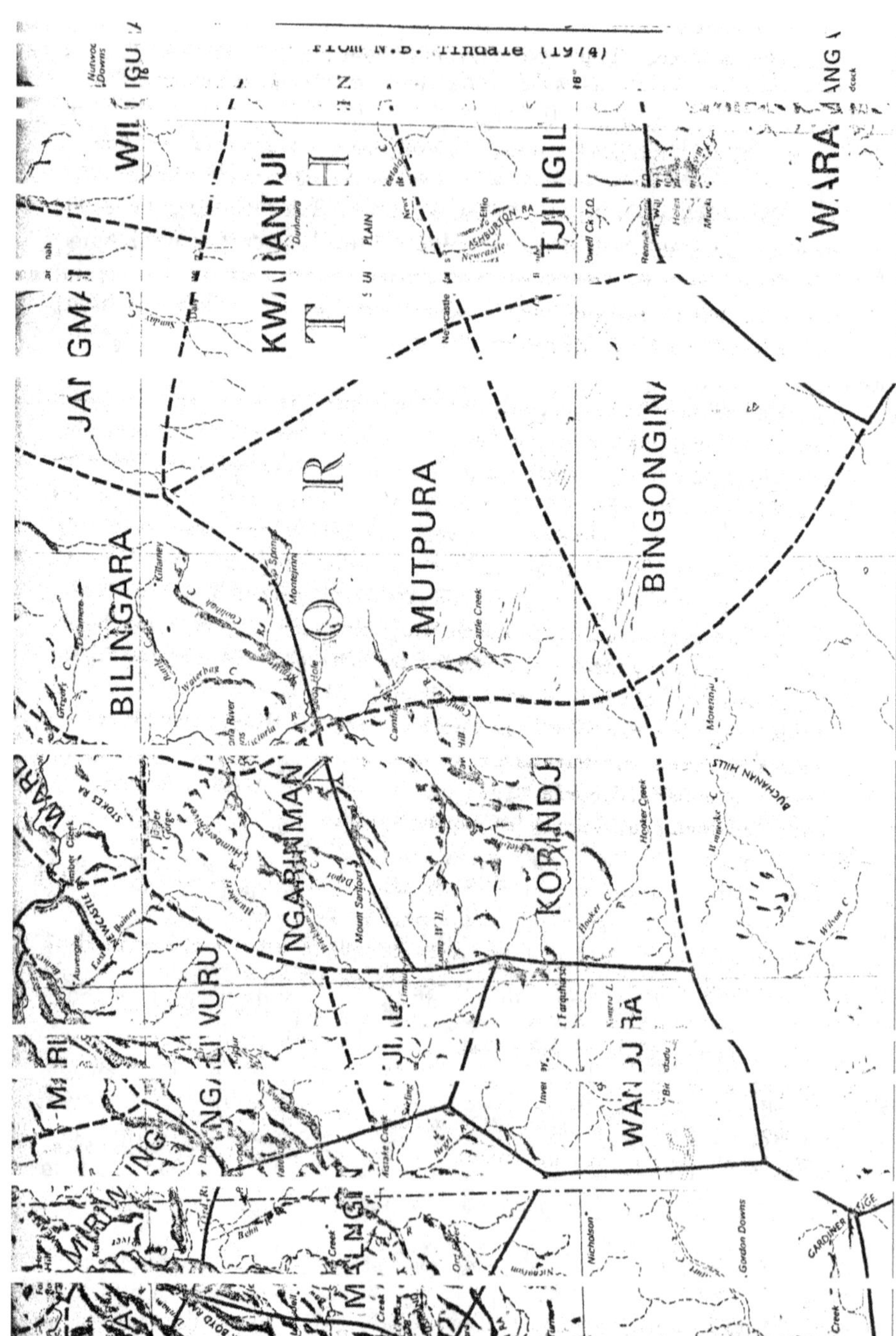

Figure 6: Section of Tindale's (1974) tribal map including Gurindji.

The formulation in the fieldnotes cited earlier prefigures the mistakes of the published version although the specification of Biri Hill as the northern boundary is closer to current ideas among Gurindji people than other aspects.

Part of the cause of Tindale's overestimation of Gurindji territory may have been the following circumstance, which he himself notes:

> Gurindji land generally lies to the south of Camfield station although there is a degree of uncertainty over the boundary delineation as historically Gurindji have been moving into Mudburra areas from the south-west. (Tindale, 1952–54, p. 1008)

This probably refers to Gurindji working on Wave Hill Station and its eastern outstation Cattle Creek. Gurindji seems to have become a *lingua franca* on Wave Hill by 1930. However, this did not imply any change in traditional custodianship of these areas. These eastern areas of Wave Hill Station are still acknowledged by everybody as Mudburra country, although a number of those traditionally connected to these areas east of the Victoria River had become predominantly Gurindji speakers. There was no "uncertainty" about the Gurindji / Mudburra traditional boundary in 1923 and 1934 when Terry and Stanner respectively surveyed the situation, nor was there in the 1960s-1980s when McConvell investigated the matter, so it is unlikely that there was uncertainty in the 1940s-1950s. People who primarily spoke Gurindji were and are traditional custodians of parts of Wave Hill Station east of the Victoria River, but everybody is well aware that their ancestry is Mudburra, and it is from this identity that their rights in land derive. None of this affects the status of the Kalkaringi area as Gurindji, a fact recorded by all the observers of the situation over the past 120 years.

Another major problem with Tindale's map of this region is the position of 'Tjial' (Tindale, 1974, pp. 235–236). It seems that in this case Birdsell who travelled to the north gathered first-hand information on the Jiyil/Jiyiljurrung group. As we have seen, Stanner was only informed of this term's usage as a name for a location and was not made aware that the term also denotes a distinct group of people and a separate language. What appears to have occurred is that Tindale used only older sources (Willshire, Mathews) and decided that Jeelowng (Jiyiljurrung) and Tjial (Jiyil) were one and the same group, despite the fact that they are clearly located in different areas nearly 200km apart (West Baines/Lower Victoria and Wattie Creek/Wave Hill, respectively) even in the old sources. He then placed this chimera group halfway between the source locations, around Limbunya, naturally causing a knock-on effect of errors in the position of other groups in the Victoria River District.

1.5 Previous work, sources and methodology on the Gurindji language

The earliest references to languages in the Victoria River District are from the infamously brutal policeman Constable W. H. Willshire. He was stationed at Gordon Creek

Police Station in the northern Victoria River District in the 1880s (see also §1.7.2). Willshire mentions the Jael as being the group associated with Wave Hill (present-day Kalkaringi). This was probably a reference to the Jiyiljurrung, a Gurindji group who lived in the Seale Gorge area. Although he did not produce a word list for Gurindji, he did provide a mixed list containing Bilinarra and Ngaliwurru words (discussed extensively in Meakins & Nordlinger, 2014, p. 15 onwards), and an impressively unsuccessful attempt at a description of the subsection system (called 'skin names' by present Gurindji generations), which was probably a reflection of his lack of real communication with the Bilinarra he kept prisoner at Gordon Creek.

From the 1900s onwards, Gurindji language and culture received attention from many of the anthropological and linguistic luminaries of the last century. We order this section according to these non-Indigenous anthropologists and linguists, rather than by the Gurindji consultants, only as a reflection of the order and periods that work was undertaken. The first real documentation of Gurindji language and culture began with R. H. Mathews who described the tribal boundaries of the region as he understood them (see also §1.4) and gave a detailed and accurate account of the subsection system (§1.8.4). His information came from correspondence with Mr. N. H. Stretch at Sturt Creek Station between 1899–1901. In 1924, Michael Terry visited the original Wave Hill Station (which later moved to Jinparrak following the 1924 flood (Bulngari, 2016; Nyurrmiari, 2016)). He focussed on aspects of ceremonial life, which are discussed in §1.5.1, and in detail in Turpin and Meakins (2019). Gerhard Laves, an American anthropologist-linguist, made notes of Gurindji language with a Gurindji man called Anyumarla in 1931 in Darwin. Very soon after in 1934, Stanner wrote down a partial vocabulary of Gurindji (§1.5.3), and in 1939, Arthur Capell also made some fieldnotes on Gurindji at Wave Hill. In 1953, Joseph Birdsell[19] collected details of language and genealogies from Dougal and his wife at Inverway Station on neighbouring Wanyjirra country. He also took a series of anthropological photographs and made notes of anatomical information of a number of Aboriginal station workers, many of whom are ancestors of current Gurindji people at Kalkaringi. He then briefly visited the Wave Hill Police Station, but did not undertake the same descriptive work or photography (§1.5.4). The first extensive documentation work was undertaken by Catherine and Ronald Berndt in 1945 at Wave Hill Station. They were sent to report on the condition of station workers who at the time were living in appalling conditions (as shown in Figure 7). Details of their work are given in §1.5.5. A decade later, Meggitt (1955) made a brief visit to Limbunya, a neighbouring station on Malngin country, and made notes on Malngin and Gurindji tribal boundaries and kinship.

The first audio recordings of Gurindji (apart from a lost film reel by Terry, and inaccessible, possibly irreparably deteriorated recordings by the Berndts) were made

19 This work at Inverway Station is commonly attributed to Norman Tindale who is the more famous of the two who often worked together. Nonetheless it was Birdsell who undertook this work, not Tindale.

Figure 7: Men and boys on the newly built airstrip. It is possible that Dandy Danbayarri is one of the children pictured, 8 April 1929. (Photo: Courtesy of the National Library of Australia).

by Kenneth Hale, an American linguist, who worked with Smiler Major in 1959 (see §1.5.6). He made 100 pages of field notes with Smiler Major. In July-August 1971, Velma Leeding spent eight weeks at Kalkaringi making word lists of Gurindji, Ngarinyman, Jaminjung and Ngaliwurru, eliciting simple sentences, conducting cognate counts, making a census of people on Wave Hill Station, Kalkaringi and Daguragu, documenting the kinship system, and making general observations about tribal boundaries (see §1.5.7).

Major documentation began with Patrick McConvell in the 1970s through AIATSIS (then AIAS) (§1.5.8) and in the 1980s with Helen and Norm McNair, through the Summer Institute of Linguistics (§1.5.9). Documentation work continued with Erika Charola in the 1990s (§1.5.10), Felicity Meakins (§1.5.11) and Lauren Campbell (§1.5.12) in the 2000s, first through Diwurruwurru-jaru Aboriginal Corporation in Katherine 500km from Kalkaringi, and later through a series of grants and Karungkarni Art and Culture Aboriginal Corporation, which was established in Kalkaringi in July 2011. It is this work that this grammar draws from (and indeed the dictionary and text collections discussed in §1.1).

1.5.1 Michael Terry

Michael Terry, pictured in Figure 8, travelled across Australia in 1924 and stopped off at several locations in the Victoria River District, including Wave Hill, collecting notes of the culture and language of the local Aboriginal people. He collected 23 vocabularies in 6 languages, including a set in 'Cooringi' (Gurindji) from a man called 'Naragoo'[20] (Terry, 1926, p. 194). This vocabulary is a near-perfect match for present-day Gurindji and shows the distinctive differences from the 'Mootburra' (Mudburra) vocabulary also collected, still familiar today, for example, 'woman' is written as 'giri' (*kirri*) in Mudburra but 'janga' (*janka*) in Gurindji.

Figure 8: Michael Terry and a unnamed man painted up ready to perform Wangka ceremony at the old station in 1925. (Photo: Michael Terry Collection, courtesy of the National Library of Australia).

Terry also observed ceremonies being performed at Wave Hill Station in August 1925 (see Figure 9). He noted "the didjijirri-du being played by a piccaninny" and "three boys doing the wonga [sic] corroborree [sic], with one playing the didjiri-du standing by" (Terry, 1925; 1927, pp. 109–110).

20 This name may actually be *narraku* 'namesake' in which case, his original name is not known.

Figure 9: Men performing Wangka at Wave Hill Station in 1925 (Michael Terry collection, courtesy of the National Library of Australia).

Terry was accompanied by a cinematographer, M. Redknap or 'Wag' (Terry, 1927: 28), who recorded this ceremony among other activities at the station on celluloid film. Terry recalls:

> Wag soon got busy with his movie camera. He routed around the blacks' camp; he perched on the stockyard where horse-breaking was in full swing; he ascended the hill for a 'pan' of the countryside; he wandered by the waters of the river. He 'shot' an afternoon tea-party among lubras seated beneath a bush shade, all drinking out of the same pannikin. During this he discarded a few inches of film . . . At another camp, there was a lubra with her piccaninny squatting on her shoulders, tightly grasping mother's locks. Attention was attracted by the talisman around the baby's ankle. Fond mother had saved a piece of Wag's discarded film and had tied it around her infant's limb. (Terry, 1927: 109)

The footage of Terry's expedition, including the Wangka ceremony, was later turned into a documentary, *In the Grip of the Wanderlust* (Pathé 1927), which showed to the Prince of Wales at New Gallery Kinema in London's West End on 31 May 1927.[21] The documentary did not play in Australia, apparently because of an American stranglehold on film distribution.[22] We have been unable to locate the footage, sadly, and do not

21 Berndt and Berndt 1987: 55; *Recorder* (Port Pierie, SA) 2 June 1927: 1; *News* (Adelaide, SA) 3 Sept 1927: 8.
22 *The West Australian* (Perth, WA) 24 August 1927: 12; *Northern Star* (Lismore, NSW) 25 August 1927: 5; *Daily Mercury* (Mackay, QLD) 2 September 1927: 6.

know if it has survived. For more discussion about Terry's expedition and the history of ceremonial life on Wave Hill Station, see Turpin and Meakins (2019, pp. 7–18).

1.5.2 Gerhard Laves

Gerhard Laves (1929–31), the American anthropologist-linguist, took down notes on a language he called 'Anyumarla' in 1931, with a man from Wave Hill, who was resident in Darwin at the time, suffering from tuberculosis. This language turns out to be a form of Gurindji, with grammar and vocabulary almost exactly matching current Gurindji, but with some apparent influence from Bilinarra – possibly this represents the Jiyiljurrung dialect of Gurindji. The language name 'Anyumarla' is a misunderstanding as it was actually the name of the man he was talking to. In 2000, Engineer Jack Japaljarri of Ali-Curung supplied David Nash and Patrick McConvell with the probable explanation for the term: there was a man Nganyimarla, also known as Fred Anyimarla, who lived at Wave Hill station in the 1930s when Engineer was there. Anyimarla is recorded on a genealogy in Stanner's fieldnotes of 1934 and in Kalkaringi Police records in 1928–29. Engineer says that Anyimarla was Mudburra from Jinpiya, an area east of Wave Hill. The fact that he was speaking Gurindji to Laves indicates that Gurindji was already a *lingua franca* for Wave Hill people including Mudburra, by the 1920s. There is little other information on people or culture in the Laves source.

1.5.3 William E. H. Stanner

In 1934, William E. H. Stanner briefly visited the Victoria River District. He kept a journal and fieldnotes (1934) which he later turned into a report (1935 [1979]) which omitted much of the detail. He arrived at Wave Hill Station (Jinparrak, the second station, about 12km east of Kalkaringi) on August 10 and spent a week there and a week at the Wave Hill Police Station 'Compound' (now Kalkaringi). At this stage, the population at Wave Hill Station was Mudburra and Gurindji, and a few others:

> The Koworindji are to be found at present camped seven or eight miles west of the Wave Hill cattle station in a large permanent camp adjoining the police station [present-day Kalkaringi] I spent a week amongst them (Stanner, 1935 [1979], p. 55)

Stanner recorded in his fieldnotes the names of most of the men and women at these locations, together with their subsection and matrilineal totem (*ngurlu*) affiliation, and in most cases, their patrilineal totems (*Mangaya*, Dreamings) and birthplaces. In addition, there are fragments of genealogies for many of them and other notes on kinship and belief systems. The genealogies stretch back up to six generations from the present to the early nineteenth century, before first contact and settlement. They confirm that much of Gurindji law and specific forms of law and custom have remained unchanged (Figure 10).

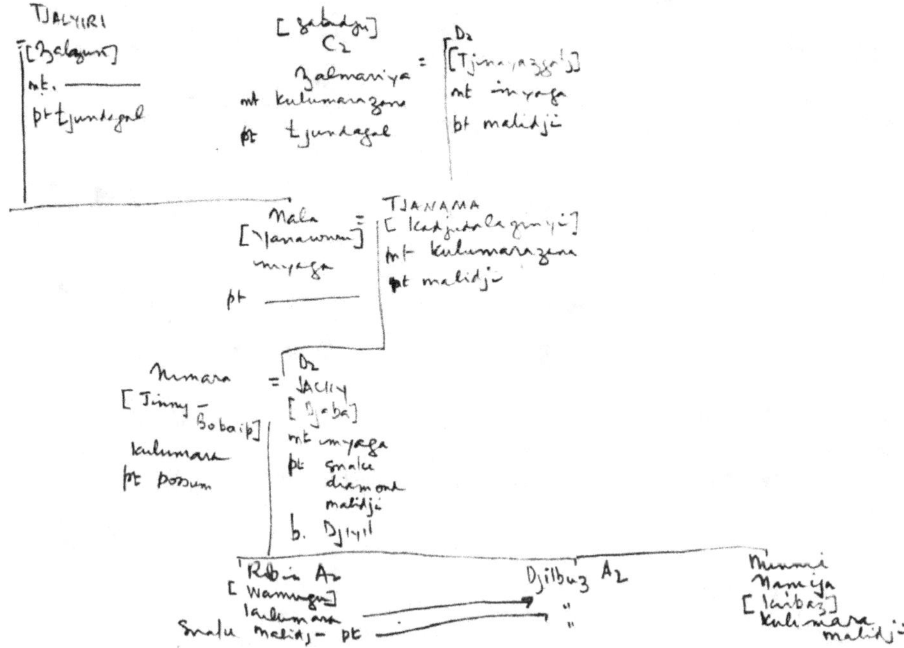

Figure 10: Partial genealogy of one family taken by Stanner at Wave Hill Police Station Camp (present-day Kalkaringi) in 1934.

The people recorded by Stanner in 1934 were King Jimmy Tiwanayirri Jangari, Jerry Jutpa Jiwaljarung, Old Man Micky Kurumbu Jangala, Mick Dulubu Jampijina, Lumpy-eye Ngirntama Jampijina, Jimmy Tinyurruk Jangala, Dolly Marlngarri Nangala, Rose Larriri Nalyirri, Mona Jarrmangali Nawurla, Waringinyi Jangari, Sambo Jatawuny Jimija, Sandy Moray Jangala,[23] Supper Yankurumurlung Jangari, Lizzie Yintangali Namija, Tommy Dodds Pirmiyari Jampijina, Daisy Ramangkarni Nampijina, Ida Malyik Nampijina. Tinyurruk can be seen in a photo from 1924 in Figure 11.

23 Sandy Moray was born 1905 and was the first Gurindji man to agitate for a better deal on the cattle stations and land rights in the 1950s before the next generation who were to lead the Wave Hill strike took over (Hokari, 2000; Rose, 1991, p. 226).

Figure 11: Unknown man, Tinyurruk (with king plate which may read 'Jimmy, King of Wave Hill'), Manyjuka Sambo who was Dandy Danbayarri's father, Minipa, Paliya in 1924 at Wave Hill Station. (Photo: Courtesy of National Archives of Australia; names from Lewis 1997).

1.5.4 Joseph Birdsell

Joseph Birdsell collected details of tribal territories, cultural features and genealogies throughout Australia. He visited Wave Hill in 1953. Before arriving at Wave Hill from the west, Birdsell interviewed Dougal and his wife at Inverway Station on 14 October 1953. Dougal was Wanyjirra born at Munpu (McConvell, 1993). He outlined the Wanyjirra boundary. On the east the boundary, with the Gurindji is Para (Cockatoo Well) in the north and O:lajan (Wurlayin; Hooker Creek Well) in the south (Tindale, 1952–54, p. 1097).

Birdsell took photographs of many of the station workers and filled out anatomical cards which was a demeaning practice of anthropologists of the time (Figure 12). The people have since been identified by Violet Wadrill, Ena Oscar and others at Kalkaringi with Felicity Meakins. The identified people are Jack Pingkiyarri Jurlama; Tiny McCale Wadja Nawurla; Lulu Nampin; Mona Wirtpaya Nanaku and her husband George Manyu Jungurra; Minnie Litiya Nawurla and her husband Duncan Walman Janama and their children Ray Duncan Jangari; Douglas Nigger Jangari who is Duncan's brother; Ruby Namija; Big George Nitji Jampin and his father General; Bandy Ripngayarri; Thomas Monkey Yikapaya Jungurra Jangala, his wife Topsy Tapayi Nangari and his sister Rosie Jilngarri Namija; Ringo Splinter Paja Jampin; Rona Rarrkngarri Nimarra; Nancy Yurrungali Nampin; Old Joe Kurtuwuti Japarta; Thunderer Mamati Jangala; Mick Wangkali Pinaya Jangari; Ruby Pawungali Nanaku; Minnie Wakarl

Nimija; and Lizzie Yanyjaya Langngarri. Sadly, there are others in the photographic collection who are unnamed and no longer recognised by current Gurindji elders at Kalkaringi.

Figure 12: Mick Wangkali Pinaya Jangari, father of Violet Wadrill, a major consultant for this grammar. (Photo: Courtesy of South Australia Museum).

Birdsell then visited Wave Hill Police Station in October 1953 and spoke with a number of Gurindji men including 'Old Crocodile' [identified as 'Crocodile Paddy' Malatulu by people at Kalkaringi 2002 pers. comm. to McConvell], at the Wave Hill native camp "a quarter mile North of the Police Station" which is the camp where many Gurindji lived just inside the eastern boundary of the present Kalkaringi block. Crocodile Paddy's primary affiliation was to country in the southern part of Daguragu. Birdsell obtained a short word list which is identical to present-day Gurindji except for the use of the term *jawi* 'fire', which is today more associated with Bilinarra and Ngarinyman (a preference also evident in the earlier notes of Laves and Stanner).

1.5.5 Catherine and Ronald Berndt

Catherine and Ronald Berndt carried out ethnographic work among the Gurindji in 1944–46. They were mainly employed to carry out a survey of Aboriginal labour on Vestey's Stations and centred their research on Wave Hill Station (the second station at Jinparrak). The report on this issue was never made publicly available

(R. Berndt & C. Berndt, 1948), but some elements of it eventually appeared edited in *End of an Era* (R. Berndt & Berndt, 1987). Their work is housed at the Berndt Museum at the University of Western Australia and is largely inaccessible due to the embargo imposed after Catherine Berndt's death, which is set to be lifted in 2024. This embargo is currently being contested by Gurindji people (Croft, Toussaint, Meakins, & McConvell, 2019, see also §1.1). It is likely that the fieldnotes contain considerably more information than they published because they were unlikely to have been able to make sense of it all at the time due to their inexperience with the Gurindji.

Catherine Berndt (1950) wrote a monograph on Gurindji women's ceremonies, which shows an active ritual life led by various Gurindji women. Wave Hill and neighbouring Limbunya were centres for such activity and the travels of the beings sung about seem to converge on this area. Berndt (1950, pp. 10, 25) notes that men's Yilpinji, the male equivalent of Jarrarta, was being performed at the time, as well as Pantimi, Yaluju and Wogeia, which are different stages of boys' ceremony. Berndt (1950) also reports that women were actively performing Jarrarta (women's love songs) and Yawulyu ceremonies in the evenings on the station. Information about the content and music of these genres is restricted and will not be discussed here; suffice to say that verses recorded by Catherine Berndt were still being sung by Gurindji women at Daguragu in the 1980s (Lauridsen, 1990) and at Daguragu, Jinparrak and Pigeon Hole in more recent years (recordings were made by Rachel Nordlinger in 1990, Felicity Meakins in 2004 and 2007, and Meakins and Myfany Turpin in 2015). The songs and song styles which Berndt recorded (Jarrarta and Yawulyu) are still used both in secret women's ceremonies and for public performance today, the major change being that the song type which was secret is now public and vice versa.

At the time that Berndt was there, and into the 1960s, areas near Jinparrak (the second Wave Hill Station), about 10km from Kalkaringi were the ceremony grounds for these ceremonies. The women's ceremonial site Warntanu on Jinparrak is still in use (Myfany Turpin & Meakins, 2019, p. 16). In later years after the 1966 Walk Off, other areas near Kalkaringi and Daguragu were and are also used (Lauridsen, 1990; Myfany Turpin & Meakins, 2019, pp. 16–17).

Ronald Berndt (1974) published a few notes on Gurindji men's ritual with photographs taken in 1944–45 at Wave Hill and neighbouring stations, but little else on the culture and society of the Gurindji.[24] The photographs and minimal captions were insufficient for Gurindji men who would have been alive at that time to identify individuals when McConvell showed them to them in 2002. They did identify the nature

24 There are copious fieldnotes of the Berndts from their work at Wave Hill, which would be immensely valuable in filling in the history between Stanner in the 1930s and anthropological work in the 1970s – 1980s, as well as for the Gurindji community, in preserving their heritage. Under the terms of their wills, however, nobody can view their fieldnotes, held at the Berndt Museum of Anthropology at UWA, until 30 years after their deaths (2020 for Ronald and 2024 for Catherine). By that time all those Gurindji who had been alive at the time of their fieldwork and could elucidate the notes will be dead (Croft et al., 2019).

of the ceremonies, and the location (south of Wave Hill Station) in some of the photographs when interviewed about it in 2002. One photograph is of a Jurntakal snake ritual with dancers decorated with a design representing traditional football called *pulyja* (R. Berndt, 1974, p. 32).

A series of crayon drawings, an anthropological practice from this time, is openly available at the Berndt Museum (Figure 13). McConvell worked with Ronnie Wavehill and Robbie Peter in 2016 to identify some of the designs and meanings depicted in the drawings, however the passing of time means that much of the import of the drawings could not be elucidated (Croft et al., 2019).

Figure 13: Annotated drawing from the Berndt Museum held at the University of Western Australia. The drawing was made by a Jaru and Gurindji senior man Smiler Kartarta Jangala at Jinparrak (old Wave Hill Station) on 20 October 1944. It shows three 'wantingarna' or 'yuungku' who were devils, possibly related to the Karu (Child) Dreaming. This information was interpreted by Ronnie Wavehill with McConvell in 2006. Smiler was a senior ceremony man who famously brought the Freedom Day *wajarra* songs from Wave Hill Station to Daguragu in 1966 during the Gurindji Walk-Off (Turpin & Meakins, 2019, pp. 29–31).

1.5.6 Ken Hale

The first audio recordings of Gurindji (apart from a lost film reel by Terry and inaccessible, possibly irreparably deteriorated recordings by the Berndts) were made by Kenneth Hale, an American linguist, who worked with Smiler Major in March and April 1959 at Wave Hill Station. Smiler gives his Gurindji name as Purrarnngarna, although it is possible this is his nickname since *-ngarna* is an associative suffix often used to create nicknames. We do not know what *purrarn* means, however.

Smiler Major was the brother of Captain Major who was one of the Gurindji Walk-Off leaders and also led the Newcastle Waters Walk-Off near Elliott (Hardy, 1968, p. 29). He did not live at Wave Hill Station at the time of the Walk-Off. He seems to have lived in different places at different times. Indeed he is listed in the 1966–68 census in Alice Springs as 45 years old.[25] Velma Leeding gives his age in 1971 as 61 and his location as Amoonguna, 15km south-east of Alice Springs (§1.5.7). He may have lived at 'the Bungalow' (Telegraph Station) in Alice Springs before then. People moved from the Bungalow to the newly established Amoonguna in the early 1960s. Smiler was also recorded as a patrol assistant in Katherine in 1977 and 1980 in the Electoral Rolls. Lady Anna Cowen (2017) described him as "famous" in her 1978 visit to Katherine.[26]

Smiler was well known as an activist and his name comes up in connection with various Aboriginal rights movements over the decades.[27] In 1961, he gave evidence to the Select Committee, which was set up to investigate the Electoral Act, saying that few Aboriginal people were well enough educated to vote (Griffen-Foley & Scalmer, 2017). He also appears quoted alongside Indigenous leader Charlie Perkins in *The Canberra Times* 7 August 1974 "'the dark and the white' must 'pull together' and that he saw no point in Europeans and Aborigines in Australia being 'separated'", which reflects the philosophy of Gurindji people during the Gurindji Walk-Off where they joined with the Northern Australian Workers Union and the Communist Party of Australia to gain equal wages and have some of their traditional lands returned (§1.7.2).

The 120 pages of fieldnotes are a very dense set of word and clause elicitation with one short text. The coverage is impressive! Most of the notes do not contain anything different from subsequent work on Gurindji, however there are very nice examples of nasal cluster dissimilation and complex bound pronouns where the dual neutralisation rule does not apply. The multilingualism of Smiler Major was also apparent. Table 1 is a set of words from p. 7 of the fieldnotes plus some other selected words which shows the mix of vocabulary Smiler drew on in his brief work with Hale.

---

25 http://www.cifhs.com/ntrecords/ntcensus/alicesprings.html

26 Thanks to David Nash for the research on Smiler Major.

27 In fact the first reference to him was in 1955 when he was 42 and sentenced for 35 seconds for illegally killing cattle, as reported in *The Argus* on 17 Nov 1955 (thanks to David Nash for finding this reference).

Table 1: Word elicitation from p. 7 of the Ken Hale fieldnotes + other selected words with our added notes about words origins.

Word	English gloss	Language source
walu	head	Ngarinyman, Eastern and Lander Warlpiri
kartpi	hair	Gurindji
langa	ear	Gurindji
mila	eye	Gurindji
jitji	nose	Gurindji
kangarnta	mouth	Gurindji
kingmarna	tooth	?
jalany	tongue	Gurindji
jangarnka	chin	(Ngardi, Warlmanpa, Warlpiri, from *ja* 'mouth' + 'steep bank/slope'). Note that *ngarnka* means 'chin' or 'beard' in many Pama-Nyungan languages including Gurindji.
jiika	beard	Gurindji
kuyuwan	bone	Gurindji
ngirlkirri	neck	Gurindji
laparn	shoulder	Gurindji
parntawurru	back	Gurindji
mangarli	chest	Gurindji
wartan	arm	Gurindji
jukupurtu[28]	elbow	Gurindji
murna	hand	Warlpiri
lipi	fingernail	Gurindji
munta	stomach	Warlpiri
kala	thigh	Gurindji
tingarri	knee	Gurindji
yunpa	foot	Mudburra and also *yuparn* in old Gurindji
kurturlu	heart	Warlpiri
marlumpa	liver	Gurindji
kurrunyu	skin	Mudburra
jatukal	kangaroo	Ngarinyman
purta	hear	Warlpiri, Jaru, Ngardi, Gurindji has pura by regular lenition from **purta*

28 In Hale's notes, this word is written as *jukupiti* which is Warlpiri but Smiler pronounces it with the /u/ vowels. It is possible that Hale was influenced by his knowledge of Warlpiri in the transcription. *Juurtu* was also used by some Gurindji speakers in the past and is formed by lenition of /k/ and /p/.

Table 1 (continued)

Word	English gloss	Language source
nguku	water	Mudburra
warnan	lie, sleep	Ngarinyman
paru	stand	Nyininy
maya[29]	many	Ngarinyman
murruru	cold	Western Mudburra
larrmularrmu	skinny	?

1.5.7 Velma Leeding

In July-August 1971, Velma Leeding spent eight weeks at Kalkaringi. She worked with a group of people:[30] Alex Japarta, Dandy Danbayarri, Mick Inverway, Mick Glasgow, Doris Warnmalngali Namija, Clara Juduwurr Namija,[31] Daisy Namija, Jerry Rinyngayarri Jurlama,[32] Charlie Pincher Jangari, Hoppy Mick Rangiari Janama, Konkaman,[33] Pincher Nyurrmiari Janama, Elsie Pincher, Lily,[34] Melva Hector Nanaku, Violet Wadrill Nanaku and Victoria Timothy Pukaka.[35]

Leeding made a 15 page comparative wordlist, a 15 page ethnographic report, a five page phonological analysis aimed at developing an orthography, a one page comparison of Gurindji and Ngarinyman. She also made 50 pages of transcription of simple Gurindji clauses and morphology, 27 pages of Ngarinyman phonology, morphology and simple clauses, and a two page cognate list for different languages represented by different people. She also produced nine pages of notes on kinship (§1.8.1) and a 13 page census of the local stations and settlements with names and ages.

Leeding also worked with Albert Bertie and his wife Ida at Montejinnie Station on a language she wasn't sure whether to classify as Gurindji or Mudburra. At a glance her four pages of notes looks like Western Mudburra which has some similarities with Gurindji.

29 In Hale's notes on p. 15, this word is written as *jarrwa* which is Gurindji but Smiler actually says *maya* (13:12min) which is from the Ngarinyman spoken in Amanbidji.

30 Where possible, Meakins has tried to identify named people based on her own genealogical work.

31 Doris and Juduwurr later worked with McConvell on Bilinarra and their work is included in the Bilinarra grammar (Meakins & Nordlinger, 2014)

32 His photo taken by Leeding appears on the front cover of *Mayarni-kari Yurrk: More Stories from Gurindji Country* (Charola & Meakins, 2016b).

33 It is not known who this was.

34 This is either Lily Punayi Namija who was married to Pincher Nyurrmiari's brother Johnny Kijngayarri, or Lila Jipuku Nalyirri who is identified in one of Leeding's photos.

35 This is Patrick McConvell's namesake. The name Pukaka was given to him after he camped with Tim on his first visit to Daguragu.

She also worked at Victoria River Downs briefly on Jaminjung and Ngaliwurru (13 pages of notes) and Mudburra and Ngarinyman (14 pages of notes). A set of 120 photos also exists. All fieldnotes and photos have been digitised but not archived at this point (Figure 14).

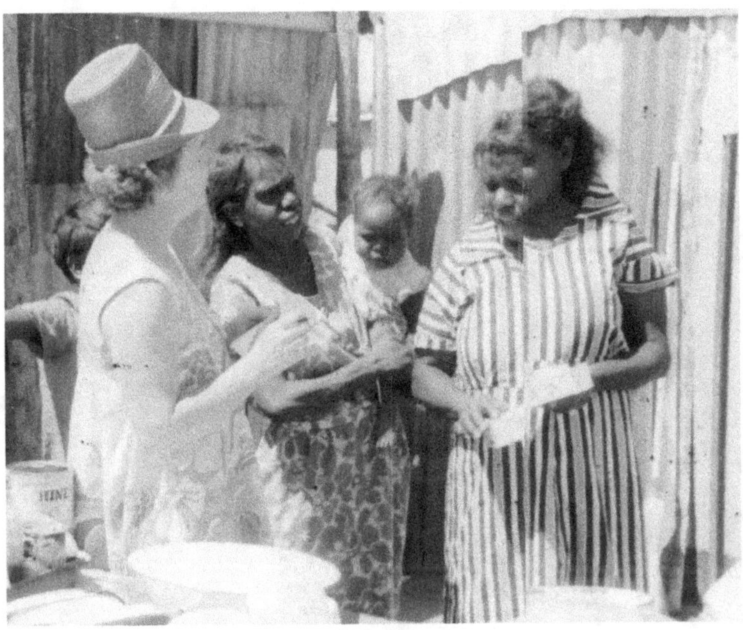

Figure 14: Velma Leeding with Violet Wadrill (holding Serena Donald) and Vera Tulyngarri Nawurla-Nangala in 1971.

1.5.8 Patrick McConvell

From 1973–77, McConvell worked as a Research Fellow in Linguistics where he conducted two years of fieldwork at Daguragu in northern Australia on Gurindji, Mudburra and Bilinarra. His recordings and transcriptions which consist of around 17.5 hours of elicitation, narratives, conversations and procedural texts are the earliest comprehensive documentation of these languages. McConvell primarily worked with Johnny Kijngayarri (Figure 16), Nugget Jinpal, Splinter Manguari, Blanche Bulngari Nawurla, Doris Warnmal Namija and Jimmy Manngayarri Kurrajnginyi Japalyi (Figure 15).[36] Further work with Johnny Kijngayarri and Marie Japan formed the basis of *Gurindji to English Dictionary* (Meakins et al., 2013). He also wrote numerous papers on language

36 Jimmy Manngayarri also worked extensively with historians Darrell Lewis (1993, 1997, 2012; Rose, 1991) and Minoru Hokari (2011) on the colonial history of Gurindji and Malngin country. A video discussing his work can be found at https://aiatsis.gov.au/gallery/video/aiatsis-audio-collections-gurindji-language.

contact, historical linguistics and kinship. McConvell's extensive publications on Gurindji language and culture are detailed in the preface of Meakins and O'Shannessy (2016, pp. xxvi-xxxiii).

Figure 15: Jimmy Manngayarri carving a boomerang in 1997. (Photo: Hokari collection).

McConvell also enlisted filmmaker Kim McKenzie in the 1970s to make a series of films about Gurindji and Mudburra language and culture. Felicity Meakins and Jenny Green repatriated these videos to current Gurindji elders in 2017 who identified the people in them. The first video is of McConvell documenting the local sign language with Albert Crowson Lalka and Sambo Crowson (two Mudburra brothers from Montejinnie Station were at Daguragu because the Montejinnie mob were on strike at the time) in a 60

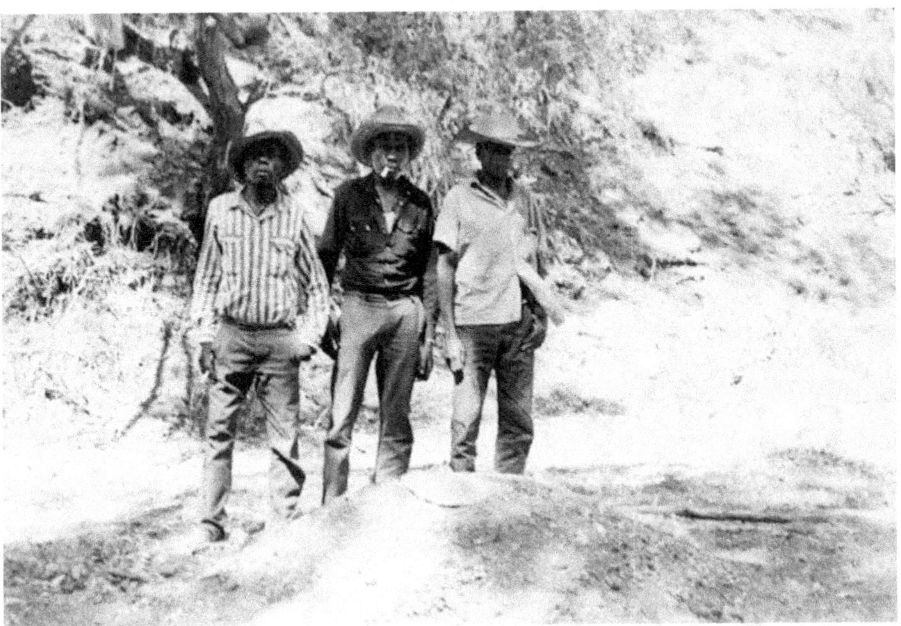

Figure 16: Long Johnny Kijngayarri with Mick Rangiari (left) and Vincent Lingiari (right) (Photo: Brian Manning 1966).

minute film (Green, Meakins, & Algy, forthcoming). McKenzie and McConvell also filmed a number of people making hawk traps including Rook Julkiyarri, Pincher Nyurrmiari (Figure 17), Blanche Bulngari, Victoria Tim Pukaka Jampin, Johnny Kijngayarri and Jimmy Manngayarri. Another video, referred to as the 'Killer' video, shows a number of stockmen killing a cow and included Jerry Rinyngayarri, Charlie Pincher, Jock Vincent, Robbie Peter, Big George Nyitji, and Kennedy. The 'Killer' video includes mostly code-switching between dialects of Gurindji and Kriol and provided empirical evidence for the claim that mixed languages, such as Gurindji Kriol, can derive from code-switching (McConvell & Meakins, 2005). A final video shows open aspects of Karungka ceremony and includes Blanche Bulngari, Mitinyngala Nimarra (from Elliott), Lizzie Ngilyawurru Nawurla, Elsie Jalyawuk Nangala, Marjorie Barry Nalyirri, Noelene Newry, Doris Minyminyngali Nangala (from Elliott) and Violet Wadrill. These videos are held at AIATSIS.

During his time at Daguragu, McConvell, referred to as Pukaka[37] by Aboriginal people in the VRD, became involved the Aboriginal land rights movement which was centred around a number of groups, including the Gurindji (§1.7). Vincent Lingiari's response (1986 (1975)) to then Prime Minister Gough Whitlam's speech at the hand back of Gurindji land in 1975 remains one of the important political speeches of this

37 Pukaka is the name of an important site for Ngarinyman people on the Wickham River in Judbarra/Gregory National Park.

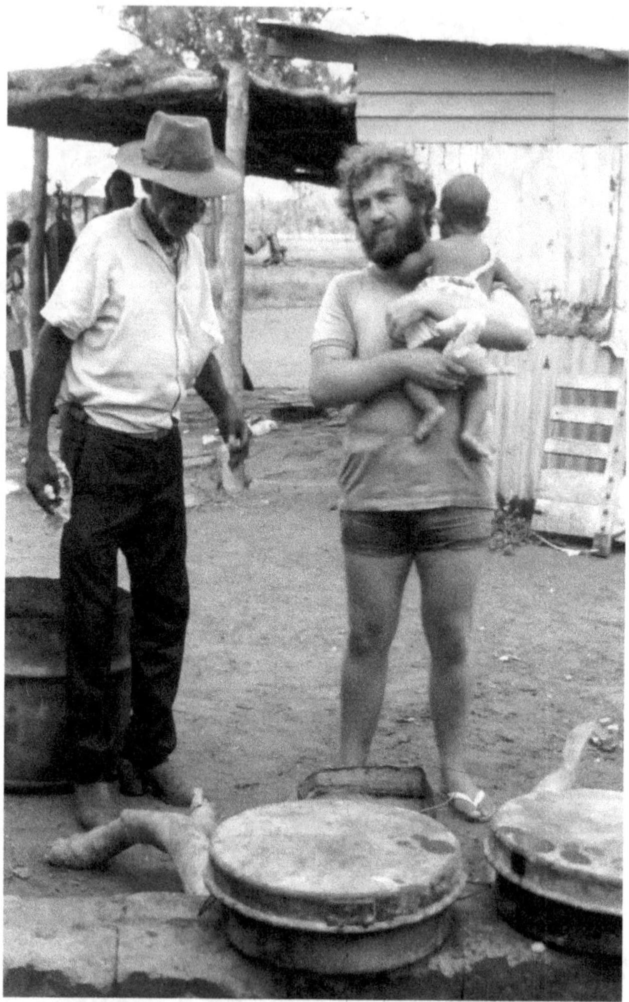

Figure 17: Pincher Nyurrmiari and Patrick McConvell at Daguragu in the mid 1970s.

era. It was delivered in Gurindji and McConvell's translation, which has appeared in many activist contexts, gave the broader Australian public access to Lingiari's words.

Following Whitlam's visit to Daguragu, the Aboriginal Land Rights (Northern Territory) Act (1976), which provides the basis upon which Aboriginal people are able to claim rights to traditional land, was legislated by the Fraser government. McConvell worked on the first land claim conducted by the Central Land Council (CLC) as the anthropologist for the Gurindji claimants to areas of their traditional lands (Peterson, McConvell, Wild, & Hagen, 1978). He was also the principal anthropologist on seven other land claims and native title cases in the Victoria River District (VRD) which together form a comprehensive and coherent ethnography of Gurindji, Malngin,

Nyininy, Bilinarra, Ngarinyman and Mudburra people including their interconnected Dreamings, shared land tenure and kinship systems.

McConvell moved back to Canberra in January 2000 where he was a Research Fellow at AIATSIS (2000–2008) and most recently at ANU (2008–2012). During his time at AIATSIS, he was involved in setting up and supporting the Australian Research Council-funded Aboriginal Child Language project (2004–2007)[38] and associated PhD projects, for example Meakins' work with Gurindji mothers and children (§1.5.11).

McConvell (1985a, 1988a) brought his background in anthropological linguistics to the task of language description and was one of the first people in Australia to begin documenting community language practices in his work on code-switching between Gurindji dialects and Kriol. This research provided the basis for McConvell and Meakins (2005) who claimed that the mixed language, Gurindji Kriol, derived from these code-switching practices, refuting previous claims that mixed languages could not find their origins in normal language contact processes.

McConvell's work on Gurindji and language contact also looks back into the deep historical past. McConvell (2009a) is a careful lexico-semantic case study of Gurindji which shows an unusually high borrowing rate of 45.6% which he details by word class, semantic domain, lexical semantics and structure. Despite the fact that high rates of borrowing have been claimed by R. M. W. Dixon to create too much noise in the historical signal, McConvell and Laughren (2004) convincingly justify the Ngumpin-Yapa language family.

This interest in language contact extended to discoveries of how complex kinship systems, including the Gurindji system, have evolved in Australia. McConvell (1985b) shows how the eight term subsection system, which classifies members into socio-centric categories necessary for understanding descent and marriage relations, developed from contact between two linguistic systems across northern Australia. This work is an example of how bilingualism and contact scenarios can lead to the complexification of pre-existing linguistic and kinship systems.

1.5.9 Helen and Norm McNair

From 1977–1984, Helen and Norm McNair (Figures 18–19) worked extensively with Dandy Danbayarri, Roy Yunga, Valerie Tasman, Blanche Bulngari, Lorna Bird, Susan Cebu, Doris Butler, Pincher Nyurrmiari, Horace Walman and Barbara Yalyural through the Summer Institute of Linguistics (now AuSIL). This work provided a very dense 6.5 hour corpus of mostly narratives which they transcribed, translated and glossed, and which we draw on extensively in this grammar. This work was also a significant

38 https://arts.unimelb.edu.au/school-of-languages-and-linguistics/research/past-research-projects/aclal

contribution to the *Gurindji to English Dictionary* (Meakins et al., 2013) and many of these stories have been published in Charola and Meakins (2016b, 2016c). They also produced many children's story booklets and translated some songs, Bible stories and sections of the Bible. Helen McNair also ran a Gurindji language program in the school and trained Gurindji literacy workers including Susanne Ronnie, Josepha Kitnari, Faye Albert, Anne Robbo, Sarah Booth, Valerie Tasman, Dawn Rook, Melva Hector and Joanne Stevens.

Figure 18: Blanche Bulngari and Helen McNair talking together. (Photo: Norm McNair 1977).

1.5.10 Erika Charola

Since the mid-1990s most of the work on Gurindji has been undertaken through Diwurruwurru-jaru Aboriginal Corporation or Katherine Regional Aboriginal Language Centre (now called Mimi Ngurrdalingi Aboriginal Corporation). From 1996 Erika Charola worked with Ronnie Wavehill Wirrpnga, Dandy Danbayarri, Ida Malyik Nampin, Violet Wadrill, Molly Tupngali Nawurla and Biddy Wavehill Yamawurr (Figure 20). They recorded many Dreaming stories and oral history accounts of the Victoria River District region and their corpus totals 8.5 hours, again a very dense corpus mostly consisting of narratives. Many of the oral histories have been published in two text collections (Charola & Meakins, 2016b, 2016c) and three stories won prizes in the 2004 Central Land Council (CLC) – Institute of Aboriginal Development (IAD) story competition. One of Ronnie Wavehill's stories *Wawirrilu Karu Warrkuj Mani 2019 – (The*

Figure 19: Dandy Danbayarri and Norm McNair working together. (Photo: Helen McNair 1982).

Kangaroo Stole Our Brother) was animated in 2019.[39] Charola also facilitated a Gurindji language program in Kalkaringi CEC from 1996–2000, and worked on the Gurindji dictionary with Dandy Danbayarri and Ronnie Wavehill. They checked a lot of the lexical content, added many example sentences which also feature in this grammar, and filled in some of the more complex paradigms including the tri-relational kinship terms.

1.5.11 Felicity Meakins

Felicity Meakins has worked with Violet Wadrill Nanaku, Topsy Dodd Ngarnjal Nangari and Biddy Wavehill Yamawurr Nangala since 2001 (Figure 21), first through Diwurruwurru-jaru Aboriginal Corporation, then through various grants held at the University of Melbourne, the University of Manchester and currently the University of Queensland. She has collected 42.5 hours of audio and video recordings which are transcribed and translated.

Her initial work involved documenting bush medicine and food collection and preparation practices. The result was a series of short films, now freely available through ICTV Play (see §1.1 for details and a URL), *Kawarla: How to Make a Coola-*

39 https://www.monash.edu/arts/monash-indigenous-studies/wunungu-awara/animations/karu-warrkuj-mani-2019-the-kangaroo-stole-our-brother,-gurindji-dreaming-story-ancestral-narrative,-northern-territory.

Figure 20: Ronnie Wavehill and Erika Charola at the site of the old Afghan shop. (Photo: Brenda L Croft 2014).

Figure 21: Biddy Wavehill, Felicity Meakins and Violet Wadrill at Warrijkuny. (Photo: Brenda L Croft 2014).

mon and *Karu: Growing up Gurindji* (Wadrill et al., 2019; Wadrill et al., 2015). She then worked extensively with Violet Wadrill to check the draft version of the Gurindji dictionary and bring it to publication. Together with a number of Gurindji elders, Meakins also collaborated with Glenn Wightman, a biologist with the Northern Territory Herbarium to write *Bilinarra, Gurindji and Malngin Plants and Animals* (Hector et al., 2012), which was started by Lauren Campbell (see §1.5.12). This work was then extended to the production of four posters of fish, birds, bush medicine and foods with the local ranger group (see §1.2 for URLs).

Meakins also worked with Ronnie Wavehill, Topsy Dodd Ngarnjal and linguist/musicologist Myfany Turpin to document public Gurindji songs called *wajarra* including the Freedom Day songs, Laka (known widely as Wanji-wanji), Kamul and Mintiwarra. They made a half hour documentary which aired on NITV in 2018 and wrote the book *Songs from the Station: Wajarra as sung by Ronnie Wavehill Wirrpnga, Dandy Danbayarri, Topsy Dodd Ngarnjal* (Turpin & Meakins, 2019). During this project they also recorded many hours of women's songs and produced a DVD for the Kalkaringi and Nitjpurru women. Meakins has also collaborated with Cassandra Algy and sign specialist Jenny Green to record the sign language used by the Kalkaringi community. They produced a series of four posters and 15 short films which aired on ICTV and are again available on ICTV Play (see §1.2 for URLs). Since 2008, all of these projects have been run through Karungkarni Art and Culture Aboriginal Corporation and the Murnkurrumurnkurru Central Land Council ranger group, both of which are Gurindji-controlled organisations based locally at Kalkaringi.

Meakins has also worked extensively with young Gurindji women and their children to document the new language, Gurindji Kriol, which is the main language of Gurindji people born after the 1970s. In 2001, she joined the Aboriginal Child Language (ACLA) project at the University of Queensland and, together with Samantha Smiler, recorded young mothers and their children interacting. They created a 60 hour corpus. During this time, Meakins (2011b) also collected an additional 20 hours of data of adult Gurindji Kriol and completed a PhD in 2008 on case-marking in Gurindji Kriol. Between 2014–2017, Cassandra Algy and Felicity Meakins then collaborated to document the children's Gurindji Kriol and compare it with their parents' language (Figure 22). The Gurindji Kriol corpus is now 165 hours (transcribed, translated, anonymised, annotated including the ACLA data) representing 157 speakers and 405,027 words of mostly picture-based elicitation (narratives and picture-prompts). Algy and Meakins have published papers on spatial relations (Dunn, Meakins, & Algy, 2021; Meakins, 2011c; Meakins & Algy, 2016; Meakins, Jones, & Algy, 2016), verbs (Meakins, 2010a, 2016b; Meakins & O'Shannessy, 2012) and case-marking (Meakins, 2009, 2014, 2015a; Meakins, Disbray, & Simpson, 2020; Meakins & O'Shannessy, 2010; Meakins & Wilmoth, 2020). Most recently Meakins has been working with biologists to map language change across multiple variables (Bromham, Hua, Algy, & Meakins, 2020; Meakins, Hua, Algy, & Bromham, 2019).

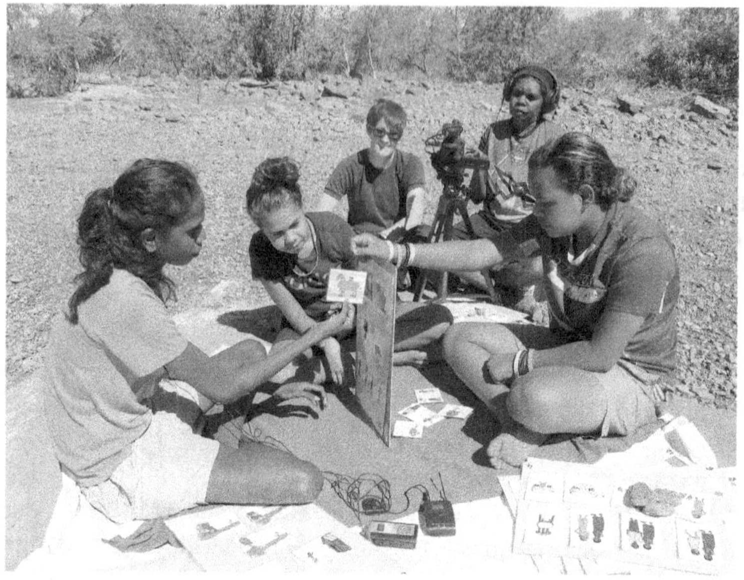

Figure 22: Cassandra Algy Nimarra and Felicity Meakins record director-matcher tasks with Jamieisha Barry Nangala, Regina Crowson Nangari and Quitayah Frith Namija (Photo: Jennifer Green 2017).

1.5.12 Lauren Campbell

Lauren Campbell was a linguist at Diwurruwurru-jaru Aboriginal Corporation (Katherine Language Centre) who supported Gurindji language work from late 2006 to early 2009. She worked closely with Dandy Danbayarri and Helen Morris in Katherine, and with Violet Wadrill, Biddy Wavehill Yamawurr and Ronnie Wavehill Wirrpnga at Kalkaringi (Figure 23). The key Gurindji language projects at the time were the ethnobiology (plant and animal book) and recording stories (and sometimes songs) that elders wanted recorded for documentation and resource production, with the hope of building up more language in the school. Helen and Lauren also developed and ran Gurindji Language Awareness courses for Kalkaringi CEC staff and Katherine West Health Board and worked on an AIATSIS project to make old Gurindji recordings from the archives accessible online with transcriptions. These projects also contributed to building entries for the dictionary and example sentences for the grammar.

In 2019, Lauren worked with Gurindji people, who grew up without access to Gurindji language, and their Gurindji-speaking families in community to compile an introductory online language course. The 'Gurindji Learners Project' was funded by the ARC Centre of Excellence for the Dynamics of Language through the ANU. These materials included fun casual-style learner videos and online flashcard games to introduce words, phrases and basic interactions and conversations in Gurindji and Gurindji Kriol. Brenda L Croft initiated this project and Leah Leaman and Cassandra Algy were key Gurindji and Gurindji Kriol contributors, amongst many others.

Figure 23: Bernard Puntiyarri, Lauren Campbell and Dandy Danbayarri discussing plant and animal terms. (Photo: Glenn Wightman 2007).

1.6 Gurindji in relation to other Ngumpin-Yapa languages

Gurindji is very closely related to the other Victoria River languages of the Ngumpin branch: Bilinarra, Ngarinyman, Wurlayi, Wanyjirra and Malngin (see the language phylogeny in Figure 2). From the perspective of linguists, these six would be considered dialects of a single language, however, they are considered different languages by the respective communities (see Dixon, 1980, p. 33ff on the different uses of 'language' reflected here). Despite their similarities, there are nonetheless a number of grammatical differences that separate the languages and the other Ngumpin-Yapa languages.

The main grammatical differences between Gurindji[40,41] and the other Victoria River languages are (i) pronominal clitic placement and catalysts, (ii) structure of the

40 Gurindji orthography uses voiceless stops /p, t, k/ where Bilinarra uses voiced stops /b, d, g/. Gurindji orthography is used here for both languages for ease of comparison.

41 Note also some minor phonological differences. While coverbs in both Gurindji and Bilinarra can be one syllable (§7.2.1), impressionistically Bilinarra tends to have more of these forms (observation from FM not agreed to by PMcC), perhaps due to the closer proximity of Bilinarra to Jaminjung from which

bound pronoun systems, (iii) structure of the free pronoun system, (iv) the lack of hither and thither suffixes on verbs in Gurindji, (v) TAM categories and forms, and (vi) the complexity of the cardinal paradigm. See Meakins et al. (2021) for a comparison of grammatical structures in the Ngumpin-Yapa family.

In most Ngumpin languages, bound pronouns attach to a catalyst. In Gurindji (1), Malngin and Wanyjirra, the default catalyst base is *ngu* (Capell, 1940, p. 428; Ise, 1998, p. 37; Senge, 2016, pp. 308–309).[42] The catalyst *ngu* may come from the Ngarinyman purposive *ngu* with loss of that meaning (or could be a retention from an earlier stage). In Bilinarra and Ngarinyman, the bound pronoun instead attaches to a prominent topic or focus element at the beginning of the clause, as shown in (2).

(1) Kajijirri-lu **ngu**=yinangulu Gurindji
old.woman.REDUP-ERG CAT=3AUG.S>3AUG.NS

warra ka-nga-na karu.
look.after take-IMPF-PRS child
"The women are looking after their children."
(🔈 VW: FM17_a442: 5:37min)

(2) [Ka-ngku=**wula**=nga,] munuwu-ngkurra Bilinarra
take-POT=3UA.S=DUB camp-ALL

taj-pa=**wula**=nga pa-rru marntaj.
smash-EP=3UA.S=DUB hit-POT OK
"Those two might take it back to camp, and pound them, OK."
(🔈 IH: BIL05aud: 2003: 6:38min)

In Gurindji, pronominal clitics are sometimes found attached to a first position constituent, but generally only when it is marked with a discourse clitic such as *=ma* (which we analyse as a prominent topic marker, see §10.1.2), as in (3). Other possibilities are imperative verbs, interrogatives, negation and a number of complementisers.

many of these coverbs were borrowed historically. Bilinarra seems to tolerate single syllable coverbs more than Gurindji, despite the fact that single syllable words are not found elsewhere in the language. For example, Gurindji has a tendency towards non-productive reduplication and fused suffixes such as *-karra* 'iterative' or *-ap* 'activity'. Some examples are *jap* (Bilinarra) vs *japkarra* (Gurindji) 'trim, skin', *taj* (Bilinarra) vs *tajkarra* (Gurindji) 'pound'.

42 Wanyjirra also has *nga*, as a neutral catalyst. In the other Ngumpin languages, Jaru has *nga* for declarative clauses (Tsunoda, 1981, pp. 68, 124–125) and Ngardi has the sequential *ngu/nga* (Ennever, 2021). The neutral catalyst *pa* occurs in Walmajarri and Mudburra (Capell, 1940, p. 427; 1965, pp. 68–69; Osgarby, 2018a, pp. 103–104).

(3) Nyila=ma=**wula** ma-na-ni warrkuwarrkuj. Gurindji
that=TOP=3UA.S do-IMPF-PST pick.up.REDUP
"They would gather them up." (🔈 VW: FM11_a161: 01:01min)

The structure of the bound pronoun system is another place which shows some variation. Gurindji has a two-way distinction between subject and non-subject pronouns, which is similar to Bilinarra and Ngarinyman. Other Ngumpin languages such as Wanyjirra, Jaru and Ngardi have an additional locational series (Ennever, 2021, pp. 304–305; Senge, 2016; Tsunoda, 1981, p. 69). Walmajarri has a four-way bound pronoun series: subject, object, oblique and locational (Hudson, 1978).

The free pronoun system also shows differences across Ngumpin languages. In Gurindji, they make the same person (1st inclusive and exclusive, 2nd and 3rd) and number (minimal, unit-augmented, augmented) distinctions as the bound pronouns. They do not have distinct subject and non-subject forms, instead using the same form for subjects and objects, but with a separate dative series. The free pronouns also do not inflect on the bare stem for case. Bilinarra, Ngarinyman, Malngin and Wanyjirra have the same system (Ise, 1998, pp. 126–127; C. Jones, Schultze-Berndt, Denniss, & Meakins, 2019, p. 36; Meakins & Nordlinger, 2014, p. 217; Senge, 2016, p. 315). On the other hand, free pronouns in Ngardi are directly case-marked, albeit optionally in the case of the ergative. There is no distinct oblique set of stems (Ennever, 2021). In Jaru, case-markers also attach directly to the stem (Tsunoda, 1981, pp. 64–65).[43] Warlmanpa and Mudburra show a much reduced free pronoun system (McConvell, 1980; Nash, 1996). Warlmanpa only distinguishes person and not number *ngayu* '1' *nyuntu* '2' and *nyantu* '3' which also have genitive forms. They optionally also take number suffixes. Warlmanpa free pronouns do not inflect for core case other than dative case, and so the form of free pronouns is the same regardless of whether it is the transitive subject, intransitive subject or object. They can also take non-core cases directly on the stem (Browne, 2021). Mudburra also only distinguishes person *ngayu* '1'*nyuntu* '2' and *nyana* '3' which also have genitive forms. Number markers are also possible, but optional (Capell, 1940, p. 427; Green, Algy, & Meakins, 2017, pp. 45–46; McConvell, 1980, p. 33).

43 Note that Ennever also analyses Ngardi has not having a third person pronoun, but instead considers *nyantu* a demonstrative, whereas Tsunoda analyses it as a free pronoun. This is the same form found in Gurindji and the other Victoria River Ngumpin languages. A point of difference with the Victoria River Ngumpin languages is that *nyanung-* is the third person stem for all non-ergative case inflections in Jaru and *nyanungu-* is the stem for all case inflections in Ngardi (including ergative). Also of relevance is that in Jaru there is a dual form *nyanpula* whereas in Ngardi *nyanungu-* simply takes the dual suffix used by other nouns or demonstratives, i.e., *nyanungu-kujarra*. The Jaru form is still a little defective in the free pronoun paradigm because there is no distinct plural third person form. There's simply an opposition between dual and unmarked ('general') number. (Thanks to Thomas Ennever for these observations).

Differences in the inflecting verbs can also be observed between Gurindji, Wanyjirra, Malngin, Bilinarra and Ngarinyman. Gurindji has 34 inflecting verbs. 18 inflecting verbs have been reported for Ngarinyman (Jones, Schultze-Berndt, Denniss, et al., 2019, p. 38), 23 for Bilinarra (Meakins & Nordlinger, 2014, p. 271) and 38 for Wanyjirra (Senge, 2016, p. 399).[44] Although the roots are largely similar, the inflectional forms differ in the present tense and imperfective forms across the five classes of verbs,[45] as shown in Tables 2 and 3, and in the position of the imperfective marker, as shown in Table 3.

Table 2: Present tense inflections in Gurindji, Wanyjirra, Malngin, Bilinarra and Ngarinyman.

	Class 1	Class 2	Class 3	Class 4	Class 5
Gurindji[1]	*-nana*	*-rnana*	*-ngana*	*-rnana*	*-nana*
Wanyjirra	*-nana*	*-rnana*	*-ngana*	*-rnana*	*-nana*
Malngin	*-nana*	*-rnana*	*-ngana*	*-rnana*	*-nana*
Bilinarra	*-rra*	*-la*	*-nga*	*-la*	*-na*
Ngarinyman	*-rra(ny)*	*-la(n)*	*-nga(n)*	*-la(n)*	*-na(n)*

[1] Note that the Gurindji forms are really present imperfective forms, e.g. *ya-na-na* 'go-IMPF-PRS' (Class 5). No present perfective equivalents exist.

Table 3: Past imperfective inflections in Gurindji, Wanyjirra, Malngin, Bilinarra and Ngarinyman.

	Class 1	Class 2	Class 3	Class 4	Class 5
Gurindji [-IMPF-PST]	*-na-ni*	*-rna-ni*	*-nga-ni*	*-rna-ni*	*-na-ni*
Wanyjirra [-IMPF-PST]	*-na-ni*	*-rna-ni*	*-nga-ni*	*-rna-ni*	*-na-ni*
Malngin [-IMPF-PST]	*-na-ni*	*-rna-ni*	*-nga-ni*	*-rna-ni*	*-na-ni*
Bilinarra [-PST-IMPF]	*-ni-rra*	*-rni-rra*	*-nya-rra*	*-rni-rra*	*-ni-rra*
Ngarinyman [-PST-IMPF]	*-ni-rra*	*-rni-rra*	*-nya-rra*	*-rni-rra*	*-ni-rra*

44 Note also that around 40 have been recorded for Walmajarri (Dixon, 1980, p. 387), and 40 odd for Jaru (Tsunoda, 1981, p. 76). Warlpiri which is a Yapa language has a larger class of verbs, numbering around 130 (Nash, 2008, p. 221). The other Yapa language, Warlmanpa has 45 verbs (Browne, 2021).
45 The imperfective form found in Bilinarra and Ngarinyman *-rra* is likely to be related to the thither suffix found in other Ngumpin-Yapa languages.

The TAM categories marked by the inflecting verbs also differ between Gurindji and Bilinarra (and Ngarinyman), as shown in Tables 4 and 5. Gurindji (and Malngin and Wanyjirra) make an im/perfective distinction across past and present tense and potential mood whereas Bilinarra (and Ngarinyman) only makes an aspectual (imperfective/perfective) distinction in the past tense.

Table 4: Gurindji, Malngin and Wanyjirra conjugation for 'yanana' (go).

	Infinitive	**Finite**			
		Imperative	**Past**	**Present**	**Potential**
Perfective	*yanu*	*yanta*	*yani*		*yanku*
Imperfective	*yananu*	*yananta*	*yanani*	*yanana*	*yanangku*

Table 5: Bilinarra conjugation for 'yana' (go).

Infinitive	**Finite**				
	Imperative	**Past**		**Present**	**Potential**
		Perf	**Imperf**		
yanu	*yanta*	*yani*	*yanirra*	*yana*	*yanku*

Another point of difference between Gurindji, and the other Ngumpin languages is the presence/absence of hither and thither suffixes on verbs. Gurindji actually does not mark these categories but is unusual in this respect. Eastern Walmajarri also does not mark these categories, however all other Ngumpin-Yapa languages do in some form or other. Bilinarra and Ngarinyman uses *-rni* 'hither' on inflecting verbs (Jones, Schultze-Berndt, Denniss, et al., 2019, p. 40; Meakins & Nordlinger, 2014, pp. 308–309) and Jaru possesses *-rni* 'hither', but it only occurs with imperative and purposive verbs (Tsunoda, 1981, p. 208). Warlpiri, Warlmanpa and Ngardi have both *-rni* 'hither' and *-rra* 'thither' on verbs and cardinals (Ennever, 2021; Laughren, 1978, p. 2; Nash, 2008). Gurindji uses *-rni* on cardinals to indicate relative elevation or 'up' and *-rra* as a frozen locative form on cardinals (Laughren & McConvell, 1999).[46]

46 This audio excerpt was taken from a stretched recording hence the poor sound quality.

(4) Ka-nya-rra-**rni**=rnalu lurrpu Bilinarra
take-PST-IMPF-HITH=1EXC.AUG.S return

na jiwirri na, yala-ngka=rni.
SEQ cooked SEQ that-LOC=ONLY
"Then we would return there bringing the cooked (meat)."
(IH: FM08_a086: 2003: 05:25min)

This inability to encode deixis in the inflecting verb distinguishes Gurindji from other Ngumpin languages (McConvell, 1983, p. 30). Allative and ablative marked demonstratives are required to make this distinction in Gurindji, as shown in (5) and (6).

(5) Wurlpun-jirri ya-nku-rra=yi Gurindji
lap-ALL go-POT-HORT=1EXC.MIN.NS

murla-ngkurra, karu=ma nyila=ma.
this-ALL child=TOP that=TOP
"Let the child come here to my lap." (TD: FM10_a166: 14:05min)

(6) Murla-ngurlu na ngu=rlaa yurra Gurindji
this-ABL FOC CAT=1INC.AUG.S startle

ma-ni kurrarntal nyamu=waa ya-ni.
do-PST brolga REL=REL go-PST
"We hunted the brolga away from here which took off then."
(VW: FM07_a058: 04:13min)

Another difference between Ngumpin languages is in the demonstrative system. Gurindji has four sets of demonstratives: *nyawa* and its suppletive stems *murla-* and *murlu-* 'PROXimal, this', *nyila* and its suppletive stems *yala-* and *yalu-* 'DIStal, that', *kuya* 'thus' and *nyanawu* 'RECOGnitional, you know the one'. Identical systems are found in Bilinarra, Ngarinyman, Malngin, Jaru and Wanyjirra (Ise, 1998, p. 27; Jones, Schultze-Berndt, Denniss, et al., 2019, p. 27; Meakins & Nordlinger, 2014, pp. 169–171; Senge, 2016, pp. 110–111; Tsunoda, 1981, pp. 61–62). Also of interest, Mudburra, Western Walmajarri and Ngardi have *minya* 'this' as a stem, as well as *murla-/murlu-* (though note that *murla-/murlu-* is only found in the Western dialect of Mudburra not the Eastern dialect). They are the only Ngumpin languages which use this stem which is curious given the distance (phylogenetic and physical) between the languages. In general, Eastern Mudburra has three-way system *minya/nginya* 'this', *kadi* 'close' and *yali* 'there', which are distinct from Gurindji (Green et al., 2019, p. 38). Warlmanpa also has a three-way system *yimpa* 'this', *yarri* 'that' and *yali* 'that (removed)' (Browne, 2021).

Finally, a number of differences between Gurindji and other Ngumpin-Yapa languages can be seen in the cardinal paradigms. Gurindji has over 30 different inflections per cardinal point (north, south, east and west). In addition, cardinals agree with other nominals in the NP. This level of complexity seems to be the highest among the Ngumpin-Yapa languages (§5.2.1).

1.7 The socio-political and linguistic history of the Gurindji people

Gurindji people earned a place in Australian history as the result of their nine year workers' strike (1966–75) against the poor employment and living conditions on the cattle stations (Figure 24). They were successful in first gaining a pastoral lease over some of their land (1975). They were later successful in a land claim (1985) under the Aboriginal Land Rights (Northern Territory) Act 1976 and in 2020 received Native Title over Wave Hill Station and Limbunya Stations. In fact, the strike provided the catalyst for the Aboriginal Land Rights (Northern Territory) Act 1976 and heralded a fresh wave of Aboriginal activism and non-Indigenous interest in the well-being of Aboriginal people.

Figure 24: Gurindji strikers in the dry riverbed of the Victoria River (Kalkaringi): Mick Tulupu, Billy King, Dexter Daniels, Banjo Ryan, Long Steven, Robert Tudawali, Mick Rangiari, Splinter Manguari, Vincent Lingiari, Long Johnny Kijngayarri, Gus George, Douglas King, Gerry Ngalgardji, Roger King, Tommy Wajipi, Ronny Wilson, George Kalibidi, Robbie and Rook Julkigari (Photo: Brian Manning 1966).

Extensive work has focussed on Gurindji history since colonisation, largely due to the Gurindji Walk-Off from Wave Hill Station in 1966. A number of accounts of colonial times come from Gurindji people (Charola & Meakins, 2016c; Daguragu-Community-Council, 2000; Donald, 1998; Frith, 1998; Kijngayarri, 1986 (1974); Lingiari, 1986 (1975); Rangiari, 1997, 1998), as well as historians (Doolan, 1977; Hokari, 2000, 2002, 2011; Long, 1996; Mulligan, 1999; Riddett, 1997; Ward, 2016), anthropologists (Lauridsen, 1990; McConvell & Hagen, 1981), and activists (Dodson, 2000; Hardy, 1968).

Gurindji is now an endangered language, which is closely tied to the current social circumstances and recent history of its people. In the last 100 years, the Gurindji population has decreased dramatically as a result of massacres and killings by early colonists and the poor treatment on the cattle stations where the Gurindji were eventually brought to work. The decline of the Gurindji language was further exacerbated by the situation on the cattle stations because different language groups including Mudburra, Warlpiri, Gurindji, Bilinarra, Malngin and Ngarinyman were made to live in much closer proximity than was traditionally found. Gurindji was the dominant language in the mix so the result was a certain levelling of differences between Gurindji, Bilinarra, Malngin and Ngarinyman. Cattle station pidgin was also introduced into this mix during this period, further endangering the use of Gurindji, but also giving rise to the contact language, Gurindji Kriol, which allowed the use of Gurindji to be maintained. These following sections tell this story. Much of this story is drawn from Gurindji accounts in *Yijarni: True Stories from Gurindji Country* (2016).

1.7.1 Pre-contact linguistic situation

Gurindji history begins with the formation of the landscape during a period called the *Puwarraj*[47] or Dreaming. Dreaming creatures traversed the land, shaping its features in a series of journeys referred to as Dreaming tracks or lines. These creatures took many forms. They were animals, humans or natural phenomena such as rain or lightning, and were responsible for the creation of hills, rocks, waterholes and clusters of trees. A number of Dreaming tracks criss-cross Gurindji country including Ngawa/Nguku (Rain), Wampana (Hare-Wallaby), Jurntakal (Western Taipan) and Yiparrartu (Emu).

The maintenance of these lines and their associated sites is essential for the physical and spiritual well-being of the Gurindji people. Some sites are imbued with procreative powers such as Karungkarni, a hill near Kalkaringi which is visited by prospective mothers (Wadrill et al., 2019, pp. 2–6). Visiting or disturbing other sites can affect the health of visitors or the Gurindji people responsible for their mainte-

47 Note *Puwarraj* also means 'body painting designs'. The word does not mean 'dream' in Gurindji although it does in other languages which is where the term 'Dreaming' comes from. For example, in Arrernte, the word for 'Dreaming' is built on the word for 'dream in other languages'.

nance by causing anything from minor ailments to major epidemics. Land and language are tightly interwoven. The Dreaming creatures sang the land into being, and the stories of the Dreaming are recounted in songs which also act to help maintain the land. These songs are passed down through family lines.

Gurindji society is divided into two patrimoieties: Jarlwawuny (Lirraku) – Heron moiety and Warlawurruwuny (Yilyiku) – Eaglehawk moiety (McConvell & Hagen, 1981).[48] The Dreaming story about Warlawurru (Eagle) and Jarlwa (Heron) begins with Warlawurru stealing and eating Jarlwa's sister. In revenge, Jarlwa lures Warlawurru into a cave. Jarlwa builds a fire at the entrance of the cave hoping to suffocate Warlawurru. But Warlawurru escapes, gathers a war party and attacks Jarlwa's family. In some versions of the story Warlawurru shows mercy to Jarlwa because they are related through marriage. These moieties are not of wide public significance like the Yirrija and Duwa moieties of North East Arnhem Land. They are mainly used in certain types of secret ceremonies.

Land ownership and management is divided between different groups. Any one area is in the custodianship of one group people called *ngurramala*, known colloquially as 'traditional owners' or 'TOs', and cared for by people from the other called *kurtungurlu* (a term from Warlpiri, which is not always used by Gurindji), called 'workers', 'policemen' or 'stockmen'. These patrimoieties are further divided into four subsections each, eight in total. The subsection system maps onto kinship relations which dictate behaviour between family members and designate appropriate marriage partners (see §1.8.1). The main view on land custodianship and management is that there is a hierarchy of importance in the lines of descent from which rights are inherited, as follows:

1. From one's father (*ngaji*) and father's father (*kaku*),
2. From one's mother (*ngamayi*), (maternal) uncle (*ngamirni*) and mother's father (*jawiji*),[49]
3. From one's mother's mother (*jaju*) and her brothers, and
4. From one's father's mother (*ngapuju*) and her brothers.

Where there are no direct descendants, the care of land is allocated to a senior person of the correct patricouple of subsections who has extensive knowledge of the country, for example through work on the cattle stations (in the case of Limbunya Native Title claim) or a collective ownership system whereby the entire community cares for the land.

---

48 Note that in two published works – McConvell (1982) and Meakins et al (2016), these moieties are recorded as Jarlwawuny (Yilyiku) and Warlawurruwuny (Lirraku), which is not correct. The confusion over these terms might relate to how little currency moieties have in everyday life, unlike the Yirrija and Duwa moieties in Arnhem Land. It is the subsection system which underlies the structure of everyday life for the Gurindji, still today.

49 Only 1 and 2 are important for ownership.

In the Warlpiri organisation, the prototypical *kurtungurlu* is the sister's son of the owner. Gurindji see the relationship primarily as that of *parnkurti* 'cross-cousin'. While quite similar in effect the emphasis is on the junior owner (the son of the senior male owner) who is cross-cousin to the workers.

There is a complementary and equal relationship between the patrilineal owners or *ngurramala* and their matrilateral relations or *kurtungurlu*. *Ngurramala* have the role of singing the songs of the Dreamings, enacting the Dreamings in ceremony and channelling their power; the *kurtungurlu* assist them in making sure the songs are correct, in organising ceremonies and protecting their rights and symbols. In practice a much broader group may assist in singing and performance, with permission from the owners and workers.

There is another type of dual division, the *Purnturtu*, or generational moiety, which is of more significance in forming 'teams' in dancing at the Marntiwa/Pantimi initiation ceremonies (and in earlier times, in traditional football game *pulyja*) (for details see McConvell & Hagen, 1981, pp. 26–27). This division is based on a generational divide and cuts across the patrimoiety division. Within each father-son couple of subsections like Jangala-Jampijina, which belong to the same patrimoiety (Heron), one (Jangala) is on one *Purnturtu* side and the other (Jampijina) is on the other side, for instance. The generational moieties are not named (see Figure 31). This type of division is not directly related to rights in land.

A final division is inherited matrilineally. This is a person's *ngurlu*.[50] McConvell (1982a, p. 92) notes that "members of different *ngurlu* are said to have differing physical characteristics; for example *kalanypuka* people are supposed to have light skin and 'chestnut' (*karrakarrak*) hair, while *kulumarra-ngarna* people are said to have dark skin and 'really black' (*mumpung-nyiyarni*) hair." Gurindji people practised exogamy outside of their *ngurlu*.

Table 6: Gurindji matrimoieties or 'ngurlu'.

Matrimoiety A/C	kulumarra-ngarna	brolga, sky-dweller
	kalanypuka	yellow rain clouds
Matrimoiety B/D	ngarin-nyung	emu, meaty-one
	yimayaka[51]	kurrajong

Before European contact, Gurindji people travelled mostly within their own nation and in neighbouring nations. Their closest neighbours were Bilinarra and Ngarinyman people to the north-west, Jaru people to the west, the Karrangpurru to the north-

50 This word also means 'seed' (McConvell, 1998).

51 This word relates to *miyaka* which is from Mudburra. The equivalent Gurindji word is *kinyjirrka*.

east, the Mudburra people to the east and the Kartangarurru (Pirlingarna) to the south. Warfare between the Gurindji and nearby desert people occurred (Danbayarri, 2016b; Ryan, 2016b), however the neighbouring groups also shared many cultural practices and would come together once a year for ceremony time (Wadrill, 2016b; Wavehill, 2019). The Gurindji characterise this time before European invasion as an unchanging, but cyclical period of social and natural order, and predictability. For a fuller account of pre-colonial Gurindji society see McConvell (1976, 1985b) and for Ngarinyman and Bilinarra people see Rose (1991, 2000).

Gurindji people refer to 'law and custom' as *yumi*. This includes systems of group and individual rights and responsibilities and norms of social and ritual behaviour and belief. Much of *yumi* was handed over to Gurindji people by their ancestors in the ancient past by the creative Dreamings (*Puwarraj, Mangaya*) (McConvell & Hagen, 1981, p. 43). Later, humans have interpreted and elaborated on the law, but it is generally thought to have an origin in the Dreaming. The Dreamings and spirits of ancestors are present and able to watch over humans and may become disturbed if the Law is not followed. Untoward consequences can follow, either sickness or injury caused by spirits, or punishment meted out by humans based on perceived breaking of the Law. For example, when entering country which has not been visited in some time, or is being visited for the first time, or which is considered dangerous, it is important for a *ngurramala* 'traditional custodian' to douse the forehead, forearms and chest of a *kaluyawung*[52] 'visitor' with water from the local water source. This procedure introduces the visitor to the deceased *ngurramala* of the site and the relevant Dreaming creatures thereby not inviting their wrath. Country is also often *ngak* or scolded by *ngurramala*. This procedure includes berating deceased traditional custodians and Dreaming creators and throwing stones at country. The aim is to prevent deceased and Dreamings from harming visitors. The practice of introducing visitors to country remains an important practice, and one where 'hard' or traditional Gurindji must be spoken (Wadrill et al., 2019, pp. 32–33).

Gurindji country, particularly the northern areas and along the Victoria River and its tributaries, was rich with a diversity of foods and medicinal plants. Kangaroos, wallabies and smaller marsupials were an important source of protein, as well as fish and large birds. Gurindji diet was further supplemented by fruit, root vegetables and grains which were made into bread. Like most Aboriginal people, Gurindji society has been characterised as a hunter-gatherer society, however this ignores the fact that they actively shaped the landscape to catch prey and propagate plants. Recently, Pascoe (2014) has drawn attention to these types of cultivation practices. For example, Gurindji people built fish traps from stone called *puul* (also the word for pouch):

52 *Kaluyawung* is transparently *kalu* 'walk' + *-yawung* 'proprietive, with'.

(7) Puul-la ngulu manani ngawa-ngka yapawurru-la. Narlirlip yanana ngawa-ma yapakaru-ma. Nyila-ma-lu-rla yuwanani wumara na, jartit ngulu-rla yuwanani, puul-la na karrinyani yawu-ma. Nyila-ma puul-la. Tirrip ngulu wanyjanani. Yanana ngawa-ma nyila-ma yapakaru, yawu-ma. Tirrip ngulu wanyjanani. Kaputkaput ngulu-rla wirra nyangani. Nyangani ngulu yawu na. Yawu-ma-nga karru jintaku-la-rni kurlpap. Turturturlarra karru-nga yapakayi-la ngawa-ngka-ma yalangka-rni kurlpap nyamu-rla kuya wirri jartirt karrinyana wumara. Pilyayarrkarra kuyangku-ma. Nyila-ma-lu manani, panani ngulu karnti-yawung-kulu na tam-pangap. Nyila-ma-lu manani pirlnyip. Yapakaru-la-ma nyila-ma-lu manani yawu na warrwarrkuj. Yuwanani ngulu waj pakara-yirri. Warrkuj ngurnalu manani jaartkarra-wu na ngurra-ngkurra. Karu-ngku na ngurnayinangulu nyangani karrap pinarrik. Murlangka kanyjurra nyamu-rnalu Compound-ta kayirra karrinyani.

In the old days, people would catch fish in traps in the shallow water (near the Victoria River Crossing). Shallow water always flows there. They would heap up stones, blocking the flowing water so the fish would get stuck there. They would go away for a couple of days while the water and fish were flowing through it. Then they come back and check the trap. Fish would be heaped up in one place, thrashing around, gasping for breath. They would get sticks and kill them then. Then they'd collect the fish – those stuck in the trap and throw them out of the water. We would pick them up and take them home to eat. I watched and learnt this as a kid, when we used to live north at the Wave Hill Welfare Compound. (Violet Wadrill to Meakins in 2015)

Figure 25: Men using a fish trap in the Victoria River at Wave Hill Settlement around 1933 (Photo: Charlie Schultz, courtesy of Darrell Lewis).

Another hunting practice involving stone structures was hawk traps called *larrkan* or *pantirij*, which is again described by Violet Wadrill. A short film also exists of men making a trap in the 1970s (see §1.5.8) and Mathews (1901, p. 76) also details the use of *larrkan* 'hawk-traps'.

(8) Nyila-ma wumara-ma kurlpakurlpap-ma kankula karrinyana karlaniyinpa. Ngulu yuwanani ngarin-ku. An warlu ngulu-rla pirrkap manani. Warlu-ma nyawa-ma jiyarnani-ma yalangka-ma. Jungkart, jungkart na yanani. Maiti ngulu yunparnani du kamparrijang-kulu-ma. Ngarin-murlung-kula na ngulu panani nyampayirla na jurlak. Jurlak-ma yanani yalangka-wu-ma jungkart-ta-wu-ma, jiwawu-warra. Panani kata punpa-lu wirlwirlkkarra, turi-yawung-kulu karnti-yawung-kulu. Panani ngulu wirlwirlkkarra-ma kuya, nyamu-lu yanani yalu-wu-ma jungkart-ku-ma. Nyatparra-wayi nyarrulu-rni kamparrijang-kulu. Kula-rnalu pina nguma-yijang-ma. Onli nyawa-ma-nga yurrk ngantipa ngurnalu marnani.

There's a pile of rocks heaped up [on a hill] west of here [along the Halls Creek road]. They used to pile them up like that to get meat. They would light a fire in it. The fire would burn inside that one. The smoke would rise then. Maybe they would also sing it in the old days [to make the smoke rise]. They used to kill birds in the old days when they didn't have meat. The birds would fly for that smoke, smelling around for meat. Then they would hit the backs of their necks with a short piece of wood. They would hit them on the back of the neck when they flew for the smoke. That's how they used to do it in the old days. Our generation don't know how to do it. We only talk about it now.
(VW: FM12_a193: 0:06min)

Other hunting practices using fire were also common. Fire was used to herd kangaroos and to clean up the country before the wet season and encourage germination after the rains came. Lewis (2002) has collected archive photos from the early colonists and taken them again at the same site with the camera approximately re-positioned. Aside from the obvious devastation to the landscape from cattle, the other striking difference is increased size and density of trees and vegetation, which Lewis (2002, pp. 50–62) attributes to the unpeopling of the land and lack of burning.

Little is known about language practices of the Gurindji before European settlement, however McConvell (1988a) suggests that the Gurindji and other Aboriginal groups have probably always been highly multilingual, with language mixing an unmarked form of communication. Indeed, Gurindji has some of the highest levels of borrowing in the world. Gurindji (Ngumpin) has borrowed 48.8% of its nouns and 49.7% of its verbs from Wardaman and the northern Mirndi languages, Ngaliwurru and Jaminjung, and Jarragan languages (McConvell, 2009a, p. 795).

1.7.2 The language situation since European invasion

First contact with *kartiya* (European people) was a brutal period. This had a harsh and lasting effect on the language and culture of the Gurindji. The black soil plains of the Victoria River District were attractive to *kartiya* who were looking for good pastoral land to set up cattle stations. The first party of *kartiya* was led by the Gregory brothers, Francis and Henry. In late 1855 they arrived from the north. They followed the Victoria River and its tributaries and came upon what is now referred to as the Victoria River District, which they decided was suitable grazing land (Makin, 2002 [1970], p. 43 onwards). Wave Hill Station was established by Nat 'Bluey' Buchanan in 1882 at Malyalyimalyalyi and Lipanangku (Lipananyku), an area of the Victoria River just downstream from what is now the Kalkaringi township. Gurindji country was first stocked with cattle in 1883 by Nat Buchanan and Sam Croker. Then, between 1903 and 1913, a number of small stations were built on what is now Limbunya Station, first by Jack Beasley who, along with Owen Cummins, is named as one of the main perpetrators of massacres in the southern Victoria River District (Manngayarri, 2016b; R. Wavehill, 2016a).

The first murder of a Gurindji person recorded by pastoralists occurred just after Nat 'Bluey' Buchanan established Wave Hill Station in 1882. Gordon Buchanan, Nat Buchanan's son, reports that Sam 'Greenhide' Croker, one of the men accompanying his father, shot an Aboriginal man for stealing a bucket and a couple of billies from the station. He was shot in the back while trying to escape. Killings became more frequent as Gurindji people started killing cattle, which began to severely undermine the economy of the cattle enterprise. Gurindji elder Ronnie Wavehill (2016a) and others detail the killings which occurred at the hands of the early colonists, for example at Tartarr (Blackfellows Knob), Warluk in Seale Gorge, where the bones of Gurindji ancestors lie today, and another massacre near Yurruj (Burtawurta). One reason the Gurindji people set up a new settlement at Daguragu after the 1966 Walk-Off was to repatriate bones from the Tartarr massacre to Palngarrawuny in Seale Gorge.

The wave of death continued west into neighbouring Malngin country with the establishment of a number of small stations on land that is now Limbunya Station. Jack Beasley is one name still remembered by Malngin and Gurindji people. Together with William Patterson, Beasley took up a grazing permit on Stirling Creek in 1903, which they named Mt Stirling. It was one of the small stations established between 1900 and 1913. Jimmy Manngayarri considers Beasley to have been the worst perpetrator of massacres in this area. Manngayarri (2016b) attributes the Yurruj (Burtawurta) and Ngima (Neave Gorge) massacres described by Ronnie Wavehill and Violet Wadrill to Beasley. Beasley also had a reputation for taking Aboriginal women against their will for his own sexual gratification. According to Manngayarri, one such woman, whom Beasley had beaten, escaped up a hill called Janpa. Beasley followed her up there, shot her and burnt her body with kerosene. Manngayarri also attributes the Kurturtu massacre to Beasley in another story. This massacre was also reported to

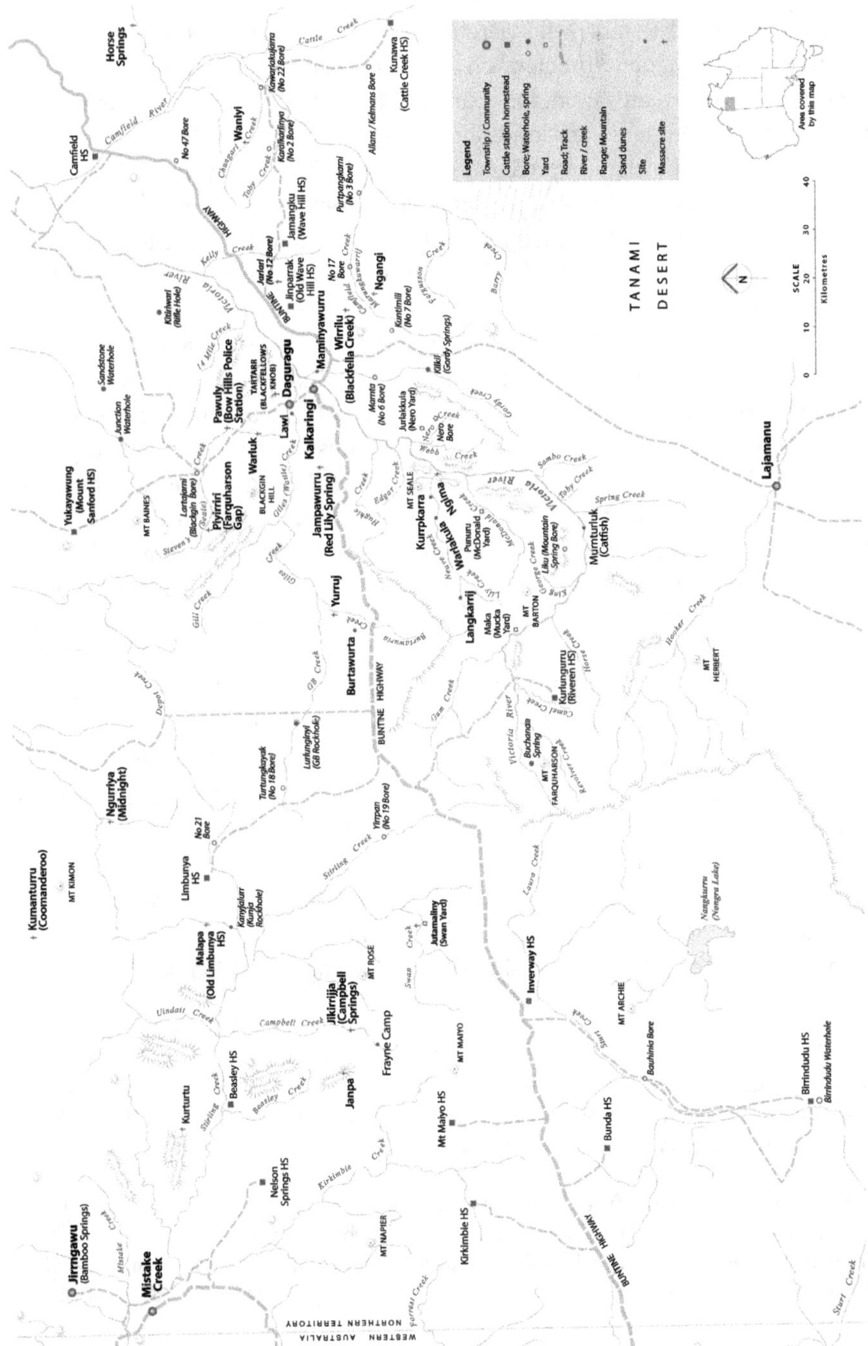

Figure 26: Massacres on Gurindji country during the early colonial period (Map: Brenda Thornley; Charola & Meakins, 2016c, pp. 28–29).

Catherine and Ronald Berndt, who were anthropologists employed in the 1940s to assess the Aboriginal labour 'problem' on the Vestey-owned cattle stations.

In the process of colonisation, the colonists also brought with them diseases that Aboriginal immune systems and traditional bush medicines could not cope with. These diseases actually slightly predated the arrival of the colonists in the Victoria River District as a wave of illness which came from already-settled areas in the north. Rose (1991, p. 75) suggests that small pox almost completely devastated the Karrangpurru before the settlers virtually wiped out this group in a series of massacres. Now only a handful of people from one family claim some Karrangpurru heritage.

Massacres became an officially sanctioned method of population control when a police station was set up in 1894. The site of the police station was on Bilinarra country at Balarrgi (Police Hole) on Gordon Creek which is a tributary of the Victoria River. Constable Willshire was the first police officer posted and he was later replaced by Sergeant O'Keefe who was stationed there until 1898 before the police station was moved to its current location at Timber Creek (Rose, 1991, p. 29). Constable Willshire kept diaries and in 1896 published an account of his time spent in the area. Although Willshire was condemned by pastoralists for interfering with their bloody attempts to secure land, he himself freely admitted to instigating and participating in numerous massacres.

On Gurindji country, Bow Hills Police Station was established in 1913 to quell the violence in the southern Victoria River District area. But, as with Willshire, the police acted on behalf of the pastoralists and little protection was afforded to the Gurindji, Malngin and Bilinarra people of the area. The policemen were Mounted Constable MacDonald and Mounted Constable Frank Keating, and Charcoal Pirtirtkunyu Jampin was their 'police boy'. Frank Keating was stationed at Bow Hills from June 1916 until his death there on 5 November 1916 and was buried there.[53,54] After his death, the station was moved to the current site and was renamed Wave Hill Police Station. At that time, it was close to the original site of Wave Hill Station at Lipanangku.[55]

> Kartiya-lu policeman-tu-ma nguyini nyawa-ma tipit-karra manani taiimap dragim. Tartartap nguyini kanya, tartartap nguyina kanya. Tartartap-warla big-chain-jawung-ma karnti-ka tipit. Tipit karnti-ka-ma policeman-tu-ma. Tipit. Na beltim kartapun beltim-parla. Beltim-ma warapik-ma luwanu-ma karlwarra-ma, kula kalu-warla nyampa-warla kungulu-ma kuyangka-ma running. Kuya-ngka-ma wangani wangani jurlimap.
>
> The policeman at Bow Hills used to tie Aboriginal people up. He would drag them along to the police station by chains and secure them to a tree. The policeman would chain them to a tree. Then he used to beat them. He beat them so badly that they couldn't get away and there'd be blood everywhere. That's when they'd set the dogs on them. (Manngayarri, 2016a, p. 198)

53 Northern Territory of Australia. *Report of the Administrator* 1918. Entry 30/9/1917.
54 Rose (1991: 71) gives the date as 1918 but that is too late.
55 Older Gurindji people pronounce this Lipananyku.

Mounted Constable Gordon Stott, who was posted to Timber Creek in the 1940s, continued this practice of police violence. He is notorious for his patrols of Waterloo and Limbunya Stations with the black tracker Kurnmali. Stories of his brutal acts against Gurindji, Malngin and other people are recounted by Banjo Ryan in Chapter 7 of *Yijarni: True Stories from Gurindji Country* (2016).

Gurindji people did not passively accept the onslaught of colonists. Ambushes and murders of pastoralists by Aboriginal men were not uncommon in the early years of occupation (Charola & Meakins, 2016a). Lewis (2012, p. 111) believes that the end of the 1890s seemed to mark the peak of Aboriginal resistance in the Victoria River District. After the 1890s, the reports of violence perpetrated by Aboriginal people became scarcer. Lewis speculates that Aboriginal numbers had decreased so much by this time that it had become difficult to maintain an active resistance to the occupation of Gurindji, Bilinarra, Malngin and Ngarinyman lands. By 1901, Wave Hill Station had a 'blacks camp' (Lewis, 2012, p. 115) and by 1910 there were 30 Aboriginal station hands working on the station. Ronnie Wavehill (2016b) recounts that a young boy was captured and trained as an interpreter, which is how Aboriginal people in the region came to work on the station located at Malyalyimalyalyi and Lipanangku, near present day Kalkaringi. Certainly, they were afforded more peace on the stations than remaining in the bush, although living and working conditions were undoubtedly appalling (Figure 27).

Figure 27: Children on Wave Hill Station in July 1920. Station conditions are evident from this photo. (Photo: Vestey Collection, courtesy of Charles Darwin University Library).

The original station at Malyalyimalyalyi and Lipanangku flooded in 1924 (see Figure 4) and then moved to Jinparrak. Most Gurindji people lived and worked at Jinparrak, along with Mudburra, Warlpiri, Bilinarra, Malngin and Ngarinyman people. This station was owned by the English lord, William Vestey, who was the largest land holder in Australia at the time, owning a number of cattle stations across the north of Australia (and in Argentina). The conditions of the Aboriginal people working and living on the stations were appalling, as recounted extensively by Gurindji people (Daguragu-Community-Council, 2000; Donald, 1998; Kijngayarri, 1986 (1974); B. Wavehill, 2016b). A report by Berndt and Berndt (1948), which was commissioned by the Vesteys to investigate the welfare of Aboriginal employees, concurs. It describes the working and living conditions as substandard. 250 people including 92 men lived in a small area. Gurindji people received no wages for their work. They worked as station hands and stockmen in exchange for goods such as tobacco, salted meat, flour, sugar, tea and occasionally clothes and blankets.

> When we were working there at the stock camp, Vestey said we were doing a good job. But we were living on just bread and corned beef at the stock camp. And every Friday we used to get four sticks of tobacco, one box of matches . . . When we used to go back to the station after two or three months of being out bush . . . we would try and ask the manager for blankets. But we couldn't just go into the store and ask for blankets or shirts or trousers or boots.
>
> (Roy Yunga in Daguragu-Community-Council, 2000)

Gurindji women were often forced into sexual liaisons with *kartiya* stockmen and many *pilyingpilying* children (<'red', now meaning 'part white heritage') resulted from these relationships who were subsequently taken by Native Welfare Officers, particularly Ted Evans and Creed Lovegrove, under the 1910 *Aborigines Act*. These children now constitute the Stolen Generations (Meakins, 2016a; M. Ryan, 2016; Wadrill, 2016a; B. Wavehill, 2016a). Gurindji children were taken to a number of places in the Northern Territory. The first, established in 1913, were Kahlin Compound (Darwin) and the Bungalow (Alice Springs Half-Caste Institution). Others were taken to Croker Island Mission, set up in 1941; the Retta Dixon Home, established by the Aborigines Inland Mission (AIM) in 1946; and Garden Point Catholic Mission and Snake Bay on Melville Island (Meakins, 2016a). Children were taken well into the 1970s. Some returned and found their families again, but many did not.

On Jinparrak, Gurindji people lived in humpies which were constructed from discarded material from the station. Fresh water had to be drawn and carried some distance from a well.

> We were treated just like dogs. We lived in humpies. You had to crawl in and out on your knees. There was no running water. The food was bad – just flour, tea, sugar and bits of beef – like the head or feet of a bullock.
>
> (Billy Bunter Jampijinpa in CLC, 1994)

Kula-ngantipa-kurlu punyuk jayingani mangarri-ma nyampa-ma nyila-ma money-ma lawara. Ngungantipangulu treatim manani warlaku-marraj, kamparrijang-payin-ma, ngayiny-ma ngaji-ma, ngamirni-ma ngayiny-ma. Ngumayijang-ma ngurnalu jirtart-parla karrinya kuya-wu-ma.

They never gave us enough food and that kind of thing, and no money. They treated us like dogs, the older people, my fathers and my mother's brothers. We younger ones got angry about that. (Kijngayarri, 1986 (1974): 306, 308–09)

As a result, the general health of people was low and the infant mortality rate very high. The Gurindji commonly liken these conditions to being treated like dogs, and despite Berndt and Berndt's candid report, little was changed.

Discontent ran high amongst the Aboriginal workers. Although many seemed resigned to their predicament, one Gurindji stockman, Sandy Moray Tipujurn, started agitating amongst the Gurindji. He had spent time travelling to other cattle stations in Queensland and Western Australia and had seen better examples of race relations and employment conditions. Tipujurn had big ideas which went beyond an industrial dispute. He wanted the Gurindji to retrieve their land and run their own cattle station. The opportunity to begin this process arose when another Gurindji stockman, Vincent Lingiari, was thrown from his horse and sent to Darwin to be treated. There he met unionists, Dexter Daniels, Bobby Tudawali and Brian Manning, who said that the NAWU (North Australian Workers Union) would support the Gurindji if they decided to strike. When Lingiari returned to Wave Hill station, he informed the station manager, Tom Fisher,[56] of their intention to strike. Then on the 23 August 1966, Lingiari gathered his people and they walked 16 kilometres to Jurnarni (Gordy Creek) and later to Daguragu which is a Ngamanpurru (Conkerberry) Dreaming place (eight kilometres from Kalkaringi and now an established Gurindji settlement). This event is now known as the Gurindji Walk Off. Various attempts over the years to convince the Gurindji *en masse* to return to the station failed. Some workers were sent back by Gurindji leaders to supplement welfare incomes, but most did not return. Eventually they were offered wages equal to those of *kartiya* stockmen. However, the Gurindji stood their ground.

Jurlukut ngungantipa yani yalangkuwarni yangkarra. 'Yanku-warla-nta wart-ma kaarnirra-ma?' 'Lawara! Kula-rnalu yanku. Kula-nngantipa ngarin nyampa-ma punyu jayinya. Wumara-ma, mangarri kula-nngantipa jayinya. Kula-rnalu yanku wart-ma, ngurnalu ngajik-parni murlang-kurra.' Ngurnalu karrinya yalangka kanyjurra ngajik. Namata ngungantipangulu yanani. Kula-rnalu wart-ma yani.

Tom Fisher (the manager of Wave Hill station) came to us. (He asked us), "Do you want to come back?" (We said), "No. We're not coming back. You didn't give us good meat or proper food or money. We're not coming back. We're going to stay right here". It didn't matter that they came to us. We didn't go back. (Donald, 1998)

56 Gurindji people used to call Tom Fisher *Jurlukut* which means 'big stomach' due to his pauch.

Although their protest had taken the form of a workers' strike, they had not stopped talking about reclaiming their traditional lands which had been taken over by the Vesteys. The NAWU, and in particular, a union activist from Sydney called Frank Hardy, continued to support the Gurindji. He helped them petition the federal government and raised money to fly Vincent Lingiari and other Gurindji stockmen including Mick Rangiari and Captain Major Lapngayarri to Sydney on a couple of occasions to talk to union and university crowds about station conditions and land issues.

Figure 28: Building new houses near the *partiki* (nut tree) at Daguragu: Long Johnny Kijngayarri, Captain Major Lapngayarri and Hoppy Mick Rangiari (Photo: Brian Manning 1967).

In 1975, after nine years of persistent campaigning and a change to a more liberal federal government, the then Australian Prime Minister Gough Whitlam flew to Daguragu to grant the Gurindji a lease for 3236km^2 of land around Daguragu. This event has been immortalised by Indigenous photo journalist Mervyn Bishop's photo of Gough Whitlam pouring soil into Vincent Lingiari's hands who was, by this stage, a much older man, and blind. Gurindji people saw this moment as a turning point in white-black relations in Australia, believing that they had finally won the respect of non-Indigenous people. Lingiari addressed a mixed crowd of Gurindji people, non-Indigenous supporters and Government officials, saying:

Nyawa jangkakarni kartiya-ma ngaliwanguny ngumpit-ku murlangkurra patati-yirri warik-karra ngulu yani nyampayila-rni kula nyampa-wu kuyawu-warla. Ngurlaa ngali jimarri karru kartiya ngumpin nyawa karrwa=lu langa-ngka-ma . . .Ngurra ngungalangkulu kanya ngulu linkarra kanya wart.

These important whitefellas have come here to our ceremonial ground and they are welcome, because they have not come for any other reason, just this handover. We will be mates, whitefellas and blackfellas. You (Gurindji) must keep this land safe for yourselves . . . They took our country away from us, now they have brought it back ceremonially.

(Lingiari, 1986 (1975), pp. 313–315)

Figure 29: A representative of the Vesteys speaks at the hand-back ceremony with Gough Whitlam, Les Johnston, Splinter Manguari, Vincent Lingiari and Goff Letts (Photo: Brian Manning 1975).

Ten years later, in 1986, they were granted the security of inalienable freehold title under the Northern Territory Land Rights Act. In 2020, Gurindji, Mudburra and Malngin were granted Native Title over Wave Hill Station and Limbunya Station. For a more detailed personal account of this sequence of events, see Frank Hardy's (1968) *The Unlucky Australians*. Other oral accounts from Gurindji people and interpretations of this period can be found in two articles by Minoru Hokari (2000, 2002). The period following the Walk-Off where the Gurindji attempted to take control of their lives, but were thwarted by various government responses, is described in detail by Ward (2016).

Little is known about the language situation at Wave Hill Station during the cattle station days, however reports from Berndt and Berndt (1987) paint a picture of multilingualism, with Gurindji and Mudburra as the dominant languages, and an Aboriginal variety of English emerging from contact with white station labour. The contact English variety described was probably the cattle station pidgin which was spoken across northern Australia at the time.

> Wave Hill was a centre of gradual but continuous intermingling of what have sometimes been called tribes with differing language, territorial and cultural affiliations ... for general purposes the *lingua franca* was either Gurindji or Mudbara (Mudburra) or usually a mixture of both. Few of the non-Walbiri (Warlpiri) people could either speaker or understand more than a few words of the language spoken by the Walbri . . . On account of their contact with Europeans, by whom so many of them were employed, most of the station people found it necessary to learn a certain amount of English. (Berndt & Berndt, 1987: 59)

Thus, it is likely that there were a number of pressures on Gurindji. First, other traditional languages spoken in the same community were either related to Gurindji, for example Mudburra, or mutually intelligible such as Bilinarra and Ngarinyman. Given this interaction, it is likely that some levelling between the languages took place. Additionally, an English-based cattle station pidgin was introduced probably by the Europeans and also by imported Aboriginal labour from Queensland. In many other areas of northern Australia, the pidgin was nativised into what is now known as Kriol and has replaced traditional languages in the process (Munro, 2000).

More information about the language situation after the Walk-Off is available. In 1970s McConvell was living and working at Daguragu with Gurindji people. He observed that the common discourse practice was code-switching between different dialects of Gurindji and a contact variety of English. In a recording of a conversation between Gurindji men who were slaughtering a cow for meat, called the 'Killer' video (see §1.5.8), he found that a third of all utterances contained code-switching. It is likely that this code-switching stabilised incrementally to form the youth variety of Gurindji called Gurindji Kriol. Gurindji Kriol has gained momentum among younger people and has spread north into Bilinarra and Ngarinyman country (McConvell & Meakins, 2005; Meakins, 2011b).

1.7.3 Gurindji life and language today

Nowadays most Gurindji people live on their traditional lands at Kalkaringi and Daguragu, with diaspora living in surrounding communities, regional centres such as Katherine and Darwin, and many other parts of Australia. Despite the dispersal of people, Kalkaringi and Daguragu remain the hub for Gurindji people. Therefore, this section will focus on Gurindji life and culture in these communities.

The name of the community, 'Kalkaringi', relates to a waterhole nearby called 'Kalkarriny'. It was originally given to the airstrip as 'Kalkurung' which was first built near this waterhole. Later when the airstrip was re-positioned on the other side of the Daguragu road, it was re-named. The township was originally named Libanangu (after the waterhole below the police station, Lipanangku) but the name was changed to 'Kalkaringi' after the airstrip was re-named and then 'Kalkarindji' in 1986. The '-dji' seems to have been added at some point to indigenise it (ironically) or to accommodate to the then majority Warlpiri residents who do not have consonant-final words, hence 'Kalkarindji' (McConvell, 2002a, p. 52). This was common practice at the time, for example Kildurk (see map in Figure 1) was renamed Amanbidji which is actually based on *ngamanpurru* 'conkerberry' with an added '-dji'. The Gurindji community themselves spell the name 'Kalkaringi' (although pronounced /j/) so we follow this spelling in this grammar. Gurindji people themselves refer to Kalkaringi as 'Wave Hill' (if they are away travelling) or 'Settlement' (if they are in the communities) which is in reference to the old Wave Hill Welfare Settlement. On the other hand, Daguragu is the original Gurindji name for the location of this community.

Kalkaringi and Daguragu are small remote Aboriginal communities located eight kilometres apart (see map in Figure 1). They are reached from a mostly single lane sealed road called the Buchanan Highway. Kalkaringi has a reasonable-sized shop, a small hospital run by Katherine West Health Board, a creche and a school which caters for primary and secondary students. Kalkaringi is also the location of Victoria Daly Shire Office, a Federal government office (originally set up during the Intervention, see below), and a number of Gurindji-controlled organisations including Karungkarni Arts, Gurindji Corporation and the Central Land Council office. For the past decade, mobile phone coverage has been available in a 25km radius. Daguragu consists only of houses, the Murnkurrumurnkurru CLC ranger office, a basketball court and football field. A school bus and shop bus make regular trips between Daguragu and Kalkaringi. The community also used to have a small clinic, shop, bakery and some Batchelor Institute buildings, but they no longer exist. Gurindji people regularly travel to Lajamanu (1.5 hrs drive), Nitjpurru (Pigeon Hole) (2 hrs drive) and Yarralin (5 hrs drive) to visit family. There is a commercial bus service to Katherine (5 hrs) and Darwin (9 hrs).

Gurindji attempts to direct and control their own lives have been undermined at various points since their resistance to colonisation in the late 1800s and the 1966 Walk-Off. Most recently, the community faced the double blow of the Intervention and the establishment of Shires, which diminished local control of Aboriginal communities in the Northern Territory and centralised governance to a Federal and Shire level. In 2007 the Intervention (later known as the Northern Territory National Emergency Response) began under John Howard, the then Prime Minister of Australia. The premise for the Intervention was the alleged rampant child abuse in remote Northern Territory communities, publicised in a news story that was later found to be fabricated. No prosecutions for so-called paedophile rings were ever made, but increased numbers of children were taken away by the Family and Children's Services (FACS) under the premise of neglect. Shires were established at the same time which meant the local Gurindji-governed Daguragu Community Council was disbanded. All of the community-owned buildings were taken over by the Victoria Daly Shire, the bakery was shut down and much of their equipment including large machinery was distributed among other communities in the Shire.

Due to the isolation of Kalkaringi, Gurindji children spend time on their country and are continuing to learn about Gurindji country, its associated Dreamings, stories and practices associated with country such as gathering bush foods and medicines. Gurindji people spend time during Wet Season, fishing, hunting and finding traditional foods. This time coincides with the two month school holiday break. Employment of Gurindji men as stockmen by surrounding cattle stations such as Wave Hill, Camfield and Delamere has also ensured that traditional knowledge about country is being passed down. In particular, the ranger program at Kalkaringi has ensured there is a continuity in passing on ecological and cultural knowledge because the program is structured around elders and intergenerational transmission. Similarly, Karungkarni Arts is usually a hub of artists painting their Dreamings and country surrounded by members of younger generations listening to the associated stories and knowledge. Nonetheless the fixed nature of the station roads and the extensive use of vehicles and horses, rather than walking, has had a significant impact on the transmission of traditional knowledge about Gurindji country. Station roads have ensured continuing access to many sites while others are now rarely visited.

Similarly, isolation from Western medicine, despite the presence of a small hospital, ensures that traditional medicinal practices are relatively strong. For example, Gurindji women still 'cook babies'.[57] This procedure involves heating *tamarra* 'termite mound' on a fire and smoking babies' backs and bottoms. The *tamarra* is also burnt down on a fire of *ngirirri* wood (Hakea arborescens) and mixed with water to create a muddy mixture which is slathered on the babies and also fed to them. After the mixture dries, children are then bathed in washes involving *kupuwupu* 'native lemon grass' and other plants. This style of medicine treats immediate ailments such as skin sores and diarrhoea, and is also a preventative measure aimed at helping babies develop strong backs, legs and hips in preparation for crawling and walking. Gurindji women practise many other treatments and are proud of the health of their children and adults (Wadrill et al., 2019, pp. 19–34). Advice about ailments which are not cured by traditional medicines is often sought from local medicine men and women called *kurrwararn* (known locally as 'witchdoctors') who deal with the supernatural causes of illness.

---

57 This term often has newcomers to the community worried about the treatment of children, however the Gurindji verb *kamparnana* which translated as 'cook' is also used to mean 'treat with heat' (§7.1.1.2). The Kriol word *kukim* is now used in its place but expresses a similar semantic range. Similarly, the Gurindji verb *jiyarnana* which is generally translated as *barnim* 'burn' or *jumokim* 'smoke' in Kriol also extends to the practice of smoking babies using leaves with medicinal properties (§7.1.1.2).

The current status of the Gurindji language is similar to Gurindji culture – maintenance occurs, but in a fragmented manner. Although the traditional language of Kalkaringi and Daguragu is Gurindji, the mixed language Gurindji Kriol is now the main language of the younger generations born after the 70s (Meakins, 2008). Kriol, Aboriginal English and Standard Australian English are also found, although their use is less frequent. A lot of cross-over exists in the sounds, grammar and vocabulary of these languages. Gurindji Kriol is the most radical amalgam of these languages, combining equal elements from the grammar and vocabulary of Gurindji and Kriol. The Aboriginal English spoken at Kalkaringi is also influenced by the Gurindji sound inventory and some grammar (Jones, 1978; Jones & Meakins, 2013b; Jones, Meakins, & Muawiyath, 2012; Stewart, Meakins, Algy, Ennever, & Joshua, 2020; Stewart, Meakins, Algy, & Joshua, 2018). Finally, Kriol contains grammatical structures which later developed under the influence of Gurindji. This influence is schematically shown in Figure 30.

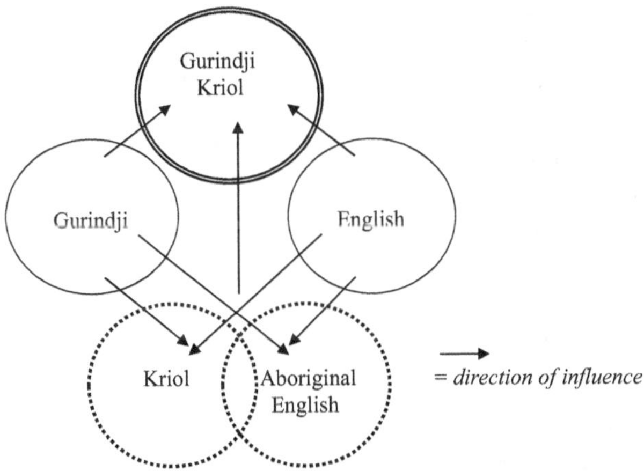

Figure 30: Language ecology of Kalkaringi (Meakins, 2011b, p. 59).

The following example is a snapshot of the type of speech between 40 year old and 20 year old women, which is characteristic of conversation from Kalkaringi. This conversation was recorded in the nearby Ngarinyman community of Yarralin on an overnight trip from Kalkaringi in August 2005. The first topic of conversation is about where another group of people have gone fishing. The second excerpt is a discussion about a type of ashes which are used to flavour chewing tobacco and where to find them around Yarralin. The speakers are SS (19 ys old), CA (21 yrs old), EO (48 yrs old) and FO (43 yrs old). The women have close relationships with each other. FO and EO are sisters. CA is the adopted daughter of FO, and she also calls EO "mother". SS calls both FO and EO "sister" because her adopted mother was the classificatory sister of the mother of EO and FO. All Gurindji words and morphemes are italicised, with Kriol elements remaining in plain font.

(9) (a) SS: Chloe-mob weya dei bin gon bij-in-bat?
Chloe-GROUP where 3PL.S PST go fish-CONT-ATEL
"Chloe and that lot – where did they go fishing?"

(b) EO: *Marntaj* wi kan *liwart* hiya wi *ngurra*
OK 1PL.S can wait here 1PL.S camp

nyawa-ngka=rni.
this-LOC=ONLY
"OK we can wait here, we'll camp here."

(c) FO: *Wanyji-ka=warla nyila ngu=lu ya-ni*?
which-LOC=FOC that CAT=3AUG.S go-PST
"Where did they go?"

(d) CA: Dei neba tok *ngayiny* dei bin jas tok
3PL.S NEG talk 1MIN.DAT 3PL.S PST just talk

"ai-m gon bij-in".
"1SG.S-PRS go fish-CONT
"They didn't talk to me, they just said 'I'm going fishing'."

(e) FO: Wal *yangki pa-rra nganayirla.*
well ask hit-IMP whats.it.name
"Well ask whats-his-name."

. . ..

(f) CA: Milktin-*ta* raitful *kawurn=ma*,
milk.tin-LOC full ashes=TOP

kuya-ny na wait-wan-*walija.*
thus-NMLZ now white-NMLZ-PAUC
"There's loads of ashes in the milk tin, lots of that white stuff now."

(g) EO: *Wanyji-ka=warla* dei ged-im-bat *kawurn*?
which-LOC=FOC 1PL.S get-TR-ATEL ashes
"Where are they getting ashes from?"

(h) CA: Hiya la Lingara Road-*ta* jamweya dei bin ged-im-bat.
here LOC Lingara Road-LOC somewhere 1PL.S PST get-TR-ATEL
"Here on the Lingara road, they've been getting it."

(i) CA: Dei bin ged-im-bat Kawurla-mob-*tu=ma*.
they PST get-TR-ATEL name-GROUP-ERG=TOP
"They got it, Kawurla and that lot."

. . ..

(j) EO: *Ngu=lu* *ma-nku* na *purrinyji-ngka* na ib dei
CAT=3AUG.S get-POT SEQ afternoon-LOC SEQ if 1PL.S

kam.
come
"They can get it in the afternoon, if they come back in time."
(Meakins, 2008, pp. 285–286)

In this conversation, the older women, EO and FO speak Gurindji and Gurindji Kriol, and switch between these languages. For example, in (c) and (e), FO speaks only Gurindji when asking where a group of people have gone fishing. EO uses Gurindji Kriol in (b) to suggest that they wait for the group and camp overnight. CA speaks Gurindji Kriol predominantly, for example in (f) when she describes where to find some ashes. The speech of SS is very similar to CA. Both the older and younger women also switch between languages in various ways. Language switching can occur between speakers of different generations. For example, in (c) FO asks CA where some people have gone in Gurindji. CA replies in Gurindji Kriol in (d) and FO follows with a command in Gurindji. Switching also occurs within a sentence. In (j) EO tells CA when some other people can collect ashes. She begins in Gurindji and then switches to Kriol halfway through. Another pattern of switching is the insertion of a single word or suffix into a sentence of a different language. For instance, in (e) FO uses a Kriol discourse marker *wal* 'well' in an otherwise Gurindji sentence. CA also uses this mixing strategy in (d), (h) and (i), however these sentences represent a more grammaticalised form of mixing, Gurindji Kriol (Meakins, 2008, pp. 286–287). The differences between Gurindji Kriol and code-switching between Gurindji and Kriol are discussed in Meakins (2012).

The mixed language Gurindji Kriol is characterised by a split in the verb and nominal structure. The core of the Gurindji clause including the inflecting verb (§7.1) and bound pronouns (§6.2) has been replaced by Kriol verbs. Gurindji bound pronouns are no longer used but the free pronouns are. The only part of the Gurindji two-part complex verb remaining are coverbs (§7.2) which are used as main verbs in the mixed language clause, and an asymmetrical serial verb construction has also developed (Meakins, 2010a). Tense, aspect and mood categories are marked by free Kriol morphemes such as *bin* 'past' and *garra* 'potential', with only little Gurindji morphology remaining (Meakins, 2016b). Despite the dominance of Kriol in the verb structure, much of the Gurindji nominal structure remains in the form of case marking (e.g. ergative, dative, locative, allative and ablative) albeit with some allomorphic reduction and change (Meakins, 2011a). Also present is other inflectional morphology and derivational morphology (§4.5.3). Lexically both Gurindji and Kriol contribute to the mix. Approximately 1/3 of vocabulary is Gurindji-derived, 1/3 of vocabulary is Kriol-derived and the remaining 1/3 contains synonymous forms which can be expressed by either language.

The structural split of the mixed language is given below. The same sentence is given in Kriol, Gurindji and the mixed language. The relevant contributions of Gurindji and Kriol are in plain font and optional elements are given in brackets:

(10) 'The man speared the goanna with a stick.'

Kriol:

Det	man	im=in	spiya-im	(im)	det	guana	gat	jik.
the	man	3SG=PST	spear-TR	3SG	the	goanna	PROP	stick

Gurindji Kriol:

Man(*-tu*)	(i)	bin	*jarrwaj*	(im)	dat	guana	*karnti-yawung.*
man-ERG	3SG	PST	spear	3SG	the	goanna	stick-PROP

Gurindji:

Ngumpit-tu	*ngu-ø-ø*	*jarrwaj*	*pu-nya*	*kirrawa*	*karnti-yawung-kulu.*
man-ERG	CAT-3SG-3SG	spear	poke-PST	goanna	spear-PROP-ERG

(Meakins & O'Shannessy, 2010, p. 1697)

In (10), the core Gurindji Kriol VP structure *i bin jarrwaj im* 'he speared him' is drawn from Kriol, while the nominal structure including case marking originates from Gurindji. Note, however, that a Gurindji coverb is used in the Kriol-based VP structure, and similarly a Kriol noun occurs with Gurindji inflectional morphology *man-tu* 'man-ERG'. The structural split of Gurindji Kriol has been described in more detail elsewhere (Meakins, 2011a, 2011b).

1.8 The Gurindji kinship system

As is common across Indigenous Australia, the kinship system determines Gurindji social organisation and family relationships. Gurindji kinship is very complex and underlies how people behave with each other, who marries whom, responsibilities and obligations with respect to family, ceremonial business, and land ownership and management.

Despite the changes to many aspects of the Gurindji language and culture, the kinship system and subsection membership are still fully understood and used by all members of the community (even the youngest children) (§1.8.1). Note that that the tri-relationship kinterms are little used and understood now. The patrimoiety system is also little used, but probably always only played a role in ceremonial life, with little currency more broadly. The kinship system is also expressed through *takataka* 'sign language', discussed in §1.8.2. Mother-in-law speech is an interesting linguistic aspect of the kinship system, but is no longer used (§1.8.3). We also include a section discussing the historical documentation of the kinship system. As with the historical notes on tribal boundaries, this section is included mostly for historical interest and also to help direct Gurindji people to archival sources (§1.8.4). Chapter 4 includes more detail about linguistic aspects of kinterms and the tri-relational kinship system which is very complex.

1.8.1 Gurindji subsections, moieties and kinterms

Subsections, which are called 'skin names' locally by Gurindji people, are an important part of the kinship system. The Gurindji community is divided according to a system of eight subsections. All Gurindji people have a skin name, reflecting their subsection grouping, which they generally inherit through their mother. For example, the children of a woman belonging to the Nawurla subsection will be Nangari (for a girl) and Jangari (for a boy). Each of the eight subsections has a different name for its male and female members, which typically differs in the initial consonant ('J' for male and 'N' for female). There are therefore eight male skin names and eight female skin names, which are divided into two patrimoiety sets, which relate to the Warlawurruwuny and Jarlwawuny moieties, and two Purnturtu generations (§1.7.1). They are given in brother-sister pairs below, e.g. Jampijina and Nampijina are brother and sister. People are often addressed and referred to by their subsection names, rather than personal names. The subsections are given in Figure 31. The letter-number codes come from Radcliffe-Brown (1930–31) and have been widely used by anthropologists to show equivalence of different terms in different groups, including by Stanner (1934).

	Warlawurruwuny Yilyiku Eagle patrimoiety		Jarlwawuny Lirraku Heron patrimoiety	
A1	Janama (m)	B1	Jurlama (m)	Purnturtu generational division
	Nanaku (f)		Nawurla (f)	
A2	Jukurtayi (m)	B2	Jangala (m)	
	Namija (f)		Nangala (f)	
D1	Japalyi (m)	C1	Japarta (m)	Purnturtu generational division
	Nalyirri (f)		Nimarra (f)	
D2	Jangari (m)	C2	Jampin (m)	
	Nangari (f)		Nampin (f)	

Figure 31: Skin groups (subsections) and their patrimoieties in Gurindji (based on McConvell, 1982a, p. 90).

Note that some skin names have alternatives, which come from other languages in some cases:
- Jukurtayi (Jimija, Jungurra)[58]
- Japalyi (Japanyi, Jalyirri)
- Jampin[59] (Jampijina)
- Nampin (Nampijina)

A few short forms of the skin names also exist. Some of them may have originally been something like the 'junior' skin names observed for other groups which are given to children, but they are not explained by the Gurindji as this.
- Nanaku (Nana)
- Namija (Namij)
- Nimarra (Nima)
- Nalyirri (Nyanyi)
- Jukurtayi (Jukurt)

Figure 32 below shows how skin names are inherited through the mother. It also shows the first and second choice marriage partners for the skin names. These marriages are referred to as *jutu*[60] or *linku* or 'straight marriages' in the local English variety. A man who is a woman's 'straight skin' or correct marriage partner is called *manyjiwan*.

58 The canonical form for this subsection was Jungurra when McConvell first began his work, but shifted to Jukurtayi sometime afterwards. Jukurtayi is currently the canonical form.
59 Actually, it is likely that 'Jampin' is really a long vowel i.e. 'Jampiyin' and the same for Nampin, but the community write these without the long vowel, an orthographic practice which we follow here.
60 The word *jutu* more generally refers to 'straight, correct'.

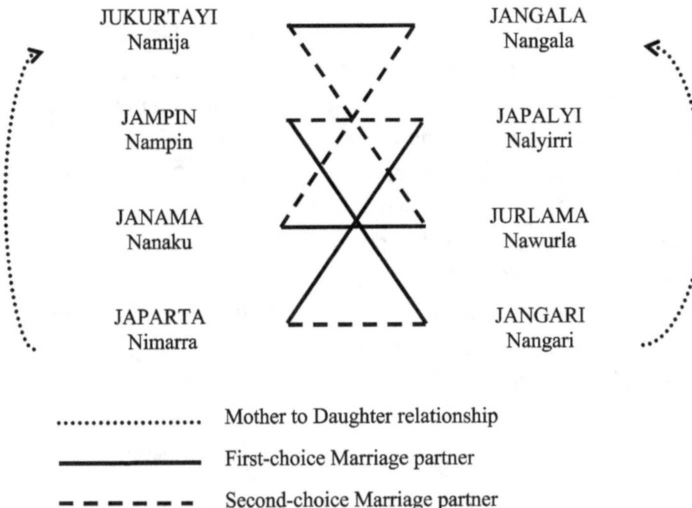

Figure 32: The subsection system in Gurindji.

Many Gurindji people have two skin names. This has come about as the older promised marriage system, whereby a young girl was promised to an older man called *luku*, has been replaced by love matches. The practice has been going on for generations, perhaps forever. It is not a new phenomenon. As a result, often young people marry outside of the traditional confines of first and second choice marriage, called *waji* 'wrong-way marriage'.[61] Children who result from 'wrong-way marriage' then inherit a skin name through their mother and also through their father. Usually, they use their skin name from their mother, but sometimes from their father if he is Gurindji and their mother is not.

Gurindji family relations map onto this skin system. A list of the main kinship terms is given in Figure 33. Gurindji family relations are based on kinship which the skin system summarises. A list of the main kinship terms was given in Figure 33, and how they relate to skin groups is demonstrated in the family tree in Figures 34 and 35. The family tree is given for just two subsections – Nangari and Jangari. Note that same-sex siblings are treated alike in this system (since they will belong to the same subsection), so the same term is used to refer to one's mother and one's mother's sisters, for example. In the grandparent generation, this gender divide disappears with all siblings related to one's mother's mother including great-uncles referred to as *jaju*.

A number of Gurindji family relations require specific behaviour. For example, mothers-in-law and sons-in-law who call each other *mali* have an avoidance relationship, which means that they cannot talk to each other, name each other, make eye contact, or be within each other's physical proximity. They must pass things to

61 Interestingly, *waji* is also the word for 'rainbow' – the general semantics is probably 'crooked'.

each other with two hands (the left hand supporting the right). A lesser avoidance relationship occurs between opposite sex siblings after the brother has gone through initiation ceremony. They cannot touch each other, say each other's names or make eye contact. They also generally avoid talking to each other. This behaviour among Gurindji people has been described in more detail by McConvell (1982a, pp. 93–94). In earlier times, when communication between people who were in a *mali* relationship was necessary, a particular speech register ('mother-in-law speech') was used. More information this register can be found in §1.8.3.

Other relationships have joking behaviour associated with them. For example, Gurindji people joke with their *ngamirni* 'uncle, mother's brother'. Upon approaching an uncle, the niece or nephew playfully hits him. The uncle tolerates this, only retaliating with obscene propositions and strong language. Again more detail about these relationships can be found in McConvell's (1982a, pp. 97–99) description of Gurindji kinship behaviour.

kawurlu, kapuku	sister (and FaBrDa, WiBrWi)	*ngalawuny*	man's child (and BrCh and man's SiCh
ngapa,[62] *papa*	older brother (and FaBrSo, WiSoHu)	*kurturtu*	woman's child
karlaj	younger sibling	*mukurl*	aunt (FaSi, MoBrWi, FaFaFaSi)
ngamayi[63]	mother (and her sisters, MoBrDa[64])	*ngamirni*	uncle (MoBr, FaSiHu, MoBrSo[35])
ngaji[65]	father (and FaBr, FaFaFa, FaFaFaBr)	*ngumparna*	husband (and his brothers)
pakutu, parnku, parnkuti	cousin (FaSiCh, MoBrCh)	*mungkaj*	wife (and her sisters)
lamparra	man's father-in-law (and his siblings and DaHu)	*ngapuju*	father's mother and siblings (woman's SoCh, SiSoCh)
kurriji	woman's mother-in-law (and her siblings and a woman's DaHuS)	*jawiji*	mother's father and siblings (man's DaCh, BrDaCh)
mali	man's mother-in-law (and her siblings and woman's son-in-law, HuMoBr)	*kaku*	father's father and siblings (man's SoCh, BrSoCh)
punkarli	WiMoMo (and her siblings), HuMoMo	*jaju*	mother's mother and siblings (woman's DaCh, SiDaCh), MoMoBrCh[35]
ngajala	sister-in-law (HuSi, WiSi)	*ngunyarri*	MoMoMo (and her siblings)
ngunang	brother-in-law (WiBr, HuBr)	*kaminyjarr*	woman's DaCh, SiDaCh
kanyirri	MoBrDaCh		

Figure 33: Gurindji kinterms and their English glosses.

A number of exclamations are also associated with particular kin. For example, *wangkawangka* is exclaimed by a man to his uncle if the latter swears at him. *Ngakuny* is an exclamation said to a wife's brother if the mother's brother swears at him. *Wartiwarti* is said to a sister if she swears.

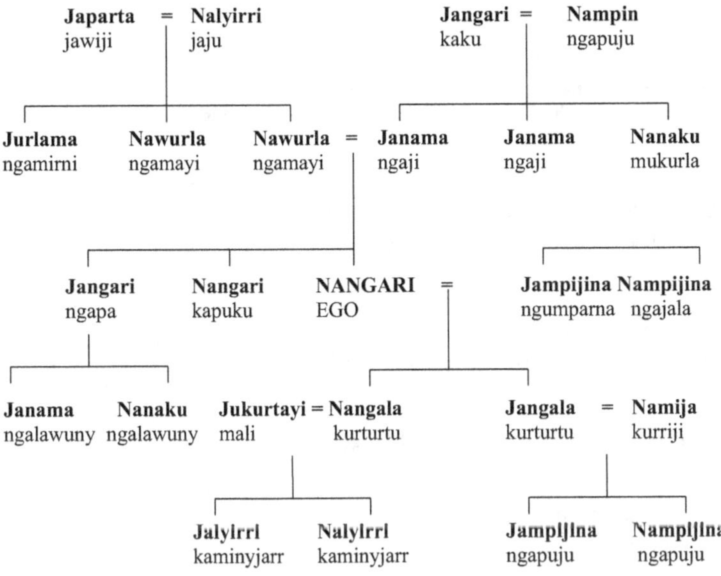

Figure 34: A basic Gurindji family tree for any woman called 'Nangari'.

1.8.2 Kin signs

Gurindji sign language is used alongside a number of spoken languages as an auxiliary language, although it is a primary language for some Gurindji deaf. This form of communication is known locally as Takataka.[66] The work reported here was under-

62 This term is no longer in use, perhaps because the Warlpiri word for 'water' is *ngapa* which is more widely known.

63 This kinterm has an old *-yi* suffix which is now frozen, although *ngama* can still be used as an address form (vocative). The *-yi* suffix has the *-ji* cognate in other languages where it has not been lenited. This suffix *-yi* is more productive in the western Ngumpin languages such as Wanyjirra (Senge, 2016, pp. 160–161). Nash (1992, p. 128) suggests the suffix is probably an old 1st person minimal non-subject form.

64 This classification comes about from a matrilineal skewing rule.

65 This term is not used by younger generations who understand it to mean 'God'.

66 The word Takataka is borrowed from Warlpiri *rdakardaka* 'sign language' which relates to *rdaka* 'hand'. The Gurindji word for hand is *wartan*, but it is not used to describe sign language. *Takataka* is recognised as a Gurindji word (Meakins et al., 2013, p. 353).

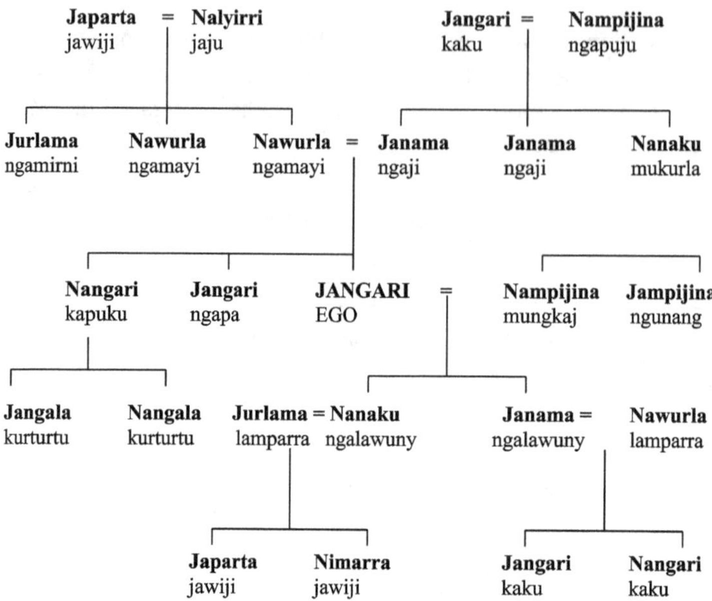

Figure 35: A basic Gurindji family tree for any man called 'Jangari'.

taken by Jenny Green, Cassandra Algy and Felicity Meakins and some of it is reported in Green, Meakins and Algy (forthcoming).

Kinship signs constitute an important domain of Takataka. In many sign languages in Australia, kinship signs are anchored in the body (Green, Bauer, Gaby, & Ellis, 2018; Kendon, 1988). Kendon (1988, p. 352) observes that almost all kinship signs consist of "pointing to some part of the body". This is in part related to the cultural practice of observing bodily sensations associated with particular kin, and to embodied practices of interaction – carrying, suckling, sitting side by side, and the converse – the avoidance of direct contact with particular kin.

There are eight common kin signs and several variations that may reflect individual or regional differences. A single sign encodes FATHER-NGAJI/AUNT-MUKURLA/MAN'S CHILD-NGALAWUNY (Figure 36)(a).[67,68] It is formed by touching the chin. The handshape varies and may be an index finger (characteristic of older generations) or a loosely cupped hand or fist. Some signers stroke the chin downwards, as if outlining an imaginary beard. The polysemy of signs MOTHER-NGAMAYI and WOMAN (Figure 36) (b) is typologically common in sign languages of the world (Wilkinson, 2009). The sign is formed by touching the chest with a fist (Green et al., 2019, p. 400; Kendon, 1988, p. 339).

67 We follow sign language conventions by referring to signs using small caps.
68 Note that all sign images contain QR codes which link to a video showing the signer demonstrating the sign.

Some variation is evident in the Gurindji signs for siblings and cross-cousins. The sign for SISTER-KAPUKU articulates with the nose (Figure 36)(d), is typologically unusual, and, to our knowledge this sign is not attested in other Australian Indigenous sign languages.[69] The sign BROTHER-PAPA (Figure 36)(e) articulates with either shoulder (although predominately the left). Some signers contrast the sibling signs with those for CROSS.COUSIN-PAKURTU (Figure 36)(f), while others group male cross-

Figure 36: Gurindji signs for kin a) FATHER-NGAJI/AUNT-MUKURL/MANS.CHILD-NGALAWINY (demonstrated by Georgina King) b) MOTHER-NGAMAYI (demonstrated by Jeffrey Barry) c) MOTHERS.MOTHER-JAJU (demonstrated by Cassandra Algy) d) SISTER-KAPUKU (demonstrated by Junior King) e) BROTHER-PAPA f) CROSS.COUSIN-PAKURTU (both demonstrated by Tara Long) (Green et al., 2017).

69 The only other reported Australian Indigenous kin sign that articulates to the nose is a Ngatajara [Ngaatjatjarra] one for FATHER (Kendon, 1988, p. 348). Our recent research with Ngaatjatjarra speakers shows that the current sign FATHER articulates with the chin as does the Gurindji sign (Green et al., 2018, p. 22). In Ngaatjatjarra pointing to the nose indicates the 1st person pronoun.

cousins with the BROTHER-PAPA sign (shoulder) and female cross-cousins with SISTER-KAPUKU (nose). The most significant variation in the sibling signs is found with older signers who employ the left and right sides of the body to distinguish between 'sister' and 'brother', with the right calf used for 'brother' and the left for 'sister'.[70] This use of the body is aligned with spoken language terminologies that lexicalise the sides of the body on the basis of embodied actions typically associated with men and women. In spoken Gurindji *warrara-wu-ny* 'brandish.spear-DAT-NMLZ' refers to the right side of the body and *juluj-ku-ny* 'carry.on.hip-DAT-NMLZ' (e.g. coolamon, child) to the left side. These terms are different from the *jutu(mparra)* 'right' and *jampu(karra)* 'left'[71] which are words referring to the hand and forearm, and which do not extend to other parts of the body or are projected more abstractly to position objects in space (see §5.2 for more information about spatial relations).

The sign SPOUSE-/SISTER IN LAW/FATHER'S MOTHER is formed by touching the back of the left hand with the palm of the right Figure 37(a). This is a commonly used sign throughout the desert regions. The sign for avoided kin such as mothers-in-law or sons-in-law is also common, formed by a flat hand that moves close to or touches the side of the face, signifying the action of turning away or averting the eyes to avoid direct contact with such kin Figure 37(b).

Figure 37: a) SPOUSE-/SISTER.IN.LAW/FATHERS.MOTHER (demonstrated by Nigel Bernard) b) MOTHER.IN.LAW/SON.IN.LAW-MALI (demonstrated by Tara Long) (Green et al., 2017).

70 Archival session: SIGN-20180607-03.

71 Another word for 'right-hand' is *jutungarrka* and other words for 'left-hand' are *wartiwarti, wirlkirri* and *jirrpintikarra*. Note that *jutu* also means 'correct, straight' (Meakins et al., 2013).

1.8.3 Mother-in-law speech

Gurindji, like many Australian languages, has a specialised speech register called *pirntika* used between a *malirlang* 'mother-in-law and son-in-law'. The term *pirntika* derives from *pirnti* 'side' and *-ka* 'locative', which indicates the indirectness of the language. Gurindji mother-in-law speech is no longer used, but is described in detail by McConvell (1982a) and see also Meakins and Nordlinger (2014, pp. 41–42) for a description of Bilinarra mother-in-law speech based on recordings made by McConvell in the 1970s.

As stated before, Gurindji people generally do not address their *mali*, but when it is necessary to communicate, speech is highly indirect. Mother-in-law register can be characterised by four features: (i) the replacement of some vocabulary items, particularly nouns and coverbs, see Table 7; (ii) the use of a general inflecting verb *luwa-* 'strike', which is a Class 2 verb in Eastern dialects and a Class 1 verb in Western dialects (see also §7.1.1), see (11) and (13); (iii) the use of the interjection *wartirri* 'sorry', see (13); (iv) the avoidance of second person pronouns, (11) and (13); and (v) the replacement of minimal pronouns with augmented pronouns, (11) and (13). These adjustments are also found in Malngin and Jaru (Ise, 1998, p. 53; Tsunoda, 1981, p. 215).

Table 7: Some Gurindji avoidance speech terms documented by McConvell (1982a, p. 95).[72]

Normal Gurindji	Pirntika	English gloss
ngawa	wirrija	water
ngarin	jarrurrung	meat, animal
mangarri	mayingarn	vegetable food
mila	ngapanyji	eye
jamana	yanu-yawung	foot → go-PROP
yawu	pinka-ngarna	fish → river-ASSOC
kuljany	jawurl	snake → saliva
ngurra	purnturr	camp
janga	kumuyung	sick

Mother-in-law register (Pirntika):

(11) Wirrija luwa=yina pilirli-marnany-ku.
water VERB=them grandmother-your-DAT
"Take water to your maternal grandmother." (McConvell, 1982a, p. 94)

72 Ise (1998, p. 52) also records some avoidance words in Malngin: *mayingany* 'vegetable food', *jarrurrung* 'meat', *wirrija* 'water', *walayira* 'tobacco'.

Equivalent in standard Gurindji:

(12) Ngawa ka-ngka=rla nyununy-ku jaju-wu.
water take-IMP=to.her your-DAT grandmother-DAT
"Take water to your maternal grandmother." (McConvell, 1982a, p. 94)

Mother-in-law register (Pirntika):

(13) Wartirri nganta=lu luwa-wu kuya-partak.
sorry perhaps=they VERB-POT thus-THITH
"Oh dear! Maybe they will go that way." (McConvell, 1982a, p. 96)

Equivalent in standard Gurindji:

(14) Ya-nta kayirra.
go-IMP north
"Go north!" (McConvell, 1982a, p. 96)

Mother-in-law register (Pirntika):

(15) Ngayu-wayin nyamu=yi=nga paya-rna-nta kuya=ma jawurl-lu=ma.
me-too REL=me=DUB bite-IMPF-IMP this=TOP saliva-ERG=TOP
"If saliva had been biting me like that." (McConvell, 1982a, p. 96)

Equivalent in standard Gurindji:

(16) Ngu-ngku paya-rni kuljany-ju?
CAT=you bite-PST snake-ERG
"Did a snake bite you?" (McConvell, 1982a, p. 96)

Mother-in-law speech also shows the replacement of second person pronouns with first person minimal inclusive pronouns =*ngali* or =*rli* 'you and I', as shown in (17) and (19).

Mother-in-law register (Pirntika):

(17) Nyawa ngu=ngali purnturr.
this CAT=you&me camp
"The camp." (Literally: The camp of ours) (McConvell, 1982a, p. 97)

Equivalent in standard Gurindji:

(18) Nyawa ngurra.
this camp
"The camp."

Mother-in-law register (Pirntika):

(19) Nyawa ngu=rna=ngali kumuyung.
this CAT=I=you&me sick
"I am sick." (Literally: I am sick for us) (McConvell, 1982a, p. 97)

Equivalent in standard Gurindji:

(20) Ngayu=ma=rna janga.
me=TOP=I sick
"I am sick."

1.8.4 Earlier work on kinship

Gurindji kinship has been of interest to anthropologists since the late 1800s. Mathews (1901, p. 71) lists some of the common socio-cultural characteristics of the Victoria River Groups, including the eight subsection system, with terms very similar to current Gurindji terms and the patrimoieties White Necked Heron and Eaglehawk which are the same in meaning as the current patrimoieties Jarlwa-wu-ny ('belonging to Heron') and Warlawurru-wu-ny ('belonging to Eagle') respectively. For the functions of subsections and moieties, see §1.7.1 and §1.8.1. In the case of subsections, each language group (Gurindji, Bilinarra, Ngarinyman, Malngin etc) has slightly different forms of the terms and these too have largely been maintained without change by the Gurindji from the 1890s when this information was collated.

Mathews (1901, p. 71) also notes the fact that "patches of country are said to belong to certain totems" ('totems' are mostly what current Gurindji people refer to as 'Dreamings'). Specific examples of the latter pattern of country belonging to 'totems' are not given for Gurindji or Jiyil. Here again this pattern has been strongly maintained to the present in the estate groups system, and its key role in determining land interests.

Table 8 below compares the Gurindji subsection terms, as recorded by Mathews in 1901, Stanner in 1934 and McConvell in 1981, which are the terms given in Figure 31. The convention used by Stanner of putting male terms in capitals and female terms

Table 8: Gurindji subsections recorded from 1900.

Patrimoiety: Warlawurruwuny Yilyiku Eagle	A1			B1	Patrimoiety: Jarlwawuny Lirraku Heron
		Mathews 1901	JANNA Nannakoo	JOOLAMA Nowala	
		Stanner 1934	TJANA Nana	TULA Nala	
		McConvell 1982	JANAMA Nanaku	JURLAMA Nawurla	
	A2			B2	
		Mathews 1901	JIMIDJA Namaja	JUNGALLA Nungalla	
		Stanner 1934	TJIMIJA Namija	DJANGALA Nangala	
		McConvell 1982	JIMIJA Namija	JANGALA Nangala	
	C1			D1	
		Mathews 1901	JEEMARA Neemara	DHALYEREE Nalyeree	
		Stanner 1934	TJIMARA Nimara	TJALYIRI Nalyiri	
		McConvell 1982	JAPARTA Nimarra	JALYIRRI Nalyirri	
	C2			D2	
		Mathews 1901	JAMBIJAN Nambean	DHONGAREE Nongaree	
		Stanner 1934	TJAMBIDJINA Nambijina	DJANGARI Nangari	
		McConvell 1982	JAMPIJINA /JAMBIYIN Nampijina/ Nampiyin	JANGARI Nangari	

(their classificatory 'sisters') in lower-case is followed here. The subsection between which the preferred marriage is made (*jutu* 'straight') are aligned with each other in the same row (e.g. A1:B1). Each patrimoiety (in the outer columns) contains four subsections, each with a male and female form.

2 Phonology

2.1 Phonemes

2.1.1 Phoneme inventory

The Gurindji consonant phonemes are set out in Table 9. This is a typical Australian language inventory containing stops (with no voicing distinction), nasals, laterals, glides and no fricatives. Five places of articulation are distinguished among the stops and nasals, with fewer distinctions made by the laterals and glides. This includes a retroflex series, but no interdental. It is the same as other members of the Ngumpin sub-group, and the same as its southern neighbour Warlpiri except Gurindji lacks the distinct retroflex flap (*rd* in the practical orthography) which occurs in some Warlpiri dialects.

Table 9: Gurindji consonant phonemes.

	Bilabial	Apico-alveolar	Retroflex	Lamino-Palatal	Velar
Stop	p, b (p)	t, d (t)	ʈ, ɖ (rt)	c, ɟ (j)	k, g (k)
Nasal	m	n	ɳ (rn)	ɲ (ny)	ŋ (ng)
Lateral		l	ɭ (rl)	ʎ (ly)	
Tap/Trill		ɾ, r (rr)			
Glide	w		ɻ (r)	j (y)	

The apico-alveolar and the retroflex are difficult to discriminate for non-native speakers, which is not uncommon for Australian languages. In Tabain, Butcher, Breen and Beare (2020)'s study of three Central Australian languages, Arrernte, Pitjantjatjara and Warlpiri, they compare the alveolar vs retroflex contrast in stops, nasals and laterals. They find a lower F3 and F4 in the preceding vowel signals a retroflex consonant which is most clearly seen in the context of an /a/ vowel, and least clearly realised in the context of an /i/ vowel, and most clearly evident in the stop consonant. Tabain and Beare (2018) give articulatory reasons for this difference. It is possible that Gurindji is similar, but an instrumental study is required to fully understand these variations.

The inventory of vowels is also typically Australian with only three short vowels distinguished. Corresponding long vowels are present, but marginal, as shown in Table 10.

https://doi.org/10.1515/9783110746884-002

Table 10: Gurindji vowel phonemes.

	Front	Central	Back
High	i, ii		ʊ (u), ʊː (uu)
Low		ɐ, (a), ɐː (aa)	

2.1.2 Practical orthography

The Gurindji practical orthography uses the English alphabet for ease of keyboard use. As a result, a number of sounds are represented by diagraphs: *ny* (palatal nasal), *ng* (velar nasal), *rt* (retroflex alveolar), *rl* (retroflex laminal) and *ly* (palatal laminal). As with most Australian languages, there is no voicing distinction in stops. The *p-t-k* voiceless stop series was adopted by McConvell to be consistent with Walmajarri and Warlpiri, both of which had literacy programs and materials at the time when Gurindji started to be written in the late 1970s. This system was adopted by Norm and Helen McNair in the late 1970s and 1980s when they taught Gurindji literacy and produced a number of Gurindji readers. Note that other Ngumpin languages use the *b-d-g* system (Bilinarra and Ngarinyman) and the *b-d-k* system (Mudburra).

We also follow the Australianist orthographic convention for retroflex nasal-stop and lateral-stop clusters, only indicating retroflexion on the first element of the cluster, for example *karnti* 'tree' (not *karnrti*). There is no contrast between retroflex and non-retroflex stops in this position – they are always retroflex. This spelling convention applies even when clusters cross morpheme boundaries, for example *lungarn-ta* 'face-LOC', where /rta/ is retroflex. The distinction between word-initial alveolar and retroflex consonants is also neutralised, and the alveolar symbol (without the preceding /r/) is always used for word-initial consonants of this kind.

In the practical orthography as used in this grammar, full reduplication is indicated by a hyphen between the reduplicated elements. In such cases if the initial consonant is retroflex but represented by alveolar, the first consonant of the second part, preceded by the hyphen, is also represented by an alveolar without an /r/, although it is phonetically retroflex.

(21) *nang-nang* 'stick.on-REDUP, repeatedly sticking on'

(22) *taka-taka*[73] 'sign language'

73 This word is derived from Warlpiri with the same meaning, and ultimately from the Warlpiri word for hand *rdaka*.

2.1.3 Phonemic oppositions

Phonemic oppositions are demonstrated here by sets of minimal pairs. Some phoneme distinctions are difficult to hear for the non-native speaker, in particular contrasts between alveolar and retroflex consonants, /t, rt/, /n, rn/ and /l, rl/, as introduced in §2.1.1. Because there are so few minimal pairs in Gurindji, in many cases the distinction makes little difference to understanding an utterance and actually there seems to be quite a lot of variation in production. In the production of the dictionary over a 40 year period by multiple compilers, there had been a lot of variation in the way that linguists represented these sounds. This variation has been standardised, however the practical orthography used is not meant to be definitive. More acoustical work is required to truly characterise retroflexes.

Note that the retroflex distinction is crucial in some cases because it can make a dramatic difference to comprehension, as (23) and (24) demonstrate, for example, the coverbs *tal* 'call a name' and *tarl* 'hit together', which both combine with the inflecting verb 'hit'. When Violet Wadrill produced (23), it was interpreted at first as (24) by Meakins who was not aware of the coverb *tal* 'to name' at that time. The result was a very different interpretation of the intended meaning!

(23) Ngu=lu **tal** pa-na-ni kamparri-jang-kulu=ma
CAT=3AUG.S call hit-IMPF-PST before-TIME-ERG=TOP

nyampayirla, **Langa** nganta.
whatsitcalled place.name ALLE
"They used to call it Langa in the old days, I think."
(🔈 VW: FM09_15_2a: 00:54min)

(24) Ngu=lu **tarl** pa-na-ni kamparri-jang-kulu=ma
CAT=3AUG.S hit.together hit-IMPF-PST before-TIME-ERG=TOP

nyampayirla, **langa** nganta.
whatsitcalled ear ALLE
"They used to hit his ears in the old days, I think."
(VW: FM09_15_2a: 00:54min)

Another crucial minimal pair involving retroflexes are the inflecting verbs *marnana* 'talk' and *manana* 'do, get' which are used frequently both individually and in combination with coverbs. They never combine with the same coverbs so there is never any confusion when a complex predicate is used, but there can be confusion when they are used as the sole verb.

It is not possible to give whole sets of distinctions between whole series, for example, the stop series /p, t, rt, j, k/. Nonetheless, pairs of contrasts can be found, for example /p, t/, /p, rt/, /p, j/ etc. In the following sections, consonant phonemes are distinguished by place of articulation (§2.1.3.1.1) (bilabial, alveolar, retroflex, palatal, velar) and manner of articulation (§2.1.3.1.2) (stop, nasal, lateral and glide). Vowel phoneme categories are set up according to height (§2.1.3.2.1), backness (§2.1.3.2.2) and length categories (§2.1.3.2.3).

2.1.3.1 Consonants

2.1.3.1.1 Place of articulation contrasts

Gurindji distinguishes five places of articulation for stops and nasals, and three for laterals and glides, as was shown in Table 9. These distinctions are demonstrated in the following sections.

2.1.3.1.1.1 Stop series /p, t, rt, j, k/

Although there is not a single set of words which demonstrates the place of articulation contrasts for the stop consonant series, the series of minimal pairs below presents evidence for these phonemic distinctions. Note that strong minimal pair distinctions should come from the same word class (Meakins, Green, & Turpin, 2018, p. 101), but we are unable to follow this protocol at all times.

/p, t/

pat	'feel about'
tat	'on top, above'
japarlng	'frog species'
jatarlng	'join'

/p, rt/

tupa	'windbreak'
turta	'freshwater mussel'

/p, j/

wap	'look back over shoulder'
waj	'throw away'
ngapa	'big brother'
ngaja	'ADMON'
purrp	'finish'
jurrp	'middle'
kalypa	'soft'
kalyja	'shallow'

/p, k/

part	'fall hard'
kart	'sleep soundly'
parnngirri	'bark'
karnngirri	'guts'

/t, rt/

kataj	'cut'
kartaj	'strangle'
pat	'feel about'
part	'fall hard'
tut	'in a line such as smoke, snakes, ridges'
turt	'hold'
lurtju	'land mass, ridge of a hill, island, country overseas'[74]
lutju	'heel, back of an axe'
tirrmit	'in a bundle'
tirrmirt	'freshwater crocodile'[75]

/t, j/

kata	'THOugh'
kaja	'bush, desert'

/t, rt, j/

jutu	'straight'
jurtu	'dust'
juju	'sacred song'

/t, k/

tarru	'spider'
karru	'be.POT'
turrp	'pierce'
kurrp	'stab'

---

74 Note that we're not convinced about this minimal pair. It is possible that they are the same word with multiple semantic extensions. On the other hand, this t/rt pair could be the same recognising the use of words for parts of small things as geographical terms.

75 This word is in fact a Malngin term but Malngin can also be considered a dialect of Gurindji which is why we include it here.

/rt, j/

wart 'return'
waj 'throw'

wirti 'stop, block'
wiji 'tata lizard'

/rt, k/

turtu 'happy'
tuku 'freshwater mussel'

/j, k/

jaru 'language'
karu 'child'

2.1.3.1.1.2 Nasal series /m, n, rn, ny, ng/

Like the stops, the nasals also contrast five places of articulation. The following minimal pairs demonstrate these distinctions.

/m, n/

manta 'get.IMP'
nanta 'small or young animal, plant or object'

ngama 'mother'
ngana 'who, whoever'

/m, rn/

kamali 'strange place'
karnali 'small of back'

/m, ny/

mila 'eye'
nyila 'that'

/m, ng/

manta 'get.IMP'
nganta 'ALLEgedly'

-murlu(ng) 'PRIVative'
-ngurlu(ng) 'ABLative'

/n, rn/

mapan 'hollow log'
maparn 'spiritual healer'

manana 'do, get'
marnana 'say'

pina 'know'
pirna 'termite eggs'

juntu 'make camp'
jurntu 'wood for tool'

pinti 'bush banana'
pirnti 'side'

kanganta 'should keep taking'
kangarnta 'teeth, mouth'

mana 'young barramundi'
marna 'tree base'

jarnak 'small flowering plant'
janak 'earless lizard'

/n, ny/
puna 'ashes'
punya 'pierced'

wanji[76] 'alive'
wanyji 'which'

/n, ng/
nama 'bee'
ngama 'mother'

karan 'scratch, dig'
karang 'salt'

/rn, ny/
nyirn 'lose something'
nyiny 'blow nose, immerse'

/rn, ng/
marna 'small barramundi'
manga 'girl'

76 This is in the dictionary as *wanyji* but *wanji* is actually correct. The distinction between *nj* and *nyj* is important as Hale maintains it does not exist in Warlpiri. Tsunoda shows it does exist in Jaru.

/ny, ng/

marany	'rub, wipe'
marang	'top grindstone'
nyawa	'this'
ngawa	'water'
puljuny	'death adder'
puljung	'put onto a fire'

2.1.3.1.1.3 Lateral consonant series /l, rl, ly/

Lateral consonants make a three-way distinction between alveolar /l/, retroflex /rl/ and palatal /ly/ places of articulation, as the following minimal pairs demonstrate. The distinction between alveolar and retroflex is made clearly in the first three examples. The phoneme /ly/ does not occur in initial position in words, and there is no contrast between /l/ and /rl/ in initial position. Note that in child-directed speech, both /l/ and /rl/ are often palatalised to /ly/ (Jones & Meakins, 2013a, pp. 178–180) (§2.5).

/l, rl/

jangala	'subsection term'
jangarla	'spring corkwood, Sesbania formosa'
tal	'name'
tarl	'hit together'
kula	'NEGation'
kurla	'bee eggs or larvae'
pilap	'look over shoulder'
pirlap	'tied around the neck'
walawuru	'wet-season wind'
warlawurru	'wedge-tailed eagle'
yulu	'ground; red kangaroo'
yurlu	'untrimmed boomerang'
tul	'throw boomerang'
turl	'chop bark'
jungkul	'disbelieve'
jungkurl	'from lack of food'

/l, ly/

kalp	'grasp, catch onto'
kalyp	'soften'

kumpali 'gecko'
kumpalyi 'native cockroach'

/rl, ly/
tarlap 'chop'
talyap 'slow'

purrurl 'let go; go fast'
purruly 'miss'

2.1.3.1.1.4 Glide and tap/trill series /r, rr, w, y/

The glide series also makes a three-way contrast, as shown in the following minimal pairs. The tap/trill /rr/ is also included in this section because it is often weakened to /r/, particularly by older speakers. Nonetheless it should be considered a separate phoneme. The glide /r/ is also often weakened to /w/ or /y/ in child-directed speech, however in adult speech these sounds should be considered separate phonemes (Jones & Meakins, 2013a, p. 179) (§2.5.2). The distinction between /w/ and /y/ is clearly phonemic and distinguishes lexical items, such as between *kawa* 'worn out vision' and *kaya* 'monster'. In other cases, however, the two appear to be in free variation with no difference in meaning observed (*tiwu/tiyu* 'fly'). This variation might be because /w/ can be realised as /y/ after an /i/. Indeed, a new dative allomorph *-yu* has emerged among some Gurindji speakers. It is used only following /i/. Most older speaker use *-wu* after all vowels (Meakins, 2011b, p. 27) (§4.3.1).

/r, rr/
karu 'child'
karru 'will be'

kura 'faeces'
kurra 'fast flow of river'

maru 'buttocks'
marru 'house'

paraj 'find, born'
parraj 'chafed, skin rubbed sore'

/r, w/
karu 'child'
kawu 'intend'

rawurru 'three-pronged spear'
wawurru 'kindling'

tawuk 'crack'
taruk 'bathe'

/r, y/
kura 'faeces'
kuya 'thus'

/rr, w/
parru 'will hit'
pawu 'persist'

/rr, y/
karra 'be'
kaya 'monster'

/w, y/
kawa 'worn out vision'
kaya 'ghost, monster'

2.1.3.1.2 Manner of articulation contrasts

Consonant phonemes can also be distinguished in terms of manner of articulation. Five manner contrasts exist: stop, nasals, laterals, a tap/trill, and glides. These are shown across five places of articulation: bilabial (§2.1.3.1.2.1), alveolar (§2.1.3.1.2.2), retroflex (§2.1.3.1.2.3), palatal (§2.1.3.1.2.4) and velar (§2.1.3.1.2.5).

2.1.3.1.2.1 Bilabial place of articulation /p, m, w/

A phonemic contrast between stops, nasals and glides is made in the bilabial place of articulation, as the following words demonstrate.

/p, m, w/
ngapa 'older brother'
ngama 'mother'
ngawa 'water'

Interestingly, manner of articulation does not always produce minimal pairs with a meaning distinction, as the following demonstrate.

kurlpam 'heap up'
kurlpap 'heap up'

2.1.3.1.2.2 Alveolar place of articulation /t, n, l, rr/

The alveolar place of articulation distinguishes four manners of articulation: stop, nasal, lateral and tap/trill. The first distinction between /t, n/ most often creates differences in word meaning, as shown by the first example, however in a number of examples either consonant can be used with no difference in meaning. This /t, n/ alternation is discussed further in §2.1.3.3.

/t, n/

jamata ‘old news’
jamana ‘foot’

ngumpit ‘man, Indigenous person’[77]
ngumpin ‘man, Indigenous person’

purrngut ‘shake, tremble from fear or sickness’
purrngun ‘sugarleaf from river red gum’

/t, l/

mutura ‘headdress including turbans’
mulura ‘maggot’

/n, l/

pina ‘know’
pila ‘chase’

wajal ‘cut meat’ (verb)
wajan ‘black spinifex wax’ (noun)

The tap/trill /rr/ is realised as a tap intervocalically. It is often difficult to distinguish between /t/ and /rr/ in this position. Nonetheless, this is a meaningful contrast, as demonstrated through the following minimal pairs. Similarly, a contrast between /rt, rr/ is often hard to hear intervocalically, but can be demonstrated, as shown in §2.1.3.1.2.3.

/t, rr/

kutij ‘stand’
kurrij ‘dig with stick’

/n, rr/

lina ‘remember’
lirra ‘tooth’

77 The *-t* variant is due to NCD, see §2.3.4.2.

/l, rr/
kalu 'walk'
karru 'will be'

/rl, rr/
kururl 'long yam'
kururr 'ignore'

2.1.3.1.2.3 Retroflexes /rt, rn, rl, r/ and /rr/

Four retroflex phonemes exist which contrast stops, nasals, laterals and glides, as the following set of words demonstrates.

/rt, rl, r/
kurta 'seed pod, pouch'
kurla 'bee eggs or larvae'
kura 'faeces'

lamparra 'father-in-law, son-in-law or daughter-in-law'[78]
lampura 'axe'

Other minimal pairs support this distinction.

/rt, rl/
kartaj 'strangle'
karlaj 'younger sibling'

purrurl 'release, let go'
purrurt 'shock, scare'

/rl, rn/
marlarl 'pelt someone'
marlarn 'river red gum'

mukurl 'aunty, father's sister'
mukurn 'mother's older sister'

Although /rr/ is not a retroflex consonant, it is included in this section because the contrast between /rt/ and /rr/, and /rl/ and /rr/ is one of the more difficult to hear intervocalically since both are often reduced to flaps. Nonetheless this contrast can be demonstrated, as the following examples show.

78 This word is a well-known Wanderwort so is not the best example for a minimal pair since it is a borrowing (McConvell, 2016).

/rt, rr/
mirlirti 'hook of spear-thrower'
mirlirri 'walking stick'

wapurt 'unconcerned'
wapurr 'distract with noise'

yawarta 'horse'
yawarra 'rest'

/t, rr/
tipirr 'break off a piece'
tipit 'tie up'

/rl, rr/
mangarli 'chest, brisket'
mangarri 'bread, fruit, vegetables'

pakurl 'rotten, bad, decayed'
pakurr 'load up, store'

/l, rr/
punpulu 'dog, dingo'
punpurru 'everyone'

2.1.3.1.2.4 Palatal place of articulation /j, ny, ly, y/
Four manner of articulation contrasts are observed for palatal consonants, as shown in the following sets.

/j, ny, y/
kaja 'bush, desert'
kanya 'took'
kaya 'monster'

kapaj 'let go of something, lose, die'
kapany 'beckon, summon'

tirtij 'camping at different place'
tirtiny 'ghost bat'

/j, ly/
jajarra 'expectant sibling'[79]
jalyarra 'dip'

79 This is a child who no longer receives milk from his/her mother because she is expecting another child.

jipij 'cover, bury, cook in hot ground'
jipily 'poke'

/ny, y/
punya 'pierced'
puya 'body'

/ny, ly/
punyja 'dung beetle'
pulyja 'traditional football game'

Similar to the /t, n/ contrast, there are some examples in which an alternation between /j/ and /ny/ does not result in a change of meaning. These will be discussed in more detail in §2.1.3.3.

waj 'throw away'
wany 'throw away'

2.1.3.1.2.5 Velar place of articulation /ng, k, w/

The velar place of articulation shows a manner contrast between stops, nasals and glides. No minimal pairs could be found for /k, w/.

/ng, k/
ngaja 'ADMONitive'
kaja 'bush, desert'

/ng, w/
langa 'ear'
lawa 'lemon wood, Dolichandrone heterophylla'

2.1.3.2 Vowels

As was shown in Table 10, Gurindji vowels are distinguished by height, backness and length. These dimensions are contrasted in the following sections as evidence of distinct vowel phonemes.

2.1.3.2.1 Height

The low vowel /a/ is contrasted with the high vowels /i/ and /u/.

/a, i/
jak 'drop'
jik 'emerge'

kartiya 'someone of European descent, non-Indigenous'
kartiyi 'deep wide coolamon, basket, boat, dish, drum'

milyamilya 'slow, lag behind'
milyimilyi 'many, large number'

yingka 'stone spearhead, stone knife'
yingki 'northern kurrajong'

/a, u/
japaka 'old woman'[80]
japuka 'Butler's grunter or sharp nose grunter'

jurlkap 'push together'
jurlkup 'straight away'

kunka 'do something on behalf of someone'
kunku 'bag, sack, cover'

karlarra 'west'
kurlarra 'south'[81]

tiwa 'forehead'
tiwu 'fly, throw'

yungkaj 'dream'
yungkuj 'tree falling down'

2.1.3.2.2 Backness

The front vowel /i/ is contrasted with the back vowels /a/ and /u/.

/i, a/
jak 'drop'
jik 'emerge'

larrmaj 'take up weapons'
larrmij 'fetch, keep, pick up'

/i, u/
jupu 'just'
jipu 'extinguish'

80 This word is actually a borrowing from Mudburra so not the best example for a minimal pair.
81 This phonological closeness of these cardinal terms causes some confusion for younger generations of Gurindji people (Dunn et al., 2021).

mampit	'put together, mix'
mamput	'unshaven'
tuwi	'grow, form'
tuwu	'swell up'

2.1.3.2.3 Length

Long vowels are not common in Gurindji or other Ngumpin languages. Nonetheless some evidence for the existence of long vowels can be presented, as shown by the following minimal pairs.

/a, aa/	
jaj	'lenient'
jaaj	'beg, humbug'
ngu=rla	'CAT=3OBL'
ngu=rlaa	'CAT=1INC.AUG.S'
/i, ii/	
jika	'chin, beard'
jiika	'finch'
pirnti	'side'
pirntii	'rib'
pitpit	'drawing on ground'
piitpiit	'bird species'
/u, uu/	
jutu	'straight'
juutu	'elbow'
puny	'kiss'
puuny	'marsupial mouse'
kurturtu	'woman's child'
kuurturtu	'cramp'
purrk	'stamp feet (dance)'
puurrk	'rain heavily'

The difference between long and short vowels is more clearly discernible through case allomorphy. For example, in Gurindji the locative allomorph *-ngka* is used in stems of two syllables and the *-la* form attaches to stems of three syllables or more (§4.3.4.1). Thus, the following minimal pair is good evidence for long vowels behaving as two syllables.

(25) pirnti-ka[82] pirntii-la
side-LOC rib-LOC

(26) maarta-lu
'young man-ERG'

Allative case marking also offers some evidence (note that variation is present in the use of case allomorphs). Two allative allomorphs exist: *-ngkurra* attaches to disyllabic stems and *-yirri* to multisyllabic stems (§4.3.5.1). When the stem *munuwu* is marked allative, the *-yirri* allomorph is always used, providing evidence that the long vowel counts as two syllables. For example, in (27), *munuwu-yirri* 'house-ALL' is contrasted with two-syllable *ngaji-ngkurra* 'father-ALL'.

(27) Nyawa=ma=wula jumpun-jumpun=parla kampa-rni. Jamana=ma
this=TOP=3UA.S smoke-REDUP=FOC cook-PST foot=TOP

wankaj. Janga jujuju-marraj. Ngu=wula purlurluj waninya
bad sick sore.REDUP-COMP CAT=3UA.S ambush fall.PST

ngarlu=parla. Kula=wula karrwa-rna-ni na yala-ngka=ma.
honey=FOC NEG=3UA.S hold-IMPF-PST FOC that-LOC=FOC

Nyila=ma=wula ka-nya na **munuwu-yirri**, **ngamayi-yirri**,
that=TOP=3UA.S take-PST FOC house-ALL mother-ALL

ngaji-ngkurra na, lurrpu na. Yala-nginyi=wula=ma
father-ALL FOC return FOC that-SOURCE=3AUG.S=TOP

langa-langa-lu ngu=wula karrinya, kuya.
ear-REDUP-ERG CAT=3UA.S be.PST thus

"The two of them treated him with smoke. His feet were no good. They took him over to the shade. They didn't keep him there though, they took him back to the camp, back to their mother and father. After that, they had learnt their lesson."
(🔈 PB: EC98_a021: 5:42min)

These long vowels are sometimes written as a vowel-glide-vowel sequence to make the syllable structure clear.

82 Here *-ngka* is reduced to *-ka* under a nasal-cluster dissimilation rule which is discussed in §2.3.4.1.

/ii/ vs /iyi/
wiit 'point, show'
wiyit

/uu/ vs /uwu/
munuu 'camp, house'
munuwu

Nonetheless McConvell (1988b, p. 137) suggests that it may be necessary to recognise a difference between long vowels and vowel-glide-vowel sequences as such triplets occur in Gurindji:

/a, awa, aa/

jaj	'to favour, treat especially well'
jawaj	'grass in ruminant's stomach'
jaaj	'beg, plead'

2.1.3.3 Alternation between phonemes /j, ny/; /t, n/

There are two stop/nasal pairs which alternate word-finally in certain words with no meaning difference. In some cases, McConvell (1988b, p. 149) suggests that the denasalisation of the final consonant is the result of a nasal-stop cluster in the stem, for example *ngumpin* vs *ngumpit* 'man, Indigenous person' or *nangkaliny* vs *nangkalij* 'ground honey'. Historical effects of earlier applications of the denasalisation of the final consonant can be seen in morphologically frozen forms in Gurindji too, for example *kumpuwuj* < *kumpu-wu-ny* 'urethra, urine-DAT-NMLZ' and *pankaluj* < *pankal-u-ny* 'Bat Dreaming, bat-DAT-NMLZ'. This process relates to nasal-stop cluster denasalisation (see §2.3.4.2). Note that the denasalisation process is not always the result of a nasal-stop cluster in the stem.

/j, ny/
-warij 'alone'
-wariny

waj 'throw away'
wany

nangkalij 'ground honey'
nangkaliny

/t, n/
ngumpin 'man, Indigenous person'
ngumpit

jarrwalun 'many'
jarrwalut

jipurn 'extinguish'
jipurt

nyiwun 'dive under'
nyiwut

In other words ending in either of these phonemes, this alternation does not occur. Indeed, many of these alternations produce minimal pair contrasts.

/j, ny/
jalaj 'knead'
jalany 'tongue'

jalij 'freshwater prawn'[83]
jaliny 'male plains kangaroo'

nguj 'pluck, make sick through supernatural power'
nguny 'grumpy'

/t, n/
lut 'kneel'
lun 'deposit'

pirtpirt 'brush off'
pirnpirn 'bloat'

An alternation between these two pairs of phonemes in certain words is also found in Jaru (Tsunoda, 1981, p. 31) and Bilinarra (Meakins & Nordlinger, 2014, pp. 54–55). We have no explanation for why this pattern exists for some words and not others, except that these words may have been borrowed after the denasalisation rule ceased to apply.

83 McConvell recorded this word as *jaalij* originally so it might not be the best example of a minimal pair. Current speakers do use a short vowel, however.

2.1.4 Allophony: Consonants

2.1.4.1 Stops and voicing

There is no phonemic distinction between voiced and voiceless consonants in Gurindji, as in most Australian languages. As a general rule, for oral stops, the voiced allophone tends to be found in syllable-initial position (onset), particularly when it is word initial, and the voiceless in syllable-final position (coda). Phonetically, VOT values are generally short-lag (0–20 ms) for word-initial stops and negative for word-medial stops. VOT in word-initial stops is also slightly longer (approximately 10 ms) in utterance-initial position than in postvocalic or post-consonantal position (Jones & Meakins, 2013b, p. 215). There is some variation in the extent to which voicing occurs in syllable-initial position for different stops, /k/ being particularly distinguished from the others by having less voicing. Oral stops immediately following nasal consonants are always voiced. Stops are usually unreleased word-finally and, consequently, their place of articulation is often difficult to discern in this position, but we present them as voiceless since this is consistent with their use in syllable-final position more generally. Finally, although /j/ is classified as a stop in our description of Gurindji, it has more affricate-like qualities phonetically (Ennever et al., 2017).

The voiced stops which are found in syllable-initial position include word-initial stops (28), intervocalic stops (29) and stops which follow nasals (30) and liquids (31).

(28) *ṯarukap* = [ˈɖɐɹʊgɐp] ‘bathe’

(29) *paṯawan* = [ˈbɐdɐwən] ‘hard’

(30) *kangarnṯa* = [ˈkɐŋɐɳɖɐ] ‘teeth, mouth’

(31) *kumarlawurlṯa* = [ˈkʊmɐɭauɭɖə] ‘magpie, butcherbird’

In some contexts, syllable-initial stops are voiceless, for example where they follow a syllable-final voiceless stop.

(32) *jartpurru* = [ˈɟɐʈpʊru] ‘bloodwood species’

The voiceless stops which are found in word-final position include (released) word-final stops (33) and stops which follow laterals (34) and taps (35).

(33) *partaj* = [ˈpɐɖɐc] ‘climb’

(34) *wumparlp̱* = [ˈwʊmbɐɭp] ‘float’

(35) *turrp* = [ˈdʊrp] ‘pierce’

An exception to these generalisations is the velar stop /k/ where the voiceless unaspirated allophone is often heard in syllable or word-initial position.

(36) *k̲ungulu* = [ˈkʊŋʊlʊ] 'blood'

2.1.5 Allophony: Vowels

The three major vowel phonemes /a/, /i/ and /u/, all exhibit allophonic variation in different phonological environments. Much of the following discussion of vowel phonemes and their allophones is based on Jones, Meakins and Muawiyath's (2012) acoustic analysis of Gurindji vowels. In addition to the allophonic variation, in many cases, /a/, /i/ and /u/ are reduced to a schwa [ə] in unstressed syllables.

2.1.5.1 Allophones of /a/

The phoneme /a/ is generally realised as [ɐ] in both stressed and unstressed syllables.

(37) *paka* = [ˈbɐgɐ] 'prickle'

Before or after a palatal consonant, /a/ is often raised and realised as [e, æ, ɛ] and sometimes [ɪ].

(38) *yamak* = [jæmɐk], [jɛmɐk], [jemɐk] 'steadily'

(39) *kajirri* = [kæɟɪrɪ], [kɛɟɪrɪ], [keɟɪrɪ] 'old woman'

(40) *nyangka* = [ɲæŋkɐ], [ɲɛŋkɐ], [ɲeŋkɐ] 'look!'

Before or after a velar consonant, /a/ is often backed and rounded, and realised as [ʊ, ɔ].

(41) *tarukap* = [dɐɻʊgɔp], [dɐɻʊgʊp] 'bathe'

(42) *jangkarni* = [ɟʊŋkɐɳi], [ɟɔŋkɐɳi] 'big'

(43) *warlaku* = [wʊɭɐgʊ], [wɔɭɐgʊ] 'dog'

2.1.5.2 Allophones of /i/

The phoneme /i/ occurs in the greatest range of consonantal contexts as [i]. Some examples are given below.

(44) *kajirri* = [kæɟɪrɪ] 'old woman'

(45) *ngali* = [ŋɐli] '1UA, the two of us'

In the environment of a bilabial consonant, /i/ is often backed and rounded and realised as [ʊ, ʉ].

(46) *liwart* = [lʉwɐd] 'wait'

(47) *jarrpip* = [ɟɐrbʉp] 'lift, carry'

2.1.5.3 Allophones of /u/

The phoneme /u/ occurs in the greatest range of consonantal contexts as [ʊ]. Some examples are given below.

(48) *tarukap* = [dɐɻʊgɔp] 'bathe'

(49) *nyuntu* = [ɲʊndʊ] 'you'

Before or after a palatal consonant, the phoneme /u/ is often centralised [ʉ] or even fronted [ɪ].

(50) *nyununy* = [ɲʉnʉɲ] 'your'

(51) *nyuntu* = [ɲɪndʊ] 'you'

(52) *kanyjurra* = [kɐɲɟɪrɐ] 'down'

2.2 Phonotactics

2.2.1 Syllable structure

The most common syllable structure is an open syllable CV, such as *ja+ju* 'maternal grandmother'. Closed syllables can end with one consonant, CVC, for example *jarr+pip* 'carry on hip', or with two consonants, CVCC, for example *jurrp* 'middle'.

In the case of CVC syllables, all consonants except glides are permissible syllable-finally (whether the syllable is stem-medial or stem-final), for example stops *jalij* 'freshwater prawn', nasals *jipurn* 'extinguish', laterals *jawul* 'split' and the tap/trill *jakarr* 'cover'.

The syllable structure CVCC is found less commonly than the CVC structure. It is generally restricted to the coverb word class (§7.2.1), although a very few nominals also have CVCC syllables. Syllables of this type are usually found in monosyllabic words or as the final syllable of a disyllabic word. The consonant clusters always consist of a liquid: /rr/, /l/ or /rl/, followed by a peripheral consonant /p/, /k/ or /ng/, for example *janyarrp* 'baby talk', *yurrk* 'tell a story', *kurlng* 'form cloud', *kalp* 'understand, catch onto', *nurlk* 'crack knuckles'. The *ng*-final consonant clusters are also found in nominals such as *jarnparrng* 'rainstone' and *jawurlng* 'hamstring'.

2.2.2 Stem syllabicity

Most words in Gurindji are minimally disyllabic. Of the few monosyllabic words, almost all are coverbs, and have closed syllables, for example CVC *tup* 'pluck', and CVCC *turrp* 'pierce'. This unusual phonology is largely because the Ngumpin languages have borrowed 40–50% of their coverb inventory from Jaminjung, Wardaman and also the Jarragan languages (McConvell, 2009a) (also see §7.2.1 for a discussion of coverb phonotactics).

There are very few monosyllabic words consisting solely of a single open syllable, CV, *yu* 'yes', *ma* 'OK' and *ngu* 'catalyst'. Additionally, many inflecting verb bound stems are monosyllabic, such as *ya-* 'go', *ma-* 'do, get' etc, however they always occur with TAM suffixes, for example *ya-na-na* 'go-IMPF-PRS', *ma-na-na* 'do/get-IMPF-PRS'. The word structure of inflecting verbs is discussed further in §7.1.1.

2.2.3 Stem-initial position

A word can begin with any consonant or glide except for /ly/ or /rr/. Words cannot begin with a consonant cluster or a vowel. The two exceptions are *ankaj* 'poor thing' and *anyan* 'dear thing' which are interjections. These might have derived from *janyarrp* 'baby talk' which deletes initial consonants (§2.5). Other cases of /y/ or /w/ elision occur, but only in the environment of /u/ or /i/, respectively, for example *yipu* 'rain' is usually pronounced [ipu] and *wutu* 'lice' is almost always pronounced [utu] (but not in the environment of a preceding vowel). Nevertheless, these words are still analysed phonemically as beginning with a glide because in citation speech, the glide is always heard. This would lend some support to the idea that the glide is present at some underlying level.

The contrast between the apical consonants /t, rt/, /n, rn/, and /l, rl/ is neutralised word initially, as is common across most Australian languages with such a phonological contrast (Dixon, 1980, p. 167). It seems likely, however, that the initial apical series is underlyingly retroflex as they have retroflex articulation following a vowel-final word in rapid speech. Again, as was discussed in §1.8.5, more instrumental work on Gurindji is required to discern differences between apical-alveolar and retroflex consonants.

The symbols for the alveolar series are used in the orthography to represent these neutralised consonants, for example *tikap* 'chop', *nakurr* 'ground oven, hole, grave' and *laja* 'shoulder'. Note that the bound pronoun forms such as *=rna* 'I', *=rla* 'for her, him, it', *=rli* 'we' are always found after a vowel so that the retroflex nature of their initial consonant is always heard. For this reason, they are written with the corresponding retroflex symbol.

2.2.4 Stem-final position

A word can end with any vowel or consonant except the glides /y/, /r/ and /w/. The phoneme /m/ is marginal word-finally. In the *Gurindji to English Dictionary* (Meakins et al., 2013), only 19 examples out of the 5696 main entries can be found. Coverbs and some nominals can also end in consonant clusters containing two members, as discussed in §2.2.1.

2.2.5 Consonant clusters

2.2.5.1 Intra-morphemic consonant clusters

Consonant clusters found within morphemes, called intra-morphemic clusters, consist of two phonemes. Three-member clusters only occur across morpheme boundaries (see §2.2.5.2). The intra-morphemic clusters are laid out in Table 11. The vertical column shows the first consonant in the cluster and the horizontal row shows the second consonant. Note that /p/ and glides are never found as the first consonant in the cluster. Laterals, the glides /r/ and /y/, the tap/trill /rr/ and nasals /n/ and /rn/ are never found as the second consonant.

A number of observations can be made based on Table 11. Firstly, there are generally no geminate consonants. Related to this, there are no clusters involving a retroflex and alveolar stop despite the fact that stop-stop clusters are permissible. This apparent restriction again brings into question whether there really is a distinction between these stop consonants (see also §1.8.5). Also related to stops, if a stop occurs as the first member in the cluster, it must be followed by another stop. Finally, clusters cannot contain more than one lateral or glide. Tsunoda (1981, pp. 38–39) notes similar patterns for Jaru, and Meakins and Nordlinger (Meakins & Nordlinger, 2014, p. 61) for Bilinarra.

2.2.5.2 Inter-morphemic consonant clusters

The possibilities for combinations of consonants are much greater in inter-morphemic consonant clusters, partly because Gurindji allows consonant-final syllables. There are two main differences between intra-morphemic and inter-morphemic consonant clusters: (i) inter-morphemic clusters can contain geminate consonants, for example *jamu**t-t**u* 'bush turkey-ERG' and *jali**j-j**awung* 'prawn-PROP', and (ii) inter-morphemic clusters can have three consonants in the cluster, for example *pu**rrp-p**a=rni* '(finish-EP=ONLY), whole lot'.

The possible inter-morphemic clusters are shown in Table 12. The vertical column shows the first consonant in the cluster and the horizontal column shows the second

Table 11: Intra-morphemic consonant clusters.

	p	**t**	**rt**	**j**	**b**	**m**	**ny**	**ng**	**w**
t	tp *nyatpa* 'how'			tj *jitji* 'nose'	tk *kutkukutku* 'pigeon sp.'				
rt	rtp *jirtpirtpi* 'gumnut'			rtj *lurtju* 'ridge'	rtk *ngarlaartku* 'chisel'				
j	jp *jijpart* 'tuck in'				jk *lajkut* 'land hard'				
k	kp *jikparn* 'bush turkey'								
m	mp *Jampin* 'SUBSECT'								
n	np *jinparl* 'kestrel'	nt *jantura* 'bush turkey'		nj *kunjirt* 'bloodwood'	nk *pinka* 'river'	nm *panmarra* 'young teenager'		nng *parranganngan* 'throat'	
rn	rnp *jarnpij* 'smoke tree'		rnt *jurnta* 'bush onion'		rnk *kurnka* 'raw'			rnng *karnngirri* 'guts'	

Table 11 (continued)

	p	t	rt	j	b	m	ny	ng	w
ny	nyp *wanyput* 'lip'				nyk *nunykuwarra* 'hungry'	nym *nganyman* 'cradle'			
ng	ngp *wirnangpurru* 'kangaroo'				ngk *jingki* 'bone type'	ngm *ngungmarta* 'quiet person'			
l	lp *jalpiny* 'spear'			lj *kaljak* 'sink in'	lk *warnpalk* 'break open'	lm *jilmung* 'break'	lny *walnyirr* 'twist ankle'	lng *wulngarn* 'sun'	lw *jilwarr* 'tear'
rl	rlp *kurlpak* 'vomit'			rlj *jirlja* 'desert'	rlk *wirlka* 'axe'	rlm *marlmurru* 'short spear'		rlng *parlnguk* 'square with'	rlw *jarlwa* 'heron'
ly	lyp *mulypu* 'calm'			lyj *malyju* 'boy'	lyk *talykip* 'knap'				lyw *kalywarr* 'swelling go down'
rr	rrp *turrp* 'pierce'			rrj *karrjan* 'double tongue'	rrk *jurrk* 'tired'	rrm *wirrminy* 'turn over'		rrng *jarnparrng* 'rainstone'	rrw *jarrwa* 'many'

consonant. Consonant clusters are generally only restricted by allomorphic rules relating to consonant-final stems and possibilities for stem-final consonants and the initial consonants on suffixes. For example, no suffixes begin with /ly/, /n/ or /r/. Additionally, those suffixes which begin with /l/, /rl/, /rn/ or /rr/ never attach to consonant-final stems. The phonemes /r/, /y/ and /w/ are not found stem-finally. Note that we have included enclitics as well as suffixes in the inter-morphemic clusters. Although enclitics are not a part of the morphological word, they are a part of the phonological word, hence their inclusion.

Table 12: Inter-morphemic consonant clusters.

	p[1]	**t**[2]	**rt**[2]	**j**[3]	**k**[4]	**m**[5]	**ny**[6]	**ng**[7]	**w**[8]
p	p-p *jakap-pa* 'sneak.up-EP'			p-j *jakap-jirri* 'sneak.up-ALL'	p-k *jakap-ku* 'to sneak up'	p-m *jakap-murlung* 'don't sneak up'	p-ny *pilkip=nyiyarni* 'really white'	p-ng *jakap-nginyi* 'after sneaking up'	p-w *pilkip-walija* 'white objects'
t	t-p *jamut-pa* 'turkey-EP'	t-t *jamut-tu* 'turkey-ERG'		t-j *jamut-jawung* 'with the turkey'	t-k *jamut-ku* 'turkey's'	t-m *jamut-murlung* 'without turkeys'	t-ny *jamut=nyiyarni* 'proper turkey'	t-ny *jamut-nginyi* 'from turkeys'	t-w *jamut-walija* 'turkeys'
rt	rt-p *jawart-pa* 'tail-EP'		rt-rt *jawart-ta* 'on the tail'	rt-j *jawart-jawung* 'with a tail'	rt-k *jawart-ku* 'for tails'	rt-m *jawart-murlung* 'without a tail'	rt-ny *jawurt=nyiyarni* 'proper tail'	rt-ng *jawart-nginyi* 'from the tail'	rt-w *jawart-walija* 'tails'
j	j-p *jalij-pa* 'prawn-EP'			j-j *jalij-jirri* 'to the prawn'	j-k *jalij-ku* 'prawn's'	j-m *jalij-murlung* 'without prawns'	j-ny *jalij=nyiyarni* 'proper prawn'	j-ng *jalij-nginyi* 'from the prawn'	j-w *jalij-walija* 'prawns'

Table 12 (continued)

	p[1]	t[2]	rt[2]	j[3]	k[4]	m[5]	ny[6]	ng[7]	w[8]
k	k-p *kartak-pa* 'cup-EP'			k-j *kartak-jirri* 'into the cup'	k-k *kartak-ku* 'for the cup'	k-m *kartak-murlung* 'without a cup'	k-ny *kartak=nyiyarni* 'proper cup'	k-ng *kartak-nginyi* 'from the cup'	k-w *kartak-walija* 'cups'
m	m-p *mum-pa* 'dark-EP'			m-j *mum-jirri* 'into the dark'	m-k *mum-kula* 'at night'	m-m *mum-murlung* 'without darkness'	m-ny *mum=nyiyarni* 'properly dark'	m-ng *mum-ngarna* 'night animals'	m-w *lamlam-walija* 'placentas'
n	n-p *kampun-pa* 'sinew-EP'	n-t *kampun-tu* 'sinew-ERG'		n-j *makin-jirri* 'while sleeping'	n-k *makin-gu* 'to sleep'	n-m *kampun-murlung* 'without sinew'	n-ny *kampun=nyiyarni* 'proper sinew'	n-ng *makin-nginyi* 'after sleep'	n-w *kampun-walija* 'sinews'
rn	rn-p *kawurn-pa* 'ashes-EP'		rn-rt *kawurn-ta* 'in the ashes'	rn-j *lamarn-jirri* 'to the river'	rn-k *kawurn-ku* 'for the ashes'	rn-m *kawurn-murlung* 'no ashes'	rn-ny *lamarn=nyiyarni* 'proper river'	rn-ng *lamarn-ngarna* 'river things'	rn-w *lamarn-walija* 'rivers'
ny	ny-p *jalany-pa* 'tongue-EP'			ny-j *jalany-ju* 'with the tongue'	ny-k *jalany-ku* 'tongue's'	ny-m *jalany-murlung* 'tongueless'	ny-ny *jalany=nyiyarni* 'proper tongue'	ny-ng *jarriny-ngarna* 'bush tobacco'	ny-w *jalany-walija* 'tongues'
ng	ng-p *karang-pa* 'salt-EP'			ng-j *karang-jawung* 'salty'	ng-k *karang-ku* 'for the salt'	ng-m *karang-murlung* 'saltless'	ng-ny karang=*nyiyarni* 'properly salty'	ng-ng *karang-ngarna* 'something' salty'	ng-w *kilang-walija* 'new moons'

Table 12 (continued)

	p[1]	t[2]	rt[2]	j[3]	k[4]	m[5]	ny[6]	ng[7]	w[8]
l	l-p *jawul-pa* 'split-EP'			l-j *jawul-jawung* 'with spit'	l-k *jawul-ku* 'for spit'	l-m *majul-murlung* 'no guts'	l-ny *majul=nyiyarni* 'proper stomach'	l-ng *majul-ngarna* 'of the stomach'	l-w *majul-walija* 'stomachs'
rl	rl-p *jinparl-pa* 'kestrel-EP'			rl-j *jinparl-jawung* 'with the kestrel'	rl-k *jinparl-ku* 'kestrel's'	rl-m *jinparl-murlung* 'without the kestrel'	rl-ny *jinparl=nyiyarni* 'proper kestrel'	rl-ng *jinparl-ngurlu* 'from the kestrel'	rl-w *jinparl-walija* 'kestrels'
ly	ly-p *pilyily-pa* 'young-EP'			ly-j *jaly-jirri* 'while cold'	ly-k *pilyily-ku* 'for the young'	ly-m *pilyily-murlung* 'without young'	ly-ny pilypily=*nyiyarni* 'proper young'	ly-ng *jaly-ngarna* 'something cold'	ly-w *pilyily-walija* 'young ones'
rr	rr-p *karlarr-pa* 'crab-EP'			rr-j *rurr-jirri* 'while sitting'	rr-k *karlarr-ku* 'crab's'	rr-m *rurr-murlung* 'don't sit'	rr-ny *karlarr=nyiyarni* 'proper crab'	rr-ng *rurr-nginyi* 'after sitting'	rr-w *karlarr-walija* 'crabs'

[1] The inter-morphemic clusters in this column are best demonstrated by the epenthetic *-pa* (§2.3.5), for example *warlakap-pa=rni* 'search-EP=ONLY', the nominal clitic *=purrupurru* 'AND', for example *ngumpin=purrupurru* 'man=AND, and men' (§4.8.3), the adjectival suffix *-pari* for example *ngarrap-pari* 'heat-ADJ, hot' (§4.7.21), the factitive suffixes *-pijik* 'FACT' and *-pirrji* 'FACT' (§7.2.4.5), the nominal suffixes *-piya* 'BIT' (§4.7.22), *=pirak* 'REALLY' (§4.8.2), and *-piti* 'SITE' (§4.7.25) and the focus clitic *=parla* (§10.1.7).

[2] The inter-morphemic clusters in these columns are best demonstrated by the locative and ergative alveolar stem-final allomorphs *-ta, -rta* and *-tu -rtu*, respectively, for example *ngumpin-tu* 'man-ERG' (§4.3.2.1).

[3] The inter-morphemic clusters in this column are best demonstrated by the consonant-final proprietive allomorph *-jawung*, for example *ngumpin-jawung* 'man-PROP, with a man' (§4.6.2.1), the palatal-final locative and ergative allomorphs *-ja* and *-ju* respectively (§4.3.4.1 and §4.3.2.1) and also the consonant-final allative allomorph *-jirri* (§4.3.5.1).

[4] The inter-morphemic clusters in this column are best demonstrated by the consonant-final dative allomorph *-ku*, for example *ngumpin-ku* 'man-DAT' (§4.3.3.1), the nominal suffixes *-kujarra* 'DU' (§4.4.4), *-kuk* 'FACT' (§7.2.4.5), *-kula* 'LOC' (§4.3.4.1), *-kulu* 'ERG' (§4.3.2.1), *-kurra* 'ALL' (§4.3.5.1), and *-kuwang* 'AND'; (§4.4.7) and the coverb suffix *-karra* (§7.2.4.1).

[5] The inter-morphemic clusters in this column are best demonstrated by the adnominal privative suffix *-murlung*, for example *wartan-murlung* 'hand-PRIV, without hands' (§4.6.3), the topic clitic *=ma*, for example *nyawa=ma* 'this=TOP' (§10.1.2), *-mala* 'OWNer' (§4.7.11), *-marraj* 'COMParative' (§4.8.12), *-mawu* 'DWELLer' (§5.1.2.3), *-mayin* 'PERLative' (§4.3.11), *-mirntij* 'SEASON' (§4.7.13) and *-mungkuj* 'OWNer' (§4.7.14).

[6] The inter-morphemic clusters in this column are best demonstrated by *-ny* 'NMLZ' (§4.7.20), the kinship suffixes *-nyan* '3POSS' (§4.5.4), *-nyanparra* '2POSS' (§4.5.4) and *-nyarrarra* 'ETC' (§4.4.8); and the clitics *=nyiyang* 'PROPERly' (§10.1.3) and *=nyiyarni* 'PROPERly' (§10.1.3).

[7] The inter-morphemic clusters in this column are best demonstrated by the associative suffix *-ngarna*, for example *Yarralin-ngarna* 'placename-ASSOC, someone from Yarralin' (§4.7.16). The case suffixes *-ngurlu* 'ABLative' (§4.3.7), *-nginyi* 'SOURCE' (§4.3.8) and *-nganayak* 'MOTivative' (§4.3.12); *-nganyju(k)* 'GROUP' (§4.7.15) and =nga 'DUBitative' (§8.3.1.3) are other examples.

[8] The inter-morphemic clusters in this column are best demonstrated by *-walija* 'PAUC' (§4.4.5), *-warij* 'ALONE' (§4.7.24), *-wariny* 'ALONE' (§4.7.24) and *=warluk* 'FIRST' (§10.1.8).

A number of tri-consonantal clusters are also possible. They are generally made up of a coverb stem with a nominal suffix. Possible clusters are shown in Table 13. The vertical column shows the initial consonant cluster and the horizontal column shows the final consonant. Note that there are no columns for /t/ or /rt/ because there are no stem-final consonant clusters ending in /t/ or /rt/. There are also that no /y/ columns because suffixes such as *-yawung* 'PROPrietive' do not attach to consonant-final stems. Similarly, there is no column for /w/ as the only w-initial morpheme *=warla* does not attach to consonant-final stems.

Table 13: Tri-consonantal clusters.

	p[1]	**j**[2]	**k**[3]	**m**[4]	**ng**[5]
rrp	rrp-p *kurrp-pa* 'stab-EP'	rrp-j *kurrp-jirri* 'while stabbing'	rrp-k *kurrp-ku* 'to stab'	rrp-m *kurrp-murlung* 'don't stab it'	rrp-ng *kurrp-nginyi* 'after stabbing'
rlp	rlp-p *kurlp-pa* 'splatter-EP'	rlp-j *kurlp-jirri* 'while splattering'	rlp-k *kurlp-karra* 'splattering'	rlp-m *kurlp=ma* 'splatter'	rlp-ng *kurlp-nginyi* 'after splattering'
lp	lp-p *pilp-pa* 'open eyes'	lp-j *pilp-jirri* 'while opening eyes'	lp-k *pilp-ku* 'to open eyes'	lp-m *pilp=ma* 'open eyes'	lp-ng *pilp-nginyi* 'after opening eyes'
rrk	rrk-p *murrk-pa* 'crunch'	rrk-j *murrk-jirri* 'while crunching'	rrk-k *murrk-karra* 'crunching'	rrk-m *murrk-murlung* 'don't crunch'	rrk-ng *murrk-nginyi* 'after crunching'
rlk	rlk-p *jampurlk-pa* 'squash-EP'	rlk-j *jampurlk-jirri* 'while squashing'	rlk-k *jampurlk-ku* 'to squash'	rlk-m *jampurlk-murlung* 'don't squash it'	rlk-ng *jampurlk-nginyi* 'after squashing'

Table 13 (continued)

lk	lk-p *palk-pa* 'stamp-EP'	lk-j *palk-jirri* 'while stamping'	lk-k *palk-ku* 'to stamp'	lk-m *palk-murlung* 'don't stamp'	lk-ng *palk-nginyi* 'after stamping'
rrng	rrng-p *parrng-pa* 'bark-EP'	rrng-j *parrng-jirri* 'while barking'	rrng-k *parrng-ku* 'to bark'	rrng-m *parrng=ma* 'bark'	rrng-ng *parrng-nginyi* 'after barking'
rlng	rlng-p *jatarlng-pa* 'join-EP'	rlng-j *murlng-jawung* 'private'	rlng-k *jatarlng-ku* 'to join'	rlng-m *jatarlng=ma* 'join'	rlng-ng *jatarlng-nginyi* 'after joining'
lng	lng-p *wilng-pa* 'persuade-EP'	lng-j *wilng-jirri* 'while persuading'	lng-k *wilng-ku* 'to persuade'	lng-m *wilng=ma* 'persuade'	lng-ng *wilng-nginyi* 'after persuading'

[1] The inter-morphemic clusters in this column are best demonstrated by the adjectival suffix *-pari*, for example *walp-pari* 'clear-ADJ, clearing' (§4.7.21), the epenthetic *-pa*, for example *walp-pa=rni* 'clear-EP=ONLY' (§6.2.3.5.2) and the focus clitic *=parla*, for example *turrp=parla* 'poke=FOC' (§10.1.7).
[2] The inter-morphemic clusters in this column are best demonstrated by the consonant-final proprietive allomorph *-jawung*, for example *murlng-jawung* 'private-PROP, with (her) own e.g. car' (§4.6.2), the palatal-final locative and ergative allomorphs *-ja* and *-ju* respectively (§4.3.4.1 and §4.3.2.1) and also the consonant-final allative allomorph *-jirri* (§4.3.5.1).
[3] The inter-morphemic clusters in this column are best demonstrated by the iterative suffix *-karra*, for example *murrk-karra* 'rub-ITER, rubbing' (§7.2.4.1), and the consonant-final dative suffix *-ku*, for example *murrk-ku* 'rub-DAT, in order to rub it' (§4.3.3.1).
[4] The inter-morphemic clusters in this column are best demonstrated by the adnominal privative suffix *-murlung*, for example *kuturrp-murlung* 'rattle-PRIV, stop rattling!' (§4.6.3) and the topic clitic *=ma*, for example *jatarlng=ma* 'join=TOP' (§10.1.2).
[5] The inter-morphemic clusters in this column are best demonstrated by the associative suffix *-ngarna*, for example *wumparlp-ngarna* 'float-ASSOC, something which floats' (§4.7.16). The ablative case suffix *-ngurlu* (§4.3.7), the source case suffix *-nginyi* (§4.3.8) and the dubitative clitic *=nga* (§7.1.3.13) are other examples.

2.3 Phonological rules

2.3.1 Stop-glide lenition

2.3.1.1 w-lenition

Stop>glide lenition affects the suffixes and clitics with initial /p/ and /k/ whereby they lenite to /w/ after a vowel.

p>w

(53) *=parla* ~ *=warla* 'FOCus'

(54) *-piti* ~ *-witi* 'SITE'

(55) *=pula* ~ *=wula* 'unit augmented'

(56) *=paju* ~ *=waju* 'BECAUSE'

(57) *=payin* ~ *=wayin* 'ETCetera'

In the case of /p/ and /k/, the preceding environment of lenition includes /rr/, /l/, and /rl/ as well as vowels.

(58) *-kaji* ~ *-waji* *pamarr-waji* 'money-AGENT'

(59) *=parla* ~ *=warla* *yantaly=warla* 'slip=FOC'

(60) *=payin* ~ *=wayin* *juwal=wayin* 'tall=ETC'

Another element which lenites after liquids is the initial /p/ of the epenthetic syllable *-pa-*, which is inserted before some consonant-initial suffixes following stem-final consonants (including some liquids). Following this rule, lenition applies converting *-pa* to *-wa*. This process does not occur following vowels as *-pa* is not inserted following vowels.

(61) *ngarin-**pa**=rni* 'meat-EP=ONLY'

(62) *wararr-**wa**=rni* 'fat-EP=ONLY'

(63) *ngawa=rni* 'water=ONLY'

k>w

(64) *-kaji* ~ *-waji* 'AGENT'

(65) *-karra* ~ *-warra* 'ITERative'

(66) *-ku* ~ *-wu* 'DATive'

(67) *-kunyja* ~ *-wunyja* 'COMitative'

(68) *-kumpal* ~ *-wumpal* 'AVERSive'

(69) *-kurt* ~ *-wurt* '(a number of) TIMES'

The lenition also affects suffixes following liquids in all cases where /u/ follows the initial vowel of the suffix, and in the case of the coverb/verb suffix *-karra* (see below).

(70) *-ku* ~ *-u* *wararr-u* 'fat-DAT'

(71) *-kunyja* ~ *-unyja* *mukurl-unyja* 'father's sister-COM'

(72) *-karra* ~ *-arra* *yantaly-arra* 'slip-ITER'

Note that not all *k*-initial suffixes lenite to /w/. A number of suffixes such as the case suffix *-kijak* 'TERMinative' (§4.3.10), and derivational suffixes *-kari* 'OTHER' (§4.7.8) and *-k* 'FACTitive' (§7.2.4.5) do not lenite. There is no strictly phonological explanation for the behaviour of these suffixes; they are best regarded as lexical exceptions to lenition. It is likely that these suffixes were borrowed into the language after lenition ceased to be a totally productive rule (as many lexical items have been); *-kari* and *-piya* are morphemes in Warlpiri, a neighbouring language without a lenition rule, and could be the source of these suffixes in Gurindji (although the meaning of *–piya* in Warlpiri is different). McConvell believes the *-kari* influence is possibly from further west.

2.3.1.2 y-lenition

Lenition also affects suffixes beginning with /j/ which lenite to /y/ after a vowel.

(73) *-jawung* ~ *-yawung* 'PROPrietive'

(74) *-jayi* ~ *-yayi* 'LATE, i.e. deceased'

(75) *-jirri* ~ *-yirri* 'ALLative'

(76) *=jina* ~ *=yina* 'them, 3AUG.NS'

Of suffixes which start with /j/, only the homophonic first person exclusive unit augmented pronominal clitic *=ja* and the topic clitic *=ja* do not lenite.

(77) *nyampa=ja* 'what=TOP'

(78) *ngu=ja* 'CAT=1EXC.UA.S'

The rule for converting /j/ to /y/ is similar to w-lenition except that the preceding environment does not include liquids:

(79) *turturl-jirri* 'cook.in.earth-ALL'

(80) *wilmurr-jawung* 'wire-PROP'

2.3.1.3 Lenition in reduplicated forms

Both the lenition rules sometimes operate to lenite the first consonant of the second copy in a reduplicated form.

(81) *purtu-wurtuj* < *purtuj-purtuj* < *purtuj* 'set fire to'

Lenition does not necessarily operate over all reduplication boundaries. Its operation may be optional or apparently impossible, but not on predictable phonological or grammatical grounds. Once again, this differential behaviour probably relates to the time of borrowing of elements into the language.

(82) *pirrka-pirrka* < **pirrka-wirrka* < *pirrka* 'make'

2.3.2 Vowel-glide deletion

In vowel-glide-vowel sequences involving /y/ or /w/, the glide is often deleted resulting in a long vowel or diphthong.

Some examples of vowel lengthening across morpheme boundaries are /awa/>[ɐː], /uwu/>[ʊː] and /iyi/>[ɪː]. Thus, it affects many of the suffixes also affected by lenition. Note that we do not represent this long vowel orthographically across morpheme and clitic boundaries in the rest of the grammar, but include the glide in the suffix.

(83)	*nyampa=warla*	>	*nyampa=arla*	'what=FOC'
(84)	*karu-wu*	>	*karu-u*	'child-DAT'
(85)	*paya-rni=yi*	>	*paya-rni=i*	'bite-PST=1EXC.MIN.NS'

Examples of vowel lengthening through glide deletion can also be found within morphemes. Long vowels such as these were discussed in §2.1.3.2.3. Where the glide is found in vowel-glide-vowel sequences in a stem, we often represent this as a long vowel.

(86)	*nyawa*	>	*nyaa*	'this'
(87)	*kupuwupu*	>	*kupuupu*	'lemon grass'
(88)	*wiyit*	>	*wiit*	'show, point'

In other vowel-glide sequences, phonetic diphthongs are often the result, for example /aw/ > [ɐʊ], /ay/ > [ɐɪ] and /uy/ > [oɪ].

(89)	*parnt<u>aw</u>urru*	>	[baɳɖɐʊru]	'back'
(90)	*yapak<u>ay</u>i*	>	[jɐbɐgɐɪ]	'small'
(91)	*wuyurrunkarra*	>	[woɪurunkɐrɐ]	'fishing'

In some cases, the vowel becomes a phonetic diphthong and the glide is deleted, and in other cases, the vowel-glide sequence creates a phonetic diphthong with the glide retained.

(92)	*ja<u>w</u>iji*	>	[ɟɐʊwɪɟi]	'grandfather'

(93) *kaya* > [kɐɪjɐ] 'monster'

(94) *muying* > [moɪjiŋ] 'black plum'

2.3.3 Vowel assimilation

Vowel assimilation only plays a minor role in Gurindji, compared with its close Ngumpin-Yapa neighbour, Warlpiri (Nash, 1986, p. 84 onwards) and the unrelated neighbouring language Jingulu (Pensalfini, 2002), which both exhibit vowel harmony. Bilinarra and Mudburra also have slightly more extensive vowel assimilation which affects the ergative *-lu* ~ *-li* and also the third person plural bound pronoun in Mudburra *-lu* ~ *-li*. Pensalfini (2021) gives an overview of this phenomenon in Australia, including the more extensive vowel harmony processes.

In Gurindji, vowel assimilation only affects the suppletive demonstrative stems *murla-* 'this' and *yala-* 'that'. First, when the ergative or dative case suffix *-ngku* or *-wu* attach to a demonstrative stem *murla-* 'this' or *yala-* 'that', the final vowel of these stems assimilates to /u/ (§5.1.1). Round (2021) refers to this as 'non-iterative assimilation'. Note that the process of vowel assimilation is only triggered by these two suffixes which are monosyllabic. Other case suffixes which contain the vowel /u/ are disyllabic, for example *-ngkurra* 'ALL' and *-ngurlu* 'ABL' do not cause a change in the stem. Table 14 shows the suppletive stems in combination with the different case suffixes. The demonstrative forms are discussed further in (§5.1.1).

Table 14: Vowel assimilation in the suppletive demonstrative stems.

	this	**that**
ERGATIVE	*murl**u**-ngku* 'this (one) did it'	*yal**u**-ngku* 'this (one) did it'
DATIVE	*murl**u**-wu* 'for this (one)'	*yal**u**-wu* 'for that (one)'
LOCATIVE	*murl**a**-ngka* 'here'	*yal**a**-ngka* 'there'
ALLATIVE	*murl**a**-ngkurra* '(to) here'	*yal**a**-ngkurra* '(to) there'
ABLATIVE	*murl**a**-ngurlu* 'from here'	*yal**a**-ngurlu* 'from there'
SOURCE	*murl**a**-nginyi* 'from here'	*yal**a**-nginyi* 'from there'
PERLATIVE	*murl**a**-mayin* 'through here'	*yal**a**-mayin* 'through there'
TERMINATIVE	*murl**a**-kijak* 'as far as here'	*yal**a**-kijak* 'as far as there'

2.3.4 Nasal cluster dissimilation

One striking morpho-phonological process found in Gurindji and other Ngumpin languages is the nasal cluster dissimilation (NCD) rule (McConvell, 1988b),[84] which has been noted for its resistance to straightforward treatments in autosegmental theory (cf. Evans, 1995a, p. 734).

There are two forms of NCD rule: NCD deletion (§2.3.4.1) and NCD denasalisation (§2.3.4.2); both have the effect of preventing the appearance on the surface of a nasal coda (a syllable-final nasal) following a nasal-stop cluster in consecutive or neighbouring syllables, by deleting or denasalising, respectively, the second nasal coda.

This rule is found in the Eastern Ngumpin languages, including Bilinarra, Ngarinyman, Mudburra, Wanyjirra (McConvell, 1988b; Meakins & Nordlinger, 2014; Senge, 2016) and in an attenuated form in Jaru (Tsunoda, 1981, pp. 48–49), but it is not observed in the western-most Ngumpin languages, such as Walmajarri, and it is not found in the Yapa languages, such as Warlpiri. The rule is described in detail, with discussion of theoretical implications in McConvell (1988b) and framed (somewhat unsuccessfully) in terms of Optimality Theory in Stanton (2019).

2.3.4.1 NCD deletion

NCD deletion is a rule which deletes the nasal from a homorganic nasal-stop cluster when it is preceded by another nasal cluster, either homorganic or heterorganic. NCD deletion is most commonly seen in adjacent syllables where, for example, the locative case suffix *-ngka* is replaced by *-ka* where a nasal cluster occurs within the noun to which the suffix is attached, as in (95) and (96). This rule also applies to the ergative and allative case suffixes (97)–(100), the perlative and edge (in the directional subclass of nominals) (101)–(103), and a minor derivational suffix (104).

-ngka ~ *-ka* 'LOCative' (see also §4.3.4.1)

(95) *pinka-ka* **pinka-ngka* 'river-LOC'

(96) *winyji-ka* **winyji-ngka* 'spring-LOC'

-ngku ~ *-ku* 'ERGative' (see also §4.3.2.1)

(97) *karnti-ku* **karnti-ngku* 'stick-ERG'

(98) *munpa-ku* **munpa-ngku* 'sorcery.murder-ERG'

-ngkurra ~ *-kurra* 'ALLative' (see also §4.3.5.1)

84 This was renamed nasal coda dissimilation by McConvell in subsequent work.

(99) *pampu-kurra* **pampu-ngkurra* 'didgeridoo-ALL'

(100) *wanyji-kurra* **wanyji-ngkurra* 'alive-ALL'

-mpal ~ *-pal* 'EDGE' (see also §5.2.1)

(101) *kanyju-pal* **kanyju-mpal* 'below-EDGE'

(102) *kankulu-pal* **kankulu-mpal* 'up-EDGE'

-mpa ~ *-pa* 'PERLative' (see also §5.2.1)

(103) *kanka-pa* **kanka-mpa* 'upstream-PERL'

-rntarn ~ *-rtarn* 'having EXCESS of' (see also §4.7.23)

(104) *tanku-rtarn* **tanku-rntarn* 'food-EXCESS'

There are also three pronominal clitics which have initial homorganic nasal clusters and are also affected by this rule, as shown in (105)–(107). An example from the corpus can also be heard in (108).

(105) *=ngku* ~ *=ku* '2MIN.NS, you'

(106) *=nyjurra* ~ *=jurra* '2AUG.NS, you mob'

(107) *=nta* ~ *=ta* '2AUG.S, you'

(108) Nya**mp**a=**ta** nga-rna-na?
what=2AUG.S eat-IMPF-PRS
"What are you mob eating?" (🔈 VW: FM07_a058: 5:45min)

NCD deletion can also operate on a nasal-stop cluster across a morpheme boundary. In this case, a cluster formed by a final nasal of a stem and the initial stop of a suffix determines deletion of a nasal in a nasal cluster internal to a suffix. This rule is shown by *-kunyja* 'COMitative' in (109) where the cluster formed by the final nasal in *ngarin* 'meat' and the initial stop in *-kunyja* causes the /ny/ to be deleted. In comparison, this rule does not apply to *jurlak* 'bird' which ends in a final stop, as shown in (110). This rule is also demonstrated using *-kumpalng* 'AVERSive', shown in (111) and (112).

-kunyja ~ *-kuja* 'COMitative' or 'LACKing' (§4.3.9 and §4.7.10)

(109) *ngari**n-k**uja* 'meat-LACK'

(110) *jurla**k-k**u**ny**ja* 'bird-LACK'

-kumpalng ~ *-kupalng* 'AVERSive' (§9.3.2)

(111) *nyi**rn-k**upalng* 'drown-AVERS'

(112) *lirla**j-k**u**m**palng* 'swim-AVERS'

The epenthetic syllable *-pa-* can also form a nasal-stop cluster with the stem it attaches to inducing a NCD deletion in the following clitic or suffix, as shown in (113).

(113) *nyatja**ng-pa**=jurra* **nyatja**ng-pa**=**ny**jurra* 'how.many-EP=2AUG.NS'

NCD deletion can also operate long distance from left to right across a number of syllables in the same word provided these contain only vowels, glides and liquids; if the intervening syllables contain any other consonant, it cannot apply (for some dialectal variation on this, see McConvell, 1988b).

=nta ~ *=ta* '2AUG.S, you'

(114)

Nyampa-wu=yi=**n**ta	ngayiny	kajakaja	wulaj
what-DAT=1EXC.MIN.NS=2AUG.S	1EXC.MIN.DAT	spurs	hide

yuwa-ni	nyurrulu?
put-PST	2AUG

"Why did you mob hide my spurs?" (🔈 SM: HALE_K06-004553: 42:31min)

-ngku- ~ *-ku-* 'EPenthetic'

(115) *ngu=**nyj**urra-ku=lu* **ngu=**nyj**urra-**ng**ku=lu* 'CAT=2AUG.NS-EP=3AUG.S'

Glides which permit NCD to apply across them include /w/ and /y/ derived by lenition from /p/, /k/ and /j/, as shown in (116)–(120). This shows that the lenition rule precedes the NCD deletion rule.

-kunyja ~ *-wunyja* ~ *-wuja* 'COMitative or LACKing'

(116) *nyampa-wuja* 'what-LACK'

1. Input *nyampa-kunyja*
2. W-lenition *nyamp**a-w**unyja*
3. NCD deletion *ny**ampa**-wuja*

(117) *jawurra-ny-kari-wuja* 'steal-NMLZ-OTHER-COM, with another thief'

1.	Input	*jawurra-ny-kari-kunyja*
2.	W-lenition	*jawurra-ny-kar**i-w**unyja*
3.	NCD deletion	*jawurra-**ny-k**ari-wuja*

=ngku ~ *=ku* '2MIN.NS, you'

(118)

Yala-**ngk**a=warla=**ngk**u	nyununy-pa=rni	aeroplane-ta=rni.
that-LOC=FOC=2MIN.NS	2MIN.DAT-EP=ONLY	aeroplane-LOC=ONLY

"He passed away on the plane on you." (🔈 BR: FM15_52_1a: 17:00min)

1.	Input	*yala-ngka=**p**arla=ngku*
2.	W-lenition	*yala-**ngk**a=warla=**ngk**u*
3.	NCD deletion	*yala-ngka=warla=ku*

Note that the NCD deletion does not apply to the following example because the stop-cluster in the stem /tp/ is not a nasal-stop cluster.

(119)

Nya**tp**a=warla=**ngk**u	ma-rni,	"Lawara	ngarin-pa=rni
how=FOC=2MIN.NS	say-PST	nothing	meat-EP=ONLY
puntanup	ma-ni	warrij	ya-ni."
gather	do-PST	leave	go-PST

"'What did he say to you?' 'Nothing he just collected the meat and left.'"
(🔈 DD: McNair_C2A: 5:57min)

=nta ~ *=ta* '2AUG.S'

(120)

Nyampa-wu=**w**arla=yi=**t**a	nya-nya?
what-DAT=FOC=1EXC.MIN.NS=2AUG.S	intake-PST

"Why did you lot look at me?" (McConvell, 1988b, p. 140)

1.	Input	*nyampa-**k**u=**p**arla=yi=nta*
2.	W-lenition	*nyampa-**w**u=**w**arla=yi=nta*
3.	NCD deletion	*nya**mp**a-wu=warla=yi=**t**a*

For a full set of examples showing blocking of NCD by stops and nasals, see McConvell (1988b).

If more than two nasal clusters appear in a word in the environment in which NCD deletion normally applies (i.e. without blocking consonants intervening), only the first cluster has the nasal deleted, e.g. in (121) only the ergative suffix *-ngku* becomes *-ku*; the pronominal clitic *=ngku* does not change to *=ku*. This is likely because the NCD deletion rules apply iteratively from left to right thus in (121) in the first step *ng* is deleted from the first suffix; only then does the opportunity arise for NCD deletion to apply again between the first and second suffixes but there is an intervening *k* consonant.

(121) Ngantu-~~ng~~ku=warla=**ng**ku nyawa tarltarl pa-ni timana
who-ERG=FOC=2MIN.NS this shoot hit-PST horse

nyununy.
2MIN.DAT
"Who shot that horse of yours?" (🔊 MS: HALE_K06-004553: 50:17min)

2.3.4.2 NCD denasalisation

NCD denasalisation converts the nasal to a corresponding non-nasal stop with the same place of articulation where it is preceded by a nasal-stop cluster. The main morpheme affected by NCD denasalisation is *=npula* '2UA.S, you two'. As with NCD deletion, the left-hand environment must contain a nasal cluster, homorganic or heterorganic for the rule to apply and the nasal which is denasalised is followed by a heterorganic stop. In (122) and (123) the determining nasal cluster is in the adjacent syllable to the clitic *=npula* which changes to *=tpula*. (124) is a contrastive example showing where the rule does not apply because there is no nasal-stop cluster in the preceding stem.

(122) *nya**mpa**=**t**pula* *nyampa=npula 'what=2UA.S'

(123) *nyatja**ng-pa**=**t**pula* *nyatjang-pa=npula 'how.many-EP=2UA.S'

(124) *ngana=**np**ula* *ngana=ntula 'who=2UA.S'

Like NCD deletion, NCD denasalisation can apply long distance over syllables containing vowels, glides and liquids, but not over other consonants (125); and it does not apply where its left-hand environment has been removed by the operation of NCD deletion, for example (126) where *-wuja* derives from underlying *-wunyja* which means that the following *=n-ku* does not undergo dissimilation.

(125) Nya**mp**a-wu=warla=**t**pula timana wirnput luwa-rni.[85]
what-DAT=FOC=2UA.S horse whip strike-PST
"Why did you two whip that horse?" (🔊 MS: HALE_K06-004553: 49:07min)

85 Major Smiler conjugates this verb as a Class 2 verb, but Malngin speakers conjugate it as a Class 1 verb (see §7.1.1).

(126) *ngantu-wuja=n-**ku**=rla* 'who-COM=2MIN.S-EP=3OBL'

The major difference between the environments of the two NCD rules is that if the right-hand nasal of NCD denasalisation is the final segment of a word, it can be denasalised, whereas final nasals cannot be deleted by NCD deletion. NCD denasalisation applies in the environment of a following word beginning with a non-nasal consonant (127) *-n* ~ *-t*, even if the initial consonant is homorganic (128) *-n* ~ *-t*. If the following consonant is nasal, it does not usually apply (129), and there is variation in the cases where the following initial segment is a glide or liquid, or if there is no immediately following word (see McConvell 1988 for details).

(127) Nyampa-wu=**t** pa-ni?
what-DAT=2MIN.S hit-PST
"Why did you hit it?" (McConvell, 1988b, p. 145)

(128) Nyampa-wu=**t** tak karrinya?
what-DAT=2MIN.S sit be.PST
"Why did you sit down?" (McConvell, 1988b, p. 146)

(129) Nyampa-wu=**n** nga-rni?
what-DAT=2MIN.S eat-PST
"Why did you eat it?" (McConvell, 1988b, p. 146)

In some other suffixes with final nasals, NCD denasalisation occurs without the need of a right-hand conditioning environment, with the same left-hand conditions as other NCD rules. Example (130) shows a case in which NCD does not operate. Example (131) shows it applying in adjacent syllables, and (132) and (133) show it operating across intervening liquids, /l/ and /rr/ respectively.

-yin ~ *-yit* 'ABLative' (with directional terms)

(130) *kaarra-yi**n*** 'east-ABL'

(131) *kanka-yi**t*** 'upstream-ABL'

(132) *kankuli-yi**t*** 'up-ABL'

(133) *kaarra-ngkarra-yi**t*** 'east-DOWN-ABL'

This alternation only occurs optionally, for some speakers, and for some may vary according to the presence of a following stop environment.

-ny ~ *-j* nominaliser 'NMLZ'

(134) *janka-wu-ny* ~ *janka-wu-j* 'woman-DAT-NMLZ; belonging to women'

(135) *parnkal-u-j* 'Bat-DAT-NMLZ; Bat Dreaming place'

The suffix *-rntarn* was used to illustrate NCD deletion of the first /rn/ in the previous section. It is also subject to denasalisation of the final /rn/ where followed by another suffix beginning with an oral consonant, i.e. *-rntarn* ~ *-rntart* EXCESS, e.g. *walu-rnta**rt**-karra* 'head-EXCESS-ITER; having a headache'.

(136) Ngantu=warla=**t**-ku=rla jayi-nya nguku?
who=FOC=2MIN.S-EP=3OBL give-PST water
"Who did you give water to?" (🔊 SM: HALE_K06-004555: 3:24min)

By comparison with related languages, and in some cases by the existence of alternative forms in Gurindji, it can be shown that NCD rules have operated to change stem forms e.g. NCD denasalisation has occurred in *ngumpin*, as shown in (137).

(137) *ngu**mpit*** 'man, Indigenous person'

NCD denasalisation in stems also applies long-distance across any number of vowels, glides, and liquids, as can be seen from alternative forms, shown in (138).

(138) *pi**np**alarri**j*** ~ *pi**np**alarri**ny*** 'snake sp.'

NCD cannot be given the status of an absolute phonotactic constraint however, as there are a number of exceptions in the lexicon, probably relatively recent loanwords, for example (139).

(139) *mu**mpung*** **mumpu**k*** 'black'

2.3.5 Epenthesis

Gurindji has a number of epenthetic syllables. The epenthetic *-ngku-* is only found in sequences of bound pronouns and is discussed in §6.2.3.5.1. The epenthetic *-pa-* is found in more places (§6.2.3.5.2). Where a stem ends in a stop, it allows a clitic with no consonant-final allomorph to attach. For suffixes and clitics which have consonant-final allomorphs, the consonant-final allomorph is used. In general, *-pa-* is used far less frequently than in other Ngumpin languages such as Bilinarra.

2.3.6 Reduplication

Reduplication is found with nominals to indicate plurality. In some adjectives, it functions derivationally to create new nominals (§4.4.9). Coverbs are also reduplicated to mark participant plurality or distributed action over multiple participants, referred to as a type of 'pluractionality' (§7.2.4.4) (cf. Schultze-Berndt, 2012). In this respect, reduplication of coverbs contrasts with the use of the iterative suffix *-karra* (§7.2.4.1). In other Ngumpin languages, Jaru and Mudburra, reduplication is also found with inflecting verbs (Osgarby, 2018a, pp. 70–88; Tsunoda, 1981, p. 172), but this has not been observed for Gurindji, or indeed its close neighbours, Bilinarra or Ngarinyman (Meakins & Nordlinger, 2014, pp. 75–77).

The first type of reduplication in Gurindji is full reduplication which involves copying the entire stem and placing it to the right of the stem. Primary stress is retained on the first syllable of the first part and the first syllable of the second part takes secondary stress. Most monosyllabic stems, and many disyllabic stems are subject only to full reduplication.

(140) *murlng-murlng* 'one each, some each' < *murlng* 'one's own'

(141) *pat-pat* 'feel around' < *pat* 'touch'

(142) *pirrka-pirrka* 'repeatedly make' < *pirrka* 'make'

Partial reduplication is the other type of reduplication. It takes a number of forms. They are dealt with in an order which reflects the number of segments by which the reduplication is reduced.

Firstly, in some cases of partial reduplication, the final consonant of the stem is lost. For example, monosyllabic coverb stems with final /p/ immediately following a liquid can have the final /p/ of the first part of the reduplication deleted. The deletion is required because full reduplication would result in an illicit consonant cluster (see §2.2.5.2 for consonant cluster possibilities). It is also possible that because *-p* used to be an active suffix, it is just added to the end of the reduplicated stem.

(143) *turrturrp* < *turrp-turrp* < *turrp* 'pierce'

In some examples, the final consonant is not copied, even though a licit consonant cluster would result, as with *jirrip* > *jirri-jirrip* 'tear up something-REDUP'. Since /pj/ is a permissible inter-morphemic cluster (see §2.2.5.2), it is not clear why the reduplicated form is not *jirrip-jirrip* here.[86]

86 Note that historically *-p* was a suffix on coverbs. So the reduplication without *-p* on the first element would not have resulted from loss of *p* but use of the form with the *-p* suffix.

In disyllabic consonant-final stems, partial reduplication most frequently results in the deletion of the final consonant of the first part.

(144) *jalnga-jalngak < jalnga**k**-jalngak < jalngak* 'ride'

(145) *kiji-kijik < kiji**k**-kijik < kijik* 'tickle'

(146) *tipa-tipart < tipa**rt**-tipart < tipart* 'jump'

(147) *wula-wulaj < wula**j**-wulaj < wulaj* 'hide'

Such reduction cannot occur if the final consonant is nasal:

(148) **kara-karan < kara**n**-karan < karan* 'scratch'

(149) **maki-makin < maki**n**-makin < makin* 'lie, sleep'

The next type of partial reduction involves deletion of the final consonant of the first part, as in the above type, and additionally, the deletion of the first consonant and vowel of the second part:

(150) *partartaj < partaj-partaj < partaj* 'climb'

Other examples with different first and second vowels show that it is the first vowel of the second part that is lost, and the second vowel of the first part is retained:

(151) *kutitij < kutij-**ku**tij < kutij* 'stand'

(152) *lirlarlaj < lirlaj-**li**rlaj < lirlaj* 'swim'

(153) *walilik < walik-**wa**lik < walik* 'around'

However, in examples where the first vowel of the stem is /a/ and the second vowel is /u/, /a/ is retained and /u/ lost:

(154) *wartartuj < wart**uj-w**artuj < wartuj* 'be lost'

(155) *warrkarrkuj < warrk**uj-w**arrkuj < warrkuj* 'pick up'

In vowel-final words of three syllables and more, the final consonant and vowel of the first part of the reduplication may be deleted:

(156) *jika-jikarna < jika**rna**-jikarna < jikarna* 'whirlwind'

(157) *kaji-kajirri < kaji**rri**-kajirri < kajirri* 'old woman'

The more radical type of reduction for vowel-final trisyllables involves the deletion of the final VCV sequence of the first part and the initial consonant of the second part:

(158) *jangkakarni* < *jangk**arni-j**angkarni* < *jangkarni* 'big'

(159) *kajajirri* < *kaji**rri-k**ajirri* < *kajirri* 'old woman'

(160) *kartartiya* < *kar**tiya-k**artiya* < *kartiya* 'non-Indigenous person'

(161) *mananungka* < *man**ungka-m**anungka* < *manungka* 'single man'

(162) *marlarluka* < *mar**luka-m**arluka* < *marluka* 'old man'

This type of reduction also applies in four-syllable words:

(163) *waringaringarri* < *waring**arri-w**aringarri* < *waringarri* 'raiding party'

2.4 Stress

Primary word stress falls on the first syllable of the phonological word. In words of two and three syllables the remaining syllables do not receive stress. In words of more than three syllables, the first and penultimate syllables generally receive stress.

(164) ***pa**ka* 'thorn'

(165) ***pa**karli* 'paperbark, paper'

(166) ***pa**karli-la* 'paperbark-LOC'

(167) ***wa**rnta**ma**rri* 'in a line'

In a polysyllabic word with a stem and suffix of more than one syllable, however, the stress falls on the first syllable of the suffix. This follows the common Australian stress pattern whereby suffixes and clitics of more than one syllable begin a new stress domain (B. Baker, 2014).

(168) *pakarli-**ya**wung-kulu* 'paperbark-PROP-ERG'

(169) *warntamarri-**ngi**nyi* 'in.line-SOURCE'

In reduplicated forms, it is the initial syllable of the reduplication which takes the secondary stress, and this syllable usually retains the stress even when the form is reduced by loss of internal segments.

The only exceptions to initial syllable stress are words and suffixes beginning with /pir/, where stress is on the second syllable beginning with /r/ and the first vowel /i/ is often not heard:

(170) *ngaji=pi**rak*** 'father=CORRECT'

Unstressed /i/ also tends to very weak or inaudible between medial consonants and /r/.

(171) ***war**niriri* 'small grasshopper'

2.5 *Janyarrp* – Gurindji babytalk

In many cultures, adults modify their speech when talking to infants and young children, which is often called 'baby talk' (Ferguson, 1964: 103). *Janyarrp* is a Gurindji term that refers both to how adults speak to young children, and how young children themselves speak. In this section, we outline some of the modifications which adults make in their speech when talking to children. This description of *janyarrp* is drawn from Jones and Meakins (2013a).

Cross-linguistically, it has been observed that adults tend to respond to children once they begin talking by using imitations of their immature speech forms (Casagrande, 1948; Chew, 1969; Cruttenden, 1994; Ferguson, 1964, 1977; Grimes, 1955; Shankara Bhat, 1967). The segmental features of baby talk include consonant cluster reduction, consonant harmony (place or nasality), consonant fronting, labialisation, replacement of rhotics, stopping of fricatives and initial or final deletion. Coronals are palatalised in baby talk in Japanese (Chew, 1969), South Estonian (Pajusalu, 2001) and Huichol (Grimes, 1955).

In Australian languages, there are a small number of papers on baby talk which observe a number of features: neutralisation of coronal place contrasts, replacement of rhotics (and laterals) and consonant cluster reduction. In speech to Warlpiri children (Laughren, 1984; O'Shannessy, 2011), adults reduce the three-way coronal place contrast (apical alveolar, apical post-alveolar, and laminal palatal) to laminal palatals in stops, nasals and laterals. Similarly, in babytalk in Kaytetye and other Arandic languages, coronal stops, nasals and laterals are pronounced as laminal dentals or laminal palatals, in free variation (Turpin, Demuth, & Campbell, 2012). (These languages have up to a four-way coronal contrast unlike Gurindji which only has three.) In Warlpiri and the Arandic languages, adults report that this style copies how young children first articulate coronals. In Arandic baby talk to older children, adults introduce a coronal distinction between apical alveolars and laminals (Turpin et al., 2012). Rhotic replacement in Southern Warlpiri results in all three rhotics being replaced by the palatal glide /j/, except in the common diminutive suffix *-pardu*, where the flap is replaced with /w/ (Laughren, 1984). For very young children up to three or four years of age, the apical laterals are replaced by /w/ in at least two common words (*wawa* for *lawa* 'no, nothing', and *wawu* for *warlu* 'fire, heat, hot'). In Arandic baby talk, the postalveolar approximant is replaced by /w/ initially and /j/ finally, and the alveolar trill is replaced by /j/ finally and elided in onset of stressed syllable (Turpin et al., 2012). Consonant cluster reduction in Warlpiri baby talk (Laughren, 1984) sees liquid+stop clusters delete the liquid (i.e. the lateral or trill/flap); in Arandic languages, in addition, liquid+stop clusters can be replaced with nasal+stop clusters (Turpin et al., 2012).

Before learning to talk, Gurindji children are usually encouraged to use an auxiliary sign language called *takataka* (see §1.8.2). The first hand signs include single signs for important commodities such as food, money and tobacco, important kin relations and queries about a person's whereabouts. At this preverbal stage, their understanding of language is often tested with commands to perform different tasks, from kinship-based demands such as fetching objects for grandmothers or playfully hitting uncles, to simple acts of dancing or kissing. Around the age of 2–3 years old, children are expected to be producing intelligible short utterances. Where children are slow to develop linguistically, adults use a number of methods to speed up their progress. The eggs of a bird called a *panaka* can be collected and smeared on children's tongues, or an adult will warm her thumb and index finger over a fire in a gun-like gesture and pull a child's tongue out. These techniques are said to shock children into speaking. Where children continue muteness into adulthood, they are referred to as *amama* 'mute one'.

Of course most Gurindji children successfully acquire language. As they learn language, Gurindji adults modify their speech in particular ways which is the basis for *janyarrp*. The follow sections describe these modifications.

2.5.1 Coronal place neutralisation (palatalisation)

Palatalisation is a common process in CDS (child-directed speech) form alongside ADS (adult-directed speech). Palatalisation affects any apical stop, nasal or lateral, in initial, medial, or final position, in singletons or clusters.

(172) Coronal place neutralisation (palatalisation)

	word	CDS	ADS		
a)	*langa*	ʎɐŋɐ	lɐŋɐ	'ear'	(CE: FM031A: 6:57min)
b)	*karnti-ngku*[87]	kɐɲɟɪŋgʊ	kɐɳɖɪŋgʊ	'stick-ERG'	(SS: FM009B: 68:27min)
c)	*partaj*	bɐɟɐɟ	pɐɖɐc	'climb'	(CE: FM019A: 31:01min)

Palatalisation is a salient aspect of *janyarrp*. Violet Wadrill responded to an excerpt of baby talk to a child of about 2 years with a demonstration of how an adult would talk *janyarrp*, and then switched to imitate the child. Both parts included extensive palatalisation, rhotic replacement, and some nasal harmony (bolded in IPA below; underlined in orthography).

ɲʊ**ɲɟ**ʊŋgʊ jʊ bɪn kɐmɐp **ɟej**ʊgɐp**k**ɪɲɪ kʊjɐ. kʊjɐrɐ kʊjɐ**l**ɐ. ɲʊ**ɲɟ**ʊŋgʊ wɐ**c** **cej**ʊgɐpŋɪɲɪ wɐ, kɐɲɟɪlɪjɪt pɪnkɐŋɪɲɪ kʊjɐ. **ɲæɲ**ɪ, ɲʊ**ɲ**ʊ**ɲ**ʊ gɔn wɐ? ɲʊ**ɲɟ**ʊmɐ jænɪ, **ɟej**ʊgɐpkʊ ŋɐjɪmɐ. kɐɲɟ**ɪj**ɐ pɪnkɐ kʊjɐ. æn ŋʊɳɐ wɔʈɭɐ jænɪ **ɟej**ʊgɐpŋɪɲɪmɐ. **cæɲ**gʊ nɐ. **cæɲ**gʊ nɐ ŋʊɳɐ, ŋɐɭʊ kʊjɐ.

'Nyuntu-ngku yu bin kamap tarukap-nginyi,' kuya. Kuyarra kuyarra. 'Nyuntu-ngku wart tarukap-nginyi wayi, kanyjuliyit pinka-nginyi?' Kuya. (Wi tok bo jem kuya karu-wu-ma hmm.) '[name], nyuntu-ngku gon wayi?' Nyuntu-ma yani, tarukap-ku ngayu-ma. Kanyjurra pinka,' kuya. "An ngurna wart yani tarukap-nginyi-ma. Tanku na. Tanku na ngurna, ngarlu," kuya.

"You just came back from swimming," said like this. We say it like this. "You came back from swimming, did you, from down at the river?" That's how we say it? (We talk to the kids like this.) "[name], are you leaving? You went for a swim? Down at the river," is how it is said. (imitates child): "And I came back from swimming. Food now. I want to have some food now," says the child.

2.5.2 Rhotic replacement

In *janyarrp*, the rhotics /ɻ, ɹ/ can be replaced by /w/ or /j/ in Gurindji words, as shown in (173).

(173) Rhotic replacement

	word	CDS	ADS		
a)	*tarukap*	gɐwʊgɐ	ɖɐɻʊgɐp	'swim'	(CS: BT1: 90:11min)
b)	*karu*	kɐjʊ	kɐɻʊ	'child'	(CE: FM019A: 42:44min)
c)	kɐwʊ	*karu*	kɐɻʊ	'child'	(CE: BT4: 3:31min)

The intervocalic trill /r/ is also replaced by /w/ and /l/ intervocalically or pre-consonantally, as shown in (174).

(174) Rhotic replacement of trill, and replacement by lateral

	word	CDS	ADS		
a)	*warrija*	wɐlɪɟɐ	wɐrɪɟɐ	'crocodile'	(MS: FM005B: 19:26min)
b)	*turrp*	tʊlp	tʊrp	'poke, stab'	(VR: FM009A: 8:50min)

87 Note that the NCD deletion has not applied to the ergative marker. This process is not present in current Gurindji adults under 40 years old.

2.5.3 Cluster simplification

Consonant clusters are simplified either by deletion of liquid in clusters, of stop and liquid or by assimilation in manner and/or place of the first consonant, resulting in homorganic nasal+stop clusters from liquid+stop and fricative+stop, and oral or nasal geminates or homorganic nasal+stop from stop+stop sequences. Rarer patterns are vowel epenthesis and coalescence.

2.5.4 Other modifications

Four other modifications are present in *janyarrp*: initial and final deletion, consonant harmony, replacements of apical postalveolars, and specific lexical items. Examples of initial and final deletion include initial deletions of velar nasal or other sonorant segment or syllable, medial sonorant syllable deletion, final deletions of liquid or nasal, or sonorous syllable. Initial deletion results in vowel-initial words even though this violates the phonotactics of Gurindji-derived words (no vowel-initial words in Gurindji).

(175) Initial and final deletion

	word	CDS	ADS		
a)	*yapakayi*	æbɐgeɪ	jæbɐgeɪ	'small'	(SS: FM031A: 10:12min)
b)	*ngapulu*	ɐbʊlʊ	ŋɐbʊlu	'milk, breast'	(CS, SS: BT1: 80:06min)
c)	*murnungku*	nʊnʊ	mʊɳʊŋgʊ	'policeman'	(CS, SS: BT1: 87:12min)
d)	*ngapulu-yu*	nɐbʊjʊ	nɐbʊlujʊ	'milk-DAT'	(CE: BT4: 32:19min)
e)	*puny*	ʊ:	pʊɲ	'kiss'	(KS: FM001A: 33:12min)

Consonant harmony patterns are also present in *janyarrp*. Typically, this is regressive place assimilation, although manner harmony is also apparent. Examples can be analysed as progressive assimilation of continuancy. Nasality/orality also shows increased domain.

(176) Consonant harmony

	word	CDS	ADS		
a)	*tarukap*	gɐwʊgɐp	ɖɐɻʊgɐp	'swim'	(CS: BT1: 90:11min)
b)	*jurlaka*	kʊɭɐgɐ	ɟʊɭɐkɐ, ɟʊɭɐk	'bird'	(SS: FM009B: 59:40min)
c)	*jurlaka*	tʊɭɐkɐ	ɟʊɭɐkɐ, ɟʊɭɐk	'bird'	(SS: BT1: 82:00min)
d)	*kumpu*	bʊmbʊ	kʊmbʊ	'urine'	(CS: BT1: 81:37min)
g)	*kura*	kʊkɐ	kʊɻɐ	'faeces'	(CS: BT1: 80:39min)
i)	*mangarri*	mɐɲɐɲɪ	mɐŋɐrɪ	'bread'	(CS: BT5: 7:56min)
j)	*kungulu*	kʊkʊlʊ	kʊŋʊlʊ	'blood'	(CE: BT4: 36:50min)

3 Parts of speech

3.1 Introduction

Gurindji has nine word classes or parts of speech which can be distinguished using inflectional and distributional criteria. In most cases, each word only belongs to one word class, although a small set of nouns and coverbs can shift word classes through zero derivation, for example *kuli* 'fight' or 'to fight', *janga* 'sickness, sore' or 'to be sick', *kumpu* 'urine' or 'to urinate', *ngurra* 'a camp' or 'to camp' and *jarrakap* 'a meeting' or 'to talk'. More generally words can change their class through the use of derivational morphology (see §4.7 for nominals and §7.2.4 for coverbs).

3.2 Nominals

Nominals are one of the largest word classes in Gurindji, the other being coverbs. This word class is large because the nouns and adjectives are open subclasses, but note that the directionals, temporals, free pronouns, demonstratives and interrogatives are closed subclasses. Noun and adjective borrowings, particularly from Kriol, supplement the Gurindji vocabulary with names for introduced European items and concepts, such as *culture* in (177), for which there is no equivalent Gurindji word. Borrowings are fully integrated into the morphological structure of Gurindji nominals, in terms of case etc.

(177) Ngantipany **kaltja** ngu=rnayinangkulu
1EXC.AUG.DAT culture CAT=1EXC.AUG.S>3AUG.NS

pinak-pinak ma-na-nku.
teach-REDUP do-IMPF-POT
"We want to be teaching them our culture."
(🔈 TD: FM08_11_4: 0:39min) (Meakins, 2014, p. 303)

Nominals are distinguished from other word classes by their ability to be inflected for case, although not all nominal subclasses can be inflected with the full range of cases, as discussed for directionals (§3.2.3), temporals (§3.2.4) and free pronouns (§3.2.5). Coverbs can also host case inflections in reduced subordinate clauses, nonetheless they can be distinguished from nominals on the basis of their inability to act as arguments in clauses. This criterion is discussed further in §3.5 and §7.2. The various subclasses of nominals show different syntactic and morphological behaviours, as discussed in the following sections.

https://doi.org/10.1515/9783110746884-003

3.2.1 Nouns

Nouns are typically referential, denoting objects and entities. They consist of common nouns, proper nouns such as personal names and place names, and kinship terms. All nouns can be case-marked according to their grammatical role (ergative, dative, locative, allative, purposive, ablative, source, comitative, perlative, terminative and motivative) (§4.3). An example of a noun receiving allative case is given in (178). (The noun *kartipa* is unmarked as it is the nominative subject of an intransitive clause). Nouns can also receive additional number suffixes (§4.4), adnominal case (proprietive and privative) (§4.6) and derivational morphology (§4.7).

(178)	Jirrpu	waninyana	kartipa	**ngawa-ngkurra.**
	dive	fall.IMPF.PRS	non-Indigenous	water-ALL

"The *kartipa* dives into the water." (🔊 VW: FHM146: 4:45min)

Nouns primarily function as arguments, such as the ergative-marked and accusative nominals (unmarked) in (179); and as complements and adjuncts, as shown by the allative-marked goal in (178) and locative-marked location in (179).

(179)	**Marluka-lu**=ma	**yalu-ngku**=ma	**ngalyakap-kaji**
	old.man-ERG=TOP	that-ERG=TOP	lick-AGENT

jak	wuya-rni	ngu	**tak-kaji-la.**
drop	throw-PST	CAT	sit-AGENT-LOC

"That man dropped the ice cream on the chair." (🔊 BW: FM07-a043: 21:07min)

Within a noun phrase, nouns typically function as the head, as shown in (179), where *marluka* 'old man' is the head of the noun phrase, modified by the demonstrative *yalu-* 'that'. Nouns may also act as modifiers in noun phrases, as in (180) where *kumpulyu* 'white currant' modifies *karnti* 'tree' to produce a single meaning of 'white currant tree'.

(180)	Nyawa=ma=kata	**karnti**	**kumpulyu=ma**
	this=TOP=IMM	tree	white.currant=TOP

kuni	ngu=rna	ma-ni.
dream	CAT=1EXC.MIN.S	do-PST

"I dreamt about that white currant tree." (🔊 VW: FM09_16_1b: 1:17min)

Nouns can also function as the predicate of a verbless clause, as demonstrated by (181), where the subject is *karu* 'child' and the predicate is *wartiwarti* 'left-hand'.

(181) Nyawa=ma **wartiwarti**-said ngu **karu**=ma.
this=TOP left.hand-SIDE CAT child=TOP
"This child is left-handed." (◀)) VW: FM10_a143: 9:09min)

Two types of nouns show some minor variation from this subclass in general. Firstly, place names are only optionally marked allative in goal constructions, whereas such marking is obligatory for all other nouns (note that animate goals are marked dative (§4.3.3.2)). For example, while an allative marker is used in (182), it is not always found. Note that the ablative and locative are obligatory, as shown in (183) and (184).

(182) Ya-nku=rlaa warrij nyawa-ngurlu=ma,
go-POT=1INC.AUG.S leave this-ABL=TOP

kurlarra nganayirla-yirri **Palyilarra-yirri**.
south whatsitcalled-ALL place.name-ALL
"Let's go from here south to Palyilarra."
(◀)) VW: FM10_30_1a: Karu Dreaming Story: 2:12min)

(183) Nyila na ya-ni kayirra-ngkarra-jirri
that FOC go-PST north-DOWN-ALL

Palyilarra-ngurlu=ma ngu=lu.
place.name-ABL=TOP CAT=3AUG.S
"They went down and north from Palyilarra [to Karungkarni]."
(◀)) VW: FM07_01_2a: 2:38min)

(184) Winyji-ka na kayirri-ngkarra ngu=lu
spring-LOC FOC north-DOWN CAT=3AUG.S

waninya **Palyilarra-la**.
fall.PST place.name-LOC
"They came north down to a spring at Palyilarra."
(◀)) VW: FM10_30_1a: Karu Dreaming Story: 2:28min)

Kinship terms also differ from other nominals because they are the only noun type which can co-occur with specific kinship suffixes, for example *–rlang* 'DYAD' which marks kinship pairs (§4.5). For instance, *parnku-rlang* 'cousin-DYAD' refers to a pair of cousins (185). Tri-relational kinterms which group the speaker, hearer and a referent in one term, also have specific morphology, shown in (186) (§4.5.4). Skin names also have different morphology, specifically a dedicated plural marker *-jpan* which is not found on other nominals (§4.4.6). An example is given in (187).

(185) Ngarnjal=ma ma-rni ngu, "**Parnku-rlang**,
NAME=TOP say-PST CAT cousin-DYAD

nomo pa-rra=wula kankulu-pal.
NEG hit-IMP=3UA.S up-EDGE
"Topsy said, 'Hey you two cousins, don't cut above the hole.'"
(◀)) VW: FM07_a021: 2:58min)

(186) **Murrwali-marnany**-ku wanyja-rra=rla.
mother.in.law-2MIN.POSS-DAT leave-IMP=3OBL
"Give room for your mother-in-law who is my child." (◀)) VW: FM12_a172: 2:21min)

(187) **Nimarra-jpan** **Japarta-jpan**
SUBSECT-PL.SKIN SUBSECT-PL.SKIN

parnkuti ngu=rla nyanuny.
cousin CAT=3OBL 3MIN.DAT
"All of the Nimarras and Japartas are her cousins." (◀)) VW: FM10_23_1b: 7:30min)

Finally, personal names associated with the action of Dreamings in particular tracts of country also have male and female endings not found on other nouns, for example *Tupngali* (f) vs *Tupngayarri* (m), which is derived from the coverb *tup* 'pluck' and describes a Dreaming's action in a particular place.

3.2.2 Adjectives

There is little formal distinction between nouns and adjectives in Gurindji, which is the case with many Australian languages (Bittner & Hale, 1995; Dixon, 1980; Simpson, 1991). Both nouns and adjectives are inflected for case and other nominal morphology, as shown in (188) where *wankaj* is marked dative. Adjectives generally modify heads, as in (188) and (189), but like nouns, they can also function as the head of a noun phrase (190) and as the predicate of a verbless clause (191). These roles are shown for the adjective *wankaj* 'no good'.

(188) Kulmarrk, waninyana, ngu=rnalu=rla kulmarrk,
work.hard fall.IMPF.PRS CAT=1EXC.AUG.S=3OBL work.hard

kajirri-wu=ma **yalu**-wu=ma **wankaj**-ku kula kalurirrp-kaji.
old.woman-DAT=TOP that-DAT=TOP sick-DAT NEG walk.around-AGENT
"We work hard for that sick old lady who can't walk about herself."
(◀)) VW: FM12_a177: 3:41min)

(189)

Warrwaraj-karra	yuwa-na-na	**nyila=ma**	**wankaj=ma.**
separate.husks-ITER	put-IMPF-PRS	that=TOP	bad=TOP

"She is separating out the bad bits." (🔈 VW: FM11_a165: 5:36min)

(190)

Wankaj	ngu	karrij	ma-na-na.
disabled	CAT	decrepit	do-IMPF-PRS

"That disabled person is decrepit." (🔈 VW: FM12_a174: 19:08min)

(191)

Wankaj	nyila=ma	jurlak=ma.
no.good	that=TOP	bird=TOP

"That bird is no good." (🔈 VW: FM11_a167: 2:22min)

Some semantic, syntactic and morphological differences between nouns and adjectives warrant them being treated as separate subclasses. Syntactically, although both nouns and adjectives can be a head or modifier of a noun phrase, it is more common for nouns to function as heads, and adjectives, as modifiers, shown in (188) and (189). In addition, nouns generally refer to entities or objects, and adjectives typically denote attributes such as qualities or quantities, for example *wankaj* 'no good'. This semantic difference leads to different derivational possibilities between adjectives and nouns. Adjectives can be derived from coverbs using *-pari* (consonant-final stems) or *-wari* (vowel-final stems) (§4.6.21). For example, the coverb *kirturlk* 'to be crooked' becomes an adjective *kirturlkpari* 'crooked' with the addition of this suffix, as in (192).

(192)

Ngu=rlaa	paya-rna-ni	<u>jeya</u>	<u>na</u>
CAT=1EXC.AUG.S	bite-IMPF-PRS	there	FOC

kayirra=ma	ngurra-ngka	**kirturlk-pari**=ma.
north=TOP	camp-LOC	crooked-ADJ=TOP

"We cut the crooked one in the [women's centre] place at Daguragu."
(🔈 VW: FM09_a120: 2:24min)

Different constructions may also affect whether an adjective refers to a state or property. Within a noun phrase, an adjective refers to the properties of an entity whereas in verbal clauses an adjective describes a state. For example, in (191) *wankaj* 'no good' refers to a property of *jurlak* 'bird', whereas in (193) *punyu* describes the state of the speaker. Nouns within verbless and verbal clauses do not show this distinction.

(193)

Kurrurij-murlung	**punyu**	ngu=rnalu	**karrinya.**
car-PRIV	good	CAT=1EXC.AUG.S	be.PST

"We were happy enough without cars."
(McConvell corpus: Meakins et al., 2016, p. 339)

Interestingly, in the speech of Gurindji Kriol speakers (see §1.7.3 for an explanation of Gurindji Kriol), the distinction between nouns and adjectives emerges more strongly. Adjectives are treated as a different word class from nominals in that they cannot function as the head of an NP and do not take case-marking. Before they can be case-marked, they are turned into a noun using the Kriol nominalising suffix *-wan* (< one) e.g. *jangkarni-wan* 'something big', as shown in (194).

(194) Ngakparn=ma im karrap jem Gurindji Kriol
frog=TOP 3SG stare 3PL.O

nyila-ngku=ma **jangkarni-wan-tu**=ma.
that-ERG=TOP big-NMLZ-ERG=TOP
"The big one stared at the frog." (◀)) CE: FM08_a068: 4:36min)

3.2.3 Directionals

Directional nominals consist of three sets of absolute terms, which refer to fixed bearings. Two of these sets are orientated on the horizontal axis: (a) the cardinal set: *kayirra* 'north', *kurlarra* 'south', *kaarnirra* 'east'[88] and *karlarra* 'west' (195); and (b) the river drainage set: *kankarra* 'upstream' and *kanimparra* 'downstream' (196) (McConvell, 2001; Meakins, 2011c). Gurindji is unusual in having both systems, but it is probably an old contact feature, which is the result of its position between languages to the north which use river drainage systems exclusively (e.g. Jaminjung) (Schultze-Berndt, 2006b) and those to the south which use cardinal directions exclusively (e.g. Warlpiri) (Laughren & McConvell, 1999) (see map in Figure 1 §1.1). Additionally, the span of Gurindji country from the black soil plains of the Victoria River District to the northern edge of the Tanami desert may have played some role in reinforcing the use of both systems. A final set of directionals orientate on the vertical axis: *kankula* 'up' and *kanyjurra* 'down' (197). Like most Australian languages, relative terms for 'left' and 'right' do not exist.

(195) **Kayirra** wulngarn jik.
north sun emerge
"In the north the sun came out." (◀)) RW: EC97_a003: Yipu-waji: 6:29min)

(196) **Kanimparra** nyawa=ma kuwart-jawung=ma.
downstream this=TOP gorge-PROP=TOP
"Downstream is the place with a gorge." (◀)) TD: FM07_a058: 0:11min)

88 Note that *kaarnirra* was originally 'east and up' (with the up suffix *-rni*). The stem was *kaarra* with a reduplicated form *karrawarra*. This form is now associated with Mudburra people, but was not when McConvell did his original work in the 1970s.

(197) Nyantu Yiparrartu **kaninyjal-a** ya-na-ni
3MIN Emu underneath-LOC go-IMPF-PST

an Pangarra **kankulu-pal-a.**
and Corella up-EDGE-LOC
"Emu ran below with Corella above." (🔈) VW: FM07_08_4e: 0:48min)

Directional nominals are distinguished from other nominal subclasses as they are inherently locative and therefore do not take locative-marking (except in agreement with a head nominal (199)), as shown in (195) and (196). Like place names, goals are also only optionally marked allative, as in (198). Where they are case-marked, the forms of the case-markers bear no relation to the usual forms of case-markers. For example, in (199), the ablative is *-yin*, where the usual forms for a nominal are *-yirri*, *-jirri* or *-ngkurra*. Another point of differentiation with other nominals is that directionals can be additionally inflected for normal case-markers in agreement with the head noun, shown by the locative in (199), a feature which they share with adverbs.

(198) **Kayirra** ngu=rna ka-ngku.
north CAT=1EXC.MIN.S take-POT
"I've got to take her north." (🔈) VW: FM07_a021: 12:58min)

(199) Ngu=rnalu ma-na-na nyawa=ma
CAT=1EXC.AUG.S do-IMPF-PRS this=TOP

kayili-yin-karra-la tirnung=ma.
north-ABL-SIDE-LOC sap=TOP
"This sap from a bloodwood tree sits on the northside [of the tree]."
(🔈) TD: FM09FM07_17_2d: 0:30min)

The cardinal directions constitute a particularly rich paradigm, with 31 different forms identified for each cardinal thus far. Inflections include the usual case distinctions, as well as land features (river, summit, shade), facets (side/edge) and orientational features (up/down, along, turning, across). This complex paradigm, and directionals in general, are discussed in detail in §5.2.

3.2.4 Temporals

Time nominals are distinguished from other nominals as they are only found marked with the locative case, and even this is optional. In this respect they differ from temporals found in Warlpiri which can take ergative agreement with a transitive subject (Simpson, 1991, p. 208). They also tend to have co-occurrence restrictions with the tense of the verb in the clause. Some examples are *kaputa* 'night' (200), *ngijingka* 'night' (201) (probably a borrowing from Bilinarra), *kaput* 'tomorrow' and *puriny* 'yesterday, late afternoon' (202). Note that in contemporary Gurindji speech, *puriny* does not occur on its own and has a *-jirri* ending, i.e. *purinyjirri*. It then optionally inflects for locative case, i.e. *purinyjirri-la*. The *-jirri* is perhaps a fused allative marker although it is odd that it is the allative and not the locative that has fused. Similarly *ngijingka* is historically *ngiji* 'night' + *ngka* 'locative'.

(200) Jajalya, murla-ngka kankulu-pal-a nyamu karrinyana, **kaputa-la**.
star this-LOC up-EDGE-LOC REL be.IMPF.PRS night-LOC
"Stars are [found] up here at night time." (◀)) VW: FM12_a171: 0:42min)

(201) Maitbi nyurrun ngu=rnayinangulu
maybe forget CAT=1EXC.AUG.S>3AUG.NS

ma-na-ni, **ngijingka-la**.
do-IMPF-PST night-LOC
"Maybe we would lose them during night time." (◀)) VW: FM12_a175: 07:40min)

(202) Ngu=rna pa-ni ngurrakin **puriny**.
CAT=1EXC.MIN.S hit-PST dingo yesterday
"I killed a dingo yesterday." (◀)) SM: HALE_K06-004553: 12:38min)

3.2.5 Free pronouns

Free pronouns form a closed class which makes a three-way distinction between person: 1st, 2nd and 3rd person; and number: minimal (MIN), unit augmented (UA) and augmented (AUG). As is typical for Australian languages, first person pronouns also make a distinction between inclusive (including the hearer) and exclusive (excluding the hearer) and no gender distinction is made. The presence of three inclusive forms is unusual for Pama-Nyungan languages. The minimal inclusive *ngali* refers to two people ('you and me'); the unit augmented inclusive *ngaliwula* refers to three people ('you, me and one other'), and augmented inclusive *ngaliwa* refers to a group of four or more (§6.1). Bound pronouns are obligatory for animates except in rare situations (§6.2.4).

The free pronouns are grammatically non-obligatory like all nominals. They work in conjunction with the bound pronoun clitics, as shown in (203), where both *ngantipa* and *=rnalu* reference the subject of a transitive clause.

(203) **Ngantipa** ngu=**rnalu** nya-nga-na
1EXC.AUG CAT=1EXC.AUG.S intake-IMPF-PRS

ngumayi-jang-kulu na kuya, jalayi-lang-kulu.
behind-TIME-ERG FOC thus now-TIME-ERG
"We who have been left behind [older generation] know about this now, and the present generation." (🔈) BW: FM07_01_1a: 4:45min)

The free pronouns case system differs from that of other nominals. Nouns/adjectives operate in an ergative-absolutive marking system, whereas free pronouns use one unmarked form for all three core grammatical functions: A, S and O.[89] For example, (203) shows a free pronoun *ngantipa* referencing the A role, although it is not ergative-marked. Free pronouns do, however, have a distinct dative form which covers a range of functions including possession, as shown in (204), benefactives, indirect objects and animate goals (see also §6.1.1).

(204) Karu-walija marturtukuja **ngantipany**
child-PAUC female.REDUP 1EXC.AUG.DAT

ngu=rnayinangulu ka-ngku, kuya, warrwarrkap.
CAT=1EXC.AUG.S>3AUG.NS take-POT thus dance.REDUP
"We will take our young girls out dancing." (🔈) VW: FM08_11_3: 2:09min)

Dative pronouns can also act as nominal modifiers. In this role, they exhibit the full case-marking range (ergative, dative, locative, allative and ablative etc) in agreement with the head noun they modify. For example, in (205) *ngantipanguny* 'our' is marked ergative in agreement with *nungkiying* 'family'.

(205) Pinak jayi-nga-ni ngu=ngantipangulu
teach give-IMPF-PST CAT=3AUG.S>1EXC.AUG.NS

kampa-rnu-p-ku=ma, **ngantipanguny**-ju nungkiying-kulu.
cook-INF-CV-DAT=TOP 1EXC.AUG.DAT-ERG family-ERG
"They taught us to cook them, our family did." (🔈) VW: FM09_12_5d: 1:22min)

While formally, free pronouns are considered to be part of the class of nominals, for the rest of this grammar free pronouns will be discussed separately from other nominals. Thus, the use of 'nominals' in this grammar excludes free pronouns. Free pronouns are discussed more fully in §6.1.

89 We use Dixon's (1979) syntactico-semantic distinctions of A (transitive subject), S (intransitive subject) and O (transitive object).

3.2.6 Demonstratives

Demonstratives are another closed class of nominals. Four series of demonstratives exist: *nyawa* 'this', *nyila* 'that', *nyanawu* 'recognitional' and *kuya* 'thus' (§5.1). The first two make a proximal and distal distinction in relation to the speaker and can function as either deictic or anaphoric demonstratives (§5.1.4). They inflect for the full range of case markers, sometimes using the free stems *nyawa* and *nyila*, but often using the suppletive forms *murla-* 'this' and *yala-* 'that', which undergo regressive vowel harmony depending on the vowel in the case-marker, for example *murlu-ngku* 'this-ERG' and *murla-ngka* 'this-LOC, here', as shown in (206), and *yalu-wu* 'that-DAT' in (207).

(206) **Murlu-ngku=ma** janginyina-lu=ma pa-ni ngu
this-ERG=TOP lightning-ERG=TOP hit-PST CAT

ngawa=ma ngakparn na **murla-ngka=ma** walyak.
water=TOP frog FOC this-LOC=TOP inside
"The lightning struck the water [when] the frog was in here."
(🔈 BW: FM07_06_2a: 2:24min)

Demonstratives also have other suffixes which are not found with other nominals, specifically *-rra* 'plural' (207), *-mawu* 'dweller', *-rniny* 'hither', and *-partak* 'thither' (§5.1.2).

(207) **Nyila-rra**=ma kirri-walija=ma ya-nku=ngantipangulu
that-PL=TOP woman-PAUC=TOP go-POT=3AUG.S>1EXC.AUG.NS

liwurrap-karra yalu-wu=rni.
humbug-ITER that-DAT=ONLY
"Lots of women will come humbugging us for just those [ashes]."
(🔈 VW: FM07_a089: 9:33min)

Nyawa, *nyila* and their inflected forms function as nominals, nominal modifiers, or adverbials (§5.1.3). For example, *murla-* 'this' may act as an adnominal agreeing with the nominal head, e.g. *murlu-ngku janginyina-lu* 'this lightning' or it may be interpreted as an adverbial, e.g. *murla-ngka* 'here' (206).

The recognitional demonstrative *nyanawu* functions as a sole argument or adnominally (208), and is used to draw attention to a time, place or entity that the speaker and hearer share a knowledge of (§5.1.4.5). As with all nominals, it inflects for the full range of case markers.

(208) **Nyanawu** kapuku ngu=rnangkulu wiit jayi-nya
RECOG sister CAT=1EXC.AUG.S>2MIN.NS show give-PST

tirrip=ma tirrip karrinya waninya karu.
overnight=TOP overnight be.PST fall.PST child
"You know the place sister where we showed you where Emu camped overnight and gave birth to her children?" (◀) TD: FM08_a08_4b: 1:09min)

The demonstrative *kuya* 'thus' is included in the discussions of demonstratives because it shares many properties with this subclass of nominal, for example it takes hither and thither suffixes (209) and case-marking. Nonetheless it is better classified as an adverb because it modifies verbs and optionally agrees with the case marking of other nominals (§5.1.3).[90] It is also used as a quotative, often found marking direct speech (233) (§5.1.4.4).

(209) Kilka waninyani ngu **kuya-partak**, purnku=ma.
clean fall.IMPF.PST CAT thus-THITH good.grain=TOP

Nyawa waninyani jilipija=ma **kuya-partak**, jurlurl.
this fall.IMPF.PST husks=TOP thus-THITH spill
"The good part would fall down that way clean. And the husks would spill over the other way." (◀) VW: FM10_a147: 0:11min)

3.2.7 Ignoratives

Ignoratives, sometimes termed 'epistemes' are classified as nominals because they are inflected with case suffixes appropriate to their function within the noun phrase (§5.3). Ignoratives are a closed class consisting of five stems *nyampa* 'what', *wanyji* 'which', *ngana* 'who', *ngatjang* 'how much' and *nyangurla* 'when'. They can be used as interrogatives or indefinites. For example, *ngana* is used to mean 'who' or 'someone, anyone'. Both functions are demonstrated in (210), which uses the ergative stem *ngantu*. When they are followed by the clitic =*wayi* they mean 'I don't know wh-'.

(210) **Ngantu-ku**=wayi=lu pu-nya nyila=ma?
who-ERG=Q=3AUG.S pierce-PST that=TOP
"Which mob killed [the manager]?"

Ngantu-ku=wayi=lu pu-nya.
someone-ERG=Q=3AUG.S pierce-PST

90 We include the discussion of this adverb in nominals, however, as to keep the discussion of demonstratives in one place.

"I don't know which mob killed him."
(🔊 DD: EC98_a011: Nyamulu Tampang Pani Kalpuman: 12:09min)

3.3 Bound pronouns

Bound pronouns are distinguished from nominals on the basis that they are clitics, whereas nominals including free pronouns are all free forms. Bound pronouns are generally obligatory while overt nominals are often omitted, leaving the bound pronoun alone to provide the information about the person, number and grammatical function of a referent. They generally attach to the catalyst *ngu* which is mostly positioned first (211) or second (212) in the clause, although exceptions exist, as shown in (214) and (215). Unlike second position Warlpiri auxiliaries which include bound pronouns, bound pronoun position and attachment in Gurindji is largely determined by the information structure of the clause (see §6.2.6 for a discussion).

(211)

Ngu=rna	ma-rna-na	"Nana
CAT=1EXC.MIN.S	say-IMPF-PST	SUBSECT

nyawa	jintara	partiki-la".
this	another	nut.tree-LOC

"I said to Nanaku – here's this other one in a nut tree." (🔊 TD: FM07_a28: 4:34min)

(212)

Wuukarra	**ngu=lu=rla**	karrinyana
afraid	CAT=3AUG.S=3OBL	be.IMPF.PRS

nyanawu-wu	kuliyan-ku.
RECOG-DAT	dangerous-DAT

"They're too afraid of crocodiles." (🔊 VW: FM11_a163: 3:27min)

Bound pronouns cross-reference the person (1st inclusive, 1st exclusive, 2nd, 3rd), number (minimal, unit augmented, augmented, see §3.2.5) and the grammatical relation (subject, non-subject) of the referent it cross-references. Bound pronouns, unlike nominals, follow a nominative/accusative pattern of marking, as shown in (213) where *=rna* cross-references the nominative transitive subject and *=ngku* cross-references the accusative object. The non-subject pronoun refers to a number of grammatical roles including objects (213) and (214), indirect objects, beneficiaries (215) and animate goals.

(213)

Ngayu=ma=**rna=ngku**	wanyja-na-na	nyiwunnyiwun-karra.
1MIN=TOP=1EXC.MIN.S=2MIN.NS	leave-IMPF-PRS	dive-ITER

"I'm going to leave you diving away."
(🔊 VW: FM10_23_2a: Warrija Kirrawa: 3:30min)

(214) "Jarrmip-kulu karu=ma karrwa=**yinangulu**" kuya.
together-ERG child=TOP hold=3AUG.S>3AUG.NS thus
"'You two look after the kids together,' she said." (🔈 VW: FM12_a172: 0:26min)

(215) Nyanuny-ku=ma ngumparna-wu=ma=**rla**
3MIN.DAT-DAT=TOP husband-DAT=TOP=3OBL

pirrkap ma-na-ni.
make do-IMPF-PST
"She used to make it for her husband." (🔈 VW: FM08_a08_1a: 22:07min)

In many cases, two pronouns combine to form a complex pronoun, as shown in (214) and (215). There are particular sequencing conditions that come into play when two bound pronouns occur together, as discussed in §6.2.2.2. In examples in this grammar, we present such combinations as single complex forms, for ease of exposition. For example, in (214) and (215), =*yinangulu* indexes a third person augmented subject and third person augmented non-subject. Individually these pronouns are =*lu* '3AUG.S' and =*yina* '3AUG.NS', yet the form of the complex pronoun is =*yinangulu*. The same complex pronoun form can also cross-reference a third augmented oblique or adjunct as shown by (215). A unit augmented neutralisation rule also means that these pronouns can refer to dual referents (§6.2.3.4).

A separate third person oblique form =*rla* also exists, as shown in (211) and (212). It is used to cross-reference all third person indirect objects, as well as third person oblique arguments and some adjuncts. This bound pronoun always appears in the final position of the bound pronoun complex (§6.2.2.3). Generally, only two core arguments are cross-referenced within one bound pronoun complex, however three pronouns are possible if =*rla* is included. In fact, up to four bound pronouns may be found if =*rla* and the second oblique =*nyanta* are used. These cases are very rare, but one example is given in (216) and these are discussed further in §6.2.2.5.

(216) Ngu=yi$_{PSR1}$=lu$_{PSP}$=rla$_{PSR2}$=nyanta$_{BEN}$ ka-nya
CAT=1EXC.MIN.S=3AUG.S=3OBL=3OBL2 take-PST

ngarin [ngumparna-wu nyanuny-ku$_{PSR2}$]$_{BEN}$.
meat husband-DAT 3MIN.DAT-DAT
"[The children of mine] take the meat for her husband."
(🔈 VW: FM13_a195: 6:20min)

Generally, only nominals with human referents are cross-referenced by bound pronouns, however on a very few occasions lower order animates and inanimates are also cross-referenced (§6.2.4). An example is given in (217) where the birds are accorded sentience through the use of the pronoun.

(217) **Kuya-ny-ju** na ngawa=ma=**yinangulu**
thus-NMLZ-ERG FOC water=TOP=3AUG.S>3AUG.NS

wiit=ma jayi-nga-na.
show=TOP give-IMPF-PRS
"Those kind [of birds] can show them where water can be found."
(🔈 VW: FM09_13_2e: 8:03min)

The morphological and syntactic rules concerning bound pronouns are quite complex; a full and detailed discussion is given in §6.2. Some of the issues involved are: the order of bound pronouns (§6.2.2.1), unit augmented neutralisation (§6.2.3.4), bound pronouns in sentences with more than one oblique argument (§6.2.3.3) and pronominal clitic placement (§6.2.6).

3.4 Inflecting verbs

The class of inflecting verbs is very small, containing only 34 verbs. This is not unusual for the Victoria River Ngumpin languages. Bilinarra and Ngarinyman have 23 (Meakins & Nordlinger, 2014, p. 89), Wanyjirra has around 38 (Senge, 2016, p. 391). Further west, but still in the Ngumpin subgroup, Jaru has around 40 verbs (Tsunoda, 1981, p. 76). A neighbouring Yapa language, Warlpiri, has a bigger set of 120 inflecting verbs.

Inflecting verbs encode basic meanings. They also contribute tense (past, present), aspect (perfective, imperfective) and mood (imperative, potential) information to the clause. They can occur as the sole verbal predicate or can combine with a coverb (§3.5) to form a complex predicate with more semantic information. Inflecting verbs in their infinitival form can also take a further *-p* suffix which creates a coverb, enabling the verb to then take derivational suffixes and case in reduced subordinate clauses (§7.2.4.2). Example (218) illustrates the combination of the inflecting verb *yunparnana* 'sing' with its derived coverb counterpart *yunparnup* (note that a second coverb *kilkilp* is also present).

(218) Ngu=rnalu yunpa-rna-na yunpa-rnu-p=ma
CAT=1EXC.AUG.S sing-IMPF-PRS sing-INF-CV=TOP

kilkilp Yawulyu-la=ma.
hit.together woman.ceremony-LOC=TOP
"We sing and play the clapsticks during the Yawulyu ceremony."
(🔊 VW: FM08_a101: 9:34min)

Inflecting verbs are discussed in more detail in §7.1.

3.5 Coverbs

Like nominals, coverbs form an open class of words and include many recent loanwords from Kriol, as shown in (219) and (220). These loanwords are fully integrated into Gurindji complete with Kriol morphology such as the transitive marker *-im* (< 'him'), atelic suffix *-bat* (< 'about') and adverbial suffixes such as the completive *-ap* (< 'up'). With the exception of *-bat* 'atelic', these Kriol suffixes are not productive in Gurindji, therefore Kriol verbs are treated as monomorphemic in Gurindji.

(219) Karrinyana ngu, Malapa-la **waruk** pa-na-na.
stay.IMPF.PRS CAT Limbunya-LOC work hit-IMPF-PRS
"He's staying at the old station and working there at old Limbunya Station homestead." (🔊 BR: FM15_52_1a: 11:42min)

(220) Ngu=rnangkulu **jou-im-bat**
CAT=1EXC.AUG.S>2MIN.NS show-TR-ATEL

ka-nga-na, nyawa=ma tuku=ma.
take-IMPF-PRS this=TOP mussel=TOP
"We take [and] show you these mussels." (🔊 TD: FM10_21_1c: 1:36min)
(Meakins, 2014, p. 301)

Like nominals, coverbs may also take case-marking, but only in reduced subordinate clauses (221), however, unlike nominals, they never index core arguments in a clause and cannot form a noun phrase together with demonstratives functioning as determiners or nominal modifiers such as adjectives.

(221) Nyawa na ngu=rna kampa-rna-na Nangari, yirrijkaji,
this FOC CAT=1EXC.MIN.S cook-IMPF-PRS SUBSECT plant.sp

yirrijkaji, karu-wu **tarukap-ku**, mantara-yawung-ku.
plant.sp child-DAT bathe-DAT sore-PROP-DAT
"I'm cooking *yirrijkaji*, Nangari, to bathe the kids who have sores."
(🔊 BW: FM07_06_2a: 0:31min)

Coverbs differ from inflecting verbs in that they are relatively uninflected. Unlike inflecting verbs, they do not take regular verbal inflections; apart from a continuative marker –*karra* (§7.2.4.1). They also combine with a number of different nominalising suffixes including -*pari* or -*wari* which form adjectives (§3.2.2), an agentive suffix -*kaji* or -*waji* (e.g. *rarraj* 'run' > *rarraj-kaji* 'car') (§4.7.6), an associative suffix -*ngarna* (e.g. *tiwu* 'fly' > *tiwu-ngarna* 'aeroplane') (§4.7.16), and a privative suffix -*murlung* (e.g. *taruk* 'bathe' > *taruk-murlung* 'bathe-PRIV, dirty') (§4.6.3).

The class of coverbs is also quite distinct from the other Gurindji word classes phonologically, morphologically and syntactically. It contains the only monosyllabic words in Gurindji and the large majority of words where final consonant clusters occur, for example *turrp* 'pierce' and *turlk* 'shoot' (§7.2.1).

Coverbs are a grammatically non-obligatory part of the Gurindji clause. Where they occur, they combine with inflecting verbs to create a complex predicate. Their main contribution to the verb complex is in providing the primary lexical semantics, expressing spatial path (e.g. *jawurruk* 'descend'), manner of motion (e.g. *kalu* 'walk'), change of state (e.g. *kiturlk* 'make crooked'), impact (*pangkily* 'hit on head'), bodily functions (*jipuluk* 'blink'), talking (*janyarrp* 'baby talk'), perception (*malany* 'taste') and so forth (§7.2.3).

Many coverbs can combine with more than one inflecting verb to encode differences in, for example, transitivity or aspect (§7.2.2.1.2). For example, *tarukap* 'bathe' combines with *karrinyana* 'be' to mean 'bathe (intrans)' (222), but also with *kangana* 'take' to mean 'take swimming' (transitive) (223). Other combinations include *tarukap waninyana* 'bathe fall, swim underwater' (224), *tarukap manana* 'bathe cook, treat skin with medicine' (225).

(222)

Ngu=wula	**karrinyani**	**tarukap-karra.**
CAT=2UA.S	be.IMPF.PST	bathe-ITER

"They were swimming about." (VW: FM10_23_2a: 1:12min)

(223)

Tarukap-karra	**ka-nga-ni**	yala-nginyi=ma
swim-ITER	take-IMPF-PST	that-SOURCE=TOP

ka-nga-ni	ngu	wart,	ngurra-ngkurra.
take-IMPF-PST	CAT	return	home-ALL

"She took it swimming and then took it back home again."
(VW: FM10_27_1a: Kurraj Story from Halls Creek: 2:14min)

(224)

Ngu=rna	**tarukap**	**waninyana,**	kanyjurra	ngawa-ngka=ma.
CAT=1EXC.MIN.S	swim	fall.IMPF.PRS	down	water-LOC=TOP

"I'll swim underwater." (VW: FM10_23_2a: Warrija Kirrawa: 3:30min)

(225) **Tarukap** ngu=rnayinangulu **ma-na-na** marlarn-tu.
bathe CAT=1EXC.AUG.S>3AUG.NS do-IMPF-PRS riv.red.gum-ERG
"We bathe them using the red river gum mix." (🔈 KM: FM09_14_3: 1:10min)

The combinatorial possibilities of coverbs are restricted and form the basis of coverb classes. These classes follow similar patterns to Bilinarra (Meakins & Nordlinger, 2014, pp. 318–338) and ultimately Schultze-Berndt's (2000) very detailed work on Jaminjung coverb classes. A full discussion of coverbs is given in §7.2.

3.6 Adverbs

For other Ngumpin languages, the criteria for distinguishing adverbs from nominals and coverbs are: (i) marking only a subset of case in main clauses, and (ii) only optionally doing so (see Browne, 2021 for Warlmanpa; see Ennever, 2021 for Ngardi; see Meakins & Nordlinger, 2014, p. 91 for Bilinarra; see Senge, 2016, p. 115 for Wanyjirra). Osgarby (2018a, p. 17) for Mudburra classifies adverbs as a subtype of coverb due to their lack of referential properties. They differ from other coverbs by not being able to be nominalised using *-pari* 'adjectival'. For some neighbouring languages which also contain coverbs, such as Wardaman (Merlan, 1994, p. 59), there are no formal criteria for distinguishing adverbs from coverbs. For other languages such as Jaminjung, some morphological criteria can be applied: adverbs do not occur with the iterative suffix and have more restricted occurrence with case-markers than do coverbs (Schultze-Berndt, 2000, p. 72). Each of these criteria is discussed in turn.

Adverbs are very similar to coverbs in that they are generally uninflected, modify an inflecting verb and are grammatically non-obligatory. However, like Jaminjung, Gurindji adverbs do not combine with the iterative suffix *-karra*, which is found marking coverbs. For this reason, we do not classify adverbs as a subclass of coverbs.

Adverbs also share some features with nominals because they can be marked with case in agreement with the head of the noun phrase, as shown in (226). Unlike nominals, however, case-marking is optional. The case-marking property is also shared with coverbs, however, in the case of adverbs, it is agreement whereas for coverbs it only occurs in reduced subordinate clauses in switch-reference constructions (§3.5). Finally, the only case-marking found is ergative for manner adverbs (226) or locative for locationals (227).

(226) Narra-yawung-kulu ngu=rna yirrirr
hook-PROP-ERG CAT=1EXC.MIN.S pull.REDUP

ma-ni kuya-ngku **yamak-kulu**.
do-PST thus-ERG gently-ERG
"I pulled it out with the hooked stick very gently like this."
(🔈) VW: FM08_a099: 7:10min)

(227) An ngamayi-lu ngu=yina nguru jayi-nga-ni
and mother-ERG CAT=3AUG.NS prepare.food give-IMPF-PST

walyak-kula=ma nanta-nanta=ma nyila=ma.
inside-LOC=TOP small-REDUP=TOP that=TOP
"The mother prepares to give food to the little ones inside."
(🔈) VW: FM10_a149: 2:17min)

There are few adverbs in Gurindji, and they can be categorised as time, positional, iterative and manner adverbs:

Time adverbs:

jala	'now, today'
jurlkup	'straight away'
karaparr	'all night'
ngajik	'long time' (229)
purrp	'completely'

Positional adverbs:

kamparri	'front, ahead' (228)
ngumayila	'behind'
walyak	'inside'
warraj	'outside'

Iterative adverbs:

jiwarn	'on and on'
mayarni	'more'
yilmij	'in turn'

Manner adverbs:

jirrimarna	'intensely, loudly, fast'
kulmarrk	'do something intensely e.g. work hard'
majka	'try'
wajija	'quickly'
yamak	'steadily, gently, slowly' (226), (227) and (228)
yipurrk	'in vain' (253)

(228) **Kamparri-jang** nyamu=lu karrinyani,
before-TIME REL=3AUG.S be.IMPF.PST

karu=ma=yinangulu ma-rna-ni,
child=TOP=3AUG.S>3AUG.NS talk-IMPF-PST

"Karra=lu **yamak** kirrp na."
be.IMP=3AUG.S quiet quiet FOC

"In the old days when they lived there, they would tell the kids, 'Stop quiet you mob.'" (🔈 VW: FM12_a178: 9:12min)

(229) Ngu=rna karrwa-rna-ngku na
CAT=1EXC.MIN.S have-IMPF-POT FOC

ngajik nyamu=yilu=nga
long.time REL=3AUG.S>1EXC.MIN.NS=DUB

pirrkap=ma ma-na-nku punyu-k=ma.
make=TOP do-IMPF-POT good-FACT=TOP

"I'll have it for a long time when they fix it for me."
(🔈 VW: FM07_a021: 6:27min)

(230) Ya-na-na ngu=rla kurrwararn-ku
go-IMPF-PRS CAT=3OBL doctor-DAT

kankarra-k **walyak** jarriny-ja.
upstream-ALL inside room-LOC

"He goes to the doctor entering his office." (🔈 BW: FM07_a043: 14:00min)

Adverbs are discussed further in §7.3.

3.7 Clitics

This class includes a range of clitics which generally have semantic or discourse functions. They are positioned after inflectional and derivational morphology (231), but before the pronominal clitics, with the exception of *=nga* 'DUBitative' (231) and (232), which occurs in the final clitic position (§7.1.3.13).

(231) Nyamu=ngantipa=**nga** ka-ngku Nangari-lu=**rningan**.
REL=1EXC.AUG.NS=DUB take-POT SUBSECT-ERG=AGAIN
"When Nangari might take us again." (🔈 VW: FM07_a021: 8:19min)

(232) Jala=**ma**=rna=**nga** karrwa-wu pirrkap-pirrkap-kula na.
now=TOP=1EXC.MIN.S=DUB keep-POT make-REDUP-LOC FOC
"Now I might keep [the wood] to make [the artefacts]." (🔈 VW: FM08_a101: 2:35min)

There are two types of clitics, referred to as 'restricted' and 'unrestricted' respectively. Unrestricted clitics can be attached to any part of speech and include *=ma* 'TOPic' (233), (235) and (184) (§10.1.3), *=parla/warla* 'FOCus' (233) (§10.1.8), *=nga* 'DUBitative' (231) and (232) (§7.1.3.13), *=purrupurru* 'AND' (234) (§4.8.3), *=kata* 'IMMediate' (235) (§10.1.1), *=rningan* 'AGAIN' (231) (§10.1.6) and *=nyiyang* 'PROPER' (§10.1.4) (236).

(233) "Ah nyawa=**rni=warla** mangarri=**ma**," kuya.
Ah this=ONLY=FOC veg.food=TOP thus
"'Ah and here's the potato,' someone said." (🔈 BW: FM09_12_6b: 1:06min)

(234) Ngu=rna=ngku ma-lu=**warluk**-pa=**rni**.
CAT=1EXC.MIN.S=2MIN.NS talk-POT=FIRST-EP=ONLY
"I want to tell you something first." (🔈 VW: FM10_23_2: Warrija Kirrawa: 6:29min)

(235) Nyila=**ma=kata** karrinyana mirntaarraj-jawung kuya-ny.
that=TOP=IMM be.IMPF.PRS waterlily-PROP thus-NMLZ
"That place has this kind of water lilies growing right here."
(🔈 VW: FM09_a13_2a: 2:24min)

(236) Nyuntu ngu=n jangkarni=**nyiyang**.
2MIN CAT=2MIN.S big=PROPER
"You are really big." (McConvell corpus: Meakins et al., 2016, p. 296)

Restricted clitics are typically constrained in their use such that they attach only to certain parts of speech. They include the expectation modifiers *=rni* 'ONLY' which attaches to all word classes except inflecting verbs (233) and (241) (except where other clitics are attached first (185)) (§10.1.5) and =*wayin/payin* 'ETC' (237), =*pirak* 'CORRECT' and =*purrupurru* 'AND' (238) which only attach to nominals.

(237) Ngaja nganta kayi-kayi pa-na-na
ADMON ALLE chase-REDUP hit-IMPF-PRS

maiti pulngayarri-lu=**wayin**.
maybe bull-ERG=ETC
"Maybe a bull or something started chasing it." (🔈 VW: FM12_a179: 6:15min)

(238) Tanku=**ma** nyawa, warlayarra=**purrupurru**. Marntaj.
food=TOP this tobacco=AND OK
"Here's some tucker, and tobacco too. OK."
(🔈 DD: EC98_a025: Rawuyarri: 11:54min)

3.8 Complementisers

Complementisers do not decline at all but provide a base to which pronominal clitics may attach. In this sense, they are similar to *ngu*, but they head finite subordinate clauses. The exception is *ngaja* 'ADMONitive' which can also head a main clause to mean 'might' (237). This main clause use is the result of a historical process of insubordination (§9.2.2). The complementisers found in Gurindji mark and identify finite subordinate clauses: *nyamu* 'RELativiser' (45) and (239) (§9.2.1), *ngaja* 'ADMONitive' (240) (§9.2.2), *kata* 'THOugh' (241) (§9.2.3), *kayi* 'SURP' (65) and (241) (§9.2.4), *kuyangka* 'that's when' (§9.2.5) and a Kriol borrowing *tumaji* 'beCAUSe' (§9.2.6).

(239) **Nyamu**=rna=nga purrp pa-rru, kawarla
REL=1EXC.MIN.S=DUB finish hit-POT coolamon

na ngu=rna=nga pirrkap ma-nku.
FOC CAT=1EXC.MIN.S=DUB make do-POT
"Maybe when I finish knocking the bark off, I'll make the coolamon."
(🔈 VW: FM07_a050: 6:39min)

(240) Ngarranginy-ju **ngaja**=ngku paya-rru.
frill-neck.lizard-ERG ADMON=2MIN.NS bite-POT
"The frill necked lizard might bite you." (VW: FM10_a152: 1:02min)

(241) **Kata**=yin=nga ma-rni ngajik-ku
THO=2MIN.S>1EXC.MIN.NS=DUB talk-PST long.time-DAT

ya-nu-wu, **kayi**=n ya-na-na wart-pa=rnirni
go-INF-DAT SURP=2MIN.S go-IMPF-PRS return-EP=ONLY.REDUP

wajija=rni.
quickly=ONLY
"I thought you told me you would go for a long time, but here you are coming back quickly." (McConvell corpus: Meakins et al., 2016, p. 444)

3.9 Particles

Gurindji contains ten particles *jupu* 'just' (242) and (243) (§10.2.1), *kula* 'NEGative' (188), (243), (250) and (251) (§10.2.2), *kutikata* 'maybe' (244) (§10.2.3), *marri* 'but' (245) (§10.2.4), *na* 'SEQ, FOC' (10.2.5), *nganta* 'ALLEgedly' (246) (§10.2.6), *palarni* 'better' (247) (§10.2.7) and *waku* 'well, except' (248) (§10.2.8), *walima* 'Question' (10.2.9) and *wayi* 'Question' (249) (§10.2.10). Particles can occur anywhere in the sentence, but when they are found in first position they often attract pronominal clitics e.g. (243) but not always e.g. (242).

(242) **Jupu** ngu=rnalu ya-ni.
JUST CAT=1EXC.AUG.S go-PST
"We just went for a little while." (🔈 TD: FM07_021: 4:33min)

(243) **Kula**=rnalu wumara ma-na-ni lawara.
NEG=1EXC.AUG.S money do-IMPF-PST nothing

Jupu ngu=ngantipa tanku na jayi-nga-ni.
JUST CAT=1EXC.AUG.NS food FOC give-IMPF-PST
"We didn't used to get money. He just used to give us food."
(🔈 VW: FM09_12_5b: 2:52min)

(244) **Kutikata** ngu=rna nya-ngku=nga=yi=rni
MAYBE CAT=1EXC.MIN.S intake-POT=DUB=1EXC.MIN.NS=ONLY

ngayiny-ju mila-ngku.
1EXC.MIN.DAT-ERG eye-ERG
"Maybe I'll go see for myself with my own eyes."
(RW: HM070529GUR.DAGU_01rw: Warrija Kirrawa)

(245) Kayi=n ma-rni ya-nu-wu **marri**
chase=2MIN.S say-PST go-INF-DAT BUT

wanyji=warla=n ya-ni?
which=FOC=2MIN.S go-PST
"You said you were going to go so then why didn't you go?"
(McConvell corpus: Meakins et al., 2016, p. 231)

(246) Kaput-kaput=ma warrij **nganta**=wula ya-na-ni.
morning-REDUP=TOP leave ALLE=3UA.S go-IMPF-PST
"Early in the morning they had apparently left them then."
(🔈 VW: FM10_30_1a: Karu Dreaming Story: 4:22min)

(247) Ngu=ja palki-ny=ma karrwa-wu
CAT=1EXC.UA.S cover-NMLZ=TOP keep-POT

murla-ngka **palarni.**
this-LOC BETTER
"It's much better if we keep the blanket over here."
(RW & DD with ECh: Meakins et al., 2016, p. 301)

(248) Ka-nga-ni ngu ngantipa=ma[91] Mud Spring-kulawu **waku**
take-IMPF-PST CAT 1EXC.AUG=TOP place.name-PURP WELL

ngu=rla yala-nginyi=ma wart ya-ni.
CAT=3OBL that-SOURCE=TOP return go-PST
"She maybe took it to Mud Spring but [the baby Rainbow Spirit] came back to her." (🔈 VW: FM10_27_1a: Kurraj Story from Halls Creek: 4:20min)

(249) **Wayi**=rna yuwa-ni ngawa-ngka kanyjurra japurr.
Q=1EXC.MIN.S put-PST water-LOC down soak
"Did I throw it into the lake?" (🔈 VW: FM10_23_1a: Luma Kurrupartu: 1:06min)

Jupu is the sentential equivalent of *=rni* 'ONLY' (§10.1.4) because it modifies expectations about the whole sentence, the verb or the predicate. The clitic *=rni* only has scope over individual parts of speech.

91 This free pronoun is a bit baffling here but isn't the non-subject pronoun because it has a topic marker attached.

3.10 Interjections

The interjections found in the corpus are *yuwayi* and *yuu* 'yes' (250), *lawara* 'no, nothing, not at all' (251) (often code-switched to Kriol as *najing* (250)), *marntaj* 'alright, well, O.K, etc.' (252), *ankaj* 'poor thing' (253), *wartarra, wartayi, warta* 'hey, goodness' (254), *kayuwa* 'can't be' (254), *ngartung* 'fortunately' (255), *yijarni* 'true' (256), *kawayi* 'come here'. Affective interjections include *wartiiti* 'oh dear', *wartayi* 'hey, goodness', *yakayaka* and *yakatayi* 'ouch' and *kawayi* 'come here' and *kala* 'leave it'. Like particles, interjections may attract pronominal clitics, however interjections are distinguished by the fact that they alone can constitute a complete utterance.

(250) **Yuwayi** kula yilarrp=ma ya-nku **najing**.
yes NEG come.off=TOP go-POT nothing
"Yes, it won't come off." (🔊 TD: FM10_a146: 11:00min)

(251) Jungkuwurru=ma kula=lu nya-ngku
echidna=TOP NEG=3AUG.S intake-POT

ngarturr-lu=ma **lawara**.
pregnant-ERG=TOP nothing
"Pregnant women should not eat echidnas, not at all."
(🔊 BW: FM09_a122: 5:04min)

(252) Ngu=rlaa nya-nya tanku jaartkarra, **marntaj**.
CAT=1INC.AUG.S intake-PST food eat OK
"We ate our lunch, OK." (🔊 BW: FM09_a121: 0:37min)

(253) Yipurrk ngu pinyinyip ma-na-na **ankaj**.
in.vain CAT twirls.stick do-IMPF-PRS poor.thing
"She twirled one stick in the groove of another in vain, poor thing."
(🔊 VW: FM09_a127: 17:18min)

(254) **Warta** **kayuwa** ngawa=rni jilngjilng-karra
hey can't.be water=ONLY seep-ITER

jiya-rna-na warlu-ngku=ma.
burn-IMPF-PRS fire-ERG=TOP
"Hey it can't be true – the fire is making water seep out even."
(🔊 VW: FM10_23_4: 7:44min)

(255)

Ngartung	ngu=yi	ka-nga-ni.
good.thing	CAT=1EXC.MIN.NS	bring-IMPF-PST

"Good thing he brought it for me."
(RW & DD with ECh: Meakins et al., 2016, p. 275)

(256)

Yijarni!	Murla-ngka=ma=lu	kayirra	karrinyani
true	this-LOC=TOP=3AUG.S	north	be.IMPF.PST

kula	yangujpa	kajijirri=ma.
NEG	few	woman.REDUP=TOP

"True! Women used to live in the north [at Pawulyji], lots of women."
(🔊 TD: FM09_17_1a: 0:09min)

Two interjections are used in conflict: *jiwilyngarri* which is used when a murder has been committed and payback is complete and *yawaliwali* which is a plea for people to stop fighting. Other interjections relate to specific kinship roles, for example *ngakuny* which is an exclamation said to a wife's brother if mother's brother swears at him, and *wangkawangka* which is said by a man to his uncle if the latter swears at him (see also §1.8.1).

4 Nominals

Nominals in Gurindji are one of the largest word classes but are not always present in the clause because they are grammatically optional, with much of the argument role borne by the pronominal clitics instead (see §4.2 for a theoretical discussion on the status of nominals vs bound pronouns in Gurindji). For illustrative purposes, we provide some of the few fully expressed clauses in the corpus to provide a sense of some of the features of nominals before discussing them in detail. Example (257) shows a clause with an ergative-marked transitive subject and an unmarked accusative object. Both arguments are cross-referenced in the complex pronoun *=yinangkulu* 'they do it to them'. In (258), the transitive subject is an ergative marked nominal. The constituents of the object NP are unmarked for case. Again, both arguments are cross-referenced in the complex pronoun *=yinangkulu* 'they do it to them'. The clause in (259) is an example of a semi-transitive clause with the subject unmarked and the indirect object marked dative. In (260), the dative marks a possessive relationship between *marluka* 'old man' and *kurrurij* 'car'.

(257)	**Waringarri-lu**$_{A}$=ma	ngu=**yinangkulu**$_{A,O}$
	warrior-ERG=TOP	CAT=3AUG.S>3AUG.NS

	turt-turt	ma-ni	**kirri-walija**$_{O}$=ma.
	grab-REDUP	get-PST	woman-PAUC=TOP

"The warriors grabbed the women." (◀)) DD: EC98_a013: 10:34min)

(258)	Ngu=**yinangkulu**[92]$_{A,O}$	[**nyila**=ma	**kartipa**=ma]$_{O}$	kaarra-yin-ta
	CAT=3AUG.S>3AUG.NS	that=TOP	non-Indigenous=TOP	west-ABL-LOC

	nya-nga-ni	[**yarrulan-kujarra-lu**]$_{A}$.
	intake-IMPF-PST	young.man-DU-ERG

"The two young men were watching the *kartiya* from the west."
(◀)) RW: EC98_a027: 6:44min)

(259)	Nyamu=**Ø**$_{S}$=**rla**$_{IO}$=nga	ma-nyja	**kartiya=ma**$_{S}$	**yalu-wu**$_{IO}$
	REL=3MIN.S=3OBL=DUB	say-IMP	non-Indigenous=TOP	that-DAT

	"Waku	ngu=**rli**$_{S}$	karru	jaliji."
	WELL	CAT=1INC.UA.S	be.POT	friend

"The *kartiya* should have talked to the *ngumpin* and said, 'Let us be friends'."
(◀)) JK: MCCONVELL_P04-012073)

92 Note that this pronoun is cross-referencing a dual subject. This occurs as a part of the process of unit augment neutralisation (see §6.2.3.4).

https://doi.org/10.1515/9783110746884-004

(260) [**Ngayiny**$_{PSR}$**-ju** **karu**$_{PSM}$**-ngku**]$_{PSP}$ ngu=yi$_{PSR}$=lu$_{PSP}$
1EXC.MIN.DAT-ERG child-ERG CAT=1EXC.MIN.NS=3AUG.S

tawirrjip pa-ni marluka-wu kurrurij.
throw.rock hit-PST old.man-DAT car
"The children of mine threw rocks at the old man's car."
(◀) VW: FM13_a194: 15:55min)

These examples show some of the grammatical relations expressed by nominals and the general structure of the clause. The structure of the nominal word which includes not only case but other inflections and derivational morphology is discussed in §4.1 and details of the structure of the NP is given in §4.2. The individual morphemes are then discussed in turn, including case (§4.3), number (§4.4), kinship suffixes (§4.5), adnominal case (§4.6), derivational morphology (§4.7) and restricted clitics (§4.8)

4.1 Word structure

The structure of the nominal word is as follows:

ROOT + (DERIV) + (DERIV) + (KIN) + (NUM) + (ADNOM)[93] + (CASE)[94] + CASE + *ny* + CASE # [= (DISCOURSE CLITIC) = (PRONOMINAL CLITIC) = (DUBITATIVE CLITIC)]

- DERIV = derivational suffix (see §4.7)
- NUM = number suffix (see §4.4)
- ADNOM = adnominal case (see §4.6)
- KIN = kinship suffix (see §4.5)
- CASE = case inflection (see §4.3)
- *ny* = nominaliser (see §4.7.20)

The various clitic possibilities do not belong to the nominal word in the morphological sense but are included here as they occur frequently on nominals, and form part of the nominal word phonologically. Some are specific to nominals (§4.8) and some are found on many different parts of speech (§10.1). Pronominal clitics are discussed in §6.2.

No example containing all elements exists in the corpus, but a number of examples of nominals with different morphological structures, including combinations of suffixes

93 In fact, the corpus contains no example of a nominal inflected with both a number marker and an adnominal case marker, so we cannot be sure about the relative ordering of these two in the template.
94 In fact, this first CASE slot can *only* be filled with locative case, and *only* if it is followed by dative case – see below.

and clitics, are given below. In (261), the stem *lamparra* 'father-in-law' has a kinship suffix, ergative case then a discourse clitic and pronominal clitic. Example (262) gives an example of an oblique free pronoun (discussed further in §6.1) plus an adnominal case (privative), locative case and discourse clitic. In (263), the nominal word *kartipa-walija-wunyja=ma* consists of a nominal root + number suffix + comitative case suffix then an additional discourse clitic. The nominal in (264) *lurr-panu-waji-yawung-kulu* is a coverb + infinitive form of the 'hit' inflecting verb which is then nominalised with an agentive suffix to create the word 'grader', a type of earth moving vehicle. It then takes the proprietive which is an adnominal case suffix and finally an ergative marker in agreement with the transitive subject. In (265), the nominal *karu-walija-kari-lu=ma* consists of a root + number suffix + derivational morpheme + case + discourse clitic. Example (267) *ngarturr-jawung-kulu=ma* consists of a nominal root + adnominal case + ergative + topic clitic. In (268) the nominal word *kuya-ny-jawung-kulu-pa=rni* shows the adverbial demonstrative *kuya* which is nominalised with *-ny* and then takes the proprietive adnominal case suffix, ergative case and finally hosts a discourse clitic preceded by the epenthetic *-pa-*.

(261) Hey **lamparra-marnany-ju=ma=ngku** jayi-nya,
hey father.in.law-2MIN.POSS-ERG=TOP=2MIN.NS give-PST

kujarra kirri-kujarra nyununy.
two woman-DU 2MIN.DAT
"Hey your father-in-law who is my son gave two girls to you."
(🔈 VW: FM10_a155: 10:48min)

(262) **Ngantipanguny-murlung-kula=rni** pa-na-ni
1EXC.AUG.DAT-PRIV-LOC=ONLY hit-IMPF-PST

wurrungarna-lu tirriny-pa=rni larrpa.
clever.man-ERG make.doctor-EP=ONLY long.ago
"One made Tinker into a clever man long before we were born."
(PN: McNair_K2J: 0:30min)

(263) Ngu=yinangkulu nyila=rni karrinyani
CAT=3AUG.S>3AUG.NS that=ONLY be.IMPF.PST

kajirri kujarra **kartipa-walija-wunyja=ma.**
woman two non-Indigenous-PAUC-COM=TOP
"Two women were with several *kartiya* there." (Appendix: Fishing: Text 2, Line 9)

(264) Lurr pa-na-ni nyawa=ma, wurruma,
go.everywhere hit-IMPF-PST this=TOP road

lurr-pa-nu-waji-yawung-kulu.
go.everywhere-hit-INF-AGENT-PROP-ERG
"They used to level off this one, the road, with the grader."
(🔈 VW: FM12_a175: 7:19min)

(265) Nyamu=lu yingi ma-rna-ni **karu-walija-kari-lu=ma**. . .
REL=3AUG.S tease talk-IMPF-PST child-PAUC-OTHER-ERG=TOP
"When the other kids teased him . . ."
(🔈 VW: LC080305GUR.KALK_02VW.mp3: 3:01min)

(266) Ngunti ngu=n pirrkap ma-nku nyanuny-ja
light CAT=2MIN.S make do-POT 3MIN.DAT-LOC

karrap-kula, **Nangari-wu-ny-ja**.
watch-LOC SUBSECT-DAT-NMLZ-LOC
"You can make the light while Nangari watches on."
(🔈 VW: FM09_17_2a: 1:24min)

(267) Juyirna ngu=lu karrinyana
prohibited CAT=3AUG.S be.IMPF.PRS

ngarturr-jawung-kulu=ma kula nya-ngku.
pregnant-PROP-ERG=TOP NEG intake-POT
"Pregnant women are not allowed. They can't eat it."
(🔈 BW: FM09_a122: 5:13min)

(268) Ngu=rna paya-rna-ngku na
CAT=1EXC.MIN.S bite-IMPF-POT FOC

kuya-ny-jawung-kulu-pa=rni, pirrkapirrkap.
thus-NMLZ-PROP-ERG-EP=ONLY make.REDUP
"I will be making [artefacts] only with this kind [of tool]."
(🔈 VW: FM08_a101: 2:53min)

Two derivational suffixes are also possible, as shown in (269), which shows the derivational suffix *-yayi* 'LATE' followed by *-nganyju* 'GROUP'.

(269) Marlarluka-lu=purrupurru lajalajap
old.man.REDUP-ERG=AND carry.on.shoulder.REDUP

kaku-yayi-nganyju-lu=ma.
FF-LATE-GROUP-ERG=TOP
"And the old men used to carry them–including my grandfather."
(🔊 VW: FM09_17_1d: 5:02min)

Derivational and number morphology always occurs before inflectional morphology. Example (265) illustrates the derivational suffix *-kari* 'OTHER' occurring after a number marker and before the ergative. Similarly, (270) shows *-kari* followed by an ergative and (271) shows *-waji* followed by a locative case marker. Example (271) also has a number suffix *-kujarra* 'DU' combined with the ergative case suffix.

(270) Ngurrku pa-na-na ngu, yalu-ngku=ma **kirri-kari-lu=ma.**
suspect hit-IMPF-PRS CAT that-ERG=TOP woman-OTHER-ERG=TOP
"Another woman suspects her [of something]." (🔊 TD, VW: FM10_a163: 7:41min)

(271) **Mangarri-waji-la** ngu=wula wanyja-na-na
veg.food-AGENT-LOC CAT=3UA.S leave-IMPF-PRS

na kamparri-la warrkawarrkap **wamala-kujarra-lu.**
FOC front-LOC dance.REDUP girl-DU-ERG
"The two girls danced in front of the shop." (🔊 BW: FM07_a043: 21:24min)

The only exception to the ordering of derivational and inflectional morphology in the corpus seem to be body part instruments where the derivational coverbaliser *-p* can follow the ergative suffix. These types of examples are odd because ergative-marked instruments also do not appear in intransitive clauses. The proprietive is used instead. We do not have an explanation for these types of examples. They also occur in Bilinarra (Meakins & Nordlinger, 2014, p. 440).[95] An example is given in (272) and another example is *lutju-ngku-p* 'heel-ERG-CV, walk on your heels' (see also §7.2.4.2).

(272) **Tingarri-lu-p** mingip ya-na-na.
knee-ERG-CV crawl go-IMPF-PRS
"She is crawling on her knees."
(McConvell corpus: Meakins et al, 2016, p. 365)

95 Note that in Warlpiri, an ergative-marked nominal can be the coverb with causative *-mani* as in *yurlpulypa-rlu-ma-ni* 'ash-ERG-CAUS-Vinfl, cover with ash' or *ngamurlu-kurlu-rlu-ma-nu* 'hug-COMIT-ERG-CAUS-PST, embraced, hugged' or *wangkanamarra-rlu-ma-nu*' dance_with_long_leafy_poles-ERG-CAUS-PST, perform leafy pole dance (for initiate)' (thanks to Mary Laughren for these examples and the observation).

Gurindji has no case-stacking (see Dench & Evans, 1988 for a discussion of case-stacking in Australian languages), except in a minor context in purposive subordinate clauses (§9.3.1). Locative-marked and allative-marked NPs in subordinate purposive clauses can be marked dative following the allative (273) or locative (274). In these instances, both case-markers are syntactically active. The allative marks the clause as subordinate and indicates that the subject of the subordinate clause is the same as the object of the main clause. The additional dative-case marker indicates that it is further embedded within a purposive clause. In this respect, the allative is looking across two levels of embedding. In the case of the locative, there is no switch reference function, but there is also a double embedding. In Gurindji, this is the only time you find case-stacking of this kind. On the other hand, Warlpiri shows similar case-stacking within main clauses where the inner case suffix has a relational function and the outer case suffix serves to demonstrate a predicational relationship between the spatial-case marked NP and another clausal argument by agreeing in case (Simpson, 1991).

(273) Ngu=rna=ngku ma-rni ka-nga-nu-wu
CAT=1EXC.MIN.S=2MIN.NS say-PST bring-IMPF-INF-DAT

wart-ku lun-ku **murla-ngkurra-wu**.
return-DAT drop-DAT this-ALL-DAT
"I told you to bring it back and drop it here."
(McConvell corpus: Meakins et al., 2016, p. 209)

(274) Kurla-mpa ngu=lu langkarna-yirri
south-PERL CAT=3AUG.S billabong-ALL

yuwa-ni kaputa-la=ma kaput-ku
put-PST tomorrow-LOC=TOP tomorrow-DAT

yuwa-nu-wu=ma **kurrpu-ngka-wu**=ma.
put-INF-DAT=TOP grave-LOC-DAT=TOP
"They put [the body] south of the billabong intending to bury it / for it to be buried the next day." (No source)

It is also possible in Gurindji to sequence case-markers by re-nominalising the nominal using *-ny*. The only case-markers which can follow the nominaliser are non-core cases including locative and allative case. For example in (275), the nominal consists of a sequence of DAT + *ny* + ALL. Example (276) shows both case-markers in direct sequence which seems to be permitted by the fact that the oblique pronoun is already a re-nominalised form: compare *nyuntu* 'you' and *nyunu**ny*** 'your'. The use of *-ny* is discussed in detail in §4.7.20.

(275) Waj yuwa-ni jamana-yirri nyanuny-jirri
throw put-PST foot-ALL 3MIN.DAT-ALL

kapuku-wu-ny-jirri.
sister-DAT-NMLZ-ALL
"He threw it where his sister's foot is." (🔈 VW: FHM098: 21:21min)

(276) Nyuntu nyamu=yi=n ma-rni kuli,
2MIN REL=1EXC.MIN.NS=2MIN.S talk-PST fight

kuya-ngka ngu=rna=ngku ngarru=ma
thus-LOC CAT=1EXC.MIN.S=2MIN.NS argue=TOP

ma-rni ngayu=ma, **nyununy-jirri-la.**
talk-PST 1EXC.MIN=TOP 2MIN.DAT-ALL-LOC
"When you swore at me, that's when I told you off."
(🔈 VW: FM10_a152: 1:32min)

The only other cases of apparent case-stacking involve the locative+dative, except we analyse this as a single purposive case-marker (§4.3.6). Dative case also has an adnominal function to encode possession, discussed in §4.6.1. In this case, we assume that the dative case appears in the adnominal slot in the above template.

This same basic structure of the word is also found in Bilinarra and Wanyjirra (Meakins & Nordlinger, 2014, pp. 98–101; Senge, 2016, p. 145).

4.2 NP structure

The existence of NPs in Australian languages has been questioned by a number of people including Blake (1983) for Kalkatungu, Hale (1983) for Warlpiri, Nordlinger (1998a) for Wambaya and Heath (1986) for Nunggubuyu. Sequences of nominals have instead been analysed as being in apposition rather than being in a structural relationship with each other. However, in other languages there are clear structural criteria for the existence of an NP constituent. For example, in languages such as Wambaya (Nordlinger 1998b) and Warlpiri (Simpson 1991), the auxiliary must appear in second position in the clause. In most examples, the auxiliary follows the first word, however the auxiliary may also follow a complex NP which lends support to the analysis of a single NP unit, at least in these contexts (Nordlinger, 1998b, p. 131). Although pronominal clitics in Gurindji can attach in various positions in the clause (see §6.2.6), they are most commonly found attached to the catalyst *ngu* in second position which can be similarly used to support the existence of complex NP constituents. Usually the catalyst + pronominal clitics appear clause initially, as in (268), or follow the first word, as in (267), however it is also possible for the pronominal clitic to follow a sequence of nominals, suggestive of a complex NP as shown in (277)–(279). We consider such examples evidence for the existence of an NP in these cases.

(277) [Ngamanpurru wurruja]$_{NP}$ **ngu=rnalu** yuwa-na-na.
conkerberry dry CAT=1EXC.AUG.S put-IMPF-PRS
"We put the dry conkerberry wood in." (🔈 VW: FM07_a085: 4:03min)

(278) [Nyila=ma kajkuru=ma]$_{NP}$ **ngu=rnalu** pa-na-na
that=TOP pandanus=TOP CAT=1EXC.AUG.S hit-IMPF-PRS

tajkarra pamarr-jawung-kulu=ma kalypa-k.
pound stone-PROP-ERG=TOP soft-FACT
"We pound the pandanus [root] with a stone until it is soft."
(🔈 TD: FM10_a146: 0:21min)

(279) [Ngayiny-ju karu-ngku]$_{NP}$ **ngu=yi=lu**
1EXC.MIN.DAT-ERG child-ERG CAT=1EXC.MIN.NS=3AUG.S

tawirrjip pa-ni marluka-wu kururij.
throw.stone hit-PST old.man-DAT car
"The children of mine threw rocks at the old man's car."
(🔈 VW: FM13_a194: 15:55min)[96]

Another criterion used for defining NPs is intonation. This criterion is used by Schultze-Berndt (2000, p. 43) and Merlan (1994, p. 226) for neighbouring languages, Jaminjung and Wardaman, respectively. They suggest that the term NP can be used to refer to nominals which fall under a single intonation contour. This criterion says little of a hierarchical relationship between the elements of the NP, however it provides a criterion for the presence of the constituent as a whole. This criterion is also used in our analysis of Gurindji. Coreferential nominals which are separated by a pause are not considered to belong to a single NP, but are treated as nominals in apposition. For example, in (280) *ngurra-ngka ngayiny-ja yarti-ngka* 'at my camp in the shade' is considered to be a single NP because the nominals occur within a single intonation contour, however *kaarra-yin-karra-la* is separated by a pause (as indicated by a comma) and is therefore considered a separate nominal in apposition with this NP. If it were not separated by a pause, this nominal would be considered a part of the NP. Similarly, in (281) *janga-ngkawu* is considered to be a separate NP because it is separated by a pause.

96 This sentence is the result of some ill-conceived elicitation rather than describing an actual event.

(280) Nyila na ngu=rna pa-na-na pirrkap
that FOC CAT=1EXC.MIN.S hit-IMPF-PRS make

ngayu=ma jala=ma, **ngurra-ngka**
1EXC.MIN=TOP today=TOP camp-LOC

ngayiny-ja yarti-ngka, kaarra-yin-karra-la.
1EXC.MIN.DAT-LOC shade-LOC west-ABL-SIDE-LOC
"I'm making that one today, I am, at my camp in the shade on the west side of my house." (🔈 VW: FM07_a050: 2:25min)

(281) Punyu kukij-karra-wu du, **janga-ngkawu,**
good drink-ITER-DAT too sick-PURP

kulykulya-lawu nyampa-kawu yala-ngkawu.
congestion-PURP what-PURP that-PURP
"It's good for drinking too when you are sick with a congestion [bad cold] or whatever." (🔈 VW: FM08_a089: 3:18min)

The structure of the NP is (brackets indicate optionality):

(MODIFIER) + (MODIFIER) + HEAD + (MODIFIER) + (MODIFIER)

Potential heads are any category of nominal, however the prototypical head is a noun or a free pronoun. Potential modifiers can also be any category of nominal, however prototypical modifiers are demonstratives, numerals and adjectives. The order of modifiers is relatively free. Demonstratives tend to appear before nouns (282) and (283), however they can also occur after the noun (284) and (285). Dative pronouns also tend to appear before nouns (286), although examples of post-nominal dative pronouns can also be found (287).

97 When a speaker is at Daguragu and refers to the 'south', it is a conventionalised reference to Kalkaringi. When a speaker is at Kalkaringi and refers to Daguragu, they use *kanyjurra* 'down' as a conventionalised reference to Daguragu.

98 Note that parts of a tool are treated like parts of the body with no dative used in the manner of an inalienable possessive construction (see §8.3.1).

(282) Ngu=yi ma-rni Yibwoin=ma
CAT=1EXC.MIN.NS talk-PST NAME=TOP

yala-ngka **yarti-ngka=ma** kurlarra.[97]
that-LOC shade-LOC=TOP south
"That's what Yibwoin told me there in the shade at Kalkaringi."
(🔈) VW: FM09_a120: 2:41min)

(283) Nangala-lu=ma lutju-ngku pa-na-na
SUBSECT-ERG=TOP heel-ERG hit-IMPF-PRS

yalu-ngku=ma **wirlka-ngku=ma** **lutju-ngku.**[98]
that-ERG=TOP axe-ERG=TOP heel-ERG
"Nangala uses the back [heel] of the axe to hit off the bark."
(🔈) VW: FM08_a089: 6:41min)

(284) Ngu=rnalu kampa-rna-na na, **wumara-lu** **yalu-ngku**.
CAT=1EXC.AUG.S cook-IMPF-PRS FOC stone-ERG that-ERG
"We cook it using those stones." (🔈) TD: FM10_a134: 1:45min)

(285) Ngu=rna yuwa-na-na japurr **ngawa-ngka** **murla-ngka**.
CAT=1EXC.MIN.S put-IMPF-PRS dip water-LOC this-LOC
"I'm dipping it in this water." (🔈) VW: FM07_01_1e: 1:46min)

(286) Lamparra-lu ngungu ma-rni nyanuny-ju
father.in.law-ERG promise talk-PST 3MIN.DAT-ERG

mali-ngku **ngalawuny-ku**.
mother.in.law-ERG mans.child-ERG
"His father-in-law and mother-in-law promised her to the son."
(McConvell corpus: Meakins et al., 2016, p. 285)

(287) Karu-ngku nyanuny-ju waral ma-na-na.
child-ERG 3MIN.DAT-ERG delay do-IMPF-PRS
"Her child is slowing her down." (🔈) VW: FM11_a164: 3:57min)

Adjectives show more freedom, appearing before the head, as in (288), and after the noun, as shown in (289), with no clear preference for either pattern. Similarly, numerals are found preceding and following the head, although they mostly appear after the noun, for example (290).

(288) **Jangkarni warlu** ngu=lu pirrkap ma-na-ni.
big fire CAT=3AUG.S build do-IMPF-PST
"They'd build a big fire." (🔈 VW: FM12_a175: 07:40min)

(289) **Nyawa pinka jangkarni** ngapirrngapirrp-karra
this river big full.of.water-ITER

nyamu=waa ma-na-na purruyip=ma.
REL=REL do-IMPF-PRS blow=TOP
"The big river has waves when the wind blows." (🔈 VW: FM10_a152: 3:11min)

(290) Kapuku papa ngu=lu karrinyana nyurraluwirri
sister brother CAT=3AUG.S be.IMPF.PRS bro.sis.pair

nyila=ma=lu. **Ngaji jintaku,**
that=TOP=3AUG.S father one

ngamayi jintaku, jaju jintaku kuya.
mother one MM one thus
"Sisters and brothers together. They have one father, one mother, one mother's mother." (🔈 VW: FM10_a154: 1:28min)

4.2.1 Properties of NPs

Noun phrases in Gurindji show agreement in case-marking across all members of the NP, which is like neighbouring Ngumpin languages, Bilinarra, Ngarinyman, Wanyjirra and Mudburra; Yapa language, Warlmanpa; but unlike neighbouring Yapa language, Warlpiri, which exhibits edge-marking. Interestingly this agreement marking has changed in Gurindji Kriol which is also an edge-marked language (Meakins, 2012, p. 127). Examples (291) and (292) show ergative agreement across the transitive subject NPs. Note that in (291), the free pronoun *nyurrulu* is not ergative-marked because free pronouns do not decline for case in the same way as nominals (see §6.1.2).

99 Note that there is no traditional Gurindji word for 'and'. See §9.1.

(291) **Karu-walija-lu, marturtukuja-lu** an[99] **kirri-walija-lu nyurrulu**
child-PAUC-ERG female.REDUP-ERG and woman-PAUC-ERG 2AUG

jangkakarni-lu karrap ngu=nta nya-nga-na.
big.REDUP-ERG look CAT=2AUG.S intake-IMPF-PRS
"Only you mob, female children and women are allowed to see the pictures."
(🔈 VW: FM07_a085: 19:27min)

(292) Tapu-k ngu=lu yuwa-na-na **karu-ngku**
blunt-FACT CAT=3AUG.S put-IMPF-PRS child-ERG

ngayirrany-ju ngapuju-walija-lu.
1EXC.UA.DAT-ERG grandchild-PAUC-ERG
"Our grandkids make [the axe] blunt." (🔈 VW: FM07_a050: 13:10min)

Agreement is also a property of adnominal suffixes, as shown in (293) and (294), which both show the proprietive agreeing across the NP.

(293) Karlirriyinyja nyila=ma ngumpit=ma, **jarrwa-yawung kirri-yawung**.
polygamist that=TOP man=TOP many-PROP woman-PROP
"A polygamist is a man with many wives." (🔈 VW: FM11_a161: 4:40min)

(294) Kanyjurra waninya ngawa-ngka jirrpu nyantu=ma
down fall.PST water-LOC dive 3MIN=TOP

wurinykurr-jawung karnti-yawung.
stick.tool-PROP stick-PROP
"He dived down into the water with his stick."
(🔈 RW: EC97_a003: Yipu-waji: 1:17min)

Nonetheless adnominal suffixes are distinguishable from case suffixes because case morphology follows adnominal suffixes where they occur, as shown in (262) and (264) above. Although the oblique form of free pronouns combines with the ergative, dative or local case markers, in these instances, the dative functions adnominally rather than as a case suffix, as shown in (262).

Derivational morphology does not show such concord across the NP, which is one feature that distinguishes derivational affixes from case and adnominal morphology (see §4.3 and §4.6). For example, in (295) the agentive *-kaji* doesn't show concord with *karu* or *ngalyapa* which makes sense of course because these nominals do not need to be derived.

(295) Ngu=yi jamurruruk ma-na-na murlu-ngku
CAT=1EXC.MIN.NS annoy do-IMPF-PRS this-ERG

karu-ngku **lungkarrap-kaji-lu** **ngalyapa-lu**.
child-ERG crybaby-AGENT-ERG constant.crier-ERG
"This crybaby is driving me crazy [with his constant crying]."
(🔊 VW: FM12_a171: 23:11min)

Gurindji also allows discontinuous NPs, where elements relating to the same referential entity are discontiguous in the clause, as in (289), (296), (297) and (305). In this case we consider them to belong to separate NPs in terms of constituent structure, although they are clearly related functionally and semantically. Further discussion of discontinuous NPs can be found in §8.1.

(296) **Mangarri-waji-la** ngu=wula wanyja-na-na
veg.food-AGENT-LOC CAT=3UA.S leave-IMPF-PRS

na **kamparri-la** warrkawarrkap wamala-kujarra-lu.
FOC front-LOC dance.REDUP girl-DU-ERG
"The two girls are dancing outside the shop." (🔊 BW: FM07_a043: 21:43min)

(297) Ngu=lu=rla ya-ni na nganta
CAT=3AUG.S=3OBL go-PST FOC ALLE

karu-walija=ma karrap-ku na **jarrwalut**.
child-PAUC=TOP look-DAT FOC many
"A big mob of kids came over for a look, people reckon."
(🔊 VW: FM10_27_1a: Kurraj Story from Halls Creek: 3:09min)

4.2.2 Functions of nominals within the NP

4.2.2.1 Heads

Although the prototypical head of an NP is a noun, all other nominals may act as heads, as demonstrated by their sole use in a noun phrase.

(a) noun as the head:

(298) **Kumpaying** na nya-nga-na ngu
honeycomb FOC intake-IMPF-PRS CAT

Nangala-lu=ma waninya **janyja-kurra**.
SUBSECT-ERG=TOP fall.PST ground-ALL
"Nangala is eating the honey [that] fell to the ground."
(🔊 TD: FM07_a028: 11:59min)

(b) free pronoun as the head

(299) Kalnguniny ngu=yi ma-na-na. Nyila=ma
deceive CAT=1EXC.MIN.NS do-IMPF-PRS that=TOP

ngayiny ngu=yi, jalak yuwa-ni.
1EXC.MIN.DAT CAT=1EXC.MIN.NS send put-PST
"He deceived me. That was for me. Someone sent it."
(🔊 VW: FM11_a160: 2:00min)

(300) **Ngayu**=ma=rna kula nga-rna-ni jaartkarra=ma.
1EXC.MIN=TOP=1EXC.MIN.S NEG eat-IMPF-PST eat=TOP
"I never used to eat it [when I was a young girl]." (🔊 VW: FM09_a123: 9:42min)

(c) adjective as the head

Adjectives may also function as the head of the NP (the addition of a 'dummy' noun is not necessary as is the case in English i.e. 'the ripe *one*'). In such contexts, however, the nominal which they modify semantically is usually understood from context.

(301) **Jiwirri** na ngu=rnalu pa-na-na
ripe FOC CAT=1EXC.AUG.S hit-IMPF-PRS

tajkarra kuya-ny-ja na wumara-la.
pound thus-NMLZ-LOC FOC rock-LOC
"We pound the ripe [black plum] on this kind of rock."
(🔊 VW: FM09_15_2a: 8:18min)

(302) **Kuliyan**-ta=ma nyamu=rnalu yuwa-na-na ngajik,
cheeky-LOC=TOP REL=1EXC.AUG.S put-IMPF-PRS long.time

purunyjirri igin, karrwa-rna-na ngu=rnalu.
late.afternoon again hold-IMPF-PRS CAT=1EXC.AUG.S
"If we use 'cheeky' ashes the flavour lasts all day."
(🔊 VW: FM08_a089: 10:20min)

(d) numeral as the head

In situations where the referent(s) are clear from context, a numeral may also function as the head of the NP:

(303) Ngu=rnalu=nyunu yuwa-na-na **murrkun**
CAT=1EXC.AUG.S=RR put-IMPF-PRS three

maitbi murla-ngka=ma.
maybe this-LOC=TOP
"We put three [lines of ochre] on ourselves here." (◀) VW: FM07_a085: 18:05min)

(304) **Jarrwa-ngku** ngu=lu ma-na-na kuya=ma.
many-ERG CAT=3AUG.S do-IMPF-PRS thus=TOP
"Lots of people do this." (◀) VW: FM08_08_1a: 8:52min)

(e) demonstrative as the head

(305) Kuurrinyji-yawung ngu=rna ma-rna-na
Gurindji-PROP CAT=1EXC.MIN.S talk-IMPF-PRS

nyawa=ma, jaru-yawung.
this=TOP language-PROP
"I am saying this in Gurindji." (◀) VW: FM07_a050: 9:12min)

(306) **Nyila**[100] ngu=ngalang jalpirri-lu nya-nga-na.
that CAT=3AUG.S>1INC.AUG.NS squat-ERG intake-IMPF-PRS
"That one is watching us while he [that one] is squatting down."
(McConvell corpus: Meakins et al., 2016, p. 76)

(307) Nyila-rra=ma kirri-walija=ma ya-nku=ngantipangulu
that-PL=TOP woman-PAUC=TOP go-POT=3AUG.S>1EXC.AUG.NS

liwurrap-karra **yalu-wu**=rni.
humbug-ITER that-DAT=ONLY
"Lots of women will come humbugging us for just those [ashes]."
(◀) VW: FM07_a089: 9:33min)

100 Note that we might have expected *yalu-ngku* 'that-ERG' here. It could be that *nyila* is acting as a dislocated topic but we don't have the audio any longer to check the prosodic contour.

4.2.2.2 Modifiers

(a) nouns as modifiers

Although nouns are prototypically heads, they can also occasionally act as modifiers. These can be nouns expressing the type of something, for example generic-specific constructions combining animal or plant names with generic nouns such as *mangarri* 'vegetable food', *ngarin* 'meat', *ngarlaka* 'seed' or *karnti* 'tree'. In (308) *pilyily* is a noun which modifies *wirnangpurru*.

(308) An **wirnangpurru** **yapawurru** **pilyily** kula=rla ma-nku
and kangaroo small pinky NEG=3OBL do-POT

turt karu-ngku=ma, ngaja=lu karrinyana tingarri wankaj.
hold child-ERG=TOP ADMON=3AUG.S be.IMPF.PRS knee bad
"Little kids shouldn't hold joeys with no hair because they might end up with bad knees." (🔈 VW: FM09_a122: 3:31min)

These NPs are different from identifier constructions where the generic noun receives topic marking, as in (309) (see §5.1.4.3 for more discussion).

(309) Nyawa=ma=kata **karnti** **kumpulyu=ma**
this=TOP=IMM tree white.currant=TOP

kuni ngu=rna ma-ni.
dream CAT=1EXC.MIN.S do-PST
"I just dreamt about that white currant tree." (🔈 VW: FM09_16_1b: 1:17min)

Nouns can function as modifiers in inclusory constructions, which involve a free pronoun as the head and a modifying noun usually a name, kinship term or subsection term (skin name).

(310) Ngu=ja kampa-rni **ngayirra** **Kitty-ngku.**
CAT=1EXC.UA.S cook-PST 1EXC.UA NAME-ERG
"Both Kitty and I treated her." (🔈 VW: FM12_33_1: 1:22min)

(b) adjectives as modifiers

The prototypical use of an adjective is as a modifier. Some examples are given in (288), (289), (311) and (312). Note that (311) is another example of a discontinuous noun phrase (see §4.2.1).

(311)

Yarti	ngu=yinangkulu	ma-ni	**karu-kujarra**	**winkilying.**
photo	CAT=3AUG.S>3AUG.NS	do-PST	child-DU	colour

"They took a colour photograph of the children."
(McConvell corpus: Meakins et al., 2016, p. 440)

(312)

Kapartkarra-la	ya-na-na	kalu	**nyila=ma**	**karu=ma**	**yapakayi=ma.**
stumble-LOC	go-IMPF-PRS	walk	that=TOP	child=TOP	small=TOP

"The toddler is stumbling around." (🔊 VW: FM12_a174: 3:40min)

(c) pronouns as modifiers

Pronouns can only act as modifiers when they are in the dative form. In this situation they form alienable possessive constructions, as shown in (266), (275), (279), (287) and (313), which will be discussed in §8.3.2.

(313)

Kawarla	pirrkap	ma-ni	ngu	kaput-pa=rni
coolamon	make	do-PST	CAT	morning-EP=ONLY

ngayiny-ju	**marluka-lu.**
1EXC.MIN.DAT-ERG	man-ERG

"My husband made the coolamon early in the morning."
(🔊 BW: FM07_04_1d: 0:33min)

(d) demonstratives as modifiers

Demonstratives can function as nominal modifiers in NPs, as shown in (258), (259), (270), (282), (284), (285), (295) and (314), discussed further in §5.1.3.

(314)

Marluka-lu=ma	**yalu-ngku=ma**	ngalyakap-kaji
old.man-ERG=TOP	that-ERG=TOP	lick-AGENT

jak	wuya-rni	ngu	tak-kaji-la.
drop	throw-PST	CAT	sit-AGENT-LOC

"That man dropped the ice cream on the chair." (🔊 BW: FM07_a043: 21:07min)

4.2.3 Nominal modifiers, secondary predicates or subordinate clauses?

Various properties of clauses in Ngumpin-Yapa languages have led to debates about clause structure and non-configurationality (discussed in detail in §8.1) and the structure of NPs which we focus on here. As was noted in §4.2.1, NPs may contain discontinuous nominals and they must agree in case, as shown in (315). There are two interpretations of this structure. Firstly, they are simply discontinuous nominals with a merged interpretation (i.e. me, an adult) or that the modifier is predicated of the subject (i.e. me, as an adult). This is a secondary predicate analysis. Similarly, in (316), *kurnka* can be interpreted as a modifier (i.e. raw [snake]) or a secondary predicate where it is predicated of the object hence the lack of case-marking (i.e. ate the [snake] raw).

(315) **Ngayu** ngu=rna karrap nya-ngku **jangkarni-lu.**
1EXC.MIN CAT=1EXC.MIN.S look intake-POT big-ERG

"Me, an adult, will see it." (discontinuous NP)
"As an adult, I will see it." (secondary predicate)
(McConvell corpus: Meakins et al., 2016, p. 207)

(316) Tampang pa-na-ni **kurnka**=rni jaartkarra.
dead hit-IMPF-PST raw=ONLY eat

"He killed and ate the raw one." (NP agreement)
"He killed it and ate it raw." (secondary predicate)
(🔊 BB: McNair_H2D: 3:24min)

There is some disagreement in the literature as to how to deal with these types of structures in Warlpiri (Laughren, 1992; Simpson, 2005). Although they have the semantics of secondary predicates, particularly through the lens of English translations, they are not structurally different from other more 'normal' discontinuous nominals. There are many other examples of discontinuous NPs where the nominals seem to have a more straightforward reading as an NP, than as a secondary predicate. In (317), the discontinuous NP is also a transitive subject which might have a merged reading (i.e. the mermaid) or a secondary predicate reading (i.e. that one who is a woman). Note also that instruments and body parts are similarly indistinguishable with similar structures of discontinuous NPs and case agreement. In (318) and (319) there are no explicit subject nominals but the instrumental and body part agree in ergative case. Also note that there are agreeing adverbs in (318).

(317) **Yalu-ngku=ma** ngu karrap=ma nya-nga-ni **janka-ku=ma.**
that-ERG=TOP CAT look=TOP intake-IMPF-PST woman-ERG=TOP

"The mermaid was looking at something." (discontinuous NP)
"That one was looking at something [who is] a woman." (secondary predicate)
(Charola texts: DB)[101]

101 These interpretations would be disambiguated by the speaker and context normally.

(318)

Narra-yawung-kulu	ngu=rna	yirrirr
hook-PROP-ERG	CAT=1EXC.MIN.S	pull.REDUP

ma-ni	**kuya-ngku**	**yamak-kulu.**
do-PST	thus-ERG	gently-ERG

"I pulled it out with the hooked stick very gently like this."
(🔈 VW: FM08_a099: 7:10min)

(319)

Janyja	ngu=rna	ma-na-na	nyila=ma
dirt	CAT=1EXC.MIN.S	do-IMPF-PRS	that=TOP

larlup-karra	**wartan-tu**,	karan.
scoop-ITER	hand-ERG	dig.with.hands

"I'm scooping the dirt out with my hands and digging some more."
(🔈 VW: FM07_a054: 8:17min)

We leave this debate about the status of these types of nominals for discussion elsewhere but just note that they have been the subject of some controversy. Finally, we note that case-marking is also used on coverbs to indicate subordinate clauses and, in a sense, coverbs have a similar surface structure since they share many properties with nominals. For example, (320) has an ergative-marked coverb *kutij* which indicates that the subject of the subordinate clause is the same as the subject of the main clause.

(320)

Kutij-ju	na	warra	ka-nga-ni.
stand-ERG	FOC	watch	take-IMPF-PST

"She$_i$ watched her$_j$ as she$_i$ stood." (🔈 VW: FM10_23_1b: 6:04min)

4.3 Case morphology

In Gurindji, case functions both to encode grammatical relations (core and non-core) and to mark different types of reduced subordinate clauses. Thus, much of the grammatical structure of Gurindji hinges on case. Gurindji is a 'split-ergative' language (c.f. Silverstein, 1976) which exhibits a three way split in core case-marking between nominals, bound pronouns and free pronouns. Nominals are marked on an ergative/absolutive pattern, bound pronouns according to a nominative/accusative pattern and free pronouns do not distinguish the transitive subject (A), intransitive subject (S) and object (O) roles (although a separate oblique series exists). Since the nominals show syncretism between the S and O roles, and the pronouns show syncretism between the S and A roles, we analyse the system as a whole as tripartite with three core cases: nominative, accusative and ergative, following Goddard (1982). This is shown abstractly in Table 15:

Table 15: Gurindji tripartite case system.

	Ergative	Nominative	Accusative
Nominals			
Bound pronouns			
Free pronouns			

Gurindji nominals also distinguish another grammatical case – dative – and nine non-core cases: locative, allative, purposive, ablative, source, perlative, terminative, comitative and motivative. Gurindji also has proprietive and privative suffixes, which have been analysed in some other Australian languages as case markers, but are regarded as adnominal case here for reasons outlined in §4.2.1, and elaborated further in §4.6.

All case markers are suffixed on the nominal stem, following derivational, number and adnominal suffixes if they are present (see template in §4.1). Most case forms show allomorphic variation determined by whether the stem is consonant or vowel-final, and the number of syllables in the stem. Example (321) shows a number (but not all) of the ergative allomorphs including *-kulu* (which attaches to peripheral-consonant stems), *-ju* (palatal-final stems), *-lu* (2+syllable, vowel-final stems), and *-ku* (nasal-stop cluster stem).

(321) Ngu=rnalu ma-na-na kamparri-jang-**kulu** nyamu=lu
CAT=1EXC.AUG.S do-IMPF-PRS before-TIME-ERG REL=3AUG.S

ma-na-ni, ngantipanguny-**ju**, ngunyarri-**lu**
do-IMPF-PST 1EXC.AUG.DAT-ERG MoMoMo-ERG

nyampa-**ku** jaju-ngku nungkiying-**kulu**.
what-ERG MoMo-ERG family-ERG
"We're doing the way the old people did it before, our great-grandparents, grandmothers and family." (🔈 VW: FM07_01_1e: 2:21min)

Allomorphy for the case-markers is given in the following figures. Note that the ablative (*-ngurlu(ng)*), source (*-nginyi*), terminative (*-kijak*), perlative (*-mayin*) and motivative (*-nganayak*) case suffixes are invariant and so are not given in the following figures. Allomorphs for multisyllabic vowel-final stems are given in Figure 38. The term 'multisyllabic' is used here to mean stems of more than two morae (i.e. including disyllables with a long vowel). The two forms of the allative appear to be free variants.

The full range of case allomorphy for two syllable vowel-final stems are given in Figure 39:

Example: *warlmayi* 'woomera'

Absolutive:	-Ø	*warlmayi*
Ergative:	*-lu*	*warlmayilu*
Dative	*-wu*	*warlmayiwu*
Locative:	*-la*	*warlmayila*
Allative:	*-yirri, -ngkurra*	*warlmayiyirri, warlmayingkurra*[102]
Purposive	*-lawu*	*warlayilawu*

Figure 38: Case allomorphy for multisyllabic vowel-final stems.

Example: *karu* 'child'

Absolutive:	-Ø	*karu*
Ergative:	*-ngku*	*karungku*
Dative	*-wu*	*karuwu*
Locative:	*-ngka*	*karungka*
Allative:	*-ngkurra*	*karungkurra*
Purposive	*-ngkawu*	*karungkawu*

Figure 39: Case allomorphy for two syllable vowel-final stems.

A nasal-stop cluster dissimilation rule whereby *ng* is deleted from the *-ngkV* case allomorph in the ergative, locative and allative applies to stems which contain nasal-stop clusters (§2.3.4.1), as shown in Figure 40:

Example: *karnti* 'tree, branch'

Absolutive:	-Ø	*karnti*
Ergative:	*-ku*	*karntiku*
Dative	*-wu*	*karntiwu*
Locative:	*-ka*	*karntika*
Allative:	*-kurra*	*karntikurra*
Purposive	*-kawu*	*karntikawu*

Figure 40: Case allomorphy for stems containing nasal-stop clusters.

Number of syllables is irrelevant for consonant-final allomorphy. Case allomorphs for stems containing peripheral-final allomorphs are given in Figure 41. These are the suffixes which occur when the final consonant is *-p*, *-k*, *-m* or *-ng*. What is involved here is the insertion of *-ku-* between the final consonant and the case suffixes appropriate to multisyllabic vowel-final stems, for the ergative and locative forms; for the other cases the same forms are used as for all consonant final stems.

102 The *-ngkurra* form is only used by younger Gurindji speakers and also adult Gurindji Kriol speakers.

Example: *kartak* 'cup, tin'

Absolutive:	-∅	*kartak*
Ergative:	*-kulu*	*kartakkulu*
Dative	*-ku*	*kartakku*
Locative:	*-kula*	*kartakkula*
Allative:	*-jirri*	*kartakjirri*
Purposive	*-kulawu*	*kartakkulawu*

Figure 41: Case allomorphy for peripheral-final stems.

Coronal consonant-final allomorphs attach to stems which end in *-t*, *-rt*, *-j*, *-n*, *-rn* or *-ny*. In the ergative and locative, it optionally involves assimilation of the place of articulation of the initial oral stop of the suffix to that of the final consonant of the stem, such that *-t* → *-j* in stems ending in *-j* or *-ny*, shown in Figure 42.

Example: *ngumpit* 'man, person, Aboriginal'

Absolutive:	-∅	*ngumpit*
Ergative:	*-tu, -rtu, -ju*	*ngumpittu*
Dative	*-ku*	*ngumpitku*
Locative:	*-ta, -rta, -ja*	*ngumpitta*
Allative:	*-jirri*	*ngumpitjirri*
Purposive	*-tawu*	*ngumpittawu*

Figure 42: Case allomorphy for other consonant-final stems.

Liquid-final allomorphs are used when the stem-final consonant is *-l*, *-rl*, *-ly* or *-rr*. The ergative and dative suffixes are usually both realised by *-u*, but some speakers geminate the liquid for the ergative, shown in Figure 43.

Example: *wararr* 'fat'

Absolutive:	-∅	*wararr*
Ergative:	*-u**	*wararru*
Dative	*-u*	*wararru*
Locative:	*-a*	*wararra*
Allative:	*-jirri*	*wararrjirri*
Purposive	*-awu*	*wararrawu*

Figure 43: Case allomorphy for liquid-final stems.

These case forms are identical with Jaru, Wanyjirra, Malngin,[103] Ngarinyman and Bilinarra (Ise, 1998, p. 25; C. Jones, Schultze-Berndt, Denniss, et al., 2019, pp. 13–18; Meakins & Nordlinger, 2014, pp. 112–116; Senge, 2016, p. 168; Tsunoda, 1981, p. 54). On a whole, Mudburra case forms are the same with some dialectal differences between

103 Note that Ise does not identify the *-tu/-ta* allomorphs for the ergative and locative but it is likely that these are forms unidentified in the corpus.

Western and Eastern Mudburra. One major difference in Mudburra are *-li*, *-ji* and *-ti* forms for the ergative, and sometimes *-lu* after /u/-final stems (Green et al., 2019, pp. 25–26). Warlpiri and Ngardi also have the two ergative and locative forms *-lu/-la* and *-ngku/-ngka* for vowel-final stems. Warlpiri does not have consonant-final stems so there is no relevant allomorph. Ngardi has a number of consonant-final forms which assimilate to the final consonant of nominal stems and are identical to Gurindji in this respect, but no *-kulu/-kula* form. The *-kulu* form is a proprietive in Ngardi instead (perhaps from Western Desert) (Ennever, 2021). In Warlmanpa, the ergative and locative forms are slightly different: *-lu/-la* and *-ngu/-nga* (Browne, 2021). Warlpiri and Ngardi only have the *-ku* and *-kurra* forms for the dative and allative cases, respectively. Warlmanpa also only has *-ku* for the dative (similar to Warlpiri), but *-ka* for the allative. The Jaru allative forms are the same as the Gurindji purposive forms. The purposive in Jaru is *-wurru* (Tsunoda, 1981, pp. 59–60), which is the comitative in Mudburra. Each of the forms and functions of the Gurindji case forms will be discussed in turn in the following sections.

4.3.1 NOMinative and ACCusative

Nominative case (for intransitive subjects) and accusative case (for transitive objects) are always unmarked. Example (322) shows a discontinuous intransitive subject *karu-walija . . . jarrwalut* which is cross-referenced by the subject pronoun *=lu* 'they', and (323) shows an unmarked object of a transitive clause, also cross-referenced in the complex bound pronoun *=yinangkulu* which also encodes the transitive subject.

(322) Ngu=**lu**$_{S}$=rla   ya-ni   na   nganta
CAT=3AUG.S=3OBL   go-PST   FOC   ALLE

karu-walija-Ø=ma$_{S}$ karrap-ku   na   **jarrwalut**$_{S}$.
child-PAUC-NOM=TOP   look-DAT   FOC   many
"A big mob of kids came over for a look, I reckon."
(🔊) VW: FM10_27_1a: Kurraj Story from Halls Creek: 3:09min)

(323) Waringarri-lu$_{A}$=ma   ngu=**yinangkulu**$_{A,\ O}$
warrior-ERG=TOP   CAT=3AUG.S>3AUG.NS

turt-turt   ma-ni   **kirri-walija**-Ø$_{O}$=ma.
grab-REDUP   get-PST   woman-PAUC-ACC=TOP
"The warriors grabbed the women." (🔊) DD: EC98_a012: 10:34min)

A zero (-Ø) to reflect this case marker is not included in the glosses in this grammar, unless it is necessary in order to exemplify a point. We remain agnostic as to whether there is no case form present or whether the case form is -Ø (see Legate, 2002 for some discussion of Warlpiri).

4.3.2 ERGative

The ergative case suffix marks the subject of a transitive sentence and optionally marks the subject of a semi-transitive sentence. The ergative suffix can also be used to mark instruments.

4.3.2.1 Form

The ergative case has a number of allomorphs, which were introduced in §4.3, and are shown in detail in Table 16.

Table 16: Different forms of the ergative.

Form	Environment	Gurindji	English gloss
-ngku	When the stem is two syllables and ends in a vowel	*karu-ngku*	'child-ERG'
-lu	When the stem is more than two syllables and ends in a vowel	*wamala-lu*	'girl-ERG'
-kulu	When the stem ends in 'p', 'k', or 'ng'	*ngarra**p**-kulu* *karta**k**-kulu* *milarra**ng**-kulu*	'heat-ERG' 'container-ERG' 'spear-ERG'
-ku	When the stem has 'mp', 'nka', 'nt', or 'nyj' in it	*ka**rnt**i-ku* *ja**nk**a-ku* *ja**nyj**a-ku*	'tree-ERG' 'woman-ERG' 'dirt-ERG'
-ju	When the word ends in 'j' or 'ny'	*jikirri**j**-ju*	'willy-wagtail-ERG'
-tu	When the word ends in 't', 'rt', 'n' or 'rn'	*linya**t**-tu* *jungka**rt**-tu*	'hot coals-ERG' 'smoke-ERG'
-u	When the word ends in 'rl', 'ly', 'rr' or 'l'	*maju**l**-u* *wara**rr**-u* *muku**rl**-u*	'stomach-ERG' 'fat-ERG' 'aunt-ERG'

Some examples of the different allomorphs are given in (321), (324)–(331).

(324) Nangala-**lu** paraj pu-nya ngu ngarlu.
SUBSECT-ERG find pierce-PST CAT honey
"Nangala found the honey." (🔈 VW: FM07_a021: 2:39min)

(325)

Wirlka-**ngku**	jangkarni-**lu**,	ngu=rna
axe-ERG	big-ERG	CAT=1EXC.MIN.S

paya-rna-na	nyila=ma.
bite-IMPF-PRS	that=TOP

"I cut it with the big axe." (🔈) VW: FM07_a027: 3:10min)

(326)

Aaah	ngu=rnayinangkulu	ngantipa=ma
Ah	CAT=1EXC.AUG.S>3AUG.NS	1EXC.AUG=TOP

janka-**ku**=ma	kayi	pa-na-ni.
woman-ERG=TOP	follow	hit-IMPF-PST

"Us women used to follow them too." (🔈) BW: FM09_12_5a: 0:33min)

(327)

Jarrwaj	pu-nya	ngu	mirlarrang-**kulu**.
spear	pierce-PST	CAT	spear-ERG

"He got it with a spear." (🔈) TD: FM10_27_1b: 0:52min)

(328)

Tarukap	ngu=rnayinangulu	ma-na-na	marlarn-**tu**.
bathe	CAT=1EXC.AUG.S>3AUG.NS	do-IMPF-PRS	river.red.gum-ERG

"We bathe them using the red river gum mix." (🔈) KM: FM09_14_3: 1:10min)

(329)

Yeah	ngarlapi	pa-na-na	ngurra-ngka	na,	Ngarnjal-**u**=ma.
yeah	carve	hit-IMPF-PRS	camp-LOC	FOC	NAME-ERG=TOP

"Yeah Topsy is carving the wood at her camp now."
(🔈) VW: FM08_a101: 17:38min)

(330)

Tapu-k	ngu=lu	yuwa-na-na	karu-**ngku**
blunt-FACT	CAT=3AUG.S	put-IMPF-PRS	kid-ERG

ngayirrany-**ju**	ngapuju-walija-**lu**.
1EXC.UA.DAT-ERG	grandchild-PAUC-ERG

"Our paternal grandchildren make the axe blunt."
(🔈) VW: FM07_a050: 13:10min)

(331)

Ngu=rnalu	kampa-rna-na	na,	wumara-**lu**	yalu-**ngku**.
CAT=1EXC.AUG.S	cook-IMPF-PRS	FOC	stone-ERG	that-ERG

"We cook it using those stones." (🔈) TD: FM10_a134: 1:45min)

4.3.2.2 Function

Examples (324), (326), (329) and (330) all show the use of the ergative case to mark the subject of a transitive sentence. In many of these examples the subjects are animate, however inanimate transitive subjects are also possible and are also marked ergative, as shown in (325), (327), (328) and (331). In many cases it is quite difficult to distinguish between an inanimate transitive subject and an instrument, however examples where the agent cannot be wielded by an animate subject (and therefore could not be an instrument) provide clear cases. The use of the ergative case is not the only possible way to mark an instrument. Instruments may be also marked with the proprietive suffix with the ergative suffix added in agreement with a transitive subject, see (264), but the ergative suffix is optional, as shown in (342).[104] In this respect, instrumentals behave more like adverbs where ergative-marking is optional. Body part instruments are always marked ergative, as in (332), which can be considered agreement with the subject nominal it is semantically related to. See the discussion of the proprietive suffix in §4.6.2.

(332) Janyja ngu=rna ma-na-na nyila=ma
dirt CAT=1EXC.MIN.S do-IMPF-PRS that=TOP

larlup-karra **wartan-tu**, karan.
scoop-ITER hand-ERG dig.with.hands
"I'm scooping the dirt out with my hands and digging some more."
(🔊 VW: FM07_a054: 8:17min)

An ergative-marked body part instrument can be derived into a coverb using the coverbalising suffix *-p* (§7.2.4.2), as shown in (333). In (334), the *-lu* allomorph is used for a two syllable word where *-ngku* might be expected. Additionally, a different suffix is used *-jayak* which we have not observed in the rest of the language. The *k* ending makes it look suspiciously like an inchoative, perhaps from another language. Note that these examples do not follow the nominal word template outlined in §4.1 because they are examples of derivational morphology following inflection. These types of examples are odd because ergative-marked instruments also do not appear in intransitive clauses. The proprietive is used instead.

104 This pattern is the same as in Warlpiri (Nash, 1986, pp. 35, 227; Simpson, 1991, p. 247).

105 It is possible that *-jayak* is a form of the motivative case suffix *-nganayak* but it is not clear. Gurindji does not normally allow case-stacking so this would be an unsatisfactory analysis in any case. This suffix is not found elsewhere in surrounding Ngumpin-Yapa languages or in Jaminjung therefore it remains a mystery.

(333) **Tingarri-lu-p** mingip ya-na-na.
knee-ERG-CV crawl go-IMPF-PRS
"She is crawling on her knees."
(McConvell corpus: Meakins et al., 2016, p. 365)

(334) Jakap-karra ya-na-na **jina-lu-jayak.**[105]
sneak-ITER go-IMPF-PRS foot-ERG-XXX
"He is sneaking up [on someone] by walking on his tiptoes."
(McConvell 1970s wordlist; but not sourced from McConvell)

The ergative is also used to mark the subject of some semi-transitive sentences (i.e. sentences with an indirect object marked with the dative case, as shown in (335), however not all semi-transitive clauses are marked ergative, see (346) (see §8.4.3).

(335) Ngu=yi **Nangari-lu** liwart pa-ni.
CAT=1EXC.MIN.NS SUBSECT-ERG wait hit-PST
"Nangari waited for me." (🔈 VW: FM09_13_3a: 0:57min)

The ergative marker is also found optionally marking adverbs in agreement with a transitive subject, as shown in (336) and (337). This is discussed further in §7.3.

(336) **Narra-yawung-kulu** ngu=rna yirrirr
hook-PROP-ERG CAT=1EXC.MIN.S pull.REDUP

ma-ni **kuya-ngku** **yamak-kulu.**
do-PST thus-ERG gently-ERG
"I pulled it out with the hooked stick very gently like this."
(🔈 VW: FM08_a099: 7:10min)

(337) **Kajijirri-lu**=ma ngu=lu
old.woman.REDUP-ERG=TOP CAT=3AUG.S

pa-na-ni **kamparri-jang-kulu**=ma.
hit-IMPF-PST before-TIME-ERG=TOP
"The women used to pound them like this in the old days."
(🔈 VW: FM09_15_2a: 8:34min)

The ergative is also used to mark intransitive coverbs in reduced subordinate clauses to indicate that the subject of the subordinate clause is the same as the subject of the main transitive clause. This function is shown in (338) and (339) and discussed in more detail in §9.3.4.2.

(338) **Kutij-ju** na warra ka-nga-ni.
stand-ERG FOC watch take-IMPF-PST
"She$_i$ watched her$_j$ as she$_i$ stood." (🔈 VW: FM10_23_1b: 6:04min)

(339) **Lurlu-ngku** ngu=rna pa-na-na, ngarlapi-la.
sit-ERG CAT=1EXC.MIN.S hit-IMPF-PRS carve-LOC
"I'm sitting down cutting [the wood], shaping it." (🔈 VW: FM08_a101: 13:59min)

4.3.3 DATive

The dative case has a large number of functions. It marks indirect objects, beneficiaries/maleficiaries, purposes, alienable possessions and animate goals. It also marks coverbs in reduced subordinate clauses to indicate purpose.

4.3.3.1 Form

The dative case has four allomorphs, which are shown in Table 17.

Table 17: Different forms of the dative.

Form	Environment	Gurindji	English gloss
-ku	When the stem ends in a consonant	*kuliya**n**-ku*	'for the dangerous one'
-wu	When the stem ends in a vowel 'a', 'i' or 'u'	*wamal**a**-wu*	'for the girl'
-yu	When the stem ends in 'i'	*kajirr**i**-yu*	'for the woman'
-u	When the word ends in 'l', 'rl', 'ly' or 'rr'	*maju**l**-u* *wara**rr**-u* *muku**rl**-u*	'for the stomach' 'for the fat' 'for the aunt'

These allomorphs are shown in (340)–(342). Note that the *-yu* allomorph is somewhat curious. It was used by Major Smiler in his 1959 recordings (341) in variation with *-wu*, but was not observed by McConvell in the 1970s. It is apparent in Meakins' recordings and entrenched in Gurindji Kriol (van den Bos, Meakins, & Algy, 2017) (342).

(340) Ngu=rnayina jayi-ngku
CAT=1EXC.MIN.S>3AUG.NS give-POT

ngayiny-**ku** mali-**wu.**
1EXC.MIN.DAT-DAT son.in.law-DAT
"I'm going to give it to my sons-in-law." (🔈 VW: FM07_05_1a: 7:32min)

(341) Nyawa=ma ngu=rla ngaji-**yu** ngayiny-**ku** ngurra.
this=FOC CAT=3OBL father-DAT 1MIN.DAT-DAT camp
"This is my father's camp." MS: HALE_K06-004553: 58:26min)

(342) Kulmarrk, waninyana, ngu=rnalu=rla kulmarrk,
work.hard fall.IMPF.PRS CAT=1EXC.AUG.S=3OBL work.hard

kajirri-**yu**=ma yalu-**wu**=ma wankaj-**ku** kula
old.woman-DAT=TOP that-DAT=TOP sick-DAT NEG

kalurirrp-kaji. Ngu=rnalu puj-im yuwa-na-na
walk.around-AGENT CAT=1EXC.AUG.S push-TR put-IMPF-PRS

na wheelchair-yawung. Karrwa-rna-na ngu=rnalu
FOC wheelchair-PROP keep-IMPF-PRS CAT=1EXC.AUG.S

pakara-la karla-yin-karra-la, warlu-ngka.
outside-LOC west-ABL-SIDE-LOC fire-LOC
"We work hard for that old lady who is sick and can't walk about herself. I push her around in a wheelchair. We keep her outside on the westside of the house next to the fire." VW: FM12_a177: 3:41min)

4.3.3.2 Function

The dative case is used to mark the indirect object of ditransitive verbs, (343) and (344), and semi-transitive verbs, as shown in (345)–(349). Where the indirect object is animate, it is cross-referenced by a non-subject pronoun or third person oblique pronoun (343), (344) and (346), and where it is inanimate, it is generally not cross-referenced (345), although note that a third person oblique pronoun *=rla* is present in (347). It is possible that this pronoun is referencing *kamara* 'long yam', but it is also possible that it refers to an unexpressed purpose. See §6.2.4 for more information about pronominal clitic cross-referencing, animacy and discourse.

(343) Nguku[106] ngu=**rla** jayi-nya **karu-wu**.
water CAT=3OBL give-PST child-DAT
"She gave some water to the kid." VW: FHM098: 33:03min)

106 Note that *nguku* 'water' is a Mudburra word.

(344) Wilarr ngu=**rla** jayi-nga-ni **Yawarlwarl-u**=ma.
seed CAT=3OBL give-IMPF-PST Crested.Pigeon-DAT=TOP
"She was giving Pigeon the seed." (🔊 TD, VW: FM08_a072: 1:54min)

(345) **Junction-ku** **murlu-wu** ngu=rna=ngku ma-rna-na.
junction-DAT this-DAT CAT=1EXC.MIN.S=2MIN.NS talk-IMPF-PRS
"I'm talking to you about this junction." (🔊 VW: FM07_a058: 0:16min)

(346) Ngu=**rla** ma-rna-ni Yawarlwarl=ma **Wayil-u**=ma.
CAT=3OBL say-IMPF-PST Crested.Pigeon=TOP Wallaby-DAT=TOP
"That's what Pigeon said to Wallaby." (🔊 VW: FM10_23_1b: 2:23min)

(347) **Kamara-wu** na ngu=**rla** nya-nga-na
long.yam-DAT FOC CAT=3OBL intake-IMPF-PRS

Ngarnjal-lu warlakap.
NAME-ERG search
"Topsy was looking around for yams." (🔊 VW: FM07_a054: 2:33min)

The dative is also used in possessive function to mark a relationship between two alienable entities, as shown in (348). In this example, *Wadrill* is marked dative to indicate that she is related to *daddy*, and the dative pronoun *ngayiny* 'my' is also used to indicate a relationship with *papa-kujarra* 'two brothers'. In these examples, the dative has an adnominal function as shown by the fact that the dative-marked noun is in agreement with the head noun.

(348) **Ngayiny** ngu=wula karrinyani
1EXC.MIN.DAT CAT=3UA.S be.IMPF.PST

papa-kujarra **Wadrill-u** **daddy**.
brother-DU NAME-DAT father
"My two brothers were here – including Violet's father."
(🔊 TD: FM10_22_1b: 0:23min)

The dative marker is also used in benefactive constructions, where the benefactor is overt, and is also cross-referenced by a non-subject pronoun if the referent is animate. Examples are given in (349) and (350).

(349) Nyila=ma=rla ka-nga-na mungkaj-ku nyanuny-ku.
that=TOP=3OBL take-IMPF-PRS wife-DAT 3MIN.DAT-DAT
"He takes it back for his wife." (🔊 VW: FM09_a123: 13:11min)

(350) Ngu=**rnayinangkulu** pirrkap-pirrkap ma-na-na
CAT=1EXC.AUG.S>3AUG.NS make-REDUP do-IMPF-PRS

kawarla=ma **kaminjarr-u** **nyampa-wu,**
coolamon=TOP grandchild-DAT what-DAT

ngapuju-wu, **kurturtu-nginyi**[107]**-yu.**
grandchild-DAT woman.child-SOURCE-DAT
"We make the coolamons for our maternal grandchildren."
(🔊) BW: FM07_2_1a: 1:19min)

Datives also mark malefactives, as shown by (351). Malefactives are the negative corollary of benefactives. In (351), no free nominal is present, but it would be an oblique pronoun. Instead, the bound pronoun indexes the malefactive (and the *=rla* likely cross-references an unexpressed purposive e.g. 'for some reason').

(351) "Ngaja=**yi**=n-ku=rla kirt
ADMON=1EXC.MIN.NS=2MIN.S-EP=3OBL break

yuwa-na-na," ngu=rla ma-rna-ni.
put-IMPF-PRS CAT=3OBL say-IMPF-PST
"'You might break it on me for some reason,' she was saying to her."
(🔊) VW: FM10_23_1b: Yawarlwarl Wanyil: 3:54min)

Datives also mark animate goals, as shown in (352)–(355). Because these goals are animate, a cross-referencing pronoun is also found.

(352) **Ngarnjal-ku**[108] ngu=**rla** ya-ni.
NAME-DAT CAT=3OBL go-PST
"She went after Topsy." (🔊) VW: FM09_a127: 21:37min)

(353) **Nyanuny-ku** <u>rain</u> jak waninya.
3MIN.DAT-DAT rain drop fall.PST
"Then the rain fell on his [camp]." (🔊) VW: FM09_12_5b: 1:51min)

107 Note that this is a derivational use of *-nginyi*, discussed further in §4.7.18.

(354) **Nyanuny-ku** **jaju-wu** ngu=**rla** ka-nga-na,
3MIN.DAT-DAT MM-DAT CAT=3OBL take-IMPF-PRS

mangarri punyu, yarti-ngkurra makin-ta-wu.
bread good shade-ALL sleep-LOC-DAT
"She takes a cake to her grandmother who was sleeping in the shade."
(🔊 VW: FHM146: 1:12min)

(355) Ngu=**rla** wany yuwa-na-na nyila=ma
CAT=3OBL throw put-IMPF-PRS that=TOP

majapula=ma **nyanuny-ku** **kapuku-wu**.
football=TOP 3MIN.DAT-DAT sister-DAT
"He throws the football to his sister." (🔊 BW: FM07_a043: 3:04min)

The distinction between beneficiary constructions, goal constructions and possessor dissension constructions is not always clear because these three constructions do not differ in the use of the dative marker and the coreferential pronoun. For example, (355) may be interpreted as 'throw it for his sister' (benefactive) or 'throw it to the sister of his' (possessor dissension) rather than 'throw it to his sister' (goal). This similarity is discussed in detail in §8.3.3.

Animate goals can also be marked with the allative case, which is shown in §4.7.20, using a sequence of dative, nominaliser and allative marker, as shown in (356). The animate is rendered as a place in this expression of goal.

(356) Kajirri-**wu-ny-jirri**, ngu=rla yapart
old.woman-DAT-NMLZ-ALL CAT=3OBL sneak

ya-na-na nyila=ma wari=ma.
go-IMPF-PRS that=TOP snake=TOP
"That snake sneaks up to the place where the old woman is [or the woman's place]." (🔊 VW: FHM146: 2006: 8:05min)

The dative case may also occur in purposive constructions. This function differs from the other dative functions discussed above in that it is never cross-referenced with an oblique pronoun, regardless of animacy.

Where the dative combines with a non-finite verb (either the infinitive form of the inflecting verb or a coverb), it creates a reduced subordinate clause which is used to indicate that the event of the subordinate clause is the purpose of the main clause.

108 Note that the allomorph *-u* can also follow *l*.

Other elements in the subordinate clause agree with the non-finite verb/coverb in dative marking (see also §9.3.1), see (357)–(360).

(357) Jululuj na ma-na-na
carry.hip.REDUP FOC do-IMPF-PRS

Nangala-lu=ma, **wartart-ku**=ma.
SUBSECT-ERG=TOP dry.out-DAT=TOP
"Nangala carries it back in order to dry it out." (🔈) VW: FM08_a089: 9:01min)

(358) Ngu=rna=rla parnngirri-la kiya-rru **majul-u**
CAT=1EXC.MIN.S=3OBL bark-LOC put-POT stomach-DAT

yura-k-ku **ngayiny-ku** **kapuku-wu**
good-FACT-DAT 1EXC.MIN.DAT-DAT sister-DAT
"I will put it in the bark dish for my sister to make her feel better."
(🔈) TD: FM07_a028: 10:58min)

(359) Ngu=lu=rla ya-ni na nganta
CAT=3AUG.S=3OBL go-PST FOC ALLE

karu-walija=ma **karrap-ku** na jarrwalut.
child-PAUC=TOP look-DAT FOC many
"A big mob of kids came over for a look."
(🔈) VW: FM10_27_1a: Kurraj Story from Halls Creek: 3:09min)

(360) Ngu=rna=rla nya-ngku **pakipaki-wu,**
CAT=1EXC.MIN.S=3OBL intake-POT chisel-DAT

kawarla-wu **pirrkap-pirrkap-ku**.
coolamon-DAT make-REDUP-DAT
"I'm going to look for chisel metal so I can make coolamons."
(🔈) VW: FM07_a021: 5:54min)

4.3.4 LOCative

The locative case typically indicates place, location or static spatial relations. It is also used, however, in time expressions and to express the means by which some action is performed.

4.3.4.1 Form

The locative case has similar allomorphic variation to the ergative case, except that the locative forms end in 'a' rather than 'u' (Table 18):[109]

Table 18: Different forms of the locative.

Form	Environment	Gurindji	English gloss
-ngka	When the word is two syllables and ends in a vowel	*malyj**u**-ngka* [109]	'with the boy'
-la	When the word is more than two syllables and ends in a vowel	*makurr**u**-la*	'in cold weather'
-kula	When the word ends in 'p', 'k' or 'ng'	*ngarra**p**-kula* *karta**k**-kula* *milarra**ng**-kula*	'in hot weather' 'in the billy' 'on the spear'
-ka	When the word has 'mp', 'nk', 'nt', or 'nyj' in it	*ka**rnt**i-ka* *ja**nk**a-ka* *ja**nyj**a-ka*	'by the tree' 'with the woman' 'in the dirt'
-ja	When the word ends in 'j', or 'ny'	*kurruri**j**-ja*	'in the car'
-ta	When the word ends in 't', 'rt', 'n' or 'rn'	*linya**t**-ta* *jungka**rt**-ta*	'on the hot coals' 'in the smoke'
-a	When the word ends in 'l', 'rl', 'rr' or 'ly'	*maju**l**-a* *wara**rr**-a* *muku**rl**-a*	'in the stomach' 'in the butter' 'with the aunt'

Examples of the different forms of the locative allomorphs are given in (361)–(372).

(361) Ngu=rna paya-rni ngu=rna yuwa-ni **parnngirri-la.**
CAT=1EXC.MIN.S bite-PST CAT=1EXC.MIN.S put-PST bark-LOC
"I chopped it and put it in the bark." (◀) VW: FM07_a021: 3:16min)

(362) Ngaja=ngku=rla **ngapanyji-la** waninya=ma.
ADMON=2MIN.NS=3OBL eye-LOC fall.PST=TOP
"In case splinters get in your eye." (◀) VW: FM07_a050: 9:24min)

(363) Nga-rna-ni purrp-karra **kamurr-kamurr-a**=rni.
eat-IMPF-PST finish-ITER middle-REDUP-LOC=ONLY
"He was finishing all of the food half-way back."
(◀) VW: FM10_a155: Ngarlking Karu: 5:41min)

109 Note that this is usually expressed with comitative DAT-ny-LOC not the plain LOC.

(364) Ngu=rna yuwa-na-na japurr **ngawa-ngka** **murla-ngka**.
CAT=1EXC.MIN.S put-IMPF-PRS dip water-LOC this-LOC
"I'm dipping it in the water." (◀) VW: FM07_01_1e: 1:46min)

(365) **Karnti-ka** partaj ya-na-na.
stick-LOC climb go-IMPF-PRS
"It climbs up the stick." (◀) VW: FM10_a133: 9:34min)

(366) Yurtup na ngu=lu kiya-rna-ni
grind FOC CAT=3AUG.S put-IMPF-PST

palwany-ja=ma **winyji-ka**=ma.
flat.rock-LOC=TOP spring-LOC=TOP
"They used to grind it down on a flat rock by the spring."
(◀) TD: FM10_a147: 3:15min)

(367) Ngu=rnalu karrinyana=ma **wulngarn-ta**, warrart.
CAT=1EXC.AUG.S be.IMPF.PRS =TOP sun-LOC bask
"We're basking in the sun." (◀) VW: FM09_a127: 13:01min)

(368) Ngu=yi yuwa-rru **kurrurij-ja**.
CAT=1EXC.MIN.NS put-POT car-LOC
"She will put it in the car for me." (◀) VW: FM08_a089: 2:54min)

(369) **Jinparrak-kula**=ma nyawa=ma ngu=rna
Wave.Hill-LOC=TOP this=TOP CAT=1EXC.MIN.S

ma-rna-na **Jinparrak-kula**.
talk-IMPF-PRS Wave.Hill-LOC
"I'm talking at old Wave Hill station." (◀) BW: FM07_a021: 0:30min)

(370) An ngamayi-lu ngu=yina nguru jayi-nga-ni
and mother-ERG CAT=3AUG.NS prepare give-IMPF-PST

walyak-kula=ma nanta-nanta=ma nyila=ma.
inside-LOC=TOP small-REDUP=TOP that=TOP
"And the mother prepares to give food to the little ones inside."
(◀) VW: FM10_a149: 2:17min)

(371) An **kartak-kula** ngu=rna yuwa-ni ngayu=ma.
and cup-LOC CAT=1EXC.MIN.S put-PST 1EXC.MIN=TOP
"And I put it in the cup, I did." (◀) VW: FM07_a021: 3:19min)

(372) Nyanawu pilyily yapakayi **majul-a** nyamu
RECOG pinky small stomach-LOC REL

ka-nga-na **puul-a** walyak.
take-IMPF-PRS pouch-LOC inside
"You know the hairless joey that is still in its mother's pouch."
(🔊 VW: FM09_a123: 6:27min)

4.3.4.2 Function

The main function of the locative case in Gurindji is to mark static location, i.e. the location of an object in relation to a person, place, object or event; i.e. relationships often expressed in English by the use of prepositions such as 'at, in, on,' etc. The examples in (361)–(372) demonstrate its use in this function. If further specification about the spatial relation is required, adverbs, cardinal directions, river drainage terms or vertical terms may be used.

This use of the locative case to mark static location has been grammaticalised to produce many place names using the sequence 'stem+LOC+ONLY'. Evidence for the fossilisation of these suffixes is seen in many place names on Wave Hill Station which end with the sequence: *-kula+rni*, *-ngka+rni*, *-ja+rni*, *-ka+rni*, *-ta+rni* or *la+rni*, for example Kurrpakarralarni. This sequence is composed of *kurrpakarra* 'jumping into the water with a splash' with a locative case-marker (*-la*) and a restrictive clitic (*=rni*) which combine to mean "right at the place of . . . ". This sequence is common to many place names in the Victoria River District (McConvell, 2009b). Other place names endings include *-yawung* or *-jawung* (with, having) e.g. Kalngayawung (with red ochre), *-wu* 'dative' + *-ny* 'nominaliser' e.g. Luwarrawuny 'place of riflefish' and Japuwuny 'place of the head (of the river)' and *–murlung* 'privative' e.g. Ngawa-murlung 'waterless'. The sequence of locative + *=rni* attaches to a noun or verb, for example Karungkarni 'right at the place of the children' or Purtpangkarni 'right at the place of thigh clapping'. In some cases, only the locative ending is found on its own, for example Jalminta.

In some cases, the name is so old that the meaning of the original word is no longer known. Jalminta is one example, where it is not clear what *jalmin* means. Another is the name Kurlpunta is suggestive of the sequence *kurlpun* + *-ta*, however the meaning of *kurlpun* is unclear. It is not known from Gurindji or Mudburra. Similarly, it is not clear what *jama* from Jamangku refers to despite the likelihood that *-ngku* is an ergative marker.

In cases where the meaning of the original word is known the name is often associated with a Dreaming story about the site. For example, Ngilyipurr, which means 'drown', is a place on a stretch of the Camfield River (Japuwuny) where a Dreaming Emu from Bilinarra country drowned. Some places have two names. In these cases, the second name is usually descriptive and involves one of the endings described above. Other examples of sites are places where traditional custodians receive their name. For example, a bore on the border of Wave Hill Station and Cattle Creek Station is called Wijina. The name Wijina is also often used to refer to Starlight Kipiyarri Japarta who was the traditional custodian of the site.

The locative case may also be found in other functions. Firstly, it can be used to express the means by which an action is performed, as shown in (373).

(373)

Ngara-ngka	kankula,	ngu=n	ya-na-na,	yala-ngka=ma
height-LOC	up	CAT=2MIN.S	go-IMPF-PRS	that-LOC=TOP

tiwu-waji-la=ma	kuya.	Kanyjurra=ma=n
fly-AGENT-LOC=TOP	thus	down=TOP=2MIN.S

nya-nga-na	karrap	yikili.
intake-IMPF-PRS	look	long.way

"You travel in a plane at great heights. You can see down a long way."
(🔊 VW: FM12_a175: 13:47min)

This use of the locative contrasts with the use of *-yawung* 'proprietive', for example *tiwu-waji-yawung* 'fly-AGENT-PROP', which is used to describe situations where the agent has control over the action, such as when the participant is a pilot, rather than a passenger (see also §4.6.2.2).

Locative case may also be used to express the source of an object, for example where something is kept (374).

(374)

Karu-ngku	kawarla	warrkuj	ma-ni	**marru-ngka**	mangarri-wu.
child-ERG	coolamon	pick.up	do-PST	house-LOC	veg.food-DAT

"A child got a coolamon from the house for [collecting] food."
(McConvell corpus: Meakins et al., 2016, p. 405)

The locative case is also used to denote a transformative relationship where one entity is made out of another, as seen in (375) and (376). (Note that (376) has Kriol as a matrix clause.) The ablative marker can also be used in this function, see §4.3.7.

(375)

Mangkaya	ngu=lu	pirrkap	ma-ni
shelter	CAT=3AUG.S	build	do-PST

ngamanpurru-la,	yalu-ngku	kirri-kujarra-lu.
conkerberry-LOC	that-ERG	woman-DU-ERG

"They built a shelter out of a conkerberry tree – the two women did."
(🔊 VW: FM10_23_4: 5:21min)

(376) On the olden time dei bin pirrkap mangarri, **yala-ngka**=ma,
on the olden time 3PL.S PST make bread that-LOC=TOP

nyampayirla-la=ma, **seed-ta**=ma nganta wayi?
whatsitcalled-LOC=TOP seed-LOC=TOP ALLE TAG
"In the old days they used to make bread out of seeds, didn't they?"
(🔈 VW: FM09_13_2a: 4:32min)

Another use of the locative case is as a comitative or an expression of accompaniment, as in (377) and (378). It has the meaning 'with' in these examples. When two entities are accompanying each other in movement, the proprietive case *-yawung* can be used instead.

(377) Kula=rnalu **ngumpit-ta** karrinyani karlarra
NEG=1EXC.AUG.S man-LOC be.IMPF.PST west

ngu=rnalu karrinyani purirripurirri-la kuya.
CAT=1EXC.AUG.S be.IMPF.PST birth.camp-LOC thus
"We never used to stay with the men [after giving birth]. We used to stay in the west in the birth camp." (🔈 VW: FM10_a133: 15:44min)

(378) Ngayu=ma ngu=rna ya-nku marru-ngkurra **ngayiny-ja**
1EXC.MIN CAT=1EXC.MIN.S go-POT house-ALL 1EXC.MIN-LOC

ngapa-ngka.
brother-LOC
"I'm going to the house with my brother." (🔈 MS: HALE_K06-004553: 59:17min)

Alternatively, the comitative can be used to express accompaniment, however this is rarer. The comitative derives from an historical combination of the locative with the dative and nominaliser to produce the forms *-wunyja* or *-kunyja* (see §4.3.9). An example is given in (379). It is cross-referenced by a non-subject pronoun. Here we separate the suffixes to show the historical source, but analyse them as a single suffix.

(379) Ya-nku=rliwula=rla Kurrpi-**wu-ny-ja** marru-ngkurra
Go-POT=1INC.UA.S=3OBL NAME-DAT-NMLZ-LOC house-ALL
"Let's go with Kurrpi to the house." (🔈 MS: HALE_K06-004553: 01:02:18hr)

The locative case is also used to mark time periods such as days, weather or ceremonies. The use of the locative case is similar to the use of 'on' in English time expressions such as "on Saturday". For some ceremony names this use has fossilised such as Karungka which is the boy's first initiation ceremony.

Another use of the locative marker is in aversive function as a warning, as in (380), where it marks something immediately dangerous. Tsunoda (1981, p. 58) observed this use in Jaru and it is also found marking warnings in Bilinarra (Meakins & Nordlinger 2014, p. 129).

(380) Kawayi! kurrurij-**ja**!
come.here car-LOC
"Come here, look out car!" (Meakins et al., 2016, p. 23)

Finally, the locative marker is used in non-finite subordinate clauses. The locative functions to indicate that the event described by the subordinate clause is simultaneous with the event described by the main clause, and that the subject of the subordinate clause is coreferential with the intransitive subject of the main clause, as demonstrated by (381). The locative marker can also be used in alternation with the ergative when the subject of the subordinate clause is co-referential with the transitive subject of the main clause (382). It can also alternate with the allative when the subject of the subordinate clause is co-referential with the object of the main clause (383)–(385).

(381) Yala-ngka=kata=rnalu karrinyani, **pirrka-pirrka-la**=ma.
that-LOC=IMM=1EXC.AUG.S be.IMPF.PST make-REDUP-LOC=TOP
"We used to sit down just there making wooden artefacts."
(🔈 VW: FM09_a120: 2:54min)

(382) Ngu=rna=ngku=rla ka-ngku
CAT=1EXC.MIN.S=2MIN.NS=3OBL take-POT

tirrip-karra-la=ma kayirra nyila.
overnight-ITER-LOC=TOP north that
"I'll take you north for that one, and we will camp out overnight."
(🔈 VW: FM09_13_2a: 5:03min)

(383) **Lurlu-ngka** jiya-rna-na ngu kanyjuli-yit na kuya.
sit-LOC burn-IMPF-PRS CAT down-ABL FOC thus
"(The baby) is smoked from below while she sits there."
(🔈 VW: FM08_a085: 4:50min)

(384) Ngu=yi=npula **makin-ta** wanyja-ni.
CAT=1EXC.MIN.NS=2UA.S sleep-LOC leave-PST
"You left me while I was sleeping."
(🔈 VW: FM10_a155: Ngarlking Karu: 10:21min)

(385) **Makin-ta**=ma wirra nya-nga-na ngu.
sleep-LOC=TOP look.over.shoulder intake-IMPF-PRS CAT
"I look over my shoulder at someone who's lying down."
(🔈 TD: FM10_a165: 10:18min)

Note too that there is one curious derivational use of the locative in the corpus where *nganymanta* 'new-born baby' is derived from *nganyman* 'wooden cradle' plus the locative *-ta*.

4.3.5 ALLative

4.3.5.1 Form

There are four forms of the allative: *-ngkurra, -kurra, -jirri* and *-yirri*. Table 19 gives the forms and some examples. Note that the allomorph *-yirri* is only found with multisyllabic stems and *-ngkurra* with both multisyllabic and disyllabic stems. The use of *-ngkurra* with multisyllabic stems is probably a recent phenomenon. Also note that where the stem contains a nasal-stop cluster, *-kurra* is used which corresponds with the locative *-ka* and the ergative *-ku*. Examples of the allative in clauses are given in (386)–(394).

Table 19: Different forms of the allative.

Form	Environment	Gurindji	English gloss
-yirri	When the multisyllabic stem ends in a vowel	*Daguragu-yirri*	'to Daguragu'
-ngkurra	When the word ends in a vowel	*Daguragu-ngkurra*	'to Daguragu'
-kurra	When the stem contains 'mp', 'nt', 'nk' or 'nyj'	*kar**nt**i-kurra* *pi**nk**a-kurra* *marri**nyj**i-kurra*	'to the tree' 'to the river' 'to the big town'
-jirri	When the stem ends in a consonant	*kurruri**j**-jirri* *jalmi**n**-jirri* *karta**k**-jirri*	'to the car' 'to the log' 'to the cup'

(386) **Ngurra-ngkurra** ngu=rna ka-ngku
home-ALL CAT=1EXC.MIN.S take-POT

nyawa=ma, kampij=ma.
this=TOP egg=TOP
"I'll take this egg back home."
(🔈 VW: FM10_27_1a: Kurraj Story from Halls Creek: 1:06min)

(387) Ngu=rlaa kA-ngku kankarra **ngawa-ngkurra**
CAT=1INC.AUG.S take-POT upstream water-ALL

na, kanyjurra **Karna-ngkurra**.
FOC down place.name-ALL
"We'll take them upstream to Karna." (VW: FM10_22_1d: 1:36min)

(388) Nyamu=waa=ngantipangulu **langa-ngkurra**
REL=REL=3AUG.S>1EXC.AUG.NS ear-ALL

ma-ni ngantipanguny.
do-PST 1EXC.AUG.DAT
"When they used to give us ideas." (VW: FM07_01_1b: 1:54min)

(389) Kaa-nu-k ngu=rna ya-nku, **Jamangku-yirri**
east-CROSS-ALL CAT=1EXC.MIN.S go-POT place.name-ALL

nyila=ma Puwarraja Mangaya=ma, nyawa=ma.
that=TOP Dreaming Dreaming=TOP this=TOP
"I'm going east crossing the river to Jamangku, that place with a Dreaming story." (DD: EC98_a017: Karnati-lu: 0:34min)

(390) **Winyji-kurra** ya-na-ni ngu=wula, **jarrwa-ngkurra.**
spring-ALL go-IMPF-PST CAT=3UA.S many-ALL
"Then the two of them went to the spring back to the big group [of children]." (VW: FM10_30_1a: Karu Dreaming Story: 3:44min)

(391) Ya-ni ngu=rnalu, kalu ngu=rnalu
go-PST CAT=1EXC.AUG.S walk CAT=1EXC.AUG.S

ya-ni **yala-ngkurra** **karnti-kurra**.
go-PST that-ALL tree-ALL
"We walked that way to the tree." (VW: FM07_a027: 0:18min)

(392) Yalu-ngku wamala-lu ka-nga-na ngu mangarri
that-ERG girl-ERG take-IMPF-PRS CAT bread

murla-ngkurra, **Settlement-jirri** **mangarri-waji-yirri**.
this-ALL Kalkaringi-ALL veg.food-AGENT-ALL
"The girl takes the cake to the Kalkaringi shop." (BW: FM07_a043: 33:50min)

(393) Jipurlp ya-na-na ngu=wula **ngaliwanguny-jirri.**
join go-IMPF-PRS CAT=3UA.S 1INC.AUG.DAT-ALL
"The two of them come over to where we're sitting [to join us]."
(🔈 VW: FM12_a173: 6:59min)

(394) Nyila=ma wamala=ma ya-na-na kurlarra **Lajaman-jirri.**
that=TOP girl=TOP go-IMPF-PRS south place.name-ALL
"That girl walks south to Lajamanu." (🔈 BW: FM07_a043: 30:48min)

A new allative allomorph *-ngkirri* has emerged among speakers of Gurindji Kriol, which is the result of phonological coalescence between *-ngkurra*, and *-jirri/-yirri*. This form attaches to vowel-final stems and *-jirri* is still used for consonant-final stems (Meakins, 2012, p. 121). This form is stigmatised by Gurindji speakers. Biddy Wavehill, a Gurindji elder, describes her concerns about the use of the new allative allomorph.

> Ngurnayinangkulu kurru karrinyana karu yu nou kula-lu marnana jutup. Ngulu marnani 'Nyawangkirri'. 'Nyawangkirri-ma', nyampayila ngulu marnana 'Murlangkurra'. 'Kawayi murlangkurra,' kuya yu nou . . . 'Nyawangkirri,' dat not rait word jaru. Ngurnayinangkulu kurru karrinyana kuya laik ngurnayinangkulu jutuk kuya-rnangku jarrakap brobli-wei.
>
> We listen to the kids, you know, and they don't talk properly. For example, they are always saying *nyawangkirri* for 'that way'. They always say *nyawangkirri* not *murlangkurra* which is wrong. You should say *murlangkurra* . . . *Nyawangkirri* is not proper Gurindji. We listen to the kids and they don't talk as well as I am talking to you. (Meakins, 2010b, p. 230)

4.3.5.2 Function

The main function of the allative is to mark inanimate goals, as shown in (386)–(394). Nonetheless there are some differences in the marking of inanimate goals. Places, including features of the landscape and buildings, are obligatorily marked with the allative case. On the other hand, place names are only optionally marked allative. In fact, they are most commonly found unmarked. Example (395) gives a place name which is unmarked *Inverway* and one which is marked *Limbunya*.

(395) Kankarra ngu=rnalu ya-na-ni kankula
upstream CAT=1EXC.AUG.S go-IMPF-PST up

Inverway kayirra-k **Limpanyung-jirri.**
place.name north-ALL Limbunya-ALL
"We used to walk upstream and uphill to Inverway and northwards to Limbunya." (McConvell corpus: Meakins et al., 2016, p. 157)

Recall also that animate goals are marked dative, however they can also be marked with the combination of a dative + *ny* + allative (§4.3.3.2). In the case of free pronouns, as in (393), the allative attaches to the oblique form of the pronoun, although in (396), an additional dative is used on *nyanuny*. An allative-marked animate is conceptualised more as a place than a person in these cases, 'where X is'. This is similar to the use of the English possessive form 'I'm going to the doctor's' or 'Let's go back to mine'. Further examples are given in (396)–(398).

(396) **Kapuku-wu-ny-jirri** **nyanuny-ku-~~ny~~[110]-jirri,**
sister-DAT-NMLZ-ALL 3MIN.DAT-DAT-NMLZ-ALL

malyju-ngku ngu wany yuwa-ni.
boy-ERG CAT throw put-PST
"The boy throws it to where his sister is." (VW: FHM098: 2:07min)

(397) Tamarra-nginyi wart ya-na-na **jija-wu-ny-jirri**
antbed-SOURCE return go-IMPF-PRS nurse-DAT-NMLZ-ALL

kuya yilmiyilmij **medisin-jirri.**
thus exchange.REDUP medicine-ALL
"After the antbed, she returns to the nurse's place, like that."[111]
(BB: McNair_E1A48: 3:55min)

(398) Lawara ngu=yina piyarr ka-nga-ni
nothing CAT=3AUG.NS report take-IMPF-PST

marluka-wu-ny-jirri.
old.man-DAT-NMLZ-ALL
"But he kept reporting back to where his father was." (DD: McNair_C2B: 3:50min)

The allative-marked nominal can also be used in conjunction with a transitive impact verb such as *panana* 'hit', *pungana* 'pierce' or *yuwanana* 'put', where the locative would usually be found. The meaning difference is subtle, but seems to suggest an action of 'into' not just 'on' or 'at', see (399). Note that it's not clear what the *=rla* '3OBL' pronoun is cross-referencing in this sentence.

110 Note that *-ny* has been deleted due to the NCD rule. We only show it here for grammatical explicitness.
111 This translation is a bit unsatisfactory.

(399) **Kala-ngkurra**, jarrwaj ngu=rla pu-nya,
thigh-ALL spear CAT=3OBL pierce-PST

karrinyana kakapara-warra na kuya.
be.IMPF.PRS crippled-ITER FOC thus
"Someone speared him in the thigh. He gets about crippled now."
(🔊 VW: FM12_a173: 18:33min)

The allative is used when a location is predicated of an object in transitive sentences. For example in (400), the use of *-kurra* 'ALL' indicates that the bird is in the tree, not the observer, which would be expressed by the use of the locative instead, as shown in (401) (McConvell & Simpson, 2012; Meakins et al., 2020).

(400) Ngu=rna karrap nya-nya jurlak **karnti-kurra**.
CAT=1EXC.MIN.S look intake-PST bird tree-ALL
"I saw a bird which was in a tree." (McConvell & Simpson, 2012, p. 165)

(401) Ngu=rna karrap nya-nya jurlak **karnti-ka**.
CAT=1EXC.MIN.S look intake-PST bird tree-LOC
"I saw a bird when I was in a tree." (McConvell & Simpson, 2012, p. 165)

Finally, the allative marks a non-finite verb in reduced subordinate clauses to indicate that the subject of the subordinate clause is co-referential with the object, indirect object or oblique argument of the main clause, and that the action denoted in the subordinate clause occurs at the same time as the action of the main clause. Examples are given in (402) and (403). In this function, the allative has some overlap with the locative (§4.3.4.2) and is described further in §9.3.4.3. The use of allative marking in non-finite clauses is related to allative marking on NPs, which are semantically locative, but which are construed as complements of objects, as was shown in (400).

(402) Ngu=rna=rla Jangala-wunyja karrinyani
CAT=1EXC.MIN.S=3OBL SUBSECT-COM be.IMPF.PST

kurrupartu-yirri **pirrkap-jirri**.
boomerang-ALL make-ALL
"I was sitting with Jangala while he made a boomerang."
(McConvell corpus: Meakins et al., 2016, p. 191)

(403) Karrap ngu=rna=yina
watch CAT=1EXC.MIN.S=3AUG.NS

nya-nga-ni	**pirrkap-jirri**=ma.
intake-IMPF-PST	make-ALL=TOP

"I watched them while they made it." (🔈 VW: FM07_05_1a: 0:33min)

4.3.6 PURPosive

4.3.6.1 Form

The purposive in Gurindji consists historically of the sequence of a locative and dative suffix. Its allomorphs are based on the locative allomorphs and their conditioning environments. Thus: *-lawu* following multisyllabic vowel-final stems (404), *-ngkawu* following disyllabic vowel-final stems (405), *-jawu* following palatal consonant-final stems (405) and (406), *-kawu* following stems with nasal-stop clusters (406), *-tawu* following alveolar and retroflex consonant-final stems (407) and *-kulawu* following peripheral consonant-final stems (408).

(404)

Yukurrukurru	nyila=ma	**Yarluju-lawu**.
dancing.stick	that=TOP	ceremony-PURP

"This singing stick is for Yarluju ceremony time." (🔈 BW: FM07_02_1a: 1:32min)

(405)

Ka-nga-ni	ngu	ngurra-**ngkawu**	nyanuny-**jawu**.
take-IMPF-PST	CAT	home-PURP	3MIN.DAT-PURP

"She took it back to her place for some reason."
(🔈 VW: FM10_27_1a: Kurraj Story from Halls Creek: 1:12min)

(406)

Kula	piyarr	ka-ngka=ngantipangulu
NEG	tell	take-IMP=3AUG.S>1EXC.AUG.NS

pinka-kawu=rni	**wulaj-jawu**.
river-PURP=ONLY	hide-PURP

"Don't tell on us about hiding by the river."
(McConvell corpus: Meakins et al., 2016, p. 332)

(407)

Ngayu	ngu=rna	pa-ni	kuturu,	wartu	ngayiny
1MIN	CAT=1EXC.MIN.S	hit-PST	nullanulla	nullanulla	1EXC.MIN.DAT

ngu=rna=yi[112]	**wartan-tawu**.
CAT=1EXC.MIN.S=1EXC.MIN.NS	hand-PURP

"I chopped wood to make a nullanulla, and a stick to keep for myself later on."
(🔈 TD: FM07_a028: 7:29min)

---

112 Note that the use of *=yi* as a reflexive pronoun is restricted to the 1EXC.MIN pronoun. See §6.2.2.4 for some discussion.

(408) Waki-waki na ngu=rnalu yuwa-na-na warrkap-**kulawu**.
white-REDUP FOC CAT=1EXC.AUG.S put-IMPF-PRS dance-PURP
"We're putting the white paint here to use at dancing ceremony time."
(BW: FM08_11_2a: 16:51min)

4.3.6.2 Function

The function of this case-marker is three-fold. Firstly, it is used to mark inanimate goals where there is a purpose, such as (405). In this respect, it is an extension of the allative which simply marks goals, but not with a specific purpose. Secondly, it is used to express a purpose with a location in mind. For example, in (407) *wartan-tawu* 'hand-PURP' literally means to keep something at hand for a purpose. In (406), people are hiding at the river for a particular reason (not stated but implied). Three other examples are given in (409)–(411). In this function, it has some overlap with the dative which more generally marks purposes without location encoded.

(409) Ngu=rlaa ka-nga-ni na kayili-yarra
CAT=1INC.AUG.S take-IMPF-PST FOC north-SIDE

yala-ngkawu ngurra-ngkawu.
that-PURP camp-PURP
"We took it to northside [of Daguragu] to the women's centre [for some reason]."
(VW: FM09_a120: 2:14min)

(410) Kaa-rni-yin ngu=rnalu ya-na-ni, murla-ngka
east-UP-ABL CAT=1EXC.AUG.S go-IMPF-PST this-LOC

kanimparra **Junction-tawu nganayirla-lawu,**
downstream place.name-PURP whatsitcalled-PURP

Jurnarni-lawu, Marlanjangku-lawu.
Gordy.Creek-PURP place.name-PURP
"They used to come from Jinparrak, from the east to here to Gordy Creek and Marlanjangku [to get some]." (VW: FM07_a054: 1:39min)

(411) Ka-nya ngu=lu **Palmer Spring-kulawu**.
take-PST CAT=3AUG.S place.name-PURP
"Then they took it to Palmer Spring [for some purpose]."
(VW: FM10_27_1a: Kurraj Story from Halls Creek: 3:59min)

Thirdly, this case suffix also marks a purpose which also has a location in time in mind. This function is common for ceremony words. For example, in (404), the purposive attaches to *Yarluju* 'ceremony' to encode that the dancing stick is for the time when this ceremony is to be performed. In (412) and (413), the purposive marks a time of sickness.

(412)

Nyawa-rra=ma	bush-medicine=ma,	**janga-ngkawu**	**nyampa-kawu**.
this-PL=TOP	bush-medicine=TOP	sick-PURP	what-PURP

"This lot of bush medicine is for times when you're sick or whatever."
(🔈 VW: FM10_a136: 10:40min)

(413)

Punyu	kukij-karra-wu	du,	**janga-ngkawu,**
good	drink-ITER-DAT	too	sick-PURP

kulykulya-lawu	**nyampa-kawu**	**yala-ngkawu**.
congestion-PURP	what-PURP	that-PURP

"It's good for drinking too when you are congested or whatever."
(🔈 VW: FM08_a089: 3:18min)

It is possible to analyse this suffix as case-stacking since it is transparently built from the locative+dative. However, they are not examples of 'true' case-stacking where the case-markers are individually and syntactically active at different levels in the clause. For this reason, we treat these LOC-DAT sequences as a single complex case form, thereby also complying with our nominal template since we assume they jointly appear in the single CASE slot.

Note though there is one context where the case-markers are separately syntactically-active. In (414) and (415), the case-markers are doubly embedded in a reduced subordinate clause. These are discussed in §9.3.4.4.

(414)

Ngu=rna	ma-ni	pujtilip,	**kukij-karra-wu,**
CAT=1EXC.MIN.S	do-PST	bush.tea.leaf	drink-ITER-DAT

janga-ngka-wu,	**tarukap-ku**	**nyampa-wu,**
sick-LOC-DAT	bathe-DAT	what-DAT

karu-wu=purrupurru,	jangkakarni-wu.
child-DAT=AND	big.REDUP-DAT

"I got some bush tea leaf then to make into a medicine for the kids and adults to drink when they're sick." (🔈 VW: FM09_14_1a: 5:32min)

(415) Jurlaka=ma tiwu ya-ni ngu=rla
bird=TOP fly go-PST CAT=3OBL

kajirri-wu **makin-ta-wu.**
old.woman-DAT sleep-LOC-DAT
"The bird flies to the old woman who is asleep." (🔈 BW: FM07_a043: 30:30min)

Indeed in this combination, the purposive is analysed as an allative in the Western Ngumpin languages: Walmajarri, Ngardi, Jaru, Wanyjirra and Malngin (Hudson & Richards, 1978, p. 375; Ise, 1998, p. 25; Meakins & Nordlinger, 2014, pp. 100–101; Senge, 2016, pp. 166–168; Tsunoda, 1981, pp. 60–61). In Jaru, it is clearly an allative since there is not an alternative form and *-wurru* is the purposive marker. Note though that Tsunoda (1981, p. 181) does observe purposive uses of the allative. In the other languages, there are separate allative forms. In Ngardi, the combination of locative+dative is treated as another type of allative, called a lative. Ngardi also has *-kurra* as an allative which is one of the allomorphs found in Gurindji. Wanyjirra and Malngin also have a separate allative form which is the more usual Gurindji allative form, however for Wanyjirra this is the form which is analysed as a purposive, although the examples given appear to be normal allatives so the analysis as a purposive is not convincing (Senge, 2016, pp. 184–185). Finally, Meakins and Nordlinger (2014, pp. 100–101) analyse the purposive in Bilinarra as a limited form of case-stacking, however it is likely that it is also a single case form in Bilinarra.

4.3.7 ABLative *-ngurlu(ng)* 'from'

There are two ablative forms, *-ngurlu* and *-ngurlung*, which are used in free variation across all generations of Gurindji speakers. It is not clear whether these represent once differentiated dialects or perhaps sociolects, but are no longer current. Examples can be seen in (416) and (417).

(416) **Kurlumpukpurru-ngurlu** ngu=rnalu ya-ni,
place.name-ABL CAT=1EXC.AUG.S go-PST

ngurra-ngkurra, Wave Hill-jirri.
home-ALL place.name-ALL
"From Kurlumpukpurru we went home to old Wave Hill station."
(🔈 VW: FM09_14_1a: 3:24min)

(417) Purtuyi-warra ngu=rna=rla karrinyana
goose.bumps-ITER CAT=1EXC.MIN.S=3OBL be.IMPF.PRS

pakarturtup.	Ngantu	kuya-ngarrang	karrap
hair.standing.up	someone	thus-??	watch

nya-nga-na	**yikili-ngurlung**	**ngumayila-ngurlung**.
intake-IMPF-PRS	far-ABL	behind-ABL

"My hair is standing on end from something. Maybe someone was watching from a long way away behind me." (🔊 VW: FM10_a154: 3:06min)

The ablative is typically used to mark direction from a place (418), from an (inanimate) location (419) or from a point in time (420). It can also indicate an action which is directed away from the object (421). Where the source is a person, the *-nginyi* suffix is used instead, as discussed in §4.3.8.

(418)	**Jurnarni-ngurlu**	ngu=rnalu	ya-ni	kanimparra.
	place.name-ABL	CAT=1EXC.AUG.S	go-PST	downstream

"From Jurnarni we came downstream." (🔊 VW: FM07_a058: 1:01min)

(419)	Purrngpurrng	karrinyana	<u>na</u>	ngawa=ma	**janyja-ngurlung**.
	spurt.out	be.IMPF.PRS	FOC	water=TOP	ground-ABL

"Water comes out from the ground there [at Jampawurru]."
(🔊 BW: FM09_13_2c: 1:11min)

(420)	Jiwarn-jiwarn	ngu=lu	yunpa-rna-na
	all.night-REDUP	CAT=3AUG.S	sing-IMPF-PRS

kaput-ngurlu	juny-pa=rni.
morning-ABL	sunset-EP=ONLY

"They sing all night, from the evening until sunrise." (RW: ECh corpus)

(421)	Ma-nku	ngu=nta	**jawurt-ngurlung**	yirr.
	do-POT	CAT=2AUG.S	tail-ABL	pull

"You mob can pull it by the tail." (🔊 VW: FM10_a154: 4:44min)

It is worth noting that the source morpheme *-nginyi* (discussed in §4.3.8 and §4.7.18) is also used to mark the place of origin (422). For reasons given below, it is analysed as a separate case suffix, however it seems to be used in free variation with *-ngurlu* in the contexts where *-ngurlu* is found. Nonetheless *-nginyi* is used in many contexts where *-ngurlu* is never found.

(422)	Ngu=rnalu	ya-na-ni	**Jinparrak-nginyi**=ma.
	CAT=1EXC.AUG.S	go-IMPF-PST	Wave.Hill-SOURCE=TOP

"We used to come from old Wave Hill station." (🔊 VW: FM09_15_2d: 0:20min)

4.3.8 SOURCE *-nginyi(ng)* 'from'

There are two allomorphs of the source marker *-nginyi* and *-nginying*. Again, it is not clear whether any dialect or sociolectal meaning is the source of the allomorphs, but if so, this distinction is not currently discussed by Gurindji people. Impressionistically, the *-nginying* variant is now more common among Gurindji Kriol speakers which are a younger generation (Meakins, 2011b, pp. 33–34). Indeed, McConvell does not remember *-nginying* being used in the 1970s or 1980s. Younger generations no longer use the ablative *-ngurlu*, instead using *-nginyi* in all contexts. This is not believed to be the source of the *-nginying* form however, but a new sociolect distinction.

The morphological status of *-nginyi* is also not straightforward. It can occur after derivation (423), shows agreement across the NP (424), and attaches to the dative form of free pronouns (425), which supports an analysis of it as an inflectional morpheme, however it is also used to derive nouns, which is discussed in detail in §4.7.18. Often morphemes which have features of inflectional and derivational morphology in Australia are best described as adnominal case, but *-nginyi* is not used to relate nominals. We choose to remain agnostic about its status and split its discussion into two sections under case (this section) and derivation (§4.7.18), according to its dual distributions. Wanyjirra and Bilinarra also have this suffix and it similarly shows multiple functions (Meakins & Nordlinger, 2014, pp. 139–143; Senge, 2016, pp. 189–193).

(423) **Karnti-kari-nginyi** na ngayu=ma=rna
tree-OTHER-SOURCE FOC 1EXC.MIN=TOP=1EXC.MIN.S

pa-na-na, parnngirri=ma.
hit-IMPF-PRS bark=TOP
"I'm cutting bark from another tree." (🔈 VW: FM08_a089: 11:23min)

(424) Yala-nginyi=ma **dinner-nginyi** ngu=lu
that-SOURCE=TOP lunch-SOURCE CAT=3AUG.S

ya-nku wuyurrunkarra.
go-POT fishing
"After lunch they'll go fishing." (🔈 EO: FM07_03_1a: 0:20min)

(425) **Nyununy-nginyi**[113] ngu=rna ma-ni.
3MIN.DAT-SOURCE CAT=1EXC.MIN.S get-PST
"I got it from you." (McConvell corpus: Meakins et al., 2016, p. 280)

The source marker *-nginyi* covers some of the same functions as the ablative *-ngurlu* in marking the source of motion, as shown in (426)–(432) where *-ngurlu* is also used.

(426) Ngu=rnalu ya-na-ni **Jinparrak-nginyi**=ma.
CAT=1EXC.AUG.S go-IMPF-PST Wave.Hill-SOURCE=TOP
"We used to come from old Wave Hill station." (🔈 VW: FM09_15_2d: 0:20min)

(427) Pirrk wapakurru ma-ni **wirrkala-nginyi**.
snatch club do-PST hair.belt-SOURCE
"He snatched a club from his belt."
(McConvell corpus: Meakins et al., 2016, p. 392)

(428) **Puul-nginyi** warrkuj ngu=rli
fish.trap-SOURCE pick.up CAT=1INC.MIN.S

ma-na-na yinarrwa=wayin.
get-IMPF-PRS barramundi=ETC
"We even get barramundi from the fish-trap."
(McConvell corpus: Meakins et al., 2016, p. 347)

(429) Ya-ni ngu nyila=ma nganayirla=ma Yiparrartu=ma
go-PST CAT that=TOP whatsitcalled=TOP Emu=TOP

kayili-yin **Mantijka-nginyi**.
north-ABL place.name-SOURCE
"Emu came from the north from a place called Mantijka."
(🔈 VW: FM08_08_4e: 0:10min)

(430) Kalypa **kanyjal-nginyi** ngu=lu=rla kirrip pu-nga-ni.
soft below-SOURCE CAT=3AUG.S=3OBL strip.off pierce-IMPF-PST
"They would strip off some of the [bark] from the soft part [of the paperbark] closest to the trunk." (🔈 VW: FM10_23_3: 2:37min)

---

113 Note that the form is *nyununy-nginyi* not *nyuntu-nginyi* which is also the case for other pronouns and demonstratives where the dative form must be the base for attaching *-nginyi*.

(431) Ya-nku ngu nyampayirla na, **kampij-nginyi**=ma
go-POT CAT whatsitcalled FOC egg-SOURCE=TOP

yala-nginyi=ma nanta na.
that-SOURCE=TOP small FOC
"A little creature is going to come out of the shell now."
(🔈 VW: FM10_27_1a: Kurraj Story from Halls Creek: 1:45min)

(432) Jurlurl yuwa-na-na **kartak-nginyi**=ma ngapulu.
pour put-IMPF-PRS jug-SOURCE=TOP milk
"She pours milk from the jug." (🔈 BW: FM07-a043: 19:45min)

Another function of *-nginyi* is to mark time periods which also overlaps with the ablative. Example (424) is a straightforward case of *-nginyi* marking a NP to mean 'after lunch'. In (433) it attaches to *karu* 'child' with the meaning of 'further generations' which is somewhat more esoteric. Given that the ergative-marker follows *-nginyi*, it might be considered derivational in this context.

(433) Ngu=yinangulu pa-na-ni parturu kataj, kajijirri
CAT=3AUG.S>3AUG.NS hit-IMPF-PST scar cut old.woman.REDUP

an marlurluka. Nyamu=lu kula yirrap-kulu karrwa-rna-ni
and old.man.REDUP REL=3AUG.S NEG group-ERG have-IMPF-PST

parturu. Yirrap-ku ngu=yinangkulu yuwa-na-ni.
scar group-DAT CAT=3AUG.S>3AUG.NS put-IMPF-PST

"Ngayiny yuwa-rra=yi=rla marntaj ngu=rna
1EXC.MIN.DAT put-IMP=1EXC.MIN.NS=3OBL OK CAT=1EXC.MIN.S

karrwa-wu. Ngu=yi=lu nya-ngku, wanyji-kijak,
have-POT CAT=3AUG.S=1EXC.MIN.NS intake-POT which-TERM

karrap, ngumayi-jang-kulu, **karu**[114]**-nginyi-lu**
watch behind-TIME-ERG child-SOURCE-ERG

114 This could also be a reference to the first boys initiation ceremony which is public.

nyampa-nginyi-lu kuya, parturu-yawung.
what-SOURCE-ERG thus ceremony.scar-PROP
"They used to cut the women and men in the old days to make ceremony scars. When they didn't have ceremony scars, they used to cut it for that mob. 'Put them on me. I'll have [the marks] then. Future generations of children will see me with ceremonial scars everywhere'." (🔈 VW: FM11_a161: 1:40min)

In some cases, *-nginyi* combines with the locative in a minor case-marking construction to mean after a particular time period, for example in (434) *rein-nginyi-la* 'after the rain time (wet season)'. Although *-nginyi* has derivational functions (§4.7.18), it does not seem correct to analyse it as such here.

(434) Ngiing-kaji-lu ngu=yi paya-rna-na, kaja-ngka,
buzz-AGENT-ERG CAT=1EXC.MIN.S bite-IMPF-PRS bush-LOC

makin-ta=ma. Parlng-karra ngu=rna pa-na-na
sleep-LOC=TOP slap-ITER CAT=1EXC.MIN.S hit-IMPF-PRS

ngiing-kaji. Kula yapayapa. Billabong-kula parlkij-ja maitbi
buzz-AGENT NEG small billabong-LOC level-LOC maybe

ngawa-ngka parlkij-ja. Kuliyan ngiing-kaji=TOP
water-LOC level-LOC aggressive buzz-AGENT=TOP

kuya-ny-ja=ma. **Rein-nginyi-la**=**ma**.
thus-NMLZ-LOC=TOP rain-SOURCE-LOC=TOP
"A mosquito bites me in the bush when I'm sleeping. So I am slapping the mosquito. It isn't a small one. At the billabong where you are level with the water. There are aggressive mosquitoes there after it has rained."
(🔈 VW: FM10_a152: 5:34min)

The source suffix also indicates the source of a change of state. In (435), two pieces of wood are cut from one long one, and in (436) a road is widened from a narrow one.

(435) **Juwal-nginyi**=ma, kujarra ngu=rna pirrkap ma-na-na.
long-SOURCE=TOP two CAT=1EXC.MIN.S make do-IMPF-PRS
"I cut the long piece of wood in two." (🔈 VW: FM08_a101: 8:57min)

(436) Payal-kuk ngu=lu ma-na-na nyila=ma wurruma=ma.
wide-FACT CAT=3AUG.S do-IMPF-PRS that=TOP road=TOP

Tartpu-nginyi **yapakayi-nginyi**, jangkarni-k.
narrow-SOURCE small-SOURCE big-FACT
"They make the road wider. From being narrow, to bigger."
(🔈 VW: FM11_a161: 3:40min)

The source suffix can also indicate a transformational relationship which overlaps with one of the functions of the locative. In (437) Violet Wadrill describes someone making a firestick from river fig wood and (438) is a description of extracting sinew from kangaroo tail to bind a spear to its shaft.

(437) Yala-nginyi na **wutuyawung-nginyi**
that-SOURCE FOC river.fig-SOURCE

pinyinyip ma-nku ngu, majka.
rub.between.palms do-POT CAT try
"She will twirl the wood to try and make [fire] out of that river fig wood."
(🔈 VW: FM09_a127: 0:27min)

(438) Ngu=lu ma-na-na **jawurt-nginyi**.
CAT=3AUG.S do-IMPF-PRS tail-SOURCE
"They make it out of the tail." (🔈 TD: FM10_a146: 11:04min)

A related function is transformational relationships which involve the change of form, either through sorcery (439) or a natural process (440), *-nginyi* is also used.

(439) Warntaj wankurriny **ngumpit-nginyi**.
transform crow man-SOURCE
"He transforms from a man into a crow."
(McConvell corpus: Meakins et al., 2016, p. 401)

(440) **Kupilyipilyi-nginyi** warntaj waninya ngakparn.
tadpole-SOURCE transform fall.PST frog
"The tadpoles turned into frogs." (McConvell corpus: Meakins et al., 2016, p. 401)

A unique function of *-nginyi* is in conjunction with personal names where the object of *tal* is source-marked and has the meaning 'by', as shown in (441).

(441) **Pirri-pirri-nginyi** ngu=yi=lu
nickname-REDUP-SOURCE CAT=3AUG.S=1EXC.MIN.NS

tal pa-na-na.
call hit-IMPF-PRS
"They're calling me by my nickname." (DD with ECh: Meakins et al., 2016, p. 329)

This form is also found in Bilinarra and Malngin (Ise, 1998, p. 30; Meakins & Nordlinger, 2014, pp. 139–142). Mudburra also has the form *-nginyi* but its functional range is slightly different. It can mark association and causation, like Gurindji, but also possession (Green et al., 2019, p. 31). Jaminjung also has a similar form *-ngunyi* 'ablative' (Schultze-Berndt, 2000, p. 58).

The derivational uses of *-nginyi* will be discussed further in (§4.7.18).

4.3.9 COMitative *-kunyja* 'with'

The comitative is marginal since it is in the process of grammaticalising. It is historically built from dative+NMLZ+locative and has two forms *-wunyja* (vowel-final) and *-kunyja* (consonant-final). Although the dative and locative suffixes each have their own function synchronically, there is reason to believe that they are not always syntactically active in the comitative combination. In (442), we show these suffixes separately, but analyse them as a single comitative suffix because if they were separate suffixes, you would expect the free pronoun form to be *ngayiny-ja* '1EXC.MIN.DAT-LOC' because the dative pronoun is already nominalised with *-ny*. In this respect, the dative pronoun simply has the comitative *-kunyja* added a single case-marker.

(442) Ngu=rna=**rla** ya-nku **ngayiny-ku-~~ny~~[115]-ja**
CAT=1EXC.MIN.S=3OBL go-POT 1EXC.MIN.DAT-DAT-NMLZ-LOC

jaju-wu-ny-ja.
MM-DAT-NMLZ-LOC
"I will go with my grandmother." (McConvell corpus: Meakins et al., 2016, p. 72)

Compare (442) with (443) where the same sequence of suffixes is in fact syntactically active. This is demonstrated by the free pronoun which is already dative and appears with the required nominaliser and thus, receives only the locative and not the additional dative+NMLZ sequence.

115 The *-ny* would be deleted as a result of the NCD rule but we show it here for grammatical explicitness.

(443) Ngu=**rla**=nyanta karrinya **nyanuny-ja**
CAT=3OBL=3OBL2 be.PST 3MIN.DAT-LOC

na **marluka-wu-ny-ja** **yalu-wu-ny-ja,**
FOC old.man-DAT-NMLZ-LOC that-DAT-NMLZ-LOC

ngayiny=ma kapuku=ma Mayawi=ma.
1EXC.MIN.DAT=TOP sister=TOP NAME=TOP
"My sister Mayawi used to stay at that old Afghan man's camp."
(🔊 VW: FM10_22_1a: 4:08min)

The existence of both (442) and (443) suggests that the comitative is still in the process of grammaticalising. Thus in examples such as (444) which do not have a free pronoun, it is not clear whether the dative+NMLZ+locative represents a synchronically analysable sequence or a single case marker.

(444) Ngu=rna=**rla** tak karrinya **marluka-wunyja** ngurra-ngka.
CAT=1EXC.MIN.S=3OBL sit be.PST old.man-COM camp-LOC
"I sat down with the old man at the camp."

OR

Ngu=rna=**rla** tak karrinya **marluka-wu**-ny-ja
CAT=1EXC.MIN.S=3OBL sit be.PST old.man-DAT-NMLZ-LOC

ngurra-ngka.
camp-LOC
"I sat down at the old man's camp." (McConvell 1996 sketch grammar)

One argument for the grammaticalisation of the comitative in (444) is the comparison with (445). In (444), the comitative-marked noun is cross-referenced by the oblique bound pronoun =*rla*, whereas in (445), the suffixes are synchronically analysable as a dative+nominaliser+locative because locative-marked nominals in complements are not cross-referenced by bound pronouns.

(445) Ngu=rna tak karrinya **marluka-wu-ny-ja** ngurra-ngka.
CAT=1EXC.MIN.S sit be.PST old.man-DAT-NMLZ-LOC camp-LOC
"I sat down **at the old man's** camp."
(McConvell corpus: Meakins et al, 2016, p. 352)

A similar problem is found with the dative + nominaliser sequence with the allative, as shown in (446), where the case-marking attaches to the dative pronoun. Again, this may represent a grammaticalisation process.

(446) **Kapuku-wu-ny-jirri** **nyanuny-ku-~~ny~~**[116] **-jirri,**
sister-DAT-NMLZ-ALL 3MIN.DAT-DAT-NMLZ-ALL

malyju-ngku ngu wany yuwa-ni.
boy-ERG CAT throw put-PST
"The boy throws it to where his sister is." (🔊 VW: FHM098: 2:07min)

The comitative function is also expressed using a single locative case-marker, as discussed in §4.3.4.2. Note also that the dative+*ny*+locative sequence is used as a derivational suffix meaning 'lacking' which is discussed in §4.7.10. We discuss the different grammaticalisation paths which led to these opposite meanings. Malngin and Wanyjirra have this same form which acts both as a comitative and derivational suffix meaning 'lacking' (Ise, 1998, p. 30; Senge, 2016, pp. 195–201).

4.3.10 TERMinative *-kijak* 'as FAR as'

This case marker has only one form, *-kijak*. It indicates the limit, extent or termination of movement, usually in terms of location. In this regard, it can be translated as meaning 'as far as', as shown in (447)–(450).

(447) Palngana, Pirntipirnti, **yala-kijak**
Flora.Valley Sturt.River that-TERM

ngu=lu ya-na-ni ngarin-ku.
CAT=3AUG.S go-IMPF-PST meat-DAT
"They used to go hunting as far as Flora Valley and Sturt River."
(Appendix: Echidna and the Big Shade: Text 2, line 6)

(448) **Yala-kijak** karla-yarra nyawa na
that-TERM west-SIDE this FOC

ngu=rnalu kayi pa-ni kankuli-yit.
CAT=1EXC.AUG.S follow hit-PST up-ABL
"We followed the old road right up to there on the westside up on the ridge."
(🔊 BW: FM09_a121: 1:25min)

116 The *-ny* would be deleted as a result of the NCD rule but we show it here for grammatical explicitness.

(449) **Karla-yarra-kijak**=ma kula=lu pinarri, lawara.
west-SIDE-TERM=TOP NEG=3AUG.S knowledgeable nothing
"As far as the west they are not very knowledgeable."
(🔈 VW: FM08_08_4a: 1:03min)

(450) Yala-nginyi wirrminy ngu=rnayinangulu yuwa-na-na
that-SOURCE turn.over CAT=1EXC.AUG.S>3AUG.NS put-IMPF-PRS

kuya, kankulu-pal parntawurru jiya-rna-na ngu **maru-kijak.**
thus up-EDGE back burn-IMPF-PRS CAT bottom-TERM
"After that we turn [the babies] over and heat treat their backs as far as their bottoms." (🔈 VW: FM07_a085: 1:58min)

This suffix can also have a comparative function when it is attached to the adverbial demonstrative *kuya* 'thus', as shown in (451), where the speaker indicates with her hands how big the egg was. This function is discussed further in §5.1.2.8.

(451) Paraj pu-nya nyila=ma kampij=ma. Jangkarni
find pierce-PST that=TOP egg=TOP big

kuya-kijak dat kampij jangkarni.
thus-TERM the egg big
"Then she found that egg. It was as big as this."
(🔈 VW: FM10_27_1a: Kurraj Story from Halls Creek: 1:12min)

Bilinarra and Ngarinyman also have this suffix (Jones, Schultze-Berndt, Denniss, et al., 2019, p. 18; Meakins & Nordlinger, 2014, p. 143), and the nearby but unrelated language Ngaliwurru (Jaminjungan, Mirndi, non-Pama-Nyungan) has an ablative suffix *-kijak* (Schultze-Berndt, 2000, p. 54). It is not clear whether these suffixes bear any relation. They are both local case suffixes, but are concerned with movement in different directions. Jaminjung also creates a terminative reading by combining the dative and ablative, as in the following example (many thanks to Eva Schultze-Berndt for this example):

(452) Jalyarri=biya waya=wung ga-yinji, **lany-gu-ngunyi.**
JAM SUBSECT=SEQ call=RESTR 3SG-IV.go:IPFV sunrise-DAT-ABL
"Jalyarri kept calling out right up to the sun rising." (ES97_A01_03.127)

4.3.11 PERLative *-mayin* 'though, around, past, in the vicinity'

The perlative case has only one allomorph: *-mayin*. It occurs only rarely in the data, with the locative or allative a more common alternative. The perlative has the meaning of 'across', 'through' or 'near', although it can also have the meaning of 'among', as shown in (453)–(455). Most of the examples in the corpus involve place names, but it can also attach to body parts with the meaning 'by way of, through, around', for example, *mangarli-mayin* 'around the chest'.

(453) Ka-nya kanka-yit murla, karla-rni-yin, kurla-yarra,
take-PST upstream-ABL this west-UP-ABL south-SIDE

nyawa=rni wurrumu=ma, kurla-yarra **Maka-mayin** thru
this=ONLY road=TOP south-SIDE place.name-PERL through

kankuli-yit nyawa na **Nero-mayin,** kankula murla-rniny
up-ABL this FOC place.name-PERL up this-HITH

past... **Donkey Gully-mayin**=parla ka-nga-ni ngu=lu.
past place.name-PERL=FOC take-IMPF-PST CAT=3AUG.S

"They took them down here from the west, coming south here, along the road through Maka, down here through Nero [Yard] down here... Through Donkey Gully they took them." (🔈 DD: EC98_a025: Rawuyarri: 1:49min)

(454) Ya-ni ngu nyawa na kaa-rni-rra, **Ngangi-mayin**=ma.
go-PST CAT this FOC east-UP-LOC place.name-PERL=TOP

"[Emu] went east and up through Ngangi." (🔈 VW: FM09_15_1a: 6:16min)

(455) Kayili-yin ngu=lu ya-ni **Jilinypuk-mayin.**
north-ABL CAT=3AUG.S go-PST place.name-PERL

"They came from the north past Jilinypuk.[117]"
(🔈 VW: FM10_30_1a: Karu Dreaming Story: 0:20min)

Warlmanpa and Ngardi have *-wana* as the perlative form (Browne, 2021; Ennever, 2021). Interestingly, Ngardi also has a derivational morpheme of *-mayin*, which is glossed as 'expert', but seems to only relate to activities involving herding or mustering (Ennever, 2021). It is possible that these forms are related where it may have developed into an inflectional suffix in Gurindji and Bilinarra from a concrete meaning of 'herding' to a conceptual meaning of 'around, through, in the vicinity of'.[118]

117 Black Gin Bore is the non-Indigenous name given to this site. We only mention it in this footnote because the name 'Jilinypuk' is not known to most younger generations of Gurindji people who use the name 'Black Gin Bore' themselves. Sadly, non-Indigenous names such as this one exist right across Australia. We are aware that continuing to use them only perpetuates racist ideologies.

118 Note that the authors depart on this idea with McConvell sceptical of this grammaticalization path.

(456) *kukunyja-mayin* 'sheep-EXPERT, shepherd' (Ngardi[119])
kunyarr-mayin 'dog-EXPERT, dog handler'
puliki-mayin 'cow-EXPERT, stockman'
timina-mayin 'horse-EXPERT, horse-tailer'

4.3.12 MOTivative *-nganayak*

The motivative is unique to Gurindji. It is neither found in form nor function in any other Ngumpin-Yapa language and is indeed rare in Gurindji. It was not observed during McConvell's work. It only turns up in the corpus around coverbs of jealousy or suspicion. It is not clear what its full functional range is. It is possible that this suffix is built from *-ngarna* 'associative' (§4.7.16), but *-ngarna* is derivational and it is not obvious where the rest of the suffix originates.

(457) Ngu=ngku ngurrku pa-na-na, yalu-ngku=ma,
CAT=2MIN.NS suspect hit-IMPF-PRS that-ERG=TOP

yala-nganayak **ngumparna-nganayak.**
that-MOT husband-MOT
"That one suspects you of [having an affair with] her husband."
(🔈 VW: FM10_a154: 1:04min)

(458) Nyila=ma tupa=ma, pumpurrng ka-nga-na
that=TOP windbreak=TOP break take-IMPF-PRS

ngu, ngumpit-tu yala-ngku. Nyamu=waa maitbi
CAT man-ERG that-ERG REL=REL maybe

purturr ma-na-na, **kirri-nganayak.**
go.in.a.huff do-IMPF-PRS woman-MOT
"That man busted up the windbreak, when he went off in a huff over his girlfriend." (🔈 VW: FM11_a162: 10:53min)

Although no other Ngumpin-Yapa language has this case-marker either in form or function, Jaminjung has a motivative case-marker *-garni* or *-warni* (thanks to Eva Schultze-Berndt for the following example).

(459) Burru-ma-ji nguyung-**warni.** (Jaminjung)
3pl-IV.hit-REFL husband-MOT
"They are fighting over a husband."

119 Examples courtesy of Tom Ennever.

4.4 Number

Number marking is not obligatory in the Gurindji NP; an unmarked nominal is unspecified for number and can refer to any number of entities. For example, in (460) *kajirri* 'old woman' is not marked for number but it is clear that the clause involves more than one old woman since it is reduplicated and cross-referenced by a third person augmented bound pronoun. Similarly, in (461) it is clear that more than one left-hander is encoded in the clause, and in (462), the unit augmented bound pronoun indicates that there is just one pigeon and kangaroo. In (463), *nantananta* 'little ones' is reduplicated and cross-referenced by an augmented pronoun.

(460) Ngu=**rnayinangulu** wart ka-nga-na namawurru=ma
CAT=1EXC.AUG.S>3AUG.NS return take-IMPF-PST honey=TOP

majul yura-k **kajijirri-wu.**
stomach good-FACT old.woman.REDUP-DAT
"We bring back the sugarbag to the old ladies to make them feel better."
(🔈 TD: FM07_a028: 11:41min)

(461) Ngu=**yinangulu** pirrkap ma-na-na **wartiwarti-wu.**
CAT=3AUG.S>3AUG.NS make do-IMPF-PRS left.handed-DAT
"They make (boomerangs) for left-handers." (🔈 BW: FM10_a143: 4:32min)

(462) **Yawarlwarl** **Wanyil** ngu=**wula**
Crested.Pigeon Nail-Tail.Kangaroo CAT=3UA.S

karrinyani, yala-ngka=ma.
be.IMPF.PST that-LOC=TOP
"Both Pigeon and Nail-Tail Kangaroo lived there." (🔈 VW: FM10_23_1b: 0:33min)

(463) Nyila=ma ngu=rlaa=rla pa-na-ni tikap,
that=TOP CAT=1INC.AUG.S=3OBL hit-IMPF-PST chop

mapan-ta-waji nyamu=**yina** **nanta-nanta**=ma karrwa-rna-ni.
hollow-LOC-AGENT REL=3AUG.NS little-REDUP=TOP hold-IMPF-PST
"We would chop at the hollow tree, like this, which held the baby ones."
(🔈 VW: FM10_a149: 2:25min)

Despite these examples, it is possible to specify number on the nominal through numerals, the use of morphology and reduplication, as will be discussed in the following sections.

4.4.1 Numerals

There are only a small number of numerals in Gurindji, given below, which can act as a modifier in an NP (465) or act as a sole head (466). The word *jarrwa* 'many' and *jangkarni* 'much' may be a part of the same semantic system, but grammatically they are more like a typical adjective than the other numerals:

jintaku	'one'	*jintakurt*	'once'
kujarra	'two'	*kujarrawurt*	'twice'
murrkun	'three'	*murrkunkurt*	'thrice, three times'
kujarrarnikujarrarni	'four'	*jarrwa*	'lots– count nouns'
kujarrarnikujarrarnijinta	'five'[120]	*jangkarni*	'lots– non-count nouns'

(465) Marluka **jintaku** karrinyana.
old.man one be.IMPF.PRS
"The old man sits there." (🔈 BW: FM07_a043: 7:38min)

(466) **Jintaku-ngku=ma** nya-nga-na ngu wirlpip-kula=ma.
one-ERG=TOP intake-IMPF-PRS CAT hit.in.grief-LOC=TOP
"One [person] sees her hitting herself in mourning."
(🔈 TD: FM10_a165: 10:03min)

There is also a counting system of 50 numerals used for counting small items such as berries, and as a game, e.g. counting footsteps when tracking. It is said that this system was borrowed from Aboriginal people to the west within living memory of older people. The numerals were chanted in sequence, and not used as qualifiers of head nouns, with the possible exception of *lurr*, the last number of the set (Meakins et al., 2013, p. 593).

1. Panturru
2. Yurr[121]
3. Kangunya
4. Parnti
5. Ngarra
6. Karni
7. Yama

---

120 This style of compounding is probably quite marginal or has gone out of use with the introduction of English numerals. It is only found in the speech of Smiler Major (Hale MS864(1): p. 14). Note also his use of the Warlpiri number for one *jinta*.

121 This word also means 'rub'

8. Murru
9. Tulu
10. Ngamirri
11. Mulyarri
12. Yanu
13. Nganayi
14. Nyirralu
15. Winimal
16. Kampiya
17. Rrangulu
18. Yiliji
19. Timpina
20. Yawara
21. Wankarrka
22. Tima
23. Pulanma
24. Yini[122]
25. Marla[123]
26. Yurulwa
27. Nila
28. Marnturrunga
29. Marnturrunga
30. Ngarlka
31. Lapipan
32. Jirri[124]
33. Malyingka
34. Rayani
35. Yawarta[125]
36. Jinpilya
37. Kalyurrka
38. Lanyura
39. Purtipa

122 This word also means 'name'
123 This word also means 'hand'
124 This word also means 'love potion'
125 This word also means 'horse'

40. Panana[126]
41. Jingarrpa
42. Nila
43. Kuyana
44. Lanyanta
45. Kalijpa[127]
46. Wakartpa
47. Ngarni[128]
48. Yulya
49. Ngangkunu
50. Lurr

4.4.2 Time spans

There are three words in Gurindji which are used to refer to days, months and years. Some examples are given in (468) and (469).

(467) *wulngarn* 'sun, day'
jakiliny 'moon, month'
ngurra 'country, camp, year'

(468)

Jakiliny=ma	nyatjang-pa=n	karrwa-wu?
month=TOP	how.many-EP=2MIN.S	hold-POT

"How many months will you spend?"
(McConvell corpus: Meakins et al, 2016, p. 73)

(469)

Ngu=ja=nga	ya-nku	marri	nyatjang-kurt	**jakiliny**
CAT=1EXC.UA.S=DUB	go-POT	BUT	how.many-TIMES	month

marri	jintaku-wurt	**jakiliny,**	yuu	maiti	kujarra.
BUT	one-TIMES	month	yes	maybe	two

"We'll be back in how many months? Maybe one, or let's say two."
(🔊 RW: EC97_a005: 16:10min)

126 This word also means 'hit'
127 This word also means 'yellow kapok'
128 This word also means 'ate'

4.4.3 *-kurt, -wurt* TIMES

This suffix has two forms *-kurt* (consonant-final stems) and *-wurt* (vowel-final stems). It attaches to numerals to indicate how many times something happened, as shown in (471) and (472). It is also found attached to the interrogative *nyatjangkurt* to mean 'how many times?' (§5.3.6). Note that it is not clear if this suffix has a broader function but it has been found with *kanyjurra* 'down' to create the lexeme *kanyjurrawurt* 'traditional custodian, people who belong to a particular place or a Dreaming' (Meakins et al., 2013, p. 140)

(470)	*jintaku*	'one'	*jintaku-wurt*	'once'
	kujarra	'two'	*kujarra-wurt*	'twice'
	murrkun	'three'	*murrkun-kurt*	'thrice, three times'

(471)	Karrinyana	ngu	maitbi	**kuya-ny-kurt**	ngurra	murrkun-kurt.
	be.IMPF.PRS	CAT	maybe	thus-NMLZ-TIMES	camp	three-TIMES

"It stays in the sun for maybe three days." (🔈 VW: FM07_a089: 6:18min)

(472)	Kankarra	ngu=rnayinangulu	ka-nga-ni	Seven Mile-la
	upstream	CAT=1EXC.AUG.S>3AUG.NS	take-IMPF-PST	place.name-LOC
	ngurra	ngu=rnayinangulu	karrwa-rna-ni	**jintaku-wurt.**
	country	CAT=1EXC.AUG.S>3AUG.NS	keep-IMPF-PST	one-TIMES

"We used to take them out to the country around Seven Mile and keep them there one night." (🔈 VW: FM08_01_3: 1:08min)

This suffix is not found in Ngardi or Warlmanpa.

4.4.4 *-kujarra* DUal

This is the first of the number suffixes which attaches to a range of nominals. It developed from the numeral *kujarra* probably through its head-modifier collocation where the numeral grammaticalised into a suffix.[129] See (473) for an example of NP where the numeral occurs before and after the noun. Alternatively, the post-head nominal could be analysed as a suffix. The suffix analysis is evidenced elsewhere through other examples by the lack of agreement across the NP which would be expected if the numeral were a separate word. For example, in (474), the noun phrase would be

129 McConvell also notes that a lenited form *-wujarra* was in use during his work but it is no longer used.

wamala-lu kujarra-lu 'girl-ERG two-ERG' if *kujarra* were a numeral. Similarly, in (475), *-kujarra* is clearly attached to *janka* 'woman' because *janka* is not ergative marked. In (476), the demonstrative *yalu-* 'that' is ergative-marked but *kirri* 'woman' is not which again suggests that *-kujarra* is a suffix not a numeral. Dual-marked nominals are cross-referenced by the unit augmented bound pronoun, as shown in (474)–(475), but not always, as shown in (476).

(473) Hey lamparra-marnany-ju=ma=ngku jayi-nya,
hey father.in.law-2MIN.POSS-ERG=TOP=2MIN.NS give-PST

kujarra **kirri** **kujarra** nyununy.
two woman two 2MIN.DAT
"Hey your father-in-law who is my son gave two girls to you."
(🔊 VW: FM10_a155: 10:48min)

(474) Mangarri-waji-la, ngu=**wula** wanyja-na-na
veg.good-AGENT-LOC CAT=3UA.S leave-IMPF-PRS

na kamparri-la, warrkawarrkap **wamala-kujarra-lu**.
FOC front-LOC dance.REDUP girl-DU-ERG
"The two girls are dancing outside the shop." (🔊 BW: FM07_a043: 21:43min)

(475) Ngu=**wula**=rla wuyurrunkarra yuwa-na-na **janka-kujarra-lu.**
CAT=3UA.S=3OBL fishing put-IMPF-PRS woman-DU-ERG
"Two women are throwing fishing lines in."
(McConvell corpus: Meakins et al., 2016, p. 169)

(476) Mangkaya ngu=**lu** pirrkap ma-ni
shelter CAT=3AUG.S build do-PST

ngamanpurru-la, **yalu-ngku** **kirri-kujarra-lu**.
conkerberry-LOC that-ERG woman-DU-ERG
"They built a shelter out of a conkerberry tree – the two women did."
(🔊 VW: FM10_23_4: 5:20min)

The suffix *-kujarra* also encodes a dispersed meaning, as shown in (477), when it attaches to *walik* 'around'.

(477) Ngu=rna ma-lu, kurru
CAT=1EXC.MIN.S talk-POT listen

nya-ngka=yi=lu wanyjiwurrajarra
intake-IMP=1EXC.MIN.NS=3AUG.S everybody

nyamu=nta karrinyana **walik-kujarra**.
REL=2AUG.S be.IMPF.PRS around-DU
"I'm going to speak, listen everybody [who is] around."
(DD with ECh: Meakins et al., 2016, p. 391)

This suffix is also found in Bilinarra, Ngarinyman, Mudburra, Malngin and Ngardi (Ennever, 2021; Green et al., 2019, p. 33; Ise, 1998, p. 29; Jones, Schultze-Berndt, Denniss, et al., 2019, p. 21; Meakins & Nordlinger, 2014, p. 145). In Wanyjirra and Jaru, the form is lenited to *-kuyarra* and it also as a vowel-final stem counterpart *-wuyarra* (Senge, 2016, pp. 210–211; Tsunoda, 1981, p. 233). Warlmanpa uses *-ja(rra)* and *-jima* (Browne, 2021).

4.4.5 *-walija* PAUCal

Gurindji does not have a plural suffix except on demonstratives (§5.1.2.1). It does have the paucal suffix *-walija* which occurs on many nominals. It is mainly used with human nouns, see (478) and (479) and other animate nouns e.g. *pingi-walija* 'a few ants', however it is also sometimes used with inanimates, as shown in (480). Another less used paucal suffix is *-nyaliny* e.g. *puka-nyaliny* 'rotten-PAUC; (group of) rotten (nasty) people'.

(478) Nyamu=lu karrinyana marntara **karu-walija**
REL=3AUG.S be.IMPF.PRS sores child-PAUC

ngu=rnayinangkulu yuwa-na-na murlu-ngku
CAT=1EXC.AUG.S>3AUG.NS put-IMPF-PRS this-ERG

na tarukap=ma ngarlaka, marntara, karan-kaji.
FOC bathe=TOP head sores scratch-AGENT
"When kids have sores or scabies on their heads, we bathe their head sores with this [*yirrijkaji*]." (🔊 BW: FM07_01_1c: 2:12min)

(479) Waringarri-lu=ma ngu=yinangkulu
warrior-ERG=TOP CAT=3AUG.S>3AUG.NS

turt-turt ma-ni **kirri-walija**=ma.
grab-REDUP do-PST woman-PAUC=TOP
"The warriors grabbed the women." (🔊 DD: EC98_a012: 10:34min)

(480) Ngu=rnalu yuwa-na-na nyila=ma **kuruwarran-walija**=ma.
CAT=1EXC.AUG.S put-IMPF-PRS that=TOP cook.rock-PAUC=TOP
"We put those cooking rocks [on the fire]." (🔊 VW: FM10_a148: 17:37min)

This suffix is also found in Bilinarra, Ngarinyman, Malngin and the Western variety of Mudburra (Ise, 1998, p. 29; Jones, Schultze-Berndt, Denniss, et al., 2019, p. 22; Meakins & Nordlinger, 2014, p. 146). It is also found in Wanyjirra, but Senge (2016, p. 211) speculates it might be a recent borrowing from Gurindji since it is not present in the Tsunoda corpus. Eastern Mudburra and Warlmanpa use *-tarra* instead (Browne, 2021; Green et al., 2019, p. 33). Warlmanpa also has *-panji* (but only with human referents) (Browne, 2021). Ngardi has *-ngampurr* as its paucal suffix (Ennever, 2021).

4.4.6 *-jpan* SKIN group

This suffix is only found marking subsection terms, commonly known as 'skin names' (see §4.4). An example is given in (481). Its presence indicates more than one person of that subsection group. Skin names can also be reduplicated to indicate more than one person of that skin group, for example *Nangarijpan* but also *Nangangari*. This suffix is also found in Bilinarra, Ngarinyman and Mudburra (Green et al., 2019, p. 32; Jones, Schultze-Berndt, Denniss, et al., 2019, p. 22; Meakins & Nordlinger, 2014, p. 145), but not other Ngumpin languages. Ngardi has the form *-warnu* in this function, but its use extends beyond subsection terms (Ennever, 2021).

(481) **Nimarra-jpan Japarta-jpan** parnkuti ngu=rla nyanuny.
SUBSECT-SKIN SUBSECT-SKIN cousin CAT=3OBL 3MIN.DAT
"All of the Nimarras and Japartas are her cousins."
(🔊 VW: FM10_23_1b: 7:30min)

4.4.7 *-kuwang* AND someone else

This suffix is not found in other Ngumpin-Yapa languages. In Gurindji it is only found rarely with the meaning 'and someone else'. It was not observed during McConvell's work. It is only found on skin names (482) and personal names (483). Often the other referent indicated by *-kuwang* is also present in the clause as these examples demonstrate.

(482) Wiit jayi-ngku ngu=rnayinangulu
show give-POT CAT=1EXC.AUG.S>3AUG.NS

Nangari-kuwang-ku **Nimarra**-wu.
SUBSECT-AND-DAT SUBSECT-DAT
"We can show Nangari and Nimarra." (🔈 VW: FM07_a085: 8:42min)

(483) An ngayiny pakurtu-walija nyila
and 1EXC.MIN.DAT cousin-PAUC that

Ngarnjal-kuwang-ku **Tup**-ku nyamu=waa=rnalu.
NAME-AND-DAT NAME-DAT REL=REL=1EXC.AUG.S
".. who are my cousins and for Topsy and Molly." (🔈 VW: FM10_23_1a: 5:58min)

4.4.8 *-nyarrarra* ETC

Another Gurindji number suffix is *-nyarrara* 'etc' which has not been found elsewhere in Ngardi, Bilinarra, Warlmanpa or Mudburra. An example is given in (484).

(484) Mangarri=ma nyampa=ma, nyila=ma finish kaa-rni-mpa
bread=TOP what=TOP that=TOP finish east-UP-PERL

murla yuwa-ni, ka-nga-ni ngu pulngayit-tu milker-**nyarrarra**
this put-PST bring-IMPF-PST CAT floodwater-ERG dairy.cow-ETC

milker=ma nganta jintaku=ma kaa-rni-mpa=ma, Nitjpurru-la
dairy.cow=TOP ALLE one=TOP east-UP-PERL=TOP place.name-LOC

waninya tungkurlp-kaji-yawung-pa=rni, tungkurlp-kaji-yawung-pa=rni,
fall.PST rattle-AGENT-PROP-EP=ONLY rattle-AGENT-PROP-EP=ONLY

come out ya-ni TVH,[130] Wave Hill-nginyi milker
come out go-PST Wave Hill place.name-SOURCE dairy.cow

ka-nga-ni, nyila=rni ngu ya-na-ni.
bring-IMPF-PST that=ONLY CAT go-IMPF-PST
"The bread etc was deposited on the eastside. The floodwaters were bringing milking cows on the eastside of Pigeon Hole and goats appeared there from Wave Hill brought by the waters, travelling along in the flood."
(🔈 RW: EC97_a003: 6:53min)

4.4.9 Reduplication

Number in Gurindji can also be indicated by reduplication. This section deals with nominal reduplication, but the reduplication of coverbs also indicates plural objects, shown in (485) by *wajajarra* 'play' (§7.2.4.4). Reduplication of full nominal stems is shown in (485)–(488), but partial reduplication is also common, as in (489) and (490). For a discussion of phonological aspects of reduplication, see §2.3.6.

(485) Ngayu=ma **wajajarra,** kayili-yarra-la ngu=rnalu
1EXC.MIN=TOP play.REDUP north-SIDE-LOC CAT=1EXC.AUG.S

ngantipany, **malyju-malyju** na, playin' aroun'.
1EXC.AUG.DAT boy-REDUP FOC playing around

Kayilirra karlarra kayirra-k ngu=rna nya-nya.
north west north-ALL CAT=1EXC.MIN.S intake-PST
"I was off to the north playing with the other boys. I looked around the north, west and to the north [again]."
(◀)) DD: EC99_a029: Kinyjirrka-wu Murtap: 2:58min)

(486) **Nanta-nanta** ngu=yina, ngajarr ngaya-na-na
small-REDUP CAT=3AUG.NS increase excrete-IMPF-PRS

murlu-ngku=ma warlaku-lu=ma jarrwalut **nanta-nanta.**
this-ERG=TOP dog-ERG=TOP many small-REDUP
"The dog gave birth to a lot of puppies." (◀)) VW: FM12_a175: 13:36min)

(487) **Jitirni-jitirni**[131] ngu=rla jayi-nga-na nya nya nya.
half.ground-REDUP CAT=3OBL give-IMPF-PRS this this this
"She gave her half-ground seed, like this this and this."
(◀)) VW: FM10_23_1b: 3:10min)

(488) **Parturu-parturu** nyila ma-ni pirrka ma-ni
marking-REDUP that do-PST make do-PST

130 TVH is the brand used on Wave Hill Station cattle.
131 In actual fact, although this form is phonologically reduplicated, *jitirni* does not exist on its own in the corpus, so it might be better to analyse *jitirnijitirni* as a single form.

nyila na, kankulu-pal nyila jawurt-ta nyila=ma.
that FOC up-EDGE that tail-LOC that=TOP
"He made those markings [with the gum] on his tail."
(🔊 RW: HM070529GUR.DAGU_01rw.mp3: Warrija Kirrawa: 2:57min)

(489) **Jangkakarni**[132] ngu=rnalu ma-na-ni,
big.REDUP CAT=1EXC.AUG.S get-IMPF-PST

muying, ngamanpurru=ma.
black.plum conkerberry=TOP
"We used to get many black plums and conkerberries there."
(🔊 VW: FM09_16_2: 2:10min)

(490) Ngu=lu yala-ngka=rni pa-na-ni
CAT=3AUG.S that-LOC=ONLY hit-IMPF-PST

karnti-ku=warla **tampatampang** purrp.
stick-ERG=FOC dead.REDUP finish
"They killed lots of fish with a stick right there." (🔊 PN: McNair: K1H: 1:31min)

In other cases, reduplication has a derivational function in that it creates new lexemes. For example, the reduplicated form of *kajirri* 'old woman' is *kajijirri* but it does not simple mean multiple old women, but women from the past (491). A similar derived meaning occurs with *marluka* 'old man'.

(491) Ngu=rnayinangulu **kajijirri**=ma
CAT=1EXC.AUG.S>3AUG.NS old.woman.REDUP=TOP

kayi pa-na-ni.
follow hit-IMPF-PST
"We would follow in the footsteps of the old ladies from the past."
(🔊 VW: FM09_15_2d: 0:20min)

A number of adjectives and nouns arose from reduplications, but can no longer be regarded as such because the unreduplicated stem is no longer attested. For example, *jakayaka* 'lame' probably arose from *jaka-jaka* with lenition changing its form, but *jaka* is not used.

132 'Big' is used in conjunction with non-count nouns to express 'many'. In this example, the reduplication of *jangkarni* also contributes to this interpretation.

4.5 Kinship morphology

In this section, we describe morphology found on kinship terms, proper names, and the set of possessive markers found on tri-relationship terms.

4.5.1 *-rlang* DYADic

This suffix form pairs of relatives such as *jaju-rlang* 'mother's mother and her daughter's child', as shown in (492). Such pairs of relatives are very important culturally and are given expression also in the local Kriol by the morpheme *-geja*, from English 'together', as in Kriol *greni-geja* 'granny together'. In this case the term is reciprocal, that is, the grandchild is called *jaju* by the grandparent as well as the grandparent being addressed in this way.

(492) Ngu=wula **jaju-rlang**=ma ya-na-ni pungkulung-kula
CAT=3UA.S MM-DYAD=TOP go-IMPF-PST deep.coolamon-LOC

juluj ka-nga-ni ngawa=ma.
carry.under.arm take-IMPF-PST water=TOP
"The two of them, he and his granny, went along, she's carrying the coolamon under her arm." (🔈 RW: EC97_a006: Jajurlang & Ngawa: 0:26min)

Dyadic terms are also found with kinterms which are not reciprocal. Usually the stem preferred is that of the senior relation, for example *ngamarlang* refers to a 'mother and child' and uses a truncated form of *ngamayi* 'mother'. Dyadic terms dealing with different-sex relatives show some variation. The term for 'brother and sister' is usually *papa-rlang* based on *papa* 'brother' but *kawu-rlang*, a truncated form based on *kawurlu* 'sister' can be used, as shown in (493).

(493) Nyawa=ma=npula=nyunu jala=ma yini=rni
this=TOP=2UA.S=RR now=TOP name=ONLY

ma-nku **kawu-rlang**-kulu=ma.
do-POT sister-DYAD-ERG=TOP
"You sister and brother call each other by your names [which is not allowed]." (McConvell 1996 sketch grammar manuscript: Speaking to young people)

This suffix is also found in Bilinarra, Ngarinyman and Wanyjirra (Jones, Schultze-Berndt, Denniss, et al., 2019, p. 20; Meakins & Nordlinger, 2014, pp. 163–165; Senge, 2016, pp. 165–167). Senge notes for Wanyjirra that it only attaches to kinterms which do not end in the suffix *-yi*, which is an old 1st person singular pronoun (Nash, 1992). Ngardi and Jaru have the form *-rlangu* (Ennever, 2021; Tsunoda, 1981, p. 233).

4.5.2 *-rlangkurla* DYAD.PLural

The plural morpheme used with *-rlang* 'DYAD' and not for any other plural formation, is *-kurla*, as in as in *jaju-rlang-kurla* 'MM-DYAD-PL, mother's mother and daughter's children, or mother's mother and her sibling or siblings and daughter's child." It is probably formed by the reduplication of *-rlang* with a *-ku-* epenthetic and the final *-ng* deleted by nasal cluster deletion.

4.5.3 *-rra* DYAD.PLural

There is also an irregular DYAD morpheme, exemplified by *-rra* in *ngumparna-rra* 'husband and wife; two siblings-in-law' and shown in (494) (note we do not know what the extra *-ri* encodes). This suffix is also found in Mudburra and more kinterms receive this suffix in Warlpiri. It could be related to the *-rra* 'plural' found on demonstratives (§5.1.2.1) Note that Western Desert also has *-rra* more broadly as a dyadic suffix on kinterms which might indicate an inheritance historically.

(494) Ngu=lu ya-na-ni kaput=ma
CAT=3AUG.S go-IMPF-PST morning=TOP

ngumparna-rra-ri warlakap tanku-wu.
husband-DYAD.PL-?? search food-DAT
"They used to go out early in the morning, hunting and looking for food in the bush." (🔈 RW: EC97_a007: 0:15min)

4.5.4 Tri-relationship term morphology

The kinship morphology in this section relates to the complex paradigm of Gurindji tri-relational kinship terms. Tri-relational kinship terms have been described for a number of other Australian languages (see Blythe, 2018 for Murrinth-patha; Garde, 2013 for Binij Gun-wok; Hansen, 1974 for Pintupi; Mervyn Meggitt, 1962 for Warlpiri; O'Grady & Mooney, 1973 for Nyangumarta), however McConvell's (1982a) paper on Gurindji tri-relational kinship terms was pioneering in Australia and much of the information in this section is drawn from that paper.

Tri-relational kinship terms specify a relationship between the referent X, reference point Y, as in X is Y's brother, but also specify the speaker's relationship to both X and Y. In actual fact it is only necessary to specify the speaker's relationship to either X or Y since from the knowledge of the speaker's relationship to X and X's relationship to Y, we can compute the speaker's relationship to Y. For example in (495), *murrwali* refers to a person the hearer refers to as 'son-in-law' who is the speaker's child (female speaker) or niece/nephew (male speaker) (the speaker's *kurturtu*, the hearer's *mali*). This relationship is represented schematically in Figure 44.

(495) **Murrwali**-marnany-ku wanyja-rra=rla.
mother.in.law-2MIN.POSS-DAT leave-IMP=3OBL
"Give room for your mali." (🔊 VW: FM12_a172: 2:21min)

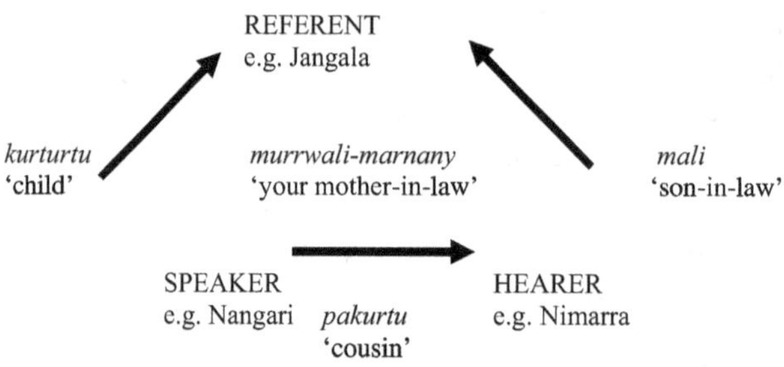

Figure 44: A schematic diagram of the referents of 'murrwali'.

The paradigm of tri-relational kinship terms is defective in the sense that only about half of the logical possibilities are covered by a shared kinterm and the normal kinterms are used in other cases (see §1.8.1 for a table of kinterms). This paradigm is given in McConvell (1982a, p. 101) and the full set is also distributed throughout the Gurindji dictionary as main entries (Meakins et al., 2013). This paradigm was possibly the first to go out of use among Gurindji people.

Tri-relational kinship terms often occur with a number of possessive suffixes, which are not found on other kinterms (when they are used in a non-tri-relational sense) or nominals. Ordinary possessive pronouns may be used instead of these suffixes with plain kinship terms e.g. *jawiji nyanuny* instead of *jawiji-nyan* for 'his mother's father'. The *-parra* suffix on *-marnany* is probably a combination of the epenthetic *-pa* and the *-rra* plural suffix discussed in §4.5.3. Some examples are given in (496)–(499).

-nyan	all dialects	'3MIN.POSS, his, hers'
-marnany	Eastern dialect	'2MIN.POSS, your'
-ngu	Western dialect	'2MIN.POSS, your'
-marnanyparra	Eastern dialect	'2AUG.POSS, you mob's'
-nguwuyarra	Western dialect	'2AUG.POSS, you mob's'
-ngaliny	all dialects	'1INC.MIN.POSS, yours and mine'
-ngayirrang	all dialects	'1EXC.UA.POSS, 'hers/his and mine'

(496) Hey **lamparra-marnany**-ju=ma=ngku jayi-nya,
hey father.in.law-2MIN.POSS-ERG=TOP=2MIN.NS give-PST

kujarra kirri kujarra nyununy.
two woman two 2MIN.DAT
"Hey your father-in-law who is my son gave two girls to you."
(🔈 VW: FM10_a155: 10:48min)

(497) **Murrwali-marnany**-ja jarrngan ma-nyja=rla.
mother.in.law-2MIN.POSS-LOC avoid talk-IMP=3OBL
"Talk indirectly to him when your *mali* is there." (🔈 VW: FM12_a172: 1:15min)

(498) Jarrngan-karra karrinyani nyila=ma ngu, **murrwali-nyan**-ta,
avoid-ITER be.IMPF.PST that=TOP CAT son.in.law-3MIN.POSS-LOC

maitbi mali-ngka yu nou.
maybe son.in.law-LOC you know
"She was keeping her distance because of her son-in-law."
(🔈 VW: FM12_a172: 01:00min)

(499) Ngu=wula=rla warlu pirrkap ma-ni nyawa,
CAT=3UA.S=3OBL fire make do-PST this

yalu-ngku **ngarlmurang-kulu**, Nangala-ngku=purrupurru.
that-ERG trirel.kin-ERG SUBSECT-ERG=AND
"Your two cousins who are my sisters made this fire for (damper) – and Nangala too." (🔈 VW: FM09_13_3a: 1:18min)

The suffixes *-nyan, -nyanparra* and *-ngu* are also found in Wanyjirra and Jaru (Senge, 2016, pp. 162–165; Tsunoda, 1981), and *-marnany* '2MIN.POSS', *-nyan* '3MIN.POSS' and *-nyanparra* '2MIN.POSS.PL' are also found in Bilinarra (Meakins & Nordlinger, 2014, pp. 165–167). The suffixes *-marnany(a)* '2MIN.POSS' and *-nyan(a)* '3MIN.POSS' are found in Mudburra (Green et al., 2019, p. 32).

4.6 Adnominal case

The adnominal function of case-marking is defined as relating one NP to another. We refer to this type of morphology as 'adnominal case' in this grammar using common terminology (cf. Dench & Evans, 1988, p. 7; Meakins & Nordlinger, 2014, p. 149). Elsewhere in the Ngumpin-Yapa literature, this type of morphology is referred to as 'derivational case' for Warlpiri (Nash, 1986, p. 16) and Wanyjirra (Senge, 2016, p. 201); or 'stem forming suffixes' for Jaru (Tsunoda, 1981, p. 221).

The two adnominal case suffixes in Gurindji are the proprietive *-jawung* (§4.6.2) and the privative *-murlung* (§4.6.3). The dative case also has an adnominal function in alienable possessive phrases, both with nominals and free pronouns (§4.6.1).

Adnominal suffixes, like case suffixes, must be marked on all members of the NP; in this respect they are different from derivational suffixes.

(500) Ngu=rli ya-na-ngku rarrarraj
CAT=1INC.MIN.S go-IMPF-POT run.REDUP

murrng-jawung **kurrurij-jawung**.
own-PROP car-PROP
"We'll travel around in our own car."
(McConvell 1996 sketch grammar manuscript: Speaking to young people)

Like case, adnominals can also occur after other inflectional morphology such as number suffixes. For example, in (501), the proprietive attaches after *-walija* 'paucal' to create the nominal word *karu-walija-yawung* 'with the children'.

(501) Kamparri-jang wanyja-ni **karu-walija-yawung**=ma.
before-TIME leave-PST child-PAUC-PROP=TOP
"A long time ago, he left the female emu there with her kids."
(🔈 VW: FM09_15_2a: 3:47min)

Nonetheless these adnominal suffixes can be distinguished from case suffixes because nominals marked with adnominal suffixes are additionally marked for case, whereas case-stacking is not a possibility otherwise (see §4.1). For example in (502) and (503), *tanku-murlung* receives an additional locative marker and *kurrupartu-yawung* is also marked ergative, respectively.

(502) Ngantipa du ngu=rnalu=nga nya-nga-ni
1EXC.AUG too CAT=1EXC.AUG.S=DUB intake-IMPF-PST

tanku-murlung-kula=ma, larrpa-larrpa=ma.
food-PRIV-LOC=TOP before-REDUP=TOP
"Us too, we might have eaten it when we were hungry in the old days."
(🔊 VW: FM09_12_6a: 1:41min)

(503) **Kurrupartu-yawung-kulu** kayi pa-na-na jamut.
boomerang-PROP-ERG chase hit-IMPF-PRS bush.turkey
"He chases the bush turkey with a boomerang." (🔊 BW: FM07_a043: 15:40min)

In the case of the dative, it is possible for more than one adnominal suffix to attach to the same stem. Thus, the dative in possessive function can combine with the proprietive or privative, or two datives can co-occur in embedded possession constructions (504). For semantic reasons the proprietive and privative are never found in combination.

(504) Nyila=ma **ngayiny-ku** jawiji-wu ngamayi-wu
that=TOP 1EXC.MIN.DAT-DAT MF-DAT mother-DAT

ngamarni-wu ngu=yina nyila=ma ngurra=ma,
uncle-DAT CAT=3AUG.NS that=TOP country=TOP

kankula nyawa na karla-ngkarla Jijaljawung.
up this FOC west-DOWN place.name
"This story is about my mother's, uncle's and mother's father's country which is down and west of here called Jijaljawung."
(🔊 VW: FM08_a071: 0:34min)

4.6.1 Dative in possessive function

The dative in possessive function is used to relate two nominals, and in this respect is classified as adnominal case. This function was introduced in §4.3.3.2 and will be discussed in detail in §8.3. The clause in (505) shows an example of a simple possessive phrase where the dative pronoun *ngayiny* 'my', the dependent, marks the relationship with the head *kapuku Mayawi* 'sister Mayawi'. The rest of the clause has an embedded possessor phrase 'that old Afghan man's camp' where *=rla* cross-references *nyanuny* and *marluka-wu* and the second oblique *=nyanta* cross-references the entire comitative noun phrase which is indicated by the locative case suffix.

(505) Ngu=rla=nyanta karrinya nyanuny-ja
CAT=3OBL=3OBL2 be.PST 3MIN.DAT-LOC

na marluka-wu-ny-ja yalu-wu-ny-ja,
FOC old.man-DAT-NMLZ-LOC that-DAT-NMLZ-LOC

ngayiny=ma kapuku=ma Mayawi=ma.
1EXC.MIN.DAT=TOP sister=TOP NAME=TOP
"My sister Mayawi used to stay at that old Afghan man's place."
(VW: FM10_22_1a: 4:08min)

4.6.2 PROPrietive

4.6.2.1 Form

The proprietive has two allomorphs *-jawu(ng) /-jaru(ng)* (consonant-final stems) and *-yawu(ng) /-yaru(ng)* (vowel-final stems). Examples are given in (506)–(509).

(506) Ngu=yi pa-ni kurturu-**yawu**.
CAT=1EXC.MIN.NS hit-PST nullanulla-PROP
She hit me with a nullanulla. (SM: HALE_K06-004554: 3:25min)

(507) Wararr-**jawung** ngu=rnalu nga-lu.
fat-PROP CAT=1EXC.AUG.S eat-POT
"We want to eat the fatty [meat]." (VW: FM09_a123: 4:00min)

(508) Majarti-**yawung**=ma kanka-yit im-in baj-im-ap
underwear-PROP=TOP upstream-ABL 3SG-PST bust-TR-ATEL

traujij-**jarung** pulngayit-tu=ma ngu yuwa-ni draund-im=ma.
trousers-PROP floodwater-ERG=TOP CAT put-PST drowned-TR=TOP
"From up there the floodwaters took his trousers and submerged them."
(JK: McConvell_A3463_G: 14:08min)

(509) Nyangurla=rli ya-nku nyila karu-**yarung**.
when=1INC.MIN.S go-POT that child-PROP
"When will we go with the child?" (TN: McConvell_A3463_K: 0:53min)

These forms are also found in Bilinarra, Ngarinyman and Malngin (Ise, 1998, p. 30; Jones, Schultze-Berndt, Denniss, et al., 2019, p. 18; Meakins & Nordlinger, 2014, pp. 151–153). Malngin uses *-jaru(ng)* and *-yaru(ng)* which also are described for Wanyjirra and Jaru without the final nasals (Senge, 2016, p. 204; Tsunoda, 1981, pp. 227–229).

Mudburra has different forms for the proprietive (*-wurru*) and comitative (*-yaru*, *-jaru*) (Green et al., 2019, pp. 29–30). Ngardi has one instance of *-jarungu* in the corpus which is probably related (Ennever, 2021). The proprietive form in Warlmanpa is *-parna* and Eastern Warlpiri has *-parnta* (Browne, 2021).

4.6.2.2 Function

The first function of the proprietive is as a comitative indicating accompaniment, as shown in (510) and (511) which describe a Dreaming Emu accompanied by her chicks in different clauses. This is often translated as 'with'.

(510) **Nanta-nanta-yawung** ya-na-ni ngu.
small-REDUP-PROP go-IMPF-PST CAT
"She came with her chicks." (🔈 VW: FM08_08_4e: 0:17min)

(511) Kamparri-jang wanyja-ni **karu-walija-yawung**=ma.
before-TIME leave-PST child-PAUC-PROP=TOP
"A long time ago, he left [the female Emu there] with her kids."
(🔈 VW: FM09_15_2a: 3:47min)

The proprietive is also used to indicate a possessive relationship between two nouns and is often translated as 'having'. For example, in (512), a billabong is described as having water. In (513), a pregnant woman is described as bearing a child and similarly in (514) a goanna is described as having eggs (gravid).

(512) "Warta yijarni yijarni langkarna. Langkarna **ngawa-yawung**."
hey true true billabong billabong water-PROP
"Hey true there's a billabong. A billabong full of water."
(🔈 VW: FM09_13_2f: 0:36min)

(513) Kula nga-lu yiparrartu du, **karu-yawung-kulu**=ma.
NEG eat-POT emu too child-PROP-ERG=TOP
"An expectant mother can't eat emu either." (🔈 VW: FM09_a123: 2:23min)

(514) Kula nga-lu **kampij-jawung**=ma kirrawa=ma.
NEG eat-POT egg-PROP=TOP goanna=TOP
"She can't eat a gravid goanna." (🔈 VW: FM09_a123: 0:13min)

In some cases, with the possessive use of the proprietive, additional case marking may occur. In (515), the proprietive-marked nominal is also marked locative to indicate that the seed-bearing plants are a location. The locative agrees with *kayirra* 'north' which is inherently locative (see §5.2.1).

(515) Nyawa na kayirra karrinyana **mangarri-yawung-kula**.
this FOC north be.IMPF.PRS veg.food-PROP-LOC
"Other ones in the north have good sized seeds." (◀) VW: FM09_13_2e: 1:56min)

The proprietive is also used to mark instruments and is usually translated as 'with'. In intransitive clauses, no other case-marking occurs in agreement with the nominative subject, as in (516) and (517); and in transitive clauses the ergative marker is often used in agreement with the transitive subject, as in (518) and (519).

(516) Ngu=rla ya-na-ni na **wirlka-yawung**=ma.
CAT=3OBL go-IMPF-PST FOC axe-PROP=TOP
"She went up to it with her axe." (◀) CN: FM10_29_3b: 4:48min)

(517) Nyamu=lu=nga ngana=wayin ya-nku **kurrurij-jawung**, marntaj.
REL=3AUG.S=DUB anyone=ETC go-POT car-PROP OK
"If anybody wants to go by car, that's all right."
(McConvell 1996 sketch grammar manuscript: Speaking to young people)

(518) Tamarra-yawung-kulu, ngarlaka, majul
antbed-PROP-ERG head stomach

ngu=rnayinangulu kampa-rna-na.
CAT=1EXC.AUG.S>3AUG.NS cook-IMPF-PRS
"We treat their heads and tummies with the antbed." (◀) VW: FM08_a085: 6:48min)

(519) Ngu=lu kampa-rna-ni **ngapulu-yawung-kulu**.
CAT=3AUG.S cook-IMPF-PST breast-PROP-ERG
"They used to cook it with milk." (◀) VW: FM09_17_1d: 6:21min)

A more abstract instrumental use of the proprietive is in descriptions of language use. People are described as speaking using a particular language, as shown in (520)–(522). Often speaking a traditional language is more obliquely described as simply 'language' rather than a specific language.

(520) **Kuurrinyji-yawung** ngu=rna ma-rna-na
Gurindji-PROP CAT=1EXC.MIN.S talk-IMPF-PRS

nyawa=ma, **jaru-yawung**.
this=TOP language-PROP
"I am saying this in Gurindji." (◀) VW: FM07_a050: 9:12min)

(521) Jarrakap ngu=rnayinangulu ma-rna-ngku, **jaru-yawung**.
talk CAT=1EXC.AUG.S>3AUG.NS talk-IMPF-POT language-PROP
"We'll be talking to them in language." (🔈 VW: FM08_11_3: 2:27min)

(522) **Jaru-yawung** ma-nyja=rla.
language-PROP talk-IMP=3OBL
"Talk to her in language (i.e. in Gurindji)"
(McConvell corpus: Meakins et al., 2016, p. 93)

A proprietive can attach to a noun or coverb to create an oblique argument in a detransitivised clause. For example, in (523), the main clause is intransitive and the proprietive attaches to the coverb *juluj*. The equivalent transitive clause would use the coverb *juluj* with the transitive inflecting verb *kangana* 'carry'.

(523) Ngana=warla nyila **juluj-jawung** karrinyana kutij.
who=FOC that carry.under.arm-PROP be.IMPF.PRS stand
"Who's that standing up [with a bundle] under their arm."
(RW & DD with ECh: Meakins et al., 2016, p. 113)

Finally, there is one derivational use of *-yawung* in the corpus: *kalu-yawung* 'walk-PROP, newcomer'.

This suffix is also found in the same form (with variation) and function in Wanyjirra and Bilinarra (Meakins & Nordlinger, 2014, pp. 151–153; Senge, 2016, pp. 204–207; Tsunoda, 1981).

4.6.3 PRIVative

The privative has one form *-murlung*, although *-murlu* is also used, as shown in (524) and (525).

(524) Ngu=rna karru **janga-murlung**.
CAT=1EXC.MIN.S be.POT sick-PRIV
"I won't be sick then." (🔈 TD: FM09_17_2d: 0:55min)

(525) Kawayiwayi, karu-walija, **yilying-murlu**
come.here.REDUP child-PAUC make.noise-PRIV

muk karra=lu.
quiet be.IMP=3AUG.S
"Come here all you kids. Stop being noisy. Keep quiet now!"
(🔈 DD: EC97_a002: 10:19min)

This privative suffix is opposite of the proprietive suffix, indicating that the head lacks something. For example, in (524), the speaker lacks an illness and in (526), the speaker lacks food.

(526)

Tanku-murlung-kulu	ngu=yi	paya-rni.
food-PRIV-ERG	CAT=1EXC.MIN.NS	bite-PST

"The hungry one bit me." (🔈 SM: HALE_K-6-004554: 16:37min)

When the privative combines with the locative suffix it produces the meaning 'in the time without'. In (527), this combination expresses times when the speaker and others felt thirsty and needed to follow finches to find water. In (528), *matches-murlung-kula* refers to the time before colonisation when there were no matches and Gurindji people used fire drills to create fire.

(527)

Nyamu=lu=nga	wanku	yirrp-karra=ma	kuya=ma
REL=3AUG.S=DUB	fall.POT	converge-ITER=TOP	thus=TOP

wal	ngu=rnalu	kurru	nya-nga-na.	Maiti
well	CAT=1EXC.AUG.S	listen	intake-IMPF-PRS	maybe

kaja-ngarna	yu	nou.	**Ngapuku-murlung-kula**.
bush-ASSOC	you	know	water-PRIV-LOC

"When the finches are flying down like this, well we hear them now.
Maybe in the bush you know. [When we were feeling] thirsty."
(🔈 VW: FM09_13_2f: 0:11min)

(528)

Tea-wu=ma,	mangarri-wu=ma,	pinyinyip=ma=lu
tea-DAT=TOP	damper-DAT=TOP	rub.between.palms=TOP=3AUG.S

ma-na-ni.	**Warlu-murlung-kula**	**matches-murlung-kula**=ma	kuya.
do-IMPF-PST	fire-PRIV-LOC	matches-PRIV-LOC=TOP	thus

"They used to rub sticks together to make fire for cooking tea and damper.
When they had no fire or matches." (🔈 TD: FM09_17_2b: 2:43min)

In some constructions *-murlung* has the meaning of negation rather than privation. A specialised use of this is where it is followed by the clitic *=nyiyang/nyiyarni* 'real, proper' thus X *-murlung=nyiyarni* means 'not an ordinary X' and, most often , 'a secret-sacred type of X', for example *tanku-murlung=nyiyang* 'meal-WITHOUT=PROPER; really hungry' (§10.1.3).

The privative also attaches to adverbs and coverbs to express negative commands. An example was given in (525) where children were directed to stop being noisy. Another example is given in (529). It can also be used instead of *kula* 'NEG' to express an action that did not happen, as shown in (530).

(529) Minyirri-warra-murlung yunpa-wu.
shy-ITER-PRIV sing-POT
"(They'd never seen a little boy) not too shy to sing."
(Turpin & Meakins, 2019, p. 50)

(530) Murnungku=ma warlakap=ma jamana=ma kuya-rniny=kata.
policeman=TOP search=TOP footprint=TOP thus-HITH=IMM

Pirlimatjurru ngu=lu ya-ni **paraj-murlung**-pa=rni,
place.name CAT=3AUG.S go-PST find-PRIV-EP=ONLY

paraj-murlung murnungku=ma kula=lu kururij-jawung
find-PRIV policeman=TOP NEG=3AUG.S car-PROP

murnungku=ma ya-ni, timana-yawung.
policeman=TOP go-PST horse-PROP
"The police were looking around for footprints. They went to Pirlimatjurru (north of Kalkaringi), but they couldn't find anything. They didn't have motor cars then so they were on horseback." (🔊 DD: EC98_a011: 12:46min)

Commands are also formed by using the imperative form of the inflecting verb with a coverb, as also shown in (525) by *muk karra=lu* 'quiet be.IMP=3AUG.S'. In these constructions, the bound pronoun lacks second person marking and only expresses number marking (see §7.1.3.8).

This suffix is also used with nominals and coverbs to create a number of idioms, which gives it a more derivational flavour. Examples are given below.

(531)

kuloj-murlung	clothes-WITHOUT	'naked'
langa-murlung	ear-WITHOUT	'stupid, inattentive'
minyirri-murlung	ashamed-WITHOUT	'shameless, not shy'
puya-murlung	body-WITHOUT	'thin'
tanku-murlung	food-WITHOUT	'hungry'

The suffix is found in the same form and functional range in Bilinarra, Ngarinyman, Malngin and Wanyjirra (Jones, Schultze-Berndt, Denniss, et al., 2019, p. 19; Meakins & Nordlinger, 2014, pp. 154–155; Senge, 2016, pp. 207–209; Tsunoda, 1981, p. 226). In Jaru, the form is *-murlungu* (Tsunoda, 1981, p. 225). In Mudburra, the equivalent is

-*wangka* (Green et al., 2019, p. 30). In Ngardi and Warlmanpa, the privative form is -*wangu* (Browne, 2021; Ennever, 2021).

4.7 Derivational morphology

Derivational morphology is used to create new lexemes. Sometimes the new lexeme is a different part of speech and in other cases it is the same part of speech. In Gurindji, nominal derivation involves adding suffixes to convert words, mostly nominals and coverbs, into new nominals (nouns or adjectives) with a different but related meaning. Other derivational processes which are used to create coverbs are discussed in §7.2.4.

The distinction between derivation and inflection was introduced in §4.1. The basic morphological criterion used here is that derivational suffixes are followed by a case suffix, except in rare examples such as (272). For example, the nominal word *turrp-kaji-yawung-kulu* 'with a needle' in (532) consists of a stem+derivation+adnominal+case. Similarly, in (533) the nominal word *murla-marraj-ngurlu* 'from somewhere like here' consists of a demonstrative stem+derivation+case. But note some variation. Further along in that same utterance is *yalu-wu-marraj* where the derivational morphology is found on the outside. We have no explanation for this.

(532)

Nyangunyangu-lu	turrp	pu-nga-na	laparn-ta
nurse-ERG	inject	pierce-IMPF-PRS	shoulder.blade-LOC

turrp-kaji-yawung-kulu	wamala.
inject-AGENT-PROP-ERG	girl

"The nurse injected the girl in the shoulder with a needle."
(🔈 BW: FM07-a043: 26:19min)

(533)

Wal	walik	ya-ni	ngu	yikili=rni	marri	**murla-marraj-ngurlu**=ma
well	turn	go-PST	CAT	far=ONLY	BUT	this-COMP-ABL=TOP

nyawa-marraj	kayi-rni	nyamu	school	jeya	kaa-rni
this-COMP	north-UP	REL	school	there	east-UP

yalu-wu-marraj	murla-ngka=ma	nyila=ma	marluka=ma.
that-DAT-COMP	this-LOC=TOP	that=TOP	old.man=TOP

"Well he turned around keeping north, a little bit of a long way, like from here to the school there up and east, he was that far away that man."
(🔈 RW: EC98_a026: Karukany II: 4:14min)

Because derivation cannot follow inflection, it attaches to a non-dative version of the pronoun, such as in (534). If it attaches to the dative pronoun, e.g. *nyununy-marraj* '2MIN.DAT-COMP' it can only mean 'like yours', not 'like you'.

(534) "Kula=rna waninyana nyiwunnyiwun=ma kanyjurra
NEG=1EXC.MIN.S fall.IMPF.PRS dive =TOP down

tarap=ma **nyuntu-marraj**=ma, lawara," kuya, ngu=rla ma-rna-ni.
dive=TOP 2MIN-COMP=TOP nothing thus CAT=3OBL talk-IMPF-PST
"'I can't dive down like you at all,' he said to him."
(🔊 VW: FM10_23_2a: Warrija Kirrawa: 1:51min)

In the following sections, 26 derivational suffixes are described plus zero derivation and reduplication processes. They are ordered alphabetically. Some derivational processes are very common and highly productive. Others have a limited use and are perhaps historically frozen. Each will be discussed in turn.

4.7.1 Zero derivation

Nominals can be derived from coverbs through a process of zero-derivation, for example *ngurra* 'camp' (n)' and to camp' (cv), *kuli* 'fight' (n) or 'to fight' (cv), *janga* 'sickness, sore' (n) or 'to be sick' (cv), *kumpu* 'urine' (n) or 'to urinate' (cv) and *jarrakap* 'language, meeting' (n) or 'to talk' (cv). In (535), *janga* is used as a coverb, and then as a nominal in (536) (noun), (537) (adjective), and (538). Note that in (538) *janga* is re-nominalised with the meaning of 'flu' rather than simply 'sickness'.

(535) Kula nga-lu yiparrartu du, karu-yawung-kulu=ma,
NEG eat-POT emu too child-PROP-ERG=TOP

ngaja **janga** karrinyana yapakayi.
ADMON sick be.IMPF.PRS small
"A pregnant woman shouldn't eat emu because her baby might become sick."
(🔊 VW: FM09_a123: 2:24min)

133 Fascinatingly, this word also means 'dragonfly, helicopter'. It is not clear where the 'bad flu' meaning comes from but Violet Wadrill reports that they used to use the word with this sense on old Wave Hill Station when they lived there.

(536) Ngu=yi=n ngunku ma-na-na,
CAT=1EXC.MIN.NS=2MIN.S hurt do-IMPF-PRS

ngu=rna **janga**-yawung.
CAT=1EXC.MIN.S sore-PROP
"You're hurting me, I've got a sore [there]." (VW: FM12_a176)

(537) Karu **janga** ngu=rnayinangulu
child sick CAT=1EXC.AUG.S>3AUG.NS

yuwa-na-na marntara-yawung.
put-IMPF-PRS sore-PROP
"We bathe sick children who have skin sores or scabies."
(VW: FM10_a145: 0:55min)

(538) Jiwarrp ngu=rnalu ma-na-na, nyamu=waa=ngantipa
gather CAT=1EXC.AUG.S do-IMPF-PRS REL=REL=1EXC.AUG.NS

piyarrp yuwa-na-ni, jangkarni **janga-ny**
report put-IMPF-PST big sick-NMLZ

na wajirrki[133] jangkarni.
FOC flu big
"We collect it because [the nurse] told us about the Swine Flu."
(🔊 VW: FM09_14_1a: 6:31min)

4.7.2 Reduplication

Reduplication is a derivational process which creates new nouns from different parts of speech. One example in the corpus of a reduplicated inflecting verb creating a noun is *nyangunyangu* 'doctor' <*nyangu* 'look'. Note though that the inflecting verb is actually *nyangana* and the non-finite version of the verb is *nyangunu* so this isn't a perfect match (although it might come from Bilinarra).

Examples of nouns derived from a coverbs are *kirinykiriny* 'skink' <*kiriny* 'slippery' and *marlumarlu* 'lame person' <*marlu* 'lame'. Other noun-noun examples are *wulngarnwulngarn* 'earless dragon, Timpanocryptis cephalus' <*wulngarn* 'sun' and *kilinykiliny* 'galah', <*kiliny* 'gravid goanna'. Some colour terms are also derived from nouns, for example *ngunyjungunyju* 'yellow' <*ngunyju* 'tobacco' and *kuntarrikuntarri* 'yellow' <*kuntarri* 'eggs and pollen of sugarbag'. In other examples, the origin of the reduplicated noun is not clear, and it might have been borrowed frozen from another language. In (539), *karrajkarraj* 'curry orange, Ziziphus quadrilocularis' is a reduplicated form but no unreduplicated form exists in the current knowledge of Gurindji speakers.

(539)

Karrajkarraj	ngu=lu	kampa-rna-ni,	yirip-karra	jurlpara-la.
curry.orange	CAT=3AUG.S	cook-IMPF-PST	warm.up-ITER	hot.coals-LOC

"They used to warm the curry orange on the hot coals."
(🔈 VW: FM09_15_2d: 2:01min)

4.7.3 *-ing* ADJectival

There are a few derivational suffixes which occur with one or two words each to produce adjectives from coverbs, for example *kalywarring* 'soft, weak, light' from *kalywarr* 'swelling gone down', *parntalying* 'slippery' from *parntaly* 'slip', *jiwilying* 'cold' from *jiwily* 'cold' (540) and *yarntalying* 'slippery' (541). In other cases, a corresponding coverb does not exist as a separate form, as in *winkilying* 'red' (542) It is possible that these are historically frozen forms or are perhaps borrowed whole from elsewhere. Indeed *parayiwiting* 'widen' is said to be a borrowing from Jaru and is used as a swear word in Gurindji.

(540)

Ngu-rnalu	kukij-karra	na,	nyamu=waa	karru	**jiwily-ing**
CAT=1EXC.AUG.S	drink-ITER	FOC	REL=REL	be.POT	cold-ADJ

na.
FOC

"We will drink it when it gets cold." (🔈 VW: FM09_16_1b: 0:29min)

(541)

Yarntaly-ing-kula	waninya	palwany-ja.
slip-ADJ-LOC	fall.PST	flat.rock-LOC

"He fell down on the slippery flat rocks."
(McConvell corpus: Meakins et al., 2016, p. 438)

(542)

Kunyini	**winkily-ing**	karrinyana.
coals	red-ADJ	be.IMPF.PRS

"The coals are red." (McConvell corpus: Meakins et al., 2016, p. 181)

There are some possible variants on *-ing*. For example, *-(rr)ang* in *kurlwarrang* 'black soil country' from *kurlwa* 'muddy, boggy'. Another possible variant is *-ung* as in *mumpung* 'black' from *mum* 'dark' (although *-pung* may be a suffix from Jarragan languages). Similarly, perhaps *-iny* as in *ngapukariny* 'strong smelling' from *ngapuk* 'smell' but this suffix could be a reduced form of *-wariny* 'alone' (§4.7.24). And again, these forms could all be frozen forms. This formation is not productive in Gurindji and these stems discussed are the only ones which exist in the Gurindji corpus. This ending and its variants are not observed in Ngardi, Warlmanpa or Mudburra.

4.7.4 *-jang* TIMEaliser

The suffixes *-jang* and *-lang* exist on three location adverbs and create nouns which relate to generations. In this respect, they act to re-map time from space: *kamparri-jang* 'front-TIME; previous generation, old' (543), *ngumayi-jang* 'behind-TIME, next generation, young', and *jalayi-lang*[134] 'today-TIME, current generation' (544). The suffix *-jang* is also used on the interrogative *nyatjang* 'how many', which does not relate to time, but more concretely to counting (545) (see §5.3.5).

(543) Ngu=lu kampa-rna-ni **kamparri-jang**-kulu kajijirri-lu.
CAT=3AUG.S cook-IMPF-PST before-TIME-ERG old.woman.REDUP-ERG
"In the old days, the women used to cook them." (🔊 TD: FM07_a059: 1:00min)

(544) Ngantipa ngu=rnalu nya-nga-na
1EXC.AUG.S CAT=1EXC.AUG.S intake-IMPF-PRS

ngumayi-jang-kulu na kuya, **jalayi-lang**-kulu.
behind-TIME-ERG FOC thus now-TIME-ERG
"We the older generation know about this now, and the present generation."
(🔊 BW: FM07_01_1a: 4:45min)

(545) "**Nyatjang**=parla ya-ni?" "Kula jarrwa, narajpurru."
how.many=FOC go-PST NEG many small.group
"How many are going?" "Not many, maybe three or four."
(McNair corpus: Meakins et al., 2016, p. 256)

It is possible that these forms have further stems, for example the nominal *kurrjalang* 'hungry' could refer to a time when a person was hungry. It has a corresponding coverb *kurrjarrp* 'full, satiated'.

Wanyjirra has the same form used in the same way, with another variant *-wart* (Senge, 2016, pp. 156–157). The *-wart* form might be related to the *-wurt* form in Gurindji discussed in §4.4.3. Bilinarra, Jaru and Malngin also have *-jang* (Meakins, 2013, p. 67; Tsunoda, 1981, p. 222). Similar suffixes appear in other Ngumpin-Yapa

134 The word for 'today' is actually *jala* so it's not clear what the *-yi* is.

languages: *-jangka* in Walmajarri (Richards & Hudson, 1990, p. 378), *-jangu* in Jaru (Tsunoda, 1981, p. 222), Ngardi and Warlpiri. In Mudburra, *-jpunga* appears on location words to create a noun encoding a person associated with that location.

4.7.5 *-jayi* LATE

This suffix has two forms *-jayi* (consonant-final) (546) and *-yayi* (vowel-final) (547) and it attaches to nouns, skin names or kinterms, as a respectful way to refer to someone who is deceased, as in 'the late so-and-so'. Examples on kinterms are given in (546) and (547).

(546) **Mukurl-jayi**-lu ngu=ngantipa pinak jayi-nga-ni
aunt-LATE-ERG CAT=1EXC.AUG.NS teach give-IMPF-PST

ngantipa=ma, Katarl-lu, mukurl-rlang-ku.
1EXC.AUG=TOP NAME-ERG aunt-DYAD-ERG
"Our aunties who have passed away showed us – Katarl – and our aunties."
(🔊 VW: FM09_14_1a: 1:34min)

(547) Marlurluka-lu=purrupurru lajalajap
old.man.REDUP-ERG=AND carry.on.shoulder.REDUP

kaku-yayi-nganyju-lu=ma.
FF-LATE-GROUP-ERG=TOP
"And the old men used to carry them – including my grandfather."
(🔊 VW: FM09_17_1d: 5:02min)

This suffix is also found in Wanyjirra in the same form and function (Senge, 2016, p. 167). Ngardi has *-puka* (Ennever, 2021).

4.7.6 *-kaji* AGENT

The agentive suffix has two allomorphs *-kaji* (consonant-final) (548) and *-waji* (vowel-final) (549). Stems ending in /rr/ are marked with either suffix. Speakers of Gurindji Kriol now tend to use the *-kaji* variant in all environments.

(548) Nyamu=n=nga wuya-wu, wuya
REL=2MIN.S=DUB throw-POT throw.IMP

marntaj **wirlng-wirlng-kaji-lu.**
OK want-REDUP-AGENT-ERG
"If you're going to throw, all right throw if you want to."
(McConvell corpus: Meakins et al., 2016, p. 431)

(549) Janka nyamu=yinangkulu ka-nga-na rarraj
woman REL=3AUG.S>3AUG.NS take-IMPF-PRS run

kuya-ngka=warla **kuli-waji.**
thus-LOC=FOC fight-AGENT
"When people run away with a woman that's when there's fighting."
(McConvell corpus: Meakins et al, 2016., p. 171)

The function of the agentive is similar to the associative marker *-ngarna* discussed in §4.7.16. In fact, often the associative and agentive suffixes are interchangeable with the same nominal. For example, *tiwu-ngarna* 'plane' is also often *tiwu-waji.*[135] There is a subtle meaning difference between these suffixes, however. The associative suffix has a broader meaning, simply marking an association between the derived nominal and the stem. The agentive suffix on the other hand has a meaning of 'the thing/person who does or is used for X'. Another way the agentive contrasts with *-ngarna* is that it is never found with place names.

The agentive suffix is found on nouns, (550) and (551), coverbs, (548), (550) and (551), and non-finite forms of inflecting verbs, (552), (554) and (555).

(550) Warlaku=ma nyila=ma kirrawa-waji paraj-kaji.
dog=TOP that=TOP goanna-AGENT find-AGENT
"That dog is a good finder (hunter) of goannas."
(McConvell corpus: Meakins et al., 2016, p. 127)

(551) Nyawa=ma **kurrupartu-waji pirrka-waji.**
this=TOP boomerang-AGENT make-AGENT
"This man is a (good) boomerang-maker."
(McConvell 1996 sketch grammar manuscript)

135 *-ngarna* in this function is more common in Mudburra; *-ngarna* tends to be restricted to 'who/which lives in place X' in Gurindji (§4.7.16).

(552) Warlaku=ma nyila=ma **ngumpit-ku** **paya-rnu-waji**.
dog=TOP that=TOP man-DAT bite-INF-AGENT
"That dog is a person biter."
(McConvell 1996 sketch grammar manuscript)

(553) Kankapa ngu=lu jarrwa kartiya **langa-wu** **nyirn-kaji**.
upstream CAT=3AUG.S many non-Indigenous ear-DAT deaf-AGENT
"Upstream there are a lot of *kartiya* who'll deafen your ears [with the noise of their machinery]." (McConvell corpus: Meakins et al., 2016, p. 137)

(554) Donkey-ku na pul-im=ma ka-nga-ni fire-plough=ma[136]
donkey-ERG FOC pull-TR=TOP take-IMPF-PST fire-plough=TOP

nyila=ma. Lurr pa-na-ni nyawa=ma, wurruma,
that=TOP go.everywhere hit-IMPF-PST this=TOP road

lurr-pa-nu-waji-yawung-kulu.
go.everywhere-hit-INF-AGENT-PROP-ERG
"Donkeys used to pull fire ploughs. They used to level off this one, the road, with the grader." (🔈 VW: FM12_a175: 7:19min)

(555) Nyila=ma **wurrwa-rnu-waji** pakajirri.
that=TOP block-INF-AGENT good.fighter
"That man is a good fighter and good blocker of weapons."
(McConvell 1996 sketch grammar manuscript)

If X is a noun, X-*kaji* describes, broadly speaking, a thing or person habitually or typically involved with an action or process which also centrally involves X. It may be useful to think of these as reduced forms of 'clausal' agent phrases as in the sentences above. So *kirrawa-waji* 'goanna-AGENT' can mean the same as what is meant by the form of the phrase with the explicit coverb 'a (good) goanna-hunter' (550). Similarly, *kurrupartu-waji* 'boomerang-maker' would most often be interpreted in the same way as the phrase with the verb in (551). This is not true of the nouns which take dative in (552) and (553): *ngumpit-kaji* alone could not be interpreted as 'person-biter' nor could *langa-waji* be interpreted as 'deafening'; this semantic information gives a clue to the different treatment of the objects in (552) and (553).

Since the verbal element is omitted from the noun-AGENT constructions instead of being included, a number of different inferences can be drawn about the nature of

136 This was a plough that was used for creating roads as a type of grader. We believe it was invented in this area.

the action involved and the semantic role of the noun from which the agent adjective is derived, in the understood clause. The probability of interpretations is regulated by the perceived naturalness of types of involvement of the noun in various events. Among common interpretations of the relation between basic noun X and the derived agent nominal are shown in (556).

(556)	*kirrawa-waji*	'goanna-AGENT; goanna hunter'	animate which gets X
	kurrupartu-waji	'boomerang-AGENT; boomerang maker'	person who makes X
	warlu-waji	'fire-AGENT; fireplace'	place for X
	wumara-waji	'money-AGENT; money-bag'	receptacle for X
	yarti-waji	'photograph-AGENT; movie-show'	thing comprising X
	yawu-waji	'fish-AGENT; fish-lover'	person who likes X

The agent suffix also attaches to coverbs. The nature of the involvement usually reflects the function of the subject of the verb as *tartartap-kaji* 'limp-NMLZ, limping person', but it can be the instrument as in *purtij-kaji* 'light fire-AGENT, matches, lighter, pyromaniac'. Involvement in the action can be of a vaguer nature, not necessarily attributable to a clear syntactic function. Thus *kuli-waji* 'fight-AGENT' would normally mean a person prone to or good at fighting, or something (like a weapon) used for fighting, but in (549) it means the cause of fighting. This suffix often combines with *-karra* 'ITER' on coverbs, for example *turlk-karra-waji* 'bang-ITER-AGENT, someone who is always shooting; place where bangs are continually heard'. The instrument 'rifle' is expresses without the iterative *turlk-kaji.*

(557)	*jakarr-waji*	cover-AGENT	'blanket, nappy'
	jarrakap-kaji	talk-AGENT	'telephone, tape-recorder, chatter-box'
	karrap-kaji	look-AGENT	'glasses'
	kataj-kaji	cut-AGENT	'knife'
	kilkilp-kaji	click-AGENT	'clapsticks'
	kulyurrk-kaji	cough-AGENT	'cough medicine'
	lingi-waji	persistent-AGENT	'irritating child'
	lurlu-waji	sit-AGENT	'chair, baby who is at sitting up stage'
	makin-kaji	sleep-AGENT	'mattress, bed'
	nang-kaji	stick.on-AGENT	'sticker, band-aid'
	ngayirrp-kaji	breath/life-AGENT	'pulse'
	rarraj-kaji	run-AGENT	'vehicle'
	tiwu-waji	fly-AGENT	'aeroplane'
	wumpulung-kaji	roll.over-AGENT	'baby at rolling over stage'

When the agent suffix attaches to an infinitive form of a verb, as in (552) and (555), the resultant nominal from the verbal type of derivation indicates an entity, animate or inanimate, which is habitually or typically involved in the action referred to by the verb. This suffix can also be used with infinitival forms of inflecting verbs followed by the coverb suffix *-p*, for example *kampa-rnu-p-kaji* 'cook-INF-CV-AGENT' which refers to a cook, or with a coverb prefixed to the inflecting verb root, for example *lurr-pa-nu-waji* 'go.everywhere-hit-INF-AGENT', as in (554).

Adjective phrases may also be built with a verb/coverb head + *-kaji* and a dependent noun phrase which stands in a syntactic relation to the infinitive verb. The relation is usually equivalent to that of a direct object in a finite sentence. There are two ways of marking this dependent object in an agent phrase: (a) by the agent suffix, as on the verb or coverb, as in (550)–(555); (b) by the dative case, as in (552) and (553).

This suffix is very commonly used to derive words for introduced items. For example, an otoscope[137] is called a *langa-waji* 'ear-AGENT', a chair is sometimes called a *rurr-kaji* 'sit-AGENT', a camera is called a *yarti-waji* 'shade-AGENT' and a vehicle is called a *rarraj-kaji* 'run-AGENT', as an alternative term to *kurrurij*. In the case of *rarraj-kaji*, the original meaning of 'fast running person or thing' is still used, although at the possible risk of ambiguity.

There is another similar but much less productive suffix *-ji* which is only found on *ngarin-ji* 'meat-AGENT; good hunter' in the corpus.

The agentive suffix *-kaji/waji* is also found in Bilinarra (Meakins & Nordlinger, 2014, pp. 159–161), Ngarinyman (Jones, Schultze-Berndt, Denniss, et al., 2019, pp. 20, 47), Malngin (Ise, 1998, p. 31), Jaru (Tsunoda, 1981, pp. 229–230) and Wanyjirra (Senge, 2016, pp. 150–154), but not Mudburra where *-ngarna* is used in this function. It is also occasionally found in Ngardi, but is probably a borrowing, with *-pirri* the more usual form (Ennever, 2021).

4.7.7 *-kilang* PROPERly

This suffix only occurs rarely in the corpus, for example *kawa-kilang* 'old.eyes-PROPER, something worn out' and *kamurr-kilang* 'middle-PROPER, middle child'. There is a possible variant *-kalang* which is seen on *mankij-kalang* 'dodge-PROPER, good dodger' and *lurruj-kalang* 'tracks and scratch marks of goannas' (although in this case, the probable coverb *lurruj* is no longer used).

A possible source of the suffix is Warlpiri which has *-kilangu* 'belongs, to do with', for example *yarla-kilangu* 'yam digger'. It is also found on non-finite verbs to encode instruments in Warlpiri. Another source might be Kija which has *-kaliny* in a similar function (*ny* is the masculine in this language).

137 An otoscope is a medical instrument used for examining ears.

4.7.8 *-kari* OTHER

This suffix has two forms *-kari* (consonant-final) and *-wari* (vowel-final) and has the general meaning which translates as 'another'. This suffix differs from other derivational suffixes in that the suffix adds a meaning qualifying the noun (referring to a subset of the entities referred to by the noun) rather than referring to an entirely different entity (not part of the subset of entities referred to by the noun) with some relationship to the noun. It is common for two nominals in discourse to be both marked with *-kari*, indicating 'one . . . the other'.

(558) Nyila **kartak-kari-la** tikily-ing; nyila **kartak-kari-la** tupurrung.
that cup-OTHER-LOC cold-ADJ that cup-OTHER-LOC hot
"That one in the one cup is cool; that one in the other cup is hot."
(McConvell 1996 sketch grammar manuscript)

The suffix *-kari* also occurs with expressions of time to mean 'the time before' with past time or 'the time after' with future time: *puriny-kari* 'afternoon-OTHER; the day before yesterday'; *kaput-kari* 'morning-OTHER; the day after tomorrow'.

Adjectival forms, optionally with this suffix, having the same meaning of 'other' are *jintapa-kari* or *jintara-kari* 'one-OTHER' and for a plural referent *yirrap-kari* 'another group'. These forms are also used where a noun 'the other one', 'another one' or 'the others' is required.

It is possible that *-wari* also acts as base for creating the form *-wariny* 'ALONE' which has an additional nominalising suffix *-ny*, since there is an underlying meaning of separation. This suffix is discussed further in §4.7.24.

This suffix is also found in Mudburra (Green et al., 2019, p. 32), Bilinarra (Meakins & Nordlinger, 2014, pp. 157–158), Ngarinyman (Jones, Schultze-Berndt, Denniss, et al., 2019, p. 20), Malngin (Ise, 1998, p. 30) and Wanyjirra (Senge, 2016, pp. 154–155). None of these languages have a lenited form *-wari* which suggests it was borrowed after lenition rules were active. Wanyjirra and Jaru also have *-wariny* and *-kariny* (Senge, 2016, p. 154; Tsunoda, 1981, p. 231), and Ngardi only has *-kariny* which can mean 'other' but also 'alone' on pronouns and 'further away' on cardinals (Ennever, 2021). Jaru has a similar functional range for *-wariny* and *-kariny*. In Gurindji and Bilinarra, the suffix *-wariny* 'ALONE' is used for these latter two functions but cannot be used to mean 'other' (§4.7.24). Warlmanpa has a completely different form *-kanyanu* (Browne, 2021).

4.7.9 *-kirlarlaj* TOY

This is another rare suffix which is only found on a few noun stems. It is possible that it originates in a coverb which has recently grammaticalised into a suffix (since it is not phonologically reduced in any respect), but no examples of its use as a coverb exist in the corpus. Another reason to believe that it is a recent innovation is that there are two forms, *-kirlarlaj* and *-kirlakirlaj*, with the latter looking like a reduplication. It attaches to a noun stem to derive the meaning 'toy' or 'pretend'. Two examples are given in (559) and (560).

(559) Ngu=rnawuliny ma-na-ni ngayu=ma
CAT=1EXC.MIN.S>3UA.NS do-IMPF-PST 1EXC.MIN=TOP

wajajarra, **kurrurij-kirlarlaj** ngu=rna ya-ni kurlarra.
play.REDUP car-TOY CAT=1EXC.MIN.S go-PST south
"I took them to play, with my toy car and I went south."
(DD with ECh: Bill Crow & Jim Crow: Appendix story 8, line 41)

(560) **Karu-kirlakirlaj** parnngirri, ngu=lu
child-TOY bark CAT=3AUG.S

pirrkap ma-na-ni karu-ngku.
make do-IMPF-PST child-ERG
"The kids used to make bark dolls." (🔊 VW: FM11_a169: 22:33min)

4.7.10 *-kunyja* LACKing

This suffix has four forms, two of which derive from a process of nasal stop cluster dissimilation: *-kunyja* (consonant-final stems), *-wunyja* (vowel-final stems), *-kuja* (consonant-final stem with a nasal-stop cluster) and *-wuja* (vowel-final stem with a nasal-stop cluster).

(561) **Ngawa-wunyja** ngu=rna.
water-LACK CAT=1EXC.MIN.S
"I'm thirsty." (RW & DD with ECh: Meakins et al., 2016, p. 181)

(562) Kuninyjirrp ngu=rna karrinyana.
hungry.for.meat CAT=1EXC.MIN.S be.IMPF.PRS

Nunykuwarra **ngarin-kuja**.
hungry meat-LACK
"I'm hungry for meat. Hungry for meat." (🔊 VW: FM12_a174: 12:00min)

(563) Warlayarra-**wunyja** ngu=rna.
tobacco-LACK CAT=1EXC.MIN.S
"I'm desperate for tobacco." (🔊 VW: FM12_a174: 12:38min)

This suffix is transparently built from dative+nominaliser+locative. The dative is not uncommonly used on its own to mean 'wanting' both in the current sense in English and in the somewhat archaic sense of 'lacking' perhaps via 'desiring'. The locative could be the result of the original structure starting out as a non-finite subordinate clause perhaps with a *karrinyana* 'be' verb in the main clause which has then been insubordinated to produce the meaning of deprivation.

Note that this suffix is homophonous with the comitative use of dative+nominaliser+locative, which was discussed in §4.3.9, but the nominals which result from this derivational process, unlike the 'lacking' suffix, show agreement across a noun phrase. The comitative use of this sequence also occurs with a verb in the main clause and is cross-referenced by a non-subject pronominal clitic. Interestingly the comitative 'with' meaning is the opposite of the 'lacking' meaning which has the potential for confusion, for example *nalija-wunyja* which means 'tea break, i.e. with tea' as opposed to *ngarinkuja* which means 'hungry for meat'. In this respect, the use is lexicalised. This difference in meaning could have come about with the comitative suffix developing from a different origin, where the locative refers to a place, which is shown in parallel allative constructions, as discussed in §4.3.5.2. Thus, this use of the locative refers to a person's place.

Note that this way of expressing the lack of something has other alternatives in Gurindji. For example, hunger is more commonly expressed in the coverb *nunykuwarra*. Another way of expressing thirst is the construction 'it is burning my throat for water', as shown in (564) and (565). The privative suffix *-murlung* is also more commonly used than the lacking suffix (§4.6.3).

(564)

Warta	ngu=**yi**	**ngawa-wu**	jiya-rna-na.
goodness	CAT=1EXC.MIN.NS	water-DAT	burn-IMPF-PRS

Ngu=rna	majul=ma	ngarrap	na.
CAT=1EXC.MIN.S	stomach=TOP	warm	FOC

"Goodness I'm really thirsty. My stomach is hot." (🔈 VW: FM11_a166: 34:04min)

(565)

Jiya-rna-ni	ngu=**ngantipa**	parunga-la
burn-IMPF-PST	CAT=1EXC.AUG.NS	hot.weather-LOC

du	nyawa=ma,	**ngapaku-wu**.
too	this=TOP	water-DAT

"We were always thirsty for water in the hot season." (🔈 VW: FM09_14_1a: 2:27min)

This suffix also appears in Wanyjirra in the same form and function. It also appears on *nyampa* to mean "what's wrong?" (Senge, 2016, pp. 157–159). (*Nyampa-wuja* "what's wrong" is also found in Gurindji). This form also appears in Jaru (Tsunoda, 1981, p. 226). In Ngardi, the 'lacking' form is *-jirraja* and in Warlmanpa it is *-jila* (Browne, 2021; Ennever, 2021).

4.7.11 *-mala* OWNer

This owner suffix only appears on *ngurra-mala* 'traditional custodian' and similarly appears in this limited function in Bilinarra and Mudburra. Ngardi and Warlpiri have another suffix *-malu* which refers to a 'group of origin x', which could be related (Ennever, 2021; Nash, 1986, p. 22). Other owner suffixes in Gurindji which are similarly lexicalised are *-mungkuj* (§4.7.14) and *-wirrirri* (§4.7.26).

4.7.12 *-marraj* COMParative

The comparative has one form *-marraj*. Its morphological status is unclear given that it sometimes attaches on the inside of case marking like derivational morphology (566) and sometimes on the outside like a clitic (567).

(566)	Kuwarnarn	jalngak	ka-nga-ni	**yawarta-waji-marraj-ju.**
	log	ride	take-IMPF-PST	horse-AGENT-COMP-ERG

"He was riding a log along like a horseman."
(McConvell 1996 sketch grammar manuscript)

(567)	Rungap	ma-rna-na	**Lawi-ngka-marraj.**
	bark	talk-IMPF-PRS	place.name-LOC-COMP

"There's barking somewhere like at Lawi."
(McConvell corpus: Meakins et al., 2016, p. 365)

(568)	Jalngak	ka-nga-ni	pulngayit-ta
	ride	take-IMPF-PST	floodwater-LOC

yawarta-marraj	kuwarnarn	jangkarni.
horse-COMP	log	big

"He was riding a big log along like a horse in the floodwater."
(McConvell corpus: Meakins et al., 2016, p. 195)

This suffix denotes similarity between the derived form and the original form. It attaches to nouns, free pronouns and demonstratives, and in this role is used to draw a comparison with another entity, or action or characteristic of this entity. Another example is given in (569).

(569) Marlmarlp-kaji nyamu=lu karrinyani,
wheeze.REDUP-AGENT REL=3AUG.S be.IMPF.PST

pujikat-marraj ngurrmilp-karra.
cat-COMP purr-ITER
"When they used to have asthma, and sound like a cat purring."
(🔊 BW: FM07_01_1a: 5:06min)

This suffix is also found in Bilinarra, Ngarinyman, Malngin, Wanyjirra and Jaru as *-marraj* (Ise, 1998, p. 30; Jones, Schultze-Berndt, Denniss, et al., 2019, p. 20; Meakins & Nordlinger, 2014, p. 161; Senge, 2016, p. 209; Tsunoda, 1981, pp. 230–231) and in Mudburra as *-marraja*. Ngardi, Warlmanpa, and Warlpiri use *-piya* (§4.7.22) (Browne, 2021; Ennever, 2021). Warlmanpa also has *-nganyja*, *-kanjarri* and *-nganjarri*. Ngardi also has *-payi*. Ennever suggests that *-payi* could be borrowed from Western Desert which also uses it as a semblative. Unrelatedly, *-marraji* in Western Desert languages means 'owner'. Gurindji has different forms for 'owner': *-mala* (§4.7.11), *-mungkuj* (4.7.14) and *-wirrirri* (§4.7.26).

4.7.13 *-mirntij* SEASON

This suffix is usually added to a coverb describing a hunting and gathering activity or an activity of animals, for example *warrartwarrart-mirntij* 'bask-SEASON, the season when crocodiles lie in the sun', *tulwarrangkarrak-mirntij* 'strip bark-SEASON; sugarbag time', *tarratarra-mirntij* 'warm-SEASON, season of warm sand [hot season]' and *tulwarrangkarrak-mirntij* 'blossom.scent-SEASON, season for sugarbag hunting or blossoms'.

4.7.14 *-mungkuj* OWNer

This suffix is added to a noun to indicate ownership, such as *ngaji-mungkuj* 'the one who calls him father'. It doesn't seem to relate to land custodianship. Instead *-mawu* is used (§5.1.2.3). An example of *-mungkuj* is given in (570). Ordinarily, ownership is expressed through possessive constructions where the dative marks this possessor (§8.3.2 and §8.3.3). In this case, *-mungkuj* marks the possessum which means it can be used when the possessor is not known.

(570) Nganayirla=rla nyila **warlaku-mungkuj?**
whatsitcalled=3OBL that dog-OWN
"Who's the owner of that dog?" (RW & DD with ECh: Meakins et al., 2016, p. 245)

4.7.15 *-nganyju(k)* GROUP

This suffix is used to refer to the group of people or things associated with the base noun e.g. *Jungurra-nganyju* 'Jungurra and his group'. It can be found with humans (571), other animates, body parts (572) and (573), and inanimates (574)–(576).

(571) **Bradley-nganyjuk** ngu=rlaa karrinyani
NAME-GROUP CAT=1INC.AUG.S be.IMPF.PST

ngurra yala-ngka=ma, outstation-ta=ma.
camp that-LOC=TOP outstation-LOC=TOP
"Bradley and others of us – well we all used to camp there at the outstation."
(🔈 CN: FM10_28_2a: 2:21min)

(572) **Ngarlaka-nganyju** ngu=rna pa-ni.
head-GROUP CAT=1EXC.MIN.S hit-PST
"I hit him all over, on the head and all."
(McConvell corpus: Meakins et al., 2016., p. 267)

(573) Nyila=ma turturl=ma ngu=lu yuwa-na-ni nyila=ma
that=TOP roast=TOP CAT=3AUG.S put-IMPF-PST that=TOP

jimirnkirt-nganyju=ma wararr=ma yuwa-na-ni lupu-ngka=ma
kidney-GROUP=TOP fat=TOP put-IMPF-PST guts-LOC=TOP

ngu=lu yuwa-na-ni walyak majul-ta.
CAT=3AUG.S put-IMPF-PST inside stomach-LOC
"They roasted all that kidney, fat and so on. They put it in the guts, inside the stomach." (VW with FM: Meakins et al., 2016, p. 268)

(574) Ngu=rnalu kampa-wu **janikeik-nganyju**, dina-wu.
CAT=1EXC.AUG.S cook-POT johnny.cake-GROUP lunch-DAT
"We will cook the little dampers for lunch." (🔈 VW: FM07_03_1a: 0:14min)

(575) Nyawa-rra=kata=rnalu ma-na-ni
this-PL=IMM=1EXC.AUG.S get-IMPF-PST

muying-nganyju ngu=lu ma-na-ni.
black.plum-GROUP CAT=3AUG.S get-IMPF-PST
"They had to collect black plums and other bush tucker then."
(🔈 VW: FM09_15_2d: 1:45min)

(576) Nyawa=ma=rli yuwa-ni **marru-nganyju** na yuwa-na-na.
this=TOP=1INC.MIN.S put-PST house-GROUP FOC put-IMPF-PRS
"Then they put up their station houses, yards and stock camps."
(🔊 PN: McNair_D2A: 1:41min)

It is not a number suffix because it can occur after other derivational morphology, as shown in (577), where it follows the deceased suffix *-yayi* and occurs before case-marker *-lu* 'ERG'.

(577) Marlurluka-lu=purrupurru lajalajap
old.man.REDUP-ERG=AND carry.on.shoulder.REDUP

kaku-yayi-nganyju-lu=ma.
FF-LATE-GROUP-ERG=TOP
"And the old men used to carry them – including my grandfather."
(🔊 VW: FM09_17_1d: 5:02min)

This suffix is also found in Ngarinyman and Mudburra (R. Green et al., 2019, p. 32; Jones, Schultze-Berndt, Denniss, et al., 2019, p. 22). Mudburra does not have the *-nganyjuk* variant and Ngarinyman does not have the *-nganyju* variant. Ngardi has the suffix *-marlu* but it is only found in kinterms, personal names, or place names to indicate a group of people from a particular place.

4.7.16 *-ngarna* ASSOCiative

The associative *-ngarna* is similar to the agentive *-kaji*, discussed in §4.7.6, where differences are discussed. The associative *-ngarna* is found deriving nominals from both coverbs and nominals. It is used to indicate a particular relationship which a noun has with another noun and/or an activity, as shown in (578) and (579).

(578) "Hey **ngawa-ngarna** nyuntu=ma ngu=n.
hey water-ASSOC 2MIN=TOP CAT=2MIN.S

Ngayu ngu=rna **kaja-ngarna**."
1EXC.MIN CAT=1EXC.MIN.S land-ASSOC
"'Hey you're a real water creature. I must be a land creature.'"
(🔊 VW: FM10_23_2a: Warrija Kirrawa: 3:10min)

(579) Ngu=rnalu ma-nku ngantipanguny,
CAT=1EXC.AUG.S get-POT 1EXC.AUG.DAT

buj-ngarna,	nyampa-kayirnikayirni	kuya.
bush-ASSOC	what-ETC	thus

"We want to get our own bush medicine, any type of medicine, we collect this lot." (🔈 VW: FM07_01_1e: 12:23min)

Some additional examples are given in (580) where nominals are derived from coverbs.

(580)	*jakarr-ngarna*	cover-ASSOC	'blanket'
	tiwu-ngarna	fly-ASSOC	'plane'[138]
	wulyuk-ngarna	wash-ASSOC	'washing day'

In some cases, the *-ngarna* suffix has fused and no other monomorphemic Gurindji word or Kriol/English borrowing is used to refer to the nominal. An example of this is *wirlangarna* 'idiot, mad person, deaf' (< dumb-ASSOC).[138]

In Gurindji, *-ngarna* can take additional plural marking *-rra*, as in *Takuraku-ngarna-rra* 'people who live at Daguragu', but this is simply a variant in Mudburra. In Warlmanpa, the form is *-ngarnarra* with no *-ngarna* variant (Browne, 2021).

Bilinarra, Ngarinyman, Malngin, Wanyjirra, Jaru and Jaminjung also have *-ngarna* in the same form and meaning (Ise, 1998, p. 30; Jones, Schultze-Berndt, Denniss, et al., 2019, pp. 20, 47; Meakins & Nordlinger, 2014, p. 158; Schultze-Berndt, 2003, p. 153; Senge, 2016, pp. 159–160; Tsunoda, 1981, p. 223). Ngardi also has the suffixes *-ngarnu* and *-ngawurr* which relate an entity to a place of habitation (ecological zone, place name, area) and are labelled 'denizen' suffixes. Ngardi also has *-jarra*, which is a more general associative suffix, with a similar functional range as *-ngarna* in Gurindji (Ennever, 2021). Warlmanpa has another associative *-palka* (Browne, 2021).

4.7.17 *-ngarri, -ngayarri* Name endings

Many traditional custodians of Gurindji country have names which are derived from sites on their country. These names are derived from an action or object associated with a Dreaming creature with the addition of a feminine or masculine ending, for example *Tupngarri* derives from the coverb *tup* 'pluck':

Women's name endings:	*-ngari, -ngarri, -ngali.*
Men's name ending:	*-ngayarri, -yarri.*

138 Recall that this is likely to be a Mudburra form and *tiwu-waji* is preferred in Gurindji.

4.7.18 *-nginyi* SOURCE

This suffix was introduced in the case section (§4.3.8) where we discussed some of the problems around its morphological classification. In this section, we discuss its derivational functions. We analyse this use of *-nginyi* as derivational because it forms new nominals and can therefore receive case-marking, as shown in (581).

(581) **Ngapaku-nginyi-lu** ngu=lu pa-ni.
grog-SOURCE-ERG CAT=3AUG.S hit-PST
"They hit him when they were drunk."
(McConvell corpus: Meakins et al., 2016, p. 268)

As a derivational morpheme, it forms adjectives from nouns, (582) and (586), and adjectives from infinitive verbs and coverbs (583)–(585). The forms resulting from adding this suffix are regarded as derived adjectives, rather than case-marked forms of nouns, because they add case suffixes, as shown in (581).

(582) **Larrpa-nginyi** yuwa-rra pakurl nyila=ma
before-SOURCE put-IMP rotten that=TOP

ngarin=ma, waj yuwa-rra.
meat=TOP throw put-IMP
"That meat is old and rotten. Throw it away." (🔊 VW: FM11_a160: 3:22min)

(583) Kataj-karra ngu=rnayinangulu pa-ni.
cut-ITER CAT=1EXC.AUG.S>3AUG.NS hit-PST

Kartpi=ma nyawa-rra=ma **katakataj-nginyi**.
hair=TOP this-PL=TOP cut.REDUP-SOURCE
"We were cutting their hair. This is cut hair." (🔊 VW: FM08_08_1a: 7:18min)

(584) Ngu=yi ma-rni Yibwoin=ma yala-ngka
CAT=1EXC.MIN.NS talk-PST NAME=TOP that-LOC

yarti-ngka=ma kurlarra, nyila nyamu **purtuj-nginyi** ngurra.
shade-LOC=TOP south that REL burn-SOURCE house
"That's what Yibwoin told me there in the shade at Kalkaringi
where there's the burnt out house." (🔊 VW: FM09_a120: 2:41min)

(585) Nyila=ma wirnangpurru=ma **turturl-nginyi**=ma ngu=lu
that=TOP kangaroo=TOP roast-SOURCE=TOP CAT=3AUG.S

ma-na-ni,	yuwa-na-ni	ngu=lu	nyampayirla-la	na,
do-IMPF-PST	put-IMPF-PST	CAT=3AUG.S	whatsitcalled-LOC	FOC

ngimal-a	ngu=lu	yuwa-na-ni,	pakarli-la
river.red.gum.leaves-LOC	CAT=3AUG.S	put-IMPF-PST	river.paperbark-LOC

or	bujij-ja.	Ngimal,	ngimal	wi	bin	kol-im.
or	bushes-LOC	gum.leaves	gum.leaves	1PL.S	PST	call-TR

Nyila=ma=rnalu	pa-na-ni	kuya-ngku=rnalu	julurrp.
that=TOP=1EXC.AUG.S	hit-IMPF-PST	thus-ERG=1EXC.AUG.S	cut.carcass

"They would get out the roasted kangaroo and put it on a bunch of leaves – some paperbark leaves. We call this bush plate 'ngimal'. Then we would cut up [the meat] like this." (🔊 VW: FM12_a178: 13:31min)

(586)	"Marntaj	ka-nga-nta=lu	tumaji	**pulngayit-nginyi**!"
	OK	take-IMPF-IMP=3AUG.S	CAUS	floodwater-SOURCE

"No worries, you can keep anything that's washed up."
(BB: Appendix: Text 4, Line 106)

Various types of semantic relationships are evident in the interpretation of SOURCE derived adjectives; thus someone who is *Kurraj-nginyi* 'Rainbow-Serpent-SOURCE' has had an encounter with that being and it has acted on him as an agent, perhaps giving him magical powers; someone who is *kurrupartu-nginyi* 'boomerang-SOURCE' may have been scarred in a boomerang fight thus the noun to which the suffix is attached in this case has acted as an instrument.

Bilinarra uses *-nginyi* in a similar manner and Warlmanpa has the suffix *-warnu* which seems to have similar functions (Browne, 2021).

4.7.19 *-ngurniny* SUPERLative

The *-ngurniny* suffix is vanishingly rare and its function is unclear. McConvell originally suggested that it encodes 'superlative', for example *jangkarni-ngurniny* 'big-SUPERL; the biggest'. In Ngardi and Jaru *-nguniny*, it is commonly found on terms for younger kin, for example children or younger siblings and also sweet or delectable food. In this sense may have a diminutive meaning which has expanded in the same way that 'sweet' has in English. In Ngardi there is also an intensifier *-nyayirniny* which is found on adverbials e.g. 'right on the back'. In Gurindji *-ngurniny* also occurs on coverbs combined with an ergative to create a reduced subordinate clause construction.

(587) Ngayu na ngu=rna **lurlu-ngurniny-ju**
1EXC.MIN FOC CAT=1EXC.MIN.S sit-SUPERL-ERG

na pa-na-na, kurla-yarra-said na, kataj-karra.
FOC hit-IMPF-PRS south-SIDE-SIDE FOC cut-ITER
"I sit down and cut the south side of the tree now." (🔈 VW: FM07_a027: 5:56min)

4.7.20 *-ny* Nominaliser (NMLZ)

This suffix is incredibly productive in Gurindji, particularly when it combines with case suffixes. Here we discuss its solo use, as well as in various combinations. We also point to other sections where we discuss its different functions.

On its own, *-ny* derives nominals from nominals and coverbs. For example, in (588) *-ny* combines with the adjective *palki* 'flat' to create the noun 'covering' and in (589) it attaches to the coverb *janga* 'sick' to create the noun 'bad flu'.

(588) **Palki-ny**-ta paku yuwa-na-na.
flat-NMLZ-LOC vomit put-IMPF-PRS
"She vomited on the tablecloth." (🔈 BW: FM07_a043: 12:53min)

(589) Jiwarrp ngu=rnalu ma-na-na, nyamu=waa=ngantipa
gather CAT=1EXC.AUG.S do-IMPF-PRS REL=REL=1EXC.AUG.NS

piyarrp yuwa-na-ni, jangkarni **janga-ny**
report put-IMPF-PST big sick-NMLZ

na wajirrki jangkarni.
FOC flu big
"We are collecting it because [the nurse] told us about the Swine Flu."
(🔈 VW: FM09_14_1a: 6:31min)

Other examples are *partikipany* 'nut-EP-NMLZ, eel-tailed catfish', *jawurrany* 'steal-NMLZ, thief', *wuukarrany* 'fear-NMLZ, scaredy cat' and *yurrany* 'herd-NMLZ, armpit sweat'. A curious example is *kulany* 'humbugging person' which may derive from the negative particle *kula*. Other examples use the epenthetic *-ku* (which in these cases is identical to the dative), for example *wiitkuny* 'show-EP-NMLZ, index finger', *karrapkuny* 'look-EP-NMLZ, prone to looking' and *kaluyany* 'walk-EP-NMLZ, prone to walking' (in this case, the epenthetic is *-ya*). The suffix *-kaji* discussed in §4.7.6 performs the same function with coverbs and is completely productive.

On its own, *-ny* also attaches to free pronouns to create dative pronouns (§6.1.1) and to the interrogative *nyatpa-ny* 'what kind?' (§5.3.6). It also attaches to demonstratives to create new nominal stems, for example *kuyany* 'thus-NMLZ, this kind', *murlany* 'this-NMLZ, this place' and *yalany* 'that-NMLZ, that place' (§5.1.2.2).

The nominaliser *-ny* is also found suffixed to dative-marked nouns in the genitive function. Both Jaru and Wanyjirra have *-kuny* as more productive genitive suffixes, as shown in (590) and (591). The moiety names were also formed through this combination: *Jalwa-wu-ny* 'heron-DAT-NMLZ, Lirraku moiety' and *Warlawurru-wu-ny* 'eagle-DAT-NMLZ, Yilyku moiety' (§1.8.1).

(590) **Marluka-wu-ny** ngu=lu jawurra ma-ni.
old.man-DAT-NMLZ CAT=3AUG.S steal do-PST
"They stole the old man's [things]."
(McConvell 1996 sketch grammar manuscript)

(591) Ngayiny-nginyi karu-nginyi ngu=rna
1EXC.MIN.DAT-SOURCE child-SOURCE CAT=1EXC.MIN.S

ka-nga-ni, **Jampin-ku-ny** Darwin-ngurlu.
bring-IMPF-PST SUBSECT-DAT-NMLZ Darwin-ABL
"I brought them from my kid Jampin's [place] from Darwin."
(🔈 LB: McNair_A1C: 1:30min)

When the dative+NMLZ then combines with the locative, two meanings are created. One is a derivational suffix 'lacking' (592), discussed in §4.7.10, and the other is a comitative (593), discussed in §4.3.9. Both have slightly different grammaticalisation paths as discussed in §4.7.10. Note that the sequence dative+NMLZ+locative in (594) is the same as the sequence making up the comitative combination (593). The difference between the two lies in the fact that the comitative combination is obligatorily cross-referenced by a non-subject pronominal. If the dative+NMLZ+locative combination is not cross-referenced, it is interpreted as a genitive, as discussed above.

(592) Warlayarra-**wunyja** ngu=rna.
tobacco-LACKING CAT=1EXC.MIN.S
"I'm desperate for tobacco." (🔈 VW: FM12_a174: 12:38min)

(593) Ngu=rna=**rla** tak karrinya **marluka-wunyja** ngurra-ngka.
CAT=1EXC.MIN.S=3OBL sit be.PST old.man-COM camp-LOC
"I sat down **with the old man** at the camp."
(McConvell 1996 sketch grammar manuscript)

(594)

Ngu=rna	tak	karrinya	**marluka-wu-ny-ja**	ngurra-ngka.
CAT=1EXC.MIN.S	sit	be.PST	old.man-DAT-NMLZ-LOC	camp-LOC

"I sat down **at the old man's** camp."
(McConvell corpus: Meakins et al, 2016, p. 252)

The dative+NMLZ+locative combination is also found in reduced subordinate clauses, as shown in (595).

(595)

Ngunti	ngu=n	pirrkap	ma-nku	**nyanuny-ja**
light	CAT=2MIN.S	make	do-POT	3MIN.DAT-LOC

karrap-kula,	**Nangari-wu-ny-ja.**
watch-LOC	SUBSECT-DAT-NMLZ-LOC

"You can make the light while Nangari watches on." (🔈 VW: FM09_17_2a: 1:24min)

The final case sequence which *-ny* participates in involves the combination of dative+ NMLZ+allative, as shown in (596). Recall that there is some variation with the free pronouns about the order of the dative (see §4.3.5.2 and §4.3.9).

(596)

Kapuku-wu-ny-jirri	**nyanuny-ku-jirri,**
sister-DAT-NMLZ-ALL	3MIN.DAT-DAT-ALL

malyju-ngku	ngu	wany	yuwa-ni.
boy-ERG	CAT	throw	put-PST

"The boy throws it to where his sister is." (🔈 VW: FHM098: 2:07min)

4.7.21 *-pari* ADJectiviser

This suffix has two forms *-pari* (consonant-final stems), (597) and (598), and *-wari* (vowel-final and liquid-final stems), (599) and (600).

(597)

Wart-pari	rarraj	nganta=wula	ya-na-na.
return-ADJ	run	ALLE=3UA.S	go-IMPF-PRS

"So they ran back again." (🔈 VW: FM10_a155: Ngarlking Karu: 5:20min)

(598)

Yibwoin-ju	maitbi	wankaj	ngu	pa-ni,	**kiturlk-pari.**
NAME-ERG	maybe	no.good	CAT	hit-PST	bend-ADJ

"Maybe Theresa cut a crooked tree down." (🔈 VW: FM09_a120: 1:51min)

(599)

Palyurr-wari	ngu,	ngu=yinangulu	tal
receding.hairline-ADJ	CAT	CAT=3AUG.S>3AUG.NS	call

pa-na-ni,	kartpi-murlung=ma	kankunungkarra-la=ma.
hit-IMPF-PST	hair-PRIV=TOP	on.top-LOC=TOP

"We say they have a receding hairline when they haven't got much hair on top of their heads." (🔈 VW: FM12_a177: 6:06min)

(600)

Karnti	karrinyana	**tuly-wari**.
tree	be.IMPF.PRS	bend-ADJ

"The tree is bent over." (🔈 TD: FM10_a166: 5:24min)

This suffix derives adjectives from some coverbs and adverbs, although it is not highly productive. One use is derivation from coverbs such as *kiturlk* 'bend' (598) *tuly* 'bend' (600) which can be used with intransitive verbs to refer to a change of state. The appropriate English translation is often a past participle such as 'bent'. Another example is *kirt-pari* 'break-ADJ, broken'. This suffix also derives a few adjectives from adverbs of location, for example *wijku-pari* 'near-ADJ, close'. Some further examples are given in (601).

(601)

jalalang-pari	upside.down-ADJ	'sloped'
jampurlk-pari	squash-ADJ	'squashed'
mum-pari	be.dark-ADJ	'darkness'
walp-pari	clear.out ADJ	'clearing'
winkily-wari	aggression-ADJ	'aggressive'

Bilinarra, Ngarinyman, Wanyjirra and Mudburra also have *-pari* and *-wari* in the same function (Green et al., 2019, p. 53; Jones, Schultze-Berndt, Denniss, et al., 2019, pp. 20, 47; Meakins & Nordlinger, 2014, p. 161; Senge, 2016, p. 159). Warlmanpa only has *-wari*, and Ngardi and Eastern Walmajarri only have *-pari*. Ngardi also has a frozen form *-pari* on some nouns (Ennever, 2021). This suffix is also found in an unrelated language of the Victoria River District, Jaminjung (Schultze-Berndt, 2003, p. 153).

4.7.22 *-piya* BIT

This suffix occurs on adjectives to indicate 'a bit more'. It is an invariant form with no allomorphs which is unusual for Gurindji. Gurindji speakers translate this suffix as 'little bit', but it can be thought of as moderating the force of an adjective or an adverb, as shown in (602) and (603). In the right context, as in (604), it can have the force of a comparative 'more'.

(602) Nyawa yirna **jangkarni-piya-lu**=warla
this flower big-BIT-ERG=FOC

nyamu nga-rna-na nyila=ma kalwaki.
REL eat-IMPF-PRS that=TOP flower.sp
"This flower which the bigger (bird) is eating is called *kalwaki.*"
(McConvell corpus: Meakins et al., 2016, p. 449)

(603) Kula karrinyana kankula-k-piya **kanyjurra-k-piya**
NEG be.IMPF.PRS up-ALL-BIT down-ALL-BIT

pa-rru=wula ngunyjung=ma.
hit-POT=3UA.S honey=TOP
"It's not up there, cut it a little bit below." (🔈 TD: FM07_a028: 4:51min)

(604) **Yamak-piya** yuwa-rra langa-wu nyirn-kupal.
quiet-BIT put-IMP ear-DAT deafen-AVERS
'Make it a bit quieter so people won't go deaf.' (RW & DD with ECh)

Bilinarra, Ngarinyman and Malngin also have this form with the same function (Ise, 1998, p. 31; Jones, Schultze-Berndt, Denniss, et al., 2019, p. 20; Meakins & Nordlinger, 2014, p. 162). In Warlpiri and Warlmanpa, the form *-piya* is a semblative.

4.7.23 *-rntarn* EXCESS

This is a highly restricted suffix (probably borrowed from Wardaman (Merlan, 1994)) which usually describes a person or animal which is always eating or drinking something, for example *ngawa-rntarn* 'water-EXCESS; always drinking'; *tanku-rtarn* 'tucker-EXCESS; always eating'. The same function is generally expressed by the agentive suffix *-kaji* which has a much wider scope (§4.7.6). Unlike the agentive suffix, the excess suffix does not attach to verbs and coverbs. It is not observed in Bilinarra, Mudburra, Ngardi or Warlmanpa.

4.7.24 *-wariny* ALONE

This suffix has two forms *-wariny* and *-warij* which might relate to NCD lenition (§2.3.4.1). Younger people use this suffix in Gurindji Kriol as *-rayiny(j)*. It is a derivational suffix, not a clitic, as demonstrated in (605), which shows case-marking attached on the outside of *-warij.*

(605) <u>Yeah</u> pampapawu ngaja=n=junu
Yeah in.trouble ADMON=2MIN.S=RR

ka-nga-na **nyuntu-warij-ju**=ma.
take-IMPF-PRS 2MIN-ALONE-ERG=TOP
"You might get yourself into trouble on your own." (🔈 VW: FM12_a177: 6:38min)

It is mostly found with free pronouns, for example (605)–(607), but it is found more rarely on nominals (608). It has the meaning 'alone'.

(606) Jala=ma Nangala=ma ya-na-na ngu Barunga-yirri.
today=TOP SUBSECT=TOP go-IMPF-PRS CAT place.name-ALL

Nyawa=ma=ja **ngayirra-warij** Nangari-wu=ma
this=TOP=1EXC.UA.S 1EXC.UA-ALONE SUBSECT-DAT=TOP

jarrakap ngu=rna=rla ma-rna-na **ngayu-warij**.
talk CAT=1EXC.MIN.S=3OBL talk-IMPF-PRS 1EXC.MIN-ALONE
"Biddy is going to Barunga today. So here it's just the two of us, with me on my own talking to Felicity." (🔈 VW: FM09_14_1a: 10:06min)

(607) Nyantu-**wariny** karrinyana ngu lurlu.
3MIN-ALONE be.IMPF.PRS CAT sit
"He's sitting down on his own." (🔈 BW: FM07_a043: 2:12min)

(608) Nyawa=rla marluka **purlka-wariny**=ma karrinyana ngu.
this=3OBL old.man old.man-ALONE=TOP be.IMPF.PRS CAT
"Here's where the old man stays alone."
(🔈 RW: EC98_a015: Marlarluka: 9:35min)

This suffix also attaches to cardinals to mean 'far away'. The link between these two meanings 'alone' and 'further away' is perhaps attenuation (see §5.2.1 for more details about the use of this suffix with cardinals).

(609) Ngu=rnawula pa-na-na kujarrap-pa=rni
CAT=1INC.AUG.S hit-IMPF-PRS pair-EP=ONLY

kaa-rni-wariny karla-rni-wariny.
east-UP-FAR west-UP-FAR
"We both cut down trees farther up east and west."
(🔈 VW: FM08_a101: 12:56min)

Ngardi has a suffix *-kariny* which often means 'other' (like Gurindji's *-kari*), but on free pronouns it also means 'alone' and can also attach to cardinals with a similar function as Gurindji. Warlpiri has *=kari* 'on and on', *-kari* 'other'; and *-kari* 'towards' on cardinals. It also has a free nominal *kari* 'other'. In Mudburra, we find *-kari* 'other', *karikari* 'a little bit far' and *kari* 'far away'. Warlmanpa has *kari* 'far away' but doesn't have the suffix.

4.7.25 *-witi* SITE

This suffix has the forms *-witi* and *-piti*. It marks places where an activity is or was regularly carried out, for example *ngurra-witi* 'camp-SITE, camping place' and *panyja-witi* 'river.edge-SITE, habitat', as shown in (610) and (611). This suffix can also form nouns from coverbs, for example *wuyurrunkarra-witi* 'fishing-SITE, fishing place'.

(610) An **ngurra-witi** ngu=ngantipa nyila,
and camp-SITE CAT=1EXC.AUG.NS that

kurla-rni-mpal-la nyawa kurla-rni-mpal-la.
south-UP-EDGE-LOC this south-UP-EDGE-LOC
"And we had a camping place on the south side." (🔊 VW: FM09_15_1a: 0:14min)

(611) **Panyja-witi-ngka** karrinya warrija=ma nyila=ma.
river.edge-SITE-LOC be.PST crocodile=TOP that=TOP
"That crocodile used to live in this habitat." (🔊 VW: FM12_a183: 23:23min)

The form and function of this suffix is not observed in other Ngumpin-Yapa languages, except Bilinarra. There is an unrelated *-witi* suffix in Jaru but it is a purposive (Tsunoda, 1981, p. 230).

4.7.26 *-wirrirri* OWNer

This is another owner suffix (see §4.7.11 for *-mala* and §4.7.14 for *-mungkuj*). It has a limited number of stems it attaches to. These include *wajarra-wirrirri* 'play-OWN, composer of corroboree'. This suffix does not appear in other Ngumpin-Yapa languages. Warlmanpa has the coverb *wirriri* 'go around in circle'.

4.7.27 *-wulp* AMONG

This suffix is only found following the locative case suffix, for example *ngumpit-ta-wulp* 'among (Aboriginal) people', and *yuka-ngka-wulp* 'in the middle of the grass'. It could be possibly analysed as a clitic since it appears on the outside of case-marking, or it is possibly a compound form *-tawulp* or *-ngkawulp*. An example in a clause is given in (612).

(612) **Karnti-ka-wulp** ngu=yina paraj pu-nya najing, wakip-jirri
tree-LOC-AMONG CAT=3AUG.NS find pierce-PST nothing white-ALL

na, wakip.
FOC white
"Then he found the white piece of fabric hanging in the trees."
(🔊 DD: McNair_G1: 12:16min)

There is also one example where it appears to be attached to a coverb *jitarttawulp* 'hate-LOC-AMONG, change promised arrangement because husband dislikes wife', although how the meaning relates to the spatial nouns isn't clear.

4.7.28 *-yukawuk* ALMOST

Another rarely occurring suffix is *-yukawuk* 'almost', for example *jangkarni-yukawuk* 'almost big'. Another example of a noun stem is given in (613). It also occurs with other stems such as case-marked coverbs *parr-wu-yukawuk* 'land-DAT-ALMOST, almost ready to land', as shown in (614).

(613) Wulngarn kankula **mangarri-yukawuk**=parla.
sun up veg.food-ALMOST=FOC
"The sun's above, it's close to lunch time."
(RW & DD with ECh: Meakins et al., 2016, p. 452)

(614) Kalpun pinparang ya-ni **parr-u-yukawuk.**
whistling.kite take.off go-PST land-DAT-ALMOST
"The raptor took off after almost landing on the grass."
(RW & DD with ECh: Meakins et al., 2016, p. 313)

4.8 Clitics

Most of the clitics in Gurindji are unrestricted in that they can occur with most parts of speech. Three clitics are specific to nominals, hence are described here. The other clitics are discussed in §10.1.

4.8.1 =*payin/wayin* ETC

Like the focus clitic =*warla/parla* (§10.1.7), this clitic also has two allomorphs: =*wayin* which follows vowels and =*payin* which follows consonants. Example (615) shows each of these allomorphs.

(615) Nyamu=n=nga karrwa-wu ngumpit-kari-wu, ngaja=ngku=rla
REL=2MIN.S=DUB have-POT man-OTHER-DAT ADMON=2MIN.NS=3OBL

jayi-nga-na **nyampa=wayin** **ngarin=payin.**
give-IMPF-PRS something=ETC meat=ETC
"If you wear another man's [body painting designs], you'll have to give him something including meat." (McConvell corpus: Meakins et al., 2016, p. 260)

It is classified as a clitic because it follows inflectional morphology, as shown in (616).

(616) Nyila=ma walaparr na ma-ni. Ngaja=nga=rla
that=TOP jump.in.shock FOC do-PST ADMON=DUB=3OBL

kayi-kayi pa-na-na maiti **pulngayarri-lu=wayin.**
chase-REDUP hit-IMPF-PRS maybe bull-ERG=ETC
"It made [the horse] jump up suddenly. Maybe a bull or something started chasing it." (🔈 VW: FM12_a179: 6:15min)

This clitic only occurs on nominals. It only occurs rarely in the corpus and is therefore difficult to discern its function. McConvell (1983, p. 8) suggests that when it is used alone it roughly has the meaning of 'x among others' where x is in the scope of =*wayin*. In this sense, it can be translated as 'etc', 'including' or 'as well as'.

(617) **Parntawurru=wayin** ngu=rna pa-ni.
back=ETC CAT=1EXC.MIN.S hit-PST
"I hit it on the back as well as other places." (McConvell, 1983, p. 8)

If =*rningan* is also used, it suggests that an action is presupposed and has the meaning of 'too'.

(618) **Parntawurru=wayin** ngu=rna pa-ni=**rningan.**
back=ETC CAT=1EXC.MIN.S hit-PST=AGAIN
"I hit it on the back too." (McConvell, 1983, p. 8)

Some further examples are given in (619)–(626). Note that it is very common on interrogatives.

(619) **Ngartung=payin** ka-nga-ni.
good.thing=ETC bring-IMPF-PST
"He brought it, and a good thing too." (ECh: RW & DD)

(620) Ngu=rna paraj pu-ngku **nyampa=wayin.**
CAT=1EXC.MIN.S find pierce-POT something=ETC
"I'll find something else." (🔈 VW: FM10_23_2a: Warrija Kirrawa: 4:33min)

(621) Nyampa-ku, **ngana=wayin** ngu=rla
what-ERG someone=ETC CAT=3OBL

maiti ma-rni nyila=ma marluka=ma.
maybe talk-PST that=TOP old.man=TOP
"Well, it was as if he was talking to someone, that old man."
(🔈 RW: EC97_a007: Warli: 2:46min)

(622) Ngumayi-jang-kulu ngu=lu **nyila=wayin** pulyjarr karru.
behind-TIME-ERG CAT=3AUG.S that=ETC crush be.POT
"The younger generations will crush that up too."
(McConvell corpus: Meakins et al., 2016, p. 335)

(623) Puul-nginyi warrkuj ngu=rli
fish.trap-SOURCE pick.up CAT=1INC.MIN.S

ma-na-na **yinarrwa=wayin**.
do-IMPF-PRS barramundi=ETC
"We even get barramundi from the fish-trap."
(McConvell corpus: Meakins et al., 2016, p. 347)

(624) Lawart ngu=rla ka-nga-na, nyila=ma, mangarri=ma,
steal CAT=3OBL take-IMPF-PRS that=TOP bread=TOP

or **ngarin=payin** **nyampa=wayin**.
or meat=ETC what=ETC
"Someone takes off with someone's bread or meat."
(🔈 VW: FM12_a175: 00:19min)

(625) Nyamu=lu=nga **ngana=wayin** ya-nku kurrurij-jawung, marntaj.
REL=3AUG.S=DUB anyone=ETC go-POT car-PROP OK
"If anybody wants to go by car, that's all right."
(McConvell corpus: Meakins et al., 2016, p. 266)

(626) Ngaja=nta taarlak-karra ya-na-na **nyampa-kurra=wayin.**
ADMON=2AUG.S danger-ITER go-IMPF-PRS something-ALL=ETC
"You mob might be in danger of something." (🔈 VW: FM12_a177: 4:35min)

4.8.2 =*pirak* CORRECT

This clitic attaches to a nominal stem to indicate that the word to which it is attached is the correct and appropriate one to use. It is particularly used with kinship terms, where correct designation of a person's many classificatory relatives is a cultural imperative.

(627) **Ngumparna-rra=pirak** ma-nyja=ngayirra.
husband-DYAD.PL=CORRECT talk-IMP=1EXC.UA.NS
"Correctly you should call us husband and wife."
(McConvell corpus: Meakins et al., 2016, p. 325)

(628) Nyila=ma kayilirra-ngarna jaru. **Jawi=pirak**=ma
that=TOP north-ASSOC language fire=CORRECT=TOP

Ngarinyman. Ngantipa=ma=rnalu ma-rna-na
Ngarinyman 1EXC.AUG=TOP=1EXC.AUG.S talk-IMPF-PRS

murla-ny-mawu, **warlu=pirak.**
this-NMLZ-DWELL fire=CORRECT
"That's from the northern language. 'Jawi' is really a Ngarinyman word. We, the people of this area, really say 'warlu'." (🔈 VW: FM11_a162: 1:33min)

4.8.3 =*purrupurru* AND someone or something else

A clitic which has a similar meaning as -*kuwang* is =*purrupurru*, but it can be found on a broader range of nominals, as shown in (629)–(633), and it can mean more than simply 'one other'. It is classified as a clitic because it occurs after inflections as shown in (630) and (631).

(629) Ngu=yi ju-ni, ngu=yi ju-ni
CAT=1EXC.MIN.NS swear-PST CAT=1EXC.MIN.NS swear-PST

ngu=yi ju-ni ngu=ngayirra ju-ni
CAT=1EXC.MIN.NS swear-PST CAT=1EXC.UA.NS swear-PST

ngayu=purrupurru	murnungku.
1EXC.MIN=AND	policeman

"He swore at me, at us, he swore at me and the policeman too."
(🔊 DD: EC98_a025: Rawuyarri: 14:12min)

(630)

Ngu=wula=rla	warlu	pirrkap	ma-ni	nyawa,
CAT=3UA.S=3OBL	fire	make	do-PST	this

yalu-ngku	ngarlmurang-kulu,	**Nangala-ngku=purrupurru**.
that-ERG	trirel.kin-ERG	SUBSECT-ERG=AND

"Your two cousins who are my sisters made this fire for [damper] – and Nangala too." (🔊 VW: FM09_13_3a: 1:18min)

(631)

Marlurluka-lu=purrupurru	lajalajap
old.man.REDUP-ERG=AND	carry.on.shoulder.REDUP

kaku-yayi-nganyju-lu=ma.
FF-LATE-GROUP-ERG=TOP

"And the old men used to carry them – including my grandfather."
(🔊 VW: FM09_17_1d: 5:02min)

(632)

Tanku=ma	nyawa,	**warlayarra=purrupurru**.	Marntaj.
food=TOP	this	tobacco=AND	OK

"Here's some tucker, and tobacco too. OK." (DD: EC98_a025: Rawuyarri: 11:54min)

(633)

Wipuwipuk	ma-nta	tanku	yala-nginyi.
take.out.REDUP	do-IMP	food	that-SOURCE

Walyawalyak	nyamu=npayi	yuwa-ni,
inside.REDUP	REL=2MIN.S>1EXC.MIN.NS	put-PST

warrayarl=purrupurru	mangarri	**an**	tinned-beef-nganyju.
sugar=AND	bread	and	tinned-beef-GROUP

"Take the tucker out of that one. Where you put the sugar, bread and tinned beef inside for me." (🔊 VW: FM12_a183: 10:35min)

This form is also found in Bilinarra and Ngarinyman as *-purrupurru* (Jones, Schultze-Berndt, Denniss, et al., 2019, p. 22; Meakins & Nordlinger, 2014, p. 222) and in Ngardi as *-purupuru*, but the meaning is slightly different: 'all of the x, many x's, as well as x' (Ennever, 2021). Ngardi has the form *=rlangu* which has some of these functions. It is also synonymous with but unrelated to the Ngardi dyad suffix *-rlangu* (Ennever, 2021). In Mudburra, the suffix *=ja* is used with that same meaning 'and, too, also'.

5 Closed class nominals

This chapter focuses on the closed class nominals which includes demonstratives (§5.1), cardinal terms (§5.2.1), river drainage terms (§5.2.2) verticality terms (§5.2.3), and ignoratives, which include the nominals that express interrogatives and indefinites (§5.3).

5.1 Demonstratives

Gurindji has four sets of demonstratives: *nyawa* and its suppletive steams *murla-* and *murlu-* 'PROXimal, this', *nyila* and its suppletive steams *yala-* and *yalu-* 'DIStal, that', *kuya* 'thus' and *nyanawu* 'RECOGnitional, you know the one'.

Note there is also a single form *kati* 'that one in the distance' which does not decline in the same way as the other demonstratives (see Table 20). This single undeclined form also appears in Ngarinyman and Bilinarra (Jones, Schultze-Berndt, Denniss, et al., 2019, p. 98; Meakins, 2013, p. 103). It is possible that the form is borrowed from Mudburra. It has a three series demonstrative system including *kati* 'that one close up' which contrasts with *yali* 'that one further away' (Green et al., 2019, p. 38). Interestingly the proximal/distal value of *kati* has flipped between Mudburra and the Victoria River Ngumpin languages.

Demonstratives decline in the same manner as other nominals with nine cases distinguished – three core cases; ergative, nominative, accusative (based on a tripartite analysis see §4.3), one additional grammatical case: dative; and five local cases: locative, allative, ablative, source and terminative. We have no examples of comitative, perlative or motivative case in the corpus, although it is possible that these exist too since they only occur rarely with other nominals. The forms of the case-markers follow the normal nominal forms for the appropriate length syllable for vowel-final stems. The demonstrative paradigms are given in Table 20. In this table, any forms not attested in our corpus are marked with # and are simply based on regularities in the rest of the paradigm.

Identical systems but not necessarily forms are found in Bilinarra, Ngarinyman, Malngin, Jaru and Wanyjirra (Ise, 1998, p. 27; Jones, Schultze-Berndt, Denniss, et al., 2019, p. 27; Meakins & Nordlinger, 2014, pp. 169–171; Senge, 2016, pp. 110–111; Tsunoda, 1981, pp. 61–62). Also of interest, Mudburra, Western Walmajarri and Ngardi have *minya* 'this' as a stem, as well as *murla-/murlu-* (though note that *murla-/murlu-* is only found in the Western dialect of Mudburra not the Eastern dialect). They are the only Ngumpin languages which use this stem, which is curious given the distances (phylogenetic and physical) between the languages. In general, Eastern Mudburra has a three-way system *minya/nginya* 'this', *kadi* 'close' and *yali* 'there', which are

https://doi.org/10.1515/9783110746884-005

Table 20: Demonstrative declension in Gurindji.

	nyawa **'this [one]'**	***nyila*** **'that [one]'**	***kuya*** **'like that'**	***nyanawu*** **'you know the one'**
Nominative / Accusative	*nyawa* 'this [one]'	*nyila* 'that [one]'	*kuya* 'like that'	*nyanawu* 'you know the one'
Ergative 'agent'	*murlungku* *nyawangku* 'this [one] did it'	*yalungku* *nyilangku* 'this [one] did it'	*kuyangku* 'do it like that [one]'	*nyanawulu* 'you know the one who did it'
Dative 'to, for'	*murluwu* *nyawawu* 'for this [one]'	*yaluwu* *nyilawu* 'for that [one]'	*kuyawu* 'like that'	*nyanawuwu* 'for the one we know'
Locative 'at, in, on'	*murlangka* *nyawangka* 'here'	*yalangka* *nyilangka* 'there'	*kuyangka* 'that's when'	*nyanawula* 'at the place we know'
Allative 'towards'	*murlangkurra* *nyawangkurra* '[to] here'	*yalangkurra* *nyilangkurra* '[to] there'	*kuyangkurra* 'like there'	*nyanawuyirri* 'to the place we know'
Ablative 'from'	*murlangurlu* *nyawanginyi* 'from here'	*yalangurlu* *nyilanginyi* 'from there'	*#kuyangurlu* 'like from there'	*nyanawungurlu* 'from the place we know'
Source 'from'	*murlanginyi* *nyawanginyi* 'from here'	*yalanginyi* *nyilanginyi* 'from there'	*kuyanginyi* 'like from there'	*nyanawunginyi* 'from the place we know'
Terminative 'up to'	*murlakijak* 'up to here'	*yalakijak* 'up to there'	*kuyakijak* 'as X as'	*#nyanawukijak* 'right up to the place we know'

distinct from Gurindji (Green et al., 2019, p. 38). Warlmanpa also has a three-way system *yimpa* 'this', *yarri* 'that' and *yali* 'that (removed)' (Browne, 2021).

The adverbial demonstrative has slightly different forms in different Ngumpin languages which reflects a dialect chain: *kuya* (Bilinarra, Ngarinyman, Gurindji, Wanyjirra and Warlmanpa), *kuwala* (Mudburra), *kuwa* (Malngin, Wanyjirra, Jaru) and *kuja* (Jaru, Ngardi). In terms of differences in the recognitional demonstratives, Wanyjirra and Ngardi has *jangu* (Ennever, 2021; Senge, 2016). Ngardi also uses the forms *nyanawu* and *yangka*. Warlmanpa has *nyanungu* (Browne, 2021).

5.1.1 Form

Nyawa and *nyila* are the nominative and accusative forms of the proximal and distal demonstratives, as exemplified by (634). On their own, *nyawa* and *nyila* can also mean 'here' and 'there' respectively. The suppletive stems, *murla-/murlu-* and *yala-/yalu-*, are generally only used when inflected, as shown in (635).

(634) Ngu=rna=rla ma-rni Nana-wu,
CAT=1EXC.MIN.S=3OBL say-PST SUBSECT-DAT

"Nyawa jintara partiki-la."
this another nut.tree-LOC
"I said to Nanaku – 'Here's this other one in a nut tree'." (TD: FM07_a28: 4:34min)

(635) **Murlu-ngku=ma** janginyina-lu=ma pa-ni ngu
this-ERG=TOP lightning-ERG=TOP hit-PST CAT

ngawa=ma ngakparn na **murla-ngka=ma** walyak.
water=TOP frog FOC this-LOC=TOP inside
"This lightning struck the water (when) the frog was in here."
(BW: FM07_06_2a: 2:24min)

Note that when McConvell documented Gurindji in the 1970s, he observed that *nyawa* and *nyila* did not decline for case and were the stems used for adnominal and derivational suffixes, for example *nyawa-yawung* (this-PROP, 'with this one'). Similarly in Jaru, Tsunoda (1981, p. 62) observed that the plain forms of the demonstratives did not decline in the 1970s. The current generation of Gurindji speakers seems to use the inflected forms of plain stems and suppletive stems interchangeably so we don't distinguish them here. Examples are given in (636) and (637). This variation is probably the result of morphological regularisation, not uncommon in language change.

(636) Yala-nginyi=ma **nyila-ngku=ma** narrinyjila-lu=ma
that-SOURCE=TOP that-ERG=TOP turtle-ERG=TOP

ngu paya-rni na warlaku=ma wartan-ta.
CAT bite-PST FOC dog=TOP hand-LOC
"After that, that turtle bit the dog on the tail." (EO: FM07_a002: 16:17min)

(637) **Nyawa-ngka**=ma=rna=nga karru ngayu-warij jarrakap,
this-LOC=TOP=1EXC.MIN.S=DUB be.POT 1EXC.MIN-ALONE talk

ngu=rna=ngku ma-rna-na ngayu nyununy=ma.
CAT=1EXC.MIN.S=2MIN.NS talk-IMPF-PRS 1EXC.MIN 2MIN.DAT=TOP
"I might be here talking on my own. I'm talking to you."
(VW: FM09_14_1a: 10:40min)

The stems *murla-* and *yala-* can also exist on their own to mean 'around here' or 'around there', but not 'this' and 'that'. An example of *murla* 'here' is given in (638).

(638) Kankula **murla**=ma=yinangkula
up this=TOP=3AUG.S>3AUG.NS

kurlng=parla yuwa-ni, maarn=ma.
form.cloud=FOC put-PST cloud=TOP
"Clouds started forming here over them." (🔊 VW: FM10_23_4: 2:05min)

A rule of regressive vowel assimilation applies to the stems *murla-* and *yala-*, where *murlu-* and *yalu-* are used when the final vowel of the suffix is a /u/ and the suffix is one syllable, as in (639) and (640). Thus the allative and ablative are the exception to this because they are longer than one syllable: *-ngkurra* 'ALL' *-ngurlu* 'ABL', as in (641) and (642). See §2.3.3 for further discussion.

(639) Namawurru=ma karrwa-rna-na **yalu-ngku** wanyarri-lu=ma.
sugarbag=TOP have-IMPF-PRS that-ERG bauhinia-ERG=TOP
"The bauhinia trees have sugarbag." (🔊 TD: FM10_a146: 1:11min)

(640) Murnungku-lu=ma ngu=lu=rla ma-rni
policeman-ERG=TOP CAT=3AUG.S=3OBL talk-PST

yalu-wu=ma kirri-wu=ma, "Ka-ngka wart."
that-DAT=TOP woman-DAT=TOP take-IMP return
"The police officers told the woman, "Take it back."
(🔊 VW: FM10_27_1a: Kurraj Story from Halls Creek: 4:04min)

(641) Kalu ngu=rnalu ya-ni **yala-ngkurra** karnti-kurra.
walk CAT=1EXC.AUG.S go-PST that-ALL tree-ALL
"We walked that way to the tree." (🔊 VW: FM07_a027: 0:19min)

(642) Yurra ngu=rnalu ma-ni **yala-ngurlu**=ma kurrarntal.
scare.away CAT=1EXC.AUG.S do-PST that-ABL=TOP brolga
"We hunted the brolga away from there." (🔊 VW: FM07_058: 4:33min)

Finally, *nyawa* is frequently heard as *nyaa* due to the phonological process by which a sequence /awa/ is often shortened to [aa] (see §2.3.2).

Kuya 'like that, thus' has a Western variant *kuwa*, but no separate suppletive form. *Nyanawu* 'recognitional' also only has one form. It inflects like other nominals which have trisyllabic vowel-final stems using the *-lu/-la* series with ergatives and locatives (§4.3).

5.1.2 Additional and interesting uses of morphology

Demonstratives combine with other nominal morphology, such as the adnominal and derivational suffixes described in §4.6 and §4.7. Some examples of demonstratives combining with the adnominal proprietive are given in (643) and (644). Note that both the suppletive stem and plain stem are used, which reflects the variation found in the case forms.

(643)

Waninyana	tarlu-tarlu-warra	karnti-yawung-pa=rni
fall.IMPF.PRS	bob.around-REDUP-ITER	tree-PROP-EP=ONLY

yalu-yawung	tarlu-tarlu-warra.
that-PROP	bob.around-REDUP-ITER

"He bobbed about with the tree." (🔊 PN: McNair_K1A: 2:57min)

(644)

Nyawa-yawung-kulu	ngu=rnalu	warrkap
this-PROP-ERG	CAT=1EXC.AUG.S	dance

wanyja-na-ni	yatu-yawung-kulu.
leave-IMPF-PST	white.ochre-PROP-ERG

"We dance painted up with this white ochre." (🔊 VW: FM08_11_2a: 17:06min)

There are also some suffixes that are only used with the demonstratives. In addition, there are a number of specialised uses of nominal suffixes which are discussed in this section. Note that not all suffixes are used with all demonstratives.

5.1.2.1 *-rra(t)* PLural

Nominals are unmarked for number, as discussed in §4.4, and demonstratives are no different. Nonetheless a special plural suffix is found attached to demonstratives where plurality is emphasised. This suffix attaches to *nyawa* and *nyila: nyawarra* 'this lot', *nyilarra* 'that lot' (645)–(646) and (692), except where the demonstrative is case-marked and then it occurs variably either on the outside (647)–(648), or inside of the case-marker (649). It is unexpected finding it on the outside because it is an unusual place for number marking, as shown in the nominal template in §4.1. Note also that the form of the demonstrative i.e. *yalu-* vs *yala-* is assimilated to the vowels in the case-marker not the plural marker. If vowel assimilation was based on the plural marker, the stem would be *yala-* not *yalu-*.[139] Note also that Gurindji speakers use the form *-rra* but Gurindji Kriol speakers use the form *-rrat*.

139 This also applies to the use of *-kujarra*, i.e., *yalu-kujarra-lu* not *yala-kujarra-lu* (SM: Hale MS864(1): p. 23); and *-walija*, i.e., *yalu-walija-lu* not *yala-walija-lu* (SM: Hale MS864(1): p. 37).

(645) Walngin ngu=yi=rla mila-ngka=ma
fly CAT=1EXC.MIN.NS=3OBL eye-LOC=TOP

karrinyana na **nyawa-rra**.
be.IMPF.PRS FOC this-PL
"This lot of flies are getting in my eyes." (VW: FM10_a133: 0:43min)

(646) **Nyila-rra**=ma kirri-walija=ma ya-nku=ngantipangulu[140]
that-PL=TOP woman-PAUC=TOP go-POT=3AUG.S>1EXC.AUG.NS

liwurrap-karra yalu-wu=rni.
humbug-ITER that-DAT=ONLY
"Lots of women will come humbugging us for just those [ashes]."
(VW: FM07_a089: 9:33min)

(647) **Yalu-rra-lu** ngu=yi=lu pa-rru ngayu=ma.
that-PL-ERG CAT=1EXC.MIN.NS=3AUG.S hit-POT 1EXC.MIN=TOP
"That mob are going to hit me." (SM: HALE_K06-004553: 23:44min)

(648) Warlakap nyamu=rla nya-nya **yalu-wu-rra** **yunanynany-ku**
search REL=3OBL intake-PST that-DAT-PL belongings.REDUP-DAT

nyanuny-ku. Ma-rni ngu=rla nyila na langarak.
3MIN.DAT-DAT talk-PST CAT=3OBL that FOC tell
"When she looked around for all of her things, that one told on him [for stealing her things]." (VW: FM12_a174: 15:59min)

(649) Jungkuwurru jangkarni ngu=yina marluka
Echidna big CAT=3AUG.NS old.man

yalu-rra-wu yapayapa-wu=ma.
that-PL-DAT children-DAT=TOP
"Echidna was the elder for a group of little ones."
(Appendix: Echidna and Big Shade: Text 1, Line 1)

This suffix can also attach to the adverbial demonstrative *kuya*. It is used to emphasise number (of both subjects and objects, but not verb iterativity).

140 Note that it is not clear why =*ngantipangulu* attaches directly to the verb and not a catalyst *ngu*.

(650)

Palman	ngu=lu	ma-na-ni	ka-nga-ni
pick.up	CAT=3AUG.S	get-IMPF-PST	take-IMPF-PST

ngu=lu	karrawarra,	**kuya-rra**.
CAT=3AUG.S	east	thus-PL

"They used to pick (the cattle) up and take them east."
(🔊 VW: FM09_17_1d: 25:00min)

(651)

Nyawa=ma=lu	kamparri-jang-kulu	kuya=ma	nyamu=rnalu
this=TOP=3AUG.S	before-TIME-ERG	thus=TOP	REL=1EXC.AUG.S

karrinyani	kaa-rni-mpa	Jinparrak-kula=rni,	**kuya-rra**.
be.IMPF.PST	east-UP-PERL	Wave.Hill-LOC=ONLY	thus-PL

"That's what they used to say in the old days when we were living right on the east side of old Wave Hill station." (🔊 VW: FM09_a123: 10:45min)

The plural suffix also occurs with *ngana* 'who' in its role as an indefinite: *ngana-rra* 'some people'. This suffix is also found in a limited form with tri-relationship kinterms (§4.5.4) where the form *-parra* incorporates the regular epenthetic syllable *-pa-* following final consonants. This suffix is also found on dyadic kinterm *ngumparna-rra* 'husband-PL, husband and wife' where *-rlang* 'dyad' is used on other kinterms (§4.5.3).

No examples of *nyanawu-rra* are found in the Gurindji corpus, so it is unclear whether such a form exists.

Bilinarra, Ngarinyman and Malngin also have this plural form *-rra* (Ise, 1998, p. 29; Jones, Schultze-Berndt, Denniss, et al., 2019, p. 23; Meakins & Nordlinger, 2014, p. 78). Warlmanpa has *-manta* which is also found on free pronouns (Browne, 2021).

5.1.2.2 *-ny* Nominaliser (NMLZ)

This suffix was discussed extensively in §4.7.20. In the context of demonstratives, it also has a nominalising function. It is used in Gurindji with the suppletive stems *murla-* and *yala-* to mean 'this place' and 'that place'. The usual nominal or adnominal case-markers can then follow, as shown in (653) and (654).

(652)

Yala-nginyi=ma	na	ngu=lu
that-SOURCE=TOP	FOC	CAT=3AUG.S

ya-na-ni	**murla-ny-jirri**	na.
go-IMPF-PST	this-NMLZ-ALL	FOC

"After that they used to come to this place." (🔊 VW: FM07_a054: 1:51min)

(653) Ngayu=ma ngu=rna ya-nku marru-ngkurra
1EXC.MIN=TOP CAT=1EXC.MIN.S go-POT house-ALL

murla-ny-jawung.
this-NMLZ-PROP
"I'm going to town with this one." (🔊 SM: HALE_K06-004554: 10:45min)

This suffix is also used with *kuya* to produce the meaning 'that kind', as shown in (654). Again, case-marking follows nominalisation.

(654) Wilmurr-jawung ngu=lu=rla pirrkap ma-na-ni
wire-PROP CAT=3AUG.S=3OBL make do-IMPF-PST

kuya-ny-ku na narrinyjila-wu warrija-wu.
thus-NMLZ-DAT FOC turtle-DAT crocodile-DAT
"They used to make it with wire to catch turtles, crocodiles and those kinds of animals." (🔊 VW: FM10_a149: 1:18min)

5.1.2.3 *-mawu* DWELLer

The suffix *-mawu* is only found on *murlany* 'this place' and *yalany* 'that place' to indicate people who inhabit an area. Some examples are given in (655)–(656). Case-marking occurs after *-mawu*, as shown in (655).

(655) Nyawa=ma ngantipa yapayapa ngu=ngantipa
this=TOP 1EXC.AUG small CAT=1EXC.AUG.NS

ka-nya mukurl-u=ma **yala-ny-mawu**-lu.
take-PST aunt-ERG=TOP that-NMLZ-DWELL-ERG
"This was when we were small when my aunty, as a traditional custodian of the country, used to take us." (🔊 VW: FM09_14_1a: 3:50min)

(656) Nyila=ma kayilirra-ngarna jaru. Jawi=pirak=ma
that=TOP north-ASSOC language fire=CORRECT=TOP

Ngarinyman. Ngantipa=ma=rnalu ma-rna-na
Ngarinyman 1EXC.AUG=TOP=1EXC.AUG.S say-IMPF-PRS

murla-ny-mawu, warlu=pirak.
this-NMLZ-DWELL fire=CORRECT
"That's from the northern language. Jawi is really a Ngarinyman word. We, the people of this area, really say 'warlu'." (🔊 VW: FM11_a162: 1:35min)

This suffix is not used with other nominals, with *-mala* (§4.7.11), *-mungkuj* (§4.7.14) and *-wirrirri* (§4.7.26) the alternatives, although note that these also have limited usage. Often *-ngarna* is used in these contexts, however *-mawu* implies a stronger and longer connection to country than *-ngarna*.

Interestingly, this same suffix is found in Murrinh-patha (a language spoken much further to the north in the Daly River area) to mark the place where someone comes from. Note that in Gurindji, *-mawu* also always refers to a group.

(657) Ngay=ka Melbourne-**mawu**. (Murrinh-patha)
1SG=FOC Melbourne-DENIZEN
"I'm from Melbourne." (example courtesy of Rachel Nordlinger)

The likely source of both of these suffixes is Jaminjung where *-mawu* is used to mean both 'traditional custodian' and 'denizen' (Schultze-Berndt, 2000, pp. 51–52). It seems that the form was borrowed with the 'denizen' meaning.

This suffix is also found in Mudburra. In Ngardi and Warlpiri, there is a suffix *-malu* which attaches to cardinal directions to mean 'people from the north', for example.

5.1.2.4 *-nganang* AXIS

This suffix only occurs once in the corpus on a demonstrative (658). It is more usually found with cardinal directions, as in (659). It is possibly simply *-ngarna* + *ng*, however the *ng* variant has not been recorded elsewhere despite the fact that many suffixes have *ng* variants.

(658) Jarrwa Jangaminyji-mayin=ma karrinyani jarrwa
many place.name-PERL=TOP be.IMPF.PST many

kuya-rniny-nganang.
thus-HITH-AXIS
"There used to be heaps around Jangaminyji." (🔈 VW: FM18_a507: 7:38min)

(659) "Wart lirlaj ya-ni nyila=rni **kanka-yit-karra-nganang**
back swim go-PST that=ONLY upstream-ABL-SIDE-AXIS

kani-yin-karra."
downstream-ABL-SIDE
"He swam back to the upstream end." (Appendix: Text 2)

5.1.2.5 *-nginyi* SOURCE

Although *-nginyi* was discussed in §4.3.8, it is mentioned here again because of some interesting uses it has when combined with demonstratives. When attached to *kuya-ny* 'thus-NMLZ', it produces the meaning 'as a result of', as shown in (660).

(660)	Tirrip	ngu=yinangulu	karrwa-rna-ni,	
	overnight	CAT=3AUG.S>3AUG.NS	keep-IMPF-PST	
	kuya-ny-ja-nginyi.	Late-bala-nginyi	yu	nou.
	thus-NMLZ-LOC-SOURCE	late-ADJ-SOURCE	you	know

"And they would keep them overnight as a result of [the cooking procedure]. From late in the afternoon." (🔊 VW: FM12_a175: 07:40min)

When combined with *yala-* 'that', the effect is a discourse connector which has roughly the meaning of the English 'and then'. It is translated into Kriol as 'after that'. An example is given in (661).

(661)	**Yala-nginyi**	wirrminy	ngu=rnayinangulu
	that-SOURCE	turn.over	CAT=1EXC.AUG.S>3AUG.NS
	yuwa-na-na	kuya.	
	put-IMPF-PRS	thus	

"After that we turn [the babies] over like this." (🔊 VW: FM08_a085: 01:12min)

5.1.2.6 *-rniny* HITHer

Two suffixes which attach to demonstrative stems and not to other nominal stems are *-rniny* 'hither' and *-partak* 'thither'. They were mistakenly analysed as irregular allative and ablative forms in Bilinarra (Meakins & Nordlinger, 2014, pp. 175–176). These endings are also found in Ngarinyman (Jones, Schultze-Berndt, Denniss, et al., 2019, p. 28). The equivalent forms in Warlpiri which also attach to the adverbial demonstrative *kuja* 'thus' are *-rnipurda* 'hither' and *-purda* 'thither' (Laughren, 1978, p. 7). Ngardi has *-purda* 'thither' which also attaches to the adverbial demonstrative *kuja* 'thus' and cardinals (Ennever, 2021).

The first suffix *-rniny* marks movement towards a location, roughly meaning 'this way'. It marks *murla-* (662), *yala-* (663) (and the plain demonstrative stems (664) and (665)), and *kuya* (666) and (667). The use of *murla-* and *yala-* adds additional proximal and distal meaning to referent, whereas *kuyarniny* is more neutral.

(662) ...ngawa-ngka nyamu karrinyana **murla-rniny**
...water-LOC REL be.IMPF.PRS this-HITH

jeya bank-kula im jidan wumara-la.
there bank-LOC 3SG stay rock-LOC
"...[this kind of turtle] which lives this way under rocks in the water on the side of waterholes." (🔊 VW: FM10_23_4: 07:34min)

(663) **Yala-rniny** ya-ni ngu karla-ngkarla Jurnarni-mayin
that-HITH go-PST CAT west-DOWN place.name-PERL

murla-ngkurra.
this-ALL
"He rode it this way down west well past Jurnarni and back here."
(🔊 RW: EC99_a030: 1:34min)

(664) Kuliyan=ma nyamu=n ma-lu kuli-kuli
aggressive=TOP REL=2MIN.S talk-POT fight-REDUP

nyila-rniny=kata=rni ngu=rnangkulu jarrara ma-nku.
that-HITH=IMM=ONLY CAT=1EXC.AUG.S>2MIN.NS follow do-POT
"If you talk aggressively that way we'll follow you up with punishment."
(McConvell 1996 grammar manuscript: Speaking to young people)

(665) **Ya-ni** ngu **nyawa-rniny** nyawa jamana=ma kuya.
go-PST CAT this-HITH this footprint=TOP thus
"It walked this way. Here are its footprints." (🔊 VW: FM10_a154: 4:31min)

(666) Ngayu=warluk **kuya-rniny** ngu=rna pa-na-na tikap.
1EXC.MIN=FIRST thus-HITH CAT=1EXC.MIN.S hit-IMPF-PRS chop
"Me first, I chop the tree this way." (🔊 VW: FM07_a027: 3:39min)

(667) Jarrwa Jangaminyji-mayin=ma karrinyani **kuya-rniny-nganang**.
many place.name-PERL=TOP be.IMPF.PST thus-HITH-AXIS
"There used to be heaps around Jangaminyji." (🔊 VW: FM18_a507: 7:38min)

Gurindji does not mark 'hither' in other places in the grammar, for example verbs (§7.1).

5.1.2.7 *-partak* THITHer

The other suffix is *-partak* 'thither'. We don't have any examples in the Gurindji corpus of *yalapartak* or *murlapartak*, however it is in the corpus marking *kuya* to indicate movement away from a place, roughly meaning 'that way' (668).

(668) Kilka waninyani ngu **kuya-partak,** purnku=ma.
clean fall.IMPF.PST CAT thus-THITH good.grain=TOP

Nyawa waninyani jilipija=ma **kuya-partak,** jurlurl.
this fall.IMPF.PST husks=TOP thus-THITH spill
"The good part would fall down that way clean. And the husks would spill over the other way." (🔊 VW: FM10_a147: 0:11min)

Gurindji does not mark 'thither' in other places in the grammar, for example verbs (§7.1).

5.1.2.8 *-kijak* TERMinative

We provide a separate discussion of *-kijak* in the demonstrative section because it has a specialised comparative usage when attached to the adverbial demonstrative *kuya*. In this context it translates as 'as X as' and it often accompanied by gestures to demonstrate size or length, for example. Some examples are given in (669) and (670).

(669) Mayarni-kari marntaj nyila=ma=lu=rla ma-na-ni yuka
more-OTHER OK that=TOP=3AUG.S=3OBL get-IMPF-PST grass

nyanawu jangkakarni yuka **kuya-kijak=kata** nyamu karrinyana.
RECOG big.REDUP grass thus-TERM=IMM REL be.IMPF.PRS
"They'd keep going then they would get some grass, you know the one, the grass which grows as big as this [accompanied by a gesture]."
(🔊 VW: FM10_a148: 9:15min)

(670) Paraj pu-nya nyila=ma kampij=ma.
find pierce-PST that=TOP egg=TOP

Jangkarni **kuya-kijak** <u>dat</u> kampij jangkarni.
big thus-TERM the egg big
"Then she found that egg. It was as big as this."
(🔊 VW: FM10_27_1a: Kurraj Story from Halls Creek: 1:12min)

Other Ngumpin languages make use of other case suffixes for comparative. Warlpiri and Warlmanpa use the dative for comparatives. Mudburra uses the ablative and dative (which have the same forms as Gurindji). (Examples courtesy of Amanda Hamilton-Hollaway and David Osgarby).

(671) Yali=ma lalija=ma hot-bala=rni yali (Mudburra)
that=TOP tea=TOP hot-ADJ=ONLY that

icecream-ngurlu=ma.
icecream-ABL=TOP
"The tea is colder than the icecream."

(672) Yali ngarrka=ma dunkuja=rni ba=rla yali (Mudburra)
that man=TOP short=ONLY CAT=3OBL that

kirri-wu=ma.
woman-DAT=TOP
"That man is shorter than that woman."

5.1.2.9 *-rntil* BELonging

This suffix is only found with demonstratives. It was described as 'belonging to' in McConvell's original sketch grammar, which indeed seems to be the case with *nyanawu-rntil* '(the tree) that used to be there at that time' in (673). Nonetheless it does not always seem to have this meaning. It occurs commonly in the speech of Malngin elder Banjo Ryan, for example in (674). Here Ronnie Wavehill describes it as the equivalent of *nyila-rra* 'that-PL'.

(673) Lawara kanyjal nyawa=ma karrinyana parramparra=warla
nothing bottom this=TOP be.IMPF.PRS plain=FOC

karnti-murlung-nginyi **nyanawu-rntil**=warla.
tree-PRIV-SOURCE RECOG-BEL=FOC
"There's nothing, down below there's a plain where there used to be [that tree]."
(Appendix: Echidna and the Big Shade: Text 1, Line 30)

(674) Ngu ya-ni nyila=ma **yala-rntil-u** ngumpit-ku stock-camp-kulawu.
CAT go-PST that=TOP that-BEL-DAT man-DAT stock-camp-PURP
"The policeman had really come for those stockmen."
(Appendix: Gordon Stott story: Text 7, Line 6)

This suffix is not observed in Bilinarra, Mudburra, Ngardi or Warlmanpa.

5.1.3 Distribution

Nyawa 'this' and *nyila* 'that' and the suppletive forms can function as (i) demonstrative pronominals, as in (675) and (676); as (ii) nominal modifiers, as shown in (677) (in which case the head noun is encoded as definite (c.f. Diessel, 1999, p. 57 onwards)); or as (iii) adverbials, such as (678).

(675) **Nyila** na ngu=rna pa-na-na
that FOC CAT=1EXC.MIN.S hit-IMPF-PRS

pirrkap ngayu=ma jala=ma.
make 1EXC.MIN=TOP today=TOP
"I'm making that one today." (🔈 VW: FM07_a050: 2:25min)

(676) Kaa-rni-yin, jawurruk ngu=rnalu waninya, **murla-ngkurra**.
east-UP-ABL descend CAT=1EXC.AUG.S fall.PST this-ALL
"We would come down here from the east." (🔈 VW: FM09_12_2a: 3:42min)

(677) Jangkarni-k jiya-rna-na **yalu-ngku=ma** **tamarra-lu=ma.**
big-FACT burn-IMPF-PRS that-ERG=TOP antbed-ERG=TOP
"The antbed treatment makes them grow up strong."
(🔈 VW: FM08_a085: 3:00min)

(678) Ngara-ngka kankula ngu=n ya-na-na
heights-LOC up CAT=2MIN.S go-IMPF-PRS

yala-ngka=ma **tiwu-waji-la=ma** kuya.
that-LOC=TOP fly-AGENT-LOC=TOP thus
"You travel there in a plane at great heights." (🔈 VW: FM12_a175: 13:47min)

Generally ergative and dative-marked demonstratives act as pronominals (unless they occur in conjunction with other nominals), and demonstratives with spatial case suffixes act as adverbials. However, this distinction is not always clear. For example, in (678), it is not clear whether *yala-ngka* 'that-LOC' should be interpreted as 'in this place' or 'there'. In general, Gurindji is a non-configurational language with discontinuous noun phrases and null anaphora (Kenneth Hale, 1983), which makes it difficult to tell whether a demonstrative is acting as an independent constituent or a nominal modifier (§8.1). Even when the demonstrative and noun are juxtaposed, it is difficult to tell whether the demonstrative is acting within the noun phrase as a modifier or acting independently as an adverbial NP. For example, (678) could be interpreted as 'in *that* plane' (one NP) or 'up *there* in a plane' (two NPs).

The demonstrative *kuya* 'thus' is only used as an adverbial (678)–(681). It has the features of an adverb (see §7.3), in that it optionally agrees with the case marking of other nominals, for example in (679) *kuya* takes ergative agreement with the transitive subject (and the instrumental *karnti-ku* 'with a stick'). Interestingly, *kuyangka* seems to be grammaticalising into a clause linker 'that's why', 'that's when', (680) and (681) (discussed further in §9.2.4).

(679)	Jimak	ngu=rnalu=rla	yuwa-na-na
	push.hot.rocks	CAT=1EXC.AUG.S=3OBL	put-IMPF-PRS

karnti-ku	na	**kuya-ngku**.
stick-ERG	FOC	thus-ERG

"We push some hot rocks up into the chest cavity with a stick."
(🔈 VW: FM10_a148: 3:33min)

(680)	Yikili	ya-na-na.	**Kuya-ngka**=ma=n	nya-nga-na
	far	go-IMPF-PRS	thus-LOC=TOP=2MIN.S	intake-IMPF-PRS

junpurlp	na	ya-na-na	ngu	kuya.
receding.figure	FOC	go-IMPF-PRS	CAT	thus

"He goes a long way away. So when you look he's a receding figure in the distance." (🔈 VW: FM12_a173: 14:08min)

(681)	Nyamu=rna	tak	karrinyani	**kuya-ngka=warla**
	REL=1EXC.MIN.S	sit	be.IMPF.PST	thus-LOC=FOC

ngu=yi	jayi-nya.
CAT=1EXC.MIN.NS	give-PST

"When I was sitting down that's when he gave it to me."
(McConvell corpus: Meakins et al., 2016, p. 196)

The recognitional demonstrative has a similar distribution to *nyawa* 'this' and *nyila* 'that', however its function is to modify a nominal to evoke mutual knowledge. It is often found as a nominal modifier (682)–(683) or adverbial (684) to check the hearer's understanding of a referent, but it is also sometimes found as a pronominal (695).

(682)	**Nyanawu**	**pilyily**	yapakayi	majul-a	nyamu
	RECOG	pinky	small	stomach-LOC	REL

ka-nga-na puul-a walyak.
take-IMPF-PRS pouch-LOC inside
"You know the hairless joey that is still in its mother's pouch."
(🔊 VW: FM09_a123: 6:27min)

(683) Juwarra karrinya ngu ngamarti,
turkey.noise be.PST CAT small.bush.turkey

yapawurru **nyanawu**, **jamut**.
small RECOG bush.turkey
"You know those small bush turkeys well they make a shhh noise in their throat."
(🔊 VW: FM10_a154: 4:56min)

(684) Jinparrak nyamu=rlaa=nga ya-nku
place.name REL=1INC.AUG.S=DUB go-POT

nyanawu-yirri **Wantany-jirri** kankarra.
RECOG-ALL birthing.place-ALL upstream
"When we'll go upstream, to Jinparrak to the birthing place I've told you about." (🔊 VW: FM08_a085: 18:59min)

5.1.4 Function

5.1.4.1 Situational use

The most basic use of the demonstratives *nyawa* 'this' and *nyila* 'that' and their inflected forms is in expressing relative distance from a deictic centre, usually the speaker. *Nyawa* and its forms are used to indicate proximity to the deictic centre (685), and *nyila*, distance. In this respect they function in much the same manner as *this* and *that* in English.

(685) **Nyawa=ma** yatu=ma **murla-nginyi** na
this=TOP white.ochre=TOP this-SOURCE FOC

ngu=lu ma-na-ni, kamparri-jang-kulu
CAT=3AUG.S get-IMPF-PST before-TIME-ERG

nungkiny-ju=ma, ngantipanguny-ju=ma.
family-ERG=TOP 1EXC.AUG.DAT-ERG=TOP
"My family used to get this white ochre from here [at Lartajarni] in the old days."
(🔊 VW: FM08_11_2b: 2:12min)

Kuya 'thus' is also used in this function when it combines with the special hither and thither suffixes, to mean 'this way' and 'that way', as shown in (662)–(664) and (668).

5.1.4.2 Anaphoric use

The demonstratives *nyawa* and *nyila* can also be used anaphorically in discourse to refer to discourse entities which have been mentioned previously. *Nyawa* has the discourse function of indicating 'that which has just been mentioned'. For example, *nyawa* in (686) is used to indicate *kumpulyu* 'white currant' thus referring back to the topic of discourse (as indicated by the topic marker *=ma*). The demonstrative *nyila* 'that' is also used in an analogous function, referring to referents further back in discourse.

(686)

Kumpulyu=ma,	janga-ngkawu	kulykulya-wu.	**Nyawa**
white.currant=TOP	sick-PURP	congestion-DAT	this

kartak-kula	ngu=rna	yuwa-na-na	kuya.
billycan-LOC	CAT=1EXC.MIN.S	put-IMPF-PRS	thus

"White currant [stems] are used to treat coughs. You put it in a billycan."
(🔈 VW: FM09_16_1a: 1:10min)

Another construction which relates to anaphora is the combination of *yala-nginyi* 'that-SOURCE', which is used to connect two events in a narrative, in a manner similar to 'then' or 'after that' in English (also discussed in §5.1.2.5). Examples of *yalanginyi* are (661) and (687). Note also the use of the derivational *-ngarna* 'associative' on the stem *yala-* 'that' (see also §4.7.16).

(687)

Yala-nginyi=ma	ngu=rnayinangulu	lurlu	yuwa-na-na
that-SOURCE=TOP	CAT=1EXC.AUG.S>3AUG.NS	sit	put-IMPF-PRS

kuya	**yala-ngarna**=ma	tarlakurru-la=ma	jungkart-ta=ma.
thus	that-ASSOC=TOP	hole-LOC=TOP	smoke-LOC=TOP

"After that we sit them in the hot pit in the smoke." (🔈 VW: FM07_a085: 1:21min)

5.1.4.3 Identifier

Diessel (1999, p. 58) uses the term 'identifier' to cover a number of other terms which have been used in the literature on demonstratives including 'predicative demonstratives', 'copulative demonstratives', 'existential demonstratives', 'pointing demonstratives' and 'deictic presentatives'. These demonstratives occur in copular or non-verbal clauses but are not restricted to them. Their function is to focus on entities in the physical or discourse context (Diessel, 1999, p. 79). In Gurindji, demonstratives used in this manner have a presentative quality, usually introducing new topics. Three constructions are discussed in this section. The first construction takes the form of specific identifier demonstrative *nyaa* which is probably a shortened form of *nyawa* 'this'. The second consists of sentence-initial topic-marked demonstratives *nyawa=ma* and *nyila=ma* (in both verbal and non-verbal clauses) and the third construction involves unmarked *nyawa* and *nyila.*

The first construction simply involves a single word utterance, *nyaa.* It is used to draw attention to something in the physical context and is usually uttered when pointing at something or holding something. It is not unlike the French deictic presentative *voilà.*

In the second construction, *nyawa* and *nyila* act as pronominals in first position in the clause. The clause may have a verbal (§8.2), (688) and (690), or a non-verbal predicate (§8.4), (689) and (691). The demonstratives are always found with a topic marker *=ma* (688)–(691) and often the pronominal clitic follows the topic marker (690) and (691). The topic-marked demonstratives present the topic of discourse, always the first mention of the topic. This construction is often used to begin narratives to identify the characteristics of something (689), and when describing pictures. Indeed, it is commonly found in the context of sentence elicitation.

(688)	**Nyila=ma**	narranyjana-la	ngu=lu	karrinyana.
	that=TOP	windbreak-LOC	CAT=3AUG.S	be.IMPF.PRS

"That's when they used to live in windbreaks." (🔈 VW: FM11_a167: 0:05min)

(689)	**Nyila=ma**	ngayiny-ku	jawiji-wu	ngamayi-wu
	that=TOP	1EXC.MIN.DAT-DAT	MF-DAT	mother-DAT

ngamarni-wu	ngu=yina	nyila=ma	ngurra=ma.
MoBr-DAT	CAT=3AUG.NS	that=TOP	country=TOP

"That's a story about my mother's, uncle's and mother's father's country." (🔈 VW: FM08_a071: 0:34min)

(690)	**Nyawa=ma**=lu	kamparri-jang-kulu	kuya	ma-rni.
	this=TOP=3AUG.S	before-TIME-ERG	thus	say-PST

"That's what they used to say in the old days." (🔈 VW: FM09_a123: 10:45min)

(691)	**Nyawa=ma**=rla	kumpu	nyanuny.
	this=TOP=3OBL	urine	3MIN.DAT

"That's her urine [referring to Emu's urine at Jampawurru which is now a spring]." (🔈 VW: FM09_15_2a: 3:29min)

The final construction consists of *nyawa* 'this' and *nyila* 'that' being used as adverbials in a presentative manner, in much the same way as 'here' and 'there' can be used in English. For example, in (692) *nyawa* is used to mean 'here' and the demonstrative was accompanied by a pointing gesture

(692)

Kayili-yin-nginyi	nyila-rra=ma	na	karu=ma.	Kayili-yin
north-ABL-SOURCE	that-PL=TOP	FOC	child=TOP	north-ABL

ngu=lu	ya-ni	Jilinypuk-mayin.	Jilinypuk	**nyawa**
CAT=3AUG.S	go-PST	place.name-PERL	place.name	this

kayirra.	Lartajarni	ngu=lu	karrinya.
north	place.name	CAT=3AUG.S	be.PST

"The Dreaming children come from the north. They came from the north through Jilinypuk. Jilinypuk is **here** north."
(🔈 VW: FM10_30_1a: Karu Dreaming Story: 0:15min)

5.1.4.4 Quotative

The adverbial demonstrative *kuya* is commonly used as a quotative following reported speech. It can be used in conjunction with the inflecting verb *marnana* 'to talk', as in (693); or it can be simply used on its own, as in (694). Often *kuya*, coupled with a change to first person, is the only indication that reported speech has occurred in a narrative, with little prosodic information marking this form of speech.

(693)

Hey,	ngantu-ku=yi	murla-nginyi
hey	who-ERG=1EXC.MIN.NS	this-SOURCE

wurraj	ya-ni	**kuya**	**ma-rni**	ngu.
take.out	go-PST	thus	say-PST	CAT

"'Hey!? Who robbed me?' he asked." (🔈 RW: EC98_a015: 20:08min)

(694)

"Ngarluk	ma-ni	ngu=n.	Kula=n
miss	do-PST	CAT=2MIN.S	NEG=2MIN.S

pa-ni	punyu-k-kulu,"	**kuya**.
hit-PST	good-FACT-ERG	thus

141 Black Gin Bore is the non-Indigenous name given to this site. We only mention it in this footnote because the name 'Jilinypuk' is not known to most younger generations of Gurindji people who use the name 'Black Gin Bore' themselves. Sadly non-Indigenous names such as this one exist right across Australia. We are aware that continuing to use them only perpetuates racist ideologies.

"'You missed it. You can't shoot properly,' he said."
(🔈 VW: FM10_a152: 0:18min, 0:28min)

5.1.4.5 Recognitional use

Like many other Australian languages, Gurindji has a specific 'recognitional' demonstrative (Diessel, 1999), *nyanawu*. The use of this demonstrative signals knowledge shared between the speaker and the hearer. It is often used to check with the hearer that they know what is being referred to. It is generally found in conversation, but also in narrative where the hearer is familiar with the content of the narrative.

A number of examples were given in (682)–(684) where the referent is also mentioned with *nyanawu* as a check for the listener. Another example is given in (695) where the referent is not mentioned. In this case, the demonstrative is also used when the speaker cannot remember the name of the place, but checks to see if the hearer has understood the referent nonetheless. In the following example, the speaker cannot remember the name of the place but uses *nyanawu* in conjunction with some descriptive information to check with her classificatory sister (Meakins who is recording the story) that she knows where it is.

(695) Kayili-yin ya-ni kayili-yin ya-ni Yiparrartu=ma.
north-ABL go-PST north-ABL go-PST Emu=TOP
"Emu came from the east."

Ya-ni ngu.
go-PST CAT
"She came."

Nyanawu kapuku ngu=rnangkulu wiit jayi-nya
RECOG sister CAT=1EXC.AUG.S>2MIN.NS show give-PST

tirrip=ma tirrip karrinya waninya karu.
overnight=TOP overnight be.PST fall.PST child
"You know the place sister we showed you [where] Emu camped overnight and gave birth to her children?" (🔈 TD: FM08_08_4b: 1:09min)

5.2 Spatial relations

Like most Australian languages, Gurindji uses fixed bearings as the primary means of describing the angular relation of a figure with respect to a ground in large-scale space. Three fixed bearing systems are in evidence: (i) verticality, (ii) cardinals, and (iii) river drainage, which are often used in tandem. Indeed, barely an utterance goes by without some use of these terms.

(696)	verticality:	*kankula*	'up'
		kanyjurra	'down'
	compass points:	*kayirra*	'north'
		kurlarra	'south'
		karlarra	'west'
		karrawarra	'east'[142]
	river drainage:	*kankarra*	'upstream'
		kanimparra	'downstream'

For example, the speaker in (697) uses cardinals (e.g. *kurlarra* 'south') and river drainage terms (e.g. *kankarra* 'upstream') to describe how she got from Kalkaringi to a large patch of medicinal lemon grass. Additional spatial relators are found including demonstratives (e.g. *nyawa* 'here', *yalangurlu* 'from there', *nyila-rra* 'those'), case marking (e.g. *-ngurlung* 'ablative'), place names (e.g. Jampawurru) and land features (e.g. *lurtju* 'ridge').

(697)

Kurlarra	ngu=rnalu	ya-ni,	Township-ngurlung=ma
south	CAT=1EXC.AUG.S	go-PST	Township-ABL=TOP

kurla-ngkurla.	**Kurlarra**	ngu=rnalu	ya-ni
south-DOWN	south	CAT=1EXC.AUG.S	go-PST

kankapa	nyawa,	Jampawurru	junction,	pinka
upstream	this	Mud.Spring	junction	river

Jampawurru-nginyi	nyawa=ma	na.	Yala-ngurlu=ma=rnalu
Mud.Spring-SOURCE	this=TOP	FOC	that-ABL=TOP=1EXC.AUG.S

ya-ni	**karrawarra-k.**	**Kaa-rni-rra**	kuya	na	lurtju-ngka
go-PST	east-ALL	east-UP-LOC	thus	FOC	ridge-LOC

nyila-rra=ma	karrinyana	yuka=ma	kupuwupu=ma.
that-PL=TOP	be.IMPF.PRS	grass=TOP	lemon.grass=TOP

"We went **south** from town. We went **south** and **upstream** (of the Victoria River) to Jampawurru junction. From Jampawurru creek. . . From there we went **eastwards. To the east** on the ridge you can find lots of lemon grass." (🔊 VW: FM08_a089: 1:05min) (Meakins, 2011c, p. 54)

142 *Karrawarra* is a reduplicated form of the stem *kaarra*. Nowadays Gurindji Kriol speakers use *kaarnirra* as the base form of east and consider *karrawarra* a Mudburra term. In fact *kaarnirra* is the 'up' form of *karrawarra*. Malngin has *karrarra* 'east' (Ise, 1998, p. 31), but this may have been *karrawarra* with the *w* deleting to produce a long vowel.

The terms in the three sets of coordinates – verticality, compass points and river drainage – are a subgroup of nominals, so-defined because they inflect for all spatial cases like other nominals. They differ from nominals because they are inherently locative, and are uninflected in a locative NP (except in agreement with a head nominal). The case suffixes of these spatial nominals also differ from the normal nominal case suffixes in form, hence their categorisation as a special subtype of nominal.

It is somewhat unusual for an Australian language to have both river drainage terms and compass points. Gurindji is sandwiched between languages to the north which use river drainage systems exclusively (e.g. Jaminjung)[143] and those to the south which use cardinal directions exclusively (e.g. Warlpiri), and it is likely the existence of both systems is an old contact feature of the Eastern Ngumpin languages (Laughren & McConvell, 1999). Additionally, the span of traditional Gurindji country from the black soil plains of the Victoria River District to the northern edge of the Tanami desert may have played some role in reinforcing the use of both systems.

A number of other Australian languages use both river drainage and cardinal systems to express absolute relations, including Gooniyandi (McGregor, 1990), Bunuba (Rumsey, 2000) and Miriwoong (Kofod p.c. cited in Schultze-Berndt, 2006b) which are non-Pama-Nyungan languages spoken in the Kimberleys; and other languages such as Martuthunira, Panyjima and Yindjinbarndi which are spoken south of the Kimberleys in the Pilbara region (Dench, 1995). Wardaman, which is located to the north-east of Gurindji country, also has a dual fixed bearing system (Merlan, 1994). Finally the Eastern Ngumpin languages, Bilinarra and Ngarinyman, which are mutually-intelligible with Gurindji, also use both systems (Jones, Schultze-Berndt, Denniss, et al., 2019; Meakins, 2013; Meakins & Nordlinger, 2014).

Most other Australian languages only employ either a river drainage system such as Jaminjung which is spoken immediately north of Gurindji in the Timber Creek area (Schultze-Berndt, 2006b); or a cardinal system which is common to the languages spoken in Central Australia, and has been described in detail for Warlpiri (Laughren, 1978) and Arrernte (Levinson & Wilkins, 2006a, 2006b; Wilkins, 2003, 2006). Cardinal systems are also found immediately west of Gurindji in the Kimberley area of north-western Australia and have been described for Jaru (Tsunoda, 1981), Ngardi (Ennever, 2021) and Warrwa (McGregor, 2006). These systems are also commonly found elsewhere in Australia. For example the use of cardinal directions in Guugu Yimithirr which is spoken in Cape York has been discussed extensively (Haviland, 1998; Levinson, 1997, 2003). Murrinh-patha is an unusual example of an Australian language which has neither river drainage terms nor cardinal terms (Blythe, Mardigan, Perdjert, & Stoakes, 2016).

143 Interestingly Schultze-Berndt (p.c.) does report that some older Jaminjung speakers have a memory of three terms for cardinal points, but they are no longer in use.

Languages such as English never use cardinal directions for descriptions of small-scale space, but rather rely heavily on the relative left/right terms. Such terms do not exist in Gurindji. Indeed, Gurindji does not express angular relations in terms of the ego in any sense. For example, speakers do not assign facets (e.g. front, back) to an inherently unfaceted object such as a tree based on their perspective. In English, speakers might say, *John is in front of the tree*, where *the tree's front* is designated based on the speaker's perspective, and John is necessarily positioned between the tree and the speaker (Levinson, 2003, p. 44). Gurindji speakers do not use these constructions for describing similar configurations of a figure and ground.

Although Gurindji has no terms for 'left' and 'right', there are words for right hand (*jutumparra*[144]) and left hand (*jampukarra, wartiwarti, ngarlkuny, ngarlkunyjirrip, wirlkirri, jirrpintikarra*[145]) (McConvell, 2010). Importantly, these terms are only used to describe handedness (698) or a specific hand (699) and have not been extended to specify the location of another entity in relation to ego.

(698) Ngu=yinangulu pirrkap ma-na-na **wartiwarti**-wu.
CAT=3AUG.S>3AUG.NS make do-IMPF-PRS left.hand-DAT
"They make [boomerangs] for left-handers." (BW: FM10_a143: 4:32min) (Meakins, 2011c, p. 61)

(699) **Wartiwarti**-lu pa-na-na karnti=ma yungkuj.
left.hand-ERG hit-IMPF-PRS tree=TOP tree.fall
"He cuts the tree down with his left-hand." (BW: FM10_a143: 5:58min) (Meakins, 2011c, p. 61)

The right and left sides of the body are also labelled in Gurindji, in this case they are derived forms of coverbs. These terms are gendered: *warrara-wu-ny* 'brandish. spear-DAT-NMLZ' refers to the right side of the body and *juluj-ku-ny* 'carry.on.hip-DAT-NMLZ' (e.g. coolamon, child) refers to the left side. A demonstration of the latter is given in Figure 45. Their gendered nature is reflected in the sign language where older signers employ the left and right sides of the body to distinguish between 'sister' and 'brother', with the right calf used for 'brother' and the left for 'sister'.

We now discuss each of the three fixed bearings systems in turn.

144 This word is built from *jutu* 'right, correct, straight' and has the same semantic extension as 'right' in English.

145 There are a surprising number of words for 'left-handed' but *wartiwarti* is the most commonly used.

Figure 45: Violet Wadrill demonstrates the side of the body 'juluj-ku-ny' with a carrying action while Topsy Dodd watches on (Green et al., forthcoming).

5.2.1 Cardinal terms

Cardinal directions are almost ubiquitous in Gurindji discourse, particularly in descriptions of travel and locations. Barely an utterance in a Gurindji conversation or narrative will go by without the use of a cardinal. They have been described in detail elsewhere (McConvell, 1991; Meakins, 2011c) and are still in use by younger generations, although the paradigm is much reduced (Dunn et al., 2021; Meakins & Algy, 2016; Meakins et al., 2016).

Cardinal directions are not grammatically obligatory, however they 'flavour' the language and people who are considered master story tellers use them liberally. Four cardinals are in evidence: *kayirra* (north), *kurlarra* (south), *karrawarra* (east) and *karlarra* (west) and they are not combined to mark deviations from the basic directions as occurs in English, for example *north-west*. When asked to point *kayirra*, Gurindji speakers will point directly north, however in conversation and narratives the term *kayirra* extends 45 degrees on either side of north to form a quadrant. Finer distinctions are indicated using hand and lip gestures, as McGregor (2006, p. 149) also observes for Warrwa speakers. Haviland (1998, p. 29) notes that, for Guugu Yimithirr speakers, the cardinal terms are rotated slightly clockwise from standard Western compass points, however in Gurindji they are aligned with these points.

Gurindji cardinal directions are highly inflected. They have a set of spatial case-markers which differ in form from the case-markers found on regular nominals. They inflect for allative, ablative, perlative and source. Additionally, they also inflect for land features (river, shade), facets (side/edge, apex) and orientational features (axis, turning, crossing). Thus far, 31 forms for each cardinal direction have been recorded, but it is possible there are more forms since this system is complex. Table 21 gives the declension for *north* and Table 22 gives the proposed suffixes.

Table 21: 'North' paradigm (McConvell, 1982b, p. 72; 2010, p. 54; Meakins, 2011c, p. 56).

kayirra	north 'north.LOC'	kayili-yin-karra	(situated) on the north side of something (hill, tree, house etc) reached when coming from the north 'north-ABL-SIDE'
kayirra-k	to the north 'north-ALL'	kayi-rni-yin-karra	from up on the northside of a river 'north-UP-ABL-RIVER.SIDE'
kayirra-mpa	in the north (long way) 'north-PERL'	kayirra-ngkarra	north and down 'north-DOWN'
kayirra-wariny	far north 'north-FAR'	kayirra-ngkarra-k	northwards and down 'north-DOWN-ALL'
kayirra-mpa-wariny	further along the north 'north-PERL-FAR'	kayikayi-rni-mpal	moving intermittently across the north on the other side of the river 'north.REDUP-UP-EDGE'
kayili-yin	from the north 'north-ABL'	kayi-nu-k	crossing a river towards the north 'north-CROSS.RIVER-ALL'
kayili-yin-nginyi	originating from a place to the north 'north-ABL-SOURCE'	kayi-rni-yin-jarrk	crossing a river from the north 'north-UP-ABL-CROSS.RIVER'
kayirra-nganang	orientated north from the south 'north-AXIS'	kayirra-la-ny	a long way to the north 'north-LOC-NMLZ'
kayili-yin-nganang	orientated from the north to the south 'north-ABL-AXIS'	kayirra-mpa-wuk	turning to the north 'north-PERL-TURN'
kayili-yarra	northside 'north-SIDE'	kayi-rni-mpa-wuk	turning to the north area and up 'north-PERL-UP-TURN'
kayi-rni	north and up 'north-UP'	kayi-rni-yin-nganang	coming from the north heading south 'north-UP-ABL-AXIS'
kayi-rni-yin	from up north 'north-UP-ABL'	kayi-rni-wariny	far on the northern end 'north-UP-FAR'
kayi-rni-rra	to the north and up 'north-UP-LOC'	kayirra-wurru	shade on the northern side 'north-SHADE'
kayi-rni-mpa	around the north and up 'north-UP-PERL'	kayirra-wuluk	on the north point of the hill 'north-APEX'

Table 21 (continued)

kayi-rni-mpal	moving or lying along the north side e.g. a river 'north-UP-EDGE'	kayi-rni-nyu	on the north point of the hill 'north-UP-??'
kayi-rni-mpal-arra	upstream or downstream towards the north 'north-UP-EDGE'		

Table 22: Cardinal suffixes.

-rra	locative
-k	allative
-yin, -yit	ablative
-nginyi	source
-mpa	perlative
-mpal	edge
-rni	up
-ngkarra	down
-karra	side (river)
-yarra	side (general)
-wuk	turn
-nganang	axis
-nu, -jarrk	cross river
-wariny	far away
-wurru	shade
-wuluk	apex, high point

Some historical and comparative comments on these suffixes are warranted:

-rra

The *-rra* component of the cardinal terms is a frozen suffix, which expresses the inherently locative nature of cardinals and other directional terms. They do not receive further locative marking to locate static objects in space (except in agreement with other nominals which will be discussed below). This suffix is likely to have originated in the thither or centrifugal suffix *-rra* which is commonly found in Ngumpin-Yapa languages, but not in Gurindji (§7.1.3.15). For example, this suffix is used in Warlpiri and Ngardi on inflecting verbs and directional terms (cardinals and verticality terms) (Ennever, 2021; Laughren, 1978, p. 2) to indicate motion away from the speaker or the fact that something is far from the speaker.

-rni

This form is likely to have derived from a hither suffix, indicating motion or proximity to the speaker. Bilinarra uses *-rni* 'hither' on inflecting verbs, Nyininy possesses the 'hither' form *-rni* but it only occurs with imperative and potential inflections. Warlpiri and Ngardi have *-rni* 'hither' on verbs and cardinals (Ennever, 2021; Laughren, 1978, p. 2). Gurindji does not have a hither suffix (§7.1.3.15), but the same form is used on cardinals to indicate relative elevation or 'up' (Laughren & McConvell, 1999).

-ngkarra

This form is found with *kayirra* 'north' and *karrawarra* 'east' (rendered *kaarrangkarra*), however the forms for 'south' and 'west' are partial reduplications, i.e. *kurlarra* 'south' → *kurlangkurla* 'south and down', and *karlarra* → *karlangkarla* 'west and down'.

-mpa

Gurindji and Warlpiri both have the perlative suffix *-mpa*. Again it is found on both Warlpiri inflecting verbs and cardinals (Laughren, 1978, p. 2). In Gurindji, it is only found inflecting cardinals. In this case, the perlative in Gurindji is true to its original meaning 'across, past'.

-mpal

We analyse this suffix as an edge suffix for Gurindji, meaning 'along a side'. For example, *kayirnimpal* means 'moving or lying along the north side'. This suffix sometimes has an additional *-a* which could be interpreted as a different form of *-mpal* or taking an additional locative suffix (since *-a* is the appropriate allomorph for laterals). Ngardi and Jaru only have *-mpala*, which Ennever (2021) and Tsunoda (1981, p. 244) analyse as meaning 'along the X side' which is essentially the same as the Gurindji edge suffix.

-yin

The ablative *-yin* becomes *-yit* as a result of the nasal-stop-cluster denasalisation in stems which contain a nasal-stop cluster (§2.3.4.2). This effects the verticality and river terms *kankula* 'up' i.e. *kankuliyit*; *kanyjurra* 'down' i.e. *kanyjuliyit*; *kankarra* 'upstream' i.e. *kankayit*. It does not affect the cardinal terms which do not contain a nasal-stop cluster. Stems often change when the ablative is used also. For example, *kayirra* becomes *kayili-* and *kanyjurra* becomes *kanyjuli-*. Jaru also has the ablative *-yin* (Tsunoda, 1981, p. 245). Ngardi also has an ablative which attaches to cardinals *-niyin*, but it is not clear whether the *-ni-* component really belongs to the stem or is the hither suffix (Ennever, 2021).

-wurru

This term is used to indicate shade cast by something on a particular side indicated by a cardinal. It is possibly related to the proprietive form found in Mudburra. The -*wurru* form of cardinals is also recorded for Malngin. A -*wurra* form is also recorded for Malngin and Jaru but neither are analysed (Ise, 1998, p. 31; Tsunoda, 1981, p. 244).

-jarrk

The use of -*jarrk* as a suffix to mean 'crossing a river' is probably a recent innovation where the coverb of the same meaning *jarrk* has grammaticalised into a suffix. Both the suffix and coverb currently coexist. The resultant form *kayirniyinjarrk* seems to have the same meaning as *kayinuk*, although the subtleties of the different cardinal forms are often difficult to elucidate. This suffix is also found in Jaru on cardinals (Tsunoda, 1981, p. 244).

-karra

This suffix specifically refers to the sides of rivers. In Ngardi it means 'around' on cardinals (Ennever, 2021).

As well as unique case forms, cardinal directions can receive additional case-markers in agreement with nominal heads. For example in (700), the cardinal *kaarnirra* receives a derivational suffix -*nginyi* 'source' followed by the ergative suffix -*lu* in agreement with the transitive subject *kajirri-lu* 'old.woman-ERG'. Other examples are given in (704), (709) and (702).

(700) Ka-nga-na ngu julujuluj **kajirri-lu,**
take-IMPF-PRS CAT carry.hip.REDUP woman-ERG

kawarla-la, **kaa-rni-mpal-a[146]-nginyi-lu[147]=ma.**
coolamon-LOC east-UP-EDGE-LOC-SOURCE-ERG=TOP
"The woman carries the baby in the coolamon using her hip from on the east-side of her body." (🔊 VW: FM10_a133: 7:12min) (Meakins, 2011c, p. 60)

Cardinal directions are common in descriptions of motion to express static location and motion in large-scale space. In (701), the speaker describes the location of other Aboriginal women who live north and north-west of Kalkaringi in Timber Creek and Kununurra, respectively. These places are 500km from Kalkaringi but are visited occasionally for familial or ceremonial purposes. Note also the additional use of the derivational suffix -*ngarna* and the terminative -*kijak* on these examples. In (702) there seems to be case-stacking of allative + locative case suffixes for which we have no explanation. The use of the allative in (703) is also not obvious. In general, the suffix sequences in Gurindji cardinal terms require further analysis.

(701) Nyila-rra=ma kirri-walija=ma **kayili-yin-ngarna=ma.**
that-PL=TOP woman-PAUC=TOP north-ABL-ASSOC=TOP

Karla-yarra-kijak=ma kula=lu pinarri, lawara.
west-SIDE-TERM=TOP NEG=3AUG.S knowledgeable nothing
"The women **from the north** and **as far as the west** are not very knowledgeable [about cultural matters]." (🔈 VW: FM08_08_4a: 1:55min) (Meakins, 2011c, p. 54)

(702) **Kaarra-ngkarra-jirri-la**=ma ngarlaka=ma kurturtu-wu
east-DOWN-ALL-LOC=TOP hill=TOP womans.daughter-DAT

nyamu=lu lungkarrap karrinyani.
REL=3AUG.S cry be.IMPF.PST
"On the east side of the hill [at Jinparrak] where they used to cry about their daughters." (🔈 VW: FM11_a167: 2:53min)

(703) Ngu=lu ma-na-ni kamparri-jang-kulu nyawa na.
CAT=3AUG.S get-IMPF-PST before-TIME-ERG this FOC

Warrkawarrkap nyamu=lu junpa=ma yunpa-rna-ni,
dance.REDUP REL=3AUG.S corroboree=TOP sing-IMPF-PST

kaarra-yin-karra-jirri nyawa kanyjurra, Compound-ta.
east-ABL-SIDE-ALL this down place.name-LOC
"They used to get this one in the old days. When they used to perform a corroboree, on the east side of the river near the Compound." (🔈 VW: FM08_11_2b: 1:29min)

146 The extra 'a' on *-mpal* looks suspiciously like a locative marker but if this were the case it would be hard to explain the source and then the ergative. It may also be an influence from Mudburra. There are many such examples which need further analysis.

147 The use of the ergative marker here is unclear. It could be functioning as an instrumental (bare ergative markers are used to mark the instrumental function in Gurindji or in conjunction with a proprietive marker) or it could be marking agreement with the subject *kajirri* 'old woman'. Schultze-Berndt (p.c.) suggests it is more likely to be the latter where the ergative is marking location as a secondary predicate. Alternatively, McGregor (p.c.) suggests that this could be an external possessive construction in which the body part is ellipsed as it is encoded in the coverb.

As is also shown in (703), cardinal directions are often used in descriptions of large-scale space in conjunction with demonstratives. Another example is given in (704) and the paradigm of demonstratives was given in Table 20.

(704) Yijarni, **murla-ngka**=ma=lu **kayirra** karrinyani
true this-LOC=TOP=3AUG.S north be.IMPF.PST

kula yangujpa kajijirri=ma.
NEG few old.woman.REDUP=TOP
"True! Lots of women used to live here in the north before."
(🔊 TD: FM09_17_1a: 0:08min) (Meakins, 2011c, p. 56)

Like many Australian languages, Gurindji also uses cardinal directions in descriptions of small-scale space, which is one of the reasons that Australian languages are unique. Cardinals are used when speakers can see each other, and the spatial context is such that other spatial resources such as gestures and deictic expressions would suffice. This is a crucial difference between different generations of Gurindji people. Gurindji people from the age of 40 years and older use compass points to describe where objects can be found in rooms or on shelves, where another person should sit in a group of people, which side of a DVD case has the opening or which part of a tabletop to shift something to. We have even observed a Gurindji speaker using cardinal directions with a blind man to explain which side of his body to find a seatbelt buckle. He had no trouble performing the task, no doubt because he had spent most of his life with sight and his mental map of the world was still obviously highly reliant on cardinal orientation.

An example of the use of cardinal directions in small-scale space is given in (705). It was uttered as three women were sitting around a 1x1m pit, digging for white ochre to use in ceremony.

(705) **Karrawarra** nyila na ngu=rna pu-nga-nku.
east that FOC CAT=1EXC.MIN.S pierce-IMPF-POT
"I want to be digging that [ochre] in the **east** [of the pit]."
(🔊 BW: FM08_01_2a: 10:27min) (Meakins, 2011c, p. 60)

The use of cardinals in small spaces is also very common in describing the location of a figure with respect to a ground which has no obvious front or back. Trees are good examples of such grounds. In Gurindji, the sides of trees are always described in terms of cardinal directions. For example, in (706) three women are chopping a tree down with an axe to make a coolamon. One woman instructs another as to where to cut the tree to make sure it falls safely away from them. Note that in this example the cardinal is double-marked with the Gurindji side suffix *-yarra* and the Kriol equivalent *-said*.

(706)

Kurla-yarra-said	na	pa-rra	Nangala,	nyuntu	na!
south-SIDE-SIDE	FOC	hit-IMP	SUBSECT	2MIN	FOC

"Chop along the south side [of the tree] Nangala, it's your turn now."
(🔊 VW: FM07_a027: 5:37min) (Meakins, 2011c, p. 60)

Cardinal directions are also found in conjunction with demonstratives in discussions of small-scale space. In the following example, the speaker describes how she will split a log in two.

(707)

Yala-nginyi=ma[148]	nyila=ma	**kurla-yarra-nginyi**	na	kataj	pa-rra.
that-SOURCE=TOP	that=TOP	south-SIDE-SOURCE	FOC	cut	hit-IMP

"Cut it from there along the south side [of the log]." (🔊 VW: FM07_a027: 7:34min) (Meakins, 2011c, p. 60)

Perhaps most striking is the use of cardinal terms to differentiate the sides of a human body or paired body parts, as is shown in (700) where the relevant hip is described as being on the east side of the woman's body. Further examples are given in (708) and (709). Note that (708) contrasts with (700) in not requiring ergative agreement because the clause is verbless so the cardinal is the head and *nyawa=ma wurturrji=ma* is the dependent. In (709), the cardinal receives ergative marking because the clause is transitive. These examples are not common as there is rarely a need to distinguish body parts, however where this distinction is required, cardinals are used. This use of cardinals to distinguish paired body parts is also observed for Malngin (Ise, 1998, p. 32).

(708)

Karla-rni-mpal-nginyi,	nyawa=ma	wurturrji=ma,	walngin
west-UP-EDGE-SOURCE	this=TOP	leg=TOP	fly

ngu=yi=rla,	nyawa	partaj	waninyana
CAT=1EXC.MIN.NS=3OBL	this	climb	fall.IMPF.PRS

wayi,	ngayiny-ja	wurturrji-la.
TAG	1EXC.MIN.DAT-LOC	leg-LOC

"The fly lands on my leg up across the westside." (🔊 VW: FM10_a133: 6:09min)

148 It is conceivable that *yala-nginyi* 'that-SOURCE' is being used here in a temporal sense 'then, after that', however given the use of the source marker on the compass point, it is most likely being used in agreement.

(709) Ngu=rla rarrarraj ya-ni nyila=ma ngu=rla
CAT=3OBL run.REDUP go-PST that=TOP CAT=3OBL

wartpaj-pa=rningan ma-ni lanti-kari-la,
throw.spear-EP=AGAIN do-PST hip-OTHER-LOC

ngu=rla pu-nya **kaa-rni-yin-tu**.
CAT=3OBL pierce-PST east-UP-ABL-ERG
"He went running over to him, threw again and got him bang in the eastern hip from the towards the river." (🔊 PP: EC98_a021: Puyukpuyuk: 4:35min)

The cardinal direction system is also utilised in the sign system. For example, Green, Meakins and Algy (forthcoming) demonstrate that signers use absolutely orientated pointing gestures to locate objects in space and indicate the orientation of actions and objects. Another way that Gurindji people use cardinal directions is in the domain of time via a time-space re-mapping. The signs TOMORROW and YESTERDAY utilise the trajectory of the sun. TOMORROW is signed with an arc movement from east to west, as if fast forwarding through the day. YESTERDAY is signed with similar arc sweeping from west to east, a 'day in reverse', as demonstrated in Figure 46. These east-west arcs may be articulated laterally across the body or over the shoulder, depending on the orientation of the signer, and so the absolute spatial anchoring of the action is preserved.

5.2.2 River drainage

The use of the river drainage terms is not as pervasive as cardinal directions in the speech of Gurindji speakers. They are fairly restricted to discussions of large-scale space particularly places and journeys where a water course (often the Victoria River and its tributaries) is salient. The river drainage terms have seven forms, as shown in Table 23. The paradigm seems to be defective, particularly for the downstream terms, although it might be the case that there is syncretism in these forms which we are not capturing in the paradigm. An example was given in (697) and further examples are given in (710)–(714).

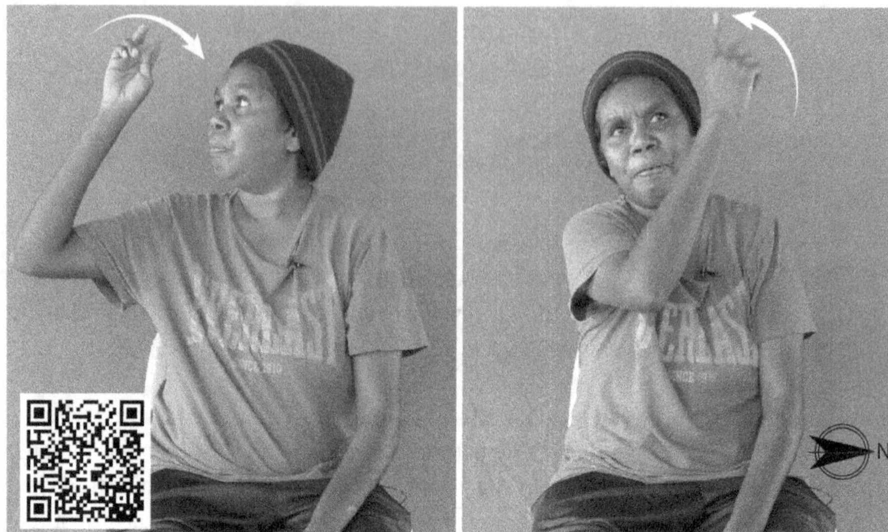

Figure 46: Cassandra Algy demonstrates the signs for TOMORROW and YESTERDAY on an east-west trajectory (the QR code is provided to watch the accompanying video) (Green et al., forthcoming).

Table 23: 'Upstream' and 'downstream' paradigm (McConvell, McNair, Charola, Meakins, & Campbell, 2010; Meakins, 2011c).

FORM	upstream	downstream
locative	kankarra 'upstream'	kani-mpa-rra 'downstream'
allative	kankarra-k 'going upstream'	kani-mpa-rra-k 'going downstream'
ablative	kanka-yit 'coming from upstream'	kani-yin 'coming from downstream'
perlative	kanka-pa[149] 'in the upstream area'	
source		kani-mpa-rra-nginyi 'from downstream'
side	kanka-yit-karra 'coming from the upstream side'	kani-yin-karra 'coming from the downstream side'
axis	kanka-yit-karra-nganang 'coming from along the upstream side'	

149 The *-pa* ending is originally *-mpa* but the nasal has been deleted due to a nasal-stop cluster dissimilation rule (§2.3.4.1).

(710) Karnati-lu=ma ka-nya **kanka-yit,** **kanka-yit**
bush.girl-ERG=TOP take-PST upstream-ABL upstream-ABL

kanka-yit lun yuwa-ni kamurr-kari.
upstream-ABL put.down put-PST middle-OTHER
"The bush-girl took it from higher up and higher and higher and put it down half-way." (🔈 DD: EC98_a017: Karnati-lu: 9:34min)

(711) Nyawa **kankapa** kupuwupu, kukij-karra-waji.
this upstream lemon.grass drink-ITER-AGENT
"The lemon grass upstream from here is drinkable."
(🔈 VW: FM09_14_1a: 6:23min)

(712) **Kanimparra** nyawa=ma kuwart-jawung=ma.
downstream this=TOP gorge-PROP=TOP
"Downstream is the place with a gorge." (🔈 TD: FM07_a058: 0:11min)

(713) **Kanimparra** kuya=warla ngawa=ma parrngany karrinyana
downstream thus=FOC water=TOP full be.IMPF.PRS

nyamu ya-na-na **kanimparra-k**=ma.
REL go-IMPF-PRS downstream-ALL=TOP
"The waterhole becomes full when [water from the spring] runs downstream."
(🔈 BW: FM09_13_2c: 1:19min)

(714) Wart lirlaj ya-ni nyila=rni **kanka-yit-karra-nganang**
back swim go-PST that=ONLY upstream-ABL-SIDE-AXIS

kani-yin-karra.
downstream-ABL-SIDE
"He swam back to the upstream end."[150] (Appendix: Text 2)

The upstream term *kankarra* has a further meaning of 'further into on the horizonal plane', such as a cave or mouth, as shown in (715) and (716). This usage has been noted in Warlpiri (Laughren & McConvell, 1999) and Warrwa also (McGregor, 2006).

(715) Jawinti-la nyawa **kankarra** walyak waninya.
hole-LOC this upstream inside fall.PST
"It went into the cave." (🔈 VW: FM10_a154: 4:40min)

150 The translation is admittedly not very revealing in this example.

(716) Ya-na-na ngu=rla kurrwararn-ku
go-IMPF-PRS CAT=3OBL doctor-DAT

kankarra-k walyak jarriny-ja.
upstream-ALL inside room-LOC
"He entered the doctor's office." (🔈 BW: FM07_a043: 14:00min)

(717) **Kankarra** ngu=rla=nyanta jimak
upstream CAT=3OBL=3OBL2 push.hot.rocks

pu-nya kuya-ngku karnti-ku na.
pierce-PST thus-ERG tree-ERG FOC
"He stuck the hot rock down her throat with a stick like this."
(🔈 VW: FM10_30_2a: Jajurlang: 6:51min)

It also provides the stem for two coverbs *kankarralaj* 'rub stick in the hole of another stick to make fire' and *kankarrarlak* 'lie on back, belly up'.

Finally, *kanimparra* also is used to mean 'head to toe', as shown (718). Note also the additional verticality term *kankunungkarra* 'on top of'.

(718) Pirrka ma-ni ngu=rla jawurt **kanimparra** kartpi
make do-PST CAT=3OBL tail head.to.toe hair

nyila, **kankunungkarra**=ma murla-ngka, kurlarla-la.
that on.top=TOP this-LOC nape.neck-LOC
"He patched him up [with bush gum] from head to toe [Lit. tail up to hair] and right on top of the back of his neck."
(🔈 RW: Warrija Kirrawa: HM070529GUR.DAGU_01rw.mp3: 3:06min)

The origin of the form *kankarra* 'upstream' is in the *kanka-* 'up' stem plus the *-rra*, which was originally a thither or centrifugal suffix (see §5.2.1). For example, *kankarra* 'upstream' in Gurindji is identical to the form simply meaning 'up' in Walmajarri. Its extension to upstream is an innovation found in Eastern Ngumpin languages, probably due to the extensive river systems. The form *kanimparra* 'downstream' comes from the proto-Ngumpin-Yapa root **kani(ny)* 'down' with the addition of the 'across' suffix *-mpa* and the thither suffix *-rra* (Laughren & McConvell, 1999).

5.2.3 Verticality

This set of terms expresses the angular relation between a figure and ground on the vertical axis and are simply translated as 'up' and 'down'. They are universal in the

Table 24: 'Up' and 'down' paradigm.

FORM	down	up
locative	kanyjurra 'down, below'	kankula 'above, on top of'
allative	kanyjurra-k 'downwards'	kankula-k 'upwards'
	kanyju 'beneath'	
	kanyju-k 'downwards'	
edge	kanyju-pal[151] 'underneath, under, below'	kankulu-pal 'above'
ablative	kanyjuli-yit 'from below'	kankuli-yit 'from above'
	kanyjal 'bottom'	
	kaninyjal 'underneath'	kankunungkarra 'on top of something'
	kanyjal-ngurlung 'from below, low in sky'	
source	kanyjurra-nginyi 'down-SOURCE'	
axis		kankuli-yit-nganang 'from the bottom to the top'

world's languages. The inflected forms are given in Table 24. The paradigm is somewhat unsatisfactory and looks incomplete. These are the forms which appear in the corpus and from elicitation, but it is not clear whether other forms exist, or the paradigm is defective. The term *kankula* is used for meanings 'on top of' and 'above' so it may be the case that this uninflected form fills out holes in the paradigm and is synchronous. On the other hand, it is perhaps not correct to consider these forms as forming a paradigm.

Some examples of the use of these forms are given in (719)–(722). In (723) *kanyjurra* 'down' and *kankula* 'up' appear in combination with a number of cardinal terms to accurately pinpoint a location, and in (724) *kanyjurra* 'down' is used in conjunction with a demonstrative and a pointing gesture.

151 The edge suffix *-pal* is formed from *-mpal* through a process of nasal-stop cluster dissimilation (§2.3.4.1).

(719)

Nyawa	na	ngu=rna=ngku	pirrkap
this	FOC	CAT=1EXC.MIN.S=2MIN.NS	make

ma-ni,	jarlaparl	karra	makin	**kanyjurra-k**.
do-PST	on.belly	be.IMP	lie.down	down-ALL

"I've made [the gum] ready for you, lie belly down."
(RW: Warrija Kirrawa: HM070529GUR.DAGU_01rw.mp3: 2:45min)

(720)

Kanyjurra	na	ngu=rna	yuwa-ni	janyja-kurra	na	lun.
down	FOC	CAT=1EXC.MIN.S	put-PST	ground-ALL	FOC	put.down

"I placed it down on the ground." (VW: FM07_a050: 3:30min)

(721)

Nyawa	ngu=rla	rail	karrinyana	parnnga
this	CAT=3OBL	rail	be.IMPF.PRS	saddle

kankunungkarra	karrinyana	partaj-ja.
on.top	be.IMPF.PRS	climb-LOC

"The saddle is sitting on the rail." (BW: FM07-043: 4:21min)

(722)

Yala-nginyi	wirrminy	ngu=rnayinangulu	yuwa-na-na
that-SOURCE	turn.over	CAT=1EXC.AUG.S>3AUG.NS	put-IMPF-PRS

kuya,	**kankulu-pal**	parntawurru	jiya-rna-na	ngu	maru-kijak.
thus	up-EDGE	back	burn-IMPF-PRS	CAT	bottom-TERM

"After that we turn them over and treat [using heated termite mound] their backs from up here to as far as their bottoms." (VW: FM08_a085: 1:12min)

(723)

Nyawa=ma	**kurla-ngkurla**	ya-nku=rli	**kanyjurra**
this=TOP	south-DOWN	go-POT=1INC.MIN.S	down

kaa-rni-rra	**kankula**.	Jurlakkula	nyawa	**kurla-rni-mpa**
east-UP-LOC	up	place.name	this	south-UP-PERL

kaa-rni-mpa	Nero Yard-ta	**kaa-rni-mpa**	ngarlaka.
east-UP-PERL	place.name-LOC	east-UP-PERL	hill

"Let's go up east along the southern side. There's a hill south east of Nero Yard, that hill on the eastern side." (RW: EC97_a003: Yipu-waji: 3:51min)

(724)

Rurruj	ngu	ma-ni	**kanyjurra**	**murla**.
dig	CAT	do-PST	down	this

"She dug a long way down here." (VW: FM09_14_1a: 2:51min)

The term *kanyjurra* 'down' is also derived into a coverb *kanyjurrap* 'bow head' and *kanyjurrawurt* 'traditional custodian or someone who lives and spends most of their time in an area and do not move away much'.

5.3 Ignoratives

There are five major ignorative words found in the corpus. They are used when the speaker does not know the identity of the referent. Like many Australian languages, ignoratives can be used as both interrogatives and indefinites (Mushin, 1995). As interrogatives, they are generally clause-initial, as shown in (725); as indefinites they occur anywhere in the clause (726), but this is not always the case for indefinites.

(725)	**Nyampa=warla=rna=ngku**	ma-lu?
	what=FOC=1EXC.MIN.S=2MIN.NS	talk-POT

“What will I tell you?” (🔈 VW: FM09_17_2a: 0:12min)

(726)	Yala-ngka	Daguragu-la	ngu=rnanyjurrakulu
	that-LOC	place.name-LOC	CAT=1EXC.AUG.S>2AUG.NS

pina	jayi-nya	Puwarraja=ma	**nyampa=ma.**
know	give-PST	Dreaming=TOP	everything=TOP

“There at Daguragu I taught you the Dreamings and everything.”
(McConvell 1996 grammar manuscript: Speaking to young people)

The six base forms are shown in (727):

(727)	*ngana*	'who/someone'
	nyampa	'what/something'
	nyangurla	'when/sometime'
	nyatjang	'how much, how many, however many'
	nyatpa(rra)	'how'
	wanyji	'which/something'

The forms *nyampa, ngana* and *wanyji* then take case inflections to express other notions. The paradigm in Table 25 contains all of the semantically logical forms which have been attested in the corpus and through elicitation. Note that *ngana* 'who' has a suppletive stem *ngantu.*

Ignoratives inflect in much the same way as nominals except no examples with adnominal case have been found in the corpus. The interrogative word tends to be more complex, largely because it is in focus position in the clause, so it receives discourse clitics:

INTERROGATIVE-(DERIVATION)-(NUMBER)-CASE=(WAYI)=(DISCOURSE) =(PRONOMINAL)=(3OBL,RR)=(NGA)

Table 25: Case forms of ignoratives in Gurindji.

CASE	Which	What	Who
Nominative Accusative	*wanyji* 'which' 'something' 'anything'	*nyampa* 'what' 'something' 'anything'	*ngana* 'who' 'someone' 'anyone'
Ergative	–	*nyampa-ku* 'what did it' 'something did it' 'anything did it'	*ngantu-ku* 'who did it' 'someone did it' 'anyone did it'
Dative	–	*nyampa-wu* 'for what purpose' 'some purpose' 'any purpose'	*ngantu-wu* 'whose' 'someone's' 'anyone's'
Locative	*wanyji-ka* 'where' 'somewhere' 'anywhere'	–	–
Allative	*wanyji-kurra* 'where to' 'to somewhere' 'to anywhere'	–	–
Ablative	*wanyji-ngurlu* 'where from' 'from somewhere' 'from anywhere'	*nyampa-ngurlu* 'caused by what' 'something cause it' 'anything caused it'	–
Source	*wanyji-nginyi* 'where from' 'from somewhere' 'from anywhere'	*nyampa-nginyi* 'caused by what' 'something caused it' 'anything caused it'	*ngana-nginyi* 'what name' 'some name' 'any name'
Purposive	*wanyji-kawu* 'where to' 'to somewhere' 'to anywhere'		
Terminative	*wanyji-kijak* 'as far as where' 'everywhere' 'anywhere'	–	–

The difference between the structure of an interrogative nominal and other nominals seems to be the lack of adnominal case,[152] as observed above, but also the addition of the question discourse clitic *=wayi* (which also occurs clause-finally as a particle, see §10.2.10) and a different form of the topic marker *=ja* 'TOP'. The use of the topic clitic produces meanings such as *nyampa=ja* 'what about X' or refers to something or someone already present in the discourse. The focus clitic is the same form found with other nominals: *=warla*/*=parla* 'FOC'. Some examples of interrogative words are given in (728)–(734). Example (728) is an interrogative with derivational morphology, which is quite rare. Similarly rare is a number marker. Only one example is observed in the corpus attaching to *nyatjang* 'how many', as in (729). The rest of the examples are all of case morphology and clitics. Further examples of indefinite words are given through the various sections.

(728) **"Wanyji-ngarna** wayi nyila=ma ngumpin=ma?" "Kaarra-yin-nginyi."
which-ASSOC TAG that=TOP man=TOP east-ABL-SOURCE
"Where's that man from?" "From the east." (🔈DD: EC98_a024: Boxer: 24:38min)

(729) Maitbi=nga **nyatjang-kurt** ngurra=ma, maitbi
maybe=DUB how.many-TIMES camp=TOP maybe

murrkun-kurt, murrkun-kurt ngurra maitbi
three-TIMES three-TIMES camp maybe

nyatjang-kurt na ngurra=ma, kangirriny-ja.
how.many-TIMES FOC camp=TOP day-LOC
"How many days? Maybe for three days." (🔈RW: EC97_a003: 4:53min)

(730) **Wanyji-ka=warla** jarrakap-kaji nyawa=rni
which-LOC=FOC talk-AGENT this=ONLY

ngu=rna karrwa-rna-na wayi?
CAT=1EXC.MIN.S have-IMPF-PRS TAG
"Where's the minidisc recorder, have I still got it?" (🔈VW: FM07_01_1d: 1:57min)

152 Note that McConvell remembers the use of the proprietive, for example, *nyampa-yawung* 'and others' but this has not been observed by Meakins and we have only one unclear example in the corpus.

(731) "Oh **ngantu-ku=wayi=lu** pu-nya manager?" "Wal
oh who-ERG=Q=3AUG.S pierce-PST manager well

kula punyu jarrakap nyawa=ma wankaj," ngu=rla
NEG good talk this=TOP bad CAT=3OBL

ma-rni nyanuny-ku ngumpin-ku.
talk-PST 3MIN.DAT-DAT man-DAT
"'Ah, who speared the manager? This is bad news, this. It looks bad,' he spoke to his Aboriginal worker." (🔊 DD: EC98_a011: 12:24min)

(732) **Ngantu=warla=n-ku=rla?** Nyuntu
who=FOC=2MIN.S-EP=3OBL 2MIN

ngayiny-ja ngayu=ma.
1EXC.MIN.DAT-LOC 1EXC.MIN=TOP
"Who are you going with? You can come with me!" (🔊 DD: EC98_a013: 10:58min)

(733) **Nyampa=warla=rna=ngku** ma-lu?
what=FOC=1EXC.MIN.S=2MIN.NS talk-POT
"What will I tell you?" (🔊 VW: FM09_17_2a: 0:12min)

(734) **Nyampa-wu=ja=n** yijkurrp yuwa-ni?
what-DAT=TOP=2MIN.S vomit put-PST
"Why are you vomiting?" (🔊 BW: FM09_a122: 10:41min)

The pronoun is generally attached to the interrogative as shown in (735) and (736).

(735) 'Hey, **ngantu-ku=yi** murla-nginyi
hey who-ERG=1EXC.MIN.NS this-SOURCE

wurraj ya-ni?' kuya ma-rni ngu.
take.out go-PST thus say-PST CAT
"'Hey!? Who robbed me?' he asked." (🔊 RW: EC98_a015: 20:08min)

(736) Wuu **ngantu-ku=yin** pu-ngku?
hey who-ERG=2MIN.S>1EXC.MIN.NS pierce-POT
"Hey! Who's trying to hit me?" (🔊 RW: EC98_a015: 20:46min)

It is possible that the ignorative word is more complex than meets the eye. There is one tantalising example in the corpus, shown in (737), where the indefinite inflects for dative 'for whatever' and then receives an agentive suffix 'the thing for whatever' and then inflects again for dative in a purposive subordinate clause.

(737) Nyamu=yi=lu ma-nku punyu-k=ma
REL=1EXC.MIN.NS=3AUG.S do-POT good-FACT=TOP

nyila=ma pakipaki=ma, pirrkapirrkap-ku
that=TOP chisel=TOP make.REDUP-DAT

yunpa-rnu-p-kaji-wu **nyampa-wu-waji-wu.**
sing-INF-CV-AGENT-DAT what-DAT-AGENT-DAT
"When they make the chisel for me, I can make singing-sticks or anything like that."
(🔊 VW: FM07_a021: 6:58min)

5.3.1 *wanyji* 'which/something'

Examples of the base form of the interrogative/indefinite *wanyji* 'why, which one, caused for what' is found in (738) and (739), but it is typically found inflected with local cases, locative (730) and (740)–(742), purposive (743), allative (744), ablative (745),[153] source and terminative (746)–(748). The locative form is the most common form and is used more than the allative form to express goals. Examples of purposive forms are only found in Smiler Major's recordings in 1959.

(738) Kayi=n ma-rni ya-nu-wu marri **wanyji**=warla=n ya-ni?
SURP=2MIN.S say-PST go-INF-DAT BUT which=FOC=2MIN.S go-PST
"You said you were going to go so then why didn't you?"
(McConvell corpus: Meakins et al., 2016, p. 231)

(739) Kula **wanyji**=warla part=ma waninya.
NEG which=FOC fall.hard=TOP fall.PST
"He didn't fall off anywhere." (McConvell corpus: Meakins et al., 2016., p. 390)

153 Note that this example takes the locative as the base form which may be a mistake because *wanyjika* is the most frequently used form with a local case marker.

(740) Turlwarrangkarrak ya-na-na ngapuk
blossom.scent go-IMPF-PRS scent

wanyji-ka, jartpurru, nyila na.
which-LOC bloodwood that FOC
"The scent of bloodwood blossoms is wafting everywhere."
(🔊 VW: FM11_a162: 14:49min)

(741) Waapatarl ya-ni **wanyji-ka**=wayi ngu=rla wangany
abscond go-PST which-LOC=Q CAT=3OBL look.around

pu-nya. Ngu=rla warlakap nya-nya yalu-ngku
pierce-PST CAT=3OBL search intake-PST that-ERG

murnungku-lu=ma. **Wanyji-ka** wayi waapatarl ya-ni?
policeman-ERG=TOP which-LOC TAG abscond go-PST
"He absconded somewhere. He looked for him. The policeman looked for him. Where did he abscond to?" (🔊 VW: FM12_a179: 3:38min)

(742) Huh **wanyji-ka**=wayi ngu=yi=lu
huh which-LOC=Q CAT=1EXC.MIN.NS=3AUG.S

wajkarra yuwa-ni, karu-ngku?
throw put-PST child-ERG
"Where on earth did the kids chuck the scissors on me?"
(🔊 VW: FM08_08_1a: 29:49min)

(743) Yangki pa-rra nyila **wanyji-kawu** ya-na-na?
ask hit-IMP that which-PURP go-IMPF-PRS
"Ask that one which way he's going?" (🔊 SM: HALE_K06-004553: 43:36min)

(744) "Nyampa=ja wal **wanyji-kurra**=npula?"
what=TOP well which-ALL=2UA.S

Nyampa=ja, ngu=wuli ma-rni kuya.
what=TOP CAT=3UA.NS talk-PST thus

Ngu=wuli ma-rni kurany-karra.
CAT=3UA.NS talk-PST lie-ITER
"'Well, you know what. Those two went somewhere,' that's what he said to them. He lied to the two of them." (🔊 DD: EC99_a028: 10:13min)

(745) "**Wanyji-ka-ngurlu**=warla nyawa ngu=lu ya-na-na?" kuya.
which-LOC-ABL=FOC this CAT=3AUG.S go-IMPF-PRS thus
"Where have you mob come from?" (🔊 BR: FM15_52_1a: 12:33min)

(746) Ngu=rlaa karrwa-rna-na kungulu **wanyji-kijak.**
CAT=1INC.AUG.S have-IMPF-PRS blood which-TERM
"We've all got the same blood." (McConvell corpus: Meakins et al., 2016, p. 180)

(747) Ngu=rna=rla warlakap nya-nya **wanyji-kijak** - lawara.
CAT=1EXC.MIN.S=3OBL search intake-PST which-TERM nothing
"I looked everywhere for her, but no luck." (RW with ECh: Meakins et al., 2016, p. 390)

(748) Ngu=yilu nya-ngku, **wanyji-kijak**,
CAT=3AUG.S>1EXC.MIN.NS intake-POT which-TERM

karrap, ngumayi-jang-kulu, karu-nginyi-lu
look behind-TIME-ERG child-SOURCE-ERG

nyampa-nginyi-lu kuya, parturu-yawung.
what-SOURCE-ERG thus ceremony.scar-PROP
"Future generations of children will see me with ceremonial scars everywhere."
(🔊 VW: FM11_a161: 1:40min)

The *wanyji* stem also combines with *-rrirniny* which bears some relation to the hither suffix found on demonstratives. The word *wanyjirrirniny* has the meaning 'which way' or 'everywhere' and seems to be used when the speaker doesn't know the location or have a location in mind.

(749) Jungkarra ngu=rna karrinyana,
decide CAT=1EXC.MIN.S be.IMPF.PRS

'**Wanyji-rrirniny**-pa=rna ya-nku?'
which-HITH-EP=1EXC.MIN.S go-POT
"I'm deciding, 'Which way will I go?'" (🔊 VW: FM12_a173: 12:44min)

(750) Ngu=rla nya-nga-ni kuya-ngku=ma,
CAT=3OBL intake-IMPF-PST thus-ERG=TOP

'**Wanyji-rrirniny**-pa=rna yuwa-ni,
which-HITH-EP=1EXC.MIN.S put-PST

wanyji-rrirniny-pa=rna=rla tarrjal ma-ni.'
which-HITH-EP=1EXC.MIN.S=3OBL landing.mark do-PST
"He kept searching for it saying, 'Which way did I throw it, where did I land it?'"
(🔊 VW: FM10_23_1b: Luma Kurrupartu: 1:21min)

(751) **Wanyji-rrirniny**-pa=rlaa ya-nku?
which-HITH-EP=1INC.AUG.S go-POT
"Which way should we go next?" (🔊 VW: FM10_30_1a: Karu Dreaming Story: 0:44min)

Another suffix which is not found marking other ignoratives or indeed nominals is *-wurrajarra/-kurrajarra*. Combined with *wanyji* it has the meaning of 'everywhere, everybody'. It is possible that this is a borrowing, since the suffix does not appear elsewhere.

(752) Ngu=rna ma-rlu, kurru
CAT=1EXC.MIN.S talk-POT listen

wanyjiwurrajarra nyamu=nta karrinyana
everyone REL=2AUG.S be.IMPF.PRS

nya-ngka=yi=lu walik-kujarra.
intake-IMP=1EXC.MIN.NS=3AUG.S around-DU
"I'm going to speak, listen everyone [who is] around."
(DD with ECh: Meakins et al., 2016, p. 391)

(753) Kungulu ngu=ngala wijku-pari **wanyjiwurrajarra**=rni.
blood CAT=1INC.AUG.NS close-ADJ everyone=ONLY
"Everyone's blood is close [we all share the same blood]."
(McConvell corpus: Meakins et al., 2016, p. 391)

(754) Nyawa ngumpit ngumpit **wanyjikurrajarra** kamparri-jang-kulu
this man man everyone before-TIME-ERG

kamparri-jang	an	jalaja-lang.
before-TIME	and	now.REDUP-TIME

"All of these people from the olden days and today." (🔊PN: McNair_K2I: 0:02min)

This ignorative can also combine with the associative *-ngarna* to associate a person with a place.

(755)

"Wanyji-ngarna	wayi	nyila=ma	ngumpin=ma?"	"Kaarra-yin-nginyi."
which-ASSOC	TAG	that=TOP	man=TOP	east-ABL-SOURCE

"Where's that man from?" "From the east." (🔊DD: EC98_a024: Boxer: 24:38min)

5.3.2 *nyampa* 'what/something'

The ignorative *nyampa* 'what, something, anything' declines regularly as for nominals. Examples of core case are accusative, as in (756) and (757), and ergative, as in (758) and (759). Note that in (758), the indefinite is marked ergative in instrumental function.

(756)

Nyampa=warla=rna=ngku	ma-lu?
what=FOC=1EXC.MIN.S=2MIN.NS	talk-POT

"What will I tell you?" (🔊 VW: FM09_17_2a: 0:12min)

(757)

"Wartayi	**nyampa**=warla=rla	nyawa	kampij?"
goodness	what=FOC=3OBL	this	egg

"Goodness what kind of egg is this?"
(🔊 VW: FM10_27_1a: Kurraj Story from Halls Creek: 0:55min)

(758)

Warlupurr	ma-na-na	ngu,	warlayarra-lu=ma	**nyampa-ku**=ma,
stingy	do-IMPF-PRS	CAT	tobacco-ERG=TOP	everything-ERG=TOP

kawurn-tu=ma,	mangarri,	ngarin	kula	jayi-ngu-waji.
ashes-ERG=TOP	bread	meat	NEG	give-INF-AGENT

Nyantu-warij=junu	nga-lu	jaartkarra.
3MIN-ALONE=RR	eat-POT	eat

"She is stingy about her tobacco, ashes and everything. She's the type of person who won't give bread or meat. She has it all on her own herself."
(🔊 VW: FM11_a164: 13:52min)

(759) Ngu=rnalu ma-na-na kamparri-jang-kulu
CAT=1EXC.AUG.S do-IMPF-PST before-TIME-ERG

nyamu=lu ma-na-ni, ngantipanguny-ju,
REL=3AUG.S do-IMPF-PST 1EXC.AUG.DAT-ERG

ngunyarri-lu **nyampa-ku** jaju-ngku nungkiny-kulu.
MMM-ERG what-ERG MM-ERG family-ERG
"We're doing the way the old people did it before, our great-grandparents, anyone, our grandmothers and family." (🔊 VW: FM07_01_1e: 2:21min)

When *nyampa* is inflected with the dative suffix *-wu* it has the meaning of 'why, with what purpose', as shown in (760).

(760) **Nyampa-wu**=ja=n kiyi nya-nga-ni?
what-DAT=TOP=2MIN.S wait.too.long intake-IMPF-PST
"Why didn't you come to see him [before he passed away]?"
(McNair corpus: Meakins et al., 2016, p. 168)

There is a subtle difference between *nyampawu* and *nyampanginyi*. The first questions the purpose and the second questions the cause, compare (734) with (761).

(761) **Nyampa-nginyi**=n kurlpak yuwa-ni?
what-SOURCE=2MIN.S vomit put-PST
"What caused you to vomit?" (McConvell corpus: Meakins et al., 2016, p. 290)

Spatial case markers are also found on *nyampa*. It is found with source (761), locative (762), allative (763), and ablative suffixes. As noted above, when *nyampa* is inflected with the ablative suffix or source suffix it is used to express the meaning of 'why, as a result of what'. It is also found with a combination of the locative and dative to form a purposeful goal, as shown in (764).

(762) Kula wupkarra-la=ma **nyampa-ka**=ma ngapuk
NEG cook.on.coals-LOC=TOP what-LOC=TOP smell

ma-nku ngarin=ma ngarturr-jawung-kulu=ma.
do-POT meat=TOP pregnant-PROP-ERG=TOP
"A pregnant woman shouldn't smell meat when some is cooking."
(🔊 VW: FM09_a123: 10:30min)

(763) Ngaja=nta taarlak-karra ya-na-na **nyampa-kurra**=wayin.
ADMON=2AUG.S danger-ITER go-IMPF-PRS something-ALL=ETC
"You mob might be in danger of something." (🔊 VW: FM12_a177: 4:35min)

(764) Nyawa-rra=ma bush-medicine=ma, janga-ngkawu **nyampa-kawu**.
this-PL=TOP bush-medicine=TOP sick-PURP what-PURP
"This lot of bush medicine is for times when you're sick or whatever."
(🔊 VW: FM10_a136: 10:40min)

The indefinite *nyampa* also combines with a suffix *-kayirnikayirni* 'ETC' which is unique to it. With this suffix it means 'and what not'. It has the same form and meaning in Ngardi. In Eastern Warlpiri, there is a form *nyayi-kanikani* and Warlmanpa has *ngana-kanikani.*[154] In this respect, the form may have been ultimately inherited not borrowed, but is highly lexicalised, since it doesn't appear elsewhere in Gurindji.

(765) Ngu=rnalu ma-nku ngantipanguny,
CAT=1EXC.AUG.S get-POT 1EXC.AUG.DAT

bush-ngarna, **nyampa-kayirnikayirni** kuya.
bush-ASSOC what-ETC thus
"We want to get our own bush medicine, any type of medicine, we collect this lot." (🔊 VW: FM07_01_1e: 12:23min)

(766) Ngu=rlaa=rla wirrin ma-nku kilka-k,
CAT=1INC.AUG.S=3OBL ?sweep do-POT clean-FACT

kilka-k yuka **nyampa-kayirnikayirni**=ma yuwa-ni.
clean-FACT grass what-ETC=TOP put-PST
"We'll clean away everything, grass and whatever else."
(🔊 DD: EC97_a002: Tiwu-waji: 0:41min)

The ignorative *nyampa* is also used to build the 'whatchamacallit' word *nyampayirla*. This word is possibly derived from *nyampa=yi=warla* 'what=1EXC.MIN.NS=FOC, what is it to me'. It could also come from *nyampa* + *yala* 'what that'. It is used to refer to inanimates, with *nganayirla* the animate counterpart. This word is used regularly in discourse, often as a filler where a speaker cannot remember the word, but also often as a stylistic discourse device. It inflects as a regular nominal, as shown in (767) and (768).

154 Thanks to David Nash for these examples.

(767)

Ngu=n-ku=rla	ngaji-wu,	jalak	yuwa-rru,
CAT=2MIN.S-EP=3OBL	father-DAT	send	put-POT

wayita,	an	**nyampayirla**	kamara,	yangunungku.
pencil.yam	and	whatsitcalled	black.soil.yam	bush.potato

"Do you want to send some pencil yams, black soil yams and bush potatoes to Dad."
(🔈 VW: FM10_a155: Ngarlking Karu: 1:55min)

(768)

Nyila=ma=wula	kartipa=ma	karrinyani	karrap
that=TOP=3UA.S	non-Indigenous=TOP	be.IMPF.PST	watch

karla-mpa-wuk-pa=rni	waninya	nyamu=yinangkulu
west-PERL-TURN-EP=ONLY	fall.PST	REL=3AUG.S>3AUG.NS

nyila	purtuj	jiya-rna-ni	**nyampayirla-lu**	warlu-ngku.
that	burn	burn-IMPF-PST	whatsitcalled-ERG	fire-ERG

"The two *kartiya* were watching, turned to the west again to where they had burnt [the bodies] with the fire." (🔈 RW: EC98_a027: Kujilirli: 7:22min)

5.3.3 *ngana* 'who/someone'

The interrogative *ngana* generally only declines for core case. Nominative examples are given in (769) and (773). Ergative and dative examples are given in respectively in (774)–(777) and (778)–(779). Recall that these case forms use the suppletive stem *ngantu*.

(769)

Ngana=warla=rla	ya-ni	nyanuny-jirri	munuwu-yirri.
who=FOC=3OBL	go-PST	3MIN.DAT-ALL	country-ALL

"Who arrived on his country."
(🔈 JM: MCCONVELL_P04-012073: 41:18min)

(770)

Wirlinyi	ya-na-ni	wiringanang,	**ngana**	jaju-rlang
hunt	go-IMPF-PST	split.up	someone	MM-DYAD

kambek	purunyjirri	tanku-yawung,	yala-ngkurra,
return	late.afternoon	food-PROP	that-ALL

ngurra-ngkurra	nyanpulany-jirri.
camp-ALL	3UA.DAT-ALL

"They used to go hunting, that .. who now .. grandmother and grandson, come back in the late afternoon with tucker and go back to their camp." (RW: EC98_a019)

(771) Wayi=ngkulu **ngana** tuwa ya-ni?
Q=3AUG.S>2MIN.NS anyone arrive go-PST
"Has anybody turned up?" (DD: EC99_a028: 13:32min)

(772) **Ngana**=wayi ngu=rla maiti ma-rni nyila=ma marluka=ma.
someone=Q CAT=3OBL maybe talk-PST that=TOP old.man=TOP
"Well, it was as if he was talking to someone, that old man."
(RW: EC97_a007: Warli: 2:46min)

(773) **Ngana**=ngku ma-rni partaj-ku=ma yala-ngkawu=ma ngarin
who=2MIN.NS talk-PST climb-DAT=TOP that-PURP=TOP meat

ngu=yi=n ngayiny purrp-karra jiya-rna-na.
CAT=1EXC.MIN.NS=2MIN.S 1EXC.MIN.DAT finish-ITER steal-IMPF-PRS
"Who told you to climb up there? You are stealing off the meat on me."
(DD: McNair_C2A: 3:51min)

(774) **Ngantu-ku**=wayi=lu pu-nya nyila=ma?
who-ERG=Q=3AUG.S hit-PST that=TOP

Ngantu-ku=wayi=lu pu nya.
who-ERG=Q=3AUG.S hit-PST
"Which mob killed [the manager]?" "Some people killed him."
(DD: EC98_a011: Nyamulu Tampang Pani Kalpuman: 12:09min)

(775) **Ngantu-ku** **ngantu-ku** murla-ngka karrawarra yunpa-rna-na?
who-ERG who-ERG this-LOC east sing-IMPF-PRS
"Who's that singing here in the east?" (BB: McNair_H2D: 5:21min)

(776) **Ngantu-ku** nyawa kutij yuwa-ni karnti
who-ERG this stand put-PST stick

ngayiny-ja ngarin-ta wijku-pari?
1EXC.MIN.DAT-LOC meat-LOC close-ADJ
"Who put this ladder next to my meat?" (DD: McNair_C2A: 3:22min)

(777) **Ngantu-ku**=wayi=lu pa-ni, kuya ngu=wula=nyunu ma-rni.
who-ERG=Q=3AUG.S hit-PST thus CAT=3UA.S=RR talk-PST
"'Who could have got her?' they were asking each other." (DD: EC98_a014: 13:57min)

(778) Ayi, timana nyawa **ngantu-wu**=rla
hey horse this who-DAT=3OBL
"'Hey, here's somebody's horse.'"

Ngantu-wu=rla=nga nyawa yawarta?
who-DAT=3OBL=DUB this horse
"'Whose horse is it?'" (🔈 DD: Nyamulu Tampang Pani Kalpuman)

(779) **Ngantu-wu**=warla nyawa ngarina?[155] Kala=yina,
who-DAT=FOC this meat leave.it=3AUG.NS

nyila=ma=yina jamayang.
that=TOP=3AUG.NS belong
"Who does this meat belong to? Leave it for them. It belongs to them."
(McConvell corpus: Meakins et al., 2016, p. 78)

This ignorative stem can also combine with the source suffix in a specific construction which elicits someone's name, as shown in (780):

(780) **Ngana-nginyi** nyila kartiya-kujarra ngu=wula?
who-SOURCE that non-Indigenous-DU CAT=3UA.S
"What was the name of those two *kartiya*?" (🔈 BW: FM10_22_1c: 0:24min)

In order to express plurality, *ngana* 'who' combines with bound pronouns. For example, in (781) it is clear that a number of people will be bringing other people. Another example was given in (774).

(781) **Ngantu-ku**=yinangkulu ka-ngku?
who-ERG=3AUG.S>3AUG.NS take-POT
"Who's going to bring them?" (🔈 DD: EC98_a024: 14:39min)

The indefinite *ngana* 'someone, anyone' can also combine with *kula* 'NEG' to mean 'no one' as an indefinite pronoun.

(782) **Kula ngana** ya-ni rarraj.
NEG anyone go-PST run
"Nobody could run." (🔈 DD: McNair_F2A: 17:17min)

155 The form *ngarina* is from Mudburra but is commonly used instead of the Gurindji form *ngarin*.

The 'whatitsname' word *nganayirla* is built on the interrogative/indefinite *ngana*. This is the animate counterpart of *nyampayirla* (discussed in §5.3.2), although it can also be used to refer to place names. This word is possibly derived from *ngana=yi=warla* 'who=1EXC.MIN.NS=FOC, who is it to me'. It could also come from *ngana* + *yala* 'who that'. It is used regularly as a filler where a speaker cannot remember the word, but also often as a stylistic discourse device. It inflects as a regular nominal, as shown in (783)–(785). Bilinarra and Ngarinyman also has both *nganayirla* and *nyampayirla* (Jones, Schultze-Berndt, Denniss, et al., 2019, p. 37; Meakins & Nordlinger, 2014, pp. 187–191), however Ngardi uses *nganayi* with both animate and inanimate referents (Ennever, 2021).

(783) Jiwawu ma-na-na ngu **nganayirla-lu**
swoop do-IMPF-PRS CAT whatitsname-ERG

kunkujuku-lu narrinyjila.
sea.eagle-ERG turtle
"The sea eagle snatches up a turtle." (🔈 VW: FM12_a173: 6:32min)

(784) Kaa-rni-yin-nginyi ngu=lu ya-ni
east-UP-ABL-SOURCE CAT=3AUG.S go-PST

nyawa **nganayirla-yirri** tarukap.
this whatsitsname-ALL swim
"From the east they went to whatsitsname and swam around."
(🔈 VW: FM10_30_1a: Karu Dreaming Story: 5:17min)

(785) Nyawa=ma ngu=rnalu nya-nga-na
this=TOP CAT=1EXC.AUG.S intake-IMPF-PRS

nganayirla-wu, tirnung-ku.
whatsitsname-DAT bloodwood.sap-DAT
"I'm looking around for the sap from the – what's its name – bloodwood tree."
(🔈 VW: FM07_01_1b: 0:36min)

5.3.4 *nyangurla* 'when/sometime'

The form *nyangurla* is used to refer to time. It does not inflect for case either as an interrogative 'when' as in (786)–(789) or as an indefinite 'sometime, anytime' as in (790) and (791). Note that in both of these examples of indefinites, it combines with the derivational suffix *-kari* to give the meaning 'at last'.

(786) **Nyangurla**=rlaa lurrpu ya-nku, marru-ngkurra?
when=1INC.AUG.S return go-POT homestead-ALL
"When are we going back to the homestead?"
(🔊 DD: EC99_a029: Kinyjirrka-wu Murtap: 29:43min)

(787) **Nyangurla**=n wart ya-nku?
when=2MIN.S return go-POT
"When are you going back?" (🔊 DD: EC98_a024: 16:08min)

(788) **Nyangurla**=rli ya-nku nyila karu-yarung?
when=1INC.MIN.S go-POT that child-PROP
"When will we go with the child?" (🔊 TN: McConvell_A3463_K: 0:53min)

(789) Ngarin-ku **nyangurla**=lu pirrka ma-nku?
meat-DAT when=3AUG.S make do-POT
"When did they make it for the meat?" (🔊 TN: McConvell_A3463_K: 24:31min)

(790) Warlu-ngka=warla warnan karrinya **nyangurla-kari** ngayirrp ma-ni.
fire-LOC=FOC sleep be.PST when-OTHER breath do-PST
"Japalyi was lying by the fire and after a while he got his breath back."
(🔊 PN: McNair_K2E: 2:32min)

(791) Nganta=lu nya-nya kaa-rni-yin jik **nyangurla-kari**.
ALLE=3AUG.S intake-PST east-UP-ABL emerge when-OTHER
"But then I think they saw him emerge from the east at last."
(🔊 BB: McNair_E2A: 7:36min)

5.3.5 *nyatjang* 'how much/some amount'

The word *nyatjang* refers to amounts (both countable and uncountable). It consists of *nyat-* plus the derivational marker *-jang* 'TIME'. *Nyat-* does not exist on its own or in any other combination hence treating *nyatjang* as a single form. It does not inflect further. Examples of it as an interrogative 'how many' are given in (792)–(794) and examples of indefinites 'however many, some amount' are given in (795) and (796).

(792) Jakiliny=ma **nyatjang**-pa=n karrwa-wu?
moon=TOP how.many-EP=2MIN.S hold-POT
"How many months will you spend?"
(McConvell corpus: Meakins et al., 2016, p. 292)

(793) "**Nyatjang**=parla ya-ni?" "Kula jarrwa, narajpurru."
how.many=FOC go-PST NEG many small.group
"How many are going?" "Not many, maybe three or four."
(McNair corpus: Meakins et al., 2016, p. 256)

(794) Ngu=rla ma-rni, 'Oh yes **nyatjang**-pa=n
CAT=3OBL talk-PST oh yes how.many-EP=2MIN.S

ka-ngku bullet=ma?'
take-POT bullet=TOP
"He said, 'Ok yes, how many bullets do you want to take?'"
(🔊 DD: EC98_a023: 4:37min)

(795) Yarrulan=ma kurlarra pirnti-witi-la olda marta, marluka
young.man=TOP south river.edge-SITE-LOC all teenage.boy old.man

nah yarrulan **nyatjang**=wayi kula=lu karrinyani
no young.man some.amount=Q NEG=3AUG.S stay.IMPF.PST

jilimi-la yikili ngu=lu karrinyani ngurra=ma.
young.girls-LOC far CAT=3AUG.S stay.IMPF.PST camp=TOP
"The young men were on the southern riverbank, all the teenage boys, the old men too, however many there were. They didn't stay near the young girls; they camped a long way away." (🔊 DD: EC97_a008: 5:17min)

(796) Kartipa **nyatjang**, maiti couple of kartipa
non-Indigenous some.amount maybe couple of non-Indigenous

eniwei dei bin gu garra yawarta.
anyway 3PL PST go PROP horse
"There were a few *kartipa*, just a couple, anyway they were going along on horseback." (🔊 RW: EC97_a005: 3:25min)

The interrogative *nyatjang* also combines with the number marker *-kurt* (see also §4.4.3) to give the meaning 'how many times', as shown in (797).

(797)

Maitbi=nga	**nyatjang-kurt**	ngurra=ma,	maitbi
maybe=DUB	how.many-TIMES	camp=TOP	maybe

murrkun-kurt,	murrkun-kurt	ngurra	maitbi
three-TIMES	three-TIMES	camp	maybe

nyatjang-kurt	na	ngurra=ma,	kangirriny-ja.
how.many-TIMES	FOC	camp=TOP	sun-LOC

"How many days? Maybe for three days." (🔊 RW: EC97_a003: 4:53min)

5.3.6 *nyatpa(rra)* 'how'

The final ignorative is *nyatpa(rra)* 'how, what sort'. Two examples are given in (798) and (799).

(798)

Nyatpa=npula	nya-nya	mila?
how=2UA.S	intake-PST	eye

"What sort of eyes did it have?"
(🔊 VW: FM10_27_1a: Kurraj Story from Halls Creek: 3:25min)

(799)

Nyatparra=warla	ngu=n	ma-na-na	wirriji	pirrkap?
how=FOC	CAT=2MIN.S	do-IMPF-PRS	hair.string	make

"How do you make the hair string?" (🔊 VW: FM08_08_1a: 9:37min)

The indefinite can combine with a nominaliser to produced *nyatpa-ny* 'what kind?' (see §4.7.20 for the nominaliser).

(800)

Nyatpa-ny=parla=lu	nyawa	marlarluka	kuya-ny
how-NMLZ=FOC=3AUG.S	this	old.man.REDUP	thus-NMLZ

kula=yi=lu	jayi-nga-na	punyu=ma	mangarri=ma
NEG=1EXC.MIN.NS=3AUG.S	give-IMPF-PRS	good=TOP	veg.food=TOP

ngu=yi=lu	jayi-nga-ni	yulu-yulu-yawung	mangarri.
CAT=1EXC.MIN.NS=3AUG.S	give-IMPF-PRS	dirt-REDUP-PROP	veg.food

"They don't offer the old men any kind of decent food, they just gave me meals with dirt in it." (🔊 RW: EC98_a015: 13:26min)

5.3.7 Discourse clitics

As introduced in §5.3, ignoratives, particularly in their function as an interrogative, can host discourse clitics. The topic and focus clitics are discussed in §10.1.2 and §10.1.7, respectively, and the pronominal clitics are analysed in §6.2. This section focuses on one clitic which is specific to demonstratives =*wayi* 'Q'. Note that =*wayin*/=*payin* is also common on interrogatives but was discussed in §4.7.1.

5.3.7.1 =*wayi* 'Question'

Ignoratives often appear with the clitic =*wayi*, which is also a particle and a tag question (see §10.2.10 for its usage as a particle). Its only function for Gurindji Kriol speakers is now as a tag question. When =*wayi* is used with ignoratives, it has the meaning 'I don't know wh-'. Examples were given above, and additional examples are provided in (801)–(807).

(801) **Nyampa=wayi**?
what=Q
"Whatever?"

(802) **Nyampa=wayi=lu** nga-lu ngurlu-k.
what=Q=3AUG.S eat-POT tasty-FACT
"They are going to eat something tasty."
(McConvell corpus: Meakins et al., 2016, p. 287)

(803) **Nyampa=wayi** ngu=lu kampa-rna-na.
what=Q CAT=3AUG.S cook-IMPF-PRS
"They are cooking something." (McConvell corpus: Meakins et al., 2016, p. 287)

(804) Lawara kula=rna pina **ngana=wayi**?
nothing NEG=1EXC.MIN.S know who=Q
"I don't know – who?" (🔊 TN: McConvell_A3463_K: 21:20min)

(805) **Ngana=wayi**=lu ya-ni.
someone=Q=3AUG.S go-PST
"Some people came but I don't know who."
(McConvell corpus: Meakins et al., 2016, p. 266)

(806) Ngu=lu jawujawurra ma-ni murla-nginyi=ma
CAT=3AUG.S steal.REDUP do-PST this-SOURCE=TOP

tanku=ma **ngantu-ku=wayi.**
food=TOP who-ERG=Q
"Some mob stole the tucker, but I don't know who."
(🔊 DD: Nyamulu Tampang Pani Kalpuman)

(807) 'Kuturu pirrkap ma-na-na, nganta=rli
nullanulla make do-IMPF-PRS ALLE=1INC.MIN.S

rarr ya-nku kurlarra.' **'Ngantu-wu=wayi**?' 'Aa
attack go-POT south who-DAT=Q ah

ngaja=lu pa-na-na, jarrwa-ngku.'
ADMON=3AUG.S hit-IMPF-PRS many-ERG
"She is making a fighting stick, in case those two rush out south for her." "Who for?" "Ah, in case a big mob [come to] attack." (🔊 DD: Karnatirlu)

This clitic is also found in Ngardi attached to ignoratives, and also =*mayi*. Ennever (2021) suggests they demonstrate uncertainty that the state depicted by its host is true, but it is unclear how they demonstrate uncertainty beyond the normal type of referent uncertainty inherent to ignoratives.

5.3.7.2 *=ja* 'TOPic'

This clitic is only found on interrogatives. It marks the category of topic. The clitic =*ma* is used on all other word classes. An example was given in (734).

6 Pronouns

Like all Ngumpin-Yapa languages, Gurindji has two sets of pronouns: free pronouns (§6.1) and bound pronouns (§6.2) (McConvell & Laughren, 2004; Meakins et al., 2021), which is also not unusual for Pama-Nyungan languages (Dixon, 1980; Mushin & Simpson, 2008). Although both sets will be discussed in this chapter, it must be noted that free pronouns are a subcategory of nominals and much of what has been said for nominals also applies to free pronouns. Although the two sets of pronouns are clearly related, one point of difference can be found in their function. While bound pronouns can reference humans and highly affected non-sentients such as animals and, in rare cases, inanimates, free pronouns only ever reference humans. The argument status of free pronouns (and other nominals) and bound pronouns is discussed further in §8.1 since this has been the focus of significant theoretical discussion.

6.1 Free pronouns

The structure of the free pronominal word is essentially the same as for other nominals, as shown below, however free pronouns do not formally distinguish the core case categories of nominative, ergative and accusative, and do not take kinship or number suffixes.

> ROOT + (DERIV) + (ADNOM) + (DAT) + *ny*[156] + (CASE) + (CASE) # [= (DISCOURSE CLITIC) = (PRONOMINAL CLITIC) = (DUBITATIVE CLITIC)]

Each component of this template will be discussed in turn in the following sections.

Like other nominals, the free pronouns are grammatically optional while the bound pronouns are (mostly) obligatory. In this respect, one of the primary functions of free pronouns is to draw attention to a discourse referent. They can be considered inherently prominent in this respect, which is discussed further in §6.2.6.

6.1.1 Form and function

The person and number categories encoded in Gurindji pronouns are shown in Table 26. As is typical for Australian languages, the first person pronouns distinguish inclusive (including the hearer) and exclusive (excluding the hearer) categories. There is also no gender distinction made in the third person pronouns. Unusually for a Pama-Nyungan language, Gurindji has a minimal-augmented number system in the

156 The nominalising suffix is required for an oblique stem.

https://doi.org/10.1515/9783110746884-006

pronouns (both free and bound), making a three-way distinction between minimal, unit augmented (i.e. minimal+1) and augmented number.[157] The system is analysed this way due to the presence of *three* inclusive forms, covering the minimal (*ngali* = two people – speaker and hearer), unit augmented (*ngaliwula* = three people – speaker, hearer and one other) and augmented (*ngaliwa* = speaker, hearer and two or more others) categories. A similar system is also described for Bilinarra and Wanyjirra (Meakins & Nordlinger, 2014, pp. 216–217; Senge, 2016, p. 304). Malngin records a trial pronoun so it is likely that the system is also a minimal-unit augmented-augmented system (Ise, 1998, p. 55).

Table 26: Free pronouns (unmarked).

	MIN	UA	AUG
1EXC	*ngayu*	*ngayirra*	*ngantipa*
1INC	*ngali*	*ngaliwula*	*ngaliwa*
2	*nyuntu*	*nyunpula*	*nyurrulu*
3	*nyantu*	*nyanpula*	*nyarrulu*

This table shows the unmarked pronominal forms, which are the pronouns used in the core ergative, nominative and accusative cases. Free pronouns do not formally distinguish case except for the dative, and therefore differ in their core case marking from both nouns (which pattern on an ergative-absolutive basis) and bound pronouns (which show a nominative-accusative pattern) (§6.2.2.1). Since we analyse Gurindji as having a tripartite system with three core cases: nominative, accusative and ergative, the free pronouns are analysed as showing syncretism across the three core cases, which means they do not distinguish transitive subject (A), intransitive subject (S) or object (O). For example in (808) and (809), the free pronouns are transitive subjects, but do not receive ergative marking. Clauses (810) and (811) show an example of an accusative and nominative subject respectively.

157 This is different from the analysis provided in McConvell (1980, pp. 49–50), in which the number system is treated as singular, dual and plural, with an additional trial form *ngaliwula* only found in the first person pronouns. He provides a number of reasons for this analysis using the bound pronoun system. For example, McConvell argues that the *=rliwula* and *=ngaliwula* forms which he analyses as '1INC.DU.S' and '1INC.DU.NS' undergo dual neutralisation like other duals. McConvell stands by this analysis. But these forms can be thought of as trial under a SG-DU-PL system. Instead, we [read Meakins] argue here that neutralisation involves unit augmented number, and not dual number, since it does not apply to the first person inclusive minimal forms (which would be dual under a SG-DU-PL system) (see §6.2.3.4).

(808) **Ngayu**=ma=**rna**=nga paya-wu katurl.
1EXC.MIN=TOP=1EXC.MIN.S=DUB bite-POT bite
"I might bite it." (RW & DD with ECh: Meakins et al., 2016, p. 153)

(809) Karnti-kari-nginyi na **ngayu**=ma=**rna**
tree-OTHER-SOURCE FOC 1EXC.MIN=TOP=1EXC.MIN.S

pa-na-na, parnngirri=ma.
hit-IMPF-PRS bark=TOP
"I'm cutting bark from another tree." (🔊 VW: FM08_a089: 11:23min)

(810) Ngu=**yi**=wula nya-nga-na karrap
CAT=1EXC.MIN.NS=3UA.S intake-IMPF-PRS watch

Nangala-kujarra-lu=ma **ngayu**=warluk pa-ni.
SUBSECT-DU-ERG=TOP 1EXC.MIN=FIRST hit-PST
"Those two Nangalas are watching me cutting first." (🔊 VW: FM07_a027: 3:34min)

(811) Maitbi **ngayu** ngu=**rna**=rla ma-lu yalu-wu
maybe 1EXC.MIN CAT=1EXC.MIN.S=3OBL say-POT that-DAT

ngayiny-ku, jaliji-yu jimarri-wu mitayi-yu . . .
1EXC.MIN.DAT-DAT friend-DAT friend-DAT friend-DAT
"Maybe I will say to my friend . . ." (🔊 VW: FM12_a171: 24:51min)

Free pronouns in core argument functions are always cross-referenced by bound pronouns. Thus, any ambiguity that may have arisen due to the lack of core case-marking on free pronouns in (808) and (809) is avoided, as the grammatical role of the free pronoun is shown by its agreement with the bound pronoun. The bound pronominal clitic *=rna* '1EXC.MIN.S' cross-references *ngayu* thereby providing information about its grammatical role as a subject.

The dative form of the pronoun is often the same form as the unmarked pronoun + *ny* (or *-nguny*), which may lead to the analysis that the *-ny* is a dative suffix. However, we argue that *-ny* is the same nominalising suffix found on nominals and coverbs §4.7.20. The full set of Gurindji pronominals is provided in Table 27

Table 27: Case forms of free pronouns.

	ERG/NOM/ACC	DATIVE
1EXC.MIN	*ngayu*	*ngayiny*
1INC.MIN	*ngali*	*ngalinguny*

Table 27 (continued)

	ERG/NOM/ACC	DATIVE
2MIN	*nyuntu*	*nyununy*[1]
3MIN	*nyantu*	*nyanuny*[1]
1EXC.UA	*ngayirra*	*ngayirrany*
1INC.UA	*ngaliwula*	*ngaliwulany*
2UA	*nyunpula*	*nyunpulany*
3UA	*nyanpula*	*nyanpulany, nyanpulanguny*
1EX.AUG	*ngantipa*	*ngantipanguny, ngantipany*
1INC.AUG	*ngaliwa*	*ngaliwanguny, ngaliwany*
2AUG	*nyurrulu*	*nyurruluny*
3AUG	*nyarrulu*	*nyarruluny*

[1] These two forms result from deleting the stop in the stem e.g. *nyuntu+ny=nyununy*. This could be a kind of regressive NCD, which is not a regular rule.

The *-nguny* variants for Gurindji are less common than the *-ny* forms. It is not clear whether there is a difference in function between the variants since both exist for some pronouns in all grammatical contexts, for example *ngantipany* and *ngantipanguny*. An example of a *-nguny* form is given in (812).

(812) Murla-ngka ngarlaka-la ka-nga-ni ngu mayingany **nyanpulanguny**.
this-LOC head-LOC take-IMPF-PST CAT veg.food 3UA.DAT
"She was carrying food on her head for the two of them."
(🔊 VW: FM10_30_2a: Jajurlang: 0:51min)

Ise (1998, p. 25) analyses similar pronouns with the *-nguny* suffix in Malngin as relating to augmented forms, but also gives this ending for some dual forms in variation with *-ny* so the analysis is not still not clear.

Dative free pronouns are cross-referenced by the non-subject series of bound pronouns. The non-subject series does not distinguish different kinds of non-subject relations such as the difference between objects and indirect objects (in all person/numbers other than third person – see §6.2.2.1 below). In these situations, the dative free pronoun helps to disambiguate the grammatical relation of the bound pronoun. For example, without the dative pronoun in the following example, the interpretation could be either 'Someone sent it to me' or 'Someone sent me'.

(813) Nyila=ma **ngayiny** ngu=**yi**, jalak yuwa-ni.
that=TOP 1EXC.MIN.DAT CAT=1EXC.MIN.NS send put-PST
"Someone sent it to me." (🔈 VW: FM11_a160: 2:00min)
*Someone sent me.

Other Ngumpin languages also show a similar person-number system and no case distinctions except in conjunction with the dative forms: Bilinarra, Ngarinyman, Malngin and Wanyjirra (Ise, 1998, pp. 126–127; Jones, Schultze-Berndt, Denniss, et al., 2019, p. 36; Meakins & Nordlinger, 2014, p. 217; Senge, 2016, p. 315). Variation in free pronoun systems is seen in other Ngumpin languages. Free pronouns in Ngardi are also directly case-marked, albeit optionally in the case of the ergative. There is no distinct oblique set of stems, as reported in other Ngumpin languages (Ennever, 2021). Jaru distinguishes first (inc/exc), second and third person pronouns, and case-markers also attach directly to the stem (Tsunoda, 1981, pp. 64–65).[158] Warlmanpa and Mudburra show a much reduced free pronoun system (McConvell, 1980; Nash, 1996). Warlmanpa only distinguishes person *ngayu* '1' *nyuntu* '2' and *nyantu* '3' which also have genitive forms. They optionally also take number suffixes. Warlmanpa free pronouns do not inflect for core case other than dative case, and so the forms of free pronouns are the same regardless of whether they are the transitive subject, intransitive subject or object. They can also take non-core cases directly on the stem (Browne, 2021). Mudburra also only distinguishes person *ngayu* '1' *nyuntu* '2' and *nyana* '3' which also have genitive forms. Number markers are also possible, but optional (Capell, 1940, p. 427; Green et al., 2019, pp. 45–46; McConvell, 1980, p. 33).

6.1.2 Pronominal morphology

Free pronouns can occur with many of the same case markers (§4.3), derivational suffixes (§4.7) and discourse clitics (§10.1), as other nominals, and they are included in these relevant sections. Here we just focus on some distributional aspects of a number of suffixes.

158 Note that Ennever also analyses Ngardi as not having a third person pronoun, but instead considers *nyantu* a demonstrative, whereas Tsunoda analyses it as a free pronoun. This is the same form found in Gurindji and the other Victoria River Ngumpin languages. A point of difference with the Victoria River Ngumpin languages is that *nyanung-* is the third person stem for all non-ergative case inflections in Jaru and *nyanungu-* is the stem for all case inflections in Ngardi (including ergative). Also of relevance, Jaru has a dual form *nyanpula* whereas in Ngardi *nyanungu-* simply takes the dual suffix of any other noun or demonstrative. i.e. *nyanungu-kujarra*. The Jaru form is still a little defective in the free pronoun paradigm because there is no distinct plural third person form. There's simply an opposition between dual and unmarked ('general') number. (Thanks to Thomas Ennever for these observations).

6.1.2.1 Case marking

Free pronouns inflect for case building on the dative form. Thus, the dative is neither relational nor adnominal in free pronouns but is simply required as a morphological stem for the case suffix. This use of the dative case is therefore 'arbitrarily required' in the sense of Libert (1988), or a type of 'derivational double case' in Austin's (1995) terms. Examples are given in (814) and (815) where the dative pronoun is the head of the NP.

(814)	Jipurlp	ya-na-na	ngu=wula	**ngaliwanguny**-jirri.
	join	go-IMPF-PRS	CAT=3UA.S	1INC.AUG.DAT-ALL

"The two of them come over to where we're sitting [to join us]."
(🔊 VW: FM12_a173: 6:59min)

(815)	Kula	**ngayiny**-jirri=ma=**yi**	ya-nta	wijku-k=ma.
	NEG	1EXC.MIN.DAT-ALL=TOP=1EXC.MIN.NS	go-IMP	near-FACT=TOP

"Don't come near me." (🔊 VW: FM12_a183: 15:55min)

Where the dative form of free pronouns is found in possessive phrases, it further declines, showing case agreement with the head noun that it modifies, for example ergative (816)–(817), dative (818), locative (819) and allative (815).

(816)	Pinak	jayi-nga-ni	ngu=ngantipangulu
	teach	give-IMPF-PST	CAT=3AUG.S>1EXC.AUG.NS

kampa-rnu-p-ku=ma,	**ngantipanguny-ju**	**nungkiying-kulu**.
cook-INF-CV-DAT=TOP	1EXC.AUG.DAT-ERG	family-ERG

"They taught us to cook them, our family did." (🔊 VW: FM09_12_5d: 1:22min)

(817)	Puntanup	ma-ni	**ngayiny-ju**	**kapuku-lu**	ngu.
	collect	do-PST	1EXC.MIN.DAT-ERG	sister-ERG	CAT

"My sister collected the hair." (🔊 VW: FM08_08_1a: 4:06min)

(818)	**Ngayiny-ku**	**jipiniya-wu**	ngu=rna=rla
	1EXC.MIN.DAT-DAT	boyfriend-DAT	CAT=1EXC.MIN.S=3OBL

jalak	yuwa-rru	jarrakap	milimili.
send	put-POT	talk	letter

"I will send a letter to my boyfriend." (DD with ECh: Meakins et al., 2016, p. 74)

(819)	Nyila	na	ngu=rna	pa-na-na	pirrkap
	that	FOC	CAT=1EXC.MIN.S	hit-IMPF-PRS	make

ngayu=ma jala=ma, ngurra-ngka
1EXC.MIN=TOP today=TOP camp-LOC

ngayiny-ja yarti-ngka, kaarra-yin-karra-la.
1EXC.MIN.DAT-LOC shade-LOC east-ABL-SIDE-LOC
"I'm making that one today at my camp in the shade on the east side of my house." (🔊 VW: FM07_a050: 2:25min)

If the dative pronoun is followed by another dative suffix (i.e. if the function of the first dative is adnominal), the form of the second dative suffix is the consonant-final variant *-ku* (see §4.3.4.1). In (820), the dative pronoun is an indirect object. In (811), *ngayiny* was additionally marked dative in agreement with the head noun which is an indirect object. In (821), the dative pronoun *ngayiny* encodes possession in the NP *ngayiny ngurra* and then receives additional locative marking in agreement with the whole adjunct *ngayiny-ja ngurra-ngka*. Again in (822), *ngayiny* encodes possession and then the comitative is added to express 'with my grandmother'. In (823), the oblique pronoun *nyununy* takes a purposive case suffix which expresses a purposeful goal.[159] In (824) the source case suffix attaches to the dative pronoun *-nginyi* '2MIN. DAT-SOURCE'.

(820) **Nyanuny** ngu=rna=**rla** jayi-ngku, Japarta-wu.
3MIN.DAT CAT=1EXC.MIN.S=3OBL give-POT SUBSECT-DAT
"I gave it to him, to Japarta." (🔊 VW: FM08_08_1a: 28:46min)

(821) Ngurra-ngka=ma **ngayiny**-ja=ma makurru
camp-LOC=TOP 1EXC.MIN.DAT-LOC=TOP cold

ngu=**yi**=rla ya-na-na.
CAT=1EXC.MIN.NS=3OBL go-IMPF-PRS
"The cold crept up on me at my camp." (🔊 VW: FM12_a177: 2:47min)

(822) Ngu=rna=rla ya-nku **ngayiny-kuja jaju-wunyja.**
CAT=1EXC.MIN.S=3OBL go-POT 1EXC.MIN.DAT-COM MM-COM
"I will go with my grandmother."
(McConvell corpus: Meakins et al., 2016, p. 72)

159 Although in examples throughout this grammar we don't segment the dative pronouns, but gloss them as a single form, e.g. *nyununy* '2MIN.DAT'.

(823) Ka-nga-ni ngu **ngurra-ngkawu** **nyanuny-jawu.**
take-IMPF-PST CAT camp-PURP 3MIN.DAT-PURP
"She took it back to her place."
(🔊 VW: FM10_27_1a: Kurraj Story from Halls Creek: 1:12min)

(824) **Nyununy-nginyi** ngu=rna ma-ni.
2MIN.DAT-SOURCE CAT=1EXC.MIN.S do-PST
"I got it from you." (McConvell corpus: Meakins et al., 2016, p. 280)

6.1.2.2 *-jawung* PROPrietive

The proprietive suffix always attaches to a dative free pronoun which marks a possessive, as shown in (825).

(825) Kartipa-lu=ma **nyanuny-jawung** **kuli-yawung**
non-Indigenous-ERG=TOP 3MIN.DAT-PROP fight-PROP

ngu=yina kampit=ma kaa-rni-yin=ma rarr
CAT=3AUG.NS XXX=TOP east-UP-ABL=TOP attack

Darwin-ngurlu=ma. Kujilirli wurlupupu yala-ngka=ma tuu-tuu.
place.name-ABL=TOP massacre wiped.out that-LOC=TOP shot-REDUP
"The *kartiya* came to them with his own aggression from up in the east and from Darwin, and wiped them all out with guns." (🔊 RW: EC98_a027: Kujilirli: 4:40min)

The only place we would expect to see a proprietive attaching to bare free pronoun stems would be in comitative constructions, however, although the proprietive is used as a comitative for inanimates, the locative or comitative is used for animates and pronouns that are inherently human. This means that *ngayu-yawung* '1EXC.MIN-PROP' is not found. Instead *ngayiny-ja* '1EXC.MIN.DAT-LOC' or *ngayiny-kunyja* '1EXC.MIN.DAT-COM' expresses the comitative relationship. *Ngayiny-jawung* as in (826) is only used where a possessive relationship is also being expressed.

6.1.2.3 *-murlung* PRIVative

In the corpus, the only examples of the privative attaching to free pronouns are found additionally marked with a locative to indicate a time period (see §4.3.4.2 for details on the functions of the locative). The dative form of the pronoun is used to attach *-murlung*, as shown in (826)–(828).

(826) "Nyawa=rla Major=ma nyamu=yina pa-ni
this=3OBL NAME=TOP REL=3AUG.NS hit-PST

Ngarlkurrun-ta=ma warlatarti kartiya, ngumpin,
place.name-LOC=TOP massacre non-Indigenous Indigenous

murnungku, murnungku boi kartiya ngu=yina
policeman policeman boy non-Indigenous CAT=3AUG.NS

pa-ni Ngarlkurrun-ta, larrpa, **ngantipany-murlung-kula**.
hit-PST place.name-LOC long.ago 1EXC.AUG.DAT-PRIV-LOC
"Here lies Major, who massacred *kartiya*, *ngumpin*, police and police boys at Ngarlkurrun, where he killed them a long time ago, before our time."
(🔈 DD: EC98_a023: 19:38min)

(827) **Ngantipanguny-murlung-kula=rni** pa-na-ni
1EXC.AUG.DAT-PRIV-LOC=ONLY hit-IMPF-PST

wurrungarna[160]-lu tirriny pa-ni larrpa.
bush.spirit-ERG make.sorcerer hit-PST long.ago
"One made [Tinker] into a sorcerer long before our time."
(🔈 PN: McNair_K2J: 0:30min)

(828) Marlurluka-wu yurrk **ngayiny-murlung-kula=rni**
old.man.REDUP-DAT recount 1EXC.MIN.DAT-PRIV-LOC=ONLY

nyamu=yi=lu yurrk yuwa-ni
REL=1EXC.MIN.NS=3AUG.S recount put-PST

ngayiny=purrupurru-wu karu-wu.
1EXC.MIN.DAT=AND-DAT child-DAT
"One of the old people's stories from before my time which they told me as a child." (🔈 DD: McNair_C2B: 2:06min)

6.1.2.4 *-warij/ny* ALONE

This derivational suffix was discussed in §4.7.24 since it attaches to other nominals. It is mostly used with free pronouns, however, and attaches to the bare form of the pronoun. A further example is given in (830). In (831), the plain form of the free pronoun receives the 'alone' clitic and then ergative case attaches on the outside. The variation between *-wariny* and *-warij* might be the result of NCD. The *-warij* form

160 This word seems to transparently consist of *wurru* 'louse' + *-ngarna* 'ASSOC' but the relationship with *wurrungarna* 'bush spirit' is not known.

commonly occurs with *nyuntu* and *nyantu* but less so with *ngayu*. This is impressionistic, however, because the operation of NCD is not regular with free pronouns.

(829) 'Wilaj-karra-waji', nyila=ma **nyantu-warij** karrinyana.
alone-ITER-AGENT that=TOP 3MIN-ALONE be.IMPF.PRS
"A *'wilajkarrawaji'* is someone who is on their own."
(🔈 VW: FM12_a183: 5:36min)

(830) Yeah pampapawu ngaja=n=junu
Yeah in.trouble ADMON=2MIN.S=RR

ka-nga-na **nyuntu-warij-ju**=ma.
take-IMPF-PRS 2MIN-ALONE-ERG=TOP
"You might get yourself into trouble on your own." (🔈 VW: FM12_a177: 6:37min)

6.1.2.5 =*warluk* FIRST

This unrestricted clitic is found on many different parts of speech (§10.1.8), but is especially common on free pronouns where it attaches to the bare form of the stem, as shown in (831)–(833).

(831) Ngu=yiwula nya-nga-na karrap
CAT=3UA.S>1EXC.MIN.NS intake-IMPF-PRS watch

Nangala-kujarra-lu=ma **ngayu=warluk** pa-ni.
SUBSECT-DU-ERG=TOP 1EXC.MIN=FIRST hit-PST
"Those two Nangalas are watching me cutting first." (🔈 VW: FM07_a027: 3:35min)

(832) **Ngayu=warluk** kuya-rniny ngu=rna pa-na-na tikap.
1EXC.MIN=FIRST thus-HITH CAT=1EXC.MIN.S hit-IMPF-PRS chop
"Me first, I chop the tree this way." (🔈 VW: FM07_a027: 3:39min)

(833) Pa-ni ngu **nyantu=warluk** Nana-ngku.
hit-PST CAT 3MIN=FIRST SUBSECT-ERG
"Nanaku started chopping first." (🔈 TD: FM07_a028: 08:07min)

Note that in (831)–(833), no case-marking is used despite the fact the nominals are transitive subjects. This is in line with the fact that non-dative forms of free pronouns don't inflect for case.

6.2 Bound pronouns

The bound pronoun system is fundamental to Gurindji grammar and is one of its most complex features. It was first described in detail in relation to Gurindji, Bilinarra and Mudburra in McConvell (1980). The function of the bound pronouns is to cross-reference the case, person and number of the core grammatical relations of a sentence, as well as some oblique arguments and adjuncts which involve highly affected entities. The following are examples of bound pronouns cross-referencing various grammatical roles with nominals marked with their appropriate case suffix.

Transitive subject:

(834) **Jarrwa-ngku** ngu=**lu** ma-na-na kuya=ma.
many-ERG CAT=3AUG.S do-IMPF-PRS thus=TOP
"Lots of people do this." (◀) VW: FM08_08_1a: 8:52min)

Intransitive subject:

(835) Ngu=**lu**=rla ya-ni na nganta **karu-walija=ma**.
CAT=3AUG.S=3OBL go-PST FOC ALLE child-PAUC=TOP
"A big mob of kids came over [for a look], I think."
(◀) VW: FM10_27_1a: Kurraj Story from Halls Creek: 3:09min)

Direct object:

(836) Yala-ngurlu=ma ngu=**yina** pangarra ju-na-ni **karu=ma**.
that-ABL=TOP CAT=3AUG.NS corella swear-IMPF-PST child=TOP
"Then the cocky would swear at the children." (IM: ECh: Pangarra)

Indirect object:

(837) **Karu-walija-wu** ngu=**yina** ma-rna-na
child-PAUC-DAT CAT=3AUG.NS talk-IMPF-PRS

nyawa=ma kirri=ma jarrakap.
this=TOP woman=TOP talk
"The woman talks to the kids." (◀) VW: FHM146: 12:52min)

(838) Wiit jayi-ngku ngu=rna**yina**ngulu
show give-POT CAT=1EXC.AUG.S>3AUG.NS

Nangari-kuwang-ku	**Nimarra-wu.**
SUBSECT-AND-DAT	SUBSECT-DAT

"We can show Nangari and Nimarra." (🔊 VW: FM07_a085: 8:42min)

(839)

Ngu=**yina**ngulu	jayi-nga-ni	tanku=ma,	**karu-wu=ma**
CAT=3AUG.S>3AUG.NS	give-IMPF-PST	food=TOP	child-DAT=TOP

nyarruluny-ku=ma,	kamparra-jang-kulu=ma.
3AUG.DAT-DAT=TOP	before-TIME-ERG=TOP

"They used to give the food to their kids in the old days."
(🔊 VW: FM10_a133: 27:24min)

Secondary object:

(840)

An	ngamayi-lu	ngu=**yina**	nguru	jayi-nga-ni
and	mother-ERG	CAT=3AUG.NS	prepare	give-IMPF-PST

walyak-kula=ma	nanta-nanta=ma	nyila=ma.
inside-LOC=TOP	small-REDUP=TOP	that=TOP

"And the mother prepares to give the little ones food inside."
(🔊 VW: FM10_a149: 2:17min)

Oblique argument (note there is no nominal in this example):

(841)

Nyila=ma=**yina**ngkula	kurlng	yuwa-ni
that=TOP=3AUG.S>3AUG.NS	form.cloud	put-PST

kankula=ma	ngawa=ma.
up=TOP	water=TOP

"The water formed into a cloud over them." (🔊 VW: FM10_23_4: 2:43min)

Inalienable possession:

(842)

Jiya-rna-na	ngu=**yina**	**kuya-ny**-kujarra	**tingarri**-kujarra=purrupurru.
burn-IMPF-PRS	CAT=3AUG.NS	thus-NMLZ-DU	knee-DU=AND

"It treats their two knees and other body parts you need for crawling."
(🔊 VW: FM07_a085: 7:05min)

Possessor dissension (note there is no free pronoun in this example):

(843) Ngurra=ma=**yina** yala-ngka karrinyani.
camp=TOP=3AUG.NS that-LOC be.IMPF.PST
"This used to be their camp." (🔊 BW: FM09_17_1c: 1:40min)

Adjunct:

(844) Nyanuny-ku=ma **ngumparna-wu**=ma pirrkap
3MIN.DAT-DAT=TOP husband-DAT=TOP make

ngu=**yina**ngulu pirrkap ma-na-ni.
CAT=3AUG.S>3AUG.NS make do-IMPF-PST
"They used to make it for their husbands." (🔊 VW: FM08_08_1a: 22:07min)

(845) Wanyja-rra=**yina**ngulu **jangkakarni-wu kajijirri-wu.**
leave-IMP=3AUG.S>3AUG.NS big.REDUP-DAT old.woman.REDUP-DAT
"They would have to leave it for the adults and old ladies."
(🔊 VW: FM09_a123: 9:25min)

(846) **Ngumparna-wu** nyamu=**yina**ngulu lungkarrap karrinyani.
husband-DAT REL=3AUG.S>3AUG.NS cry be.IMPF.PST
"Where they used to cry over their husbands [who had passed away]."
(🔊 VW: FM11_a167: 2:53min)

(847) Kajkuru=ma, **karu-wu**=ma=**yina** punyu=rningan.
pandanus=TOP child-DAT=TOP=3AUG.NS good=AGAIN
"The pandanus root is good for the children." (🔊 VW: FM10_a145: 20:10min)

(848) Ngumparna=ma=**yina**ngulu waninyani=ma.
husband=TOP=3AUG.S>3AUG.NS fall.IMPF.PST=TOP
"Their husbands used to pass away on them." (🔊 VW: FM12_a175: 3:17min)

Bound pronouns are mostly obligatory for human NPs, and are generally not used with non-humans, unless they are highly affected, as will be discussed in §6.2.4. Three clitics are not uncommon, as shown in (849).

(849) Karu-ngku$_{A}$ ngayiny$_{PSR1}$-ju$_{C}$ ngu=**yi**$_{PSR1}$=**lu**$_{A}$=**rla**$_{BEN}$
child-ERG 1EXC.MIN.DAT-DAT CAT=1EXC.MIN.NS=3AUG.S=3OBL

ka-nya ngarin marluka-wu$_{BEN}$.
take-PST meat old.man-DAT
"The children of mine took meat for the old man." (VW: FM13_a194: 1:59min)

Up to four grammatical functions (under certain conditions) may be cross-referenced, as shown in (850), although this is extremely rare (see §6.2.2.5). This extent of the use of bound pronouns has also been observed for Warlpiri:

> The approximately 60,000 lines of Warlpiri material available in machine-readable form conform absolutely to the generalisation that *-rla-jinta* cannot follow any (non-zero) non-subject pronominal clitic [FM: i.e. four pronouns are not possible]. Yet several Warlpiri speakers on different occasions have agreed that such a combination is well formed and interpretable.
>
> (Nash, 1996, p. 132)

(850) Ngu=**yi**$_{PSR1}$=**lu**$_{PSP}$=**rla** $_{PSR2}$=**nyanta** $_{BEN}$ ka-nya
CAT=1EXC.MIN.S=3AUG.S=3OBL=3OBL2 take-PST

ngarin [ngumparna-wu nyanuny-ku$_{PSR2}$]$_{BEN}$.
meat husband-DAT 3MIN.DAT-DAT
"[The children of mine] take the meat for her husband."
(VW: FM13_a195: 6:20min)

The structure of the clitic complex is discussed in detail in §6.2.2.

Bound pronouns are clearly clitics: they have clausal scope and placement, can attach to almost any part of speech including imperative verbs (851), and attach after all other inflectional and derivational morphology, and discourse clitics such as topic and focus markers (852). Only the dubitative clitic *=nga* follows pronominal clitics (853).

(851) Jarrmip-kulu karu=ma karrwa=**yinangulu** kuya.
together-ERG child=TOP hold=3AUG.S>3AUG.NS thus
"You two look after the kids together." (VW: FM12_a172: 0:26min)

(852) Hey lamparra-marnany-ju=**ma**=**ngku** jayi-nya,
hey father.in.law-2MIN.POSS-ERG=TOP=2MIN.NS give-PST

kujarra kirri kujarra nyununy.
two woman two 2MIN.DAT
"Hey your father-in-law who is my son gave two girls to you."
(VW: FM10_a155: 10:48min)

(853) Ngantu-wu=**rla=nga** nyawa yawarta?
who-DAT=3OBL=DUB this horse
"Whose horse is it?" (DD: Nyamulu Tampang Pani Kalpuman)

6.2.1 Catalyst attachment

Generally pronominal clitics attach to *ngu* which is the catalyst found in declarative clauses. The catalyst *ngu* may come from the Ngarinyman purposive *ngu* with loss of that meaning. Attachment to a neutral catalyst is not uncommon in Ngumpin-Yapa languages. The *ngu* catalyst is also found in Malngin and Wanyjirra (Capell, 1940, p. 428; Ise, 1998, p. 37; Senge, 2016, pp. 308–309). Wanyjirra also has *nga*. Jaru has *nga* for declarative clauses (Capell, 1940, p. 428), and also *wa* and *pa* for interrogative clauses (Tsunoda, 1981, pp. 68, 124–125). Ngardi has the sequential *ngu/nga*, topic *ma* and emphatic *ka* (Ennever, 2021). The neutral catalyst *pa* occurs in Walmajarri and Mudburra (Capell, 1940, p. 427; 1965, pp. 68–69; Osgarby, 2018a, pp. 103–104). Mudburra also has *nya* 'hypothetical' and *bi/bu/biya* 'apprehensive'. In Ngarinyman and Bilinarra, there is no neutral catalyst and in Warlpiri the catalyst is an auxiliary which also encodes TAM information, for example *lpa* 'imperfective' and *ka* 'present' (Nash, 1986). Warlmanpa also has auxiliaries rather than catalysts (Nash, 2008).

Bound pronouns in Gurindji also attach to a number of other complementisers and particles, for example *wayi* 'Q', *nyamu* 'RELativiser', *kula* 'NEGative' and *ngaja* 'ADMONitive' (see §10.2). The position of the catalyst + pronouns is variable and this choice is governed by complex and largely discourse-related rules (see §6.2.6).

6.2.2 Structure of the bound pronoun complex

This section describes the basic templatic structure for the clitic complex and each of the clitics which make up this complex (cf. Simpson & Withcott, 1986), as well as a number of additional constraints and morphological processes that override this basic structure under certain conditions.

The basic structure of the bound pronoun complex is given in (854); the components of this structure are explained in subsequent discussion.

(854) SUBJ.PERS – NSUBJ/RR – (*ng(k)u*)[161] – SUBJ.NUM – (*ng(k)u*) = 3OBL = 3OBL2

Where:

SUBJ	=	subject
PERS	=	person
NSUBJ	=	non-subject
-ng(k)u-	=	epenthetic
NUM	=	number
RR	=	reflexive/reciprocal
OBL	=	oblique

A rare example of a clitic complex with the full complement of four clitics was given in (850). In (855), the combination of a third person subject marker (⊘),[162] third person augmented non-subject pronoun (=*yina*), epenthetic (-*ngu*-), third person augmented number subject marker (=*lu*) and third person oblique (=*rla*) is shown. Example (856) shows the order of the subject pronoun and reflexive/reciprocal marker. In (857), the order of the non-subject pronoun and the third person oblique is shown. Example (858) is included to show the order of the subject pronoun (=*wula*), the reciprocal/reflexive (=*nyunu*), epenthetic (-*ngku*-) and finally the third person oblique (=*rla*).

(855) Ngu=**⊘-yina-ngu-lu**=**rla** karrinyani
CAT=3P-3AUG.NS=EP=3AUG.S=3OBL be.IMPF.PST

waruk, kapuku-yayi ngayiny kanyirri.
work sister-LATE 1EXC.MIN.DAT half.sibling
"Others used to work for them, like a half-sister of mine."
(🔈 VW: FM10_22_1a: 1:02min)

(856) Nganyanganyang-karra ngu=**n**=**junu** ka-nga-na.
leave.in.fear.REDUP-ITER CAT=2MIN.S=RR take-IMPF-PRS
"You're taking yourself away in fear." (🔈 VW: FM11_a165: 5:51min)

(857) Wajarra-wu=ma ngu=**ngku**=**rla** wirrp yuwa-rru.
corroboree-DAT=TOP CAT=2MIN.NS=3OBL paint.up put-POT
"He will paint it on you for the corroboree."
(McConvell corpus: Meakins et al., 2016, p. 378)

161 This is an epenthetic that appears when both the subject and the object are non-minimal number. See §6.2.2.2 below for discussion.

162 The lack or zero-marking of 3rd person singular/minimal pronouns is not unusual across Australia (Dixon, 2002, p. 363).

(858) Yawu-wu ngu=**wula=nyunu-ngku=rla** wuya-rna-na.
fish-DAT CAT=3UA.S=RR-EP=3OBL throw-IMPF-PRS
"The two of them are casting a line for fish for themselves."
(McConvell corpus: Meakins et al., 2016, p. 431)

Each of the components of the template will be discussed in turn including the subject and non-subject pronouns (§6.2.2.1), combinations of subject and non-subject pronouns (§6.2.2.2), the third person oblique =*rla* (§6.2.2.3) and the reflexive/reciprocal pronoun =*nyunu* (§6.2.2.4).

6.2.2.1 Individual subject and non-subject forms

Bound pronouns decline according to a nominative-accusative pattern in contrast to nouns, which have an ergative-absolutive declension (§4.3), and free pronouns, which have just one form for A, S and O (§6.1.1). Under a tripartite analysis (c.f. Goddard, 1982, see also §4.3), bound pronouns show syncretism between the ergative and nominative case forms – having a single category of 'subject' – but have separate accusative case forms (marking 'non-subject') in all person/number combinations except for third minimal (which is unmarked for subject and object). These non-subject forms are also used to cross-reference humans and some highly affected non-sentients and inanimates in many non-object functions, including indirect object, secondary object, oblique argument and optionally in some adjunct functions. Hence, we refer to them as non-subject forms; although note that there is a separate third person oblique form =*rla*, which is discussed in §6.2.2.3 below. The basic bound pronoun forms are presented in Table 28.

Table 28: Form of subject and non-subject bound pronouns.

	SUBJECT	NON-SUBJECT
1EXC.MIN	=*rna*	=*yi*
1INC.MIN	=*rli*	=*ngali(ny)*
2MIN	=*n*	=*ngku*
3MIN	–	–
1EXC.UA	=*ja*, (=*rnawula*)[1]	=*ngayirra*
1INC.UA	=*rliwula*	=*ngaliwula*
2UA	=*npula*	=*nkuwula*[2]
3UA	=*wula*	=*wuliny*[3]
1EXC.AUG	=*rnalu*	=*ngantipa*
1INC.AUG	=*rlaa*	=*ngala*

Table 28 (continued)

	SUBJECT	NON-SUBJECT
2AUG	*=nta*	*=nyjurra*
3AUG	*=lu*	*=yina*

[1] *=rnawula* is also an alternative subject form for '1EXC.UA.S' probably based on *=rna* (1EXC.MIN.S) +*=wula* (3UA.S).
[2] *=nkuwula* is often heard as *=nkuula*, undergoing a phonological process of vowel-lengthening after the deletion of a semi-vowel (see §2.3.2).
[3] It is possible to drop the final consonant on the 3UA object/oblique form, pronouncing it *=wuli*.

The two-way distinction in Gurindji is fairly standard for Ngumpin-Yapa languages. For example, this paradigm is very similar to Bilinarra, except it lacks the consonant-final *=pula* and *=puliny* variants for the third person unit augmented pronouns, and the *=jina* variant for the third person augmented non-subject pronoun (Meakins & Nordlinger, 2014, p. 229). Other languages such as Wanyjirra, Jaru and Ngardi have an additional locational series (Ennever, 2021, pp. 304–305; Senge, 2016; Tsunoda, 1981, p. 69). Walmajarri has a four-way bound pronoun series: subject, object, oblique and locational (Hudson, 1978).[163] For example, (859)–(861) give the forms for the first person singular: *-rna* '1SG.S, I', *-ja* '1SG.NS, me' and *-ji* '1SG.NSBL, at/with/to me'. In contrast, Gurindji (and Bilinarra) uses the same form *=yi* '1EXC.MIN.NS' for object, obliques and adjuncts.

(859) Jula-rni ma-**rna**-rla ngaju-rlu. (Walmajarri)
talk-PST AUX-1SG.S-3DAT 1SG-ERG
"I talked to him." (Hudson, 1978, p. 17)

(860) Ka-nya pa-**ja** ngamaji-rlu ngaju-kura-rlu. (Walmajarri)
bring-PST AUX-1SG.NS mother-ERG 1SG-POSS-ERG
"My mother hit me." (Hudson, 1978, p. 20)

(861) Warral-pi-nya pa-**ji** manga-ngu. (Walmajarri)
laugh-hit-PST AUX-1SG.DAT girl-ERG
"The girl laughed at me." (Hudson, 1978, p. 21)

163 Note that Hudson refers to the pronominal clitics according to their case features, i.e. nominative, accusative and dative; but I prefer to refer to them according to the grammatical relations they cross-reference, i.e. subject, object, oblique. I have adjusted Hudson's glosses accordingly.

Historically, proto-Ngumpin-Yapa was much like Walmajarri with regards to bound pronouns. Laughren (2011) reconstructs proto-Ngumpin-Yapa as containing a series of three pronouns in the first and second person which cross-referenced subjects, objects and obliques. The forms are given in Table 29.

Table 29: 1st and 2nd person pronouns in Ngumpin-Yapa (adapted from Laughren, 2011).

SUB-GROUP	LANGUAGE	SUBJ	OBJ	OBL	SUBJ	OBJ	OBL
		1st person singular/minimal			2nd person singular/minimal		
Yapa	Warlpiri	*-rna*	*-ju/ji*	*-ju/ji*	*-n(pa)*	*-ngku ~ -ngki*	*-ngku ~-ngki*
	Warlmanpa	*-rna*	*-ju*	*-ju*	*-n(ku)*	*-ngu*	*-ngu*
Western Ngumpin	Walmajarri	*-rna*	*-ja*	*-ji*	*-n*	*-nta*	*-ngu*
Eastern Ngumpin	Ngardi	*-rna*	*-yi*	*-yi*	*-n*	*-ngku*	*-ngku*
	Jaru	*-rna*	*-yi*	*-yi*	*-n*	*-ngku*	*-ngku*
	Gurindji	*-rna*	*-yi*	*-yi*	*-n(ku)*	*-ngku*	*-ngku*
	Bilinarra	*-rna*	*-yi*	*-yi*	*-n*	*-ngku*	*-ngku*
	Mudburra	*-rna*	*-yi*	*-yi*	*-n*	*-ngku*	*-ngku*
	Ngarinyman	*-rna*	*-yi*	*-yi*	*-n*	*-ngku*	*-ngku*
Proto-Ngumpin-Yapa		**-rna*	**-ja*	**-ju*	**-n*	**-nta*	**-ngku*

Laughren (2011) claims that the object pronoun series of 1st and 2nd person singular pronouns in the Eastern Ngumpin and Yapa languages are historically oblique pronouns, but now there is complete syncretism across the oblique and object forms.

Although we present the subject pronouns as monomorphemic forms in Table 28, it is possible to analyse many of them as consisting of distinct person and number morphemes, as follows:

Person:		Number:	
1EXC	*=rna*	MIN	Ø
1INC	*=rli*	UA	*=wula/=pula*
2	*=n*	AUG	*=lu*
3	Ø		

Thus, from these morphs are formed *=rna*+Ø 1EXC; *=rna+lu* 1EXC.AUG; *=n*+Ø 2MIN; *=n+pula* 2UA; =Ø+Ø 3MIN; =Ø+*wula* 3UA; =Ø+*lu* 3AUG etc. Note that we do not gloss examples with Ø where 3rd minimal forms are referenced.

As we will see in §6.2.2.2 below, these component morphemes are transparently distinguished in combination with non-subject forms, where, under certain conditions, the non-subject pronoun splits the two parts of the subject bound pronoun as shown in (862).

(862) Kula=**rna=ngku=lu**[164] ma-nku punyu-k.
NEG=1EXC.S=2MIN.NS=AUG.S do-POT good-FACT
"We can't make you better."
(🔊 VW: FM10_27_1a: Kurraj Story from Halls Creek: 5:55min)

Further evidence for the separability of person and number marking in the pronouns comes from imperative clauses. Gurindji, like many languages, has a grammatical rule of 2nd person subject deletion in imperatives. According to this rule in Gurindji, the subject PERSON marker is omitted, but the NUMBER marker remains, as shown in (863).

(863) Wilimat wanta=**lu**=rla yalu-wu, jarrwa
team.up fall.IMP=3AUG.S=3OBL that-DAT many

ya-nta=**lu**, kayi pa-rra=**lu** nyila.
go-IMP=3AUG.S follow hit-IMP=3AUG.S that
"You mob team up with that one. A big mob of you go. You mob follow him."
(🔊 VW: FM12_a183: 6:20min)

Note that this leaves the subject markers in an imperative construction appearing identical to third person subject forms (and they are glossed as such), since these have a zero person marker and are therefore formally identical to the number marker alone:

3MIN	=Ø	3UA	=*wula*	3AUG	=*lu*
2MIN	=n	2UA	=*npula*	2AUG	=*nta* (suppletive form of =*n-lu*)

See §7.1.3.8 and §7.1.3.9 for further discussion of imperatives.

As for non-subject clitics, it is worth noting that the 1st person clitics display a very strong similarity with the corresponding free pronouns as demonstrated in Table 30:

Table 30: First person object clitics and free pronouns.

	FREE PRONOUN	OBJECT BOUND PRONOUN
1INC.MIN	*ngali*	=*ngali*
1EXC.UA	*ngayirra*	=*ngayirra*
1INC.AUG	*ngaliwa*	=*ngala*
1EXC.AUG	*ngantipa*	=*ngantipa*

164 Note that in most glosses, *-rnangkulu* is just glossed as '1EXC.AUG.S>2MIN.NS'.

Finally, we have not included the third oblique pronoun =*rla* in this paradigm or discussion even though it has been included in this paradigm in other grammars including the Bilinarra grammar (Meakins & Nordlinger, 2014, pp. 227–229). Firstly, including =*rla* would treat the third oblique bound pronoun as belonging to the same category as all of the other non-subject pronouns used in oblique function. But, in fact, their position in the bound pronoun complex is quite distinct, as shown in §6.2.2. Whereas non-subject bound pronouns cross-referencing oblique functions generally appear in the second slot of the bound pronoun complex, =*rla* must appear in the second-last slot. This is demonstrated by the fact that it is possible to have a sequence of a subject + non-subject pronoun + =*rla*, as shown in (864) and (865) (with the order reversed in (865) due to the person hierarchy rule, see §6.2.3.2), but it is not possible to have a sequence of two non-subject pronouns.

(864) Kutirni kutirni karrwa=**rna=ngku=rla** yet.
soon soon keep=1EXC.MIN.S=2MIN.NS=3OBL yet
"Wait, wait I'll keep some for you for it." (🔈 DD: McNair_F2A: 2:31min)

(865) "Pu-ngka=**yi=lu=rla** kapkap," ngu=yina ma-rni.
pierce-IMP=1EXC.MIN.NS=3AUG.S=3OBL gang.up CAT=3AUG.NS say-PST
"'You mob – gang up on him for me,' he said to them." (🔈 VW: FM11_a164: 17:06min)

Furthermore, the fact that =*rla* is paradigmatically distinct from the other bound pronouns used in oblique function is reinforced by the fact that, in the event that the second position in the bound pronoun complex is already filled with a non-subject pronoun, =*rla* can be co-opted to refer to any third person oblique, even if it is non-minimal. This is a feature of =*rla* also observed in Bilinarra and Wanyjirra (Meakins & Nordlinger, 2014, p. 228; Senge, 2016, pp. 320–321). This is shown in (866) in which =*rla* cross-references the plural adjunct *marlarlarluka* 'men from the past'. The regular plural non-subject bound pronoun is not possible here since it can only appear in the second position in the clitic complex, which is already filled with an object bound pronoun =*yina* referring to *yarrulan* 'young people'.

(866) Ngu=rlaa**yina**ngku=rla ma-rna-na
CAT=1INC.AUG.S>3AUG.NS=3OBL talk-IMPF-PRS

marlarlarluka-wu=ma yarrulan-ku=ma.
old.people.REDUP-DAT=TOP young.people-DAT=TOP
"We old people tell the young people about the old people."
(McConvell corpus: Meakins et al., 2016, p. 439)

6.2.2.2 Subject and non-subject clitic combinations

The full set of subject and non-subject combinations are given in Tables 31–33. For simplicity we will gloss many of these as single complex forms throughout this grammar, despite the fact that many have transparent internal structure. Note that there are gaps in the paradigms which mostly represent logical gaps, not gaps in our corpus. Most of these combinations are identical to those in Bilinarra (Meakins & Nordlinger, 2014, pp. 252–253). Note that Hale records some complex pronouns which involve two participants acting on two participants. We do not include these pronouns in these paradigms and instead discuss them in the section on unit augmented neutralisation §6.2.3.4.

Table 31: Complex pronouns with a minimal object.

	1EXC.MIN.NS 'me'	**1INC.MIN.NS** 'us two'	**2MIN.NS** 'you'	**3MIN.NS** 'him, her'
1EXC.MIN.S 'I'	*=rnanyunu* 'I do it to myself'	*=rnangali* 'I do it to us two'	*=rnangku* 'I do it to you'	*=rna* 'I do it to her'
1INC.MIN.S 'you and I'		*=rlinyunu* 'you and I do it to ourselves'		*=rli* 'you and I do it to him'
2MIN.S 'you'	*=yin, =npayi* 'you do it to me'	*=nngali* 'you do it to us two'	*=njunu* 'you do it to yourselves'	*=n* 'you do it to her'
3MIN.S 'he, she'	*=yi* 'he does it to me'	*=ngali* 'she does it to us two'	*=ngku* 'he does it to you'	
1EXC.UA.S 'we two not you'			*=jangku* 'we two do it to you'	*=ja* 'we two do it to him'
1INC.UA.S 'we three'				*=rliwula* 'we three do it to her'
2UA.S 'you two'	*=yinpula* 'you two do it to me'			*=npula* 'you two do it to him'
3UA.S 'those two'	*=yiwula* 'those two do it to me'		*=ngkuwula* 'those two do it to you'	*=wula* 'those two do it to her'
1EXC.AUG.S 'we not you'			*=rnangkulu* 'we do it to you'	*=rnalu* 'we not you do it to him'

Table 31 (continued)

	1EXC.MIN.NS 'me'	**1INC.MIN.NS** 'us two'	**2MIN.NS** 'you'	**3MIN.NS** 'him, her'
1INC.AUG.S 'we'				*=rlaa* 'we do it to her'
2AUG.S 'you mob'	*=yinta* 'you mob do it to me'			*=nta* 'you mob do it to him'
3AUG.S 'they'	*=yilu* 'they do it to me'		*=ngkulu* 'they do it to you'	*=lu* 'they do it to him'

Table 32: Complex pronouns with a minimal subject.

	1EXC.MIN.S 'I'	**2MIN.S** 'you'	**3MIN.S** 'he, she'
1EXC.MIN.NS 'me'	*=rnanyunu* 'I do it to myself'	*=yin* 'you do it to me'	*=yi* 'he does it to me'
1INC.MIN.NS 'you and me'	*=rnangali* 'I do it to you and me'	*=nngali* 'you do it to you and me'	*=ngali* 'she does it to you and me'
2MIN.NS 'you'	*=rnangku* 'I do it to you'	*=njunu* 'you do it to yourself'	*=ngku* 'she does it to you'
3MIN.NS 'him, her'	*=rna* 'I do it to him'	*=n* 'you do it to her'	Ø 'she does it to him'
1EXC.UA.NS 'me and her/him'	*=rnangayirra* 'I do it to us not you'	*=nngayirra* 'you do it to us two'	*=ngayirra* 'he does it to us'
1INC.UA.NS 'us three'	*=rnangaliwula* 'I do it for us three'	*=nngaliwula* 'you do it to us three'	*=ngaliwula* 'she does it to us three'
2UA.NS 'you two'	*=rnangkuwula* 'I do it to you two'		*=nkuwula* 'he does it to you two'
3UA.NS 'the two of them'	*=rnawuliny* 'I do it to those two'	*=npuliny* 'you do it to those two'	*=wuliny* 'she does it to those two'
1EXC.AUG.NS 'us not you'	*=rnangantipa* 'I do it to us not you'	*=nngantipa* 'you do it to us not you'	*=ngantipa* 'he does it to us not you'
1INC.AUG.NS 'us'	*=rnangala* 'I do it to us'	*=nngala* 'you do it to us'	*=ngala* 'she does it to us'

Table 32 (continued)

	1EXC.MIN.S 'I'	2MIN.S 'you'	3MIN.S 'he, she'
2AUG.NS 'you mob'	*=rnanyjurra* 'I do it to you mob'		*=nyjurra* 'he does it to you mob'
3AUG.NS 'them'	*=rnayina* 'I do it to them'	*=njina* 'you do it to them'	*=yina* 'she does it to them'

Table 33: Complex pronouns with a non-minimal subject and non-minimal non-subject.

	1INC.NS 'us'	1EXC.NS 'us not you'	2.NS 'you mob'	3.NS 'them'
1INC.S 'we'	*=rlaanyunu* 'we do it to ourselves'			*=rlaayinangkulu* *=rlaangulu* 'we do it to them'
1EXC.S 'we not you'		*=rnalunyunu* 'we do it to ourselves not you'	*=rnanyjurrakulu* 'we do it to you mob'	*=rnayinangkulu* 'we do it to them'
2.S 'you mob'		*=nngantipangkulu* 'you mob do it to us'	*=ntanyunu* 'you mob do it to yourselves'	*=njinangkulu* 'you mob do it to them'
3.S 'they'	*=ngalangkulu* 'they do it to us'	*=ngantipangkulu* 'they do it to us'	*=nyjurrakulu* 'they do it to you mob'	*=yinangkulu* 'they do it to them'

6.2.2.3 The third person oblique *=rla*

The third person oblique form *=rla* is unmarked for number, as discussed in §6.2.2.1, when another third person augmented non-subject form is present. It most other cases, it is used to cross-reference all third person minimal non-subjects (including indirect objects, complements and animate adjuncts) except objects. Examples are given of the bound pronoun used to cross-reference a range of dative-marked obliques, including indirect objects (867)–(875), beneficiaries (876)–(878)[165] and animate goals (879), comitative (880) and purposive (881). It is only used to cross-reference purposive constructions where the purpose is encoded by a nominal.

165 Note that in most examples where there is an animate beneficiary, a full dative-marked nominal or dative free pronoun is almost always found. This is a rare case where the tendency of Gurindji to omit NPs is more constrained though this is likely to be a pragmatic rather than syntactic constraint.

(867) Ngu=rna=**rla** ma-rni **Nana-wu,**
CAT=1EXC.MIN.S=3OBL say-PST SUBSECT-DAT

"Nyawa jintara partiki-la".
this another nut.tree-LOC
"I said to Nanaku – Here's this other one in a nut tree." (🔊 TD: FM07_a028: 4:34min)

(868) Wuukarra ngu=lu=**rla** karrinyana **nyanawu-wu kuliyan-ku.**
afraid CAT=3AUG.S=3OBL be.IMPF.PRS RECOG-DAT dangerous-DAT
"They're too afraid of crocodiles." (🔊 VW: FM11_a163: 3:27min)

(869) Ngu=rna=**rla** jungkul ma-rna-na **yalu-wu ngumpin-ku.**
CAT=1EXC.MIN.S=3OBL disbelieve talk-IMPF-PRS that-DAT man-DAT
"I am disbelieving of that man." (McConvell corpus: Meakins et al., 2016, p. 116)

(870) **Ngayiny-ku jipiniya-wu** ngu=rna=**rla**
1EXC.MIN.DAT-DAT boyfriend-DAT CAT=1EXC.MIN.S=3OBL

jalak yuwa-rru jarrakap milimili.
send put-POT talk letter
"I will send a letter to my boyfriend." (DD with ECh: Meakins et al., 2016, p. 74)

(871) Kilkila ngu=rna=**rla** karrinyana,
affection CAT=1EXC.MIN.S=3OBL be.IMPF.PRS

karu-wu yapawurru-wu.
child-DAT small-DAT
"I feel affection for my little child." (🔊 VW: FM12_a174: 6:09min)

(872) **Tirnung-ku** ngu=rnalu=**rla** nya-ngku, warlakap.
bloodwood.sap-DAT CAT=1EXC.AUG.S=3OBL intake-POT search
"We will look around for bloodwood sap now." (🔊 VW: FM07_01_1a: 4:19min)

(873) Mart ngu=lu=**rla** karrinyani **wirnangpurru-wu**=ma.
stop CAT=3AUG.S=3OBL be.IMPF.PST kangaroo-DAT=TOP
"They used to stop and wait for kangaroos." (🔊 VW: FM11_a166: 16:48min)

(874) **Nyanuny** ngu=rna=**rla** jayi-ngku, **Japarta-wu.**
3MIN.DAT CAT=1EXC.MIN.S=3OBL give-POT SUBSECT-DAT
"I will give it to him, to Japarta." (🔊 VW: FM08_08_1a: 28:46min)

(875) Ngumpit-tu ngu=lu=**rla** pat-pat
man-ERG CAT=3AUG.S=3OBL feel-REDUP

ma-na-ni **warrija-wu**.
do-IMPF-PST crocodile-DAT
"The men used to feel around for crocodiles."
(McConvell corpus: Meakins et al., 2016, p. 318)

(876) Ngu=rna=**rla** kampa-wu **ngayiny-ku** **karu-wu**.
CAT=1EXC.MIN.S=3OBL cook-POT 1EXC.MIN.DAT-DAT child-DAT
"I'm going to cook it for my kid." (🔈 VW: FM07_01_1c: 6:22min)

(877) Nyila=ma=**rla** ka-nga-na **munkaj-ku** **nyanuny-ku**.
that=TOP=3OBL take-IMPF-PRS wife-DAT 3MIN.DAT-DAT
"He takes it back for his wife." (🔈 VW: FM09_a123: 13:11min)

(878) Ngu=rna=**rla** parnngirri-la kiya-wu, majul
CAT=1EXC.MIN.S=3OBL bark-LOC put-POT stomach

yura-k-ku **ngayiny-ku** **kapuku-wu**.
good-FACT-DAT 1EXC.MIN.DAT-DAT sister-DAT
"I will put it in the bark dish for my sister to make her feel better."
(🔈 TD: FM07_a028: 10:58min)

(879) Tuwa nganta=**rla** ya-na-ni **ngaji-wu**=ma.
meet ALLE=3OBL go-IMPF-PST father-DAT=TOP
"He might have met up with his father."
(🔈 VW: FM10_a155: Ngarlking Karu: 0:06min)

(880) Ngu=rna=**rla** ya-nku **ngayiny-kunyja**[166] **jaju-wunyja**.
CAT=1EXC.MIN.S=3OBL go-POT 1EXC.MIN.DAT-COM MM-COM
"I will go with my grandmother."
(McConvell corpus: Meakins et al., 2016, p. 72)

(881) Nyila jayi-ngka=yi=**rla** jamalarl **ngawa-wu**.
that give-IMP=1EXC.MIN.NS=3OBL handleless water-DAT
"Give me that handleless tin to get some water." (🔈 VW: FM12_a171: 20:19min)

166 Note that *-kuja* is expected here due to the NCD rule. We no longer have the audio to check the example.

In some situations, *=rla* is also found cross-referencing a locative-marked nominal when it is animate, for example in (882). In other examples, such as (883) and (884), it is not clear if *=rla* is cross-referencing the locative-marked nominal or an unstated purpose or person since nominals are not grammatically obligatory. For example (883) could translate as 'We sat in the shade for some reason' or 'We sat in the shade with him'. Note that in Jaru, Ngardi and Wanyjirra (Tsunoda, 1981, p. 69), examples such as these would be analysed as a separate locative series of pronouns.

(882) **Ngurra-ngka**=ma **ngayiny-ja**=ma makurru
camp-LOC=TOP 1EXC.MIN.DAT-LOC=TOP cold

ngu=yi=**rla** ya-na-na.
CAT=1EXC.MIN.NS=3OBL go-IMPF-PRS
"The cold crept up on me at my camp." (🔊 VW: FM12_a177: 0:44min)

(883) **Ngantawi-la** ngu=rna=**rla** karrinya.
shade-LOC CAT=1EXC.MIN.S=3OBL be.PST
"We sat in the shade." (🔊 VW: FM09_a120: 1:00min)

(884) Kurrij-karra na, kurrij-karra mulurrp ngu=rna=**rla**
dig-ITER FOC dig-ITER bore CAT=1EXC.MIN.S=3OBL

pu-nga-na **kankunungkarra-la**.
pierce-IMPF-PRS on.top-LOC
"I am digging away at it, boring from above." (🔊 VW: FM11_a160: 0:43min)

It is also possible that *=rla* can cross-reference a source-marked nominal and ablative-marked nominal, although it must also be noted that in both of these cases, the *=rla* could be interpreted as cross-referencing an unstated purpose or another oblique nominal.

(885) Nyila=rni ma-nta=**rla**=ma kanyjurra-nginyi-nginyi[167]
that=ONLY get-IMP=3OBL=TOP down-SOURCE-REDUP

nomo **partaj-nginyi.**
NEG climb-SOURCE
"Only collect the ones from below, not from the tree." (🔊 VW: FM09_15_2a: 9:03min)

---

167 The use of two source markers is not attested elsewhere. It could be a mistake, or it is possible that one is deriving a directional form and the other agrees with the noun phrase.

(886) Kula=n-ku=**rla** warrij ya-nku **kawurlu-ngurlu**=ma yikili.
NEG=2MIN.S-EP=3OBL leave go-POT sister-SOURCE=TOP far
"You won't walk far away from your sister."
(McConvell 1996 grammar manuscript: Speaking to young people)

The third person oblique pronoun *=rla* is also used to cross-reference a body part where it is marked locative in inalienable possession constructions, as shown in (887)–(889). The non-subject pronoun in each of these examples references the possessor. See §8.3.1, for more discussion of inalienable possessive constructions.

(887) Walngin ngu=yi=**rla**, nyawa partaj
fly CAT=1EXC.MIN.NS=3OBL this climb

waninyana wayi, **ngayiny-ja** **wurturrji-la**.
fall.IMPF.PRS TAG 1EXC.MIN.DAT-LOC leg-LOC
"The fly lands and perches on my leg." (🔈 VW: FM10_a133: 6:09min)

(888) Ngaja=ngku=**rla** **ngapanyji-la** waninya=ma.
ADMON=2MIN.NS=3OBL eye-LOC fall.PST=TOP
"Splinters might get in your eye." (🔈 VW: FM07_a050: 9:24min)

(889) Ngu=yi=**rla** ya-na-na **mila-ngka**.
CAT=1EXC.MIN.NS=3OBL go-IMPF-PRS eye-LOC
"[Flies] are getting in my eyes." (🔈 VW: FM09_13_3b: 2:13min)

The *=rla* is also used in another possessive construction, called 'possessor dissension' by Meakins and Nordlinger (2017). In this case, the bound pronouns 'look into' the possessive phrase and cross-references the possessor, as shown in (890). See §8.3.3, for more discussion of possessor dissension.

(890) Yuwart pa-rra yuwart pa-rra. Janka=ma
chase.away hit-IMP chase.away hit-IMP woman=TOP

nyanuny=ma=**rla** karrinyana ngurra-ngka.
3MIN.DAT=TOP=3OBL be.IMPF.PRS home-LOC
"Chase him away. His woman is at home." (🔈 VW: FM11_a166: 35:54min)

Finally, the third person oblique pronoun *=rla* is used to cross-reference dative-marked reduced subordinate clauses which express a purpose.

(891) Ngu=lu=**rla** ya-ni na nganta
CAT=3AUG.S=3OBL go-PST FOC ALLE

karu-walija=ma **karrap-ku** na jarrwalut.
child-PAUC=TOP look-DAT FOC many
"A big mob of kids came over for a look, I reckon."
(🔊 VW: FM10_27_1a: Kurraj Story from Halls Creek: 3:09min)

(892) Jinim ngu=rnalu=nyunu=**rla** yuwa-na-na,
decorate CAT=1EXC.AUG.S=RR=3OBL put-IMPF-PRS

yatu=ma, **warrkawarrkap-kulawu.**
white.ochre=TOP dance.REDUP-PURP
"We use the white ochre to decorate ourselves for dancing."
(🔊 VW: FM08_a100: 0:15min)

(893) **Turturl-u** pirrkap ma-nta=lu=**rla,** warlu.
roast-DAT make do-IMP=3AUG.S=3OBL fire
"You mob make a fire to roast it." (🔊 VW: FM10_22_1d: 1:49min)

(894) Wilmurr jawung ngu=lu=**rla** pirrkap ma-na-ni
wire-PROP CAT=3AUG.S=3OBL make do-IMPF-PST

kuya-ny-ku na **narrinyjila-wu warrija-wu.**
thus-NMLZ-DAT FOC turtle-DAT crocodile-DAT
"They used to make it with wire to catch turtles, crocodiles and those kinds of animals." (🔊 VW: FM10_a149: 1:18min)

In many other cases, it is impossible to tell what =*rla* is cross-referencing since no overt nominal is present. We provide one extended example in (895) but do not offer hypotheses as to the referents of =*rla* since this requires some analysis of the context of the utterance and some creativity. It is instructive for the reader to get a sense of how prevalent the use of =*rla* is in discourse.

(895) Tajkarra=ma=lu pa-na-ni, yala-nginyi=ma
pound=TOP=3AUG.S hit-IMPF-PST that-SOURCE=TOP

ngu=lu=**rla** ma-na-ni nyampayirla, jilaminy.
CAT=3AUG.S=3OBL get-IMPF-PST whatsitcalled mangrove
"[In the old days people] would get mangrove branches and would pound them."

Jilaminy nyila, nyampayirla-la nyamu
mangrove that whatsitcalled-LOC REL

karrinyana kawirri-la.
be.IMPF.PRS white.soil.plain-LOC
"The mangrove grows in white soil country."

Nyila=ma tajkarra=ma ngu=lu=**rla** pa-na-ni, marntaj.
that=TOP pound=TOP CAT=3AUG.S=3OBL hit-IMPF-PST OK
"They used to pound it."

Ngawa-ngka yapakayi-la na ngu=lu yuwa-na-ni.
water-LOC small-LOC FOC CAT=3AUG.S put-IMPF-PST
"Then they would put it in small billabongs [to poison the fish]."

Jak-im ngu=lu=**rla** yuwa-na-ni.
throw-TR CAT=3AUG.S=3OBL put-IMPF-PST
"They would throw it [in the waterhole]."

Ka-nga-ni na ngu=lu=**rla** wuringwuring wuringwuring.
take-IMPF-PST FOC CAT=3AUG.S=3OBL stir.up.water stir.up.water
"Then they would stir up the water [using the branches]."

Tartartap-karra-la ngu=lu=**rla** wuringwuring=ma ka-nga-ni.
drag-ITER-LOC CAT=3AUG.S=3OBL stir.up.water=TOP take-IMPF-PST
"They would keep dragging them [through the water] and stirring it up."

Tartartap-karra ngu=lu=**rla** ka-nga-ni, wal.
drag-ITER CAT=3AUG.S=3OBL take-IMPF-PST well
"They would keep dragging the branches [through the water]."

Babulap-karra na nyawa=ma karrinya lumutu na ngamalart.
bubble.up-ITER FOC this=TOP be.PST froth FOC froth
"Then the froth bubbled up."

Ngamalart na.
froth FOC
"Froth and scum."

Tampatampang pa-na-na, janyja-ku=purrupurru ngamalart-tu
die.REDUP hit-IMPF-PRS silt-ERG=AND froth-ERG

yalu-ngku.
that-ERG
"The silt and froth kills them."

Nyila=ma ngu=lu=**rla** kilkip ka-nga-ni.
that=TOP CAT=3AUG.S=3OBL stir.up take-IMPF-PST
"They kept stirring up that one."

Tampatampang na nyila-rra=ma yawu=ma.
die.REDUP FOC that-PL=TOP fish=TOP
"And all of the fish died."

Nya-ngku=n na tampatampang, murla-ngka=ma
intake-POT=2MIN.S FOC die.REDUP this-LOC=TOP

nyamu=**rla**=nga karru kutij=ma.
REL=3OBL=DUB be.POT stand=TOP
"You would see them all dead here where they are on the side of the bank."

Nyila=ma ngu=lu ma-na-ni na warrkuwarrkuj.
that=TOP CAT=3AUG.S do-IMPF-PST FOC collect.REDUP
"Then they collect them all." (🔈 VW: FM10_a148: 7:30min)

6.2.2.4 The reflexive/reciprocal pronoun *=nyunu/=junu*

Reflexive and reciprocal clauses encode events in which the subject and object/indirect/beneficiary are the same participant(s). The clauses are always transitive or semi-transitive. Gurindji is similar to many Australian languages and certainly all Ngumpin-Yapa languages in not distinguishing the reflexive/reciprocal which we gloss as 'RR' (Gaby, forthcoming). The reflexive/reciprocal suffix *=nyunu/=junu* occurs in the non-subject slot in the pronominal template, followed by the third oblique pronoun which attaches often using the epenthetic *-ng(k)u-* (896), but not always (897). The variant *=junu* occurs after a consonant as shown in (898).

(896) Namata ngu=yinangkulu paya-rna-ni kuya
no.matter CAT=3AUG.S>3AUG.NS bite-IMPF-PST thus

ngu=**lu=nyunu-ngku=rla** ma-na-ni nyila=ma pingi=ma.
CAT=3AUG.S=RR-EP=3OBL do-IMPF-PST that=TOP ant=TOP
"It wouldn't matter if the ants were biting them, they would just brush the ants off themselves like this." (🔈 VW: FM10_a148: 09:36min)

(897) Jinim ngu=**rnalu=nyunu=rla** yuwa-na-na,
decorate CAT=1EXC.AUG.S=RR=3OBL put-IMPF-PRS

yatu=ma, **warrkawarrkap-kulawu.**
white.ochre=TOP dance.REDUP-PURP
"We put white ochre on each other for dancing." (🔈 VW: FM08_a100: 0:15min)

(898) Nganyanganyang-karra ngu=**n=junu** ka-nga-na.
leave.in.fear.REDUP-ITER CAT=2MIN.S=RR take-IMPF-PRS
"You're taking yourself away in fear." (🔈 VW: FM11_a165: 5:51min)

The reflexive/reciprocal pronoun is most often used to cross-reference direct objects, as shown in (898) and (899)–(907). Sometimes the referent is reflexive (899)–(902) and sometimes reciprocal (903)–(907). Note that in (901) and (902), the subject is an inanimate therefore the reflexive is too. In the case of reciprocals, the subject pronoun is always plural and the reciprocal *=nyunu* is the same form therefore it does not encode number. Because *=nyunu* is both the reflexive and reciprocal, clauses like (904) are ambiguous. Although we translate it as a reciprocal, it could also just as easily be a reflexive i.e. "those two hit themselves". Context determines the interpretation. An object nominal is never found in the clause because *=nyunu* receives its semantic information from the subject nominal, for example 'that man or woman' in (900).

(899) Nyila=ma kart ma-ni ngu=n=**nyunu** makin na.
that=TOP lose.oneself do-PST CAT=2MIN.S=RR sleep FOC
"So then you lose yourself in sleep." (🔈 VW: FM12_a174: 3:53min)

(900) Taarlak ngu=**nyunu** ka-nya yalu-ngku=ma
trouble CAT=RR take-PST that-ERG=TOP

kuli-ngkurra, ngumpit-tu or janka-ku.
fight-ALL man-ERG or woman-ERG
"That man or woman got him or herself into a fight." (🔈 VW: FM11_a162: 0:33min)

(901) Ngu=**nyunu** tingkirt na ma-na-na kuya julu-ngku=ma.
CAT=RR tie.up FOC do-IMPF-PRS thus umbilical.cord-ERG=TOP
"The umbilical cord can wrap around [the baby's neck]."[168]
(🔈 VW: FM10_a143: 8:45min)

168 Because the umbilical cord is a body part, it can mean wrapping around the baby not getting tangled up in itself.

(902) Siks-kula=ma kampa=**nyunu** jumpurn warlu-ngku.
six-LOC=TOP cook.IMP=RR smoke fire-ERG.
"After six days, the fire made itself smoke." (🔈JK: McConvell_A3464_A: 4:06min)

(903) "Marntaj=parla," ngu=wula=**nyunu** nurnaj ma-ni.
OK=FOC CAT=3UA.S=RR nod do-PST
"OK, the two of them nodded at each other." (🔈DD: EC97_a001: Purnkali: 7:01min)

(904) Marntaj=parla ngu=npula=**nyunu** kungulu-k pa-ni.
OK=FOC CAT=2UA.S=RR blood-FACT hit-PST
"You two have hit each other enough now and drawn blood."
(McConvell corpus: Meakins et al., 2016, p. 258)

(905) Tilyak pa-na-na, nyila=ma, ngu=wula=**nyunu**.
love hit-IMPF-PRS that=TOP CAT=3UA.S=RR
"Those two love each other." (🔈VW: FM11_a162: 10:28min)

(906) Ngu=lu=**nyunu** ngarta ma-na-na yalu-wu ngumpit-ku.
CAT=3AUG.S=RR surround do-IMPF-PRS that-DAT man-DAT
"They gathered each other around the man."
(RW & DD with ECh: Meakins et al., 2016, p. 275)

(907) Nyila=ma=wula=**nyunu** nyanpula=rni
that=TOP=3UA.S=RR 3UA=ONLY

nyarlk-ik-karra yuwa-na-ni.
push.down-FACT-ITER put-IMPF-PST
"The two of them were still wrestling each other." (🔈PN: McNair_H2B: 2:24min)

The reflexive/reciprocal pronoun also cross-references the indirect object. Examples (908) and (909) involve 'talk' verbs which take indirect objects. Examples (896), (897) and (911) involve locative indirect objects. In (896) *yuwanana* 'put' takes an indirect object which is a locative-marked nominal in non-reflexive clauses. In all of these examples, *=nyunu* cross-references the referent nominal and *=rla* cross-references the whole locative phrase. Again, in all of these examples both a reflexive and reciprocal interpretation is possible.

(908) Juurl-juurl-wa=rni ma-nyja=wula=**nyunu**!
apologise-REDUP-EP=ONLY talk-IMP=3UA.S=RR
"You two just apologise to each other!" (McNair corpus: Meakins et al., 2016, p. 123)

(909) Yajurrp ma-rni ngu=wula=**nyunu**.
talk.politely talk-PST CAT=3UA.S=RR
"The two of them talked to each other politely." (VW: FM12_a173: 16:07min)

(910) Namata ngu=yinangkulu paya-rna-ni kuya
no.matter CAT=3AUG.S>3AUG.NS bite-IMPF-PST thus

ngu=lu=**nyunu**-ngku=**rla** ma-na-ni nyila=ma pingi=ma.
CAT=3AUG.S=RR-EP=3OBL do-IMPF-PST that=TOP ant=TOP
"It wouldn't matter if the ants were biting them, they would just brush the ants off themselves like this." (VW: FM10_a148: 09:36min)

(911) Wumara walilik yuwa-ni ngu=**nyunu**-ngku=**rla**
stone around.REDUP put-PST CAT=RR-EP=3OBL
"He put stones around himself." (Meakins et al., 2013, p. 381)

The reflexive/reciprocal pronoun can also indicate a benefactive, as in (912) and (913). In (912), the imperative verb is used which means that the person reference is deleted, giving the appearance of a third minimal referent which is ⊘ (see §7.1.3.8). Note that the *-ngku-* is an epenthetic, not the second person minimal object pronoun.

(912) Karrwa=**nyunu-ngku=rla** kurturtu. Jarti karrwa=rla, tanku.
keep.IMP=RR-EP=3OBL womans.child keep hold.IMP=3OBL food
"Keep it somewhere for yourself my child. Hold some food for someone."
(VW: FM12_a172: 3:24min)

(913) Ngayu=ma ngu=**rna=nyunu** wulyuk ma-nku wapawapa.
1EXC.MIN=TOP CAT=1EXC.MIN.S=RR wash do-POT clothes
"I will wash clothes for myself." (SM: HALE_K06-004553: 45:49min)

So far the use of the reflexive to cross-reference objects and dative-marked indirect objects and benefactives is similar to Warlpiri (Simpson, 1991, p. 163). Another grammatical context where the reflexive/reciprocal pronoun is found is comitatives. In (914), *=nyunu* cross-references a comitative which is either locative or comitative-marked for animates (see §4.2.4 and §4.2.9, respectively).

(914) Nyawa=ma=**nyunu** ya-na-ni Mudburra-ngarna Bilinarra.
this=TOP=RR go-IMPF-PST Mudburra-ASSOC Bilinarra
"Mudburra, Bilinarra and Gurindji used to travel around here with each other in the old days." (PN: McNair_D2A: 2:08min)

The reflexive/reciprocal pronoun can also be used in inalienable possession. In (915)–(918), *=nyunu* references the possessor. Note that in Gurindji, reflections, images, shadows and personal names participate in inalienable possession as well as body parts. In these cases, *=nyunu* can only be reflexive. Similar examples can be found in Warlpiri (Simpson, 1991, p. 170).

(915) Waj-karra ngu=**nyunu** wuya-rni mila.
throw-ITER CAT=RR throw-PST eye
"[The Dreaming] threw his own eyes away."
(McConvell corpus: Meakins et al., 2016, p. 235)

(916) Miyijkarra ma-na-ni ngu=**nyunu**, kuya-ny=ma ngapanyji=ma.
wipe.tears do-IMPF-PST CAT=RR thus-NMLZ=TOP eye=TOP
"He was wiping his eyes." (🔊 VW: FM10_23_1a: Luma Kurrupartu: 2:54min)

(917) Ngu=**nyunu** nya-nga-na yarti.
CAT=RR intake-IMPF-PRS reflection
"He's looking at his reflection." (McConvell corpus: Meakins et al., 2016, p. 439)

(918) Kurruman=ma, kuya ngu=**nyunu**-ngku=rla yini ma-rna-ni.
NAME=TOP thus CAT=RR-EP=3OBL name talk-IMPF-PST
"He called himself that name Kurruman." (🔊 BB: McNair_H2D: 3:30min)

Finally, the reflexive/reciprocal pronoun can combine with a free pronoun and *-warij* 'alone' to mean "on one's own". For example, (919) cannot mean "she eats herself", rather it simply reinforces the 'alone' meaning of the *-warij* suffix. The *=nyunu* pronoun must attach to the free pronoun to give this meaning. For example, in (920), it is attached to the admonitive conjunction, not the free pronoun and has the usual reflexive meaning.

(919) Nyantu-warij=**junu** nga-lu na jaartkarra=ma.
3MIN-ALONE=RR eat-POT FOC eat=TOP
"She eats on her own." (🔊 VW: FM11_a164: 14:04min)

(920) Yeah pampapawu ngaja=n=**junu**
yeah get.into.trouble ADMON=2MIN.S=RR

ka-nga-na nyuntu-warij-ju=ma.
take-IMPF-PRS 2MIN-ALONE-ERG=TOP
"You might get yourself into trouble on your own."
(🔈 VW: FM12_a177: 6:37min)[169]

As discussed above, the reflexive pronoun does not encode number. It also does not encode person. As a result, the same form is used for all person and number combinations. There is one exception. In the case of first person minimal pronouns, *=nyunu* can be replaced by the non-subject pronoun *=yi*. So both *=nyunu* (913) and (921) and *=yi* (922) and (923) are possible. This variation is also found in Mudburra. It is also the case for Bilinarra, but *=yi* is only used in benefactive reflexives (Meakins & Nordlinger, 2014, pp. 236–237). In Gurindji, *=nyunu* is also possible for benefactives, as shown in (914). In Warlpiri, the first person singular non-subject pronoun *=ju* also replaces the reflexive, although it's not clear if there is some variation with the *=nyunu* reflexive (Simpson, 1991, pp. 163–164). In Warlmanpa, the first person reflexive alternates between *=ju* and *=nyanu*. The *=nyanu* form in Warlmanpa is restricted to clauses where the first person singular occupies a syntactic role other than (direct) object – this includes benefactives indirect objects and inalienably possessed objects (Browne, 2021).

(921) Ngu=rna=**nyunu** shaving paya-rni nyawa.
CAT=1EXC.MIN.S=RR shaving bite-PST this
"I was shaving myself." (🔈 TN: McConvell_A3463_K: 3:38min)

(922) Ngayu ngu=rna pa-ni kuturu, wartu
1EXC.MIN CAT=1EXC.MIN.S cut-PST nullanulla nullanulla

ngayiny ngu=rna=**yi** wartan-tawu.
1EXC.MIN.DAT CAT=1EXC.MIN.S=1EXC.MIN.NS hand-PURP
"I cut a nullanulla, and a stick to keep for myself later on."
(🔈 TD: FM07_a028: 7:29min)

(923) Ngu=rna=**yi** na ma-rni, 'Ngu=rna
CAT=1EXC.MIN.S=1EXC.MIN.NS FOC say-PST CAT=1EXC.MIN.S

169 This example is slightly odd in the use of the ergative and the clitic/derivational status of *-warij*. This example is discussed in more detail in §6.2.6.2.

pa-na-na kuturu wartu ngu=rna pa-na-na.'
hit-IMPF-PRS nullanulla nullanulla CAT=1EXC.MIN.S hit-IMPF-PRS
"Well I said to myself, 'I will cut wood for a nullanulla and stick'."
(🔊 TD: FM07_a028: 6:09min)

Wanyjirra and Jaru have an additional use of the reflexive/reciprocal bound pronoun with intransitive verbs to give to meaning 'together', for example 'they cry together' where the subject pronoun and reflexive are used (Senge, 2016, pp. 332–334; Tsunoda, 2007, pp. 887–889). This function does not occur in Gurindji. Malngin has the form =*nyunu* (Ise, 1998, p. 46). The form =*junu* is unrecorded, but this is likely to be a limitation of the corpus. Mudburra divides the functions of reflexive and reciprocal between =*nyunu* and =*rna*, respectively (Osgarby, 2018a, pp. 122–124).

6.2.2.5 Second oblique =*nyanta*

Where two obliques are expressed, a second oblique pronoun =*nyanta* can be used which follows =*rla* in the pronoun template. In (924), the first oblique =*rla* refers to the possessive NP 'her husband' and the second refers to 'at his place', which is encoded by the locative. Similarly in (925),=*rla* refers to *nyantu* 'his' and =*nyanta* 'at him' refers to the whole locative phrase *nyanuny-ja*, which could also be translated as 'the place where he's standing'. Two other examples are given (926) and (927), but they do not include the full nominals.

(924) Ngu=**rla=nyanta** karrinya **nyanuny-ja** na
CAT=3OBL=3OBL2 stay.PST 3MIN.DAT-LOC FOC

marluka-wu-ny-ja **yalu-wu-ny-ja**,
old.man-DAT-NMLZ-LOC that-DAT-NMLZ-LOC

ngayiny=ma kapuku=ma Mayawi=ma.
1EXC.MIN.DAT=TOP sister=TOP NAME=TOP
"My sister Mayawi used to stay at that old Afghan man's place."
(🔊 VW: FM10_22_1a: 4:08min)

(925) Yikili-ngurlung, kurrupartu=ma warntarrija
far-ABL boomerang=TOP throw.boomerang

yuwa-na-na. Jartaj ma-ni
put-IMPF-PRS hit.with.boomerang do-PST

ngu=**rla=nyanta** **nyanuny-ja**=rni kuya.
CAT=3OBL=3OBL2 3MIN.DAT-LOC=ONLY thus
"He throws a boomerang from a long way away. He aimed it right at him."
(🔊 VW: FM12_a172: 2:42min)

(926) Kankarra ngu=**rla=nyanta** jimak
upstream CAT=3OBL=3OBL2 heat.up.rocks

pu-nya kuya-ngku karnti-ku na.
pierce-PST thus-ERG tree-ERG FOC
"He stuck the hot rock down her throat with a stick like this."
(VW: FM10_30_2a: Jajurlang: 6:51min)

(927) Nyamu=rla papa=ma waninyana,
REL=3OBL older.brother=TOP fall.IMPF.PRS

yapawurru=warla maitbi, nyila=ma kirri=ma wangu
small=FOC maybe that=TOP woman=TOP widow

ngu=**rla=nyanta** pirnti-ka karrinyana.
CAT=3OBL=3OBL2 alongside-LOC be.IMPF.PRS

Lirrpanti ngu=rla karrinyana.
live.with.brother.of.deceased.husband CAT=3OBL be.IMPF.PRS
"When his older brother passes away, his wife who is a widow lives with the younger brother. She goes to live with him." (VW: FM12_a178: 1:33min)

The combination of *=rla=nyanta* can also co-occur with a subject pronoun, such as in (928), where *=lu* refers to crocodile hunters. Again, the combination of *=rla=nyanta* cross-references a possessive phrase embedded in a locative phrase 'into the crocodile's back'.

(928) Tarl ngu=**lu=rla=nyanta** yuwa-na-ni, warrija-la=ma.
hit CAT=3AUG.S=3OBL=3OBL2 put-IMPF-PST crocodile-LOC=TOP
"They used to stab [the spear] into the crocodile's [back]."
(VW: FM12_a173: 4:52min)

In fact, the use of *=nyanta* means that it is possible to produce some of the very rare examples of a sequence of four bound pronouns: *=lu* 'they' (transitive subject), *=yi* 'my' (possessor), *=rla* 'her' (possessor dissension) and *=nyanta* 'for her husband' (beneficiary). The sequence of four pronouns is also possible, but rare in Warlpiri (Nash, 1996, p. 132), as discussed in §6.2.2.1.

(929) **Ngu=yi**$_{PSR1}$**=lu**$_{PSP}$**=rla**$_{PSR2}$**=nyanta**$_{BEN}$ ka-nya
CAT=1EXC.MIN.S=3AUG.S=3OBL=3OBL2 take-PST

ngarin [**ngumparna-wu** **nyanuny-ku**$_{PSR2}$]$_{BEN}$.
meat husband-DAT 3MIN.DAT-DAT
"[The children of mine] take the meat for her husband."
(🔈 VW: FM13_a195: 6:20min)

6.2.3 Combination rules

The previous sections described each of the types of bound pronouns and their position in the template. The following sections describe rules that affect combinations of bound pronouns.

6.2.3.1 Subject marking

As can be seen from the template in §6.1.1, in the presence of a non-subject pronoun, the subject marking is split with the subject person morpheme appearing to the left of the non-subject marker, and the subject number morpheme to the right, as in (930). Where the subject pronoun is minimal and therefore ⊘, the order gives the appearance of subject then non-subject pronoun (because only person is expressed), as in (931):[170]

(930) Kula=**rna-ngku=lu** ma-nku punyu-k.
NEG=1EXC.MIN-2MIN.NS-EP-AUG do-POT good-FACT
"We can't make you better."
(🔈 VW: FM10_27_1a: Kurraj Story from Halls Creek: 5:55min)

(931) Junction-ku murlu-wu ngu=**rna=ngku** ma-rna-na.
junction-DAT this-DAT CAT=1EXC.MIN.S=2MIN.NS talk-IMPF-PRS
"I'm talking to you about this junction." (🔈 VW: FM07_a058: 0:16min)

There are two augmented subject pronouns whose basic forms (given in Table 28 above) are not readily segmentable into person and number morphemes. The first of these is the second person augmented bound pronoun =*nta* (932). Although in its base form it cannot be analysed as consisting of separate person and number morphemes, the predicted forms surface when a second person augmented subject is combined with a non-subject marker, as shown in (933).

170 Note that, although we gloss the parts separately in this discussion for presentational purposes, throughout this grammar we generally gloss subject and non-subject bound pronoun combinations as single forms (to aid in the readability of glossing) or as subject>object pronouns if the forms are easily separated. Thus, a bound pronoun complex such as =*rnangkulu* is glossed as '1EXC.AUG.S>2MIN.NS' in (931) and a separable clitic complex such as =*rna=ngku* in (932) is usually glossed as '1EXC.MIN.S=2MIN.NS'.

(932)

Ma-nku	ngu=**nta**	jawurt-ngurlung	yirr.
do-POT	CAT=2AUG.S	tail-ABL	pull

"You mob can pull it by the tail." (🔈 VW: FM10_a154: 4:44min)

(933)

Nyawa=ma	warlaku=ma	jarrwa=kata	ngu=**n=jina-ngku=lu**
this=TOP	dog=TOP	many=IMM	CAT=2.S=3AUG.NS-EP=AUG

karrwa-rna-na	murla-ngka=ma.
have-IMPF-PRS	this-LOC=TOP

"You've got heaps of dogs here." (🔈 DB: McNair_A1B: 2:53min)

The other non-segmentable subject form is *=rlaa* '1INC.AUG.S'. The only overt non-subject bound pronoun with which *=rlaa* co-occurs in the corpus is the 3AUG object *=yina*. In such a combination, the augmented subject morpheme *=lu* is included in the complex, and appears to the right of the *-ng(k)u-* linker as in (934). The morph which fills the 'subject person marker' slot of the complex, however, remains as *=rlaa*, and the non-subject bound pronoun is unexpressed. The result is an irregular bound pronoun complex, *=rlaangkulu*, which is also the form found in Bilinarra (Meakins & Nordlinger, 2014, p. 245) and Mudburra (McConvell, 1980, p. 36). The fact that the clause has a non-minimal object, despite the absence of the *=yina* non-subject clitic, is evidenced by the fact that the linking element *-ngu-*, which appears only with non-minimal objects, is present in the surface form. The expected form *=rlaayinang-kulu* also appears in the Gurindji corpus, as shown in (935).

(934)

Puntanup	ma-nta	nyila-rra	warlu	yapayapa.
collect	do-IMP	that-PL	fire	small

Yuwa-rra=nga=**rlaangulu**	talwarrirn	kuya.
put-IMP=DUB=1INC.AUG.S>3AUG.NS	make.fire	thus

"Collect some small pieces of wood. Let us build up the fire for them." (🔈 VW: FM11_a162: 1:54min)

(935)

Kaput	makin-ta=rni	purlurluj	wanku=**rlaayinangkulu**
tomorrow	sleep=LOC=ONLY	ambush	fall.POT=1INC.AUG.S>3AUG.NS

makin-jirri=rni	murla-ngka	karru=rlaa,
sleep-ALL=ONLY	this-LOC	be.POT=1INC.AUG.S

karru=**rlaayinangkulu**,	na	na	kurnamirnti-la
be.POT=1INC.AUG.S>3AUG.NS	FOC	FOC	sleep.top.toe-LOC

ngurra=ma.	'Marntaj	kula=ngalangkulu	nya-ngku"!
camp=TOP	OK	NEG= 3AUG.S>1INC.AUG.NS	intake-POT

"Tomorrow morning when they're still asleep we can attack them.
'Let's sleep here tonight, top to tail like for *waringarri*. They won't see us."'
(🔈 RW: EC98_a027: 20:38min)

6.2.3.2 Person hierarchy

The bound pronoun template given in §6.2.2 accounts for the majority of clitic combinations in Gurindji grammar. However, there is also a person hierarchy in play that overrides the basic subject>non-subject ordering: 1 > 2, 3. A first person minimal bound pronoun must precede any other bound pronoun, regardless of its grammatical role. Therefore, when the subject is second or third person and the non-subject first person minimal, the surface order of the bound pronouns is non-subject-subject, as shown in (936) and (937).

(936)

Huh	wanyji-ka=wayi	ngu=**yi=lu**
huh	which-LOC=Q	CAT=1EXC.MIN.NS=3AUG.S

waj-karra	yuwa-ni,	karu-ngku?
throw-ITER	put-PST	child-ERG

"Where on earth did the kids chuck the scissors on me?"
(🔈 VW: FM08_08_1a: 29:49min)

(937)

Warta	katik	ma-na-na	ngu=**yi=n**
goodness	trick	do-IMPF-PRS	CAT=1 EXC.MIN.NS=2MIN.S

ngayiny	nyila=ma.
1EXC.MIN.DAT	that=TOP

"Goodness you tricked me. That was for me." (🔈 VW: FM11_a160: 3:52min)

Fascinatingly there is just one example in the corpus, shown in (938) where this rule is not obeyed and Violet Wadrill produces the form *=n-pa=yi* '2MIN.S-EP-1EXC.MIN.NS' instead of *=yi=n* '1EXC.MIN.NS=2MIN.S'. This would suggest that the person hierarchy rule is synchronically active, not just a historical process which went into forming now frozen complex pronouns.

(938) Wipuwipuk ma-nta tanku yala-nginyi.
take.out.REDUP do-IMP food that-SOURCE

Walyawalyak nyamu=**npayi** yuwa-ni,
inside.REDUP REL=2MIN.S>1EXC.MIN.NS put-PST

warrayarl=purrupurru mangarri an tinned-beef-nganyju.
sugar=AND bread and tinned-beef-GROUP
"Take the tucker out of that one. Where you put the sugar, bread and tinned beef inside for me." (🔊 VW: FM12_a183: 10:35min)

This rule only affects first person *minimal* objects, for example in (939), the object is first person non-minimal, yet the order remains subject-non-subject. This order also does not affect all minimal pronouns, for example in (940), the object is minimal and the subject is unit augmented, but the order remains subject-object.

(939) Nyamu=**n=ngantipa**=nga ka-ngku.
REL=2MIN.S=1EXC.AUG.NS=DUB take-POT
"When you might take us." (Unknown source)

(940) Walima=**ja=ngku** ya-nku
Q=1EXC.UA.S=2MIN.NS go-POT

wirti-wirti-wu=ma liwaya=ma?
block-REDUP-DAT=TOP keep.company=TOP
"How about we come with you to back you up?"
(🔊 RW: EC97_a007: Warli: 7:56min)

In this respect, Gurindji differs from languages such as Ngiyambaa (Donaldson, 1980) in which the person hierarchy applies irrespective of number. This person hierarchy is found in other Ngumpin-Yapa languages, however, such as Jaru (Tsunoda, 1981, p. 131).

Where there are two first person minimal bound pronouns, the ordering reverts to the expected subject-non-subject order. More of these examples were given in §6.2.2.4:

(941) Ngu=**rna=yi** na ma-rni, "Ngu=rna
CAT=1EXC.MIN.S=1EXC.MIN.NS FOC say-PST CAT=1EXC.MIN.S

pa-na-na kurturu wartu ngu=rna pa-na-na."
hit-IMPF-PRS nullanulla nullanulla CAT=1EXC.MIN.S hit-IMPF-PRS
"Well I said to myself, 'I will cut wood for a nullanulla and stick.'"
(🔊 TD: FM07_a028: 6:09min)

6.2.3.3 More than one object/oblique

It is not possible to encode more than one non-subject pronoun in the bound pronoun template. In the case of ditransitive clauses, the indirect object trumps the direct object, as shown in (942). Thus *=ngku* 'you' is present in the pronoun complex, but not the expected unit augmented *=wuliny*.

(942) Hey lamparra-marnany-ju=ma=**ngku**$_{IO}$. jayi-nya,
hey father.in.law-2MIN.POSS-ERG=TOP=2MIN.NS give-PST

[kujarra kirri kujarra]$_{O}$ **nyununy**$_{IO}$.
two woman two 2MIN.DAT
"Hey your father-in-law who is my son gave two girls to you."
(🔈 VW: FM10_a155: 10:48min)

Although it is not possible to cross-reference two objects, it is possible to cross-reference an object or indirect object and a third person dative adjunct in benefactive or purposive constructions, for example (943), or a locative complement, as in (944) where *waruk* 'work' takes a locative-marked complement which expresses the basis of the work. The dative adjunct is cross-referenced with the oblique pronoun *=rla* (§6.2.2.3).

(943) Kutirni kutirni liwart ngu=**rna=ngku=rla**
soon soon wait CAT=1EXC.MIN.S=2MIN.NS=3OBL

yuwa-rru nyawa, parnngirri-la.
put-POT this bark-LOC
"Wait now I'll wrap some for you in paperbark [to give] to her."
(🔈 VW: FM10_a155: Ngarlking Karu: 0:21min)

(944) Ngu=**yinangulu=rla** karrinyani waruk,
CAT=3AUG.S>3AUG.NS=3OBL be.IMPF.PST work

kapuku-yayi ngayiny kanyirri.
sister-LATE 1EXC.MIN.DAT half.sibling
"Others used to work for them, like a half-sister of mine."
(🔈 VW: FM10_22_1a: 1:02min)

6.2.3.4 Unit augmented neutralisation

A final rule of bound pronoun clitic complexes involves the neutralisation of unit augmented number in all non-minimal contexts (McConvell, 1980) and has been observed for other Ngumpin languages such as Bilinarra and Wanyjirra (Meakins & Nordlinger,

2014, pp. 250–252; Senge, 2016, pp. 341–346). The neutralisation of dual and plural bound pronouns to the plural form is also common in Australian languages (Blake, 1987, p. 105). Thus, we assume this is the same type of neutralisation, despite the slight difference in number categories.

In Gurindji, this process occurs in all combinations of non-minimal subjects and non-minimal non-subjects. Thus, the distinction between unit augmented and augmented number is neutralised in these contexts. For example, in (945), the subject is clearly dual as shown by the nominal *kajirri-kujarra* 'two women' and yet it is cross-referenced by an augmented pronoun. Example (946) is a bit more marginal since reflections and, by extension, probably photos, are inalienable. So, it could be that the augmented non-subject pronoun actually references plural photos, not two children.

(945) Ngu=**yinangkulu** nyila=rni karrinyani
CAT=3AUG.S>3AUG.NS that=ONLY be.IMPF.PST

kajirri-kujarra kartipa-walija-wunyja=ma.
woman-DU non-Indigenous-PAUC-COM=TOP
"Two *kartiya* women were with several *kartiya* men there."
(McConvell corpus: Meakins et al., 2016, p. 445)

(946) Yarti ngu=**yinangkulu** ma-ni **karu-kujarra** winkily-ing.
shade CAT=3AUG.S>3AUG.NS do-PST child-DU red-ADJ
"They took a coloured photograph of the children." (Meakins et al., 2013, p. 440)

Effectively, this process means that unit augmented bound pronouns only occur in the language when they are either combined with minimal bound pronouns, for example (947), or where they are the only cross-referenced argument.

(947) Ngu=yi=**wula** nya-nga-na karrap
CAT=1EXC.MIN.NS=3UA.S intake-IMPF-PRS watch

Nangala-kujarra-lu=ma ngayu=warluk pa-ni.
SUBSECT-DU-ERG=TOP 1EXC.MIN=FIRST hit-PST
"Those two Nangalas are watching me cutting first." (VW: FM07_a027: 3:35min)

The bound pronoun complexes produced by the application of this process were shown in Table 33. Note that, apart from the number neutralisation, they are otherwise completely predictable in form from the structural properties of bound pronoun complexes outlined in the previous sections.

It is clear that this neutralisation involves unit augmented number, and not dual number, since it doesn't apply to the first person inclusive minimal forms (which would be dual under a singular/dual/plural system):

(948) Wayi=**rli=yina** yangkarra ya-nku?
Q=1INC.UA.S=3AUG.NS follow go-POT
"Shall we follow them?" (DD: McNair_F2A: 12:49min)

Some dialectal and historical comments about this neutralisation process are warranted. In Hale's work with Smiler Major in 1959, McConvell (1980, p. 59) notes that "neutralisation did not occur when there is a second dual subject and a third dual oblique, which the latter is neutralised to plural". For example, Smiler Major produced the forms =*npulangkulu* '3UA.S>3AUG.NS' and =*nngayirrangkulu* '3UA.S>3UA.NS' (p. 28).[171] So this rule might not be hard and fast. Interestingly, in Capell's 1939 notes on Ngarinyman, he lists complex pronouns with dual participants acting on dual participants, for example =*wulangayirrang* '3DU.S>1EXC.DU.NS', =*jagula* '1EXC.DU.S>2DU.NS', =*jawilin* '1EXC.DU.S>3DU.NS', =*nbulangayirrang* '2DU.S>1EXC.DU.NS', =*nbulawilin* '2DU.S>3DU.NS'; and duals acting on plurals (and vice versa), for example =*wulanyurrang* '3DU.S>2PL.S', =*nbulayining* '2DU.S>3PL.NS' and =*ndangayirrang* '2PL.S>1EXC.DU.NS' (reported in McConvell, 1980, pp. 55–56). In Ngarinyman, only dual subjects may be neutralised. Note though that Capell (1940, p. 428) says that "[s]ome of the compound forms [complex bound pronouns] would naturally be very clumsy and in practice they are not made. So, in Ngarinyman, "you two . . . us" takes a particle *banbula ngairang*; 'you two gave it to us': *banbula binanyang ngairang*, the word *ngaira* being the Ngar. cardinal [free pronoun] 'we'". This suggests that Capell elicited DU>DU pronouns which may have been accepted but not used, instead with the object pronoun expressed by a free pronoun, which is a strategy different from the dual neutralisation rule where the PL>PL complex bound pronoun would be used.

Curiously in Bilinarra, this rule of UA neutralisation is also not obligatory (at least for one of the oldest speakers). In a formal elicitation session, sentences in which UA forms co-occur with other non-minimal forms were accepted, repeated and elaborated.

(949) Ka-ngku=**ngayirra=npula**. (Bilinarra)
take-POT=1EXC.UA.NS=2UA.S
"You two will take us two." (Meakins & Nordlinger, 2014, p. 251)

(950) Ka-ngku=**ngantipa=npula**. (Bilinarra)
take-POT=1EXC.AUG.NS=2UA.S
"They will take us two." (Meakins & Nordlinger, 2014, p. 251)

In the last two cases the expected (number-neutralised) form would have been:

171 Thanks to David Nash for making the Hale notes available.

(951) Ka-ngku=**nngantipangulu**. (Bilinarra)
take-POT=2AUG.S>1EXC.AUG.NS
"You two/all will take us two/all." (Meakins & Nordlinger, 2014, p. 251)

There are two interpretations of the evidence from the earlier recordings of Gurindji, Ngarinyman and Bilinarra. Firstly, it is possible that unit augmented complex pronouns may have existed at one point and the paradigm has simplified in the last 100 years, with vestiges of the system remembered by the oldest speakers. Another possibility is that the complex bound pronouns are not historically frozen forms, but their components are synchronically analysable by (some) speakers which means that it is possible to spontaneously create dual or unit augmented forms if elicited.

6.2.3.5 Morpho-phonological rules of attachment

6.2.3.5.1 Epenthetic *-(ng)(k)u-*

Where both the subject and non-subject have non-minimal number, an augment *-ngku-* (with variants *-ngu-* and *-ku-*)[172] is added to the bound clitic complex, following the non-minimal marker, and preceding the subject number marker, as shown in (952).

(952) Ngu=**rna=yina-ngu=lu** yuwa-na-na karu jangkakarni <u>du</u>.
CAT=1EXC=3AUG.NS-EP=AUG put-IMPF-PRS child big.REDUP too
"We bathe both the kids and adults using [lemon grass]."
(🔊 VW: FM07_a089: 2:15min)

The epenthetic *-ngku-* is also found linking *=nyunu* 'RR' to *=rla* '3OBL', as shown in (896) and the *-ku-* epenthetic is also found inserted between the 2MIN.S clitic and indirect object clitic *=n-ku=rla*, as in (953)–(956). The form *-ku-* is the result of NCD deletion, as discussed in §2.3.4.1.

(953) Jatkarra ngu=**n-ku=rla** yuwa-na-na.
play.frighten CAT=2MIN.S-EP=3OBL put-IMPF-PRS
"You're frightening her with it in jest." (🔊 VW: FM12_a172: 5:41min)

(954) Kurlpi-marraj ngarra=**yi=n-ku=rla**
light.coolamon-COMP ADMON=1EXC.MIN.NS=2MIN.S-EP=3OBL

172 *-ku* is most likely the old epenthetic and *-ngku* results from a combination of pronouns ending in *ng* and *-ku-*. The other variant *-ngu* occurs due to absence of the final *-ng*.

jirrmung yuwa-na-na.
break put-IMPF-PRS
"You might break it on me and make it like a light coolamon."
(🔈 VW: FM10_23_1b: Yawarlwarl Wanyil: 2:48min)

(955) Maitbi yikili-ngurlu ngu=**n-ku=rla** nya-ngku
maybe far-ABL CAT=2MIN.S-EP=3OBL intake-POT

karrap, 'Nyawa nyawa kanyjal.' Julurrp ngu=rna
look this this below roast.carcass CAT=1EXC.MIN.S

jiya-rna-na, warlu=ma=yina julurrp jiya-rna-na.
burn-IMPF-PRS fire=TOP=3AUG.NS roast.carcass burn-IMPF-PRS
"Maybe from a long way away you can look for it, 'Here down here.'
I'm cooking the carcass. The fire is cooking the carcass for them."
(🔈 VW: FM12_a173: 12:18min)

(956) Kiyi ngu=**n-ku=rla** ma-ni.
wait.too.long CAT=2MIN.S-EP=3OBL do-PST
"You hesitated too long over it." (🔈 VW: FM12_a174: 9:57min)

The epenthetic is also found linking other pronouns not always requiring the epenthetic. Example (957) shows *-ngku* linking *=ngali* and *=rla* but no phonological motivation for this sequence is obvious.

(957) Ma-nta=**ngali-ngku=rla** nalija-wu
get-IMP=1INC.MIN.NS-EP=3OBL tea-DAT

kampa-rnu-wu ngarin-ku wupkarra-wu.
cook-INF-DAT meat-DAT cook.on.coals-DAT
"Get us [some wood] to make tea and cook meat." (🔈 VW: FM11_a166: 35:36min)

This augment is also found in Bilinarra, only as *-ngu-* (Meakins & Nordlinger, 2014, pp. 245–246). The augment *-(ng)ku-* is found in Wanyjirra (Senge, 2016, p. 350). Tsunoda (1981, p. 128) also reports the existence of the element *-ngu-* in Jaru. However, Tsunoda does not describe its occurrence as being governed by the number of the non-subject bound pronoun. Rather, Tsunoda tries to explain it in terms of phonological rules, saying that it occurs immediately before /l/. We see no reason why the presence of the phoneme /l/ would in any way prompt the occurrence of this element. If that were the case, one would expect, for example, that the subject bound pronoun for '1EXC.AUG' in Gurindji would be *=rna-ngku-lu*, rather than *=rna-lu* and so on.

6.2.3.5.2 Epenthetic *-pa-*

The epenthetic *-pa-* is used to join bound pronouns to consonant-final stems, i.e. nominals (e.g. interrogatives) and coverbs rather than the catalyst *ngu* or complementisers which all end in vowels.

(958) Wanyji-rrirniny-**pa=rna** yuwa-ni
which-HITH-EP=1EXC.MIN.S put-PST

wanyji-rrirniny-**pa=rna=rla** tarrjal ma-ni?
which-HITH-EP=1EXC.MIN.S=3OBL landing.mark do-PST
"Which way did I throw it, where did I land it?"
(VW: FM10_23_1b: Luma Kurrupartu: 1:21min)

(959) Jakiliny=ma nyatjang-**pa=n** karrwa-wu?
month=TOP how.many-EP=2MIN.S keep-POT
"How many months will you spend?"
(McConvell corpus: Meakins et al., 2016, p. 73)

This epenthetic syllable is commonly found in other Ngumpin-Yapa languages such as Warlpiri, where it has been incorporated into the stem of some words which were originally consonant-final (Hale, 1973). In other Ngumpin languages such as Jaru, Mudburra and Walmajarri, it has actually become an auxiliary after it lost the consonant-final conditioning. This process has not occurred in Gurindji (and Bilinarra). In Wanyjirra it has a much more limited use, only joining bound pronouns to the interrogative *nyayang* 'how much' (Senge, 2016, pp. 350–351).

6.2.3.5.3 Lenition *ny/j, p/w*

Like other morphology in Gurindji, one pronominal clitic is sensitive to whether the final segment in the stem is a vowel or consonant: *=junu/=nyunu* 'RR'. This pronominal clitic shows allomorphic variation depending on the stem: *=junu* is used for consonant-final stems and *=nyunu* for vowel-final stems (see examples in §6.2.2.4).

The bound pronoun *=yina* '3AUG.NS' (960) also becomes *=jina*[173] when it occurs after the second person minimal subject pronoun rather than taking an epenthetic *-ku-*. Thus, the form is *=njina* (962). In Bilinarra and Wanyjirra, there are two allomorphs of the third augmented non-subject clitic *=yina/=jina*, and *=yanu/=janu*, respectively. The choice depends on whether the host is vowel-final or consonant-final (Meakins & Nordlinger, 2014, p. 254; Senge, 2016, p. 305).

173 *=jina* relates to an old form of '3PL' in Pama-Nyungan *jana*, just as *pula* was the old form of dual before lenition.

(960) Najing ngu=**yina** tilykurr-tilykurr
nothing CAT=3AUG.NS strike-REDUP

nganta pa-na-ni janginyina-lu=ma.
ALLE hit-IMPF-PST lightning-ERG=TOP
"Lightning kept striking them I think."
(🔈 VW: FM10_27_1a: Kurraj Story from Halls Creek: 4:57min)

(961) Kamparri-jang ngu=**njina** nya-nya jutu-k.
before-TIME CAT=2MIN.S>3AUG.NS intake-PST proper-FACT
"You saw them do it properly." (🔈 VW: FM09_17_2a: 2:19min)

Historically, there is another lenition process which has affected the third person unit augmented subject pronoun =*wula*. Although we separate number and person in the pronoun template, this probably really reveals the historical formation of these pronouns, not a strictly synchronic analysis of them. Nonetheless this analysis demonstrates the morpho-phonological lenition processes, which occurred in their development. The form of the third person unit augmented subject pronoun is =*wula*, but the second person equivalent is =*npula* where the person marker is originally =*n* and the number marker was =*pula* in the development of Gurindji pronouns, as shown in (962). The non-subject pronoun is =*nkuwula* which solves the consonant-final stem problem using the epenthetic -*ku*-.

(962) Nomo ngarrka ma-nta=yi=**wula**
NEG remember do-IMP=1EXC.MIN.NS=3UA.S

nyamu=yi=**npula** warlaku-marraj=ma wanyja-ni.
REL=1EXC.MIN.NS=2UA.S dog-COMP=TOP leave-PST
"Don't think you two can remember me since you left me like a dog."
(🔈 VW: FM10_a155: Ngarlking Karu: 10:12min)

Indeed, this process is still synchronically observable in Bilinarra and Wanyjirra. The third person unit augmented pronouns =*wula* and =*wuliny* still have consonant-final stem counterparts =*pula* and =*puliny* (Meakins & Nordlinger, 2014, pp. 254–255; Senge, 2016, p. 305). It is likely that Bilinarra has kept these variants because it does not have a catalyst such as *ngu* which hosts bound pronouns in declarative clauses. This means that consonant-final hosts, for example coverbs and nominals, are more common in Bilinarra than Gurindji.

6.2.4 Agency, affectedness and NP cross-referencing

A lot of attention has been given to 'null anaphora' or the common omission of nominals in Australian languages, in particular Warlpiri (Ngumpin-Yapa, Pama-Nyungan).[174] Null anaphora is one of the properties of non-configurational languages (Hale, 1983) which has generated a lengthy debate in the formalis literature about whether nominals can occupy argument positions in a clause (Austin & Bresnan, 1996; Baker, 1996; Jelinek, 1984; Nordlinger, 1998a; Pensalfini, 2004; Simpson, 1991) (as discussed in detail in §8.1). Other research has focussed on how information structure governs the variable use of nominals (Hale, 1992; Laughren, 2002; Legate, 2002; Simpson, 2007; Swartz, 1991). Much of this work assumes that the other argument marking system in languages such as Warlpiri – the bound pronoun system – is invariable, i.e. the pronouns are either obligatory or categorically absent.

In fact, bound pronouns are not always found where they are expected in Warlpiri (Meakins, 2015b). Indeed variation in the application of bound pronouns has been observed in three other languages related to Warlpiri which also exhibit null anaphora; Jaru (Tsunoda, 1981: pp. 140 onwards), Wanyjirra (Senge, 2016, pp. 323–329) and Bilinarra (Meakins, 2015b; Meakins & Nordlinger, 2014, pp. 238–242). Gurindji exhibits similar properties: bound pronouns are obligatory for first and second persons (964), categorically absent for the third person minimal (965),[175] and used only variably for third person non-minimal referents and minimal third person oblique referents. Examples (963)–(965) show the pronouns in use and (966)–(968) show the absence of bound pronouns where they would be expected. In (966)–(968), we know the referents are non-minimal because the cross-referencing nominals have either number marking or are reduplicated.

(963) Maitbi **ngayu** ngu=**rna**=**rla** ma-lu **yalu-wu**
maybe 1EXC.MIN CAT=1EXC.MIN.S=3OBL say-POT that-DAT

ngayiny-ku, **jaliji-yu** **jimarri-wu** **mitayi-yu . . .**
1EXC.MIN.DAT-DAT friend-DAT friend-DAT friend-DAT
"Maybe I will say to my friend . . ." (🔈 VW: FM12_a171: 24:51min)

(964) **Chloe-ngku**$_{A}$=ma=**Ø**$_{A}$=**Ø**$_{O}$ paraj pu-nya
NAME-ERG=TOP=3MIN.S=3MIN.NS find pierce-PST

174 Also described for many other Australian languages including Jiwarli (Austin, 2001), Wambaya (Nordlinger, 1998a) and Jingulu (Pensalfini, 2004).
175 The lack of 3rd person singular/minimal pronouns is not unusual across Australia (Dixon, 2002, p. 363).

partaj-ja, **kirrawa**$_{O}$ na.
climb-LOC goanna FOC
"Chloe found a goanna perched (on a fence post)." (🔊) SO: FM10_29_3a: 3:49min)

(965) Ngu=**yinangkulu**$_{A,O}$ [**nyila**=ma **kartipa=ma**]$_{O}$ karra-yin-ta
CAT=3AUG.S>3AUG.NS that=TOP non-Indigenous=TOP west-ABL-LOC

nya-nga-ni [**yarrulan**-tu **kujarra-lu**]$_{A.}$
intake-IMPF-PST young.man-ERG two-ERG
"The two young men were watching the *kartiya* from the west."
(🔊) RW: EC98_a027: 6:44min)

(966) [**Marlurluka** **kajijirri**]$_{S}$ ngu=**Ø**$_{S}$=ngku=rla ma-rni.
old.man.REDUP old.woman.REDUP CAT=3AUG.S=2MIN.NS=3OBL talk-PST
"The old men and women told you to (take it back)." (🔊) VW: FM10_27_1a: 4:10min)

(967) Yala=ma jawurra-ny, **nyila-rra-lu** **kujarra-lu=ma**
that=TOP steal-NMLZ that-PL-ERG two-ERG=TOP

kartiya-lu$_{A}$**=ma=Ø**$_{A}$ ngurrku pa-ni.
non-Indigenous-ERG=TOP=3MIN.S suspect hit-PST
"That thief, those two *kartiya* started to suspect." (🔊) DD: EC99_a028: 6:40min)

(968) Jiwarr-jiwarr ya-nta=lu$_{A}$=**Ø**$_{O}$ **kajikajirri**$_{O.}$[176]
gather-REDUP go-IMP=3AUG.S=3AUG.NS old.woman.REDUP
"You mob gather together all the women." (🔊) DD: EC98_a013: 6:45min)[176]

Meakins (2015b) finds that referents in Gurindji are less likely to be cross-referenced by bound pronouns if they are non-human and are also expressed by a nominal (969)–(970), and in particular are non-human objects (971). In these examples, other properties of the clause let us know that the nominals are plural. This convergence of factors, which affects the use of the pronominal clitics =*lu* 'they', =*yina* 'them', =*wula* 'those two', =*wuliny* 'the two of them' and =*rla* 'for/to/with him/her/it', is suggestive of topicality i.e. bound pronouns mark topical referents.

---

176 The plurality of the object is encoded in the reduplicated coverb *jiwarrjiwarr* 'gather' and reduplicated noun *kajikajirri* 'old women'.
177 In this example, plurality is indicated by the repeated subject nominal *yapakayi* 'small'.
178 The plurality of the subject is encoded elsewhere in the clause in the reduplicated coverb *jipujipu* 'extinguish'.

(969) Ma-na-ni ngu=**Ø**$_{A}$=yina$_{O}$ [**yapakayi-lu yapakayi-lu**]$_{A}$.[177]
get-IMPF-PST CAT=3AUG.S=3AUG.NS small-ERG small-ERG
"More and more small (drops of rain) were getting them."
(🔈 VW: FM10_23_4: 2:48min)

(970) Jipu-jipu=**Ø**$_{A}$ ma-na-ni nganta
extinguish-REDUP=3AUG.S do-IMPF-PST ALLE

warlu=ma$_{O}$ [**yalu-ngku=ma mungku-ku=ma**]$_{A}$.[178]
fire=TOP that-ERG=TOP red-faced.turtle-ERG=TOP
"Those turtles might have been extinguishing the fire." (🔈 VW: FM10_23_4: 6:16min)

(971) Ngu=rnalu$_{A}$=**Ø**$_{O}$ yuwa-na-na
CAT=1EXC.AUG.S=3AUG.NS put-IMPF-PRS

[**nyila=ma kuruwarrany-walija=ma**]$_{O}$.
that=TOP cooking.rocks-PAUC=TOP
"We put those rocks (on the fire)." (🔈 VW: FM10_a148: 17:37min)

This pattern is not unusual. It follows the cross-linguistic tendency for pronouns to be largely restricted to human referents and avoided for non-human referents. Genetti and Crain (2003) refer to this as the *Avoid inanimate pronouns* constraint.

Cross-linguistically the presence of cross-referencing affixes is commonly conditioned by factors related to information structure, for example studies of objects in Ostyak (Irina Nikolaeva, 1999, 2001) and object indexing in Yimas (Foley, 1992). In grammatical systems which show this type of variable marking, only arguments with topical referents (i.e. referents which have been previously established in discourse) get cross-referenced, while those with new referents do not. For example, Dalrymple & Nikolaeva (2011) observe that cross-referencing of objects is generally associated with old information.

In Gurindji, humans are more likely to be subjects (A or S) than objects and humans are more likely to be cross-referenced with pronominal clitics. Secondly pronominal clitics are less likely to be found cross-referenced by nominals. Thus the most common pattern found for a Gurindji clause is for a subject to be human, not expressed by a nominal, but cross-referenced by a bound pronoun, and for the object to be expressed by a nominals, as in (972) (Meakins, 2015b).

(972) Ngu=lu kampa-rna-ni turturl-arra jarlarlka=ma.
CAT=3AUG.S cook-IMPF-PST roast-ITER catfish=TOP
"They used to roast catfish." (🔈 VW: FM09_13_3a: 4:15min)

Where objects are cross-referenced, this is usually because they are humans (hence the association of animacy and bound pronouns). This association is compatible with the notion that humans are most often topical, as shown in (973) and (974).

(973) Ngu=**rna=wuliny** ka-nya lun
CAT=1EXC.MIN.S=3UA.NS take-PST deposit

na karlarra marru-ngkurra, kuya.
FOC west house-ALL thus
"Then I would take them west and leave them there at the homestead."
(🔊 CN: FM10_28_2a: 8:13min)

(974) Nyamu=**rna=wuliny**=nga ka-ngka wartuj.
REL=1EXC.MIN.S=3UA.NS=DUB take-IMP hide
"I would have taken them out bush and hidden them." (🔊 BW: FM14_a205: 2:55min)

The pattern found in (973) follows Du Bois' (1987) *Avoid lexical A* (i.e. avoid expressing a transitive subject with an NP) constraint which is related to the animacy of referent, as claimed by Everett (2009) and Haig and Schnell (2016). This effect also demonstrates a compounding of Genetti and Crain's (2003) two constraints: *Avoid inanimate pronouns* and *Avoid pronominal Ps*. This convergence of factors and resulting pattern is likely the result of the fact that humans are more likely to be topical and therefore A subjects, and thus, are not expressed by a nominal or cross-referenced by a pronominal clitic.

Despite the strong correlation between humanness and the use of bound pronouns in Gurindji, bound pronouns are not found cross-referencing 9% of human referents, (975)–(977), and are found cross-referencing 42% of non-human referents (Meakins, 2015b).

(975) Yala=ma jawurra-ny, **nyila-rra-lu kujarra-lu=ma**
that=TOP=3MIN.S steal-NMLZ that-PL-ERG two-ERG=TOP

kartiya-lu$_A$=ma=Ø$_A$ ngurrku pa-ni.
non-Indigenous-ERG=TOP=3MIN.S suspect hit-PST
"That thief, those two *kartiya* started to suspect." (🔊 DD: EC99_a028: 6:40min)

(976) **[Marlurluka kajijirri]**$_S$ ngu=**Ø$_S$**=ngku$_A$=rla$_{ADJ}$ ma-rni.
old.man.REDUP old.woman.REDUP CAT=3AUG.S=2MIN.NS=3OBL talk-PST
"The old men and women told you to [take it back]." (🔊 VW: FM10_27_1a: 4:10min)

(977) Jiwarr-jiwarr ya-nta=lu$_A$=**Ø$_O$** **kajikajirri**$_O$.
gather-REDUP go-IMP=3AUG.S=3AUG.NS old.woman.REDUP
"You mob gather together all the women." (🔊 DD: EC98_a013: 6:45min)

These cases are unexpected and suggests that the role of bound pronouns in Gurindji extends beyond the standard functions of pronouns, such as indexing arguments, tracking referents through extended discourse and providing number information for unmarked nominals. It demonstrates how these pronouns and their sensitivity to animacy can be brought into service in discourse, enabling speakers to express an attitudinal stance to referents.

Firstly, all of the non-use of bound pronouns to refer human referents appears in Gurindji stories of non-Indigenous brutality. In particular, bound pronouns are notably absent in stories of the invasion of Gurindji country by European colonists which began in the 1860s. Aboriginal people were massacred so that colonists could seize control of their land to establish cattle stations. In stories of these times,[179] the Gurindji shock at the behaviour of early colonists is expressed in a number of ways, but perhaps most subtly through the omission of bound pronouns. The strong association of bound pronouns with humans allows the story tellers to convey the savagery and animalism of the early colonists through their absence.[180]

(978)

Ngu=**Ø**$_A$=yina$_O$	papart	pu-nga-ni.
CAT=3AUG.S=3AUG.NS	massacre	pierce-IMPF-PST

"[*Kartiya*] used to massacre [*ngumpin*]." (◀) DD: EC98_a013: 11:29min)

(979)

Nya-ngka=yi$_{OBL}$=Ø$_O$	<u>na</u>	kartipa$_O$
intake-IMP=1EXC.MIN.S=3AUG.NS	FOC	non-Indigenous

ngaja=**Ø**$_A$=ngala$_O$	**kartipa-lu**$_A$	paraj	pu-ngku.
ADMON=3AUG.S=1INC.AUG.NS	non-Indigenous-ERG	find	pierce-POT

"Watch the *kartiya* for me now, otherwise they might find us."
(◀) RW: EC98_a027: 11:27min)

(980)

Nyamu=**Ø**$_A$=yina$_O$	pa-ni	ngurra-ngurlung
REL=3AUG.S=3AUG.NS	hit-PST	country-ABL

nyanuny-ngurlu=rni	wurlurturr.
3MIN.DAT-ABL=ONLY	exterminate

"When [the *kartiya*] brutally removed them from his[181] land."
(◀) PN: McNair: D2A: 4:21min)

The killings continued until station owners realised that Aboriginal people would make a good source of free labour. In stories of early station times, the lack of bound pronouns also has the effect of denying the managers and other non-Indigenous offi-

179 See Charola and Meakins (2016c) for a compilation of Gurindji historical narratives in *Yijarni: True Stories from Gurindji Country*.

180 Note that this interpretation of the data is from Meakins (2015) and McConvell remains sceptical of this line of argument.

cials their humanity. Indeed, many were perpetrators of inhumane policies. Station managers provided Aboriginal workers and their families with little food and poor accommodation, access to water and sanitation, described in (981), and children with European fathers were taken away from their Gurindji families to Croker Island, some never reunited (982). They formed what is now known as the Stolen Generations (see §1.7.2). The absence of these pronouns is in stark contrast to the Gurindji referents who are cross-referenced by pronouns in these examples.

(981) Kamparri-jang-kulu, kula=**Ø**$_{A}$=yina$_{O}$
before-TIME-ERG NEG=3AUG.S=3AUG.NS

jayi-rna-ni **kartiya-lu**$_{A}$=ma.
give-IMPF-PST non-Indigenous-ERG=TOP
"The *kartiya* didn't give them anything before." (BW: FM09_17_1c: 0:40min)

(982) Long time you know lurtju-kari ngu=**Ø**$_{A}$=yina$_{O}$
long time you know island-OTHER CAT=3AUG.S=3AUG.NS

ka-nya [pilyingpilying-walija=ma ngaliwany=ma]$_{O}$
take-PST *pilyingpilying*-PAUC=TOP 1INC.AUG.DAT=TOP

kula kajupari lurtju-kari.
NEG close island-OTHER
"A long time ago (Welfare Officers) used to take our *pilyingpilying* children to an island. The island wasn't close." (VW: FM14_a205)

The converse use of pronouns also requires some explanation, i.e. non-humans are not expressed by a bound pronoun 58% of the time (Meakins, 2015b), therefore cases where non-humans are cross-referenced are marked. The use of pronouns to cross-reference non-humans seems to accord them human-like attributes such as agency, in the case of transitive subjects (983), or affectedness in the case of intransitive subjects (984).

(983) Namata ngu=**yinangkulu**$_{A,O}$ paya-rna-ni kuya.
no.matter CAT=3AUG.S>3AUG.NS bite-IMPF-PST thus
"It didn't matter if [the ants] were biting them like this."
(🔈 VW: FM10_a148: 9:35min)

(984) Nyamu=**lu**$_{S}$ karrinyani wangiyip=ma [**yawu=ma nyila-rra=ma**]$_{S}$.
REL=3AUG.S be.IMPF.PST dizzy=TOP fish=TOP that-PL=TOP
"When the fish were dizzy then [from the silt]." (🔈 VW: FM09_13_3a: 3:21min)

181 This refers to a particular Aboriginal owner of an estate.

The cross-referencing of non-humans is particularly high in creation myths, referred to as Puwarraja or Dreaming (see §1.7.1). In these stories, Puwarraja creatures traverse the as-yet-unformed landscape, moulding its features. These Puwarraja creatures take on many forms. They are animals, humans, plants or natural phenomena such as rain or lightning, and are responsible for the creation of hills, rocks, waterholes and trees. In these stories, the use of the bound pronoun animates the Dreaming creatures or imbues them with human-like abilities such as higher order mental capacities. Bound pronouns are used to bring inanimates to life, such as in (985) where two brolgas hide yams from their grandsons which demonstrate they have an awareness of other minds, and are capable of deception for instance.

(985) Nyawa nyawa ngu=**wula**$_{A}$ wulawulaj
this this CAT=3UA.S hide.REDUP

jiya-rna-na punyunyu=ma.
steal-IMPF-PRS good.REDUP=TOP
"Here and here the two [brolgas] hid the good [yams from their grandsons]."
(BP: McNair_A1B)

Bound pronouns are also used in other genres of narrative to confer higher levels of sentience to inanimates and animals. For example, in the following two excerpts from a historical tale, the speaker amplifies the horror that human victims felt watching as clouds possessed by an evil force form over them (986) and as red-faced turtles swarm into their shelters with an air of malevolent deliberation (987).

(986) Kankula murla=ma=yinangku**lu**$_{S,\ OBL}$=rla
up this=TOP=3AUG.S>3AUG.NS=3OBL

kurlng=parla yuwa-ni, **maarn**$_{S}$=ma.
cloud.form=FOC put-PST cloud=TOP
"Then clouds started forming over them." (🔈 VW: FM10_23_4: 2:05min)

(987) **Mungku**$_{S}$=ma=yinangku**lu**$_{S,\ OBL}$ ya-na-ni.
red-faced.turtle=TOP=3AUG.S>3AUG.NS go-IMPF-PST
"The turtles were coming for them." (🔈 VW: FM10_23_4: 6:12min)

Other human characteristics are expressed by the use of bound pronouns, for example, animals become possessors of homes (not just inhabitants) (988) and insects and clumps of vegetation are individuated in (989) and (990).

(988) **Jurlaka-walija-wu**$_{OBL}$ ngu=rna$_{A}$=**yina**$_{OBL}$
bird-PAUC-DAT CAT=1EXC.MIN.S=3AUG.NS

ngurra paraj pu-nya.
home find pierce-PST
"I found the home of some birds." (🔈 VW: FM14_a228: 3:32min)

(989) **Yirrpan**$_{O}$ ngu=rna$_{A}$=**yina**$_{O}$ paraj pu-nya.
termite CAT=1EXC.MIN.S=3AUG.NS find pierce-PST
"I found some termites." (🔈 VW: FM14_a228: 4:50min)

(990) **Kurlpap**$_{S}$ ngu=**lu**$_{S}$ karrinyani.
clump CAT=3AUG.S be.IMPF.PST
"[The grass] was [growing] in clumps." (🔈 VW: FM10_a141: 2:11min)

Thus, the strong association of bound pronouns with humanness provides speakers with an anthropomorphising device which allows them to attribute human-like properties to animals and inanimates. It also provides speakers with an additional attitudinal device in discourse to express their degree of empathy with referents (Meakins, 2015b). This discourse use operates in tandem with its other morpho-syntactic functions of argument marking and number cross-reference.

6.2.5 Inclusory constructions

As is common amongst Australian languages, Gurindji has inclusory constructions (Lichtenberk, 2000; Singer, 2001), in which an overt NP 'picks out' one actor in a group referred to by the bound pronoun. Thus, the bound pronoun refers to the superset, and a free nominal refers to a member of that superset. For example, in (991) the subject bound pronoun refers to a group of people, of which one is the speaker. The overt NP *Nangari* refers to a member of this group.

(991) Ngu=**rnalu**=rla warlakap nya-nga-ni
CAT=1EXC.AUG.S=3OBL search intake-IMPF-PST

kinyuwurra-wu=ma, **Nangari-lu**=ma.
onion-DAT=TOP SUBSECT-ERG=TOP
"We, including Nangari, were looking everywhere for the bush onion."
(🔈 VW: FM07_a058: 3:49min)

Inclusory constructions are found in other Ngumpin languages including Bilinarra and Wanyjirra (Meakins & Nordlinger, 2014, p. 243; Senge, 2016, pp. 329–330).

6.2.6 Clitic placement

The Gurindji pronominal clitic complex is often found in initial or second position in declarative sentences attached to the catalyst *ngu*, however there is much variation in both position and host. The pronominal clitic complex occurs in different positions in the clause and with different parts of speech. Clitic placement is governed by complex discourse principles related to discourse prominence. A comprehensive account of clitic placement would require a good description of the information structure of Gurindji, which is not in the scope of this grammar. Our analysis in this section follows McConvell (1996) for Gurindji and is also informed by the work which has been undertaken for Warlpiri and Bilinarra in describing clitic attachment.

6.2.6.1 Parts of speech and bound pronoun attraction

The most common part of speech pronominal clitics attach to is the catalyst *ngu*. If we take a commonly occurring pronoun in the corpus *=rnalu* '1EXC.AUG.S, we', we find that of the 518 occurrences of it in the *Gurindji to English Dictionary*, 85% (n=440) occur attached to the catalyst *ngu* (992)–(993).

(992) Ngu=**rnalu** jalayi-lang tanjarri ma-ni kuya.
CAT=1EXC.AUG.S now-TIME raise do-PST thus
"We brought up the current generation." (🔈 VW: FM10_a148: 1:55min)

(993) Majul-a ngu=**rnalu**=rla kiya-rna-na.
stomach-LOC CAT=1EXC.AUG.S=3OBL put-IMPF-PRS
"And we put them in the stomach." (🔈 TD: FM10_a134: 4:37min)

Attachment to *ngu* is overridden by imperative verbs (994)–(997) (McConvell, 2012), clause-initial interrogatives (998), *kula* 'negation' (999), (1000), (1023) and (1024), subordinators such as *ngaja* 'admonitive' (1001) and *nyamu* 'relativiser' (1002) and (1003); topic-marked pronouns (1004)–(1005); and demonstratives (1006)–(1008) (Many more of the topic-marked examples occur in the following section).

(i) Imperative verbs:

(994) Jiwily-ing ngawa **jayi-ngka=yi**.
cold-ADJ water give-IMP=1EXC.MIN.NS
"Give me some cold water." (🔈 VW: FM12_a171: 1:11min)

(995) Nyila **jayi-ngka=yi=rla** jamalarl ngawa-wu.
that give-IMP=1EXC.MIN.NS=3OBL handle-less water-DAT
"Give me that handle-less tin to get some water." (🔈 VW: FM12_a171: 20:19min)

(996) **Ma-nta=ngali-ngku=rla** nalija-wu
get-IMP=1INC.MIN.NS-EP=3OBL tea-DAT

kampa-rnu-wu ngarin-ku wupkarra-wu.
cook-INF-DAT meat-DAT cook.on.coals-DAT
"Get us [some wood] to make tea and cook meat." (🔊 VW: FM11_a166: 35:36min)

(997) Ngu=yina ma-rni, murnungku=ma, **'Ya-nta=lu**
CAT=3AUG.NS say-PST policeman=TOP go-IMP=3AUG.S

karla-rni-yin-jarrk, kankulu-ngkarra-yirri'.
west-UP-ABL-CROSS up-SIDE-ALL
"The policeman used to say to them, 'You mob go across to the westside of the river and up the bank'." (🔊 BW: FM09_17_1c: 1:27min)

(ii) Clause-initial interrogatives (see §5.3 for many more examples):

(998) **Nyampa=warla=rna=ngku** ma-lu?
what=FOC=1EXC.MIN.S=2MIN.NS talk-POT
"What will I tell you?" (🔊 VW: FM09_17_2a: 0:12min)

(iii) Negation:

(999) **Kula=lu** yuwa-ni kurrku karnti-ka
NEG=3AUG.S put-PST grave tree-LOC

ngu=lu yuwa-ni jirri-ngka.
CAT=3AUG.S put-PST burial.platform-LOC
"They didn't put her in a grave, they put her on a burial platform [in a tree]." (🔊 DD: LC071220GURdd.nangala.mp3: 0:29min)

(1000) **Kula=rnalu** wumara ma-na-ni lawara.
NEG=1EXC.AUG.S money do-IMPF-PST nothing
"We didn't used to get money." (🔊 VW: FM09_12_5b: 2:52min)

(iv) Subordinating coordinators:

(1001) Kanyju-k **ngaja=ngku** waninyana.
down-ALL ADMON=2MIN.NS fall.IMPF.PRS
"In case you fall down." (🔊 VW: FM12_a178: 6:29min)

(1002) **Nyamu=rnalu**=nga kurnka-ka karru.
REL=1EXC.AUG.S=DUB die-LOC be.POT
"When we pass away." (TD: FM10_21_1c: 02:09min)

(1003) **Nyamu=rnalu** na kampa-wu nyanuny-ja waruju-la.
REL=1EXC.AUG.S FOC cook-POT 3MIN.DAT-LOC together-LOC
"When we'll burn the ashes, she'll be there with us."
(VW: FM08_a089: 13:13min)

(v) Topic-marked free pronouns:

(1004) **Nyuntu=ma=n** ya-ni murla-ngka Nangari?
2MIN=TOP=2MIN.S go-PST this-LOC SUBSECT
"Have you come here before, Nangari?" (BW: FM08_11_2a: 15:23min)

(1005) **Ngantipa=ma=rnalu** ma-rna-na
1EXC.AUG=TOP=1EXC.AUG.S say-IMPF-PRS

murla-ny-mawu, warlu=pirak.
this-NMLZ-DWELL fire=CORRECT
"We, the people of this area, really say 'warlu'." (VW: FM11_a162: 1:35min)

(vi) Topic-marked demonstratives:

(1006) **Nyawa=ma=rnalu** nganayirla-la karrinyana,
this=TOP=1EXC.AUG.S whatsitcalled-LOC be.IMPF.PRS

wuyurrunkarra, Four-Mile-la, Yurru-ngka.
fishing place.name-LOC place.name-LOC
"Here we are at Four Mile fishing." (VW: FM09_13_3a: 0:35min)

(1007) Yijarni, **murla-ngka=ma=lu** kayirra karrinyani
true this-LOC=TOP=3AUG.S north be.IMPF.PST

kula yangujpa kajijirri=ma.
NEG few old.woman.REDUP=TOP
"True – women used to live in the north [at Pawulyji], lots of women."
(TD: FM09_17_1a: 0:09min)

(1008) **Yala-ngka=warla=rnalu** karrinyani ngantipa=ma
that-LOC=FOC=1EXC.AUG.S be.IMPF.PST 1EXC.AUG=TOP

tupa-tupa-la=ma ngurra=ma.
windbreak-REDUP-LOC=TOP home=TOP
"There we used to live in windbreaks." (🔈 VW: FM09_17_1d: 1:18min)

Cysouw (2006)[182] observes that cross-linguistically bound pronouns attach to parts of speech which carry 'inherent' focus, i.e. forms which bear a focus-related meaning as a part of their semantics. Focus here is used to mean prominent information rather than new information. Cysouw suggests that interrogatives, negation, focussed nominals and clause linkers and adverbs of place and time are the most prototypical elements which are inherently prominent. Imperative and hortative verb forms also rank more highly than non-prominent nominals and other verb forms. Cysouw observes that pronominal clitics commonly attach to these inherently prominent constituents cross-linguistically. He suggests that there is a tendency for the least prominent information in a clause, in this case pronominal clitics, to be attracted to the most prominent, e.g. negatives and interrogatives. Pronominal clitics are inherently without prominence because they mark information which is already well established in discourse (topical).

Where more than one of these focus-attracting clausal elements occur, McConvell (1996, p. 320) notes that imperative verbs (1009)–(1011) outrank negative particle, i.e. where both of these constituents are present, the bound pronoun will attach to the imperative verb. Similarly, if both a hortative verb and a negative particle are present, the pronominal clitic will attach to the hortative verb (1012).

(1009) **Kula** piyarr **ka-ngka=ngantipangulu**
NEG report take-IMP=3AUG.S>1EXC.AUG.NS

pinka-kawu=rni wulaj-jawu.
river-PURP=ONLY hide-PURP
"Don't report that we're hiding by the river for a reason."
(McConvell corpus: Meakins et al., 2016, p. 124)

(1010) Ngarnjal=ma ma-rni ngu, 'Parnku-rlang,
NAME=TOP say-PST CAT cousin-DYAD

nomo **pa-rra=wula** kankulu-pal.'
NEG hit-IMP=3UA.S up-EDGE
"Topsy said, 'Hey you two cousins, don't cut above the hole'."
(🔈 VW: FM07_a021: 2:58min)

182 See also Mushin (2006) for a good overview of Cysouw's paper.

(1011) **Nomo** tirringinji-warra **wanta=rla** yalu-wu. Nyawa
NEG encroach-ITER fall.IMP=3OBL that-DAT this

ngu=rnalu=rla jayi-nya. Ngumparna=ma **wanyja-rra=rla**
CAT=1EXC.AUG.S=3OBL give-PST husband=TOP leave-IMP=3OBL

nyila=ma nyanuny ngu=rla, murlu-wu. Jayi-nya
that=TOP 3MIN.DAT CAT=3OBL this-DAT give-PST

ngu=rnalu=rla nyawa=ma kirri=ma. **Wanyja-rra=rla**
CAT=1EXC.AUG.S=3OBL this=TOP woman=TOP leave-IMP=3OBL

nyuntu. Tirringinji ngu=n-ku=rla waninya, waninya,
2MIN encroach CAT=2MIN.S-EP=3OBL fall.PST fall.PST

ngumparna-wu=ma nyanuny-ku. Nyawa-wu kirri-wu
husband-DAT=TOP 3MIN.DAT-DAT this-DAT woman-DAT

ngu=rla ngumparna=ma yala=ma **wanyja-rra=rla**.
CAT=3OBL husband=TOP that=TOP leave-IMP=3OBL

Nomo tirringinji-warra, kuya.
NEG encroach-ITER thus
"Don't cross him for his promised wife. We gave this [woman] to [another man]. That's her husband. You should leave her alone. We gave [another man] this woman. You should leave her alone. You're encroached on her husband. This is the woman's husband [not yours]. You should leave her alone. Don't cross her husband."
(🔈 VW: FM11_a162: 13:49min)

(1012) "Nyila=ma jintapa-kari=ma ya-na-na. Wal wut
that=TOP another-OTHER=TOP go-IMPF-PRS well mislead

ma-nta nyila=ma. Nomo **ya-nku-rra=rla**," kuya.
do-IMP that=TOP NEG go-POT-HORT=3OBL thus
"'That other one has gone somewhere. Well you trick this one. Don't let him go after him,' he said." (🔈 VW: FM12_a183: 12:50min)

McConvell (1996, p. 315) also notes that complementisers and interrogatives outrank *kula* in Gurindji, i.e. where a complementiser or interrogative occurs in conjunction with *kula*, the pattern is COMP=PRO *kula* or WH=PRO *kula*, as in (1013) and (1014). Topic-marked free pronouns and demonstratives also outrank *kula* in terms of attracting bound pronouns, as shown in (1015) and (1016).

(1013) **Nyamu=lu** **kula** ya-ni, ya-nku-rra=lu.
REL=3AUG.S NEG go-PST go-POT-HORT=3AUG.S
"Those who have not gone, let them go." (McConvell, 1996, p. 315)

(1014) **Ngana=lu** **kula** ya-ni?
who=3AUG.S NEG go-PST
"Who did not want to go?" (McConvell, 1996, p. 315)

(1015) **Ngayu=ma=rna** **kula** nga-ni jaartkarra=ma.
1EXC.MIN=TOP=1EXC.MIN.S NEG eat-PST eat=TOP
"I never ate it [when I was a young girl]." (🔊 VW: FM09_a123: 9:42min)

(1016) Nyila=ma=lu ka-nya, **kula** **najing** **nyila=ma=lu**
that=TOP=3AUG.S take-PST NEG nothing that=TOP=3AUG

ka-nya kaa-rni-mpal nyawa marru ngilyipurr nga-rni.
take-PST east-UP-EDGE this house drown eat-PST
"They took him then, but it wasn't for nothing they were on their way out with the bloke who had flooded the homestead here east."
(🔊 RW: EC97_a003: Yipu-waji: 8:27min)

The relative ranking of complementisers, interrogatives, imperative and hortative verbs is impossible to discern since imperative and hortative verbs do not co-occur with complementisers and interrogatives.

Finally, pronominal clitics can occur on other parts of speech, for example other inflecting verbs (1017), coverbs and nominals including nouns, place names and temporals.

(1017) Nyawa=ma=kata karnti kumpulyu=ma kuni
this=TOP=IMM tree white.currant=TOP dream

ngu=**rna** ma-ni. Ma-nku=**rna**
CAT=1EXC.MIN.S do-PST do-POT=1EXC.MIN.S

majka, kukij-karra-wu, kulyurrk-kaji-lu.
try drink-ITER-DAT cough-AGENT-ERG
"I dreamt about that *kumpulyu*. So I might try to drink it to treat my cough."
(🔊 VW: FM09_16_1b: 1:17min)

Thus, a five-tiered attraction hierarchy may be suggested:

> complementisers, interrogative pronouns, imperative and hortative verbs > negative particle > topic-marked and focus-marked free pronouns and interrogatives > *ngu* > other inflecting verbs, nominals, coverbs.

This hierarchy of bound pronoun hosts can be framed in terms of relative inherent prominence (Figure 47).

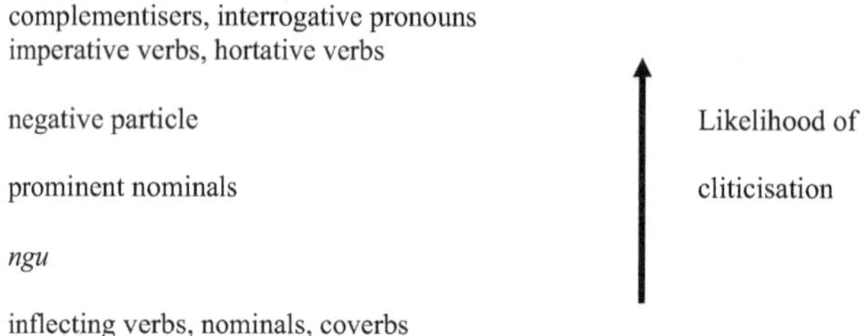

Figure 47: Hierarchy of pronominal clitic attraction.

6.2.6.2 Clause position

The tendency of clitics to attach to inherently focused or prominent elements also relates to another tendency: their tendency to be found attached to elements which occur early in the clause. Second position, or Wackernagel clitics are very common cross-linguistically (Anderson, 2005; Halpern & Zwicky, 1996). Mushin (2006, p. 296) suggests that the second position tendency of clitics is the result of two independent linguistic behaviours, "the tendency for grammatical information to gravitate to positions of focus, and the tendency for focused elements to occur clause initially". (Again, the term 'focus' here refers to prominence, not new-ness.) First position in many Australian languages, and indeed cross-linguistically, carries focus in the sense of prominence, and it is common for pronominal clitics and also TAM information to occur in this position (often in an auxiliary cluster) (Mushin, 2006; Simpson, 2007; Simpson & Mushin, 2008).

In Gurindji, the most common position for the pronominal clitic complex including the catalyst is initial position, or encliticised to the first or second element, as many of the examples in the previous section demonstrated. Bound pronouns can also be found in third position, as shown in (1019) and (1020). McConvell (1996) calls this sort of variable clitic placement a 'split-Wackernagel clitic system'.

(1018)	Nyila=ma	wararr-jawung-kulu	na	ngu=**rnalu**
	that=TOP	fat-PROP-ERG	FOC	CAT=1EXC.AUG.S

ma-na-na kuya-ngku.
do-IMPF-PRS thus-ERG
"We rub it with fat like this." (🔈 VW: FM10_a141: 2:56min)

(1019) Palangari-la kalurirrp ngu=**rnalu** ya-na-na nyila=ma.
black.soil-LOC walk.around CAT=1EXC.AUG.S go-IMPF-PRS that=TOP
"We walk around the blacksoil country." (🔈 VW: FM07_a054: 2:58min)

Although clitic placement in Gurindji looks variable with respect to position, we suggest that in fact it is consistently encliticised to a constituent which is prominent in terms of information structure and marks a transition to less prominent information. In this respect, we follow Simpson's (2007) analysis of Warlpiri auxiliaries which include pronominal clitics. Simpson builds on Legate's (2002) and Laughren's (2002) work on topic and focus phrases in Warlpiri and her paper is also a reconciliation of earlier work done by Hale (1992) and Swartz (1988) on first position (pre-AUX) in Warlpiri.

Simpson follows Choi's (1999) account of information structure by distinguishing between the accessibility of information and its prominence. Under Choi's model, the term 'focus' refers to new information and 'topic', to given information, however focus and topic can also be prominent or non-prominent. For Warlpiri, Simpson (2007, p. 420) suggests that:

> (r)elatively prominent information, whether topical or new information, occurs in the position before the AUX . . . but the span of words up until the AUX can be considered prominent. The attachment of the AUX to a constituent signals the prominence of that constituent, but also signals the transition to less prominent information. The AUX contains pronominals which indicate continuing topics. The constituent to which the AUX attaches may or may not be new information.

Thus we suggest that the left periphery of a Gurindji clause looks much like that of Warlpiri, as shown in Figure 48, with the pronominal clitic cluster in Gurindji behaving similarly to the AUX constituent in Warlpiri.

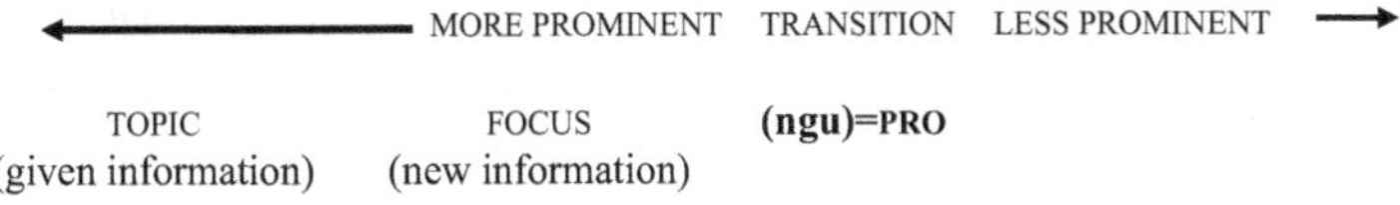

Figure 48: The left periphery (adapted from Simpson (2007)).

The topic and focus positions may or may not both be filled (given the variation stated above between second and third position for the pronominal clitics). Nonetheless the pronominal clitic attaches to what is prominent (either given or new information) and everything which occurs afterwards is less prominent. For example, if the topic position is empty, then the pronominal clitic attaches to the constituent under focus.

Question-answer sequences provide good examples of such constructions because answers to questions constitute new, focused information.

(1020) 'Nyampa-wuja=**n** wanyja-ni nyawa tanku ngarin?'
what-LACK=2MIN.S leave-PST this food meat
"What's wrong that you left this meat?"

'Majul ngu=**rna** janga,'
stomach CAT=1EXC.MIN.S sick

ngu=rla ma-rni kurany-karra.
CAT=3OBL talk-PST lie-ITER
"'I have a stomach upset,' he lied to him." (🔊 DD: McNair_F2A: 6:07min)

Pronominal clitics also commonly follow focus markers, as shown in (1021) and (1022). Note that in (1022), the Kriol *na* particle is found instead of the focus clitic. The Kriol particle has been in common use for decades now (see §10.2.5).

(1021) Yala-ngka=**warla=rnalu** karrinyani ngantipa=ma
that-LOC=FOC=1EXC.AUG.S be.IMPF.PST 1EXC.AUG=TOP

tupa-tupa-la=ma ngurra=ma.
windbreak-REDUP-LOC=TOP home=TOP
"There we used to live in windbreaks." (🔊 VW: FM09_17_1d: 1:18min)

(1022) Bow Hill-a **na** **ngu=rnalu** karrinya.
place.name-LOC FOC CAT=1EXC.AUG.S be.PST
"We were at Bow Hill." (🔊 VW: FM10_30_1a: 2:01min)

In other cases, there is no other focus marking, but an inherently focussed constituent appears initially in focus position followed by a pronominal clitic complex. Most of these inherently focussed constituents that appear in first position were discussed in §6.2.6.1, for example complementisers, the negative particle, imperative and hortative verbs. In these constructions, the transition between prominent and non-prominent information is marked by the bound pronoun.

Alternatively, the focus position may not be filled, so that the first position consists of a prominent topic to which the pronominal clitic attaches. Many of these examples are the topic-marked free pronouns and demonstratives discussed in §6.2.6.1. McConvell (1996, pp. 318–320) observes that two types of prominent topics are found in Gurindji: (i) contrastive topics, as shown in (1023)–(1027); and (ii) topic sets, as shown in (1029)–(1031). In all of these cases, the bound pronoun attaches to the prominent topic which is also marked by =*ma*.

(1023)

Kula=**ngku**	nyununy-ju	janka-ku	mayingany
NEG=2MIN.NS	2MIN.DAT-ERG	woman-ERG	veg.food

ka-ngku	**nyawa=ma=n-ku**=rla	warlu-ngkurra	jintaku-yirri=rni.
bring-POT	this=TOP=2MIN.S-EP=3OBL	fire-ALL	one-ALL=ONLY

"Your wife doesn't bring food for you because you come to the same fire with your mother-in-law."
(McConvell 1996 grammar manuscript: Speaking to young people)

(1024)

Kula=**yi=lu**	jayi-nya	ngarin=ma
NEG=1EXC.MIN.NS=3AUG.S	give-PST	meat=TOP

nyawa=ma=rna	ma-nku	tip	yarti=ma.
this=TOP=1EXC.MIN.S	get-POT	pull.out	shade=TOP

"They didn't give me meat, so I'll take away the shade."
(Appendix: Echidna and the Big Shade: Story 1, Line 20)

(1025)

Jala=ma	Nangala=ma	ya-na-na	ngu	Barunga-yirri.
today=TOP	SUBSECT=TOP	go-IMPF-PRS	CAT	place.name-ALL

Nyawa=ma=**ja**	**ngayirra-warij**	Nangari-wu=ma
this=TOP=1EXC.UA.S	1EXC.UA-ALONE	SUBSECT-DAT=TOP

jarrakap	ngu=rna=rla	ma-rna-na	ngayu-warij.
talk	CAT=1EXC.MIN.S=3OBL	talk-IMPF-PRS	1EXC.MIN-ALONE

"Biddy is going to Barunga today. So here it's just the two of us, with me on my own talking to Felicity." (🔊 VW: FM09_14_1a: 10:06min)

(1026)

Kuya-ngka=ma	**nyuntu=ma**,	ya-nta	kaja-ngkurra	na.
thus-LOC=TOP	2MIN=TOP	go-IMP	land-ALL	FOC

"Well you..... must go to the land."

Kaja-ngka	na	karra.
land-LOC	FOC	stay.IMP

"Stay on land."

Nomo	ngawa-ngkurra	ya-nta	wart-kari.
NEG	water-ALL	go-IMP	return-OTHER

"Don't go back into the water again."

Ngu=rla	ma-rni	nyila=ma	Warrija=ma.
CAT=3OBL	say-PST	that=TOP	Crocodile=TOP

"That's what Crocodile said to him."

Ngayu=ma=rna	ya-nku	ngawa-ngkurra=ma.
1EXC.MIN=TOP=1EXC.MIN.S	go-POT	water-ALL=TOP

"Me, well I'm going into the water." (🔈 VW: FM10_23_2a: 6:44min)

(1027)

Nyila=ma	kayili-yarra-ngarna	jaru.	Jawi=pirak=ma
that=TOP	north-SIDE-ASSOC	language	fire=CORRECT=TOP

Ngarinyman.	**Ngantipa=ma=rnalu**	ma-rna-na
Ngarinyman	1EXC.AUG=TOP=1EXC.AUG.S	say-IMPF-PRS

murla-ny-mawu,	warlu=pirak.
this-NMLZ-DWELL	fire=CORRECT

"That's from the northern language. 'Jawi' is really a Ngarinyman word. We, the people of this area, really say 'warlu'." (🔈 VW: FM11_a162: 1:35min)

Topic sets are commonly found in the beginning of stories or story episodes, descriptions of pictures or when something is introduced into the immediate context. Example (1028) is found at the beginning of a fishing story. Examples (1029) and (1031) mark episodic boundaries in stories.

(1028)

Nyawa=ma=rnalu	nganayirla-la	karrinyana,
this=TOP=1EXC.AUG.S	whatsitcalled-LOC	be.IMPF.PRS

wuyurrunkarra,	Four-Mile-la,	Yurru-ngka.
fishing	place.name-LOC	place.name-LOC

"Here we are at Four Mile fishing." (🔈 VW: FM09_13_3a: 0:35min)

(1029)

Nyawa=ma	**kawurn=ma**	ngu=rna
this=TOP	ashes=TOP	CAT=1EXC.MIN.S

ma-ni	kaa-rni-yin-karra	yala-ngka.
get-PST	east-UP-ABL-SIDE	that-LOC

"I got these ashes from up on the east side of the river."
(🔈 VW: FM07_01_1e: 2:47min)

(1030)

Yala-nginyi=ma	na	ngu=lu
that-SOURCE=TOP	FOC	CAT=3AUG.S

ya-na-ni murla-rniny-jirri[183] na.
go-IMPF-PST this-HITH-ALL FOC
"After that they used to come to this place." (🔊 VW: FM07_a054: 1:51min)

(1031) **Nyawa=ma=ngantipa** piyarrp yuwa-ni
this=TOP=1EXC.AUG.NS inform put-PST

kaput-pa=rni sister-ngku=ma.
morning-EP=ONLY nurse-ERG=TOP
"The nurse informed us [of the Swine Flu] this morning."
(🔊 VW: FM09_14_1a: 6:46min)

Where both the topic and focus positions are filled, pronominal clitics are found attached to the constituent under focus. In this situation, they are not second position clitics, but attach in third position. A couple of examples are given here. In (1032), Violet Wadrill is holding some white ochre and discussing how and where to collect it. She begins with a prominent topic *nyawa=ma yatu=ma* 'this white ochre', states a prominent focussed constituent *murla-nginyi* 'from here' which has the Kriol focus particle *na*, then the pronominal clitic is found attached to *ngu*. Example (1033) is a topic setting construction, like the ones above, except that the second position is filled by an NP rather than a pronominal clitic. As a result, the nominal is prominent and in focus before the boundary of prominence is marked by the pronominal clitic.

(1032) Nyawa=ma yatu=ma murla-nginyi na
this=TOP white.ochre=TOP this-SOURCE FOC

ngu=lu ma-na-ni, kamparri-jang-kulu
CAT=3AUG.S get-IMPF-PST before-TIME-ERG

nungkiny-ku=ma, ngantipanguny-ju=ma.
family-ERG=TOP 1EXC.AUG.DAT-ERG=TOP
"This white ochre from here [at Lartajarni], well my family used to get in the old days." (🔊 VW: FM08_11_2b: 2:12min)

183 Note that the use of the hither and allative suffix together is unusual.

(1033)

Nyila=ma	ngayiny-ku	jawiji-wu	ngamayi-wu
that=TOP	1EXC.MIN.DAT-DAT	MF-DAT	mother-DAT

ngamirni-wu	**ngu=yina**	nyila=ma	ngurra=ma
MoBr-DAT	CAT=3AUG.NS	that=TOP	country=TOP

kankula	nyawa	na	karla-ngkarla	Jijaljawung.
up	this	FOC	west-DOWN	place.name

"This story is about my mother's, uncle's and mother's father's country which is down and west of here called Jijaljawung." (🔊 VW: FM08_a071: 0:34min)

7 Inflecting verbs and coverbs

Gurindji, like a number of northern Australian languages (see for example McGregor, 2002 for discussion), augments its small verbal inventory with a range of complex predicates consisting of two elements: one of a limited set of 'inflecting verbs' combined with one of an open class of 'coverbs' (see §7.2.2.1). Complex predicates are an areal feature of north Australian languages, which cuts across the Pama-Nyungan/non-Pama-Nyungan divide. For example, in the Victoria River District and northern Tanami Desert region, complex predicates are found in the Pama-Nyungan languages of the Ngumpin-Yapa group such as Bilinarra, Ngarinyman, Mudburra and Warlpiri (Jones, Schultze-Berndt, Denniss, et al., 2019; Laughren, 2010; Meakins, 2010a; Meakins & Nordlinger, 2014; Nash, 1986, 2008; Osgarby, 2018a), as well as the non-Pama-Nyungan languages of the Jaminjungan subgroup, Jaminjung and Ngaliwurru, and Jarragan languages and Wardaman (Merlan, 1994; Schultze-Berndt, 2000, 2003).

Complex predicates in Gurindji are composed of two separate verbal words: an 'inflecting verb' (also known as 'finite verb' and 'auxiliary' in other north Australian languages with complex verbs) and a 'coverb' (also called 'preverb', 'uninflecting verb' and 'verbal particle') (see Schultze-Berndt, 2003, p. 146 for an overview of terminology). Inflecting verbs and coverbs can be distinguished by their morpho-syntactic behaviour and their semantic contribution to the clause. Inflecting verbs are semantically general, encoding only basic meanings such as 'do', 'take', 'hit', 'see', 'talk', 'go', 'fall' and 'cook'. They belong to a small closed class which probably numbers around 34 (see §7.1.1 for further discussion). Their main contributions to the clause are tense, aspect and mood information and they are grammatically obligatory. Coverbs, on the other hand, are an open class. They are not grammatically obligatory, but where they occur, they carry the semantic weight of the clause. They are not inflected, except for an iterative suffix (§7.2.4.1) and case in subordinate clauses (§7.2.2.3). They also receive derivational morphology, mostly converting them into nominals.

Main clauses often consist of an inflecting verb and a coverb, which can be a discontinuous unit, as shown in (1034). Nonetheless many clauses consist only of an inflecting verb as shown in (1035). In non-finite subordinate clauses in which tense, aspect and mood are not specified, coverbs are typically found alone, though infinitive forms of inflecting verbs are also found, as shown in (1036). Infinitive verbs will be discussed further in §7.1.3.6.

(1034)	**Jipij**	ngu=rnalu	**kampa-rna-na**	julpara-la.
	cover	CAT=1EXC.AUG.S	cook-IMPF-PRS	coals-LOC

"We cook it covered up in the hot coals." (🔈 VW: FM07_a058: 6:16min)

(1035)	Nyamu=rnalu	na	**kampa-wu**	nyanuny-ja	waruju-la.
	REL=1EXC.AUG.S	FOC	cook-DAT	3MIN.DAT-LOC	together-LOC

"When we'll burn the ashes together with her." (🔈 VW: FM08_a089: 13:13min)

https://doi.org/10.1515/9783110746884-007

(1036) Ka-nga-ni nganta nyila=ma wayita=ma
take-IMPF-PST ALLE that=TOP pencil.yam=TOP

kampa-rnu-nginyi=ma.
cook-INF-SOURCE=TOP
"He allegedly took the bush yams after they were cooked."
(🔈 VW: FM10_a155: Ngarlking Karu: 2:03min)

7.1 Inflecting verbs

7.1.1 Conjugations

Gurindji, like all Ngumpin languages, has a very small number of inflecting verbs. Only 34[184] inflecting verbs have been recorded for Gurindji (Meakins, 2009). 18 inflecting verbs have been reported for Ngarinyman (Jones, Schultze-Berndt, Denniss, et al., 2019, p. 38), 23 for Bilinarra (Meakins & Nordlinger, 2014, p. 271), 38 for Wanyjirra (Senge, 2016, p. 399), around 40 for Walmajarri (Dixon, 1980, p. 387) and 40 odd for Jaru (Tsunoda, 1981, p. 76). Warlpiri which is a Yapa language has a larger class of verbs, numbering around 130 (Nash, 2008, p. 221). The other Yapa language, Warlmanpa has 45 verbs (Browne, 2021). For an areal survey of inflecting verb inventories in other neighbouring language families, including Mirndi (e.g. Jaminjung), Jarragan (e.g. Gija), Worrorran (e.g. Ngarinyin) and Nyulnyulan (e.g. Nyulnyul, Bardi and Warrwa), see Schultze-Berndt (2003, p. 147).

Conjugation classes are exhibited in a majority of Pama-Nyungan languages, which may have up to seven different classes (Dixon, 1980, p. 279). There are five conjugation classes and two irregular inflecting verbs in Gurindji, each characterised by a different conjugation marker. The conjugation classes are given in Table 34. Note that we do not morphologically separate conjugation markers in glosses in example sentences instead treating them as historically frozen. The conjugation marker for each class is given in brackets in each class column. The marker is generally based on the POTential form (§7.1.3.4). The proposed underlying form for each TAM category is given in brackets after the TAM name and discussed in Meakins and Nordlinger (2014, p. 289ff) for Bilinarra, which also applies to Gurindji. Other verbal morphology such as the hortative (§7.1.3.10) and dubitative (§7.1.3.13) are discussed in the following sections.

The verbs are listed below according to their conjugation class. The citation form given is the present tense form rather than the infinitive form as this is the form given by speakers, probably because it also reflects habitual or customary aspect e.g. 'We build houses'. The two irregular verbs are *karrinyana* 'be' (§7.1.1.6.1) and *waninyana* 'fall' (§7.1.1.6.2).

184 Note that Nash (2008: 224) gives the number of inflecting verbs in Gurindji as 27, however 34 have been documented in the Gurindji dictionary (Meakins et al., 2013).

Table 34: Gurindji conjugation classes.

	Class 1 (rr)	Class 2 (Ø)	Class 3 (ng)	Class 4 (l)	Class 5 (n)
IMP PERF	*–rra*	Ø	*–ngka*	*–nyja*	*–nta*
IMP IMPF	*–na-nta*	*–rna-nta*	*–nga-nta*	*–rna-nta*	*–na-nta*
PST PERF	*–ni*	*–rni*	*–nya*	*–rni*	*–ni*
PST IMPF	*–na-ni*	*–rna-ni*	*–nga-ni*	*–rna-ni*	*–na-ni*
POT PERF	*–rru*	*–wu*	*–ngku*	*–lu*	*–nku*
POT IMPF	*–na-ngku* *–na-nyku*	*–rna-ngku*	*–nga-nku*	*–rna-ngku*	*–na-ngku*
PRS (IMPF)	*–na-na*	*–rna-na*	*–nga-na*	*–rna-na*	*–na-na*
INFIN PERF	*–nu*	*–rnu*	*–ngu*	*–rnu*	*–nu*
INFIN IMPF	*–na-nu*	*–rna-nu*	*–nga-nu*	*–rna-nu*	*–na-nu*

7.1.1.1 Class 1 – rr

The set of Class 1 inflecting verbs is given in (1037) and an example conjugation is given for the most common of these verbs, *yuwanana* 'put' in Table 35:

Table 35: Class 1 conjugations.

	Infinitive	Imperative	Indicative		
			Past	Present	Potential
Perfect	*yuwanu* 'to put it'	*yuwarra* 'put it!'	*yuwani* 'put it' 'had put it'		*yuwarru* 'will put it' 'want to put it'
Imperfect	*yuwananu* 'be putting it'	*yuwananta* 'should put it!'	*yuwanani* 'was putting it' 'used to put it'	*yuwanana* 'put it' 'is putting'	*yuwanangku* *yuwananyku* 'will be putting it, want to be putting it'

(1037)

jamanana	'grind'	*ngayanana*	'excrete'
kayanana	'kick'	*panana*	'hit'
kunyjanana	'wet' (transitive)	*papanana*	'weigh down'
wanyjanana	'leave' (transitive)	*yuwanana*	'put'
luwanana	'strike' (Malngin)		

7.1.1.2 Class 2 – Ø

The set of Class 2 inflecting verbs is given in (1038) and an example conjugation is given for the most common of these verbs, *kamparnana* 'cook' in Table 36.

Table 36: Class 2 conjugations.

	Infinitive	Imperative	Indicative		
			Past	Present	Potential
Perfect	*kamparnu* 'to cook'	*kampa* 'cook it!'	*kamparni* 'cooked it' 'had cooked it'		*kampawu* 'will cook it' 'want to cook it'
Imperfect	*kamparnanu* 'be cooking it'	*kamparnanta* 'should cook it!'	*kamparnani* 'was cooking it' 'used to cook it'	*kamparnana* 'cook' 'cooking it'	*kamparnangku* 'will be cooking it' 'want to be cooking it'

(1039)

jiyarnana	'burn, take from'	*payarnana*	'bite'[185]
kamparnana	'cook'	*tumarnana*	'grow'
karrwarnana	'have, hold'	*wurrwarnana*	'block'
kiyarnana	'put'[186]	*wuyarnana*	'throw'
luwarnana	'strike' (Gurindji)	*yinkarnana*	'trim'
minyjarnana	'make cold or wet'	*yunparnana*	'sing'

The semantics of most of these forms is straightforward and well expressed by their English translations, however some comments on the 'cook', 'sing', 'burn and take from' verbs are warranted.

First, *kamparnana* 'cook' means 'to apply heat to' more broadly. It is used to refer to food preparation (1034)–(1036) and also other activities such as treating patients with bush medicine including heated termite mound and leaves (1039). The latter activities are translated as *kukim* 'cook' in Kriol.

(1039) An majul ngu=rna **kampa-rni,**
and stomach CAT=1EXC.MIN.S cook-PST

makin-jirri warrngarlap-jirri, purinyjirri-la=ma.
lie.down-ALL lie.on.back-ALL evening-LOC=TOP
"And I 'cooked' her stomach [with heated termite mound] too while she was lying on her back in the evening." (🔈 VW: FM12_33_1: 1:14min)

185 For two speakers in the corpus, this verb is actually in the Class 1 conjugation, as shown in their use of the potential form *payarru* 'will bite'.
186 This verb is rare and probably cognate with Mudburra *kuya-* 'throw'.

The inflecting verb *yunparnana* 'sing' is used in transitive clauses to mean 'sing' and therefore always takes an ergative-marked subject. It takes a cognate object, i.e. 'sing a song', where sometimes this song is named, or if not, it is implied, as in (1040). This verb cannot be used intransitively, as in English 'she sings'. It can also be used to mean 'cast a spell' in either a good sense or malevolently, as shown in (1041). In these clauses, this verb can be translated into Kriol as *jingim* 'curse, cast a spell'.

(1040) Nyila=ma=rnalu **yunpa-rna-na** ngumpit-tu janka-ku.
that=TOP=1EXC.AUG.S sing-IMPF-PRS man-ERG woman-ERG
"That's the one that both us men and women sing."
(🔊) RW: FM17_a444: 7:18min)

(1041) Ngu=lu **yunpa-rna-ni** marlurluka-lu=ma,
CAT=3AUG.S sing-IMPF-PST old.man.REDUP-ERG=TOP

lawara. Nyantu=ma yipu=ma waninyani nyila=ma
nothing 3MIN=TOP rain=TOP fall.IMPF.PST that=TOP

waninyani yipu=ma nyilirrp, tirrip.
fall.IMPF.PST rain=TOP drizzle overnight
"The old men tried singing it away, but no luck. The rain came sprinkling down then. They camped the night." (🔊) DD: EC97_a008: 6:59min)

The semantics of *payarnana* most generally relates to oral activity, specifically biting (1042) and drinking (1043), but not eating. Some speakers use it in chopping activities to give the sense of biting into a material, for example wood, as shown in (1044).[187]

(1042) Ngarranginy-ju ngaja=ngku **paya-rru.**[188]
frill-neck.lizard-ERG ADMON=2MIN.NS bite-POT
"The frill necked lizard might bite you [for example when it has eggs and you get too close]." (🔊) VW: FM10_a152: 1:02min)

187 Strictly speaking, because this verb is actually in the Class 1 conjugation for this speaker, as shown in her use of the potential form *payarru* 'will bite', these verbs should be transcribed as *payanana*, but since the retroflex is marginal and barely perceptible in most speaker's language, we leave these as Class 2 verbs. For all other speakers, this is a Class 2 verb.

188 For this speaker, this verb is actually in the Class 1 conjugation, as shown in her use of the potential form *payarru* 'will bite'. It is possible there are two verbs with the stem paya-, one which means 'cut' and the other which means 'bite'.

(1043) Ngu=rnalu kukij-karra na **paya-rni** nyila=ma ngawa=ma.
CAT=1EXC.AUG.S drink-ITER FOC bite-PST that=TOP water=TOP
"Then we were drinking the water." (🔈 VW: FM09_14_1a: 3:07min)

(1044) Nyila na lumpung ngu=rna **paya-rni**
that FOC fish.poison.bush CAT=1EXC.MIN.S bite-PST

kuturu ngu=rna pirrkap ma-nku.
nullanulla CAT=1EXC.MIN.S make get-POT
"I cut some lumpung wood and I'll make a nullanulla out of it."
(🔈 VW: FM08_a101: 1:09min)

The verb *jiyarnana* is polysemous. It is used to mean (i) 'to apply flames, sunlight or smoke' (in a negative 'burning' sense in transitive (1045) and intransitive clauses (1047), and a positive 'reflection' sense (1046) and 'cooking' sense (1048)). It can also be used to mean 'drying out' (1049) or a related sense, 'thirst' (1050). The inflecting verb *jiyarnana* is also used transitively to mean 'apply smoke to someone as a medicinal practice' (1051) or intransitively to mean 'smoke billowing up' (1052). Interestingly, it can also be used to mean 'to take something from someone' (1053).

(1045) Ngu=yi wulngarn-tu=ma **jiya-rni**.
CAT=1EXC.MIN.NS sun-ERG=TOP burn-PST
"The sun burnt me." (🔈 VW: FM10_a152: 4:58min)

(1046) Wulngarn-tu=ma **jiya-rna-na** mirlinyiny-karra.
sun-ERG=TOP burn-IMPF-PRS reflect-ITER
"The sun reflects off it." (🔈 TD: FM10_a145: 14:48min)

(1047) Jawi ngu **jiya-rna-na**.
fire CAT burn-IMPF-PRS
"The fire burns." (🔈 VW: FM11_a162: 01:33min)

(1048) Nyila=ma puya=ma **jiya-rna-na** jipij, kuya.
that=TOP carcass=TOP burn-IMPF-PRS cover thus
"That carcass cooks in the ground like that." (🔈 VW: FM10_a148: 4:28min)

(1049) **Jiya-rna-na** wartartart nyamu=waa wurruja **jiya-wu,**
burn-IMPF-PRS dry.out.REDUP REL=REL dry burn-POT

ngu=rna kampa-wu <u>na</u>, kuliyan-pirrji.
CAT=1EXC.MIN.S cook-POT FOC aggressive-FACT
"[The sun] dries it out [the ashes] and, when it is dry, I will burn it to make it bitter." (🔊 VW: FM07_a089: 12:18min)

(1050) Warta ngu=yi ngawa-wu **jiya-rna-na.**
goodness CAT=1EXC.MIN.NS water-DAT burn-IMPF-PRS

Ngu=rna majul=ma ngarrap <u>na</u>.
CAT=1EXC.MIN.S stomach=TOP warm FOC
"Goodness I'm really thirsty. My stomach is hot." (🔊 VW: FM11_a166: 34:04min)

(1051) Yala-nginyi wirrminy ngu=rnayinangulu yuwa-na-na
that-SOURCE turn.over CAT=1EXC.AUG.S>3AUG.NS put-IMPF-PRS

kuya, kankulu-pal, parntawurru **jiya-rna-na** ngu maru-kijak.
thus up-EDGE back burn-IMPF-PRS CAT bottom-TERM
"After that we turn [the babies] over and smoke their backs right down to their bottoms." (🔊 VW: FM08_a085: 01:12min)

(1052) Jurlup ngu **jiya-rna-na** jungkart.
billow CAT burn-IMPF-PRS smoke
"The smoke billows up." (🔊 VW: FM10_a133: 10:45min)

(1053) Aa, ya-nku=rli, karu ngu=ngaliny **jiya-rni.**
oh go-POT=1INC.MIN.S child CAT=1INC.MIN.POSS steal-PST
" Oh let's go, they've taken the child from you and me."
(🔊 DD: EC98_a017: Karnati-lu: 5:05min)

The inflecting verb *wuyarnana* 'throw' can be used in a straight forward sense to mean 'throw' or 'drop' (1054), but it also expresses 'put' (1055), intransitive existential meanings where *karrinyana* 'be' might be expected (1056), 'push' (1057), and changes of emotional and physical state (1058).

(1054) Marluka-lu=ma yalu-ngku=ma ngalyakap-kaji
man-ERG=TOP that-ERG=TOP lick-AGENT

jak **wuya-rni** ngu tak-kaji-la.
drop throw-PST CAT sit-AGENT-LOC
"That man dropped the icecream on the chair." (🔊 BW: FM07-a043: 21:07min)

(1055) Yala-ngka=warla **wuya-rni** ngu ngunyjung=ma, kumpaying
that-LOC=FOC throw-PST CAT honey=TOP yellow.part

ngu=wula **wuya-rni** japajapa marntaj.
CAT=3UA.S throw-PST block OK
"She put the honey in the bark, and the yellow part she put around the outside to block the honey from dripping off." (🔊 BW: FM07_a021: 1:41min)

(1056) Ngunyjung=ma **wuya-rna-na** kanyjurra-k.
honey=TOP throw-IMPF-PRS down-ALL
"The honey is underneath." (🔊 BW: FM07_a021: 1:02min)

(1057) Pinka-kurra pulngayit-tu **wuya-rni**.
river-ALL floodwater-ERG throw-PST
"The floodwaters took everything to the river."
(🔊 JK: McConvell_A3463_G: 6:58min)

(1058) Jangkarni=rna karu **wuya-rni** wamala.
big=1EXC.MIN.S child throw-PST girl
"I become a big kid, a little girl."
(DW: MCCONVELL_P08-014877: 2:47min)

The inflecting verb *luwarnana* 'strike' is a Class 2 verb in Eastern dialects and a Class 1 verb in Western dialects. It is also in the mother-in-law register where it replaces other inflecting verbs, regardless of their class (see also §1.8.3), for example (1059).

(1059) Wartirri nganta=lu **luwa-wu** kuya-partak.
oh.dear ALLE=3AUG.S VERB-POT thus-THITH
"Oh dear! Maybe they will go that way." (McConvell, 1982a, p. 96)

7.1.1.3 Class 3 – ng

Class 3 inflecting verbs consist of the forms given in (1060) and a conjugation table for one of the most common forms *kangana* 'take' is given in Table 37.

189 Historically, this verb derives from *jaa* 'mouth' + *yung-* 'give'.

190 The inflecting verbs *pungana* and *wungana* are one and the same. Not that historically and synchronically, lenition does not occur initially, however it is clear that these forms are related.

Table 37: Class 3 conjugations.

	Infinitive	Imperative	Indicative		
			Past	Present	Potential
Perfect	*kangu* 'to take'	*kangka* 'take it!'	*kanya* 'took' 'had taken it'		*kangku* 'will take it' 'want to take it'
Imperfect	*kanganu* 'to be taking'	*kanganta* 'should take it!'	*kangani* 'was taking it' 'used to take it'	*kangana* 'take' 'taking it'	*kanganku* 'will take it' 'want to take it'

(1060) *jayingana* 'give'[189] *pungana* 'pierce, poke'
kangana 'take' *nyangana* 'intake (look, eat, hear)'
wungana 'pierce, poke'[190]

The meaning of *kangana* 'take' also extends to 'bring' (1061). In this respect, it can be thought of as having a general meaning of 'carry'. Gurindji does not have 'hither' or 'thither' markers unlike other Ngumpin-Yapa languages, so often the use of allative or ablative/source marked nominals provide the deictic information.

(1061) Nyanuny-ku jaju-wu ngu=rla **ka-nga-na,**
3MIN.DAT-DAT MM-DAT CAT=3OBL take-IMPF-PRS

mangarri punyu, yarti-ngkurra makin-ta-wu.
bread good shade-ALL sleep-LOC-DAT
"She takes a cake to her grandmother who was sleeping in the shade."
(🔊 VW: FHM146: 1:12min)

The inflecting verb *nyangana* is most often translated as 'see, look' (1062) by Gurindji speakers, but it is also used with and without coverbs to mean 'eat' (1063), 'drink' (1064), 'hear, listen' (1065) and 'know' (1066). In this respect, it could be translated more broadly as 'perceive', or perhaps 'intake'. We gloss it as 'intake' throughout the grammar.

(1062) Kururl-wu na ngu=rla **nya-nga-na.**
long.yam-DAT FOC CAT=3OBL intake-IMPF-PRS
"She was looking for the yam." (🔊 VW: FM07_a054: 3:39min)

(1063) Kumpaying na **nya-nga-na** ngu
honeycomb FOC intake-IMPF-PRS CAT

Nangala-lu=ma waninya janyja-kurra.
SUBSECT-ERG=TOP fall.PST ground-ALL
"Nangala is eating the honey that fell on the ground."
(🔈 TD: FM07_a028: 11:59min)

(1064) Nalija ngu=rnalu **nya-nga-na** kuya-ny=ma.
tea CAT=1EXC.AUG.S intake-IMPF-PRS thus-NMLZ=TOP
"We drink this kind of tea [referring to bush tea-leaf]."
(🔈 VW: FM07_01_1a: 1:34min)

(1065) Kurru **nya-nga-ni** nganta kuya-ngku=ma.
listen intake-IMPF-PST ALLE thus-ERG=TOP
"This is how she was listening to it, I reckon."
(🔈 VW: FM10_27_1a: Kurraj Story from Halls Creek: 1:34min)

(1066) Ngantipa ngu=rnalu **nya-nga-na**
1EXC.AUG.S CAT=1EXC.AUG.S intake-IMPF-PRS

ngumayi-jang-kulu na kuya, jalayi-lang-kulu.
behind-TIME-ERG FOC thus now-TIME-ERG
"We who have been left behind know about this now, and the present generation." (🔈 BW: FM07_01_1a: 4:45min)

This semantic extension of 'hearing' and 'knowing' is found in many Aboriginal languages, where the word 'hear' is also used to mean 'understand', in much the same way as 'seeing' is extended to 'understanding' in English and other European languages, i.e. a common exclamation when a person understands something is "I see!" (Evans & Wilkins, 1998). In Gurindji, while the coverb *pina* means 'know', it is the proto-Pama-Nyungan form for 'ear' which is still commonly found across Australia in different forms such as *pinang*. The notion of learning something is often expressed by putting ideas into the ear, as shown in (1067).

(1067) Jarrakap ngu=rna=ngku ma-rna-na.
talk CAT=1EXC.MIN.S=2MIN.NS talk-IMPF-PRS

Ngarrka ngu=n ma-na-na.
know CAT=2MIN.S do-IMPF-PRS

Latalata	ngu=rna=ngku	ma-rna-na
instruct	CAT=1EXC.MIN.S=2MIN.NS	talk-IMPF-PRS

langa-ngkurra	nyununy.
ear-ALL	2MIN.DAT

"I talk to you. You understand it then. I express this knowledge in your ear." (🔈 VW: FM12_a174: 17:25min)

The verb *jayingana* 'give' is used both in the sense of the transfer of possession (1068) as well as the transfer of information, and can be considered to have a broader semantics of 'transfer' (1069).

(1068)	Ngu=rla	**jayi-nga-na**	kajirri-lu=ma,	**lin-karra**.
	CAT=3OBL	give-IMPF-PRS	old.woman-ERG=TOP	give-ITER

"The woman gives him something." (🔈 BW: FM07_a043: 7:33min)

(1069)	Ngu=rnayinangulu	**pina-rrik**	**jayi-ngku**
	CAT=1EXC.AUG.S>3AUG.NS	know-FACT	give-POT

karu	jarrakap	jaru,	ngantipanguny.
child	talk	language	1EXC.AUG.DAT

"We want to teach our children to speak language."
(🔈 VW: FM08_11_3: 0:08min)

The inflecting verb *pungana* 'pierce' is translated as *pokim* 'poke' in Kriol. It is used with a range of coverbs which also express a pierce meaning, for example *jarrwaj pungana* 'spear' (1070) and *kurrij pungana* 'dig with an implement' (1071). It has another form *wungana*.

(1070)	Jamut	**jarrwaj**	**pu-nya**	karu-ngku.
	bush.turkey	spear	pierce-PST	child-ERG

"The kid speared the bush turkey." (🔈 VW: FM09_a123: 33:23min)

(1071)	Janyja-ka	ngu=rnalu	**kurrij-karra**	**pu-nya**	yirimuri-la.
	ground-LOC	CAT=1EXC.AUG.S	dig-ITER	pierce-PST	sand-LOC

"We were digging in the sandy ground." (🔈 VW: FM08_a100: 3:36min)

This inflecting verb is also used with other coverbs to express a more focused action, for example *jarrak marnana* 'talk' (< talk+talk), and *jarrak pungana* 'give a speech' (< talk+pierce) (1072). These types of inflecting verb/coverb alternations will be discussed in more detail in §7.2.2.1.2.

(1072) Ngayu=ma=rnanyjurra pa-rra-ngka=ma
1EXC.MIN=TOP=1EXC.MIN.S>2AUG.NS hit-IMP-LOC=TOP

kaputa-la=ma ngumpit-ta **jarrak** **pu-nga-na.**
night-LOC=TOP man-LOC make.speech pierce-IMPF-PRS
"I make a speech to you at night in the open space among the people."
(McConvell 1996 grammar manuscript: Speaking to young people)

7.1.1.4 Class 4 – l

Class 4 inflecting verbs consist of two lexemes: *marnana* 'talk, say' (in/semitransitive) and *ngarnana* 'eat' (in/transitive). The forms of *marnana* 'talk, say' are given in Table 38.

Table 38: Class 4 conjugations.

	Infinitive	Imperative	Indicative		
			Past	Present	Potential
Perfect	*marnu* 'to talk'	*manyja* 'talk to him!'	*marni* 'talked' 'had talked'		*malu* 'will talk to' 'want to talk to'
Imperfect	*marnanu* 'to be talking'	*marnanta* 'should put it!'	*marnani* 'was talking' 'used to talk'	*marnana* 'talk to' 'is talking'	*marnangku* 'will be talking, want to be talking'

In many surrounding north Australian languages such as Jaru and Jaminjung, 'say/do/get' are expressed by a single general speech/performance verb (Schultze-Berndt, 2000, p. 358; Tsunoda, 1981, p. 76). The 'say' (1073) and 'do/get' (1074) inflecting verbs are distinct forms in Gurindji, which belong to different conjugation classes (*manana* inflects according to the Class 5 conjugation). The clearest evidence of this difference is found in the imperative forms of these inflecting verbs: *manyja* 'talk' and *manta* 'get it, do it'.

(1073) Ngu=rna=rla **ma-rni** Nana-wu,
CAT=1EXC.MIN.S=3OBL say-PST SUBSECT-DAT

'Nyawa jintara partiki-la'.
this another nut.tree-LOC
"I said to Nanaku – 'Here's this other one in a nut tree'."
(🔊) TD: FM07_a28: 4:34min)

(1074) **Ma-ni** ngu jarrwalut.
get-PST CAT many
"She got a whole lot." (🔈 TD: FM07_a059: 3:38min)

7.1.1.5 Class 5 -n

Class 5 inflecting verbs include four forms *junana* 'swear at', *manana* 'do, get', *yanana* 'go' and the 'copulate' verb which is not given here in respect of Gurindji women elders' wishes. It is also not recorded in the dictionary for this reason. The forms of *yanana* 'go' are given in Table 39.

Table 39: Class 5 conjugations.

	Infinitive	Imperative	Indicative		
			Past	Present	Potential
Perfect	*yanu* 'to go'	*yanta* 'go!'	*yani* 'went' 'had gone'		*yanku* 'will go' 'want to go'
Imperfect	*yananu* 'to be going'	*yananta* 'should go!'	*yanani* 'was going' 'used to go'	*yanana* 'go' 'going'	*yanangku* 'will be going' 'want to go'

The inflecting verb *manana* has the basic meaning of physical manipulation at its core. It is most often used to express 'get' (1075), 'do' (1076), 'make' or 'handle' (1077).

(1075) Kawurn ngu=rna **ma-ni** nyila kankunungkarra.
ashes CAT=1EXC.MIN.S get-PST that on.top
"I just got some ashes from high up [on the riverbank at Four Mile – Yurru]."
(🔈 VW: FM09_13_3a: 0:55min)

(1076) Ngawa-ngku **ma-ni** kalypa-k.
water-ERG do-PST soft-FACT
"The water made [the white ochre] soft." (🔈 VW: FM08_11_2c: 4:14min)

(1077) Ngu=rna turt **ma-ni** ngaja wanta.
CAT=1EXC.MIN.S hold do-PST ADMON fall.IMP
"I held him in case he fell." (McConvell corpus: Meakins et al., 2016, p. 260)

Similar to *kangana* 'take', the meaning of *yanana* 'go' shifts to 'come' (1078) with the addition of deictic information provided by demonstratives, for example *nyawa-rniny*. This is one place where Gurindji differs from Bilinarra, Jaru, Wanyjirra and Warlpiri. Bilinarra and Jaru verbs encode hither on verbs using *-rni* (Meakins & Nordlinger,

2014, pp. 308–309; Tsunoda, 1981, p. 208), although note in Jaru, it is only used with imperative and purposive forms of verbs (Tsunoda, 1981: 208). Wanyjirra and Warlpiri encode both hither and thither using *-rni* and *-rra*, respectively (Laughren, 1978, p. 2; Senge, 2016, pp. 426–427). Warlpiri also has a perlative suffix *-mpa*.

(1078) **Ya-ni** ngu **nyawa-rniny** nyawa jamana=ma kuya.
go-PST CAT this-HITH this footprint=TOP thus
"It walked this way. Here are its footprints." (🔈 VW: FM10_a154: 4:31min)

7.1.1.6 Irregular verbs

In addition to the five verb conjugations, two irregular verbs exist: *karrinyana* 'be, sit' (Table 40) and *waninyana* 'fall' (Table 41).

Table 40: Gurindji 'be' verb.

	Infinitive	Imperative	Indicative		
			Past	Present	Potential
Perfect	*karrinyu* 'to be' 'to sit'	*karra* 'sit!' 'stay!'	*karrinya* 'was, sat' 'had been' 'had sat'		*karru* 'will be' 'will sit' 'want to sit'
Imperfect	*karrinyanu* 'to be sitting'	*karrinyanta* 'should be!'	*karrinyani* 'was sitting' 'used to sit' 'used to be'	*karrinyana* 'is, sit' 'sitting'	*karrinyangku* 'will be or want to be sitting'

Table 41: Gurindji 'fall' verb.

	Infinitive	Imperative	Indicative		
			Past	Present	Potential
Perfect	*waninyu* 'to fall'	*wanta* 'fall!'	*waninya* 'fell' 'had fallen'		*wanku* 'will fall' 'want to fall'
Imperfect	*waninyanu* 'to be falling'	*waninyanta* 'should fall!'	*waninyani* 'was falling'	*waninyana* 'fall' 'falling'	*waninyangku* 'will be falling, want to be falling'

7.1.1.6.1 *karrinyana* 'be'

The 'be' verb bears some resemblance to the Class 1 conjugation, however this analysis depends on the stem being analysed as *ka-* which produces the correct potential *karru* and imperative forms *karra*, which are usually the distinguishing forms in the conjugations. To produce the rest of the forms in the paradigm, the stem would need to be analysed as *karri-* with cluster reductions for the imperative and potential forms, i.e. *rri-rra* → *rra*. Indeed there is a cognate verb in Warlpiri: *karri-* 'to stand' (Nash, 1982, p. 191; 2008, p. 222). However, this leaves a spurious *-nya-* which only makes sense for past tense in Class 3 verbs, but no other paradigms, and even then this palatal *nya* does not make an appearance as a form in Class 3 verbs or elsewhere.

One interesting use of *karrinyana* involves constructions of the type that Schultze-Berndt (2012) terms 'pseudo progressive' in Jaminjung. In this construction, *karrinyana* is substituted for another inflecting verb in a complex predicate to give a sense of continuing action. These alternations are possible with many classes of coverbs including coverbs of sound emission (§7.2.3.5), as shown in (1079) and (1080); and coverbs of intake (§7.2.3.13).

(1079)	**Jarrakap**	ngu=rna=rla	**ma-rna-na**	jaru.
	talk	CAT=1EXC.MIN.S=3OBL	talk-IMPF-PRS	language

"I talk in language to her." (🔈) VW: FM07_01_1a: 3:17min)

(1080)	Ngu=rna=rla	Nangari-wu	**karrinyana**	**jarrakap**.
	CAT=1EXC.MIN.S=3OBL	SUBSECT-DAT	be.IMPF.PRS	talk

"I am talking to Nangari." (🔈) VW: FM09_14_1a: 12:18min)

It is possible that this verb is the source of the iterative suffix *-karra* which is widespread in Ngumpin-Yapa languages as a coverb suffix in various guises as an iterative marker or switch-reference marker. This hypothesis is strengthened if the Bilinarra equivalent *karra* 'be.PRS' is considered (Meakins & Nordlinger, 2014, pp. 283–284). Indeed Bybee and Dahl (1989) observe that locative verbs such as 'be' are a common source for progressive markers cross-linguistically. Another possibility is that *-karra* finds its origins in *karra* which is the adverbial demonstrative 'thus' in a number of Pama-Nyungan languages in the region.

7.1.1.6.2 *waninyana* 'fall'

The fall verb is as similarly perplexing as the *karrinyana* 'be' verb. The potential *wanku* and imperative forms *wanta* best match Class 5 verbs if the stem is analysed as *wa-*. But this does not produce the expected forms in the rest of the paradigm, for example the past form should be *wani* not the actual form *waninya*. Instead the past form also resembles the Class 3 forms with *-nya* as the past tense marker. But then the forms do not match the rest of the paradigm. In fact, the rest of the forms in the paradigm bear the strongest resemblance to the irregular *karrinyana* 'be' conjugation.

This verb is translated by Gurindji speakers as 'fall', however has a broader meaning of a 'change of locative relation' which is in line with Schultze-Berndt's (2000, p. 230) analysis of the equivalent 'fall' verb in Jaminjung. This broader meaning does not necessarily have a 'downward' component to it, although it can, as shown in (1081), but rather a change of stance (1082), location (1083)–(1086) or liminal state, for example it is used to mean 'die'[191] (1087)–(1088), 'be born'[192] (1089), 'become disabled' (1090) or 'transform into a Dreaming feature' (1091).

(1081) Jintaku=ma jak **waninya** janyja-ka.
one=TOP drop fall.PST ground-LOC
"One dropped on the ground." (🔈 VW: FM07_a185: 11:27min)

(1082) Yipurrk ngu=rna yawarta-la jalngak **waninya.**
for.nothing CAT=1EXC.MIN.S horse-LOC mount fall.PST
"I got on the horse for nothing [I got thrown off]."
(McConvell corpus: Meakins et al., 2016, p. 448)

(1083) Ngu=rnalu jawurruk **waninya.**
CAT=1EXC.AUG.S descend fall.PST
"We got out [of the car]." (🔈 BW: FM07_a021: 0:19min)

(1084) Winyji-ka <u>na</u> kayirra-ngkarra ngu=lu
spring-LOC FOC north-DOWN CAT=3AUG.S

waninya Palyilarra-la.
fall.PST place.name-LOC
"They came down to a spring on the north side of Palyilarra."
(🔈 VW: FM10_30_1a: 1:38min)

(1085) Ngu=rna kankula karrakarrap-karra nyawa
CAT=1EXC.MIN.S up look.REDUP-ITER this

<u>na</u> paraj pu-nya nama **waninya** ngu.
FOC find pierce-PST bee fall.PST CAT
"I was looking up here and there and then I saw a bee going into a tree."
(🔈 BW: FM07_a021: 2:32min)

191 The 'fall' verb is often used in conjunction with *tampang* 'dead', *papart* 'massacre', *jungap* 'die' and other death coverbs in a complex predicate express death.
192 The 'fall' verb is often used in conjunction with *paraj* 'find' in a complex predicate to express birth.

(1086) Jirrpu **waninya** nyiwunyiwun=parla ya-nku ngu.
dive fall.PST dive=FOC go-POT CAT
"He dived in and swam underwater." (🔈 BW: FM07_a043: 32:23min)

(1087) Jungap-pa=rni ngu=rla **waninya** mirlarrang.
die-EP=ONLY CAT=3OBL fall.PST spear
"He died when a spear got him." (McConvell corpus: Meakins et al., 2016, p. 115)

(1088) Ngumparna=ma=yinangulu **waninyani**=ma.
husband=TOP=3AUG.S>3AUG.NS fall.IMPF.PST=TOP
"Their husbands used to pass away on them." (🔈 VW: FM12_a175: 3:17min)

(1089) Nyamu=lu **waninyana** karu, yapakayi...
REL=3AUG.S fall.IMPF.PRS child small
"When children are born..." (🔈 VW: FM10_a143: 8:45min)

(1090) ...ngaja **waninyana** martartilyi.
...ADMON fall.IMPF.PRS disabled
"...in case it becomes disabled." (🔈 BW: FM09_a122: 5:04min)

(1091) Ngajik-pa=rni na Mamungkul **waninya**
long.time-EP=ONLY FOC Dreaming.feature fall.PST

ngu=wula, kankula nyila=ma.
CAT=3UA.S up that=TOP
"The two of them became Dreaming features permanently up there."
(🔈 VW: FM10_a151: 4:12min)

7.1.2 Gurindji verbal predicates in comparison with surrounding languages

7.1.2.1 Coverbs and their derivation

Many of the forms and semantic range of the inflecting verb roots in Gurindji virtually match the Bilinarra and Ngarinyman roots. Gurindji has more verb roots (34 as compared with 23 from Bilinarra and 18 from Ngarinyman), but where there is overlap, most of them are exact matches. The Yapa language, Warlpiri, has a much larger verb inventory with around 120 verbs. McConvell and Schultze-Berndt (2001; reported in Nash, 2008, p. 232) claim that historically Ngumpin-Yapa had about 50 simple verbs and that daughter languages, other than Warlpiri, have lost simple verbs. This includes Gurindji. In line with this picture, Nash (1982, pp. 185–200) claims that Warlpiri has gained verbs through borrowing from Arandic languages and the fusion of coverbs to inflecting verbs to create new inflecting verbs. This section discusses how Gurindji may have lost inflecting verbs to the coverb category.

Evidence for the creation of coverbs from inflecting verbs comes from synchronic derivational processes. In Gurindji and other Ngumpin languages, such as Bilinarra, coverbs are synchronically derived from inflecting verbs with the addition of *-p* to the infinitive form of the inflecting verb, for example the inflecting verb *kampa-* 'cook' becomes a coverb *kampa-rnu-p* 'cook-INF-CV'. Its status as a coverb is confirmed by the fact that *kamparnup* has the same distributional features as other coverbs, for example expressing reduced subordinate clauses with the addition of case marking, as shown in (1092). (Note also that the infinitive form of the verb without the *-p* suffix can also be used in these reduced subordinate clauses, as shown in (1036)). Both the inflecting verb and the derived coverb can even co-exist in a single clause as shown by (1093) where the inflecting verb *yunparnana* combines with the derived coverb *yunparnup*. Other examples of inflecting verbs which co-exist with derived coverbs are *jamanup manana* > *jamanana* 'grind', *yinkarnup yinkarnana* > *yinkarnana* 'plane down' and *kunyjanup manana* > *kunyjanana* 'wetten'. Thus five of the 34 inflecting verbs have coverb counterparts.

(1092) Nyila=ma ngu=lu ka-nga-ni na **kampa-rnu-p-ku** na.
that=TOP CAT=3AUG.S bring-IMPF-PST FOC cook-INF-CV-DAT FOC
"They would bring [the fish] to cook now." (🔊 VW: FM09_a16_2: 4:53min)

(1093) Ngu=rnalu **yunpa-rna-na** **yunpa-rnu-p=ma**
CAT=1EXC.AUG.S sing-IMPF-PRS sing-INF-CV=TOP

kilkilp Yawulyu-la=ma.
click.together woman.ceremony-LOC=TOP
"We sing and play the clapsticks during the Yawulyu ceremony."
(🔊 VW: FM08_a101: 9:34min)

In some cases, the equivalent inflecting verb in Gurindji is no longer found, but the derived coverb remains. These derivations can be found by comparing the Eastern Ngumpin languages with the more conservative Western Ngumpin languages, which have larger inflecting verb inventories. For example, Senge (2008, p. 126) reports *punta-* 'collect' as an inflecting verb root for Wanyjirra. In Gurindji, a related coverb *puntanup* 'collect' exists which is most likely derived from an infinitive verb plus coverbaliser: *punta-nu-p* 'collect-INF-CV' (see §7.1.3.6 and §7.1.3.7 with regard to the form and function of infinitives and §7.2.4.2 for the coverbaliser). In Gurindji, the coverb *puntanup* combines with *manana* 'do'. Similarly, there is *wingarnu* 'swim' in Gurindji and *winganup* in Wanyjirra. No inflecting verb exists, but the existence of both of these coverbs is suggestive of an earlier inflecting verb.

Comparisons can also be made between other Eastern Ngumpin languages. For example, Tsunoda (1981, p. 82) gives *pulang-* as an inflecting verb in Jaru which means 'call out' which is found in Nyininy as a coverb *pulangup*. In Warlmanpa, Ngardi, Jaru, Gurindji and Eastern Walmajarri, there is the form *ngalyanu* 'tongue' and Ngardi also has lick coverb: *ngalya-*, which is suggestive of an inflecting verb which existed at some point meaning 'lick'. In Gurindji, the 'lick' coverb is *ngalyak*.

Another path of development from coverb to inflecting verb seems to have been the fusion of the iterative suffix *-karra* to the stem of the inflecting verb, resulting in a coverb. Again, a comparison of Eastern and Western Ngumpin supports this analysis. Some inflecting verbs which are reported for the Western Ngumpin languages are expressed by coverbs in Gurindji, Ngarinyman and Bilinarra. For example, 'cry' is an inflecting verb in Wanyjirra (*lungana*) (Senge, 2008, p. 125) and Jaru (*lungan*) (Tsunoda, 1981, p. 82), but is a coverb in Gurindji, Bilinarra and Ngarinyman (*lungkarra(p)*). Hints of the existence of these coverbs as inflecting verbs can be found in older Dreaming stories which preserve more conservative forms of the language. For example, a Gurindji story about Blue Tongue and his boomerang contains an utterance where 'crying' is expressed by the coverb *lungkarrap*, but also an equivalent inflecting verb.

(1094)	**Lungkarrap**	ngu=rla	**lu-nga-ni**,	kuya.
	cry	CAT=3OBL	cry-IMPF-PST	thus

"He cried over it, like this." (🔈) KM: FM08_a073: 01:25min)

Examples like these suggest that at one point Gurindji had a 'cry' inflecting verb which coexisted with the coverb for a while until the inflecting verb was lost, and the verb complex came to be expressed with the inflecting verb 'be' as in *lungkarra karrinyana*.

7.1.2.2 Inflecting verbs, their forms and inflectional categories

The inflectional forms of the Gurindji verb conjugations also match the Malngin and Wanyjirra forms[193] and virtually match the Bilinarra and Ngarinyman forms (Ise, 1998; Jones, Schultze-Berndt, Denniss, et al., 2019; Meakins, 2013; Meakins & Nordlinger, 2014; Senge, 2016). The imperative and potential forms are the same as Malngin, Wanyjirra, Bilinarra and Ngarinyman. Where they differ is in the present tense forms, as is shown in Table 42, and the past imperfective inflections, as shown in Table 43. We do not have data for the rest of the forms because they were not documented for Bilinarra and Ngarinyman. Bilinarra and Ngarinyman differ only in the final nasal, which is variable, but more consistently found in Ngarinyman dialects around the Timber

193 Note that Senge (2016) divides conjugation classes beyond the five classes reported for Gurindji in order to accommodate the 'be' and 'fall' verbs which we classify as irregular verbs in our analysis. Wanyjirra also has more verbs in its inventory.

Creek area rather than Yarralin. The past imperfective inflections differ in both form and position. Gurindji has the form *-na* (with allomorphic variation of the initial nasal) which occurs *before* the past tense inflection, and Bilinarra and Ngarinyman have the form *-rra* which occurs *after* the past tense inflection and, as shown in Table 43.

Table 42: Present tense inflections in Gurindji, Wanyjirra, Malngin, Bilinarra and Ngarinyman.

	Class 1	Class 2	Class 3	Class 4	Class 5
Gurindji[1]	*–nana*	*–rnana*	*–ngana*	*–rnana*	*–nana*
Wanyjirra	*–nana*	*–rnana*	*–ngana*	*–rnana*	*–nana*
Malngin	*–nana*	*–rnana*	*–ngana*	*–rnana*	*–nana*
Bilinarra	*–rra*	*–la*	*–nga*	*–la*	*–na*
Ngarinyman	*–rra(ny)*	*–la(n)*	*–nga(n)*	*–la(n)*	*–na(n)*

[1] Note that the Gurindji forms are present imperfective forms, e.g. *ya-na-na* 'go-IMPF-PRS' (Class 5).

Table 43: Past imperfective inflections in Gurindji, Wanyjirra, Malngin, Bilinarra and Ngarinyman.

	Class 1	Class 2	Class 3	Class 4	Class 5
Gurindji [-IMPF-PST]	*–na-ni*	*–rna-ni*	*–nga-ni*	*–rna-ni*	*–na-ni*
Wanyjirra [-IMPF-PST]	*–na-ni*	*–rna-ni*	*–nga-ni*	*–rna-ni*	*–na-ni*
Malngin [-IMPF-PST]	*–na-ni*	*–rna-ni*	*–nga-ni*	*–rna-ni*	*–na-ni*
Bilinarra [-PST-IMPF]	*–ni-rra*	*–rni-rra*	*–nya-rra*	*–rni-rra*	*–ni-rra*
Ngarinyman [-PST-IMPF]	*–ni-rra*	*–rni-rra*	*–nya-rra*	*–rni-rra*	*–ni-rra*

Gurindji shows even more differences from Mudburra and Jaru in terms of the forms in the inflecting verb paradigm, which are not discussed here.

7.1.3 Functions of tense, aspect and mood categories

Gurindji makes two tense distinctions: past (§7.1.3.2) and present (§7.1.3.1). Future time is indicated using the potential mood, which also has desiderative and obligatory meanings (§7.1.3.4). Aspectual distinctions (perfective and imperfective) are made within past tense, potential and imperative moods, and the infinitive. Another mood category marked on the verb is the hortative (§7.1.3.10). Periphrastic constructions using a complementiser or clitic to mark other mood categories include admonitive (§7.1.3.11), interrogative (§7.1.3.12) and dubitative (§7.1.3.13).

7.1.3.1 Present tense

Present tense refers to an event time which overlaps with the speech time. The present tense uses the imperfective infix *-na-* but does not distinguish a separate perfective form. The most frequent use of the present tense is for ongoing activity, as shown in (1095) and (1096).

(1095) **Ya-na-na** jarriny-ngurlung=parla wart pakara.
go-IMPF-PRS room-ABL=FOC return outside
"She comes out of the [doctor]'s." (🔈 BW: FM07_043: 13:31min)

(1096) Jipurlp **ya-na-na** ngu=wula ngaliwanguny-jirri.
join go-IMPF-PRS CAT=3UA.S 1INC.AUG.DAT-ALL
"The two of them join us where we're sitting." (🔈 VW: FM12_a173: 6:59min)

Reduplicated coverbs (§7.2.4.4), extreme vowel lengthening and the iterative suffix on coverbs (§7.2.4.1) are also used to express ongoing activity. An example of the present tense combining with *-karra* 'iterative' is given in (1097).

(1097) Kartak-kula takurl-**arra** **kiya-rna-na**, jarrwalut.
billycan-LOC inside-ITER put-IMPF-PRS many
"She is putting them in a billycan, lots of them." (🔈 TD: FM10_a163: 4:06min)

The present tense can also be used to express habitual or customary aspect, as shown in (1098) and (1099):

(1098) Nyanawu pilyily yapakayi majul-a nyamu
RECOG pinky small stomach-LOC REL

ka-nga-na puul-a walyak.
take-IMPF-PRS pouch-LOC inside
"You know the hairless joey that lives in its mother's pouch."
(🔈 VW: FM09_a123: 6:27min)

(1099) Nyamu=yinangkulu **ka-nga-na** kaa-rni-yin
REL=3AUG.S>3AUG.NS take-IMPF-PRS east-UP-ABL

wart=ma, hospital-ngurlu=ma.
return=TOP hospital-ABL=TOP
"When [the mothers] bring [the babies] back from up in the east from [Katherine] hospital." (◀)) BW: FM07_02_1a: 0:56min)

7.1.3.2 Past perfective tense

The past perfective describes a completed past event that is viewed as a whole, as in (1100)–(1103).

(1100) Ngu=yinangkulu **yuwa-ni** ngirlkirri-la na.
CAT=3AUG.S>3AUG.NS put-PST throat-LOC FOC
"Then they chained the stockmen together by the neck."[194]
(◀)) BR: FM15_52_1a: 4:00min)

(1101) Ngu=yina **ka-nya** Timber Creek-jirri wart.
CAT=3AUG.NS take-PST place.name-ALL return
"He brought them back to Timber Creek." (◀)) BR: FM15_52_1a: 8:35min)

(1102) Ngu **nya-nya** kuya-ngku=ma, nyawa "Ngu=yi
CAT intake-PST thus-ERG=TOP this CAT=1EXC.MIN.NS

ya-ni ngayiny-jirri rait."
go-PST 1EXC.MIN.DAT-ALL right
"He saw him saying, 'Ah he's heading my way.'" (◀)) BR: FM15_52_1b: 0:54min)

(1103) Jilinypuk-kula ngu=lu **karrinya** nyila
place.name-LOC CAT=3AUG.S be.PST that

194 This was a heinous practice in early colonial times to punish Aboriginal people or stop them from running away. Example sentences like these are used throughout the grammar to remind readers of the recent colonial history of Gurindji people and its contribution to the endangerment of the language. We apologise for the upsetting nature of the content for Indigenous readers. The full story can be found in Ryan (2016a).

<u>na</u>	yatu	nyamu=lu	**wanyja-ni**.
FOC	white.ochre	REL=3AUG.S	leave-PST

"They stopped at Jilinypuk[195] where they left some white ochre."
(🔈 VW: FM10_30_1a: 0:29min)

If the focus clitic *=parla/=warla* (§10.1.7) is added to a verb inflected with the past tense, it can give the meaning of 'immediate past' which may be relative to the past being discussed (1104), or 'sequential' as shown in (1105) and (1106).

(1104)

Wumara=ma	kuya-ny	ma-ni=nyanta
rock=TOP	thus-NMLZ	get-PST=3OBL2

yuwa-ni=warla,	wararr=ma	walyak.
put-PST=FOC	fat=TOP	inside

"He got this kind of rock and immediately wrapped the fat around it."
(🔈 VW: FM10_30_2b: 1:24min)

(1105)

Ngu=lu	**ya-ni=warla**	kayirra	nyawa	karu-yawung=ma.
CAT=3AUG.S	go-PST=FOC	north	this	child-PROP=TOP

"Then they headed north with the boy."
(🔈 BR: FM15_52_1a: 13:27min)

(1106)

Kuya-ngka=warla	kula	**nya-nya=warla**	nyampayirla=ma
thus-LOC=FOC	NEG	intake-PST=FOC	whatsitcalled=TOP

nya-nya=warla	kula	nyampayirla=ma	mirlarrang=ma.
intake-PST=FOC	NEG	whatsitcalled=TOP	spear=TOP.

"That's when he stopped being able to see the spears."
(🔈 BB: McNair_D1A: 5:10min)

7.1.3.3 Past imperfective tense

Imperfective aspect is encoded in the past tense as the infix *-na-* positioned before the past tense inflection. This form is most often used to give a past habitual reading of 'used to' or 'would' and is commonly found in oral history accounts of past times, as shown in (1107) where Violet Wadrill describes past practices. It is translated into Kriol as *yusta* '<used to', *oldei* '<all day', or *bin olataim* '<been all the time'.

195 Black Gin Yard is the non-Indigenous name given to this site. We only include it in the gloss and footnote it here because the name 'Jilinypuk' is not known to most younger generations of Gurindji people who use the name 'Black Gin Yard' themselves. Sadly, non-Indigenous names such as this one exist right across Australia. We are aware that continuing to use them only perpetuates racist ideologies.

(1107) Janiki karrinya ngu=lu pirrkap

loincloth be.PST CAT=3AUG.S make

ma-na-ni possum-nginyi.

do-IMPF-PST possum-SOURCE

"They used to make loin cloths from possum fur."

(🔊 VW: FM11_a164: 13:25min)

The past imperfective is also used to mark an event in the past as ongoing with respect to another event. For example, in (1108), it is used to describe a Dreaming Emu running below a flying Dreaming Corella, and in (1109), it is used to describe collecting and eating honey at the same time.

(1108) Nyantu Yiparrartu kaninyjal-a **ya-na-ni**

3MIN Emu below-LOC go-IMPF-PST

an Pangarra kankulu-pal-a.

and Corella up-EDGE-LOC

"Emu was running below with Corella above." (🔊 VW: FM08_08_4e: 0:48min)

(1109) Ngu=ja **ma-na-ni** ngunyjung=ma,

CAT=1EXC.UA.S get-IMPF-PST honey=TOP

jaartkarra ngu=ja **nya-nga-ni**.

eat CAT=1EXC.UA.S intake-IMPF-PST

"We were getting lumps of honey and eating them."

(🔊 TD: FM07_a028: 11:10min)

7.1.3.4 Potential mood

Gurindji does not mark future tense, but rather expresses future time through the potential suffix. Both Bilinarra and Wanyjirra show a similar functional range for this category, although Senge (2016, pp. 411–414) refers to it as future tense in Wanyjirra. In the case of Gurindji, potential mood is used to refer to an action which has not yet taken place, but which the speaker feels will probably happen, or should probably happen. It can be used to refer to either the immediate or distant future. Examples are given in (1110)–(1112).

(1110) Punyu-k **ma-nku** janga-nginyi ngu.

good-FACT do-POT sick-SOURCE CAT

"The honey will make her feel better after being sick."

(🔊 TD: FM07_a028: 12:12min)

(1111) Ngu=rna=yina **jayi-ngku**
CAT=1EXC.MIN.S=3AUG.NS give-POT

ngayiny-ku mali-wu.
1EXC.MIN.DAT-DAT son.in.law-DAT
"I'm going to give it to my son-in-laws." (🔈 VW: FM07_05_1a: 7:32min)

(1112) Jungkarra ngu=rna karrinyana,
decide CAT=1EXC.MIN.S be.IMPF.PRS

"Wanyji-rrirniny-pa=rna **ya-nku**?"
which-HITH-EP=1EXC.MIN.S go-POT
"I'm deciding, 'Which way should I go?'" (🔈 VW: FM12_a173: 12:44min)

In the negative, the potential mood expresses something that could happen but will not, which can be translated as 'will not' as exemplified in (1113). It can also express an inability to do something, translated as 'could not' or 'cannot', as in (1114) and (1115).

(1113) **Kula**=ngkulu, **jayi-ngku**, kajikajirri-lu=ma,
NEG=3AUG.S>2MIN.NS give-POT old.woman.REDUP-ERG=TOP

ngaja karrinyana ngirlkirri wankaj karu=ma.
ADMON be.IMPF.PRS throat bad child=TOP
"The old ladies won't give [bush turkey] to you, in case the baby is born with a bad throat." (🔈 VW: FM09_a123: 4:06min)

(1114) Jarrnga-jarrnga-warra karrinyana=ma ngumpit=ma
stuck.in.tree-REDUP-ITER be.IMPF.PRS=TOP man=TOP

kankula, **kula** jawurruk **ya-nku**.
up NEG descend go-POT
"The man is stuck up there and can't come down."
(🔈 DD: EC97_a001: Purnkali: 3:55min)

(1115)

Karrij	na	ma-na-na.	**Kula**	**ya-nku**	na
decrepit	FOC	get-IMPF-PRS	NEG	go-POT	FOC

kalurirrp-karra=ma	yikikili=ma.
walk.around-ITER=TOP	far.REDUP=TOP

Wankaj	ngu	karrij	ma-na-na.
no.good	CAT	decrepit	get-IMPF-PRS

"He's disabled [from age]. He can't walk very far. He's no good because he's decrepit." (🔈 VW: FM12_a174: 19:08min)

If the speaker feels that there is a chance that the action will not take place, the dubitative aspect suffix is also used, as shown in (1116) and (1117) (see also §7.1.3.13). Alternatively, the potential mood can combine with the adverb *majka* 'try', as in (1118), although *majka* can combine with other tenses.

(1116)

Nyila=ma=rna	**ma-nku=nga**	yilarrp
that=TOP=1EXC.MIN.S	get-POT=DUB	pull.out

na,	nyila=ma	lamawurt=ma.
FOC	that=TOP	witchetty.grub=TOP

"I might draw it out now – the witchetty grub that is." (🔈 VW: FM08_a099: 6:28min)

(1117)

Karrawarra	**ya-nku=nga**	Nangala=ma,	Barunga-yirri.
east	go-POT=DUB	SUBSECT=TOP	place.name-ALL

"Nangala might be going east to Barunga." (🔈 VW: FM09_14_1a: 14:38min)

(1118)

Juwal	ngu=rlaa	pirrkap	**ma-nku**	**majka**.
long	CAT=1INC.AUG.S	make	do-POT	try

"We'll try to make a long [fire drill]." (🔈 VW: FM09_a127: 23:22min)

Potential mood is also used to express notions such as necessity and is translated as 'should' in these examples, as shown in (1119). In combination with *kula* the meaning becomes 'should not', as in (1120)–(1122). In these sentences, it is not ability which is in question but something which is at stake, either social conventions at risk of being breached or a physical risk.

(1119)

Jitiwu	nya-ngka	karrap.	Ngu=n	**wanyja-rru**	na	warrij.
last.time	intake-IMP	see	CAT=2MIN.S	leave-POT	FOC	leave

"See her for the last time. You should leave then." (🔈 VW: FM12_a173: 8:40min)

(1120) **Kula** wupkarra-la=ma nyampa-ka=ma ngapuk
NEG cook.on.coals-LOC=TOP what-LOC=TOP smell

ma-nku ngarin=ma ngarturr-jawung-kulu=ma.
do-POT meat=TOP pregnant-PROP-ERG=TOP
"A pregnant woman shouldn't smell meat when some is cooking."
(🔊 VW: FM09_a123: 10:30min)

(1121) **Kula**=n-ku=rla kuli **ma-lu**, purruna ngu=ngku.
NEG=2MIN.S-EP=3OBL argue talk-POT mother.in.law CAT=2MIN.NS
"You can't raise your voice to her, that's your mother-in-law."
(RW with ECh: Meakins et al., 2016, p. 344)

(1122) Nya-nga-ni ngu=lu ngarrungkap-karra ma-rna-ni
intake-IMPF-PST CAT=3AUG.S want-ITER say-IMPF-PST

yu nou jaartkarra-wu. 'Lawara, **kula**=nta **nga-lu.**
you know eat-DAT nothing NEG=2AUG.S eat-POT

Ngu=rnalu nga-lu ngantipa=rni marlurluka-lu.
CAT=1EXC.AUG.S eat-POT 1EXC.AUG=ONLY old.man.REDUP-ERG

Kajijirri-lu, jaartkarra-wu=ma.'
old.woman.REDUP-ERG eat-DAT=TOP
"They used to see it and want to be eating it. [But we said], 'You shouldn't eat it. Only us old men and women are allowed to eat it'."
(🔊 VW: FM09_a123: 3:04min)

The potential mood is also used to give polite or very indirect instructions, as in (1123). In this clause, the speaker is not expressing the hearer's ability to do something, but that she should.

(1123) Ngunti ngu=n pirrkap **ma-nku** nyanuny-ja
light CAT=2MIN.S make do-POT 3MIN.DAT-LOC

karrap-kula, Nangari-wu-ny-ja.
watch-LOC SUBSECT-DAT-NMLZ-LOC
"You can make the light while Nangari watches on."
(🔊 VW: FM09_17_2a: 1:24min)

Potential mood can also be used to express desire, as in (1124)–(1126).

(1124) Wararr-jawung ngu=rnalu **nga-lu**.
fat-PROP CAT=1EXC.AUG.S eat-POT
"We want to eat the fatty [meat]." (🔈 VW: FM09_a123: 0:13min)

(1125) Makin-ta jayi-ngka=yi tuwarrji.
lie-LOC give-IMP=1EXC.MIN.NS pillow

Ngu=rna **karru** makin.
CAT=1EXC.MIN.S be.POT sleep
"Give me the pillow when I'm lying down. I want to sleep."
(🔈 TD: FM10_a163: 2:01min)

(1126) Ngu=rna **ya-nku** wajija. Lawara nyuntu
CAT=1EXC.MIN.S go-POT quickly nothing 2MIN

waral ma-nta=yi. Karra ngumayila.
delay do-IMP=1EXC.MIN.NS stay.IMP behind
"I want to go faster. No – you're holding me up. Stay behind."
(🔈 VW: FM11_a164: 4:02min)

7.1.3.5 Potential imperfective mood

The potential imperfective expresses the same range as the perfective, with the added meaning of 'to be doing in the future'. It is used to express something ongoing in the future (1127)–(1128), as well as ongoing desire (1129), permission (1130) and ability (1131).

(1127) Ngurra ngu=rnalu **ya-na-ngku** ngarin
camp CAT=1EXC.AUG.S go-IMPF-POT meat

ngu=rnalu **pa-na-ngku**, ngu=rnalu
CAT=1EXC.AUG.S hit-IMPF-POT CAT=1EXC.AUG.S

ka-nga-nku murla-ngkawu=rni ngurra-wu.
take-IMPF-POT this-PURP=ONLY camp-DAT
"We're going to go camping out, killing some game and bringing back the meat back here for the camp."
(Appendix: Echidna and the Big Shade: Text 1, Line 4)

(1128) Wamamala ngu=rnayinangkulu wiit
girl.REDUP CAT=1EXC.AUG.S>3AUG.NS show

jayi-nga-nku	warrwarrkap-ku.
give-IMPF-POT	dance.REDUP-DAT

"We'll be showing all of the girls how to dance." (🔈 BW: FM08_11_5: 1:58min)

(1129)

Ngu=rnayinangulu	pina-rrik	**jayi-nga-nku**
CAT=1EXC.AUG.S>3AUG.NS	know-FACT	give-IMPF-POT

karu	jarrakap	jaru,	ngantipanguny.
child	talk	language	1EXC.AUG.DAT

"We want to be teaching our children to speak language."
(🔈 VW: FM08_11_3: 0:08min)

(1130)

Nyila=ma	**nya-nga-nku**	ngu=nta
that=TOP	intake-IMPF-POT	CAT=2AUG.S

nyurrulu=rni	kirri-walija-lu	karrap.
2AUG=ONLY	woman-PAUC-ERG	look

"[When you take a photo], only you women are allowed to be looking at it."
(🔈 VW: FM07_a085: 19:15min)

(1131)

Ngu=rna	**karrwa-rna-ngku**	<u>na</u>	ngajik
CAT=1EXC.MIN.S	have-IMPF-POT	FOC	long.time

nyamu=yilu=nga	pirrkap=ma
REL=3AUG.S>1EXC.MIN.NS=DUB	make=TOP

ma-nku	punyu-k=ma.
do-POT	good-FACT=TOP

(🔈 VW : FM07_a021: 6:27min)

7.1.3.6 Infinitive perfective

This verbal inflection is called the 'infinitive' by Meakins and Nordlinger (2014, p. 293) for Bilinarra, the 'subordinate' by Dixon (1980, p. 385) for Walmajarri and the 'verbid' by Tsunoda (1981, p. 78) for Jaru. The term 'infinitive' is used here.

(1132) Nyamu=waa wurruja=ma karru nyila-rra=ma
REL=REL dry=TOP be.POT that-PL=TOP

parnngirri=ma, **kampa-rnu** na ngu=rnalu
bark=TOP cook-INF FOC CAT=1EXC.AUG.S

kampa-rna-na kuliyan, kuliyan-pirrji.
cook-IMPF-PRS aggressive aggressive-FACT
"When the bark is dry we burn it make it bitey [to combine with chewing tobacco]." (🔈 VW: FM07_a089: 8:35min)

The infinitive is also used in subordinate clauses, sometimes with the coverbiliser suffix *-p* (1133)–(1135), but not always (1136)–(1138). It allows the inflecting verb to take the same range of case suffixes which can occur on coverbs in subordinate clauses. Those that are found in the corpus are often inflecting verbs which do not have coverb counterparts, for example 'cook' (1092), (1134) and (1136) and 'sing' (1093).[196] But inflecting verbs which have coverbs that express the same meaning are also used. For example, in (1135), the speaker could have used *yurtup* or *kutukutu* 'grind'. In (1137), *jarrakap* 'talk' is found more usually in subordinate clauses, and in (1138) *pirrkap-ku* 'make-DAT' would have sufficed.

(1133) Pakarli-la nyamu=rli karrinyana
river.paperbark-LOC REL=1INC.MIN.S be.IMPF.PRS

yuwa-nu-p-kula-karra[197] jarrakap-karra nyampa-ka.
put-INF-CV-LOC-ITER talk-ITER what-LOC
"Under the paperbark tree where we talk language and whatever to record it." (🔈 VW: FM11_a167: 5:37min)

(1134) Ngu=rna ka-nya **kampa-rnu-p-ku.**
CAT=1EXC.MIN.S take-PST cook-INF-CV-DAT
"Then I brought it back to cook." (🔈 CN: FM10_28_2a: 5:37min)

(1135) Karrinyani wartart na, **jama-nu-p-ku.**
be.IMPF.PST dry.out FOC grind-INF-CV-DAT
"And dried it out for grinding." (🔈 BW: FM10_a143: 24:03min)

196 See also §7.2.2.3 for coverbs in subordinate clauses and §9.2. See §7.1.2.1 for notes on how coverbs may develop from the infinitive forms of inflecting verbs.
197 Note that this is an odd reversal of the order of INF-LOC-*karra* and you would also expect the lenited form *-warra*.

(1136) Ma-nta=ngali-ku=rla nalija-wu
get-IMP=1INC.MIN.NS-EP=3OBL tea-DAT

kampa-rnu-wu ngarin-ku wupkarra-wu.
cook-INF-DAT meat-DAT cook.on.coals-DAT
"Get us (some wood) to make tea and cook meat." (🔈 VW: FM11_a166: 35:36min)

(1137) Kuya <u>na</u>, ngantipany=ma yumi=ma=ngantipa,
thus FOC 1EXC.AUG.DAT=TOP law=TOP=1EXC.AUG.NS

ma-rnu-wu karu-wu=ma.
talk-INF-DAT child-DAT=TOP
"Like that, this is our traditional practice for [getting] children to speak."
(🔈 TD: FM11_a168: 17:27min)

(1138) Ngu=lu wanyja-na-na pirrka **ma-nu-wu=ma**.
CAT=3AUG.S leave-IMPF-PRS make do-INF-DAT=TOP
"They are leaving to make it." (🔈 TN: McConvell_A3463_K: 24:43min)

Even without *-p*, infinitives are essentially coverbs and can be thought as word-class changing inflection (cf. Haspelmath, 1996), normally a property of derivational morphology. These verbs can also then take morphology normally found deriving nominals (§4.7). Some inflecting verbs have an additional coverb or nominal prefixed, as shown in Table 44. Some examples in clauses are given in (1139) and (1140).

Table 44: Nominals derived from infinitive verbs.

Derived form	Gloss	Translation
yinka-rnu-waji	grind-INF-AGENT	chisel
jama-nu-waji	grind-INF-AGENT	chisel
kampa-rnu-waji	cook-INF-AGENT	a cook
linyjarr-nga-rnu-waji	corpse-eat-INF-AGENT	murderer
lurr-pa-nu-waji	go.everywhere-hit-INF-AGENT	grader
wutu-nga-rnu-waji	louse-eat-INF-AGENT	monkey
kula-jayi-ngu-waji	NEG-give-INF-AGENT	stingy person
warlupurr-ma-nu-waji	refuse-do-INF-AGENT	stingy person
ma-rnu-murlung-kaji	talk-INF-PRIV-AGENT	mute
paya-rnu-waji	bite-INF-AGENT	bitey thing
yunpa-rnu-p-kaji	sing-INF-CV-AGENT	singing sticks

(1139) Mumpung=ma nyila=ma yapayapa nyamu karrinyana
black=TOP that=TOP small REL be.IMPF.PRS

kuliyan=ma **paya-rnu-waji=ma**. Yala-nginyi
aggressive=TOP bite-INF-AGENT=TOP that-SOURCE

na ngu=lu nga-rna-ni kampij.
FOC CAT=3AUG.S eat-IMPF-PST egg
"Those little black ants which bite. Well [people] would eat the eggs."
(◀) VW: FM10_a148: 10:19min)

(1140) Nyamu=yi=lu ma-nku punyu-k=ma
REL=1EXC.MIN.NS=3AUG.S do-POT good-FACT=TOP

nyila=ma pakipaki=ma pirrkapirrkap-ku
that=TOP chisel=TOP make.REDUP-DAT

yunpa-rnu-p-kaji-wu nyampa-wu-waji-wu.
sing-INF-CV-AGENT-DAT something-DAT-AGENT-DAT
"When they sharpen the chisel for me, I can make singing-sticks or whatever."
(◀) VW: FM07_a021: 6:58min)

Non-finite morphology in Bilinarra and Wanyjirra has a similar nominalising function and ability to take additional morphology (Meakins & Nordlinger, 2014, pp. 299–300; Senge, 2016, pp. 424–425).

7.1.3.7 Infinitive imperfective

The infinitive can also appear in the imperfective form, as shown in (1141) and (1142).

(1141) Ngu=rnangku ma-rni **ka-nga-nu-wu**
CAT=1EXC.MIN.S>2MIN.NS talk-PST take-IMPF-INF-DAT

wart-ku lun-ku murla-ngkurra-wu.
return-DAT put.down-DAT this-ALL-DAT
"I told you to bring it back and drop it here."
(McConvell corpus: Meakins et al., 2016, p. 209)

(1142) Pinarri karrinyana kurrurij-ku rarraj-ku **ka-nga-nu-wu=ma**
know be.IMPF.PRS car-DAT run-DAT take-IMPF-INF-DAT=TOP
"He knows how to drive a car fast." (McConvell 1996 grammar manuscript)

7.1.3.8 Imperative perfective mood

The imperative mood is used to express commands, orders or instructions (Lyons, 1968, p. 307). Commands may be formed with the imperative form of the inflecting verb (1143)–(1144), in conjunction with a coverb (1145)–(1149) or with a stand-alone coverb (discussed in §7.2.2.4).

(1143) **Jayi-ngka**=yi=rla ngu=rna
give-IMP=1EXC.MIN.NS=3OBL CAT=1EXC.MIN.S

jama-rru ngayu na.
grind-POT 1EXC.MIN FOC
"Give it to me so I can grind [some seed] now."
(🔊 VW: FM10_23_1b: Yawarlwarl Wanyil: 2:20min)

(1144) Yuu, marntaj, **ya-nta**=lu ngarin-ku=ma
yes OK go-IMP=3AUG.S meat-DAT=TOP

pa-rra=ngalangkulu.
hit-IMP=3AUG.S>1INC.AUG.NS
"Yes, all right [said Echidna] go for meat, kill something for us all."
(Appendix: Echidna and the Big Shade: Text 1, Line 5)

(1145) **Wilimat** **wanta**=lu=rla yalu-wu, jarrwa
team.up fall.IMP=3AUG.S=3OBL that-DAT many

ya-nta=lu, **kayi** **pa-rra**=lu nyila.
go-IMP=3AUG.S follow hit-IMP=3AUG.S that
"You mob team up with that one. A big mob of you go. You mob follow him."
(🔊 VW: FM12_a183: 6:20min)

Recall from §6.2.3.1 that the subject person marker is deleted in imperative constructions, while the subject number marker remains. This results in the subject bound pronoun in an imperative construction being formally identical with the equivalent third person subject bound pronoun (since the person marker in third person is ⊘). Thus in (1144)–(1146), the pronoun *=lu* is used which is glossed as '3AUG.S', but is really just the augmented marker.

(1146) Turturl-lu pirrkap **ma-nta=lu**=rla, warlu.
roast-ERG make do-IMP=3AUG.S=3OBL fire
"You mob make a fire and roast it." (🔊 VW: FM10_22_1d: 1:50min)

The fact that the reference is really to a second person augmented pronoun is demonstrated conclusively in (1148) where the free pronoun is the second person augmented *nyurrulu* not *nyarrulu* which is third person augmented. An identical process of person deletion/replacement is found in Jaru (Tsunoda, 1981, p. 133) and Walmajarri (Hudson, 1978, p. 80).

(1147) Kapkap nyurrulu=ma **pu-ngka=yi=lu=rla**.
gang.up 2AUG=TOP hit-IMP=1EXC.MIN.NS=3AUG.NS=3OBL
"You mob – gang up on me." (🔊 VW: FM11_a164: 15:31min)

There are two ways to negate an imperative construction. The usual way is to use the negative particle *kula*, as in (1148) and (1149).[198]

(1148) **Kula ya-nta partaj**, ngaja=n waninyana jirrjiwurntu.
NEG go-IMP climb ADMON=2MIN.S fall.IMPF.PRS high.up
"Don't climb up or else you'll fall down from up there."
(DD with ECh: Meakins et al., 2016, p. 107)

(1149) **Kula piyarr ka-ngka**=ngantipangulu
NEG report take-IMP=3AUG.S>1EXC.AUG.NS

pinka-kawu=rni wulaj-jawu.
river-PURP=ONLY hide-PURP
"Don't report that we're hiding by the river for a reason."
(McConvell corpus: Meakins et al., 2016, p. 124)

It is also possible to use the adnominal case suffix *-murlu(ng)* 'PRIV' with a coverb (see §4.6.3), to order the cessation of an action:

(1150) Kawayiwayi, karu-walija, **yilying-murlu**
come.here.REDUP child-PAUC make.noise-PRIV

muk karra=lu.
quiet be.IMP=3AUG.S
"Come here all you kids. Stop being noisy. Keep quiet now!"
(🔊 DD: EC97_a002: 10:19min)

198 In earlier work, McConvell found this strategy so it is possible it has increased. The Kriol particle *nomo* was commonly used or the other strategy of INF/CV-*murlung*.

7.1.3.9 Imperative imperfective mood

The imperative imperfective is perhaps better described as a subjunctive since it often describes a demand for a hypothetical situation or an outcome to have been different. It often gets translated in English as 'should have'.

(1151)

"**Ya-na-nta**=yi=lu=rla	nyawa
go-IMPF-IMP=1MIN.EXC.NS=3AUG.S=3OBL	this

pa-na-nta=yi=lu	kartik,"	kuya.
hit-IMPF-IMP=1EXC.MIN.NS=3AUG.S	stop	thus

"'You mob should come here for me and stop him hitting me,' he called out."
(◀)) VW: FM14_a203: 3:40min)

(1152)

"Nyangurla=warla	ya-nku?
when=FOC	go-POT

"When will the supplies arrive?"

"Nya,	nya,	**ya-na-nta**	karla-yin."
here	here	go-IMPF-IMP	west-ABL

"Here, here, it should be coming up here from the west."
(Danbayarri, 2016a, p. 120)

(1153)

"Yuwu,	maiti	nyila=ja	karu,	nyuntu	ka-ngka,
yes	maybe	that=TOP	child	2MIN	take-IMP

lajap	**ka-nga-nta,**	ngarlu	**jayi-nga-nta.**
carry.on.shoulder	take-IMPF-IMP	honey	give-IMPF-IMP

"OK, well what about the kid. Take him! You should take him with you on your shoulders and you should give him some honey."
(◀)) DD: EC97_a004: 0:55min)

(1154)

"Nyamu=n=nga	ya-nku	marralungku=ma	waruju=rni
REL=2MIN.S=DUB	go-POT	black.plum=TOP	together=ONLY

ka-nga-nta	nyila=ma	tartartap-karra	yapakaru=ma,"	kuya.
take-IMPF-IMP	that=TOP	lead-ITER	small=TOP	thus

"'When you go looking for black plums, you have to lead the little one around everywhere,' he said." (◀)) DD: EC98_a017: 10:44min)

(1155)

"Nomo	ngumayila	**wanyja-na-nta**	kula	**wanyja-na-nta**
NEG	behind	leave-IMPF-IMP	NEG	leave-IMPF-IMP

ngumayila	**ka-nga-nta**=n	marralungku-la=ma,"
behind	take-IMPF-IMP=2MIN.S	black.plum-LOC=TOP

ngu=rna=ngku	ma-rna-na.
CAT=1EXC.MIN.S=2MIN.NS	talk-IMPF-PRS

"'Don't be leaving him behind somewhere. You shouldn't just leave him behind. You have to take him right with you to that tree,' I say to you." (🔈 DD: EC98_a017: 10:50min)

(1156)

Yamak	ya-nta	**pu-nga-nta**=wula=nyunu	nyamu=npula=nyunu
calmly	go-IMP	pierce-IMPF-IMP=3UA.S=RR	REL=2UA.S=RR

pa-na-na	linyjarr	murnmurn-karra.
hit-IMPF-PRS	dead.person	fight.to.death-ITER

"Yes, go calmly! You two should give it up instead of fighting each other to the death." (🔈 RW: EC97_a007: 12:14min)

7.1.3.10 Hortative mood

Hortative mood is realised by affixing *-rra* 'HORT' on the outside of the potential mood suffix. The hortative marks permission or a polite command and translates into English as 'let'. Examples are given in (1157)–(1163).

(1157)

'**Jiya-wu-rra**=ngali	murla-ngka=rni	kanyjurra=rni,'	kuya.
burn-POT-HORT=1INC.MIN.NS	this-LOC=ONLY	down=ONLY	thus.

"'Let it burn us right down here,' she said." (🔈 CN: FM10_28_1a: 15:29min)

(1158)

Wurlpun-jirri	**ya-nku-rra**=yi
lap-ALL	go-POT-HORT=1EXC.MIN.NS

murla-ngkurra,	karu=ma	nyila=ma.
this-ALL	child=TOP	that=TOP

"Let the child come here to my lap." (🔈 TD: FM10_a166: 14:05min)

(1159)

"Kutirni	**ya-nku-rra**=yina	nyawa=ma	kamparri-nginyi	yu	nou
soon	go-POT-HORT=3AUG.NS	this=TOP	front-SOURCE	you	know

ngumayila-nginyi-wu	liwart	karra=yina	nyamu=lu=nga
behind-SOURCE-DAT	wait	be.IMP=3AUG.NS	REL=3AUG.S=DUB

ya-nku	ngumayila	kajikajirri=ma	tumaji	ngu=lu
go-POT	behind	old.woman.REDUP=TOP	CAUS	CAT=3AUG.S

yamak	ya-na-na	kajikajirri=ma.
slowly	go-IMPF-PRS	old.woman.REDUP=TOP

"Let them go ahead for a bit. Wait for them from behind when the old ladies go because they walk slowly". (🔈 DD: McNair_F2A: 15:43min)

(1160)

Yirrap-ku	kartipa-wu	ngu=yina	du	ya-ni.
other.group-DAT	non-Indigenous-DAT	CAT=3AUG.NS	too	go-PST

"He walked over to the other group of *kartiya*."

Kalpuman[199]	bin	jeya	du.
boss	PST	there	too

"The boss man was there too."

An	ngu=ngantipa	ma-rni	kalpuman=ma.
and	CAT=1EXC.AUG.NS	say-PST	boss=TOP

"The boss man said to us."

'**Ya-nku-rra**=lu	ngumpin=ma.'
go-IMP-HORT=3AUG.S	man=TOP

"'Let those men come.'" (🔈 DD: McNair_A2A: 11:30min)

(1161)

Ya-nku-rra=rlaa=rla	kuyuwan-ku=warla	warrkuj-ku.
go-POT-HORT=1INC.AUG.S=3OBL	bone-DAT=FOC	pick.up-DAT

"Let's go back to get his bones." (BB: McNair_H2D: 1:34min)

(1162)

Karru-rra=wula	murla-ngka=rni.
be.POT-HORT=3UA.S	this-LOC=ONLY

"Let the two of them stop right here." (McConvell 1996 grammar manuscript)

(1163)

Wajiwurru	karrinyana	lungkarrap.	Maralang-karra	ka-ngka=wula
crybaby	be.IMPF.PRS	cry	share-ITER	take-IMP=3UA.S

jayi-ngka=rla	kapuku-wu	du	**ka-ngku-rra.**
give-IMP=3OBL	sister-DAT	too	take-POT-HORT

"He's crying constantly. You two share it. Give it to your sister. Let her take it." (🔈 VW: FM12_a175: 11:04min)

199 This is a Kriol word which derives from 'government'.

The form varies between Ngumpin languages. Malngin and Wanyjirra also uses *-rra* (Ise, 1998, pp. 46–47; Senge, 2016, pp. 408–409). Hortative mood in Bilinarra, Ngarinyman and Mudburra is realised by affixing the imperative form of the verb with *-rla* 'HORT' (Jones, Schultze-Berndt, Denniss, et al., 2019, p. 40; McConvell, 1980, p. 90; Meakins & Nordlinger, 2014, p. 303).

7.1.3.11 Admonitive mood

Admonitive mood refers to something potentially dangerous occurring in the immediate discourse context and is usually translated as 'might'. It thus corresponds in function to what is often glossed 'LEST' in other Australian languages (Dixon, 2002).

Admonitive mood in Gurindji is expressed by a periphrastic construction involving *ngaja* which heads a main clause followed by a verb generally inflected with the present tense (1164)–(1170), but also potential mood (1171) and past tense (1172). *Ngaja* serves as the host for the bound pronoun complex (§6.2.6.1). See §9.2.2 for more information about the function of *ngaja*.

(1164) Kanyju-k **ngaja**=ngku **waninyana**.
down-ALL ADMON=2MIN.NS fall.IMPF.PRS
"It might fall on you." (🔈 VW: FM12_a178: 6:29min)

(1165) Warta **ngaja**=n **waninyana** ya-nta jawurruk.
goodness ADMON=2MIN.S fall.IMPF.PRS go-IMP descend
"Goodness you might fall down, get down!"
(🔈 VW: FM07_a085: 9:06min)

(1166) Nomo=ma jamana-lu kaya-rra nyila. Karnti, patawan.
NEG=TOP foot-ERG kick-IMP that wood hard

Ngaja=n tingarri **waninyana** lukurr.
ADMON=2MIN.S knee fall.IMPF.PRS twist
"Don't break [the branch] with your foot. The wood is too hard. You might twist your knee." (🔈 VW: FM12_a178: 2:37min)

(1167) Jawulwurntirrp ngu ngalyakap **ngaja** **ma-na-na**
salivate CAT lick ADMON do-IMPF-PRS

ngantipanguny nyila-rra kartak nyampa saucepan.
1EXC.AUG.DAT that-PL cup anything saucepan
"[The dog] is salivating and it might lick those cups of ours or anything like saucepans." (🔈 VW: FM12_a177: 7:54min)

(1168) Kula=n wanyji karra yala-nginyi=ma
NEG=2MIN.S alive stay.IMP that-SOURCE=TOP

ngaja=ngala ngawa-ngku ngilyipurr **nga-rna-na**.
ADMON=1INC.AUG.NS water-ERG drown eat-IMPF-PRS
"It won't let you stay alive, it will drown you."
(🔊 VW: FM10_27_1a: Kurraj Story from Halls Creek: 4:14min)

(1169) **Ngaja**=yi=n-ku=rla **yuwa-na-na**
ADMON=1EXC.MIN.NS=2MIN.S-EP=3OBL put-IMPF-PRS

kurlpi[200]-marraj kawurlu.
light-COMP sister
"You might make it like a light grindstone, sister [i.e. you might break it]."
(🔊 VW: FM10_23_1b: Yawarlwarl Wanyil: 2:43min)

(1170) **Ngaja**=nta taarlak-karra **ya-na-na** nyampa-kurra=wayin.
ADMON=2AUG.S danger-ITER go-IMPF-PRS something-ALL=ETC
"You mob might be in danger of something." (🔊 VW: FM12_a177: 4:35min)

(1171) Yunany **ngaja**=yi=lu **ma-nku**
belongings ADMON =1EXC.MIN.NS=3AUG.S do-POT

warrkuwarrkuj. Lalarrp karrinyana nyila=ma door=ma
pick.up.REDUP open be.IMPF.PRS that=TOP door=TOP
"That mob might take my things. The door is open."
(🔊 VW: FM12_a174: 15:11min)

(1172) **Ngaja**=ngku=rla ngapanyji-la **waninya**=ma.
ADMON=2MIN.NS=3OBL eye-LOC fall.PST=TOP
"In case splinters got in your eye." (🔊 VW: FM07_a050: 9:24min)

Note that *ngaja* does not need to come first, but a prominent topic or focus nominal can be put in focus position in the main clause, as in (1173)–(1175).

(1173) **Puntu** **ngaja**=ngku=rla wanku ngapanyji-la.
wood.chip ADMON=2MIN.NS=3OBL fall.POT eye-LOC
"Wood chips might fall in your eyes." (🔊 VW: FM07_05_1a: 8:55min)

200 *Kurlpi* is a Nyininy word.

(1174) Ngarranginy-ju **ngaja**=ngku paya-rru.
frill-neck.lizard-ERG ADMON=2MIN.NS bite-POT
"The frill necked lizard might bite you [for example when it has eggs and you get too close]." (◀) VW: FM10_a152: 1:02min)

(1175) Kanyju-k **ngaja**=ngku waninyana.
down-ALL ADMON=2MIN.NS fall.IMPF.PRS
"You might fall down." (◀) VW: FM12_a178: 6:29min)

A main clause headed by *ngaja* can also then take an embedded *nyamu* subordinate clause. Example (1176), has a main clause is 'it might not cook' followed by 'if it balls up', although the sequencing is reversed.

(1176) Nyawa ngu=rna pa-na-na palki-k
this CAT=1EXC.MIN.S hit-IMPF-PRS flat-FACT

kuya=ma. **Nyamu**=nga karru turrnyu=ma,
thus=TOP REL=DUB be.POT spherical=TOP

ngaja karrinyana kurnka.
ADMON be.IMPF.PRS half-cooked
"I'm flattening [the damper] by hitting it like this. If it balls up, it might not cook properly." (◀) VW: FM09_13_3a: 4:25min)

The admonitive *ngaja* can also take a reduced subordinate clause, as in (1177), where the main clause is 'they might get in trouble' followed by a simultaneous subordinate clause marked locative 'not looked after by you mob' where the subject of the main clause is the object of the subordinate clause. Note that *ngumpin-jirri* 'man-ALL' is an oblique argument in the main clause.

(1177) An ngumpit-jirri **ngaja**=lu taarlak ya-na-na,
and man-ALL ADMON=3AUG.S danger go-IMPF-PRS

palmurujmuruj-ja na, lawara-la=nta warra-warra-la.
dusk-LOC FOC nothing-LOC=2AUG.S look.after-REDUP-LOC
"They might get into danger from a man at dusk [if] you mob don't look after them." (◀) VW: FM12_a177: 4:59min)

The Nyininy equivalent *ngarra* is sometimes used at Kalkaringi by speakers such as Violet Wadrill who have Western connections (1178) and sometimes the Kriol particle *maitbi* 'maybe' is used in conjunction with *ngaja* (1179).

(1178) Kurlpi-marraj **ngarra**=yi=n-ku=rla
light-COMP ADMON=1EXC.MIN.NS=2MIN.S-EP=3OBL

jirrmung yuwa-na-na.
break put-IMPF-PRS
"You might break it on me and make it like a light grindstone."
(🔈 VW: FM10_23_1b: Yawarlwarl Wanyil: 2:48min)

(1179) Maitbi **kaya-ngkurra** ngaja=lu taarlak ya-nku.
maybe bad.spirit-ALL ADMON=3AUG.S danger go-POT
"They might be in danger of a bad spirit." (🔈 VW: FM12_a177: 4:52min)

The use of the *ngaja* to head a main clause may have arisen through 'ellipsis' of the main clause expressing the event that should be undertaken to avoid the negative consequence expressed by the *ngaja* clause (§9.2.2). They could exemplify a type of 'insubordination' common in Australian languages (Evans, 2007). An example of *ngaja* heading a subordinate clause is given in (1181).

(1180) Yiparrartu gigin Mamurung ngu nyawa=ma. Murla-nginyi
Emu again Dreaming.place CAT this=TOP this-SOURCE

karnti, nyawa-rra kula=rlaa pa-rru kataj-kataj=ma.
tree this-PL NEG=1INC.AUG.S hit-POT cut-REDUP=TOP

Ngaja=n janga **karru=nga** na.
ADMON=2MIN.S sick be.POT=DUB FOC
"This is an Emu Dreaming place [Jampawurru]. We can't cut down trees here, or you might get sick." (🔈 VW: FM09_13_2d: 2:57min)

For a good overview of apprehensives in Ngumpin-Yapa languages, see Browne, Ennever and Osgarby (2021). They give the following forms for other Ngumpin languages: *pi(ya)* (Mudburra), *ngaja* (Bilinarra), *ngarra* (Wanyjirra, Nyininy, Jaru, Ngardi), *ngarda* (Ngardi), *nga=* (Warlmanpa, Walmajarri).

7.1.3.12 Interrogative mood

In most of the interrogative sentences in the corpus, the interrogative mood is signalled by the use of one of the interrogative words: *nyampa* 'what', *wanyji* 'which', *ngana* 'who', *nyangurla* 'when', *nyatjang* 'how many' and *nyatparra* 'how' (see §5.3). For polar interrogatives, the particle *wayi* is used. More often than not *wayi* occurs in first position and attracts the pronominal clitic, as shown in (1181). It is also found in final position as a tag question (1182) and (1183) (McConvell, 1980, p. 74). It is also found as a clitic attached to the interrogative, as discussed in §5.3.7.1.

(1181) **Wayi**=rna yuwa-ni ngawa-ngka kanyjurra japurr?
Q=1EXC.MIN.S put-PST water-LOC down soak
"Did I throw it into the lake?" (🔈) VW: FM10_23_1a: Luma Kurrupartu: 1:06min)

(1182) **Wayi**=rlaa wart ya-nku **wayi**?
Q=1INC.AUG.S return go-POT TAG
"Shall we go back?" (🔈) VW: FM10_30_1a: Karu Dreaming Story: 1:06min)

(1183) Nyila na ngu=rna ma-nku lawa **wayi**?
that FOC CAT=1EXC.MIN.S get-POT lemon.wood TAG
"Shall I go and get lemonwood now?" (🔈) VW: FM07_01_1b: 2:59min)

It is also possible to ask a polar question by using a sentence of the same structure as the corresponding indicative sentence, but with a rising intonation. We have no recordings of such examples, but have overhead this method of questioning used.

7.1.3.13 *=nga* Dubitative mood

The clitic *=nga* marks dubitative mood and is encliticised to the end of the bound pronoun complex (1184), (1186)–(1193) or an inflecting verb (1185). It is also found in Bilinarra, Ngarinyman and Warlmanpa (Browne et al., 2021; Jones, Schultze-Berndt, Denniss, et al., 2019, p. 41; Meakins & Nordlinger, 2014, pp. 306–307). It serves three main functions in the corpus in combination with the potential mood, with imperative mood to create an irrealis clause, and in conditional clauses.

When it occurs with the potential suffix, it indicates epistemic mood, namely that the speaker has only a limited amount of confidence in the truth of their assertion. In this function, it is roughly equivalent to the English modal auxiliaries 'could' or 'might' (1184)–(1186). It also co-occurs with past tense (1187) in this function.

(1184) Jala=ma=rna=**nga** **karrwa-wu** pirrkap-pirrkap-kula na.
now=TOP=1EXC.MIN.S=DUB keep-POT make-REDUP-LOC FOC
"Now I might keep [the wood] to make [the artefacts]."
(🔈) VW: FM08_a101: 2:35min)

(1185) Wirtikwirtik ngu=wula=nyunu **pa-rru=nga**
fight.with.nullanulla CAT=3UA.S=RR hit-POT=DUB

kirri-kujarra-lu=ma kuya.
woman-DU-ERG=TOP thus
"Two women might fight each other with nullanullas like that."
(🔈 VW: FM08_a101: 6:04min)

(1186) Yirrap=ma=rna=**nga** **yuwa-rru** waj-karra.
another.lot=TOP=1EXC.MIN.S=DUB put-POT throw.away-ITER
"I might chuck the other lot of hair away." (🔈 VW: FM08_08_1a: 11:39)

(1187) Ngantipa du ngu=rnalu=**nga** **nya-nga-ni**
1EXC.AUG too CAT=1EXC.AUG.S=DUB intake-IMPF-PST

tanku-murlung-kula=ma, larrpa-larrpa=ma.
food-PRIV-LOC=TOP old.days-REDUP=TOP
"Us too, we might have eaten it when we were hungry in the old days."
(🔈 VW: FM09_12_6a: 1:41min)

Secondly, the dubitative suffix is used in combination with an imperative verb to create an irrealis clauses, as in (1188)–(1190).

(1188) Karra=**nga** punyu-k-kulawu=rni.
be.IMP=DUB good-FACT-PURP=ONLY
"She should have been better about it." (🔈 VW: FM10_30_2b: 1:14min)

(1189) Ngajik ngu=n=**nga** karra palarni.
long.time CAT=2MIN.S=DUB stay.IMP BETTER
"It's better if you stay for a long time."
(McConvell corpus: Meakins et al., 2016, p. 301)

(1190) **Nyamu**=yina=**nga** ngamayi-lu **ngaya-rra**
REL=3AUG.NS=DUB mother-ERG excrete-IMP

ngayiny-ja waruju-la=ma kuya-ngka=ma
1EXC.MIN.DAT-LOC together-LOC=TOP thus-LOC=TOP

wayi=rna=yina=**nga** **pa-rra.**
Q=1EXC.MIN.S=3AUG.NS=DUB hit-IMP
"If the mother [cat] had given birth to them while I was around, I might have killed [the kittens]." (McConvell corpus: Meakins et al., 2016, p. 277)

Thirdly, it is used in conditional clauses headed by *nyamu* where both verbs generally occur in the potential mood (1191) and (1192), although the present tense is used for habitual aspect (1193).

(1191) Ngu=rna=rla=nga wiit-wiit=ma
CAT=1EXC.MIN.S=3OBL=DUB show-REDUP=TOP

jayi-ngku, **nyamu=nga** **wanku** ngawa.
give-POT REL=DUB fall.POT water
"I'll show her if it rains." (🔊 VW: FM09_16_2: 0:38min)

(1192) Yarti-waji ngu=ngku **ma-nku** kuya,
photo-AGENT CAT=2MIN.NS do-POT thus

nyamu=rli=rla=nga paraj **pu-ngku** jalang=ma.
REL=1INC.MIN.2=3OBL=DUB find pierce-POT today=TOP
"She'll record you like this if you and I find it for her today."
(🔊 VW: FM09_17_2a: 1:34min)

(1193) Wurrk na ngu=rnalu **yuwa-na-na** **nyamu=nga**
throw.away FOC CAT=1EXC.AUG.S put-IMPF-PRS REL=DUB

tampang-tampang yawu=ma **karrinyana**. Janyja=ma
dead-REDUP fish=TOP be.IMPF.PRS dirt=TOP

nyamu=rnalu=rla jayi-nga-na, kuya, marntaj.
REL=1EXC.AUG.S=3OBL give-IMPF-PRS thus OK
"We throw the fish [out of the water hole] if they die. When we gave them dirt [to eat]." (🔊 VW: FM11_a167: 5:55min)

The clitic *=nga* also occurs in combination with *kata* 'though', as shown in (1194).

(1194) **Kata**=yin=**nga** ma-rni ngajik-ku
BUT=2MIN.S>1EXC.MIN.NS=DUB talk-PST long.time-DAT

kayi=n ya-na-na wart-pa=rni=rni wajija=rni.
SURP=2MIN.S go-IMPF-PRS return-EP=ONLY=REDUP quickly=ONLY

ya-nu-wu.
go-INF-DAT
"I thought you told me you would go for a long time, but here you are coming back quickly" (McConvell corpus: Meakins et al., 2016, p. 444)

7.1.3.14 *-ny* Nominaliser (NMLZ)

In §7.1.3.6, we discussed the use of imperative inflection as word-class changing morphology, which can then receive derivational morphology, for example *-p* 'coverbaliser' or *-waji* 'agent'. The only other derivational morphology found with inflecting verbs is the ubiquitous *-ny* 'nominaliser' which was discussed extensively in §4.7.20. One example is found in the corpus attached to an imperative verb *wanta* 'fall!' to create a place name relating to birth, which indeed the 'fall' verb can express.

(1195) Jinparrak nyamu=rlaa=nga ya-nku
place.name REL=1INC.AUG.S=DUB go-POT

nyanawu-yirri **wanta-ny**-jirri kankarra.
RECOG-ALL fall.IMP-NMLZ-ALL upstream
"One day we'll go to Jinparrak to the birthing place."
(🔈 VW: FM08_a085: 18:59min)

This nominaliser is found in this form and function in Bilinarra and Ngarinyman (C. Jones, Schultze-Berndt, Denniss, et al., 2019, p. 47; Meakins & Nordlinger, 2014, p. 340).

7.1.3.15 Absence of hither and thither

Gurindji actually does not mark these categories in verbs, only on demonstratives. However, it is unusual in this respect, thus some further comments are warranted. Eastern Walmajarri also does not mark these categories in verbs, however all other Ngumpin-Yapa languages do in some form or other. Bilinarra and Ngarinyman uses *-rni* 'hither' on inflecting verbs (Jones, Schultze-Berndt, Denniss, et al., 2019, p. 40; Meakins & Nordlinger, 2014, pp. 308–309) and Jaru possesses *-rni* 'hither', but it only occurs with imperative and purposive verbs (Tsunoda, 1981, p. 208). Warlpiri, Warlmanpa and Ngardi have both *-rni* 'hither' and *-rra* 'thither' on verbs and cardinals (Ennever, 2021; Laughren, 1978, p. 2; Nash, 2008). Gurindji uses *-rni* on cardinals to indicate relative elevation or 'up' and *-rra* as a frozen locative form on cardinals (Laughren & McConvell, 1999).

7.2 Coverbs

Coverbs are found in both Pama-Nyungan and non-Pama-Nyungan languages across northern Australia. They have been described for other Ngumpin languages of the Victoria River District: Bilinarra (Meakins & Nordlinger, 2014), Ngarinyman (Jones, Schultze-Berndt, Denniss, et al., 2019) and Wanyjirra (Senge, 2016); as well as other Ngumpin-Yapa languages such as Warlpiri (Laughren, 2010; Nash, 1982, 1986), Mudburra (Green et al., 2019; Osgarby, 2018a) and Warlmanpa (Browne, 2021); and also for unrelated neighbouring non-Pama-Nyungan languages: Wardaman (Merlan, 1994), Jaminjung and Ngaliwurru (Schultze-Berndt, 2000, 2001, 2003, 2006a). Other non-Pama-Nyungan languages such as Wambaya and Jingulu which are in the Barkly Tablelands and border Mudburra show remnants of a complex verb structure (Nordlinger, 1998b, 2010; Pensalfini, 2003). Coverbs are also found in languages spoken in the northern Kimberley such as the Jarragan languages: Gija, Miriwoong and Gajirrabeng (Kofod, 1996). Gooniyandi, Warrwa and Nyulnyul in the northern Kimberley region also exhibit complex verbs (McGregor, 1990, 1994, 1996, 2002), as do the Western Ngumpin languages spoken in the Kimberleys and Tanami: Jaru (Tsunoda, 1981), Walmajarri (Hudson, 1978) and Ngardi (Ennever, 2021). Coverbs have also been observed in the Daly River region: Ngankikurungkurr (Hoddinott & Kofod, 1988), Ngan'gityemerri (Reid, 1990), Murrinh-Patha (Joseph Blythe, 2009; Street, 1987) and Wagiman (Cook, 1988); and Arnhem Land: Nunggubuyu (Heath, 1976, 1984). For areal overviews of coverbs and complex verbs in northern Australian languages see Capell (1979), Dixon (2001), McGregor (2002) Schultze-Berndt (2000, 2003, 2006a) and Amberber, Baker and Harvey (2010).

Coverbs in Gurindji exhibit a number of properties which make them a distinct word class. Phonologically, coverbs show unusual word structure (§7.2.1). Syntactically, they combine with inflecting verbs to create complex verbs (§7.2.3). Coverbs can also act alone in reduced subordinate clauses (§7.2.2.3) and, to a limited extent, main clauses (§7.2.2.4). In terms of their contribution to meaning, they carry the semantic weight of the clause (§7.2.3). Morphologically, the only TAM marking they take is an iterative suffix, however they host a number of nominalising suffixes, and also case suffixes in reduced subordinate clauses (§7.2.4). Note also that coverbs can be formed from nominals through zero derivation and interestingly this is something reflected in the local auxiliary sign language, *takataka*, where nominals and verbs are often expressed using the same sign. Two examples are given in Figure 49 (Green et al., forthcoming).

7.2.1 Phonology

As a word class, coverbs are exceptional phonologically, which is also the case for Jaminjung (Schultze-Berndt, 2001, pp. 356–357), Bilinarra (Meakins & Nordlinger, 2014, p. 311) and Ngarinyman (Jones, Schultze-Berndt, Denniss, et al., 2019, pp. 41–46),

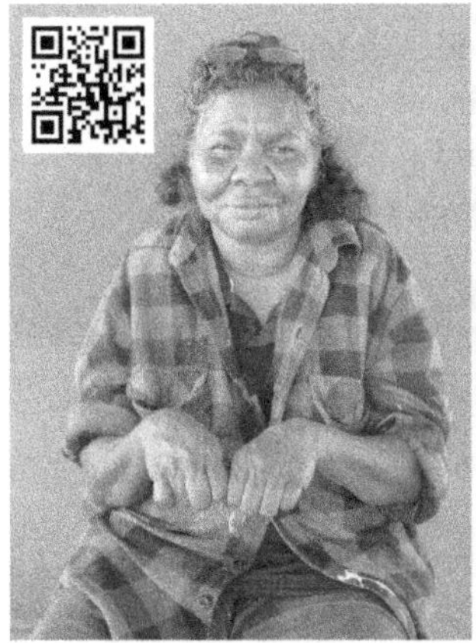

Figure 49: a) Joanne Stevens demonstrates the sign for damper/knead, and b) Gus George demonstrates the sign for gun/shoot.

largely because the Ngumpin languages have borrowed 40–50% of their coverb inventory from Jaminjung, Wardaman and also the Jarragan languages (McConvell, 2009a).

In Gurindji, many examples of monosyllabic coverbs exist. Some examples are:

juny	'sunset'	*turrp*	'pierce'
milyk	'premonition'	*wart*	'return'
tak	'sit'	*wik*	'scrape off'
tup	'pluck'	*yurrk*	'recount'

This word structure is unusual because almost all other words are minimally disyllabic. A very few words other than coverbs are monosyllabic, however they all contain long vowels, for example *maarn* 'cloud' and *muurn* 'sleep in the eye'. These long vowels can be analysed as disyllabic vowel-glide-vowel sequences (§2.1.1).

The other phonological characteristic particular to coverbs is word-final consonant clusters. The consonant clusters always consist of a liquid: [rr], [l] or [rl], followed by a peripheral consonant [p], [k] or [ng]. These consonant clusters occur in both monosyllabic and multisyllabic coverbs. Note that consonant clusters are also found in a very few nominals such as *tampurrng* 'spinifex snake' and *janyparlk* 'ripe nut' (see also §2.2.5):[201]

jampurlk	'squash, flatten'	*turrp*	'stab, poke, pierce'
janyarrp	'baby talk'	*warnparlk*	'break open'
jarrk	'go down the the river'	*wumparlp*	'float'

201 A number of the *-p* final nouns are borrowed from non-Pama-Nyungan languages.

murrk	'crunch on food'	*yanyjarlng*	'join together'
nirlk	'squash between fingernails'	*yinparrng*	'dry up'
parlng	'slap'	*yipurrk*	'in vain'
tungkurlp	'rattle a bell'	*yurrk*	'tell a story'

7.2.2 Syntax

The processes involved when coverbs and inflecting verbs combine to form complex predicates are discussed in §7.2.2.1. Also discussed are the ways in which coverbs function independently from verbs: in reduced subordinate clauses (§7.2.2.3) and in imperatives (§7.2.2.4).

7.2.2.1 Complex verbs

Although most main clauses consist only of an inflecting verb, as shown in (1196) and (1198), inflecting verbs are also found in combination with coverbs, as shown in (1197) and (1199).

(1196) Ngarnjal-ku ngu=rla **ya-ni.**
NAME-DAT CAT=3OBL go-PST
"She went after Topsy." (🔈) VW: FM09_a127: 21:37min)

(1197) **Kalu** ngu=rnalu **ya-ni** yala-ngkurra karnti-kurra.
walk CAT=1EXC.AUG.S go-PST that-ALL tree-ALL
"We walked that way to the tree." (🔈) VW: FM07_a027: 0:19min)

(1198) Kajijirri-lu kamparri-jang-kulu, ngu=lu **ma-na-ni.**
old.woman.REDUP-ERG before-TIME-ERG CAT=3AUG.S get-IMPF-PST
"A long time ago, the women used to get it." (🔈) VW: FM07_01_1a: 2:10min)

(1199) Ngu=rnalu **ma-na-na** **puntanup** nyawa-rra na.
CAT=1EXC.AUG.S do-IMPF-PRS gather this-PL FOC
"We're gathering this lot now." (🔈) VW: FM07_01_1a: 2:49min)

The following sections discuss the structure and function of these coverb-inflecting verb combinations.

7.2.2.1.1 Tight nexus and loose nexus coverbs

Where coverbs combine with inflecting verbs, they form more or less tight compounds. We distinguish two broad categories of tight and loose nexus verbs, which are so defined due to their combinatory properties: (i) the flexibility of word order, and (ii) the semantic transparency of the components versus the combination.

Firstly, the order of the coverb with respect to the inflecting verb is not always fixed, which is different from other Ngumpin-Yapa languages where the coverbs are strictly ordered before the inflecting verb and considered to be a part of the verbal word, for instance Warlpiri, Walmajarri and Ngardi (Ennever, 2021; Hudson, 1978; Laughren, 2010; Nash, 1982). Coverbs in Gurindji may precede the inflecting verb (1200) or they may follow (1201). The complex verb may also be non-contiguous, as shown in (1201). These are termed loose nexus coverbs.

(1200)	Nangala=ma	**partaj**	**ya-ni**	ngu	Yibwoin=ma.
	SUBSECT=TOP	climb	go-PST	CAT	NAME=TOP

"Nangala climbed the tree, Theresa that is." (◀)) VW: FM07_a085: 8:56min)

(1201)	Kankula	**ya-ni**	ngu	kilipi-wu	**partaj**,	kajirri=ma.
	up	go-PST	CAT	bush.banana-DAT	climb	old.woman=TOP

"The old lady climbed up to get the bananas." (◀)) VW: FM07_a085: 9:00min)

Although the order of the inflecting verb and loose nexus coverb varies, the coverb generally precedes the inflecting verb. Where it follows the inflecting verb, it often occurs after a pause in a right-dislocated afterthought construction, as in (1202). These constructions provide the hearer with more information about the action referred to in the main clause, such as the manner of motion, the type of implement used or the position on the body where the action occurred. These constructions are not possible for tight nexus complex verbs which are more non-compositional.

(1202)	Laja-ngka	ngu=yi=rla	**waninya**	walngin,	**partaj**.
	shoulder-LOC	CAT=1EXC.MIN.NS=3OBL	fall.PST	fly	climb

"The fly landed on my shoulder." (◀)) VW: FM10_a133: 3:53min)

On the other hand, tight nexus coverbs always come before the inflecting verb, and only bound pronouns and discourse clitics can split the complex verb. An example of a tight nexus coverb construction is given in (1203) for the coverb *paraj*. If the tight nexus coverb followed the inflecting verb in (1203), a hearer might become confused assuming at first that the speaker was referring to a piercing action. Coverbs such as *paraj* participate in both tight and weak nexus structures. In (1204), the coverb-inflecting verb combination seems idiosyncratic like a tight nexus structure, but 'fall' on its own can refer to birth, as well as other changes to liminal states (§7.1.1.6.2), so *paraj* simply specifies which state. In Kriol *faindim* 'find-TR' refers to birth as well.

(1203) Ngu=rnalu **paraj** **pu-nya** janangarn na.
CAT=1EXC.AUG.S find pierce-PST patch FOC
"We found a big patch of them now." (🔈 TD: FM07_a059: 0:37min)

(1204) Wal nyila=ma karu=ma nyamu **waninyana** **paraj=ma** . . .
well that=TOP child=TOP REL fall.IMPF.PRS find=TOP
"Well when the child is born . . ." (🔈 BW: FM09_a122: 10:55min)

This strict ordering of the inflecting verb and coverb makes sense given that the entire semantics of the complex predicate is reliant on the combination. Semantically, loose nexus predicates are always non-compositional, and tight nexus predicates are always compositional. When a loose nexus coverb combines with an inflecting verb, it usually carries the main semantic load of the complex verb, with the inflecting verb primarily contributing tense, aspect, mood and argument-structure information. In this respect we consider them hyponyms of their accompanying inflecting verb. For example, in (1201), although the coverb *partaj* 'climb' follows the inflecting verb *yanana* 'go', there is no potential for miscommunication. The coverb merely adds more information to the clause about the manner of motion.

Most often loose nexus coverbs combine with semantically relevant inflecting verbs, for example manner of motion coverbs combine with basic motion inflecting verbs such as *yanana* 'go' in (1205) and (1206) (§7.2.3.7).

(1205) kalu yanana 'to walk'
walk go

(1206) walik yanana 'go around'
go.around go

Tight nexus coverbs on the other hand are more idiosyncratic. In the following examples, the contribution of the inflecting verb to the complex verb is not obvious from the meaning of the inflecting verb (1207)–(1210):

(1207) kurrwara yuwanana 'blame'
blame put

(1208) ngurrku panana 'jealous of'
jealous hit

(1209) paraj pungana 'to find'
find pierce

(1210) yangki panana 'to ask'
ask hit

7.2.2.1.2 Different combinations of coverbs and inflecting verbs

Some coverbs are only found with a single inflecting verb, however many coverbs can combine with a number of different inflecting verbs to varying effects. To begin with, the use of different inflecting verbs may change the transitivity of the clause. For example, when *partaj* 'climb' combines with *yanana* 'go' it forms an intransitive complex verb (1211),[202] however in combination with *yuwanana* 'put', it forms a transitive complex verb (1212). In (1213), it combines with *waninyana* 'fall' to refer to coming into a particular stance, and in (1214), it combines with *karrinyana* to produce a stative clause.

(1211) Pinka ngu=rna **ya-na-na** **partaj**
river CAT=1EXC.MIN.S go-IMPF-PRS climb

na kankula, palypurru-la init?
FOC up slope-LOC TAG
"I'm climbing the up riverbank to the top of the slope, aren't I."
(🔈 TD: FM10_166: 8:58min)

(1212) Wumara-la na **partaj** **yuwa-ni**, wumara-la tankuj-ja.
rock-LOC FOC climb put-PST stone-LOC support-LOC
"She puts the wood on a rock for support." (🔈 VW: FM09_a127: 5:50min)

(1213) Karla-rni-mpal-nginyi, nyawa=ma wurturrji=ma, walngin
west-UP-EDGE-SOURCE this=TOP leg=TOP fly

ngu=yi=rla, nyawa **partaj** **waninyana**
CAT=1EXC.MIN.NS=3OBL this climb fall.IMPF.PRS

wayi, ngayiny-ja wurturrji-la.
TAG 1EXC.MIN.DAT-LOC leg-LOC
"The fly lands on my leg up across the westside." (🔈 VW: FM10_a133: 6:09min)

202 The complex verb takes a locative-marked complement rather than an object in these sentences (much like German).

(1214) Kuwurtpirt-ta=ma **partaj** ngu=lu=rla **karrinyani**
lie.in.wait-LOC=TOP climb CAT=3AUG.S=3OBL be.IMPF.PST

maiti tungun-ta yu jidan.
maybe hidden-LOC you sit
"They would be perched somewhere hidden from view."
(VW: FM12_a173: 2:32min)

Other coverbs are most commonly found with transitive inflecting verbs, however they can also combine with intransitive inflecting verbs. For example, coverbs of holding (1215) can be 'detransitivised' by combining with the intransitive inflecting verbs *karrinyana* 'be' or *waninyana* 'fall', or the intransitive locomotion verb *yanana* 'go'. In combination with *yanana* the subject becomes nominative and second participant is marked with the proprietive suffix *-yawung/-jawung* (see also §7.2.3.3).

(1215) Ngu=rnayinangulu **ka-nga-na**
CAT=1EXC.AUG.S>3AUG.NS take-IMPF-PRS

julujuluj, kawarla-la=ma.
carry.under.arm.REDUP coolamon-LOC=TOP
"Now we carry our children under our arms in coolamons." (VW: FM07_02_1c: 0:49min)

Different combinations of coverbs and inflecting verbs can also affect the general meaning of the complex verb, as the following examples of *tarukap* 'bathe, swim' demonstrate (1216)–(1219).

(1216) Ngayiny jawiji marluka **tarukap** **waninya.**
1EXC.MIN.DAT MF old.man bathe fall.PST
"My old grandfather bathed." (McConvell corpus: Meakins et al., 2016, p. 94)

(1217) **Tarukap-karra** **ka-nga-ni** yala-nginyi=ma
swim-ITER take-IMPF-PST that-SOURCE=TOP

ka-nga-ni ngu wart, ngurra-ngkurra.
take-IMPF-PST CAT return home-ALL
"She took it swimming and then took it back home again."
(VW: FM10_27_1a: Kurraj Story from Halls Creek: 2:14min)

(1218) Nyamu=lu karrinyana marntara karu-walija
REL=3AUG.S be.IMPF.PRS sores child-PAUC

ngu=rnayinangulu **yuwa-na-na** murlu-ngku na
CAT=1EXC.AUG.S>3AUG.NS put-IMPF-PRS this-ERG FOC

tarukap=ma karu-walija=ma ngarlaka, marntara, karan-kaji.
bathe=TOP child-PAUC=TOP head sores scratch-AGENT
"When kids have sores or scabies, we bathe their head sores and scabies."
(🔈 BW: FM07_01_1c: 2:50min)

(1219) Kaa-rni-mpa ngu=lu **karrinya** **tarukap-karra**, purrp.
east-UP-PERL CAT=3AUG.S be.PST swim-ITER finish
"They swam around on the eastern side until they had had enough."
(🔈 VW: FM10_30_1a: 5:34min)

These combinatory features of coverbs are responsible for the formation of different classes of coverbs, as will be discussed in §7.2.3.

7.2.2.2 Multiple coverbs

It is worth noting that it is possible to have multiple coverbs in a single clause, as shown in (1220) and (1221). There are possibly restrictions on this such as the ability of each verb individually to combine with the inflecting verbs, and whether you can combine coverbs from the same or different coverb classes. We leave these matters for future research.

(1220) **Tirrip**-pa=rni **kalu**=ma=lu ya-na-ni=ma karu=ma,
over.night-EP=ONLY walk=TOP=3AUG.S go-IMPF-PST=TOP child=TOP

marlurluka=ma, kajijirri=ma jangkakarni=ma.
old.man.REDUP=TOP old.woman.REDUP=TOP big.REDUP=TOP
"They were walking all through the night [looking for water] –
all of the children, men, women and adults."
(🔈 VW: FM10_a155: Ngarlking Karu: 9:19min)

(1221) Kuya, **wart** ma-na-ni ngu=lu **yirr**, tarukpirn[203]-tu=ma.
thus return do-IMPF-PST CAT=3AUG.S pull diver-ERG=TOP
"Like that the diver would pull the crocodile out of the water."
(🔈 VW: FM12_a178: 8:07min)

7.2.2.3 Coverbs in reduced subordinate clauses

As was mentioned above, when coverbs combine with inflecting verbs to form complex predicates, typically the coverb carries the bulk of the semantic load, while the inflecting verb primarily contributes tense/aspect/mood and argument-structure information. In reduced subordinate clauses, the coverb often occurs on its own and gets its temporal information in reference to the main clause. Compare (1219) in which the coverb *tarukap* 'bathe' occurs with the inflecting verb *karrinya* 'was' in a main clause, with (1222) where it occurs alone in a subordinate clause without an inflecting verb. In this clause, the dative indicates that the event of bathing will occur after 'cooking'.

(1222) Nyawa na ngu=rna kampa-rna-na
this FOC CAT=1EXC.MIN.S cook-IMPF-PRS

yirrijkaji, yirrijkaji, karu-wu **tarukap-ku**,
plant.sp plant.sp child-DAT bathe-DAT

Nangari, mantara-yawung-ku.
SUBSECT sores-PROP-DAT
"I'm cooking *yirrijkaji*, Nangari, to bathe the kids who have sores."
(🔈 BW: FM07_06_2a: 0:31min)

Structures such as these where the coverb or an infinitive form of an inflecting verb occur alone and are case-marked are referred to as non-finite or reduced subordinate clauses. These constructions are discussed in detail in §9.3.

7.2.2.4 Coverbs in imperatives

Imperatives may be formed in one of three ways: (i) using the imperative form of the inflecting verb, (ii) using a coverb in conjunction with the imperative form of the inflecting verb, (§7.1.3.8), or (iii) using a coverb on its own, as in (1223).

(1223) Kawayiwayi, karu-walija, **yilying-murlu**
come.here.REDUP child-PAUC make.noise-PRIV

muk karra=lu.
quiet be.IMP=3AUG.S
"Come here all you kids. Stop being noisy. Keep quiet now!"
(🔈 DD: EC97_a002: 10:19min)

---

203 The word *tarukpirn* 'diver' clearly consists of *taruk* 'bathe' + *pirn*. But the meaning of *pirn* is unclear.

7.2.3 Classes of coverbs

Although inflecting verbs are the only type of verb considered to have classes based on their TAM forms, different classes of coverbs can also be established on the basis of formal criteria (McGregor, 2002). Coverbs do not inflect and therefore cannot be categorised according to the form the inflection takes (see §7.1.1 inflecting verb classes), but classes can be established based on their combinatory properties, specifically the types of inflecting verbs particular groups of coverbs are found in combination with, and some derivational properties. Note that most coverbs can combine with *karrinyana* 'be' in a periphrastic progressive construction as per Schultze-Berndt (2012) so this alone is not a criteria for coverb classes. The coverb classes here are based substantially on Schultze-Berndt's (2000: Ch. 6) and Meakins and Nordlinger's (2014: §7.2.3) classification of Jaminjung and Bilinarra coverbs, respectively. The Gurindji categories follow the Jaminjung and Bilinarra categories closely which is not surprising given the extensive borrowing of Jaminjung coverbs into Bilinarra and Gurindji.

7.2.3.1 Coverbs of spatial configuration

Coverbs of spatial configuration combine with the stative inflecting verb *karrinyana* 'be' to encode a state of being in a position or configuration. Two subgroups exist: (i) posturals, and (ii) positionals.

Postural coverbs describe the configuration of parts with respect to a whole. For example, Gurindji has many different coverbs which express different manners of sitting, as shown in (1224):

(1224)	*jalngak*	'sit astride'
	jarntawa	'sit with one knee bent up'
	jarripirliny	'sit cross-legged'
	jiput	'sit with knees bent and together'
	larl	'sit with legs apart'
	lurlu	'sit'
	tartpu	'sit with knees to the side'
	wulujurr	'sit with legs out'

These coverbs really just describe leg configuration and many can be used to describe equivalent standing postures. Postural coverbs can also combine with *yuwanana* 'put' and *waninyana* 'fall'. The valency of the complex verb is increased in combination with *yuwanana* to add an agent, as in 'stand something up'; compare (1225) with (1226). The use of *waninyana* expresses the meaning of 'come to be in X position' or 'enter into X position (with respect to location)', as in (1227). See §7.1.1.6.2 for a more detailed discussion of the semantics of *waninyana*.

(1225)

Nangala-kujarra	jeya	ngu=yi=wula	**kutij**	**karrinyana.**
SUBSECT-DU	there	CAT=1EXC.MIN.NS=3UA.S	stand	be.IMPF.PRS

"The two Nangalas are standing there with me."
(🔈 VW: FM07_a027: 0:51min)

(1226)

Kutij	ngu=rna	**yuwa-ni.**
stand	CAT=1EXC.MIN.S	put.PST

"I stood [the coolamon] up." (🔈 VW: FM07_a050: 3:14min)

(1227)

Wulngarn	**kutij**	**waninyana.**
sun	stand	fall.IMPF.PRS

"The sun is coming up." (McConvell corpus: Meakins et al., 2016, p. 423)

Positional coverbs describe the configuration of a figure (an object to be located) with respect to a location. Examples are given in (1228):

(1228)

nang	'stick on'
ngurra	'camp'
takurl	'inside open container'
tirrjak	'stuck in'
walyak	'inside'
warrp	'be together'

They differ from posturals in that they entail a location, which is often unexpressed but can be encoded in a locative-marked nominal, as in (1229). Like posturals, many positionals can combine with *yuwanana* 'put' (1230) and *waninyana* 'fall', as well as *karrinyana* 'be' (1231).

(1229)

Nang-nang	na	**karrinya**	ngu=rla,	yatu-ngka=ma.
stuck-REDUP	FOC	be.PST	CAT=3OBL	white.ochre-LOC=TOP

"[Bits of dirt] were stuck to the white ochre." (🔈 VW: FM08_a100: 3:39min)

(1230)

Ngu=rla	**yuwa-ni**	nyila	na	martiya.
CAT=3OBL	put-PST	that	FOC	bush.gum

nang-nang	ngu=rla	**yuwa-ni.**
adhere-REDUP	CAT=3OBL	put-PST

"He stuck the gum onto him."
(🔈 RW: Warrija Kirrawa: HM070529GUR.DAGU_01rw.mp3: 3:00min)

7.2.3.2 Coverbs of transfer

Coverbs of transfer combine with the inflecting verb *jayingana* 'give'. Transfer is most commonly of the physical kind, however the transfer of knowledge is also expressed using this construction, as in (1232) and (1233). Some other examples of coverbs are given in (1231).

(1231)	*jalarntu*	'give as a gift'
	jirri	'promise a girl'
	jungkut	'give away'
	lin	'give formally'
	pinak	'teach'
	wiit	'show'
	yilmij	'give back'
	yuwarrap	'give only a little'

(1232)

Wamamala	ngu=rnayinangkulu	**wiit**
girl.REDUP	CAT=1EXC.AUG.S>3AUG.NS	show

jayi-nga-nku	warrwarrkap-ku.
give-IMPF-POT	dance.REDUP-DAT

"We'll be showing all of the girls how to dance." (🔊 BW: FM08_11_5: 1:58min)

(1233)

Ngu=ngantipa	pirrkap-ku=ma
CAT=1EXC.AUG.NS	make-DAT=TOP

pinak	**jayi-nya**	nyantu	na.
teach	give-PST	3MIN	FOC

"He taught us how to make the hair string." (🔊 VW: FM08_08_1a: 9:22min)

7.2.3.3 Coverbs of holding

Like coverbs of spatial configuration, coverbs of holding express a spatial configuration between two entities, however they only combine with *karrinyana* 'be' in a periphrastic progressive construction in the sense that all coverbs can as per Schultze-Berndt (2012). Instead they combine with another stative verb, *karrwarnana* 'hold, keep', forming a bivalent complex verb. Some examples are given in (1234).

(1234)	*jalngak*	'hold on back'
	jarrpip	'hold'
	juluj	'hold under arm'
	karrilili	'hold rattling'
	lajap	'hold on shoulder'

larrmij	'keep in a bundle'
murnamurna	'hold by the wrist'
put	'hold under hand'
turt	'hold in hands'
warra	'take care of'
wirt	'hold in mouth'

It is also possible for coverbs of holding to combine with *kangana* 'take' to express accompaniment and to combine with *manana* 'do/get' in a causative construction. For example, *jarrpip karrwarnana* 'hold', *jarrpip kangana* 'carry' and *jarrpip manana* 'pick up'.

Coverbs of holding can also be detransitivised by combining with the intransitive inflecting verbs *waninyana* 'fall' or the intransitive locomotion verb *yanana* 'go'. In the case of *waninyana*, the ergative subject becomes a locative complement and the object becomes the subject. In combination with *yanana* the subject is nominative and the second participant is marked with the proprietive suffix *-yawung/-jawung*.

7.2.3.4 Coverbs of state

Coverbs of state express the state or property of an entity. Like coverbs of spatial configuration, they also combine with the stative verb *karrinyana* 'be', however they can be distinguished from these coverbs because they also combine with the nominalising (adjectival) suffixes *-pari/-wari* (§4.7.21) and *-ing* (§4.7.3), as in (1235). They can also combine with *manana* 'do/get' in a causative construction.

(1235) Ngu=rnalu kukij-karra na,
CAT=1EXC.AUG.S drink-ITER FOC

Nyamu=waa karru **jiwily-ing** na.
REL=REL be.POT cold-ADJ FOC
"We will drink it when it gets cold." (◀) W: FM09_16_1b: 0:29min)

Other examples include *ngapuk* 'smell', *malany* 'taste', *parntaly* 'bend', *jarlarl* 'split, crack', *tipirr* 'break off' and *mum* 'be dark'. Unlike Jaminjung (Schultze-Berndt, 2000, p. 448), words for colour seem to be nominals in Gurindji rather than coverbs, e.g. *kikik* 'red' and *wurrkal* 'green', as shown by their ability to take case-marking as arguments, although one is clearly a coverb, for example *winkily* (cv) 'redden, angry' can be derived as *winkilying* (adj) 'red' or *winkilywari* 'anger' (adj).

7.2.3.5 Coverbs of speech and sound emission

This class of coverbs consists of those coverbs which express modes of human speech or animal/mechanical sounds.

(1236) Human speech:

jaaj	'plead'
jaalap	'bid farewell'
jamanymany	'sleep talk'
jamarlukmarluk	'chatter'
jangat	'answer'
jarrakap	'talk'
jawirtij	'talk in private'
jungjungkarra	'click tongue'
kalkalp	'talk rudely'
kapany	'beckon'
kiyap	'whisper'
nguyurrp	'hum'
takataka	'sign'
wartayip	'call out for'
wuruny	'whistle'
yangki	'ask'
yingi	'tease'
yurrk	'tell, recount'

Animal/mechanical sounds:

jiying	'flying fox call'
kukukuk	'crow crowing'
muwup	'howl, moo'
ngaak	'whine'
ngakakap	'neigh, whinny'
ngukukngukuk	'croak'
ngungung	'hum, putter'
ngurr	'buzz, growl'
nyiyu	'meow'
parrng	'loud barking'
purrngip	'snore, purr, putter'
rungap	'bark'
tirrak	'black cockatoo call'
warrawurlun	'drone, gush'
wukukwukuk	'croak'
yilyilyip	'hiss, fizz, sizzle'

This class of coverbs is distinguished from other coverbs on formal grounds by their ability to combine with *marnana* 'talk', as in (1237). They can also combine with *karrinyana* like all coverbs to form a periphrastic progressive, as shown in (1238).

(1237) **Jarrakap** ngu=rna=rla **ma-rna-na** jaru.
talk CAT=1EXC.MIN.S=3OBL talk-IMPF-PRS language
"I talk language to her." (🔈 VW: FM07_01_1a: 3:17min)

(1238) Ngu=rna=rla Nangari-wu **karrinya** **jarrakap**.
CAT=1EXC.MIN.S=3OBL SUBSECT-DAT be.PST talk
"I was talking to Nangari." (🔈 VW: FM09_14_1a: 12:18min)

7.2.3.6 Coverbs of bodily functions and emotions

This coverb class refers quite straight-forwardly to bodily functions and emotions. Some examples are given in (1239):

(1239) Coverbs of bodily function:

jaakip	'yawn'
jarrawurlp	'premonition twitch'
jilngit	'sweat'
jipuluk	'shut eyes'
jupak	'spit'

Coverbs of thought and emotion:

jalya	'feel fit'
jitart	'disgruntled'
jungkurl	'fell weak'
kuli	'angry'
marrunyu	'happy'

jupuyupu	'puffed'	*minyirri*	'shy'
kartarrp	'clear ears'	*nguny*	'grumpy, sulky'
kulykulya	'congestion'	*nguran*	'worry, grieve'
ngajirrp	'sneeze'	*pina*	'know'
ngajkula	'have diarrhoea'	*punyu*	'good'
paku	'vomit'	*wuukarra*	'afraid'
warrngun	'in pain'		

This set of coverbs only combines with the stative inflecting verb *karrinyana* 'be'. They are distinguished from coverbs of state by their inability to combine with adverbial suffixes. This is the only set of coverbs which shows such a restricted combination with inflecting verbs. Some examples are given in (1240)–(1244).

(1240) Ngu=rnayinangulu **nguran** **karrinya**
CAT=1EXC.AUG.S>3AUG.NS grieve be.PST

yalu-wu na karu-wu.
that-DAT FOC child-DAT
"We all grieved for those children." (🔈 VW: FM14_a204: 1:03min)[204]

(1241) Kurrurij-murlung **punyu** ngu=rnalu **karrinya,** **punyu.**[205]
car-PRIV good CAT=1EXC.AUG.S be.PST good
"We got on well without cars."
(McConvell 1996 grammar manuscript: Speaking to young people)

(1242) Ngu=rnalu=rla **wuukarra** **karrinya.**
CAT=1EXC.AUG.S=3OBL afraid be.PST
"We were afraid of it."
(🔈 VW: FM10_27_1a: Kurraj Story from Halls Creek: 3:56min)

(1243) Ngu=rnalu **jitart**=parla **karrinya** kuya-wu=ma.
CAT=1EXC.AUG.S hate=FOC be.PST thus-DAT=TOP
"We hated how it was." (🔈 JK: McConvell_A3464_C: 1:48min)[206]

---

204 This sentence was uttered in a story about the Stolen Generations who were children taken away for having European fathers. The full story can be found in Wadrill (2016a).

205 Another analysis of *punyu* here might be as an adjectival predicate.

206 This sentence comes from a commentary about colonisation.

(1244)

Yuwa-na-ni	jujurlk	murla-ngkurra	jujurlk,
put-IMPF-PST	push.REDUP	this-ALL	push.REDUP

nyamu=lu	**karrinyani**	**wangiyip=ma**,	yawu=ma
REL=3AUG.S	be.IMPF.PST	dizzy=TOP	fish=TOP

murla-ngkurra,	nyila-rra=ma.
this-ALL	that-PL=TOP

"[The first rain] would push the fish to the riverbank who would get dizzy from the stirred-up water." (🔊 VW: FM09_13_3a: 3:16min)

(1245)

Kartiya=ma	kula=rla	**pina**	**karrinya**	yalu-wu=ma
non-Indigenous=TOP	NEG=3OBL	know	be.PST	that-DAT=TOP

marluka-wu=ma	nyamu	ngawa	pirrka	ma-ni.
old.man-DAT=TOP	REL	water	make	do-PST

"The *kartiya* didn't know that the old man made rain."
(McConvell corpus: Meakins et al., 2016, p. 322)

The other distinguishing feature about these coverbs are that they are also often found without an inflecting verb. Compare (1244) with (1246), and (1245) with (1247). Further examples are given in (1248) and (1249). In (1250), *makurru* 'cold' also undergoes zero derivation and becomes a nominal in the second clause, as shown by the ergative-marking.

(1246)

Ngu=rna	ngarlaka	**wangiyip**.
CAT=1EXC.MIN.S	head	dizzy

"I'm feeling dizzy." (BW with ECh: Meakins et al., 2016, p. 388)

(1247)

Ngarnjal	**pina**	ngu=rla.
NAME	know	CAT=3OBL

"Topsy knows about it." (🔊 VW: FM08_11_2c: 7:54min)

(1248)

Ngu=**rna**	**makurru**,	makurru-lu
CAT=1EXC.MIN.S	cold	cold-ERG

ngu=yi	minyja-rna-na.
CAT=1EXC.MIN.NS	make.cold-IMPF-PRS

"I'm cold, the cold is making me cold."
(🔊 RW: EC98_a019: Jajurlang & Puturn: 1:22min)

(1249) Warta ngu=yi ngawa-wu jiya-rna-na.
goodness CAT=1EXC.MIN.NS water-DAT burn-IMPF-PRS

Ngu=**rna** **majul=ma** **ngarrap** na.
CAT=1EXC.MIN.S stomach=TOP hot FOC
"Goodness I'm really thirsty. My stomach is hot."
(🔊 VW: FM11_a166: 34:04min)

Emotions are also often discussed in terms of body parts. Note that not all of these are coverbs. For example:

(1250)			
	majul punyu	'happy'	<stomach good
	majul wankaj	'unhappy'	<stomach bad
	majul patawan	'brave'	<strong stomach, see also (1252)
	kujakujarram-karra-waji majul	'two-faced'	<two.REDUP-ITER-AGENT stomach
	kujarra-kujarra majul	'two-faced'	<two-REDUP stomach
	majul turrp pungana	'premonition'	<stomach stab pierce

(1251) Nya-nga-ni ngu=rla **majul-lu=ma** **patawan-tu**
intake-IMPF-PST CAT=3OBL stomach-ERG=TOP strong-ERG

patawan-tu **patawan-tu** najing yala-nginyi=ma,
strong-ERG strong-ERG nothing that-SOURCE=TOP

lawara. Lungkarra na ngu=rla lu-nga-ni.
nothing cry FOC CAT=3OBL cry-IMPF-PST
"[Bluetongue] kept looking around bravely without crying, but then it was too much. [So] he cried about it."
(🔊 VW: FM10_23_1a: Luma Kurrupartu: 2:42min)

Other coverbs are often translated into English in terms of body parts. For example, *nguny* which means 'grumpy' or 'sulky' is more often than not translated as 'mean face'.

7.2.3.7 Coverbs of motion

Coverbs of motion combine with verbs of locomotion: *yanana* 'go' (intransitive) or *kangana* 'take' (transitive), and often both. For example, *rarraj* 'run' combines with *yanana* to mean 'run' and with *kangana* to mean 'run away with' or 'elope'.

The first group of coverbs of motion are 'manner of motion' coverbs. Some examples are given in (1252).

(1252)	*jakap*	'sneak up on'	*manpurr*	'shuffle'
	jarrara	'accompany'	*mingip*	'crawl'
	jarrk	'descend to river'	*murtap*	'hunt'
	jik	'emerge, come out'	*nyiwunnyiwun*	'dive underwater'
	jiwawu	'swoop for prey'	*rarraj*	'run'
	kalu	'walk'	*takijkarra*	'limp'
	kapartkarra	'stumble'	*talip*	'walk with a stick'
	kayikayi	'chase'	*tarak*	'disappear behind'
	kiriny	'slip'	*wakarr*	'waddle'
	lajkut	'land hard'	*wumparlp*	'float'
	lurrmin	'back and forth'	*yangkarra*	'follow'

A second set of coverbs of motion are the 'direction of motion' coverbs. They are distinguished from the 'manner of motion' coverbs by their ability to combine with *waninyana* 'to fall' and *yuwanana* 'put', as well as locomotion verbs. When they combine with *yuwanana* the verb complex also encodes an oblique object. Examples for *partaj* 'ascend' were given in (1211)–(1214). Some other examples of coverbs of 'direction of motion' are given in (1253):

(1253)	*jajurrk*	'turn back half-way'	*kirti*	'climb to summit'
	jampurlk	'squash'	*parr*	'land on ground'
	japurr	'immerse'	*timpuk*	'go through'
	jawurruk	'descend'	*tipart*	'jump'
	jirrpu	'dive'	*walik*	'go around'
	kamurrk	'go past someone'	*wart*	'return'

7.2.3.8 Coverbs of leaving

A small group of coverbs combine with the 'leave' inflecting verb *wanyjanana* which is transitive. A number of these coverbs also combine with *kangana* 'take' to express the meaning 'take and leave (in some manner)'.

(1254)	*naru*	'dodge'
	parik	'leave behind'
	warrkap	'dance'

The curious coverb in this group is *warrkap* 'dance', however this coverb makes more sense given the traditional style of dancing where leaving behind footprints which are stamped into the ground or sand is important. Curiously, it is also transitive. An example is given in (1255).

(1255)

Warrkap-karra	ngu=lu	**wanyja-na-ni**	yala-ngka=ma
dance-ITER	CAT=3AUG.S	leave-IMPF-PST	that-LOC=TOP

marlurluka-lu	kajijirri-lu	ngu=rnayinangulu
old.man.REDUP-ERG	old.woman.REDUP-ERG	CAT=1EXC.AUG.S>3AUG.NS

ka-nga-ni	an	skul-ngarna-lu.
take-IMPF-PST	and	school-ASSOC-ERG

"The old men and women were dancing for them there when we used to take them out – and the school mob danced too." (🔈 VW: FM08_11_3: 1:13min)

7.2.3.9 Coverbs of cooking and burning

All of the coverbs in this class combine with *kamparnana* 'cook, apply heat' and often with *jiyarnana* 'burn, smoke, apply light'. In the following examples, *jipij* 'roast in ground' combines with *kamparnana* to mean the fish is cooked under the coals (1256), and with *jiyarnana* to indicate that the fish was cooked on the coals (1257).

(1256)

Jipij	ngu=rnalu	**kampa-rna-na**	julpara-la.
cover	CAT=1EXC.AUG.S	cook-IMPF-PRS	coals-LOC

"We cook it in the hot coals covered up." (🔈 VW: FM07_a058: 6:16min)

(1257)

Nyila=ma	puya=ma	**jiya-rna-na**	**jipij**,	kuya.
that=TOP	carcass=TOP	burn-IMPF-PRS	cover	thus

"That carcass cooks in the ground like that." (🔈 VW: FM10_a148: 4:28min)

The coverbs of cooking and burning give more specific information about the mode of heat and smoke application, for example the type of heated substance being used (e.g. ground, ashes, coals, leaves, branding iron etc) and where the cooking takes place (e.g. on the coals, in the ground etc).

Some examples of cooking coverbs are given in (1258). They include coverbs of manner of heating as well as light emission:

(1258)

janarr	'burn someone'	*purtuj*	'set alight'
jumpurn	'smoke something'	*walarrparr*	'tattoo'
kim	'sting'	*wumpu*	'singe'
kirrim	'sting'	*wupkarra*	'cook on coals'
jily	'burn, brand'	*yilyingkap*	'fry'
jipij	'cook in coals'	*yirip*	'warm up'
wanyjirr	'cook mixed ingredients'		

For more on the semantics of *kamparnana* and *jiyarnana*, see §7.1.1.2.

7.2.3.10 Coverbs of impact and intensity

Coverbs of impact and intensity combine with *panana* 'hit', *pungana* 'pierce' or *payarnana* 'bite'. We can divide this class into three groups: the first group combines with only *panana*; the second group combines with only *pungana*; and the third group only with *payarnana* 'bite'.

Coverbs which combine with *panana* 'hit' include:

(1259)	*jalkaj*	'knock down'	*kataj*	'cut'
	jataj	'scratch out'	*kirt*	'hit and break'
	jilmung	'break by hitting'	*kurakik*	'hit back of head'
	jinkirr	'break and tear'	*lurrku*	'ignite by rubbing sticks'
	julurrp	'chop up a carcass'	*pangkily*	'hit head'
	jum	'hit back of neck'	*wamip*	'spin hair string'

Coverbs which combine only with *pungana* 'pierce' include:

(1260)	*jup*	'pluck'
	jurt	'poke with a stick'
	kirlk	'squash between fingernails'
	kirrip	'strip off paperbark'
	kurrij	'dig with a stick'
	lirrp	'spear repeatedly'
	marany	'rub, wipe'
	mulurrp	'pierce with implement'
	turrp	'poke, pierce'
	yatyat	'poke ground with stick for bush potatoes'

Coverbs which combine with *payarnana* 'bite' include:

(1261)	*jangkawu*	'fish bite'
	kalp	'learn quickly'
	kamarrwa	'bite something fatally'
	kartirrk	'bite hard'
	katurl	'bite'
	kukij	'drink'
	malany	'taste'
	minykarra	'lick'
	warlwarl	'bite and shake'

Many 'bite' coverbs combine with either *panana* 'hit' and *pungana* 'pierce' as well:

(1262) *jarrwaj* 'spear'
jartirr 'injure'
jinyparlk 'spear right through'
ngamany 'stop, prevent'
papart 'massacre'
warnparlk 'chop lump off tree'

A number of other coverbs which are not specifically related to impact also form idiosyncratic complex verbs with *panana* and *pungana*. The use of these inflecting verbs seems to add a sense of intensity, a focused activity or an emphasis on the result. For example, while the act of looking for something is expressed by *warlakap nyangana* 'look around for (cv) + look (iv)' the act of finding is expressed by *paraj pungana* 'find (cv) + pierce (iv)'. Other examples are given in (1263).

(1263) *jipily* 'tell a lie' *ngurrku* 'jealous of, suspect'
jiwaj 'disagree, argue' *paraj* 'find'
kanginy 'not recognise' *wangany* 'search'
lirrkan 'step in on behalf of' *yangki* 'ask (for)'
marru 'envy'

A final set of impact coverbs can combine with either an impact inflecting verb (*panana* 'hit' or *pungana* 'pierce') or one of two manipulation inflecting verbs (*yuwanana* 'put' or *manana* 'do, get').

(1264) *jirrip* 'tear' *tarl* 'hit something on'
mirlij 'skin' *tawirrjip* 'throw stones'
ning 'break' *warnparlk* 'break open'
pinyinyip 'twirl one stick in the groove of another to create fire'

This alternation exists for one of two purposes. Firstly, it can express whether impact was the result of the use of an instrument or whether it was the result of handling and manipulation. For example, *mirlij panana* 'skin + hit' implies that a knife or axe was used to skin something whereas *mirlij manana* 'skin + do' implies that the act of skinning was performed with the hands. And *mirlij payarnana* 'skin + bite' suggests that the skin was taken off with teeth.

The second effect of the use of the manipulation inflecting verb seems to be to focus on the activity rather than the end result. For example *tawirrjip panana* 'throw stones + hit' means to pelt someone with stones (where 'stone' is encoded with an ergative or proprietive + ergative) (1265), whereas *tawirrjip yuwanana* 'throw stones + put' is not concerned with whether the target is hit, rather just with the act of throwing stones (1266).

(1265)

Wakarr	karrinyana	kirrawa=ma.	Majul=ma	murla
waddle	be.IMPF.PRS	goanna=TOP	stomach=TOP	this

kanyjurra.	Ya-nta=rla	rarraj!	Pa-rra	nyamu=nga
down	go-IMP=3OBL	run	hit-IMP	REL=DUB

ya-nku	karnti-kurra	partaj	kankula.	Nyila=ma
go-POT	tree-ALL	climb	up	that=TOP

tawirrjip	**pa-rra**	**wumara-lu**!
throw.stones	hit-IMP	stone-ERG

"A goanna is there waddling along. Its belly is right on the ground. Run after it! Shoot it when it maybe climbs up a tree. Pelt that one with stones!"
(🔈 TD: FM10_a163: 5:13min)

(1266)

Katataj	pa-na-na	ngarin	**tawirrijip**
cut.REDUP	hit-IMPF-PRS	meat	throw.stones

murlu-ngku=rni	**yuwa-na-na**.
this-ERG=ONLY	put-IMPF-PRS

"She cuts meat and throws stones with this [left-hand]."
(🔈 VW: FM18_a513: 0:17min)

A number of coverbs of impact can also combine with *waninyana* 'fall'. The differences in meaning that arise from the choice of inflecting verb are shown below:

(1267)

jungap panana	'kill'
jungap waninyana	'died'
kamarrwa panana	'mortally wound'
kamarrwa waninyana	'spear stuck in a fatal place'
kirt panana	'break off'
kirt waninyana	'get broken'
lak panana	'split a log'
lak waninyana	'open or split'

The effect of the use of the 'fall' inflecting verb is to de-transitivise the complex verb and focus on the change of state without concern for the agent. Indeed, the change of state may have come about without agentive force. For example, *turl panana* 'bark off + hit' means that someone cut bark off a tree, whereas *turl waninyana* 'bark off + fall' means that bark came off, perhaps due to natural causes (wind, dry weather etc). A similar story applies to *kirt* 'break off' as demonstrated in the following examples (1268) and (1269).

(1268)

Ngayu	<u>na</u>	ngu=rna	karnti-yawung-kulu=ma
1EXC.MIN	FOC	CAT=1EXC.MIN.S	stick-PROP-ERG=TOP

pa-ni,	**kirt**	ngu=rna	**pa-ni**.
hit-PST	break	CAT=1EXC.MIN.S	hit-PST

"Me, well, I hit [the branch] with a stick and I broke it."
(🔈 VW: FM07_a085: 11:19min)

(1269)

Kirt-kirt	**waninya**	karnti=ma.
break-REDUP	fall.PST	tree=TOP

"The tree fell and broke into pieces."
(Appendix: Echidna and the Big Shade: Text 1, Line 41)

A number of coverbs of impact can also combine with *manana* 'do, get' and *yuwanana* 'put' to produce meanings of manipulation or causation. Some examples are given in (1270) and in clauses in (1271)–(1272).

(1270)

kurrij manana	'get by digging'
kurrij panana	'stab at ground with crowbar'
langarak manana	'pass on a message'
langarak panana	'give someone a reminder'
langarak yuwanana	'pass on a message'
lurrku manana	'make a fire light up'
lurrku panana	'light a fire by rubbing sticks together'
lurrku yuwanana	'light a fire'
pinyinyip manana	'rub anything between palms of hands'
pinyinyip panana	'rub sticks together to make fire'
yirntij manana	'pinch'
yirntij payarnana	'bite, for example ants, centipedes'
yurtup manana	'grind seed'
yurtup panana	'grind a stone to sharpen it'
yurra panana	'scare out, scare away'
yurra manana	'scare away'

(1271)

Palki-k	ngu=rna	**ma-ni**.
flat-FACT	CAT=1EXC.MIN.S	do-PST

"I'm flattening it with my hands." (🔈 VW: FM09_13_3b: 3:49min)

(1272)

Nyawa	ngu=rna	**pa-na-na**	**palki-k**	kuya=ma.
this	CAT=1EXC.MIN.S	hit-IMPF-PRS	flat-FACT	thus=TOP

"I'm hitting it out flat like this." (🔈 VW: FM09_13_3b: 4:24min)

7.2.3.11 Coverbs of touch and manipulation

All of the verbs in this category combine with *manana* 'do, get' which expresses notions of handling, touch, obtainment and manipulation. The important semantic feature of these coverbs seems to be the involvement of the body in the action, particularly the hands. For example, some coverbs of impact combine with *panana* 'hit', *payarnana* 'bite' or *pungana* 'pierce' and *manana* 'do, get'. However, the digging verbs which combine with *panana* or *pungana* involve instruments, whereas the digging verbs in this category such as *karan* 'dig with hands' and *ngaraly* 'excavate' involve only the hands. Examples of coverbs of 'touch and manipulation' are given in (1273).

(1273)

Coverbs of direct contact:		Coverbs of indirect contact:	
jakarr	'cover'	*jirrkalyp*	'splash'
jalak	'knead'	*kilka*	'clean'
jalk	'hook up spear'	*kirralk*	'chip at'
jalyarra	'rub with fat'	*pinkaj*	'brush'
jawurra	'steal'	*wulyuk*	'wash something'
jinkirr	'tear with hands'		
ngaraly	'excavate'		

Coverbs of food gathering:		Coverbs of manipulation:	
jiwarrp	'gather up'	*jakarr*	'cover'
jupart	'throw dirt'	*jingiyip*	'tease apart'
karan	'dig with hands'	*jumpurlk*	'do hair, comb'
larlup	'scoop up'	*kartaj*	'choke'
lirritkarra	'stir leaves (to stun fish)'	*lukurr*	'twist'
mararap	'feel about'	*nang*	'stick on'
martmart	'feel about with hands'	*pirrka*	'make'
mijip	'scrounge'	*pulup*	'mix with water'
mirlij	'skin'	*tirrk*	'tie up'
puntanup	'collect'	*wanyjirr*	'mix'
yilirtij	'winnow'	*yirr*	'pull'

Coverbs of obtainment/loss:		Coverbs of touch:	
jak	'drop'	*july*	'squeeze pimple'
jawurra	'steal'	*kamang*	'rub out'
kup	'take out'	*karan*	'scratch'
lap	'pick up'	*kijikijik*	'tickle'
nunyju	'grab someone'	*lawurr*	'hug'
nyirn	'lose'	*ngalyak*	'lick'
palman	'pick up someone'	*pat*	'touch'
turt	'hold, grab'	*punup*	'paint up'
yilimpi	'feel around in water'	*puny*	'kiss'

yipuk	'take off'
yirajip	'rifle through'
yirlarrp	'undress'

Coverbs of memory and emotion:

kaji	'make trouble'
kajup	'deceive'
kalnguniny	'deceive'
karlunyjurr	'upset'
mapuk	'embarrass'
ngarrka	'recognise'
ngatji	'mean, selfish'
ngawululu	'pay respects'
ngawututu	'hold someone dear'
ngurruj	'copy, imitate'
nyurrun	'forget, lose'

A small number of these coverbs also combine with *yuwanana* 'put', for example *jurlurl* 'pour', *wuyurrunkarra* 'fishing' and *wurlmip* 'get water from soak'. The meaning difference is not entirely clear in all cases, although see the next section.

7.2.3.12 Coverbs of induced change of location or configuration

The name for this category comes from Schultze-Berndt (2000, p. 505). Although these coverbs involve manipulation and therefore might be expected to combine with *manana* 'do, get', they combine with *yuwanana* 'put' instead. Indeed, most coverbs in this class and the previously described class behave in an exclusive manner, i.e. coverbs which combine with *manana* do not combine with *yuwanana* and vice versa. Some exceptions exist which were given in the previous section. The difference between these two classes of coverbs seems to lie in the ability of an object to be configured. For example, the 'put' inflecting verb *yuwanana* also combines with coverbs of spatial configuration (postural and positionals) to indicate an induced change in locative relation (see §7.2.3.1). A number of these coverbs combine exclusively with *yuwanana*. Examples include:

(1274)

Coverbs of physical contact:		Coverbs of speech and thought:	
jakirtij	'block off, close'	*jaalap*	'wave goodbye'
jalarr	'join together'	*jalak*	'send'
jalaj	'knead'	*jinpuk*	'hurt feelings'
jarlaparl	'put on belly'	*kurrwara*	'blame'
kurlpap	'gather in a heap'	*kururr*	'ignore'
lakup	'scoop up'	*langarak*	'send message'

nang	'stick something on'	*latalata*	'instruct, teach'
nyanyjarlng	'join together'	*minyirri*	'shame someone'
pakurr	'put into container'	*piyarrp*	'report'

A number of other coverbs that can be described as expressing an 'induced change of location' also combine with the stative inflecting verb *karrinyana* 'be' or *waninyana* 'come to be' to express an induced change in locative relation as discussed above. Other 'coverbs of induced change of configuration' combine with intransitive verbs, for example *jijkurrp karrinyana* 'immersed', *jijkurrp yuwanana* 'immerse someone' and *jijkurrp waninyana* 'fall into water'.

A final set of coverbs relate to induced ballistic motion. They combine with *yuwanana* 'put', but also with *luwarnana* 'strike'. The difference in meaning is not clear. Examples are given in (1275) and one sentence example is given in (1276).

(1275) *janang* 'knock down'
lirrp 'spear all over'
turlk 'shoot'
wany 'throw'
warntarrija 'throw boomerang'

(1276) **Yuwa-ni** ngu **warntarrija** kurrupartu=ma,
put-PST CAT throw.boomerang boomerang=TOP

nyampayirla-lu=ma Luma-ngku=ma.
whatsitcalled-ERG=TOP Bluetongue.lizard-ERG=TOP
"Bluetongue threw a boomerang."
(🔈 VW: FM10_23_1a: Luma Kurrupartu: 0:30min)

7.2.3.13 Coverbs of intake

Coverbs of intake include coverbs of perception (hearing and looking) (1277) and (1278), and coverbs of ingestion (eating and drinking) (1279). The common link between these coverbs is their ability to combine with *nyangana* which generally is translated into English as 'look', but has a more general meaning of 'intake' (see §7.1.1.3).

(1277) **Karrap** ngu=rna=yina **nya-nga-ni**
watch CAT=1EXC.MIN.S=3AUG.NS intake-IMPF-PST

pirrkap-jirri=ma.
make-ALL=TOP
"I watched them while they made it." (🔈 VW: FM07_05_1a: 0:33min)

(1278) Nyamu=lu=nga wanku yirrp-karra=ma kuya=ma
REL=3AUG.S=DUB fall.POT converge-ITER=TOP thus=TOP

wal ngu=rnalu **kurru** **nya-nga-na.**
well CAT=1EXC.AUG.S hear intake-IMPF-PRS
"When they converge [on the waterhole] like this, well we hear them."
(🔈 VW: FM09_13_2d: 0:06min)

(1279) Ngu=rlaa **nya-nya** tanku **jaartkarra**, marntaj.
CAT=1INC.AUG.S intake-PST food eat OK
"We ate our lunch, OK." (🔈 BW: FM09_a121: 0:37min)

The first group of 'coverbs of intake' are perception coverbs. Examples are given in (1280).

(1280)	*jirrang*	'crane to see'	*lirring*	'inspect'
	jurnpulp	'squint'	*murt*	'premonition'
	kalirr	'look cock-eyed'	*ngaarrap*	'look up'
	karnkilkkarra	'look shyly'	*pilap*	'look back'
	karrap	'look at, watch'	*wap*	'look over shoulder'
	kawa	'blurred vision'	*warap*	'scan'
	kurru	'hear'	*warlakap*	'look around for'
	lawu	'see clearly'	*wirra*	'spy on'

These forms are classified as coverbs of perception because they combine with *nyangana* 'intake'. However, they also combine with *karrinyana* 'be' to form stative complex verbs, for example (1281).

(1281) Ngu=rna **kurru** **karrinyana** ngarlu, nama.
CAT=1EXC.MIN.S listen be.IMPF.PRS honey bee
"I'm listening for bees." (🔈 BW: FM07_a028: 3:33min)

The coverbs of ingestion also combine with the 'eat' inflecting verb, *ngarnana*. Coverbs related to drinking can also combine with *payarnana* 'bite'. It is not clear how the meaning changes with the use of the different inflecting verbs. Some examples of coverbs of ingestion are given in (1282) and examples in sentences are in (1283)–(1285):

(1282)	*jaartkarra*	'eat'	*ngurlu*	'salivate'
	kartaj	'choke on food'	*nyuknyuk*	'suck(le)'
	kukij	'drink'	*tarap*	'inhale water'
	ngirljik	'swallow'	*warlupurr*	'eat and never share'

(1283) Nyuk-nyuk-karra ngu=rla paya-rna-ni ngapulu=ma.
suck-REDUP-ITER CAT=3OBL bite-IMPF-PST breast=TOP
"She was suckling at her breast." (🔈 VW: FM12_33_1: 0:46min)

(1284) Ngayu=ma=rna kula nga-rni jaartkarra=ma.
1EXC.MIN=TOP=1EXC.MIN.S NEG eat-PST eat=TOP
"I never used to eat it [when I was a young girl]."
(🔈 VW: FM09_a123: 9:42min)

(1285) Ngu=rnalu **kukij-karra** na **paya-rni** nyila=ma ngawa=ma.
CAT=1EXC.AUG.S drink-ITER FOC bite-PST that=TOP water=TOP
"Then we were drinking the water." (🔈 VW: FM09_14_1a: 3:07min)

Other coverbs which combine with *nyangana* are less easy to categorise but are given as follows in (1286).

(1286) *jikilikili* 'provoke'
kiyi 'hesitate to visit when too late'
kuli 'start a fight'
piirti 'make up stories or ideas'
pujirrij 'rub nose to mean you are lying'
tapilipili 'bedridden'

7.2.3.14 Coverbs of excretion

A small number of coverbs combine only with the inflecting verb *ngayanana* 'excrete' and express different means of excretion from the body. On its own, this verb refers to giving birth, with *waninyana* 'fall' the intransitive counterpart, 'to be born'. Coverbs of excretion include: *kumpu* 'urinate', *kura* 'defecate' with two examples given in (1287) and (1288). Note they can also combine with *karrinyana* in the usual periphrastic progressive described for other coverbs.

(1287) Murla-ngka tirrip karrinya **kumpu** **ngaya-ni**
this-LOC overnight be.PST urinate excrete-PST

ngu wal nyawa na ngawa.
CAT well this FOC waterhole
"The [Dreaming Emu] camped over night and urinated here and created this spring." (🔈 VW: FM07_04_1c: 7:43min)

(1288) Nyamu=yina=nga ngamayi-lu **ngaya-rra**
REL=3AUG.NS=DUB mother-ERG excrete-IMP

ngayiny-ja waruju-la=ma kuya-ngka=ma
1EXC.MIN.DAT-LOC together-LOC=TOP thus-LOC=TOP

wayi=rna=yina=nga pa-rra.
Q=1EXC.MIN.S=3AUG.NS=DUB hit-IMP
"If the mother [cat] had given birth to them while I was around, I might have killed [the kittens]." (McConvell corpus: Meakins et al., 2016, p. 277)

7.2.4 Morphology

Coverbs host very little morphology. In this section, we discuss the little TAM morphology found on coverbs: the iterative suffix *-karra* (§7.2.4.1), the coverb-deriving suffix *-ap/-p* which may also have some aspectual properties (§7.2.4.2), the 'together' suffix *-warrp* (§7.2.4.3) and reduplication which is used to mark iterative aspect (§7.2.4.4). We also discuss the factitive suffix (§7.2.4.5).

A number of nominalising suffixes are also found marking coverbs which are dealt with in other chapters. These include the agentive *-kaji/-waji* (§4.7.7), nominaliser *-ny* (§4.7.20), associative *-ngarna* (§4.7.16) and adjectival marker *-pari/-wari* (§4.7.21). Also discussed in Chapter 4 was the adnominal case suffix *-murlung* (§4.6.3) which is used to form preventative imperative verbs from coverbs. Case-marked coverbs are also found in reduced subordinate clauses, which was introduced in various sections in Chapter 4 and will be discussed in detail in Chapter 8.

7.2.4.1 *-karra*, *-warra*, *-arra* ITERative

The iterative suffix has three forms: *-karra*, *-warra*, and *-arra*. They are shown in Table 45. When the *-warra* allomorph attaches to *a*-final stems, the result is usually a long vowel with *-w* deleted, for example *kakapara-warra* is pronounced *kakaparaarra*. Some examples are given in (1289)–(1291).

Table 45: Allomorphy for the iterative marker.

Form	Environment	Gurindji example	English gloss
-karra	When the stem ends in a consonant	*juluj-karra*	'carrying'
-warra	When the stem ends in a vowel	*jiwawu-warra* *tirringinji-warra* *kakapara-warra*	'diving for prey' 'encroaching' 'get about crippled'

Table 45 (Continued)

Form	Environment	Gurindji example	English gloss
-arra	When the stem ends in an 'l' or 'rr'	*taku**rl**-arra*	'putting in container'
		*pangki**ly**-arra*	'hitting head with rock'
		*jilwa**rr**-arra*	'tearing'

(1289) Ngu=rnayinangkulu ka-nga-na **juluj-karra** na.
CAT=1EXC.AUG.S>3AUG.NS take-IMPF-PRS carry.under.arm-ITER FOC
"And we are carrying them under our arms in the coolamons."
(◀)) BW: FM07_02_1a: 1:02min)

(1290) Kartak-kula **takurl-arra** yuwa-na-na, jarrwalut.
billycan-LOC inside-ITER put-IMPF-PRS many
"She is putting them in a billycan, lots of them." (◀)) TD: FM10_a163: 4:06min)

(1291) **Purtuyi-warra** ngu=rna=rla karrinyana
goose.bumps-ITER CAT=1EXC.MIN.S=3OBL be.IMPF.PRS

pakarturtup. Ngantu-ku=warla karrap nya-nga-na
hair.standing.up who-ERG=FOC watch intake-IMPF-PRS

yikili-ngurlung ngumayila-ngurlung.
far-ABL behind-ABL
"My hair is standing on end from something. Maybe someone was watching from a long way away behind me." (◀)) VW: FM10a_154: 3:06min)

Incomplete action in complex verbs can be indicated in a number of ways including the use of the imperfective infix *-na-* on inflecting verbs (§7.1.3.3, §7.1.3.5 and §7.1.3.7), reduplication of the coverb (§7.2.4.4), the use of the *karrinyana* inflecting verb (§7.1.1.6.1), or the addition of the *-karra* suffix to coverbs. Compare the coverb *juluj* which receives an iterative suffix in (1290) and occurs as a reduplicated form in (1292).

(1292) Ngu=rnayinangulu ka-nga-na
CAT=1EXC.AUG.S>3AUG.NS take-IMPF-PRS

julujuluj, kawarla-la=ma.
carry.under.arm.REDUP coolamon-LOC=TOP
"Now we carry our children under our arms in coolamons."
(◀)) VW: FM07_02_1c: 0:49min)

The iterative *-karra* is used to indicate iterativity, or multiple repetitions of an event, following the same arguments given for *=mayan* in Jaminjung (Schultze-Berndt, 2012, p. 22). Although it appears to be similar to the progressive, it does not have co-occurrence restrictions with stative predicates and achievement (punctual) predicates observed for progressives cross-linguistically. For example, it appears attached to *jarrgan* 'keep distance from mother-in-law' in (1293) (stative) and *kataj* 'cut' in (1294) (punctual). If it were a derivational marker of atelic lexical aspect, we would expect restrictions in the co-occurrence with activity coverbs, as shown in (1296).

(1293) **Jarrngan-karra** karrinyani nyila=ma ngu,
give.room-ITER be.IMPF.PST that=TOP CAT

murrwali-nyan-ta, maitbi
mother.in.law-3MIN.POSS-LOC maybe

mali-ngka yu nou.
mother.in.law-LOC you know
"He was keeping his distance because of her mother-in-law."
(◀) VW: FM12_a172: 1:01min)

(1294) **Kataj-karra** ngu=rnayinangulu pa-ni,
cut-ITER CAT=1EXC.AUG.S>3AUG.NS hit-PST

kartpi=ma nyawa-rra=ma katakataj-nginyi.
hair=TOP this-PL=TOP cut.REDUP-SOURCE
"We were cutting their hair, so this hair comes from hair cuts."
(◀) VW: FM08_08_1a: 7:18min)

(1295) Kula ya-nku na **kalurirrp-karra**=ma.
NEG go-POT FOC walk.around-ITER=TOP
"He can't be walking very far." (◀) VW: FM12_a174: 7:40min)

The iterative marker is used in conjunction with the past tense form of an inflecting verb, as shown in (1294) and (1297), or with present tense forms (1289) and (1290), potential forms (1295) and imperative forms (1297). Note also that there are a few examples of *-karra* co-occurring with imperfective aspect where the *-karra* is not frozen (see below), for example (1293).

(1296) Janyja-ka ngu=rnalu **kurrij-karra** pu-nya yirimuri-la.
ground-LOC CAT=1EXC.AUG.S dig-ITER pierce-PST sand-LOC
"We were digging in the sandy ground." (◀) VW: FM08_a100: 3:36min)

(1297) Walima ngu=rna=ngku jaja **tang-karra=kata**
Q CAT=1EXC.MIN.S=2MIN.NS MM open.mouth-ITER=IMM

tang-karra nyawa murla jira-wu.
open.mouth-ITER this this fat-DAT
"Guess what I've got for you granny, come quick, open your mouth, open up for this [kangaroo] fat." (🔈 RW: EC97_a006: Jajurlang & Ngawa: 7:25min)

The iterative suffix can also occur on inflecting verbs in their infinitive form, as in (1298), or adverbs or nominals which have been derived as coverbs using the factitive suffix, as in (1299).

(1298) Pirrij **ma-rnu-warra** karrinyana.
lie talk-INF-ITER be.IMPF.PRS
"He/she is making up stories." (Meakins et al., 2016, p. 329)

(1299) **Kamparri-k-karra** ngu=yinangkulu wurrwa-wu.
front-FACT-ITER CAT=3AUG.S>3AUG.NS block-POT
"They will block [boomerangs from] them by going in front of them." (Meakins et al., 2016, p. 429)

Some coverbs have *-karra* as a frozen morph, for example *tajkarra* 'pound', *jaartkarra* 'eat', *miyijkarra* 'wipe tears away', *lungkarra* 'cry', *kapartkarra* 'stumble', *japalarra* 'plop', *jarrawujarrawuwarra* 'moving light', *jarrngajarrngaarra* 'stuck in a tree' and *kartirtijkarra* 'grind teeth'. In some of these cases, the equivalent coverb without iterative marking occurs in Jaminjung and Bilinarra, for example *taj* 'pound'. It is possible they were borrowed from the north. Bilinarra tolerates single syllable coverbs to a greater extent than Gurindji, hence the frozen *-karra* in Gurindji. A curious case is *wuyurrunkarra* 'fishing' where *-karra* seems to have derived the coverb from the nominal *wuyurrun* 'fishing line' since this is a recent tool.

The iterative is also found in Bilinarra, Ngarinyman, Mudburra, Jaru and Wanyjirra, although in Nyininy and Wanyjirra it has an additional allomorph *-parra*. In Wanyjirra, it follows /p/, /rt/ and /i/. It is referred to as a 'continuative' in Bilinarra and a 'repetitive' in Wanyjirra (Meakins & Nordlinger, 2014, p. 342; Senge, 2016, pp. 433–434; Tsunoda, 1981, pp. 241–242). It is possible that the iterative suffix is derived from the Bilinarra present tense form of the inflecting verb *karra* 'to be', which forms pseudo progressive constructions with many coverbs, as discussed in §7.1.1.6.1, however it is also used as a switch reference marker in a number of Ngumpin-Yapa languages including Warlpiri (Simpson, 1988).

7.2.4.2 *-ap*/*-p* CV

This suffix is used as a derivational suffix on infinitive forms of inflecting verbs to produce coverbs (§7.1.3.7), as shown in (1300) and (1301). It also appears on the outside of case inflections in a few idiosyncratic forms, as in (1302) (see also §4.1). There is also one example of it appearing on an imperative form of an inflecting verb *yuwa-rra-p* 'put-IMP-CV' in (1303), but this might be a coincidence and a case of linguist over-analysis.

(1300)

Nyila=ma	ngu=lu	ka-nga-ni	na	**kampa-rnu-p-ku**	na.
that=TOP	CAT=3AUG.S	bring-IMPF-PST	FOC	cook-INF-CV-DAT	FOC

"They would bring [the fish] to cook now." (🔈 VW: FM09_16_2: 4:53min)

(1301)

Ngu=rnalu	yunpa-rna-na	**yunpa-rnu-p**=ma
CAT=1EXC.AUG.S	sing-IMPF-PRS	sing-INF-CV=TOP

kilkilp	Yawulyu-la=ma.
click.together	woman.ceremony-LOC=TOP

"We sing and play the clapsticks during the Yawulyu ceremony."
(🔈 VW: FM08_a101: 9:34min)

(1302)

Tingarri-lu-p	mingip	ya-na-na.
knee-ERG-CV	crawl	go-IMPF-PRS

"She is crawling on her knees." (McConvell corpus: Meakins et al., 2016, p. 365)

(1303)

Nomo	**yuwa-rra-p**	jayi-ngka=yi
NEG	put-IMP-CV	give-IMP=1EXC.MIN.NS

yapawurru,	jangkarni	jayi-ngka=yi.
small	big	give-IMP=1EXC.MIN.NS

"Don't give me a small amount, give me some more."
(🔈 VW: FM12_a183: 18:31min)

A number of coverbs in Gurindji also end with the suffix –*ap* or –*p*. Some examples are given below.

jakap	'sneak up'	*warrkap*	'dance'
pirrkap	'make'	*yikarap*	'touch lightly'
tarukap	'shower, swim'	*yurtap*	'hunt for kangaroo'
warlakap	'look around'	*yurtukap*	'shy of women'

This suffix originally derives from a Jarragan language in the north and is used to express an activity of some duration. Any aspectual qualities of this suffix are not clear in Gurindji. In a very few cases, this suffix seems to be productive, i.e. the base form of the coverb and the *–ap* form co-exist, for example *taruk* and *tarukap* 'swim'; *pirrka* and *pirrkap* 'make'; *japurr* and *japurrp* 'immerse'; *yurtuk* and *yurtukap* 'shy of women'. In one case, the suffix produces a meaning difference: *jarrak* 'shout at' and *jarrakap* 'talk'. However, in a majority of cases, the *-ap* suffix has fused to the coverb and the base form of the coverb no longer exists. For example, younger speakers of Gurindji now no longer use *taruk* or *pirrka.*

7.2.4.3 *-warrp* 'together'

This a curious suffix which is not very productive in that it only occurs on a few pairs of coverbs: *mijip* and *mijiwarrp* 'scrounge'; *mingip* and *mingiwarrp* 'crawl'; *paku* and *pakuwarrp* 'vomit'; and *tiirli* and *tiirliwarrp* 'light up'. Some further examples are given in (1304)–(1306). Note that in (1304), it appears on the outside of a locative suffix. It is also found in the infinitive form of the inflecting verb *panana* → *pa-nu-warrp.*

(1304) **Kalu-ngka-warrp**[207] ngu=rlaa ya-nku, kula=rlaa
walk-LOC-TOGETHER CAT=1INC.AUG.S go-POT NEG=1INC.AUG.S

yawarra ma-na-na Top Springs-kula.
rest do-IMPF-PRS place.name-LOC
"We'll go straight through; we won't have a break at Top Springs."
(McNair corpus: Meakins et al., 2016, p. 405)

(1305) **Jiwarrji-warrp** ma-nta=lu=nyunu murla-ngkawu.
gather-TOGETHER do-IMP=3AUG.S=RR this-PURP
"Gather yourselves together [for some purpose]."
(McConvell corpus: Meakins et al., 2016, p. 405)

(1306) **Kuli-warrp** ngu=lu=nyunu nya-nga-ni nyila
fight-TOGETHER CAT=3AUG.S=RR intake-IMPF-PST that

kaa-rni-mpa. Ngu=rnayinangkulu ya-nku karrap.
east-UP-PERL CAT=1EXC.AUG.S>3AUG.NS go-POT watch
"They were ready to fight each other on the eastside. We'll go over and watch them." (🔈 VW: FM10_a148: 13:15min)

207 Note also that this suffix appears on the outside of the case suffix so it could be a clitic.

The meaning of this suffix is not clear, but it possibly means 'together' or 'around'. There is a coverb in Gurindji *warrp* 'together' which may have grammaticalised. This coverb is found in non-Pama-Nyungan languages further north, for example the Mirndi language, Jaminjung and Jingulu. A related coverb *warrpa* is also found in Wardaman meaning 'numerous, many'. This is not the only coverb that may have grammaticalized recently. In §5.2.1, we described a cross-river suffix which attaches to directional terms that derives from the coverb *jarrk* 'cross river'.

7.2.4.4 Reduplication

Coverbs can be reduplicated to give an additional meaning of durative aspect (1307)–(1311), or encoding multiple objects (1312)–(1313).

(1307) **Wirra-wirra**, 'Kuwarl ma-nku=rli, jungkuwurru-wu=rla
spy-REDUP pretend do-POT=1INC.MIN.S echidna-DAT=3OBL

ngu walyak wanku, yala-ngka=rla ngu=rli yuwa-rru'.
CAT inside fall.POT that-LOC=3OBL CAT=1INC.MIN.S put-POT
"He looked around a few times, 'Let's pretend we're going for echidna, like that we can get him to go inside there'."
(🔈 DD: EC98_a014: Jalwa, Warlawurru, Kurlirrit: 1:54min)

(1308) **Jipu-jipu** ma-na-ni nganta warlu=ma,
extinguish-REDUP do-IMPF-PST ALLE fire=TOP

yalu-ngku=ma mungku-ku=ma.
that-ERG=TOP red-faced.turtle-ERG=TOP
"The turtle kept extinguishing the fire [but it kept flaring up]."
(🔈 VW: FM10_23_4: 6:17min)

(1309) **Lurr-lurr** ya-na-na ngu,
go.everywhere-REDUP go.IMPF-PRS CAT

nyila=ma ngarlaka wankaj maitbi.
that=TOP head no.good maybe
"He keeps going around all over the place. Maybe he's not good in the head."
(🔈 VW: FM12_a175: 5:20min)

(1310) Ngu=lu yala-ngka=rni pa-na-ni
CAT=3AUG.S that-LOC=ONLY hit-IMPF-PST

karnti-ku=warla **tampatampang** purrp.
stick-ERG=FOC dead.REDUP finish
"They killed lots of fish with a stick right there." (🔈 PN: McNair: K1H: 1:31min)
(Meakins, 2015b, p. 141)

(1311) Ngu=rla ma-rna-ni **jaajaaj**, "Jayi-ngka=yi=rla".
CAT=3OBL talk-IMPF-PST beg.REDUP give-IMP=1EXC.MIN.NS=3OBL
"She begged her again and again for it, 'Give it to me [so I can do it].'"
(🔈 VW: FM10_23_1b: 4:12min)

(1312) **Murrka-murrka** ngu=ja ka-nga-na kurrurij-jirri
drop.off-REDUP CAT=1EXC.UA.S take-IMPF-PRS car-ALL

na, nyila-rra na karnti yungkuj-karra-nginyi
FOC that-PL FOC wood cut.down-ITER-SOURCE

nyamu=ja pa-ni yapayapa.
REL=1EXC.UA.S hit-PST small
"We take the pieces of wood which we were chopping down to the car."
(🔈 VW: FM08_a101: 15:09min)

(1313) Wirnangpurru-wu=ma ngarina-wu=ma pulumanu-wu=ma
kangaroo-DAT=TOP meat-DAT=TOP cattle-DAT=TOP

ngu=rnalu **pila-pila** ma-ni.
CAT=1EXC.AUG.S chase-REDUP do-PST
"We chased around for kangaroos and cattle."
(McConvell 1996 grammar manuscript: Speaking to young people)

Where reduplication occurs, the whole form can be reduplicated, as shown in (1307)–(1309) and (1312)–(1312), or the coverb can be partially reduplicated (1310) and (1311). Partial reduplication takes a number of forms including the CVCV of the stem being prefixed to the stem, for example *juluj* becomes *julu-juluj* or the second CV is infixed into the stem, for example *partaj* becomes *pa-rta-rtaj*. Patterns of reduplication are discussed more in §2.3.6. Reduplication can also co-occur with the iterative marker, as shown in (1314).

(1314) **Kijikijik-karra** ngu ma-ni, yakyak-karra
tickle-ITER CAT do-PST burst.out.laughing-ITER

ngu yayip karrinyana.
CAT laugh be.IMPF.PRS
"He tickled him and [now] he's shrieking out with laughter."
(McConvell corpus: Meakins et al., 2016, p. 158)

Reduplication is now the frozen form for some coverbs where the durative meaning is inherent to the semantics, for example *jalarnjalarn* 'have an abundance of food', *jalngajalngaarra* 'hold up someone', *jamarlukmarluk* 'talk incessantly', *milyamilya* 'lag behind', *jilngjilng* 'seep', *jungjungkarra* 'tsk, tut' (*jungkarra* 'plan, plot') and *karrilili* 'rattle boomerangs'. The durative explanation does not make sense for other frozen forms. *Janguyunynguyuny* 'prepare ceremony ground', *jatajata* 'blame someone else', *jatijati* 'lift and give', *jikilikili* 'incite' and *jingijingi* 'crooked'.

7.2.4.5 *-k, -kuk, -kik, -k, -wuk, -irrik, -pijik* and *-pirrji* FACTitive

The factitive has many allomorphs which are lexicalised: *-k*, *-kik*, *-kuk*, *-wuk* (probably analysable as the dative *-ku* or *-wu* followed by *-k*), *-irrik*, *-pijik*,[208] and *-pirrji*.[209] Some examples are shown in Table 46. Note that although most seem to be associated with a single lexeme, there is one example of *patawan* occurring with both *-kik* (the only example with *-kik*, said by Violet Wadrill) (1322) and *-pirrji* (said by Smiler Major – 1959 Hale fieldnotes p. 81).

Table 46: Factitive allomorphs in Gurindji.[210]

Form	Gurindji examples	English gloss	Meaning
-k	*punyu-k*	'good-FACT'	'better'
	kalypa-k	'soft-FACT'	'soften'
	kungulu-k	'blood-FACT'	'bleed'
	pina-k	'know-FACT'	'teach'
	wurruja-k	'dry-FACT'	'dried out'
	jiwirri-k	'ripen-FACT'	'ripe'
-kik	*patawan-kik*	'hard-FACT'	'harden'

208 *-piji* is found in Mudburra.

209 The form *-pirrji* is from Malngin.

210 Note that it might not be the case that the different suffixes align with the morphemes they are suffixed to. It is possible that some are forms used by different speakers.

Table 46 (Continued)

Form	Gurindji examples	English gloss	Meaning
-kuk	*patawan-kuk*	'hard-FACT'	'harden'
	pulwarr-kuk	'dry-FACT'	'dried out'
	payal-kuk	'wide-FACT'	'widen'
	parntaly-kuk	'bend-FACT'	'bent'
-ik	*nyarlk-ik*	'push.down-FACT'	'wrestle'
-irrik	*wankaj-irrik*	'bad-FACT'	'worsen'
	pina-rrik	'know-FACT'	'teach'
-pijik	*nyangu-nyangu-pijik*	'doctor-FACT'	'make a doctor'
	kuliyan-pijik	'aggressive-FACT'	'make aggressive'
	minyirri-pijik	'shy-FACT'	'make shy'
-pirrji	*kuliyan pirrji*	'aggressive-FACT'	'make aggressive'
	winkilying-pirrji	'red-FACT'	'redden'
	warrngun-pirrji	'pain-FACT'	'make painful'
	ngayirrp-pirrji	'breathe-FACT'	'get out of breath'
	wanymarl-pirrji	'dry-FACT'	'dried out'
	patawan-pirrji	'hard-FACT'	'harden'
-wuk	*minyirri-wuk*	'shy-FACT'	'shame someone'

This suffix has been previously described as an inchoative, however we re-analyse it as a factitive suffix.[211] Factitive suffixes create coverbs which express the idea of making or rendering something in a certain way that they then take a direct object. On the other hand, inchoative suffixes denote the inception of something. The difference is between "make bleed" and "start bleeding", for example. A number of examples are given in (1315)–(1326).

(1315) Kuya-ngka kajijirri-lu=ma kamparra-jang-kulu=ma,
thus-LOC old.woman.REDUP-ERG=TOP before-TIME-ERG=TOP

ngu=lu=nyunu wirlpwirlpip-kulu pa-na-ni
CAT=3AUG.S=RR hit.in.grief.REDUP-ERG hit-IMPF-PST

wankaj-irrik ngarlaka=ma.
bad-FACT head=TOP
"That's when the women in the old days used to hit themselves with rocks to hurt their heads." (🔈 VW: FM11_a167: 2:53min)

211 Note that McConvell stands by its analysis as an inchoative.
212 This is a Nyininy word. The Gurindji equivalent is *punyu*.

(1316) Ngu=rnayinangulu wart ka-nga-na namawurru=ma
CAT=1EXC.AUG.S>3AUG.NS return take-IMPF-PST sugarbag=TOP

majul **yura**[212]**-k** kajirri.
stomach good-FACT old.woman
"We bring back the sugarbag to them make the old ladies feel better."
(TD: FM07_a028: 11:41min)

(1317) Ma-nku **nyangunyangu-pijik** Karrkany-ju.
do-POT doctor-FACT Chickenhawk-ERG
"Chickenhawk will make him into a doctor."
(McConvell corpus: Meakins et al., 2016, p. 188)

(1318) Jiya-rna-na wartartart nyamu=waa wurruja-k jiya-wu,
burn-IMPF-PRS dry.out.REDUP REL=REL dry-FACT burn-POT

ngu=rna kampa-wu na, **kuliyan-pirrji**.
CAT=1EXC.MIN.S cook-POT FOC bitter-FACT
"The sun will dry it out [the ashes] and when it is dry I will burn it to make it bitter." (VW: FM07_a089: 12:18min)

(1319) Ngawa-ngku yuwa-ni **parntaly-kuk**.
water-ERG put-PST bend-FACT
"The water made [a spear] bend."
(McConvell corpus: Meakins et al., 2016, p. 169)

(1320) **Pulwarr-kuk** jiya-wu talwirr-a=ma.
dry-FACT burn-POT hang-LOC=TOP
"It will get dry hanging up." (McConvell corpus: Meakins et al., 2016, p. 335)

(1321) Ngawa-ngku yu nou **wankaj-irrik** ma-ni.
water-ERG you know bad-FACT do-PST
"The water damaged it." (BW: FM08_11_2a: 15:40min)

(1322) Jayi-ngka=yi=lu=rla ngu=rna
give-IMP=1EXC.MIN.NS=3AUG.S=3OBL CAT=1EXC.MIN.S

yuwa-rru **patawan-kik**, mayarni-kari.
put-POT firm-FACT more-OTHER
"Give me some more [flour]. I want to make it firmer."
(VW: FM10_a151: 0:06min)

(1323) Walp-kulu ngu=yilu
go.toilet-ERG CAT=3AUG.S>1EXC.MIN.NS

nya-nga-na karrap **minyirri-pijik**.
intake-IMPF-PRS watch embarrassed-FACT
"They are watching me while they go to the toilet and making me embarrassed." (McConvell corpus: Meakins et al, 2016, p. 383)

(1324) Ngu=rna=nyunu pa-ni an mupiji nyawa na.
CAT=1EXC.MIN.S=RR hit-PST and swell.up this FOC

Kula=rna=nyunu pa-ni **kungulu-k**.
NEG=1EXC.MIN.S=RR hit-PST blood-FACT

Ngu=rna=nyunu pa-ni **warrngun-pirrji**.
CAT=1EXC.MIN.S=RR hit-PST ache-FACT
"I hit myself and it swells up. But I didn't make myself bleed. I just gave myself a headache." (🔊 VW: FM12_a175: 12:38min)

(1325) Mukurl-jayi-lu ngu=ngantipa **pina-k**
aunt-LATE-ERG CAT=1EXC.AUG.NS know-FACT

jayi-nga-ni ngantipa=ma, Katarl-lu, mukurl-rlang-ku.
give-IMPF-PST 1EXC.AUG=TOP NAME-ERG aunt-DYAD-DAT
"Our aunty Katarl who has passed away taught us as her nieces."
(🔊 VW: FM09_14_1a: 1:34min)

(1326) Ngayirra=rlaa[213] **punyu-k** ma-nku nyila=ma pakipaki=ma.
1EXC.UA=1INC.AUG.S good-FACT do-POT that=TOP chisel=TOP
"We will make the chisels sharp." (🔊 VW: FM07_a021: 6:01min)

Once a coverb has been derived using the factitive suffix, the stem receives coverb morphology such as *-karra*, as in (1327) and (1328), and ergatives in reduced subordinate clauses, as in (1329).

(1327) Mangarri=kata na **wurruja-k-karra** jiya-wu.
damper=IMM FOC dry-FACT-ITER burn-POT
"The damper will dry out." (🔊 VW: FM09_13_3b: 2:25min)

213 Normally you would expect a topic marker between the free and bound pronouns. This is an unusual example.

(1328) Wirlwirlp na ngu=nyunu pa-ni nyawa kuya wumara-lu.
hit.in.grief FOC CAT=RR hit-PST this thus stone-ERG

Kungulu-k ngu=nyunu pa-na-na pangkily-arra kuya.
bleed-FACT CAT=RR hit-IMPF-PRS hit.head-ITER thus

Jintaku-lu=ma nya-nga-na ngu wirlpip-kula=ma.
one-ERG=TOP intake-IMPF-PRS CAT hit.in.grief-LOC=TOP

'Warta ngu=n=junu pa-ni nyila **kungulu-k-karra**
hey CAT=2MIN.S=RR hit-PST that bleed-FACT-ITER

wirlpip,' 'pirrk jiya=rla init. Wumara pirrk jiya=rla.'
hit.in.grief snatch take=3OBL TAG stone snatch take=3OBL
"She hit herself with a rock. She is hitting herself on the head with a rock making herself bleed. One person sees her hitting herself. 'Goodness you're making yourself bleed hitting yourself on the head.' 'Take [the rock] from her. Grab the rock from her.'" (◀) TD: FM10_a165: 9:25min)

(1329) 'Ngarluk ma-ni ngu=n. Kula=n
miss do-PST CAT=2MIN.S NEG=2MIN.S

pa-ni **punyu-k-kulu**,' kuya.
hit-PST good-FACT-ERG thus
"'You missed it. You can't shoot properly,' he said."
(◀) VW: FM10_a152: 0:18min, 0:28min)

The *-k* form of the factitive is also used in Bilinarra, Ngarinyman, Malngin and Wanyjirra, although it is referred to as a translative in Wanyjirra (Ise, 1998, p. 46; Jones, Schultze-Berndt, Denniss, et al., 2019, p. 20; Meakins & Nordlinger, 2014, pp. 343–344; Senge, 2016, pp. 432–433). The forms *-piji*, *-yili* and *-pili* are found in Mudburra (Green et al., 2019, pp. 32, 53).

7.2.5 Coverbs and borrowing

The word class of coverbs is an open class and includes a large number of recent loanwords from the class of Kriol verbs. They are easily borrowed because both Kriol verbs and Gurindji coverbs are largely uninflected. These Kriol loanwords are fully integrated into Gurindji complete with Kriol morphology such as the transitive marker *-im*, atelic suffix *-bat* and adverbial suffixes e.g. *-ap* 'telic' (Meakins, 2016b; Schultze-Berndt, Meakins, & Angelo, 2013). The Kriol *-im* is not productive in Gurindji, but the others are. In Gurindji Kriol, all suffixes are productive (Meakins, 2010a, 2016b; Meakins & O'Shannessy, 2012). Note though that the Kriol suffix *-bat* and adverbial suffixes are not productive on Gurindji coverbs in either Gurindji or Gurindji Kriol. Some examples of their integration are given below in (1330)–(1333) and the references above discuss these code-switches and borrowings in more detail. The first example (1330) shows the equivalences between Gurindji coverbs and Kriol verbs.

(1330) **Kilkak** ngu=rnalu ma-na-na, kuya-ngku...
clean CAT=1EXC.AUG.S do-IMPF-PRS thus-ERG

kuya-ngku na ngu=rnalu ma-na-na **klin-im**.
thus-ERG FOC CAT=1EXC.AUG.S do-IMPF-PRS clean-TR
"We clean it off like this . . . Like this we clean (off the bark) . . ."
(🔊 VW: FM07_a058: 6:27min) (Meakins, 2010a, p. 29)

(1331) Nyawa nyampayila-yawung-kulu na wirriji-yawung-kulu
this whatsitcalled-PROP-ERG FOC hair.string-PROP-ERG

kartpi-yawung-kulu **tai-im-ap** ngu=lu
hair-PROP-ERG tie-TR-ATEL CAT=3AUG.S

ma-na-ni, kamparri-jang-kulu na.
do-IMPF-PST before-TIME-ERG FOC
"And in the old days, they used to tie it up with hair string."
(🔊 BW: FM06_06_2a: 6:30min)

(1332) Karrinyana ngu, Malapa-la **waruk** pa-na-na.
stay.IMPF.PRS CAT Limbunya-LOC work hit-IMPF-PRS
"He's staying at the old station and working there at old Limbunya Station homestead". (🔊 BR: FM15_52_1a: 11:42min)

(1333) Nya-ngka=yi=rla, kuya na ngu=rnalu
intake-IMP=1EXC.MIN.S=3OBL thus FOC CAT=1EXC.AUG.S

yus-im ma-na-na.
use-TR do-IMPF-PRS
"Look at me, this is how we use them." (🔊 VW: FM07_04_1d: 1:21min)

This integration of inflected Kriol verbs into the coverb 'slot' is a common phenomenon in the Victoria River District present in Jaminjung (Schultze-Berndt, 2007), Bilinarra (Meakins & Nordlinger, 2014, p. 347) and Wanyjirra (Senge, 2016, pp. 469–471).

7.3 Adverbs

Adverbs are a difficult part of speech to categorise and difficult to distinguish from coverbs and nominals. They share some properties with coverbs in that they modify the inflecting verb and are grammatically non-obligatory, however they can be distinguished from coverbs by the fact that they do not combine with the iterative suffix *-karra*. Adverbs also do not form subordinate clauses using case-markers (see §9.3.4). Adverbs can be case-marked, however this is a form of agreement which makes them more similar to nominals.[214] Nonetheless they do not fulfil core grammatical roles, which is a property of nominals. In this respect, they can be distinguished from nominals. Also, unlike nominals, case agreement is not obligatory. The following examples show adverbs marked ergative in agreement with transitive subjects (1334)–(1338).

(1334)	**Yamak-kulu**	ka-nga-na	kurrurij	**Jangari-lu**.
	slowly-ERG	take-IMPF-PRS	car	SUBSECT-ERG

"Jangari is driving the car slowly."
(McConvell corpus: Meakins et al., 2016, p. 435)

(1335)	**Narra-yawung-kulu**	ngu=rna	yirrirr
	hook-PROP-ERG	CAT=1EXC.MIN.S	pull.REDUP

ma-ni	kuya-ngku	yamak-kulu.
do-PST	thus-ERG	gently-ERG

"I pulled it out with the hooked stick very gently like this."
(🔈 VW: FM08_a099: 7:10min)

(1336)	**Jarrmip-kulu**	karu=ma	karrwa=yinangulu	kuya.
	together-ERG	child=TOP	hold=3AUG.S>3AUG.NS	thus

"You two look after the kids together." (🔈 VW: FM12_a172: 0:26min)

(1337)	**Kulmarrk-kulu**	ngu=n	ka-nga-na.
	go.fast-ERG	CAT=2MIN.S	take-IMPF-PRS

"You're driving too fast." (McConvell corpus: Meakins et al., 2016, p. 172)

(1338)	Kula=n	wumara-lu	wuya-wu	**wilyjiwilyjing-kulu=ma**.
	NEG=2MIN.S	stone-ERG	throw-POT	persistently-ERG=TOP

"Don't just keep chucking stones."
(RW & DD with ECh: Meakins et al., 2016, p. 412)

214 This is also observed in Warlpiri (Simpson, 1991, p. 204).

Some typical examples of adverbs are *lingi* 'persistent', *yipurrk* 'in vain', *majka* 'try',[215] *yamak* 'steadily, gently, slowly', *jirrimarna* 'intensely, loudly, fast', *wajija* 'quickly', *walyak* 'inside', *takurl* 'inside open container', *timpak* 'full', *ngumayila* 'rear, in the back, behind, go behind', *kamparri* 'in front, in front of, go first', *kamurr* 'in the middle, go past' and *julngurra* 'face away'.

(1339) Nyila=ma karu=ma lungkarrap ngu=rla karrinyana
that=TOP child=TOP cry CAT=3OBL be.IMPF.PRS

yipurrk. Nyila ngu=rla ka-nga-na lawart na.
in.vain that CAT=3OBL take-IMPF-PRS take.off FOC
"That kid is crying in vain. Someone took something from her."
(🔈 VW: FM12_a175: 0:03min)

(1340) **Majka** kungkarla-wu ngu=rnalu=rla nya-ngku.
try firestick.tree-DAT CAT=1EXC.AUG.S=3OBL intake-POT
"We'll try and look for firestick wood instead." (🔈 VW: FM09_a127: 4:28min)

(1341) Nyanawu pilyily yapakayi majul-a nyamu
RECOG pinky small stomach-LOC REL

ka-nga-na puul-a **walyak**.
take-IMPF-PRS pouch-LOC inside
"You know the hairless joey that is still in its mother's pouch."
(🔈 VW: FM09_a123: 6:27min)

(1342) Ma-nyja=rla **jirrimarna**, nyirn-pari langa ngu.
talk-IMP=3OBL loud deaf-ADJ ear CAT
"Speak up [when] talking to him, he's half-deaf."
(DD with ECh: Meakins et al., 2016, p. 295)

(1343) Nga-rna-ni purrp-karra **kamurrkamurra**=rni.
eat-IMPF-PST finish-ITER middle.REDUP=ONLY
"He was finishing all of the food half-way back."
(🔈 VW: FM10_a155: Ngarlking Karu: 5:40min)

215 Note that we have no examples of *majka* 'try' appearing with an ergative so it might not be an adverb.

8 Syntax of main clauses

Main clauses consist of a single clause without subordinate or coordinate clauses. Gurindji has two basic clause types (divided according to their predicators): verbless clauses (§8.2) and verbal clauses (§8.4). A verbal clause has a finite inflecting verb (possibly combined with a coverb) as a predicate, and a verbless clause has a nominal or coverb as a predicate, with no inflecting verb. We also include a discussion of possession after the verbless clause section since it is a type of nominal predication (§8.3). We begin with a discussion of configurationality, i.e. word order, and the status of nominals versus bound pronouns since the properties of languages such as Gurindji have figured prominently in the theoretical literature on this topic.

8.1 Non-configurationality

Gurindji exhibits all of the properties of non-configurationality, first observed by Hale (1983) for Warlpiri[216] and since described for many other Australian languages including Jiwarli (Austin, 2001), Wambaya (Nordlinger, 1998a) and Jingulu (Pensalfini, 2004). First, word order is relatively free. In the case of Warlpiri and Wambaya, constituents can occur in any order as long as the auxiliary containing pronominal clitics remains in second position (Hale, 1983, p. 6; Nordlinger, 1998a, p. 28). Similarly, in Gurindji the ordering of constituents is flexible, and determined by discourse principles, as discussed in §6.2.6. For example, (1344) and (1345) are transitive clauses with overtly expressed subjects and objects. Yet in (1344) the A argument occurs clause finally and in (1345) it occurs clause initially. The ergative case marker distinguishes the A and O arguments in these clauses, rather than word order.

(1344)

Kawarla	pirrkap	ma-ni	ngu	kaput-pa=rni
coolamon	make	do-PST	CAT	morning-EP=ONLY

ngayiny-ju	**marluka-lu**.
1EXC.MIN.DAT-ERG	man-ERG

"My husband made the coolamon early in the morning."
(🔈 BW: FM07_04_1d: 0:33min)

(1345)

Marluka-lu=ma	**yalu-ngku**=ma	ngalyakap-kaji
old.man-ERG=TOP	that-ERG=TOP	lick-AGENT

216 Laughren (1989) also outlines the features of non-configurationality in detail for Warlpiri.

https://doi.org/10.1515/9783110746884-008

jak wuya-rni ngu tak-kaji-la.
drop throw-PST CAT sit-AGENT-LOC
"That man dropped the icecream on the chair." (🔊 BW: FM07-a043: 21:07min)

Non-configurational languages differ from configurational languages with respect to word order. Configurational languages such as English are hierarchically organised, with grammatical functions associated with particular phrase structure positions. For example, the object is a daughter of V' (and a sister to the verb) whereas the subject is a daughter of the node above the maximal projection dominating the verb and object, namely S (or IP). These phrase structure positions are reflected in the strict ordering of basic sentences. In particular, constituency tests such as pseudo-cleft demonstrate that the verb and the object form a single constituent, for example [*Throw the rock into the water*] *is what he did.* In contrast, there are no tests which provide evidence for similar constituent structures in non-configurational languages. Examples (1346) and (1347) also demonstrate that the verb and object do not need to be contiguous in Gurindji, since in these examples the modifiers of the transitive subject occur between them.

(1346) **Karu-kirlikirlaj** **parnngirri**, ngu=lu
child-TOY bark CAT=3AUG.S

pirrkap **ma-na-ni** karu-ngku.
make do-IMPF-PST child-ERG
"The kids used to make bark dolls." (🔊 VW: FM11_a169: 1:06min)

(1347) **Kayi-kayi** **pa-na-na** karu-ngku **nyawa** **jamut**.
chase-REDUP hit-IMPF-PRS child-ERG this bush.turkey
"The kid is chasing this bush turkey." (🔊 BW: FM07_a043: 4:00min)

Word order in non-configurational languages such as Warlpiri and Gurindji is largely determined by information structure rather than phrasal structure. In particular, the left periphery of the clause is generally associated with prominent information (Simpson, 2007, p. 420 using Choi's (1999) model of information structure). In Warlpiri, the second position pronominal clitic provides a transition between more and less prominent information. A similar analysis of Gurindji can be made. Where pronominal clitics occur, the constituents to their left are accorded prominence, for example 'bark doll' in (1346). Even where pronominal clitics are not present, as for third person minimal pronouns, constituents are placed at the front of the sentence to receive prominence. An example is 'coolamon' found in (1344) (§6.2.6.2).

Another property Hale (1983) observed for Warlpiri, which he considered a defining feature of non-configurationality, was the presence of discontinuous noun phrases, that is nominals which refer to an entity but which are separated by other constituents. This is a feature which Gurindji shares with Warlpiri. As in Warlpiri, discontinuous nominals are related through case-marking in Gurindji. For example, in (1348) 'that woman' is referred to by two nominals which are found at opposite ends of the clause. Case concord and topic-marking agreement indicate that both nominals are referring to the same entity. Either nominal may be interpreted as the (semantic) head and, as a result, the clause may be interpreted in two ways: *That girl is looking at something* or *That girlish one is looking at something* (indeed *janka* refers to a mermaid in this example). An adjunct interpretation is also possible: *That one was looking at something, and she (that one) is a woman.* Similarly, *warlu* 'fire' and *tumpiyi* 'warmth' are discontinuous, giving different possible interpretations as well (§4.1.3).

(1349)	**Yalu-ngku=ma**	ngu	karrap=ma	nya-nga-ni	**janka-ku=ma.**
	that-ERG=TOP	CAT	look=TOP	intake-IMPF-PST	woman-ERG=TOP

"That mermaid was looking at something."
(Charola texts: DB: No source found)

(1350)	**Warlu-ngka**	ngu=rna	tanyjik	karrinyana	**tumpiyi-la.**
	fire-LOC	CAT=1EXC.MIN.S	warm.up	be.IMPF.PRS	warm-LOC

"I am sitting next to the warm fire." (◀) VW: FM12_a178: 13:14min)

Finally, NP arguments and adjuncts can be freely omitted (i.e. 'null anaphora' (Kenneth Hale, 1983)) with bound pronominal clitics obligatory (where grammatically appropriate), as shown in (1350) where the A and O argument NPs are omitted with these grammatical relations expressed by a complex pronominal clitic. Pronominal clitics always occur either alone, or doubled by a coreferential NP, as demonstrated in (1351) where the A and O arguments are expressed by both overt NPs *yarrulan-tu kujarra-lu* 'two men' and *nyila kartipa* 'those non-Indigenous people' and a pronominal clitic *=yinangkulu* 'they do it to them'.

(1350)	Kula	**ngantipa**=rni	kamparri-jang-kulu=ma=**yinangulu**
	NEG	1EXC.AUG.NS=ONLY	before-TIME-ERG=TOP=3AUG.S>3AUG.NS

kuya	na	ka-nga-ni.
thus	FOC	take-IMPF-PST

"Not only us now but they used to carry them around in the old days."
(◀) VW: FM07_02_1c: 1:15min)

(1351)	Ngu=**yinangkulu**$_{A,O}$	[**nyila=ma**	**kartipa=ma**]$_O$	kaarra-yin-ta
	CAT=3AUG.S>3AUG.NS	that=TOP	non-Indigenous=TOP	east-ABL-LOC

nya-nga-ni [**yarrulan-tu kujarra-lu**]A.
intake-IMPF-PST young.man-ERG two-ERG
"The two young men were watching the *kartipa* from the west."
(🔈 RW: EC98_a027: 6:44min)

There are a number of other contexts where arguments are not expressed by a pronominal clitic regardless of whether or not they are third minimal, for example cognate objects (1352), inanimate or non-sentient non-singular arguments (1353) and (1356), the direct object of a ditransitive verb (1354), even if it is animate (1355). For example, (1355) cannot mean 'I'm going to give them to my sons-in-law'. Additionally, some adjuncts such as animate beneficiaries are registered as pronominal clitics even though they are not a part of the thematic grid of the clause. In (1356) the inanimate object does not register on the catalyst even though it is plural, however the animate beneficiary =*yi* 'me' is found. In this respect, the use of pronominal clitics is more related to animacy rather than to argument structure (see §6.2.4).

(1352) Ngu=wula wanyja-na-na[217] na wamala-kujarra-lu yarti-ngka.
CAT=3UA.S leave-IMPF-PRS FOC girl-DU-ERG shade-LOC
"The two girls [are dancing] in the shade." (🔈 BW: FM07-a043: 20:32min)

(1353) Juwal-nginyi=ma, kujarra ngu=rna pirrkap ma-na-na.
long-SOURCE=TOP two CAT=1EXC.MIN.S make do-IMPF-PRS
"Out of a long one, I make two pieces." (🔈 VW: FM08-a101: 8:57min)

(1354) Ngu=rna=yina jayi-ngku
CAT=1EXC.MIN.S=3AUG.NS give-POT

ngayiny-ku mali-wu.
1MIN.DAT-DAT son.in.law-DAT
"I'm going to give it to my sons-in-law." (🔈 VW: FM07-a05-1a: 7:32min)

(1355) Ngu=rna=yina=rla jayi-ngku
CAT=1EXC.MIN.S=3AUG.NS=3OBL give-POT

ngayiny-ku mali-wu.
1MIN.DAT-DAT son.in.law-DAT
"I'm going to give it to my son-in-laws [so they can cut it]."
*'I'm going to give them to my son-in-laws.'

217 Note that the expression of 'dance' is usually *warrkap wanyjanana* 'dance leave', however *wanyjanana* 'leave' on its own can also mean 'dance' if the context is clear.

(1356) Nyila-rra=ma, parnngirri=ma wartartart
that-PL=TOP bark=TOP dry.REDUP

jiya-rna-na ngu=yi.
burn-IMPF-PRS CAT=1EXC.MIN.S
"[The sun] is drying those pieces of bark out for me."
(🔊 VW: FM08-a089: 12:14min)

The only situation where overt nominals are grammatically obligatory is to express direct objects when the object pronoun refers to benefactives or malefactives. The overt nominal is required to ensure the bound pronominal is not interpreted as the object.[218] For example, without the overt object nominal, (1356) would be ambiguous: '(The sun) is drying it out for me' (benefactive reading) or '(The sun) is drying me out' (object reading). Similarly, without the overt object nominal, (1357) could mean 'We'll gather it for them' (benefactive reading) or 'We'll muster them' (object reading). Some further examples are given in (1358) and (1359).

(1357) Jiwarrp ngu=rnayinangulu ma-na-na <u>bush-medicine</u>.
muster CAT=1EXC.AUG.S>3AUG.NS get-IMPF-PRS bush-medicine
"We'll gather together the bush medicine for them."
(🔊 VW: FM09-a14-1a: 7:26min)

(1358) Ngana=ngku ma-rni partaj-ku yala-ngkawu=ma ngarin
who=2MIN.NS talk-PST climb-DAT that-PURP=TOP meat

ngu=yi=n ngayiny purrp jiya-rna-na.
CAT=1EXC.MIN.NS=2MIN.S 1EXC.MIN.DAT finish steal-IMPF-PRS
"Who told you to climb up there? You are stealing the meat off me."
(🔊 DD: McNair_C2A: 3:51min)

(1359) "Ngaja=**yi=n-ku=rla** kirt
ADMON=1EXC.MIN.S=2MIN.S-EP=3OBL break

yuwa-na-na," ngu=rla ma-rna-ni.
put-IMPF-PRS CAT=3OBL say-IMPF-PST
"'You might break it on me,' she was saying to her."
(🔊 VW: FM10_23_1b: Yawarlwarl Wanyil: 3:54min)

218 Given that this claim is based on production data, it is not clear whether this observation represents a grammatical constraint or a pragmatic imperative. Grammaticality judgement tests have not been conducted to test this claim. Nonetheless, given how easily NPs are omitted, it is striking that objects are never found omitted in these benefactive constructions.

8.2 Verbless clauses

Like most Australian languages, clauses in Gurindji can have non-verbal predicates. Verbless clauses generally consist of a nominal predicate and a subject (in nominative case), but may also consist of a coverb predicate, as shown in §8.2.2 below. Where the subject is human, it must also be expressed by a pronominal clitic, usually attached to a topic-marked demonstrative or free pronoun in first position. Other non-human subjects may also be expressed by a pronominal clitic in some circumstances, as discussed in §6.2.4. No copula is needed although a copula (*karrinyana* 'to be, sit') can be used in existential constructions and in non-present tense contexts (see §8.2.5). Generally, though, these types of clauses do not have an inflecting verb (§6.1) and therefore do not express tense, aspect or mood. Tense information is given by the context, usually the surrounding discourse or the discourse participants' own mutual knowledge of events. Uttered in isolation, verbless clauses usually refer to present time. For example, (1360) has no verb and is assumed to be present tense in the habitual use of this tense, whereas (1361) explicitly has a verb placing the statement into past time.

(1360) Kaa-rni-mpal-a nyawa=ma jarrwa Cattle Creek-mayin=ma.
east-UP-EDGE-LOC this=TOP many place.name-PERL=TOP
"Ones [which are] from east near Cattle Creek station."
(🔈 VW: FM10_23_3: 3:30min)

(1361) Jangaminyji-mayin=ma **karrinyani** jarrwa kuya-rniny-nganang.
place.name-PERL=TOP be.IMPF.PST many thus-HITH-AXIS
"There used to be heaps around Jangaminyji." (🔈 VW: FM18_a507: 7:38min)

Verbless clauses are of four types: ascriptive (§8.2.1), local (§8.2.2), having/lacking constructions (§8.2.3) and possessive (§8.2.4). As well as these clauses, there is another type of verbless clause which contains what will be referred to as a nominal predicator (§8.2.6). Nominal predicators are similar to verbs in that they select non-subject arguments. As with other types of sentences, the word order of verbless clauses is determined by discourse level information rather than syntactic structure. The subject and predicate can be found in either order, with the constituent in focus usually found in first position.

8.2.1 Ascriptive clauses

The predicate of an ascriptive clause describes the subject as having a certain property. It can be a noun, for example (1362)–(1366), or an adjective, for example (1367)–(1370). In these clauses, both the subject and predicate are in nominative case.

(1362) **Puwarraja** **yurrk**[219] nyawa=ma.
Dreaming tell.story this=TOP
"This is a Dreaming story." (🔊 DD: McNair_C2B: 5:05min)[219]

(1363) Palarni ngu=rna **nguku-murlung-kaji**.
BETTER CAT=1EXC.MIN.S grog-PRIV-AGENT
"At least I'm not a drinker." (CE with FM: Meakins et al., 2016, p. 301)

(1364) Nyawa=ma **wartiwarti-said** ngu **karu=ma.**
this=TOP left.handed-side CAT child=TOP
"This is a left-handed child." (🔊 BW: FM10_a143: 9:09min)

(1365) Nyila=ma **kayili-yarra-ngarna** **jaru.**
that=TOP north-SIDE-ASSOC language
"That's from the northern language." (🔊 VW: FM11_a162: 1:35min)

(1366) **Kankula**=warla nyawa=ma wulngarn=ma.
up=FOC this=TOP sun=TOP
"The sun is high." (🔊 PN: McNair_K2G: 0:42min)

(1367) **Kuliyan** ngiing-kaji=ma kuya-ny-ja=ma.
aggressive buzz-AGENT=TOP thus-NMLZ-LOC=TOP
"Mosquitoes are aggressive in this kind of place." (🔊 VW: FM10_a152: 5:34min)

(1368) Nyila=ma **kuliyan** kartiya=ma.
that=TOP aggressive non-Indigenous=TOP
"He was a nasty *kartiya*." (🔊 DD: EC98_a023: 1:25min)

(1369) Maitbi=nga **punyu** nyawa=ma marluka=ma.
maybe=DUB good this=TOP old.man=TOP
"That old man might be generous." (🔊 RW: EC98_a015: 9:45min)

219 *Yurrk* 'recount/story' is both a coverb and a noun, but acts as a noun in this clause.

(1370)

Nyuntu	ngu=n	**jangkarni**	nyawa	kuya	**jangkarni**.
2MIN	CAT=2MIN.S	big	this	thus	big

Ngayu=ma	ngu=rna	**yapawurru**.	Nyuntu
1EXC.MIN=TOP	CAT=1EXC.MIN.S	small	2MIN

ngu=n	**pakajirri**	kuli-ngka=ma.
CAT=2MIN.S	good.fighter	fight-LOC=TOP

"You, you're big. But me, I'm small. You're a good fighter in fights."
(🔈 VW: FM10_a154: 1:56min)

Specific types of ascriptive clauses include (i) part-whole clauses where the predicate refers to a part of the subject, as in (1371), (ii) type-subtype clauses where the predicate refers to a subtype of the subject, as exemplified by (1372), and (iii) purposive ascriptive clauses where the predicate consists of a dative-marked non-finite verb, most often a coverb, which refers to the function or purpose of the subject, as shown in (1373) and (1374).

(1371)

Mila	wankaj	ngayu=ma.
eye	bad	1EXC.MIN=TOP

"I have bad eyes." (McConvell corpus: Meakins et al., 2016, p. 235)

(1372)

Nyila=ma	karnti=ma	kilipi.
that=TOP	tree=TOP	bush.banana

"That tree is a bush banana." (FM Analogical Construct)

(1373)

Kupuwupu=ma	nyila=ma	janga-ngka-wu,	kulyurrkap-kaji-wu,
lemon.grass=TOP	that=TOP	sick-LOC-DAT	cough-AGENT-DAT

kulykulya-wu,	ngarlaka-wu	nyampa-wu	tarukap-ku.
congestion-DAT	head-DAT	what-DAT	bathe-DAT

"Lemon grass is good as a cough medicine for coughs or a stuffed-up head. It's also good to bathe in." (🔈 VW: FM08_a089: 2:03min)

(1374)

Nyawa	marntaj	ngu=yi	nyawa=ma	partaj-ku=ma.
this	OK	CAT=1EXC.MIN.NS	this=TOP	climb-DAT=TOP

"This will be fine for me to climb." (🔈 DD: McNair_C2A: 2:12min)

8.2.2 Local clauses

This type of verbless clause has a predicate marked with either the locative (1375), ablative (1376), source (1377) or perlative case suffix.

(1375) Jarrwalut **yala-ngka=ma** **wirrnginy-ja=ma** **parntarl-a=ma**
many that-LOC=TOP goanna.burrow-LOC=TOP goanna.burrow-LOC=TOP
"Lots of them live there in burrows." (◀) TD: FM11_a169: 0:59min)

(1376) Warlu warlu=rni nyawa=ma **kurla-yin**.
fire fire=ONLY this=TOP south-ABL
"There was only fire coming from the south." (◀) PN: McNair_K1E: 5:23min)

(1377) **Murla-nginyi** **mana-nginyi** nyawa=ma.
this-SOURCE root-SOURCE this=TOP
"This [bush onion] is from the root of the plant." (◀) VW: FM07_a058: 1:58min)

Time rather than location can also be indicated in these clauses, as shown in (1379).

(1378) Nyawa=ma ngu=ngalang **purunyjirri** na.
this=TOP CAT=1INC.AUG.NS late FOC
"It's late for us now." (◀) BW: FM09_a119: 2:27min)

8.2.3 Having/Lacking clauses

The predicate of these verbless clauses has a nominal inflected with adnominal case, either *-jawung/-yawung* 'PROPrietive' (1379)–(1383) (§4.6.2.1) or *-murlung* 'PRIVative' (1384)–(1385) (§4.6.3). These constructions are similar to ascriptive clauses as they assign a property to the subject of the clause.

(1379) Karlirriyinyja nyila=ma ngumpit=ma, **jarrwa-yawung** **kirri-yawung.**
polygamist that=TOP man=TOP many-PROP woman-PROP
"A polygamist is a man with many wives." (◀) VW: FM11_a161: 4:40min)

(1380) Julurrk warlaku=ma nyila=ma,
pregnant.dog dog=TOP that=TOP

nanta-nanta-yawung, **ngarturr-jawung**.
small-REDUP-PROP pregnant-PROP
"A pregnant dog is a dog carrying pups." (◀) VW: FM12_a173: 11:27min)

(1381) Karrap yijarni nyawa=ma. Billabong **ngawa-yawung**.
look true this=TOP billabong water-PROP
"True have a look here. A billabong with water."
(◀) VW: FM09_13_2d: 0:06min)

(1382) Kanimparra nyawa=ma **kuwart-jawung**=ma.
downstream this=TOP gorge-PROP=TOP
"Downstream is the place with a gorge." (🔈 TD: FM07_a058: 0:10min)

(1383) Warta yijarni-yijarni langkarna. Langkarna **ngawa-yawung.**
hey true-REDUP billabong billabong water-PROP
"Hey true there's a billabong. A billabong full of water!"
(🔈 VW: FM09_13_2f: 0:36min)

(1384) Tangka-la nyila=ma parnngirri=ma **mangarri-murlu.**
empty-LOC that=TOP dish=TOP veg.food-PRIV
"There's nothing in that dish, no tucker."
(🔈 RW: EC98_a015: Marlarluka: 18:11min)

(1385) **Ngawa-murlung ngawa-murlung** nyawa=ma ngurra=ma.
water-PRIV water-PRIV this=TOP camp=TOP
"The country was in drought." (🔈 PN: McNair_K2H: 0:29min)

Another way of expressing the meaning of 'lacking' in a verbless clause is to use the interjection *lawara* which negates whole clause, as shown in (1386).

(1386) Jala=ma=rnalu wumara=ma **lawara!**
today=TOP=1EXC.AUG.S money=TOP nothing
"We don't have any money today!" (Meakins, 2013)

8.2.4 Predicative possession

In possessive verbless clauses, the subject is the possessee and the predicate is the possessor or a possessive phrase. The possessor, either a nominal or a free pronoun is inflected with a dative case suffix if it is alienable (1387)–(1389). Alienable possession is discussed further in §8.3.2. The possessor is also cross-referenced by a non-subject pronominal clitic if it is a possessive dissension construction (1391)–(1394). These constructions are discussed in some detail in §8.3.3.

(1387) Kula **ngayiny** yumi.
NEG 1EXC.MIN.DAT law
"That's not right in my law." (McConvell corpus: Meakins et al., 2016, p. 453)

(1388) Nyila=ma **karu-wu yalu-wu** na.
that=TOP child-DAT that-DAT FOC
"That place is for that child." (🔈 VW: FM10_a151: 4:22min)

(1389) Nyawa=ma=nga **ngayiny** papa.
this=TOP=DUB 1EXC.MIN.DAT brother
"This might be my brother." (🔈 DD: McNair_F2A: 8:55min)

(1390) **Ngumpit-ku** na **ngu=rla** nyawa=ma ngurra=ma.
Aboriginal-DAT FOC CAT=3OBL this=TOP land=TOP
"This is Aboriginal land." (🔈 PN: McNair_D2A: 3:44min)

(1391) Nyawa=ma yatu=ma **ngaliwany=ma=rlaa**
this=TOP white.ochre=TOP 1INC.AUG.DAT=TOP=1INC.AUG.S

kuya-ny nyawa **ngumpit-ku**=ma kuya.
thus-NMLZ this Aboriginal-DAT=TOP thus
"This white ochre [is a part of] our [culture]." (🔈 VW: FM08_a100: 1:38min)

(1392) Nyila=ma **ngantipanguny** ngurra=ma
that=TOP 1EXC.AUG.DAT country=TOP

ngu=**ngantipa** nineteen bore kankarra.
CAT=1EXC.AUG.NS nineteen bore upstream
"That country at Number 19 bore which is upstream belongs to us."
(🔈 VW: LIM07_030913: 0:47min)

(1393) Ngantipa=ma kurla-yarra-side-ta=ma Nama na
1EXC.AUG=TOP south-SIDE-SIDE-LOC=TOP Bee FOC

Dreaming=ma ngu=**ngantipa** **ngantipanguny**=ma.
Dreaming=TOP CAT=1EXC.AUG.NS 1EXC.AUG.DAT=TOP
"Us mob are on the south side (of the river). The Bee Dreaming belongs to us."
(🔈 VW: LIM07_030913: 2:13min)

In the case of inalienable possession, the possessor cannot be referred to using a free dative pronoun but is cross-referenced by a bound pronoun, as in (1394). Inalienable possession is discussed further in §8.3.1.

(1394) Karu-ngku ngu=**yi**$_{PSR}$ pat-pat
child-ERG CAT=1EXC.MIN.S feel-REDUP

ma-ni **wartan**$_{PSM}$ **ngayu**$_{PSR}$.
do-PST hand 1EXC.MIN
"The child feels my hand." (🔈 VW: FM14_a228: 10:36min)

8.2.5 Use of *karrinyana* 'sit, be' as a copula

As demonstrated in the examples in previous sections, it is possible for a clause to have no inflecting verb, but to use a nominal or coverb as a predicate instead. However, many clauses also use the inflecting verb *karrinyana* 'sit, be' as a copula in an existential construction. The use of *karrinyana* as a copula also allows the encoding of temporal information. For example, all of the examples of the verbless clauses discussed in the previous sections are implicitly in the present tense. When the speaker wants to express a different temporal frame, *karrinyana* is used with the appropriate tense inflection, for example past tense (1395)–(1396) or potential mood (1397)–(1398):

(1395) Ngapulunypuluny=ma nyila na kankarra. Ngapulu
place.name=TOP that FOC upstream Milk

Dreaming. Mangaya **karrinya** ngu=yina.
Dreaming Dreaming be.PST CAT=3AUG.NS
"Ngapulunypuluny is further upstream. It's a Milk Dreaming. It was their Dreaming [for the Dreaming children]." (🔈) VW: FM10_a151: 4:22min)

(1396) Tanku-murlung ngu=rna **karrinya** ngarin-murlung.
food-PRIV CAT=1EXC.MIN.S be.PST meat-PRIV
"I was really hungry, without any meat to eat."
(Appendix: Fishing story: Text 2, Line 21)

(1397) Ngu=rna **karru** janga-murlung.
CAT=1EXC.MIN.S be.POT sick-PRIV
"I won't be sick then." (🔈) TD: FM09_17_2d: 0:55min)

(1398) Ngu puya jangkarni **karru**.
CAT body big be.POT
"[The antbed treatment] makes the body become strong."
(🔈) VW: FM07_a085: 3:04min)

The use of *karrinyana* also conveys a sense of residence, either long term or temporary, for example (1399).

(1399) Panyja-witi-ngka **karrinya** warrija=ma nyila=ma.
river.edge-SITE-LOC be.PST crocodile=TOP that=TOP
"That crocodile lived in this habitat." (🔈) VW: FM12_a183: 23:23min)

8.2.6 Nominal predicators

Nominal predictors behave like verbs in that they may subcategorise for an object (in the accusative case) or an indirect object (in the dative case), as shown in (1400)–(1402). Their subject is always in nominative case. Nominal predicators often express concepts that are typically associated with the category of stative verbs in other languages (such as English) (Hale, 1982, p. 220). The only examples we have in the Gurindji corpus are *pina* 'knowing' and *pinarri* 'knowledgeable'.

(1400)

Ngarnjal	**pina**	ngu=rla.
NAME	know	CAT=3OBL

"Topsy knows about it." (🔈 VW: FM08_11_2c: 7:54min)

(1401)

An	ngu=rna=wuliny	**pina**	yalu-wu=ma,
and	CAT=1EXC.MIN.S=3UA.NS	know	that-DAT=TOP

Walyji	kuya-ny-ku=ma	Ajarraman-ku=ma.
NAME	thus-NMLZ-DAT=TOP	NAME-DAT=TOP

"And I knew about those two who were called Walyji and Ajarraman."
(🔈 VW: FM10_22_1a: 0:27min)

(1402)

Pinarri	ngu=n	nyuntu=ma.
knowledgeable	CAT=2MIN.S	2MIN=TOP

"You know [how to do this]." (🔈 VW: FM09_17_2a: 2:16min)

Like other verbless clauses, they can take the *karrinyana* 'be' verb in different tenses to express time periods other than the present. Compare (1400)–(1401) with (1403).

(1403)

Kartiya=ma	kula=rla	**pina**	**karrinya**	yalu-wu=ma
non-Indigenous=TOP	NEG=3OBL	know	be.PST	that-DAT=TOP

marluka-wu=ma	nyamu	ngawa	pirrka	ma-ni.
old.man-DAT=TOP	REL	water	make	do-PST

"The *kartiya* didn't know that the old man-made rain."
(McConvell corpus: Meakins et al., 2016, p. 322)

8.3 Attributive possession

There are a number of different ways to express possession in Gurindji, including the use of the proprietive suffix (1404)–(1405) (§4.6.2.1), a number of possessive suffixes specific to kinship terms (§4.4). The inflecting verb *karrwarnana* 'hold, keep' is used for predicative possession (1406) (§8.2.4). This section just deals with attributive possession.

(1404) Kula nga-lu yiparrartu du, **karu-yawung**-kulu=ma.
NEG eat-POT emu too child-PROP-ERG=TOP
"An expectant mother can't eat emu either." (🔈 VW: FM09_a123: 15:57min)

(1405) Kamparri-jang wanyja-ni **karu-walija-yawung**=ma.
before-TIME leave-PST child-PAUC-PROP=TOP
"A long time ago, he left the female emu there with her kids."
(🔈 VW: FM09_15_2a: 3:47min)

(1406) Jarrwa kirri **karrwa-rna-ni** ngu=yina karu jintaku.
many woman have-IMPF-PST CAT=3AUG.NS child one
"He had many wives and one child." (🔈 DD: McNair_C2B: 0:11min)

Like all Ngumpin languages, Gurindji also expresses possession using the dative case suffix. The dative is used to express alienable relationships, as will be discussed in §8.3.2. Gurindji also uses bound pronouns to express inalienable relationships, as will be shown in §8.3.1. Unusally Gurindji also has a third possessive construction called possessor dissension where the possessor is both dative-marked and cross-referenced by a bound pronoun. In this respect it is a hybrid of alienable and inalienable constructions. These are discussed in §8.3.3 and have been described extensively in Meakins and Nordlinger (2017) which we draw on in this grammar. We summarise the different constructions in Table 47 (also in comparison with benefactives which have a lot of structural overlap with possessor dissension).

Table 47: Summary of features of constructions.

Construction	Case on possessor	Bound pronoun cross-references	Grammatical function of bound pronoun	Function of construction
Inalienable possession	core	possessor only (argument of verb)	subject, non-subject (depending on grammatical relation of possessor)	possessum is a body part, shadow, image, name
Alienable possession	dative	whole possessive phrase (argument of verb)	subject, non-subject (depending on grammatical relation of possessive phrase)	possessum is all other potentially possessed objects

Table 48 (Continued)

Possessor dissension	dative	possessor (oblique) *and* whole possessive phrase	*possessor*: oblique only *possessive phrase*: subject, non-subject (depending on grammatical function)	preferred construction for human possessors of alienable possessums
Benefactive/ Malefactive	dative	beneficiary/ maleficiary (adjunct)	oblique only (always an adjunct)	introduces a beneficiary/ maleficiary of an event

8.3.1 Inalienable possession

Inalienable possessive constructions mark "an indissoluble connection between two entities" (Chappell & McGregor, 1995, p. 4). Cross-linguistically part-whole relationships usually involve inherent or unchangeable relationships between the possessor and possessed, for example the relationship between animate entities and their body parts, kin, position in space or closely associated objects such as tools. In Gurindji, inalienable possession marks relations involving body parts (1407), images (1408), reflections (1409), shadows and personal names (1410), but not kin.

(1407) Tamarra-yawung-kulu, **ngarlaka,** **majul**
antbed-PROP-ERG head stomach

ngu=rna**yina**ngulu kampa-rna-na.
CAT=1EXC.AUG.S>3AUG.NS cook-IMPF-PRS
"We cover their heads and tummies with the antbed."
(🔊 VW: FM07_a085: 6:48min)

(1408) Yarti ngu=**yina**ngkulu ma-ni **karu-kujarra** winkilying.
photo CAT=3AUG.S>3AUG.NS do-PST child-DU coloured
"They took a colour photograph of the two children."
(McConvell corpus: Meakins et al., 2016, p. 440)

(1409) Ngu=**nyunu** nya-nga-na **yarti.**
CAT=RR intake-IMPF-PRS reflection
"He's looking at his reflection."
(McConvell corpus: Meakins et al., 2016, p. 439)

(1410) “Kurruman=ma, kuya ngu=**nyunu**-ngku=rla **yini** ma-rna-ni.
NAME=TOP thus CAT=RR-EP=3OBL name talk-IMPF-PST
“He called himself that name Kurruman.” (🔊) BB: McNair_H2D: 3:30min)

Disembodied body parts are marked alienable. In (1411), the non-subject pronoun cross-references the beneficiary, not the disembodied hand:

(1411) **Nyila** **wartan** marluka-wu yalu-wu kurnpirlirn-ku
that hand old.man-DAT that-DAT spiritual.healer-DAT

ngu=lu=**rla** jayi-nya “Nyawa=warla ka-ngka.”
CAT=3AUG.S=3OBL give-PST this=FOC take-IMP
“They gave the hand part [of Japalyi] to the spiritual healer, ‘Take this.’”
(🔊) BB: McNair_D1B: 1:30min)

Inalienable possession in Ngumpin-Yapa languages is encoded with an ‘external possession’ (or ‘possessor-raising’) construction (McGregor, 2010; Payne & Barshi, 1999) in which the possessor is the verbal argument, rather than a dependent of the NP headed by the possessum. This is shown by (i) a pronominal clitic cross-referencing the possessor as an argument of the verb; as a subject (1412) or object (1413) (or indeed indirect object), and (ii) identical relational case marking (in the sense of Dench and Evans (1988)) on any nominals encoding the possessor$_{PSR}$ and possessum$_{PSM}$, with neither marked as a dependent. Possessors may also be expressed using a free pronoun, as shown in (1413), in which case they appear in the appropriate relational case for the argument function they perform (e.g. subject, object, indirect object, etc). Such overt nominals are grammatically optional however, and often the possessor is only expressed by a bound pronoun (1412).

(1412) Warta ngu=yi ngawa-wu jiya-rna-na.
goodness CAT=1EXC.MIN.NS water-DAT burn-IMPF-PRS

Ngu=**rna**$_{PSR}$ **majul**=ma ngarrap na.
CAT=1EXC.MIN.S stomach=TOP warm FOC
“Goodness I’m really thirsty. My stomach is hot.” (🔊) VW: FM11_a166: 34:04min)

(1413) Karu-ngku ngu=**yi**$_{PSR}$ pat-pat
child-ERG CAT=1EXC.MIN.S feel-REDUP

ma-ni **wartan**$_{PSM}$ **ngayu**$_{PSR}$.
do-PST hand 1EXC.MIN
“The child feels my hand.” (🔊) VW: FM14_a228: 10:36min)

Crucially, in inalienable possessive constructions there is no bound pronoun cross-referencing the possessum, only the possessor. For example, in (1414), only 'their' is registered with a bound pronoun, not 'two knees' (which would require a unit augmented (UA) pronominal clitic).

(1414) Jiya-rna-na ngu=**yina**$_{PSR}$ [kuya-ny-kujarra
burn-IMPF-PRS CAT=3AUG.NS thus-NMLZ-DU

tingarri-kujarra=purrupurru]$_{PSM}$.
knee-DU=AND
"It smokes their pairs of body parts (you need for crawling) including their two knees." (🔊 VW: FM08_a085: 7:05min)

8.3.2 Alienable possession

While inalienable constructions mark an intrinsic relationship between two entities, distance and free association is represented in *alienable* structures. (Regular) alienable possession in Gurindji is expressed by a phrase consisting of (i) a head nominal which encodes the possessum$_{PSM}$, (ii) a dative-marked dependent nominal/pronominal which encodes the possessor$_{PSR}$, and (iii) a pronominal clitic cross-referencing the whole possessive NP$_{PSP}$ as an argument/adjunct of the verb, for example a subject (1415), object (1416) (or indirect object).

(1415) Nyawa=ma yatu=ma murla-nginyi <u>na</u>
this=TOP white.ochre=TOP this-SOURCE FOC

ngu=**lu**$_{PSP}$ ma-na-ni, kamparri-jang-kulu=ma
CAT=3AUG.S do-IMPF-PST before-TIME-ERG=TOP

[nungkiny-ku=ma, ngantipanguny-ju=ma$_{PSR}$]$_{PSP}$.
family-ERG=TOP 1EXC.AUG.DAT-ERG=TOP
"My family used to get this white ochre from here [at Lartajarni] in the old days." (🔊 VW: FM08_11_2b: 2:12min)

(1416) **[Karu-walija marturtukuja ngantipany$_{PSR}$]**$_{PSP}$
child-PAUC female.REDUP 1EXC.AUG.DAT

ngu=rna-**yina**$_{PSP}$-ngulu ka-ngku, kuya, warrkawarrkap.
CAT=1EXC.AUG.S>3AUG.NS take-POT thus dance.REDUP
"We will take our young girls out dancing." (🔊 VW: FM08_11_3: 2:09min)

Thus, in these constructions it is the possessum, rather than the possessor, which is cross-referenced with the pronominal clitic. Cross-linguistically there is a typological tendency for nouns in alienable possession (either the head or possessor) to be marked, often morphologically, and those in inalienable possession constructions to be unmarked (Heine, 1997, p. 172). This marking distinction is common in Australian languages (Dixon, 1980, p. 293; Nichols, 1992, p. 118), and Gurindji is no exception.

8.3.3 Possessor dissension

In possessor dissension constructions, the possessor (not obligatory) is marked with the dative case, which shows it to be a modifier of the NP headed by the possessum (which is obligatory), and is cross-referenced with a non-subject pronominal clitic, as in (1417). These constructions are unusal in Australian languages and worldwide, but are found commonly in Ngumpin-Yapa languages. They are the most frequent way of expressed possession of alienable possessums in the 1959 Hale fieldnotes (e.g. pp. 21, 33, 44, 48).

(1417) Ngu=wuliny$_{PSR}$ [Japalyi-wu$_{PSR}$ kururij$_{PSM}$]
CAT=3UA.NS SUBSECT-DAT car

ya-na-na wart, jalang=ma.
go-IMPF-PRS return today=TOP
"The car of Jimmy [and Biddy]'s came back today."
(🔈 VW: FM09_14_1a: 11:03min)

It is not obligatory that the possessor be expressed with an overt NP (like inalienable possession constructions and unlike other alienable possession constructions), and often the pronominal clitic is the sole element encoding the possessor, as shown in (1418).

(1418) An ngurra-witi$_{PSM}$ ngu=**ngantipa**$_{PSR}$ nyila,
and camp-SITE CAT=1EXC.AUG.NS that

kurla-rni-mpal-a nyawa kurla-rni-mpal-a.
south-UP-EDGE-LOC this south-UP-EDGE-LOC
"Our camping place was up on the south side."
(🔈 VW: FM09_15_1a: 0:14min)

Since third person minimal objects are not cross-referenced in Gurindji, often the possessor NP in a possessor dissension construction is cross-referenced while the whole possessive NP in which it is embedded is not. This is what we see in (1417) and (1418).

However, as (1419) demonstrates, in the appropriate grammatical conditions, both the possessor NP and the whole possessive NP will be cross-referenced. In this example the whole possessive NP is cross-referenced with the subject pronominal clitic *=lu* '3AUG.S' while the embedded possessor within the subject is also cross-referenced, with *=yi* '1EXC.MIN.NS'. Thus, there are two different clitic agreement markers both relating to (parts of the) subject NP *ngayiny-ju karu-ngku.*

(1419) [Ngayiny$_{PSR}$-ju karu$_{PSM}$-ngku]$_{PSP}$ ngu=yi$_{PSR}$=lu$_{PSP}$
1EXC.MIN.DAT-ERG child-ERG CAT=1EXC.MIN.S=3AUG.S

tawirrjip pa-ni marluka-wu kurrurij.
throw.rocks hit-PST old.man-DAT car
"The children of mine threw rocks at the old man's car."
(🔈 VW: FM13_a194: 1:35min)[220]

One way to account for the fact that the possessor is cross-referenced as a clausal argument in these examples, independently of the possessive NP itself, would be to argue that the possessor is *not*, in fact, syntactically embedded in the possessive NP in this construction, but has been 'raised' out of the NP to be a clause-level argument (e.g. Payne and Barshi 1999). Such 'possessor raising' is common across the world's languages and is well-known in the literature. However, there are good reasons against this analysis for the possessor dissension construction that we discuss here. Firstly, Gurindji has a true 'possessor raising' construction that is used to express inalienable (part-whole) possession and can be shown to be morphosyntactically distinct from the possessor dissension construction in crucial ways.

Secondly, there is clear morphosyntactic evidence that the possessor (when present) remains part of the larger possessive NP in these possessor dissension constructions, despite being cross-referenced at the level of the clause. The evidence for this comes from two sources: (i) both nominals can occur together before the second position clitic complex suggesting that they are a single constituent (see §6.2.6.2); and more importantly, (ii) the possessor NP *must* show case agreement with the possessum like any other nominal modifier. Both of these structural properties are exhibited in (1420) and (1421).

(1420) **[Karu$_{PSM}$-ngku ngayiny$_{PSR}$-ju]$_{PSP}$** ngu=**yi$_{PSR}$**=**lu$_{PSP}$**=rla$_{BEN}$
child-ERG 1EXC.MIN.DAT-ERG CAT=1EXC.MIN.NS=3AUG.S=3OBL

---

220 This sentence does not reflect a true event but is the result of poor elicitation judgement on the part of Meakins.

221 Note that the *ngayu-warij* 'by myself' is crucial to the analysis of this sentence as containing an oblique possessive. Without it, this sentence could conceivably mean 'I sat down with them at their camp', which is a standard alienable construction.

ka-nya ngarin marluka-wu$_{BEN}$.
take-PST meat old.man-DAT
"The children of mine took meat for the old man." (🔈 VW: FM13_a194: 1:59min)

(1421) Ngu=rna=**yina**$_{PSR}$-nku=**rla**$_{PSP}$ ngayu-warij[221] lurlu
CAT=1EXC.MIN.S=3AUG.NS-EP=3OBL 1MIN-ALONE sit

karrinyana **[nyarruluny**$_{PSR}$**-ja ngurra-ngka]**$_{PSP}$.
be.IMPF.PRS 3AUG.DAT-LOC camp-LOC
"I'm sitting down on my own at that camp of theirs."
(🔈 VW: FM13_a196: 0:13min)

The cross-referencing of the possessor with a pronominal clitic is a feature shared by both inalienable possession and possessor dissension constructions. However, the constructions can nonetheless be clearly distinguished, as the possessor is cross-referenced differently in each case. In inalienable possession, different forms of the pronominal clitic (subject, non-subject) can be found cross-referencing the possessor, depending upon the grammatical function of the possessor in the clause. In possessor dissension constructions, however, the possessor is *always* an oblique and cross-referenced by a non-subject pronoun, irrespective of the grammatical function of the larger possessive NP. This difference follows from the fact that the bound pronoun reflects the grammatical relation of the *possessor*: in an inalienable construction, the possessor bears an argument relation to the verb (which may be subject, object, etc); whereas in a possessor dissension construction the possessor is always a dependent of the possessive NP (and therefore always an oblique).

The distinction between possessor dissension constructions and other possessive constructions is seen most clearly in clauses where the possessive phrase is non-singular, since we then see an overt pronominal clitic agreeing with the whole possessive NP as well as a non-subject pronominal clitic agreeing with the embedded possessor. Where the whole possessive phrase$_{PSP}$ is a subject, as in (1420), it is encoded using a pronominal clitic which reflects its grammatical role (here, *=lu*) while the possessor$_{PSR}$ is encoded using a non-subject pronominal clitic (here, *=yi*). In this respect the possessor dissension construction is distinguished from both inalienable *and* alienable possession constructions, with each cross-referencing only one relation (the possessor and the possessive phrase, respectively), whereas in the possessor dissension construction *both* participants in the possessive construction are cross-referenced. This results in a type of 'double-marking' whereby there are two different clause-level agreement markers corresponding to the same argument: one cross-referencing the embedded possessor and the other cross-referencing the whole argument NP.

In (1420) and (1422), the possessor is embedded in a benefactive construction which is also an oblique argument, thus both the possessor and the benefactive NP are cross-referenced as obliques.

(1422) Kajirri-lu ngu=**yi**$_{PSR}$=**rla**$_{BEN}$ kampa-wu
old.woman-ERG CAT=1EXC.MIN.S=3OBL cook-POT

[ngayiny$_{PSR}$**-ku karu**$_{PSM}$**-wu]**$_{BEN}$ ngarin.
1EXC.MIN.DAT-DAT child-DAT meat
"The old woman will cook the meat for the child of mine."
(🔈 VW: FM13_a194: 2.33min)

Since the non-subject bound pronoun series in Gurindji cross-references both objects and obliques, it is not immediately obvious that the possessor in possessor dissension constructions is functioning as an oblique rather than an object. However, if the possessor in the possessor dissension construction were a type of object, it would trigger the use of the reflexive pronoun clitic in clauses where it is coreferential with the subject. This is the case in inalienable possession constructions, as shown in (1410), but not for possessor dissension, thus providing evidence for its analysis as an oblique even in languages where this is not distinguished by the pronominal clitics.

Thus, inalienable possession and possessor dissension share the structural characteristic of cross-referencing the possessor with a bound pronoun, which differentiates them from alienable possession. In both constructions, the form of the bound pronoun indicates the grammatical role borne by the possessor. However, whereas the possessor in inalienable constructions can perform different grammatical functions (subject, object etc), since it is treated as the true verbal argument, the possessor in possessor dissension constructions is always an oblique argument.

Like alienable possession, in the possessor dissension construction, the possessor is a modifier within the larger possessive NP and is marked with the dative case when overt. As a modifier, the possessor NP in each of these constructions must also carry additional case marking in agreement with the relational case of the head nominal which it modifies. The difference between the two constructions is that in alienable possession constructions it is *only* the whole possessive NP that is cross-referenced with a bound pronominal clitic, whereas in possessor dissension the possessor is also cross-referenced, resulting in the double-marking discussed above. Furthermore, in the alienable possession construction the possessor NP is obligatory, whereas in the possessor dissension construction, the possessor NP can be omitted as the possessor is cross-referenced with a bound pronoun.

The use of the non-subject bound pronoun in possessor dissension constructions to cross-reference the possessor as an oblique argument makes them appear like benefactive/ malefactive or goal constructions.[222] These construction types also involve

222 Simpson (1991, p. 398) also notes ambiguities between possessor dissension (although she does not use this term) and causal constructions by giving alternate translations of sentences containing these constructions, for example "The horse might tread on my child while it's sleeping" or "The horse is liable to tread on the child while it's sleeping because of me".

the use of a non-subject pronominal clitic to cross-reference a human (or at least animate) participant, which is dative-marked if expressed by an overt nominal or free pronoun. As a result of this similarity in surface structure, many sentences are ambiguous (outside of context) as to whether they should be interpreted as a possessor dissension construction or benefactive/malefactive construction. For example, (1423) could be understood as 'The sun will dry out the pieces of bark of mine' (possessor dissension) or 'The sun will dry the pieces of bark out for me' (benefactive). Similarly, (1424) could be interpreted as either 'This blunt axe of mine is making it hard to cut (the wood)' (possessor dissension) or 'This blunt axe is making it hard for me to cut (the wood)' (malefactive).

(1423) Nyila-rra=ma, parnngirri=ma wartartart
that-PL=TOP bark=TOP dry.REDUP

jiya-rna-na ngu=**yi**.
burn-IMPF-PRS CAT=1EXC.MIN.S
"The sun will dry the pieces of bark out for me."
OR "The sun will dry out the pieces of bark of mine." (Meakins, 2014, p. 293)

(1424) Ngu=**yi** maral pa-na-na tuja-ngku murlu-ngku.
CAT=1EXC.MIN.S cut.badly hit-IMPF-PRS blunt-ERG this-ERG
"This blunt axe is making hard for me to cut (the wood)."
OR "This blunt axe of mine is making it hard to cut (the wood)."
(🔊 VW: FM07_05_1a: 7:01min)

Nonetheless in some examples benefactive/malefactive constructions can be distinguished from possessor dissension constructions by case agreement marking: in benefactive/ malefactive constructions the dative-marked NP has its own clausal relation and therefore never shows case agreement with another NP in the clause. In possessor dissension constructions however, the possessor shows case agreement with the possessum, as shown in (1420).

Finally, the two constructions can be shown to be distinct by the fact that they may co-occur. In (1425) the oblique possessive phrase$_{\text{PSP}}$ 'the child of mine' is embedded within a benefactive construction$_{\text{BEN}}$ 'for the child of mine'. In this sentence, the pronominal clitic =*yi* 'of mine' cross-references the possessor in the possessor dissension construction and =*rla* 'for ... ' cross-references the entire benefactive construction (which is a discontinuous NP). This sentence contrasts with (1426) which is an example of an alienable possessive phrase embedded in an inalienable possessive phrase within a benefactive construction. The crucial difference is the lack of pronominal clitic in (1426) to refer to the 1st person possessor.

(1425) [Karu-wu]$_{BEN}$ ngu=yi$_{PSR}$=rla$_{BEN}$ [ngayiny$_{PSR}$-ku]$_{BEN}$ jiya-wu.
child-DAT CAT=1EXC.MIN.S=3OBL 1EXC.MIN.DAT-DAT boil-POT
"It will boil for the child of mine." (🔈 VW: FM07_01_1e: 2:02min)

(1426) Ngu=rna=**rla**$_{PSR2}$ kampa-wu **[karu**$_{PSM1}$**-wu**
CAT=1EXC.MIN.S=3OBL cook-POT child-DAT

ngayiny-ku$_{PSR1}$**]**$_{PSR2}$ **ngarlaka-wu**$_{PSM2}$
1EXC.MIN.DAT-DAT head-DAT
"I'm cooking it for my child's head." (🔈 VW: FM07_01_1e: 1:18min)

In (1420), we see three bound pronominal clitics, one referring to the 'dissenting' possessor within the subject (*=yi*), another referring to the 3rd plural subject within which this possessor is contained (*=lu*), and the third cross-referencing the benefactive NP 'old man' (*=rla*). A particularly complex example given in (1427) demonstrates the limits of the clitic cluster in Gurindji. In this example, two possessor dissension constructions are found, one within a transitive subject (unexpressed) and one within the benefactive adjunct. As a result, an additional third oblique suffix *=nyanta* is used.

(1427) Ngu=yi$_{PSR1}$=lu$_{PSP}$=rla $_{PSR2}$=nyanta $_{BEN}$ ka-nya
CAT=1EXC.MIN.S=3AUG.S=3OBL=3OBL2 take-PST

ngarin **[ngumparna-wu nyanuny-ku**$_{PSR2}$**]**$_{BEN}$.
meat husband-DAT 3MIN.DAT-DAT
"[The children of mine] take the meat for her husband."
(🔈 VW: FM13_a195: 6:20min)

Possessor dissension constructions appear to be the preferred way of encoding alienable possession for human and other animate possessors, and less so animates. Human possessors are the main type of possessor possible in these constructions. Possessor dissension constructions seem to be the only legitimate means of expressing possession by non-humans. For example, (1428)(a) was rejected outright and corrected to (1428)(b) and (1428)(c) was consider permissible.

(1428) (a) STANDARD ALIENABLE:
*Ngu=rna paraj pu-nya jurlak-ku juru.
CAT=1EXC.MIN.S find pierce-PST bird-DAT nest
"I found a bird's nest." (🔈 FM: FM14_a231: 8:36min)

LOCATIVE CONSTRUCTION:

(b) Ngu=rna paraj pu-nya jurlak juru-ngka.
CAT=1EXC.MIN.S find pierce-PST bird nest-LOC
"I found a bird in a nest." (🔈 VW: FM14_a231: 8:59min)

POSSESSOR DISSENSION:

(c) Nyawa=ma=**rla**$_b$ jurlak-ku$_b$ juru.
this=TOP=3OBL bird-DAT nest
"This is the home of the bird." (🔈 VW: FM14_a231: 9:22min)

Thus, the use of cross-referencing bound pronouns for the animate possessors in these constructions may reflect a common cross-linguistic tendency for referents with high cognitive accessibility (such as human referents) to receive less formal encoding (such as dependent agreement marking, rather than overt NPs).

Beyond possessor animacy, however, functional differences between possessor dissension constructions and regular alienable possession are not immediately obvious. The question is – why use a possessor dissension construction instead of an alienable possessive construction to express a relation between a possessor and an alienable entity? In particular, why shift all of the available linguistic resources (i.e. dative marking, cross-referencing bound pronoun) to the expression of the possessor?

Other languages which present similar choices in encoding alienable possessors show differences relating to information structure. For example, in their brief typological survey of the phenomenon Nikolaeva, Bárány and Bond (2019) refer to this type of construction as involving 'internal prominent possessors'. Similarly Kibrik and Seleznev (cited in Dalrymple & Nikolaeva, 2011, p. 120 onwards) claim that the referent of non-subject agreement in Tabassaran (North Caucasian) is more prominent than non-agreeing referents, which means that the possessor becomes prominent. In Itelmen (Chukotko-Kamchatkan, Russia), the use of an oblique bound pronoun in intransitive sentences to cross-reference a possessor of a subject, in contrast to subject bound pronoun cross-referencing the whole possessive phrase, is likewise claimed to accord prominence to a possessor (Bobaljik & Wurmbrand, 2002, p. 24 onwards). Similarly we suggest these constructions accord prominence to the possessor in discourse, specifically encoding a type of contrastive focus which is counter-presuppositional (c.f. Dik, 1997).

In other contexts, possessor dissension constructions are used to present a possessor as the correct candidate in a set of possible possessors (either explicitly or not explicitly stated). This function is demonstrated in a major context where ownership is considered high stakes – claims about land tenure and the associated mythological Dreaming creatures who created the landscape. Identifying the custodians of particular estates and Dreamings is important in Aboriginal law. These are the people who are ceremonially responsible for maintaining the country and its Dreamings.

Poor management is considered detrimental to the well-being of tribal groups and the environment (§1.7.1). Thus, statements of custodianship are commonly found in creation myths, as well as in modern contexts such as legal evidence provided to land claims called Native Title in Australia. Some examples are given below. The speakers in (1429) and (1430) make claim to particular animal Dreamings which traversed their traditional land. In (1431), a claim about land custodianship is made in evidence given in a Native Title research trip. The statement was made to narrow custodianship to her family in opposition to another claim that included a number of families. The statement given in (1433) also makes a claim about land association in a Native Title research trip. In this case, the speaker is responding to a claim that both *ngumpit* and *kartiya* lived in a particular area.

(1429) Ngantipa=ma kurla-yarra-side-ta=ma Nama na
1EXC.AUG=TOP south-SIDE-SIDE-LOC=TOP Bee FOC

Dreaming=ma ngu=**ngantipa** **ngantipanguny**=ma.
Dreaming=TOP CAT=1EXC.AUG.NS 1EXC.AUG.DAT=TOP
"Us mob are on the south side (of the river). The Bee Dreaming belongs to us."
(🔊 VW: LIM07_030913: 2:13min)

(1430) Wampana kantri nyamu=**ngantipa**
wallaby country REL=1EXC.AUG.NS

ngantipany kantri holot-ku.
1EXC.AUG.DAT country all-DAT
"The Spectacled Hare Wallaby Dreaming country which belongs to all of us."
(🔊 CN: FM10_28_2a: 0:25min)

(1431) Yeah **ngayiny-ku** **ngamayi-wu,** **ngayiny-ku**
yes 1EXC.MIN.DAT-DAT mother-DAT 1EXC.MIN.DAT-DAT

jawiji-wu, nyila=ma ngu=**yina,** nyampayirla=ma
MF-DAT that=TOP CAT=3AUG.NS whatsitcalled=TOP

Puwarraj=ma nyila=ma.
Dreaming=TOP that=TOP
"That [Dreaming] is my mother's and mother's father's."
(🔊 VW: FM10_23_1a: 5:45min)

(1432) Nyila=ma **ngantipanguny** ngurra=ma
that=TOP 1EXC.AUG.DAT country=TOP

ngu=**ngantipa** nineteen bore kankarra.
CAT=1EXC.AUG.NS nineteen bore upstream
"That country at Number 19 bore which is upstream belongs to us."
(🔈) VW: LIM07_030913: 0:47min)

(1433) Nyamu=lu karrinyani marlurluka, kajirri-kajirri,
REL=3AUG.S be.IMPF.PST old.man.REDUP old.woman-REDUP

murla-ngka ngurra-ngka, kaa-rni-mpa nyawa
this-LOC country-LOC east-UP-PERL this

ngu=**yina** ngurra=ma karla-rni-yin-karra.
CAT=3AUG.NS country=TOP west-UP-ABL-SIDE
"When Aboriginal men and women used to live on this land in the old days, the area on the east side of the river was theirs." (🔈) BW: FM09_17_1c: 0:13min)

All of these examples single out a person or group of people from a potential set of land custodians. The shift in focus is achieved by dedicating all of the linguistic resources used in possessive constructions, i.e. the dative case suffix and the bound pronominal clitic, to encoding the possessor. In inalienable possession, the bound pronoun expresses the possessor, in alienable possession, the dative marker is used (with the bound pronoun cross-referencing the whole possessive phrase) and in possessor dissension, both the bound pronoun and the dative case suffix are co-opted for the purpose of encoding the possessor. Thus, the function of the possessor dissension construction is to bring the possessor into focus and accord that possessor prominence in discourse.

Focus has been given several treatments within the literature. Most generally it is discussed as either new information (Comrie, 1981; Halliday, 1967) or as salient information (Lambrecht, 1994). We follow the latter interpretation and suggest that a constituent in focus is one that evokes a number of alternatives that are relevant for its interpretation (Dik 1997, p. 328). In particular, we propose that possessor dissension is a type of contrastive focus in that it either sets up a restricted set of alternatives (either explicitly or not) and puts forward one of the alternatives or expands a set of potential possessors. Dik (1997, pp. 331–332) refers to this type of focus as a counter-presuppositional contrastive focus and proposes a number of subcategories.

Counter-presuppositional:

	Presupposition	Assertion
Rejecting	X	not X!
Replacing	X	(not X, but) Y!
Expanding	X	also Y!
Restricting	X and Y	only X!
Selecting	X or Y	X!

Possessor dissension can be used for *restricting* focus where the speaker presumes that the hearer has a correct piece of information X, but also incorrectly believes Y to be the case, i.e. (X and Y) only X!; and also *expanding* focus, where the speaker presumes that the hearer has a correct piece of information, but knows another piece of information which is also correct, i.e. (X) but also Y! In both cases, one possessor option is highlighted over another.

Firstly, some cases of restricting focus. In the land tenure examples given above, the custodianship of land is explicitly restricted to the stated possessor (with the presupposition of a range of potential possessors remaining unstated). In other instances, the presupposition and assertion are both stated explicitly by the speaker. For example, (1434) is a discussion of Gurindji food taboos. A particular food type has a set of potential consumers including young men and women and older adults. The speaker explicitly restricts this group, claiming that only older adults are allowed to eat this food. Similarly, in (1435) the custodianship of an area on a cattle station is under discussion, with two potential possessors, *ngumpin* and *kartiya* station owners. The speaker explicitly restricts the set of potential possessors to one, claiming that the area under contention is owned by *ngumpin* and that the *kartiya* station managers own a separate area.

(1434) 'Kula=nta nga-lu, yarrulan-tu=ma janka-ku=ma,' kuya.
NEG=2AUG.S eat-POT young.man-ERG=TOP woman-ERG=TOP thus

'Ngu=**ngantipa** **ngantipanguny** jangkakarni-lu
CAT=1EXC.AUG.NS 1EXC.AUG.DAT big.REDUP-ERG

ngu=rnalu nga-lu kajijirri-lu kuya-ny.'
CAT=1EXC.AUG.S eat-POT old.woman.REDUP-ERG thus-NMLZ
"'You shouldn't eat it, young men and women,' she said." "It is ours, as adults. Only us older women can eat that type." (🔊 VW: FM09_a123: 1:09min)

(1435) Nyila na **ngantipany**=ma **ngumpit-ku**=ma
that FOC 1EXC.AUG.DAT=TOP Aboriginal-DAT=TOP

ngu=**ngantipa** nyawa=ma kartipa-wu <u>place.</u>
CAT=1EXC.AUG.NS this=TOP non-Indigenous-DAT place
"That [place] belongs to us Aboriginal people. This is the *kartiya*'s place."
(🔈 CN: FM10_28_2a: 3:31min)

In most cases, however, the range of potential possessors is not explicitly stated. The land tenure and Dreaming ownership examples above were such cases. The example given in (1436) restricts the presumed users of a particular stone type (*ngumpin*) to the ancestors of contemporary *ngumpin*.

(1436) Nyarrulunguny kuya-ny=ma kamparri-jang-ku
3AUG.DAT thus-NMLZ=TOP before-TIME-DAT

ngumpit-ku=yina
Indigenous-DAT=3AUG.NS
"This type [of stone] belonged to *ngumpin* from before."
(🔈 VW: FM10_23_3: 4:41min)

Possessor dissension is also used to expand a possible set of possessors by foregrounding another possessor in discourse. In (1437), the use of the possessor dissension construction replaces the hearer's presupposition that the white ochre is used only by women with a statement of its use by both men and women. This presupposition is based on previous utterances which discuss its use by women in ceremonies.

(1437) **Ngumpit-ku** parlak nyawa=ma **ngu=ngantipa** **ngantipany.**
man-DAT together this=TOP CAT=1EXC.AUG.NS 1EXC.AUG.DAT
"This (white ochre) is ours, men together (with women)."
(🔈 TD: FM08_11_2b: 0:34min)

8.4 Verbal clauses

In this section, verbal clauses are discussed in terms of their predicate (whether an inflecting verb or a verb complex consisting of a coverb plus inflecting verb, see §7.2.2.1.2) and the core arguments that are subcategorised for: subject, object (direct, indirect and secondary) and subject complement. We first define the various core grammatical relations in Gurindji, and distinguish argument functions from non-argument functions (§8.4.1). A discussion of the different argument structure frames found in Gurindji is provided in §8.4.2.

8.4.1 Grammatical relations

We classify grammatical relations in a number of ways. First, we distinguish arguments from adjuncts. Arguments are subcategorisable and are selected by the verb. Arguments are the participants which are inherently involved in the nature of the relation or activity described by the predicate (Kroeger, 2005); and are specified in the predicate-argument structure. Arguments may themselves be grouped into core arguments and oblique arguments.

Core arguments are subjects and objects (direct, secondary and indirect), and are often semantically unrestricted, in that their thematic role is dependent upon the verbal predicate with which they combine.[223] In Gurindji, we define the core arguments – subject, direct object, secondary object, indirect object – according to the following basic criteria which follow those used for Bilinarra (Meakins & Nordlinger, 2014, p. 362):

(i) Subjects are the arguments cross-referenced with the subject bound pronoun clitics.
(ii) Direct objects are those arguments which are cross-referenced with the non-subject bound pronoun clitics (except with 'give' inflecting verbs in which case the indirect object is cross-referenced), and appear in unmarked (accusative) case when expressed by overt NPs.
(iii) Secondary objects are found with a small number of ditransitive verbs (see §8.4.2.14). Like direct objects, they always appear in unmarked, accusative case. Unlike direct objects, however, they are never cross-referenced by a pronominal clitic.
(iv) Indirect objects are marked with the dative case, and (when third minimal) are cross-referenced with a distinct oblique bound pronoun *=rla* (§6.2.2.3) (other person/number combinations use the non-subject bound pronouns for all types of object and indirect functions, see §6.2.2.1).

Oblique arguments are like core arguments in that they are clearly subcategorised for by the verbal predicate, as shown by the fact that they can only combine with a restricted set of predicates.[224] Unlike core arguments, however, they are generally semantically independent from the predicate and are not required for the predicate to have a complete sense. They are also more easily omitted (although, this is a hard criterion to apply in Gurindji, given that no arguments are obligatory). For example, inflecting verbs such as *panana* 'hit' have an oblique argument expressing instru-

---

223 Secondary objects are the exception as they are clearly (unmarked) objects yet are also semantically restricted to being patients/themes. See below for further discussion.

224 Oblique arguments fall, therefore, somewhere between core arguments and adjuncts. They are similar to what Bresnan (1982) calls 'complements' (Evans, 1995a; Meakins & Nordlinger, 2014; Nordlinger, 1998b). We follow Kroeger's (2005) terminology here to avoid confusion generated by multiple uses of the term 'complement' in the literature.

ment, while inflecting verbs of motion such as *yanana* 'go' can take oblique arguments in the allative or ablative cases indicating the direction of the movement. Oblique arguments are marked with a range of cases, including locative, allative, ablative, source, perlative, terminative, comitative, motivative and ergative (for instrumental), and dative (e.g. for animate goals). Oblique arguments marked with the dative case and sometimes other local cases can be cross-referenced with a non-subject bound pronoun, see §8.4.2.2. Ergative-marked subjects can be distinguished from ergative-marked oblique arguments by the fact that the latter are not cross-referenced with a subject bound pronoun.

Adjuncts represent the opposite end of the spectrum from core arguments in that they can combine with any verbal predicate with which they are semantically compatible, and are semantically independent; they have constant meanings regardless of the verbal predicate with which they combine, and their presence does not impact on the meaning of the predicate. Adjuncts in Gurindji include nominals marked with spatial case suffixes such as locative (§4.3.4), allative (§4.3.5), ablative (§4.3.7), source (§4.3.8), terminative (§4.3.10) and perlative (§4.3.11), other cases such as purposive (§4.3.6) and comitative (§4.3.9), and many of the functions of the dative such as beneficiary/maleficiary and purpose (§4.3.3).

Adjuncts are often difficult to distinguish from arguments for a number of reasons. Firstly, the same case can be used for a range of grammatical relations. The dative case, for example, is used to mark indirect object arguments (1438)–(1440), oblique arguments (such as animate goals) (1441) and adjuncts indicating a beneficiary or purpose (1442)–(1444); and the locative case is found marking both locative adjuncts, locative indirect objects and locative arguments. Furthermore, many types of adjuncts, particularly humans and highly affected non-human entities, can be cross-referenced with a non-subject bound pronoun or third person oblique *=rla*, as shown in (1438), so this can't be used as a criterion to distinguish arguments from adjuncts per se (see §6.2.4). Nonetheless, cross-referencing is only optional for adjuncts even where they are human, as shown in (1443)–(1444). In this respect they contrast with arguments where cross-referencing bound pronouns are obligatory. In fact, (1445) shows the necessity of cross-referencing an animate. Violet Wadrill begins the clause without *=rla* then corrects it in the next clause.

Dative indirect object argument:

(1438) Nguku ngu=**rla** jayi-nya **karu-wu**.
water CAT=3OBL give-PST child-DAT
"She gave some water to the kid." (🔈 VW: FHM098: 33:03min)

(1439) Ngu=rna=**rla** **Nangari-wu** karrinya jarrakap.
CAT=1EXC.MIN.S=3OBL SUBSECT-DAT be.PST talk
"I talked to Nangari." (🔈 VW: FM09_14_1a: 12:18min)

(1440) **Kamara-wu** na ngu=**rla** nya-nga-na
long.yam-DAT FOC CAT=3OBL intake-IMPF-PRS

Ngarnjal-lu warlakap.
NAME-ERG search
"Topsy was looking around for yams." (🔈) VW: FM07_a054: 2:33min)

Dative oblique argument (animate goal):

(1441) Ya-na-ni ngu=**rla** **ngamayi-wu** jik.
go-IMPF-PST CAT=3OBL mother-DAT arrive
"Then he went up to his mother." (🔈) VW: FM10_a155: Ngarlking Karu: 0:54min)

Dative adjunct (purposive):

(1442) Nyila jayi-ngka=yi=**rla** jamalarl **ngawa-wu.**
that give-IMP=1EXC.MIN.NS=3OBL handleless water-DAT
"Give me that handleless tin to get some water." (🔈) VW: FM12_a171: 20:19min)

(1443) **Jintapa-kari-wu** na ngu=rnawula
another-OTHER-DAT FOC CAT=1EXC.UA.S

pu-nga-ni nyila=ma, kurrij-karra.
pierce-IMPF-PST that=TOP dig-ITER
"We dug for another one now." (🔈) VW: FM07_a054: 8:56min)

(1444) Nyila=ma karrinyana yarti-ngka liwart **ngawa-wu.**
that=TOP be.IMPF.PRS shade-LOC wait water-DAT
"That's him standing in the shade waiting for water."
(🔈) VW: FM12_a173: 15:37min)

(1445) Jirripinang=ma, palangari-ngarna, ngu=rnalu
plant.sp=TOP black.soil-ASSOC CAT=1EXC.AUG.S

puntanup ma-na-ni wananga-la walyawalyak.
gather do-IMPF-PST bag-LOC inside.REDUP

Ngu=rnalu ma-na-ni, manager-wu
CAT=1EXC.AUG.S do-IMPF-PST manager-DAT

ngu=rnalu=rla Wave Hill-ngarna-wu.
CAT=1EXC.AUG.S=3OBL place.name-ASSOC-DAT
"This plant grows on the blacksoil. We used to collect it and put it in our bags. We used to collect it for the Wave Hill manager."
(🔈 VW: FM12_a173: 8:19min)

8.4.2 Argument structure

An overview of the core argument structures found in Gurindji are given in Table 48. Arguments in the first column are those registered with a subject bound pronoun; those in the second and third columns are cross-referenced by non-subject pronouns. All other arguments are not cross-referenced. As discussed in Chapter 6, the bound pronoun system only distinguishes objects and obliques in the third person minimal. In Table 48, we have used italics to indicate the grammatical functions encoded as obliques in the third minimal (i.e. with the oblique bound pronoun =*rla*). In all other cases, the same set of non-subject pronouns is used in all of these non-subject functions.

Table 48: Argument structure of verbal clauses.

IMPERSONAL	no arguments			e.g. *ngarrap* 'hot'
INTRANSITIVE				
simple intransitive	^{S}NOM			e.g. *rarraj* 'run'
with oblique argument	^{S}NOM		^{O}LOC	e.g. go to somewhere
with adjunct	^{S}NOM			
with subj. complement	^{S}NOM		^{S}COMP	e.g. *yany* 'turn into, become'
SEMI-TRANSITIVE				
with nom. subject	^{S}NOM	^{IO}*DAT*		e.g. *yangkarra* 'follow'
with erg. subject	^{S}ERG	^{IO}*DAT*		e.g. *warlakap* 'look for'
with cognate object	^{S}ERG	^{O}ACC	(^{IO}*DAT*)	e.g. *jarrakap* 'talk language to'
with allative object	^{S}NOM	^{O}ALL		e.g. *taarlak* 'in danger of'
TRANSITIVE				
simple transitive	^{S}ERG	^{O}ACC		e.g. *panana* 'hit'
with adjunct	^{S}ERG	^{O}ACC		
with cognate object	^{S}ERG	^{O}ACC	(^{IO}DAT)	e.g. *yunparnana* 'sing a song'
DITRANSITIVE				
O_2-theme	^{S}ERG	^{O}ACC	^{O2}ACC	e.g. *pinak* 'teach', *wiit* 'show', *jayingana* 'give'
O-theme with dative IO	^{S}ERG	^{O}ACC	^{IO}*DAT*	e.g. *jayingana* 'give'
O-theme with spatial IO	^{S}ERG	^{O}ACC	^{IO}LOC	e.g. *yuwanana* 'throw'
O-theme with mot. IO	^{S}ERG	^{O}ACC	^{IO}MOT	e.g. *ngurrku* 'suspect'

8.4.2.1 Impersonal clauses

Impersonal clauses are derived from a restricted set of coverbs (only two) which refer to weather: *ngarrap* 'to be hot' or *makurru* 'to be cold'. They combine with the inflecting verb *karrinyana* 'be' and do not take a referential subject. These complex verbs are also found in regular intransitive constructions, which do not refer to the weather.

(1446) Jawarti-la ngu murruru-la[225] karru.
tomorrow-LOC CAT cold-LOC be.POT
"It will be cold tomorrow." (🔈 SM: Hale_K06-004553: 17:44min)

8.4.2.2 Basic intransitive clauses

Intransitive verbs subcategorise for a nominative subject. The possible inflecting verbs found in intransitive clauses are *yanana* 'go', *karrinyana* 'be', *waninyana* 'fall', *marnana* 'talk' (which can also be semi-transitive), *ngayanana* 'excrete' (also transitive). The coverbs which combine with these inflecting verbs tend to be coverbs of spatial configuration (§7.2.3.1), state (§7.2.3.4), speech (§7.2.3.5), bodily functions (§7.2.3.6), motion (§7.2.3.7) and leaving (§7.2.3.8). In intransitive clauses, the subject is registered either as a subject pronominal clitic, or as both a subject pronominal clitic and an overt nominative NP, as in (1447).

(1447) Ngu=**lu** ya-na-na **kaluyawung.**[226]
CAT=3AUG.S go-IMPF-PRS stranger
"Some strangers are coming." (🔈 VW: FM12_a183: 11:20min)

The following examples demonstrate the alternative case frame where the coverb and inflecting verb remain the same i.e. *wuukarra karrinyana* 'scared be', (1448) and (1449), and *liwart karrinyana* 'wait be', (1450) and (1451). The first of each pair is a plain intransitive clause and the second is semi-transitive, as shown by the use of *=rla* '3OBL, of it' and *=ngku* '2MIN.NS, for you'. In the case of *liwart* 'wait', it can also combine with *panana* to produce a transitive sentence, as shown by the ergative-marked subject in (1452).

(1448) Wuukarra **ngu=lu** karrinyani.
scared CAT=3AUG.S be.IMPF.PST
"They were scared." (🔈 TD: FM10_22_1b: 1:55min)

(1449) Wuukarra ngu=lu=**rla** karrinyana **nyanawu-wu**
afraid CAT=3AUG.S=3OBL be.IMPF.PRS RECOG-DAT

225 The word *murruru* 'cold' is not found often and likely comes from Western Mudburra.
226 Note that this word is transparently made up of *kalu* 'walk' and *-yawung* 'PROP'.

kuliyan-ku,	**nyampayirla-wu,**	**crocodile-ku.**
aggressive-DAT	whatsitcalled-DAT	crocodile-DAT

"They're too afraid of crocodiles." (🔈 VW: FM11_a163: 3:27min)

(1450)

Jurlan-karra	jiya-rna-na.	Nyila=ma	**karrinyana**
thirsty-ITER	burn-IMPF-PRS	that=TOP	be.IMPF.PRS

yarti-ngka	**liwart**	**ngawa-wu.**
shade-LOC	wait	water-DAT

"He's really thirsty. That's him standing in the shade waiting for water." (VW: FM12_a173: 15:37min)

(1451)

Ngu=rna=**ngku**	**liwart**	**karrinya**	yipurrk.
CAT=1EXC.MIN.S=2MIN.NS	wait	be.PST	in.vain

"I waited for you, but you didn't come." (McConvell corpus: Meakins et al., 2016, p. 448)

(1452)

Ngu=**yi**	**Nangari-lu**	**liwart**	**pa-ni.**
CAT=1EXC.MIN.S	SUBSECT-ERG	wait	hit-PST

"Nangari waited for me." (🔈 VW: FM09_13_3a: 0:57min)

8.4.2.3 Intransitive clauses with oblique arguments

Intransitive verbs often co-occur with spatial oblique arguments. For example, *yanana* 'go' is often found with a locative-marked trajectory (1453) and (1454), an allative-marked goal (1455)–(1457) or an ablative-marked source (1458) and (1459).

(1453)

Karnti-ka	partaj	ya-na-na.
stick-LOC	climb	go-IMPF-PRS

"It climbs up the stick." (🔈 VW: FM10_a133: 9:34min)

(1454)

Palangari-la	kalurirrp	ngu=rnalu
black.soil-LOC	walk.around	CAT=1EXC.AUG.S

ya-na-na	nyila=ma.
go-IMPF-PRS	that=TOP

"We walk around the blacksoil country." (🔈 VW: FM07_a054: 2:58min)

(1455)

Karu-walija=ma	na	rarraj	ya-na-na	**kurrurij-jirri.**
child-PAUC=TOP	FOC	run	go-IMPF-PRS	car-ALL

"The kids run for the car [because it is raining]." (🔈 BW: FM07_a043: 31:23min)

(1456) Kalu ngu=rnalu ya-ni **yala-ngkurra** **karnti-kurra.**
walk CAT=1EXC.AUG.S go-PST that-ALL tree-ALL
"We walked that way to the tree." (🔈) VW: FM07_a027: 0:19min)

(1457) Kurlumpukpurru-ngurlu ngu=rnalu
place.name-ABL CAT=1EXC.AUG.S

ya-ni, **ngurra-ngkurra,** **Wave Hill-jirri.**
go-PST home-ALL place.name-ALL
"From Kurlumpukpurru we went home to old Wave Hill station."
(🔈) VW: FM09_14_1a: 3:24min)

(1458) **Jurnarni-ngurlu** ngu=rnalu ya-ni kanimparra.
place.name-ABL CAT=1EXC.AUG.S go-PST downstream
"From Jurnarni we came downstream." (🔈) VW: FM07_a058: 1:01min)

Where goal or source arguments of intransitive verbs are human, they are marked with the dative case and are also cross-referenced by a pronominal clitic (§4.3.3.2), as shown in (1459).

(1459) Ya-na-na ngu=**rla** **kurrwararn-ku**
go-IMPF-PRS CAT=3OBL doctor-DAT

kankarra-k walyak jarriny-ja.
upstream-ALL inside room-LOC
"She went to the doctor in her office." (🔈) BW: FM07_a043: 14:00min)

8.4.2.4 Intransitive clauses with adjuncts

Intransitive verbs are also often found with adjuncts, for example locative-marked NPs which refer to the place or time of an action, as shown in (1460)–(1461), or a dative-marked purpose, as shown in (1450) and (1462).

(1460) Warlaku karrinyana ngu **tanku-waji-la.**
dog be.IMPF.PRS CAT food-AGENT-LOC
"The dog is sitting outside the shop." (🔈) BW: FM07_a043: 4:55min)

(1461) Karrinyana nyawa=warla warlaku=ma makin **warlu-ngka.**
be.IMPF.PRS this=FOC dog=TOP sleep fire-LOC
"The dog sleeps beside the fire." (🔈) BW: FM07_a043: 5:08min)

(1462) Palngana, Pirntipirnti, yala-kijak ngu=lu
Flora.Valley Sturt.River that-TERM CAT=3AUG.S

ya-na-ni **ngarin-ku.**
go-IMPF-PST meat-DAT
"They used to go hunting as far as Flora Valley and Sturt River."
(Appendix: Echidna and the Big Shade: Story 1, line 6)

8.4.2.5 Intransitive clauses with a subject complement

Some intransitive clauses subcategorise for a subject complement. On its own, *karrinyana* 'be' can subcategorise for a subject complement as shown in (1463). In (1464), the nominal *nyantu-wariny* 'by himself' is the subject complement. Other examples such as (1465) use the intransitive *waninyana* 'fall' in combination with *yany* 'transform' to subcategorise for a subject complement.

(1463) Ngayu=ma=rna karru **kajirri.**
1MIN=TOP=1EXC.MIN.S be.POT old.woman
"I will become an old woman." (Sounce unknown)

(1464) Ngumpin=ma nyila=ma karrinyani **nyantu-wariny** liwart.
man=TOP that=TOP be.IMPF.PST 3MIN-ALONE wait
"The man was waiting there by himself."
(🔈 DD: EC98_a017: 8:00min)

(1465) Nyila marluka yany waninya **Kurraj.**
that old.man transform fall.PST Rainbow.Serpent
"That old man transformed into a Rainbow Serpent."
(McConvell corpus: Meakins et al., 2016, p. 188)

8.4.2.6 Semi-transitive clauses with a nominative subject

Semi-transitive clauses have been introduced in the previous sections in relation to their alternation with intransitive clauses, as shown in (1449), (1451) and (1478). Semi-transitive clauses consist of a case frame which includes a dative indirect object. Two types of semi-transitive clauses occur, one which takes a nominative subject and one which takes an ergative subject.

The first type is shown in (1466) which combines *yanana* 'go' with *yangkarra* 'follow' and takes a nominative subject *jintaku* 'one' and a dative-marked indirect object *janka-wu* 'woman-DAT'. The dative indirect object is also optionally cross-referenced by a non-subject bound pronoun, present in (1466) and (1467), and absent in (1468). It is more likely to appear if the referent is human, as discussed in §6.2.4. These clauses always use intransitive inflecting verbs. Further examples of semi-transitive clauses containing *yanana* 'go' and *karrinyana* 'be' are given in (1467) and (1468), respectively.

(1466) Jintaku ngu=**rla** ya-na-na yangkarra
one CAT=3OBL go-IMPF-PRS follow

yalu-wu na, **janka-wu**.
that-DAT FOC woman-DAT
"One [man] is following after that woman." (🔈 TD: FM10_a163: 1:51min)

(1467) **Ngarnjal-ku** ngu=**rla** ya-ni.
NAME-DAT CAT=3OBL go-PST
"She went after Topsy." (🔈 VW: FM09_a127: 21:37min)

(1468) Nyawa na, **manyirrkila-wu** liwart
this FOC barramundi-DAT wait

karrinyana murla-ngka kuwurtpirtta.
be.IMPF.PRS this-LOC lie.in.wait
"He waited out of sight for barramundi." (🔈 DD: EC98_a013: 1:26min)

8.4.2.7 Semi-transitive clauses with an ergative subject

The second type of semi-transitive clauses takes an ergative subject, for example (1469) and (1470). Again, the dative indirect object is optionally cross-referenced by a non-subject bound pronoun, for example it is present in (1469) and absent in (1470). These clauses use transitive inflecting verbs.

(1469) Ngu=rnalu=**rla** warlakap nya-nga-ni
CAT=1EXC.AUG.S=3OBL search intake-IMPF-PST

kinyuwurra-wu=ma, **Nangari-lu**=ma.
bush.onion-DAT=TOP SUBSECT-ERG=TOP
"We, including Nangari, were looking everywhere for the bush onion."
(🔈 VW: FM07_a058: 3:49min)

(1470) **Lamparra-lu** ngungu ma-rni **nyanuny-ju**
father.in.law-ERG promise talk-PST 3MIN.DAT-ERG

mali-ngku **ngalawiny-ku.**
mother.in.law-ERG mans.child-DAT
"His father-in-law and mother-in-law promised her to the son."
(McConvell corpus: Meakins et al., 2016, p. 285)

Many of these types of semi-transitive clauses have transitive counterparts where the semi-transitive clause marks goals or 'failed objects' while the transitive counterpart expresses an affected patient.[227] Some examples are: throwing a spear at an animal (semi-transitive) (1471) as opposed to actually spearing it (transitive) (1472), or chasing around *for* something (semi-transitive) (1473) as opposed to chasing something (transitive) (1474). Transitive clauses differ grammatically from their semi-transitive counterparts by subcategorising for an accusative object rather than a dative-indirect object.

(1471) Mirlarrang-kulu ngu=rla pu-nya jarrwaj.
spear-ERG CAT=3OBL pierce-PST spear
"He threw a spear at it." (🔈 VW: FM10_30_2a: Jajurlang: 5:15min)

(1472) Jamut jarrwaj pu-nya karu-ngku.
bush.turkey spear pierce-PST child-ERG
"The kid speared the bush turkey." (🔈 VW: FM09_a123: 33:23min)

(1473) Wirnangpurru-wu=ma ngarina-wu=ma pulumanu-wu=ma
kangaroo-DAT=TOP meat-DAT=TOP cattle-DAT=TOP

ngu=rnalu pila-pila ma-ni.
CAT=1EXC.AUG.S chase-REDUP do-PST
"We chased around for kangaroos and cattle."
(McConvell 1996 grammar manuscript: Speaking to young people)

(1474) Ngu=wula=nyunu pila-pila na ma-ni kanyjurra.
CAT=3UA.S=RR chase-REDUP FOC do-PST down
"The two of them chased after each other down to the river."
(🔈 BR: FM15_52_1b: 0:57min)

Other semi-transitive clauses have nominative subjects where semi-transitive clauses tend to express a purpose or reason behind an action, or who the action is directed towards. For example, 'waiting' as opposed to 'waiting for' (see §8.4.2.6) or 'speaking' as opposed to 'speaking to' (see §8.4.2.8).

227 A similar distinction is found in a number of Australian languages, including Kalkatungu (Blake 1987) and Warlpiri (Hale 1982).

8.4.2.8 Semi-transitive clauses with a cognate object

The inflecting verb *marnana* 'talk' subcategorises for dative indirect object (the hearer) but can subcategorise for a cognate object which refers to the language spoken, as shown in (1475).[228] Such a meaning can also be expressed using a proprietive marker, as shown in (1476). The 'talk' inflecting verb is also found as a simple intransitive verb, as in (1477), and a semi-transitive verb which takes a dative-marked indirect object, as in (1478).

(1475)

Jarrakap	ngu=rna=rla	ma-rna-na	**jaru**.
talk	CAT=1EXC.MIN.S=3OBL	talk-IMPF-PRS	language

"I talk language to her." (🔈 VW: FM07_01_1a: 3:17min)

(1476)

Jarrakap	ngu=rnayinangulu	ma-rna-na,	**jaru-yawung**.
talk	CAT=1EXC.AUG.S>3AUG.NS	talk-IMPF-PRS	language-PROP

"We talk to them in language." (🔈 VW: FM08_11_3: 2:27min)

(1477)

Wampal	karrinyana.	Kula	**ma-rna-na**	**jarrakap**.
quiet	be.IMPF.PRS	NEG	talk-IMPF-PRS	talk

"She's sitting down quietly. She's not talking." (🔈 TD: FM10_a166: 2:33min)

(1478)

Karu-walija-wu	ngu=**yina**	**ma-rna-ni**
child-PAUC-DAT	CAT=3AUG.NS	talk-IMPF-PST

nyawa=ma	kirri=ma	**jarrakap**.
this=TOP	woman=TOP	talk

"The woman was talking to the kids." (🔈 VW: FHM146: 12:51min)

8.4.2.9 Semi-transitive clauses with an allative object

Another semi-transitive clause structure subcategorises for an allative object with the complex predicate *taarlak yanana* 'in danger of'. Two examples are given in (1479) and (1480).

(1479)

Maitbi	**kaya-ngkurra**	ngaja=lu	taarlak	ya-nku.
maybe	bad.spirit-ALL	ADMON=3AUG.S	danger	go-POT

"They might be in danger of a bad spirit." (🔈 VW: FM12_a177: 4:52min)

(1480)

Ngaja=nta	taarlak-karra	ya-na-na	**nyampa-kurra**=wayin.
ADMON=2AUG.S	danger-ITER	go-IMPF-PRS	something-ALL=ETC

"You mob might be in danger of something." (🔈 VW: FM12_a177: 4:35min)

228 Saying that you are 'talking language' refers only to a traditional Aboriginal language.

Another complex predicate *ngarru marnana* 'talk rudely' involves an allative object (1481), but the two examples in the corpus also have a locative marker, which is possibly marking a reduced subordinate clause, however it's not clear.

(1481)

Ngu=rna=ngku	ngarru	ma-rni,
CAT=1EXC.MIN.S=2MIN.NS	talk.rudely	talk-PST

jupu,	**nyununy-jirri-la**.
JUST	2MIN.DAT-ALL-LOC

"I just talked rudely to you." (🔈 VW: FM10_a152: 1:23min)

8.4.2.10 Basic transitive clauses

All transitive clauses contain an ergative subject[229] and an accusative object, as shown in (1482) and (1483). Where the arguments are not third person minimal, they are also cross-referenced by bound pronouns, often a complex pronoun, as exemplified in (1484).

(1482)

[**Nangala-lu**]$_{A}$	paraj	pu-nya	ngu	[**ngarlu**]$_{O}$.
SUBSECT-ERG	find	pierce-PST	CAT	honey

"Nangala found the honey." (🔈 VW: FM07_a021: 2:39min)

(1483)

[**Wirnangpurru**]$_{O}$	pa-na-na	[**jawurt**]$_{O}$	[**kajirri-lu**]$_{A}$.
kangaroo	hit-IMPF-PRS	tail	old.woman-ERG

"The woman cuts off the kangaroo tail." (🔈 VW: FHM146: 10:52min)

(1484)

Ngu=**yinangkulu**$_{A,O}$	[**nyila=ma**	**kartipa=ma**]$_{O}$	karra-yin-ta
CAT=3AUG.S>3AUG.NS	that=TOP	non-Indigenous=TOP	west-ABL-LOC

nya-nga-ni	[**yarrulan-tu**	**kujarra-lu**]$_{A}$.
intake-IMPF-PST	young.man-ERG	two-ERG

"The two young men were watching the *kartiya* from the west."
(🔈 RW: EC98_a027: 6:44min)

Examples of inflecting verbs which are found in transitive clauses are *panana* 'hit', *pungana* 'pierce', *manana* 'do, get', *kamparnana* 'cook', *jiyarnana* 'burn, snatch', *yuwanana* 'put', *karrwarnana* 'hold, have', *payarnana* 'bite, drink', *nyangana* 'intake' and *kangana* 'take'. Categories of coverbs which typically combine with these inflecting verbs are coverbs of holding (§7.2.3.3), cooking and burning (§7.2.3.9), impact (§7.2.3.10), touch and manipulation (§7.2.3.11), induced change of location (§7.2.3.12) and intake

229 For speakers of Gurindji Kriol, the ergative marker is now optional and encodes discourse functions (Meakins, 2009, 2015a; Meakins & O'Shannessy, 2010; Meakins & Wilmoth, 2020).

(§7.2.3.13). Other coverbs such as those which express position can be transitivised using the inflecting verb *yuwanana* 'put'. Compare (1485) and (1486).

(1485) Nangala-kujarra jeya ngu=yi=wula **kutij karrinyana.**
SUBSECT-DU there CAT=1EXC.MIN.NS=3UA.S stand be.IMPF.PRS
"The two Nangalas are standing there with me." (🔈 VW: FM07_a027: 0:51min)

(1486) **Kutij** ngu=rna **yuwa-ni.**
stand CAT=1EXC.MIN.S put-PST
"I stood [the coolamon] up." (🔈 VW: FM07_a050: 3:14min)

Clauses which have reflexive/reciprocal objects behave like normal transitive clauses in that they require an ergative-marked subject and a pronominal clitic which cross-references the subject (if it isn't third person minimal). The reflexive/reciprocal pronominal clitic cross-references an object which is never explicitly expressed by a nominal (§6.2.2.4).

(1487) **[Yalu-ngku marluka-lu]**$_A$ ngu=**[lu]**$_A$=**[nyunu]**$_O$ kuli nya-nga-na.
that-ERG old.man-ERG CAT=3AUG.S=RR fight intake-IMPF-PRS
"Those two old blokes started fighting each other." (🔈 VW: FM12_a174: 16:21min)

8.4.2.11 Transitive with oblique arguments

Transitive clauses can be expanded with the addition of oblique arguments, for example allative-marked or dative-marked goals (1488), ablative or source-marked obliques (1489) of *kangana* 'take' verbs, ergative-marked instrumentals (1490) or ergative+proprietive-marked instrumentals of impact verbs (1491), and locative-marked body parts of impact coverbs such as *panana* 'hit' or *payarnana* 'bite' (1492). Such NPs can combine with these verb types, providing that they are semantically appropriate.

(1488) Nyanuny-ku jaju-wu ngu=rla **ka-nga-na,**
3MIN.DAT-DAT MM-DAT CAT=3OBL take-IMPF-PRS

mangarri punyu, **yarti-ngkurra** makin-ta-wu.
bread good shade-ALL sleep-LOC-DAT
"She takes a cake to her grandmother who was sleeping in the shade."
(🔈 VW: FHM146: 1:12min)

(1489) Karrinyani ngu=lu tanku=ma nyawa=ma
be.IMPF.PST CAT=3AUG.S food=TOP this=TOP

ka-nga-ni **Wyndham-nginyi**=ma.
take-IMPF-PST place.name-SOURCE=TOP
"They used to live here and [another Afghan] used to bring stores from Wyndham." (◀)) VW: FM10_22_1a: 4:29min)

(1490) Ngu=rnalu **kampa-rna-na** na, **wumara-lu** yalu-ngku.
CAT=1EXC.AUG.S cook-IMPF-PRS FOC stone-ERG that-ERG
"We cook it using those stones." (◀)) TD: FM10_a134: 1:45min)

(1491) Malyju-ngku **kurrupartu-yawung-kulu** kayi-kayi
boy-ERG boomerang-PROP-ERG chase-REDUP

pa-na-na jamut.
hit-IMPF-PRS bush.turkey
"The boy chases the bush turkey with a boomerang." (◀)) BW: FM07-a043: 15:53min)

(1492) **Jamana-la**=rla **paya-rni** ngu.
foot-LOC=3OBL bite-PST CAT
"It bit him on the foot." (◀)) BW: FM07-043: 1:43min)

8.4.2.12 Transitive clauses with adjuncts

Transitive clauses can also be found with adjuncts, for example locative-marked or allative-marked nominals, either locations (1493)–(1496), or temporals, and dative-marked nominals used in purposive constructions (1497) and (1498).

(1493) Jala-jala ngu=yinangulu ka-nga-na **pusher-ngka** na.
now-REDUP CAT=3AUG.S>3AUG.NS take-IMPF-PRS pram-LOC FOC
"These days they take them around in prams." (◀)) VW: FM07_05_1a: 2:00min)

(1494) Ngu=rnalu kampa-rna-na **warlu-ngka**.
CAT=1EXC.AUG.S cook-IMPF-PRS fire-LOC
"We cook it in the fire." (◀)) VW: FM07_a058: 2:21min)

(1495) Nyila na ngu=rna pa-na-na pirrkap
that FOC CAT=1EXC.MIN.S hit-IMPF-PRS make

ngayu=ma jala=ma, ngurra-ngka
1EXC.MIN=TOP today=TOP camp-LOC

ngayiny-ja **yarti-ngka,** **kaarra-yin-karra-la**.
1EXC.MIN.DAT-LOC shade-LOC east-ABL-SIDE-LOC
"I'm making that one today, I am, at my camp in the shade on the east side of my house." (◀)) VW: FM07_a050: 2:25min)

(1496) Ngu=yinangulu wanyja-na-ni, **yarrulan-jirri**
CAT=3AUG.S>3AUG.NS leave-IMPF-PST young.man-ALL

ngumpit-jirri, kirri-ngku=ma, marlurluka=ma.
man-ALL woman-ERG=TOP old.man.REDUP=TOP
"Women would leave the old men for a younger man."
(🔊 VW: FM11_a162: 15:28min)

(1497) **Tea-wu=ma, mangarri-wu=ma,** pinyinyip=ma=lu
tea-DAT=TOP damper-DAT=TOP rub.between.palms=TOP=3AUG.S

ma-na-ni.
do-IMPF-PST
"They used to rub sticks together to make fire for cooking tea and damper."
(🔊 TD: FM09_17_2b: 2:43min)

(1498) Karu-ngku kawarla warrkuj ma-ni **marru-ngka mangarri-wu.**
child-ERG coolamon pick.up do-PST house-LOC veg.food-DAT
"A child got a coolamon from the house for [collecting] food."
(McConvell corpus: Meakins et al., 2016, p. 405)

Some transitive verbs can also have alternative case frames as semi-transitive verbs. Examples of these were discussed in §8.4.2.6.

8.4.2.13 Transitive clauses with a cognate object

The transitive verbs *yunparnana* 'sing' and *wanyjanana* 'leave' and in combination with some coverbs such as *warrkap* 'dance' can occur with a cognate object which can only be the name of a ceremony. For example, (1499) contains an object *junpa* 'public corroboree' and (1500) contains an object *wajarra* 'corroboree'. These types of objects are referred to as cognate objects (Austin, 1982). These clauses also occur with no overtly expressed object, as shown in (1501), or various adjuncts including locative-marked ceremony names which translate as "X time", as in (1502).

(1499) Warrkawarrkap nyamu=lu **junpa**=ma yunpa-rna-ni.
dance.REDUP REL=3AUG.S corroboree=TOP sing-IMPF-PST
"When they used to perform a public corroboree."
(🔊 VW: FM08_11_2b: 1:29min)

(1500) **Wajarra** na ngu=lu yunpa-rna-nu wanyja-na-ni.
corroboree FOC CAT=3AUG.S sing-IMPF-INF leave-IMPF-PST
"They were performing a public corroboree together."
(🔈 BR: FM15_52_1e: 5:32min)

(1501) Ngu=lu yunpa-rna-ni, ngu=lu yunpa-rna-ni
CAT=3AUG.S sing-IMPF-PST CAT=3AUG.S sing-IMPF-PST

kurla-yarra nyarrulu murlng-pa=rni.
south-SIDE 3AUG separate-EP=ONLY
"They were singing off by themselves to the south."
(🔈 DD: EC99_a029: Kinyjirrka-wu Murtap: 16:08min)

(1502) Ngu=rnalu yunpa-rna-na yunpa-rnu-p=ma
CAT=1EXC.AUG.S sing-IMPF-PRS sing-INF-CV=TOP

kilkilp **Yawulyu-la**=ma.
click.sticks woman.ceremony-LOC=TOP
"We sing and play the clapsticks during the Yawulyu ceremony."
(🔈 VW: FM08_a101: 9:34min)

8.4.2.14 Ditransitive clauses with two accusative objects

Ditransitive verbs have three arguments – an ergative-marked subject and two objects. Two types of ditransitive clauses exist:

(i) O_2-theme ditransitive clauses: two accusative objects (direct object and secondary object).
(ii) O-theme ditransitive clauses: one accusative object (direct object) and one dative object or spatial object (indirect object).

The O_2-theme case frame is rare, but possible for 'give' verbs. The secondary object, which is the recipient, is unmarked and cross-referenced by a non-subject pronoun, as in (1503). In the case of third minimal recipients, it is not encoded. The other type of O_2-theme ditransitive clauses involves *tal* 'call', as shown in (1504). These clauses do not alternate with O-theme ditransitive clauses. Curiously (1505) has a locative-marked indirect object, but it is possible that this is =*warla* 'focus'.

(1503) An ngamayi-lu ngu=**yina** nguru jayi-nga-ni
and mother-ERG CAT=3AUG.NS prepare give-IMPF-PST

walyak-kula=ma **nanta-nanta=ma** **nyila=ma**.
inside-LOC=TOP small-REDUP=TOP that=TOP
"And the mother prepares to give the little ones food inside."
(◀) VW: FM10_a149: 2:17min)

(1504) **Ngamayak** ngu=rnalu tal pa-na-na,
diarrhoea CAT=1EXC.AUG.S call hit-IMPF-PRS

nyila=ma **mangarri=ma** **kalypa=ma**.
that=TOP bread=TOP soft=TOP
"We call soft dough 'ngamayak'." (◀) VW: FM10_a151: 0:37min)

(1505) An nyuntu Nangari ngu=n, Nangari=ma ngu=n
and 2MIN SUBSECT CAT=2MIN.S SUBSECT=TOP CAT=2MIN.S

tal pa-na-na **mali-la**=ma **Jukurtayi**=ma **Jungurra**=ma.
call hit-IMPF-PRS son.in.law-LOC=TOP SUBSECT=TOP SUBSECT=TOP
"Nangari calls her mali Jukurtayi or Jungurra." (◀) VW: FM12_a183: 15:55min)

8.4.2.15 Ditransitive clauses with an accusative object and dative indirect object

O-theme ditransitive clauses have a dative-marked indirect object cross-referenced by either a non-subject pronoun (1506) or the third oblique pronoun *=rla* (1507). In this respect, they resemble transitive clauses with beneficiary adjuncts, however in the case of O-theme ditransitive clauses the bound oblique pronoun is not optional (see also §4.3.3.2 and §6.2.2.3).

(1506) Kirt-kirt ma-ni murrkun-kari=ma,
break-REDUP do-PST three-OTHER=TOP

ngu=**wuliny** jayi-nya **Nangari-kujarra-wu**.
CAT=3UA.NS give-PST SUBSECT-DU-DAT
"She broke off three more and gave them to the two Nangaris."
(◀) VW: FM07_a085: 11:42min)

(1507) Nguku ngu=**rla** jayi-nya **karu-wu**.
water CAT=3OBL give-PST child-DAT
"She gave some water to the kid." (◀) VW: FHM098: 33:03min)

In all ditransitive clauses, the direct object is never cross-referenced with a bound pronoun. This is clear in examples where the direct object is non-singular and animate (1508) or human (1509) and a bound pronoun would therefore be expected. In these examples, neither the 'horses' nor 'woman' are cross-referenced by bound pronouns, however the recipients are.

(1508) **Murrkun yawarta** ngu=rla jayi-nya.
three horse CAT=3OBL give-PST
"He gave three horses to him." (DD: EC98_a011: 1:48min)

(1509) Hey lamparra-marnany-ju=ma=ngku jayi-nya,
hey father.in.law-2MIN.POSS-ERG=TOP=2MIN.NS give-PST

kujarra kirri kujarra nyununy.
two woman two 2MIN.DAT
"Hey your father-in-law gave two girls to you." (VW: FM10_a155: 10:48min)

Most O_2-theme ditransitive clauses in Gurindji involve the inflecting verb *jayingana* 'give' either on its own or in combination with coverbs, as shown in (1510)–(1512). Where the indirect object is a free pronoun, it is expressed by a dative pronoun and cross-referenced by a bound pronoun.

(1510) Mungamunga-lu=ma jayi-nya ngu=lu=rla wajarra.
Spirit.Women-ERG=TOP give-PST CAT=3AUG.S=3OBL corroboree
"The Mungamunga gave *wajarra* to him." (RW: FM17_a444: 4:37min)

(1511) Ngu=yinangulu jayi-nga-ni tanku=ma, karu-wu=ma
CAT=3AUG.S>3AUG.NS give-IMPF-PST food=TOP child-DAT=TOP

nyarruluny-ku=ma, kamparri-jang-kulu=ma.
3AUG.DAT-DAT=TOP before-TIME-ERG=TOP
"They used to give the food to their kids in the old days."
(VW: FM10_a133: 27:24min)

(1512) Yalu-ngku=ma karu-wu=ma ngu=wula=rla
that-ERG=TOP child-DAT=TOP CAT=3UA.S=3OBL

jayi-nga-ni marnarnarn wankawankaj.
give-IMPF-PST bad.REDUP bad.REDUP
"They gave the child the bad ones." (PN: McNair_K1E: 2:23min)

The 'give' inflecting verb occurs on its own in the above examples. It also combines with coverbs with 'give' type meanings such as *wirnan* 'trade' (1513), but also with other coverbs such as *wiit* 'show' (1514), and *pinak* 'teach' (1515) which express more abstract notions of 'giving' such as passing on knowledge or information.

(1513) Ngumpit-tu=ma **wirnan**=ma=lu=nyunu jayi-nga-ni.
Aboriginal-ERG=TOP trade=TOP=3AUG.S=RR give-IMPF-PST
"Gurindji people used to trade." (🔊 PN: McNair_D2A: 3:13min)

(1514) **Wiit-wiit** jayi-nga-ni ngu=rla nyawa=kata
show-REDUP give-IMPF-PST CAT=3OBL this=IMM

pinyinyip-kaji, warlu-wu pirrkap-ku.
rub.between.palms-AGENT fire-DAT make-DAT
"She showed her the firedrill for making fire." (🔊 VW: FM09_a127: 5:24min)

(1515) Ngu=rna=ngku **pinak** jayi-ngku.
CAT=1EXC.MIN.S=2MIN.NS teach give-POT
"I'll teach you." (🔊 VW: FM08_08_1a: 10:10min)

Although *jayingana* 'give' is the most common inflecting verb used in a ditransitive clause, other possibilities exist. The inflecting verb *yuwanana* 'put' and *panana* 'hit' are used in combination with coverbs meaning 'send' such as *jalak* and *yujuk* to create O-theme ditransitive clauses, as in (1516) and (1517).

(1516) Ngayiny-ku jipiniya-wu ngu=rna=rla
1EXC.MIN.DAT-DAT boyfriend-DAT CAT=1EXC.MIN.S=3OBL

jalak **yuwa-rru** jarrakap milimili.
send put-POT talk letter
"I will send a letter to my boyfriend."
(DD with ECh: Meakins et al., 2016, p. 75)

(1517) Ngaji, ngu=n-ku=rla kirrawa **yujuk**
dad CAT=2MIN.S-EP=3OBL goanna send

pa-rru ngamanti-wu, ngamayi-wu?
hit-POT mum-DAT mum-DAT
"Dad – do you want to send some goanna to Mum now?"
(🔊 VW: FM10_a155: Ngarlking Karu: 2:54min)

Other ditransitive clauses of the O-theme type include clauses containing 'talk' type coverbs such as *yangki* which involve the topic of discussion and a listener. In (1518) the indirect object is *jungkart* 'cigarette' and the direct object is the unmarked *nyila kajirri* 'that woman'.

(1518) Marluka-lu na yangki pa-na-na
old.man-ERG FOC ask hit-IMPF-PRS

ngu nyila=ma kajirri=ma jungkart-ku.
CAT that=TOP old.woman=TOP cigarette-DAT
"The old man asks that woman for a cigarette."
(🔊 BW: FM07_a043: 8:19min)

Another type of O-theme ditransitive clause contains *yuwanana* 'put' and a dative-marked indirect object, for example (1519)–(1521).

(1519) Ngu=rna=rla ngayu namun
CAT=1EXC.MIN.S=3OBL 1EXC.MIN help.talk

yuwa-ni **jaru-wu** **murnungku-wu**.
put-PST language-DAT policeman-DAT
"I helped him talk to the police."
(RW & DD with ECh: Meakins et al., 2016, p. 254)

(1520) Ngu=rna=rla wililip yuwa-na-na
CAT=1EXC.MIN.S=3OBL draw.out.grub put-IMPF-PRS

yalu-wu na **lamawurt-ku.**
that-DAT FOC witchetty.grub-DAT
"Then we tried to draw out the witchetty grub." (VW: FM08_a099: 1:07min)

(1521) Nyila=ma=rla kirrkirr yuwa-na-na **jintaku-wu**=rni.
that=TOP=3OBL accompany put-IMPF-PRS one-DAT=ONLY
"He is always going around with that one person."
(McNair corpus: Meakins et al., 2016, p. 165)

8.4.2.16 Ditransitive clauses with an accusative object and spatial indirect object

Yet other ditransitive clauses of the O-theme type include clauses containing the inflecting verb *yuwanana* 'put'. This inflecting verb can take a locative-marked indirect object when it is used literally to express the end point of the action of *putting*, as in (1522)–(1525). Note that in these examples, the locative-marked indirect object is never registered as an oblique pronoun *=rla* because it is inanimate.

(1522) Yuwa-na-na kajirri-lu ngu murlukurn
put-IMPF-PRS old.woman-ERG CAT bottle

partaj mangarri-wu **jaartkarra-waji-la.**
climb veg.food-DAT eat-AGENT-LOC
"The woman puts the bottle on the table." (◀) BW: FM07_a043: 6:40min)

(1523) Kurrp yuwa-na-na ngu **janyja-ka.**
stab put-IMPF-PRS CAT ground-LOC
"She stabs at the ground [with a digging stick]." (◀) VW: FM12_a174: 14:32min)

(1524) Ngu=rnayinangulu lurlu yuwa-na-na, **tarlakurru-la.**
CAT=1EXC.AUG.S>3AUG.NS sit put-IMPF-PRS hole-LOC
"We make them sit in a hole in the ground." (◀) VW: FM07_01_1c: 2:52min)

(1525) Tuturrp ngu=rna yuwa-na-na
carry.fish.on.stick CAT=1EXC.MIN.S put-IMPF-PRS

pulinyin-ta yawu=ma.
fish.stick-LOC fish=TOP
"I thread the fish on the stick [to carry home]." (◀) VW: FM12_a178: 10:58min)

Alternatively, the 'put' verb can subcategorise for allative-marked goals, with a subtle meaning difference (1526) and (1527). In the case of (1527), the meaning seems to be 'into' the water rather than 'at' the water.

(1526) Kanyjurra na ngu=rna yuwa-ni **janyja-kurra** na lun.
down FOC CAT=1EXC.MIN.S put-PST ground-ALL FOC deposit
"I put it down on the ground." (◀) VW: FM07_a050: 3:30min)

(1527) Wumara ngu waj yuwa-na-na **ngawa-ngkurra.**
rock CAT throw put-IMPF-PRS water-ALL
"He throws the rock into the water." (◀) VW: FHM146: 1:56min)

Note that 'put' verbs also take adjuncts such as sources (1528) or locations (1529). Adjuncts are never cross-referenced with *=rla*.

(1528) Jurlurl yuwa-na-na **kartak-nginyi**=ma ngapulu.
pour put-IMPF-PRS jug-SOURCE=TOP milk
"She pours milk from the jug." (◀) BW: FM07_a43: 19:36min)

(1529) Yalu-ngku=ma kirri-ngku=ma nganta, **Halls Creek-kula**
that-ERG=TOP woman-ERG=TOP ALLE place.name-LOC

ngu=ngantipangulu yurrk yuwa-ni.
CAT=3AUG.S>1EXC.AUG.NS tell.story put-PST
"Some women told us at Halls Creek."
(◀) VW: FM10_27_1a: Kurraj Story from Halls Creek: 0:10min)

8.4.2.17 Ditransitive clauses with an accusative object and motivative indirect object

Finally, the motivative case also marks an indirect object. The motivative case is not observed in other Ngumpin-Yapa languages. It only appears in the corpus subcategorised for by the complex predicate *ngurrku panana* 'suspect hit'. In this example, the subject is ergative-marked, the direct object is cross-referenced by =*ngku* 'you' and the indirect object is *yala-nganayak ngumparna-nganayak* 'that husband', which is not cross-referenced by -*rla* '3OBL'.

(1530) Ngu=**ngku** ngurrku pa-na-na, yalu-ngku=ma,
CAT=2MIN.NS suspect hit-IMPF-PRS that-ERG=TOP

yala-nganayak ngumparna-nganayak.
that-MOT husband-MOT
"That one suspects you of [having an affair with] her husband."
(◀) VW: FM10_a154: 1:04min)

9 Complex sentences

Complex sentences consist of two or more clauses. Gurindji links clauses in coordinate clauses (§9.1) and subordinate clauses. Subordinate clauses can be divided into two types: finite (§9.2) and non-finite (§9.3).

9.1 Conjoined clauses

Conjoined clauses are often formed by juxtaposing two (or more) main clauses, which is a common pattern in Australian languages. Conjoined clauses are distinguished from a sequence of two or more main clauses by intonational criteria. Complex sentences which contain conjoined clauses occur within one intonational contour, as shown in (1531) whereas two juxtaposed main clauses have an intonation break separating them, as shown by (1532) and (1533), where the intonation break is indicated with a comma. In both examples the individual clauses are delineated by square brackets.

(1531) [Jama-na-ni ngu=rla jitirnijitirni]
grind-IMPF-PST CAT=3OBL half-ground

[ngu=rla jayi-nga-ni parntaparntara=rni].
CAT=3OBL give-IMPF-PST whole.REDUP=ONLY
"She ground it a bit and gave it to her half-ground, still whole."
(🔊 VW: FM10_23_1b: Yawarlwarl Wanyil: 4:23min)

(1532) [Ngu=ja ma-na-ni ngunyjung],
CAT=1EXC.UA.S get-IMPF-PST honey

[jaartkarra ngu=ja nya-nga-ni].
eat CAT=1EXC.UA.S intake-IMPF-PST
"We were getting a lump of honey and eating it." (🔊 TD: FM07_a028: 11:10min)

(1533) [Nyanuny <u>na</u> ngu=rla ya-ni jiwawu
3MIN.DAT FOC CAT=3OBL go-PST swoop

ma-ni], [warak kurtap=ma waninya ngarlaka=ma].
do-PST dodge duck=TOP fall.PST head=TOP
"[The eagle] went for him, swooped down but he dodged, he ducked his head down." (🔊 DD: EC98_a017: Karnati: 17:12min)

Conjoined clauses can mirror each other in structure. For example, in (1535), each clause shows the structure NGU-PRO VERB. This is not a requirement, however, since

https://doi.org/10.1515/9783110746884-009

the corpus includes examples of other conjoined clauses that do not match in structure as exemplified in (1531).

(1534)

[Ngu=rnayinangulu	ma-na-ni	warrwarrkuj]
CAT=1EXC.AUG.S>3AUG.NS	do-IMPF-PST	pick.up.REDUP

[ngu=lu	ma-na-ni	kajijirri-lu
CAT=3AUG.S	do-IMPF-PST	old.woman.REDUP-ERG

warrwarrkuj,	puntanup,	kampa-rnu-p-ku	murla-ngkawu].
pick.up.REDUP	collect	cook-INF-CV-DAT	this-PURP

"Then the women used to pick them up out of the water. They would collect them to cook them." (◀) VW: FM09_13_3a: 3:16min)

Conjoined clauses have a number of functions in Gurindji. The relationship between the sentences in (1535) is simultaneous where both actions occur at the same time. In other clauses such as (1536), the actions are sequential and therefore translated with 'then'. Example (1537) shows both simultaneous juxtaposed clauses and then sequential clauses.

(1535)

[Pinyinyip	ma-na-ni	ngu=lu]
rub.between.palms	do-IMPF-PST	CAT=3AUG.S

[ngunti	kiya-rna-ni	ngu=lu].
light	put-IMPF-PST	CAT=3AUG.S

"They used to twirl one stick in the depression of another and make a light." (◀) TD: FM09_17_2b: 0:22min)

(1536)

[Ngu=rnalu	karrinyani	purinyjirri-la=rni]
CAT=1EXC.AUG.S	be.IMPF.PST	late.afternoon-LOC=ONLY

[ngu=ngantipangkulu	ya-na-ni	wart-wart]
CAT=3AUG.S>1EXC.AUG.NS	go-IMPF-PST	return-REDUP

[ngu=rnayinangkulu	kampa-rna-ni	mangarri	nyampa
CAT=1EXC.AUG.S>3AUG.NS	cook-IMPF-PST	bread	something

ngarina	jiwijiwirri-k	ngantipa=ma,	janka-ku=ma].
meat	cooked.REDUP-FACT	1EXC.AUG=TOP	woman-DAT=TOP

"We stayed here, then in the late afternoon they would return to us and us women would cook some bread and meat for them."
(◀) BW: FM09_12_5a: 00:45min)

(1537) [Ngu=lu pu-nga-na kamparri-jang-kulu=ma jart-jart]
CAT=3AUG.S pierce-IMPF-PRS before-TIME-ERG=TOP push-REDUP

[ngu=lu=rla pu-nga-ni kuya]. ["Ah nyawa na
CAT=3AUG.S=3OBL pierce-IMPF-PST thus ah this FOC

ngurnta!"] [Kurrij ngu=lu pu-nga-ni yangunungku=ma]
potato.root dig CAT=3AUG.S pierce-IMPF-PST bush.potato=TOP

[ngu=lu paraj pu-nga-ni]. ['Ah nyawa=rni=warla
CAT=3AUG.S find pierce-IMPF-PST ah this=ONLY=FOC

mangarri=ma,' kuya]. [Ngu=lu pu-nga-ni]
veg.food=TOP thus CAT=3AUG.S pierce-IMPF-PST

[ngu=lu tup ma-na-ni, mangarri=ma].
CAT=3AUG.S pull.out do-IMPF-PST veg.food=TOP

"They used to dig for it in the old days by pushing back the sand. 'Ah here's the root'. They dug and found the tuber saying, 'Ah here's the potato.' Then they would dig for the potato and pull it up." (🔈 BW: FM09_12_6b: 1:06min)

Gurindji has no conjunctive particle equivalent to English 'and' or 'but', although *an* 'and' is a well-established borrowing from Kriol. It is used to link two clauses where the temporal sequencing of the clauses is sequential (1538) and (1539).

(1538) Lurlu ngu=rna karrinyana
sit CAT=1EXC.MIN.S be.IMPF.PRS

an ngu=rna pa-rru tikap.
and CAT=1EXC.MIN.S hit-POT chop

"I sit down and then I will chop the tree." (🔈 VW: FM07_a027: 5:20min)

(1539) Jiwirri-k=ma jiya-rni **an** ngu=lu ma-ni kuya na.
cooked-FACT=TOP burn-PST and CAT=3AUG.S do-PST thus FOC

"[The bush onion] cooked, then they rubbed the skin off."
(🔈 TD: FM07_059: 01:30min)

The conjunction *an* is also used to join nominals in much the same manner as English, where the last nominal is preceded by 'and', as in (1540)–(1542), but the 'and' can also come anywhere in the sequence of nominals, as in (1543) or indeed between every nominal, as shown in (1544). It can also link NPs, not simply nominals, as shown in (1545). The conjunction *an* can also co-occur with =*purrupurru* which is the closest element Gurindji has to 'and', for example (1546) (see §4.7.3 for more information on =*purrupurru*).

(1540) Ngarnjal, ngayu, Kitty, Biddy **an** Nangari
NAME 1EXC.MIN NAME NAME and SUBSECT

ngu=rnalu ya-ni pinka-kurra kanyjurra.
CAT=1EXC.AUG.S go-PST river-ALL down
"Topsy, me, Kitty, Biddy and Felicity went down to the river."
(🔊 VW: FM09_a127: 4:55min)

(1541) Ngu=rnayinangulu jungkart jiya-rna-ni, yirrijkaji-lu
CAT=1EXC.AUG.S>3AUG.NS smoke burn-IMPF-PST plant.sp-ERG

marlarn-tu **an** lawa-ngku murlu-ngku.
red.river.gum-ERG and lemon.wood-ERG this-ERG
"We used to smoke them with the leaves of the *yirrijkaji*, bloodwood and this lemonwood [by burning a fire down to charcoal and then throwing leaves on top]." (🔊 BW: FM07_01_1c: 2:32min)

(1542) Karu-walija-lu, marturtukuja-lu **an** kirri-walija-lu nyurrulu
child-PAUC-ERG female.REDUP-ERG and woman-PAUC-ERG 2AUG

jangkakarni-lu karrap ngu=nta nya-nga-na.
big.REDUP-ERG look CAT=2AUG.S intake-IMPF-PRS
"Only you mob female children and women are allowed to see the pictures."
(🔊 VW: FM07_a085: 19:27min)

(1543) Ngu=n-ku=rla ngaji-wu, jalak yuwa-rru, wayita,
CAT=2MIN.S-EP=3OBL dad-DAT send put-POT pencil.yam

an nyampayirla kamara, yangunungku.
and whatsitcalled long.yam bush.potato
"Do you want to send some yams and whatsitcalled black soil yams and potatoes to Dad." (🔊 VW: FM10_a155: Ngarlking Karu: 1:55min)

(1544) Ngu=rna pu-nga-ni nyila kurrij-karra, karntawarra
CAT=1EXC.MIN.S pierce-IMPF-PST that dig-ITER yellow.ochre

an kalnga **an** nyila pirlkiya, ngunyjungunyju.
and red.ochre and that white.ochre brown.ochre
"I'm digging there for yellow, red and that white and brown ochre."
(🔊 VW: FM07_a085: 15:23min)

(1545) Nyantu Yiparrartu kaninyjal-a ya-na-ni
3MIN Emu underneath-LOC go-IMPF-PST

an Pangarra kankulu-pal-a.
and Corella up-EDGE-LOC
"Emu was running below with Corella above." (🔊 VW: FM08_08_4e: 0:48min)

(1546) Wipuwipuk ma-nta tanku yala-nginyi. Walyawalyak
take.out.REDUP do-IMP food that-SOURCE inside.REDUP

nyamu=npayi yuwa-ni, warrayarl=**purrupurru**
REL=2MIN.S>1EXC.MIN.NS put-PST sugar=AND

mangarri **an** tinned-beef-nganyju.
bread and tinned-beef-GROUP
"Take the tucker out of that one. Where you put the sugar, bread and tinned beef inside for me." (🔊 VW: FM12_a183: 10:35min)

It is also very common for the conjunction *an* to head main clauses. Sometimes there is a link with a previous clause, as in (1547), but in many cases new clauses will simply begin with 'and' without an obvious link to the previous clause, as shown in (1548)–(1550). This is now very common in Gurindji Kriol, particularly in the children's speech where sequences of clauses will begin with 'and'. We leave the use of *an* open for analysis in these constructions.

(1547) Jirlan-jirlan, nyanawu nyamu wulngarn kutij karrinyana.
heat.up-REDUP RECOG REL sun stand be.IMPF.PRS

An jilngit na, kalu-ngka=ma, tupurrung.
and sweat FOC walk-LOC=TOP hot
"*Jirlanjirlan* means you know when the sun is high. And you sweat when you're walking [because] you're hot." (🔊 VW: FM12_a173: 7:54min)

(1548) **An** ngamayi-lu ngu=yina nguru jayi-nga-ni
and mother-ERG CAT=3AUG.NS prepare give-IMPF-PST

walyak-kula=ma nanta-nanta=ma nyila=ma.
inside-LOC=TOP small-REDUP=TOP that=TOP
"And the mother prepares to give food to the little ones inside."
(◀) VW: FM10_a149: 2:17min)

(1549) **An** kartak-kula ngu=rna yuwa-ni ngayu na.
and cup-LOC CAT=1EXC.MIN.S put-PST 1EXC.MIN FOC
"And I put it in the cup, I did." (◀) VW: FM07_a021: 3:19min)

(1550) **An** ngurra-witi ngu=ngantipa nyila,
and camp-SITE CAT=1EXC.AUG.NS that

kurla-rni-mpal-a nyawa kurla-rni-mpal-a.
south-UP-EDGE-LOC this south-UP-EDGE-LOC
"And we had a camping place on the south side." (◀) VW: FM09_15_1a: 0:14min)

Although there are no conjunctive particles, adjacent clauses can often produce the meaning of 'but' for example in (1551).

(1551) Ngu=rna=rla ngayu=rni jayi-nya
CAT=1EXC.MIN.S=3OBL 1EXC.MIN=ONLY give-PST

jaminypurra, kula yilmij jayi-nya.
gift NEG exchange give-PST
"I gave it to him like that [but] he didn't give [anything] in return."
(McNair corpus: Meakins et al., 2016, p. 78)

9.2 Finite subordinate clauses

There are six complementisers which connect two finite main clauses and specify the relationship that exists between them: *nyamu* 'which, who, when, RELativiser' (§9.2.1), *ngaja* 'lest, in case, or else, ADMONitive' (§9.2.2), *kata* 'THOugh' (§9.2.3), *kayi* 'SURPise' (§9.2.4), *kuyangka* 'that's when, <thus-LOC' (§9.2.5) and an old Kriol borrowing *tumaj(i)* 'beCAUSe' (§9.2.6).

Complementisers constitute a distinct word class. They share a number of features: (i) they all head a finite subordinate clause, (ii) they are found in first or second position in the subordinate clause and (iii) bound pronouns always attach to them.

9.2.1 *nyamu* RELativiser

The complementiser *nyamu* occurs at the beginning of what Hale (1976) calls an 'adjoined relative clause'. This clause type has both adverbial and relative functions, and in the case of relative clauses, may be discontiguous with respect to the nominal it modifies. Nordlinger (2006, p. 6) observes that Hale's term has been (mis-)interpreted as suggesting that Australian languages do not have true syntactic embedding and are largely homogenous with respect to clause-combining strategies. She proposes a different term 'general modifying subordinate clause' (GMSC) which allows for the heterogeneous nature of these constructions across Australian languages and the fact that they may indeed form subordinate clauses. This is the term adopted by McConvell (2006a) in his discussion of *nyamu* in Gurindji. McConvell (2006a, p. 112) suggests *nyamu* is derived from an old recognitional demonstrative which is still found in Warlmanpa. He notes that, in general, recognitional demonstratives are a common source of complementisers in Ngumpin-Yapa languages.

The relativiser has two forms: *nyamu* and *nyamu=waa*. The source of =*waa* is probably Ngarinyman and Mudburra, which have the relativising clitic =*waa*/=*paa*. It is not unusual in Gurindji to find doubled particles and clitics, often constructed through borrowings. For example, *maitbi=nga* 'maybe=DUB' which is derived from Kriol *maitbi* and Gurindji =*nga*. Pronominal clitics generally attach outside of =*waa*, as shown in (1552) but are occasionally found on the inside, as in (1553).

(1552)

Jiwarrp	ngu=rnalu	ma-na-na,	**nyamu=waa=ngantipa**
collect	CAT=1EXC.AUG.S	do-IMPF-PRS	REL=REL=1EXC.AUG.NS

piyarrp	yuwa-ni,	jangkarni	janga-ny
inform	put-PST	big	sick-NMLZ

na	wajirrki	jangkarni.
FOC	flu	big

"We collect it because [the nurse] told us about the Swine Flu."
(VW: FM09_14_1a: 6:31min)

(1553)

Nyila=ma	narranyjana-la	ngu=lu	karrinyana.	Jurlujpurru,[230]
that=TOP	windbreak-LOC	CAT=3AUG.S	be.IMPF.PRS	women.birth.camp

janka	ngu=yinangulu	tal	pa-na-ni
woman	CAT=3AUG.S>3AUG.NS	name	hit-IMPF-PST

230 The word *jurlujpurru* 'new mothers' is derived from *jurluj* 'cradle' and an unlenited form of the Mudburra comitative -*wurru*.

kamparri-jang-kulu=ma. Jurlujpurru=ma **nyamu=lu=waa**
before-TIME-ERG=TOP women.birth.camp=TOP REL=3AUG.S=REL

purirripurirri-la karrinyani. Narranyjana-la, nyamu=lu
birth.camp-LOC be.IMPF.PST windbreak-LOC REL=3AUG.S

pirrkap ma-na-ni narranyjana=ma kuya. Yala-ngka=warla
make do-IMPF-PST windbreak=TOP thus that-LOC=FOC

ngu=lu karrinyani jurlujpurru. Narranyjana-la=warla
CAT=3AUG.S be.IMPF.PST women.birth.camp windbreak-LOC=FOC

nyamu=lu karrinyani tupa-tupa-la.
REL=3AUG.S be.IMPF.PST windbreak-REDUP-LOC
"That's when they used to live in windbreaks. They used to call women 'jurlujpurru' a long time ago. 'Jurlujpurru' were women who lived in the birth camps. In windbreaks, when they used to make them. It was there that the 'jurlujpurru' lived. In windbreaks was where they used to live."
(🔊 VW: FM11_a167: 0:05min)

In terms of distribution, the subordinate clause which *nyamu* heads can either precede the main clause, as shown in (1554) and (1555), or follow it, as shown in (1556) and (1557). The subordinate clause is indicated by square brackets in these examples. Bound pronouns indicating arguments in the subordinate clause attach to *nyamu*.

(1554) [**Nyamu**=rna=nga purrp pa-rru], kawarla <u>na</u>
REL=1EXC.MIN.S=DUB finish hit-POT coolamon FOC

ngu=rna=nga pirrkap ma-nku.
CAT=1EXC.MIN.S=DUB make do-POT
"Maybe when I finish knocking [the bark] off, I'll make the coolamon."
(🔊 VW: FM07_a050: 6:39min)

(1555) [**Nyamu**=rna tak karrinyani]
REL=1EXC.MIN.S sit be.IMPF.PST

kuya-ngka=warla ngu=yi jayi-nya.
thus-LOC=FOC CAT=1EXC.MIN.NS give-PST
"When I was sitting down [that's when] he gave me it."
(McConvell corpus: Meakins et al., 2016, p. 290–291)

(1556) Ngayu=ma=rna ngurra-mala
1EXC.MIN=TOP=1EXC.MIN.S country-OWN

[nyamu=rna=nga ma-nku ngarin=ma].
REL=1EXC.MIN.S=DUB get-POT meat=TOP
"I'm the traditional custodian so I should get meat."
(McConvell 1996 grammar manuscript)

(1557) Nyanawu pilyily yapakayi majul-a
RECOG hairless.joey small stomach-LOC

[nyamu ka-nga-na puul-a walyak].
REL take-IMPF-PRS pouch-LOC inside
"You know the hairless joey that is still in its mother's pouch."
(🔊 VW: FM09_a123: 6:27min)

Subordinate clauses headed by *nyamu* have a range of functions, many of which are found in other Australian languages. Examples (1558)–(1562) are instances of conditional clauses where the complementiser hosts the pronominal clitics and the dubitative clitic =*nga* (§7.1.3.13). The potential form of the inflecting verb is used. In these examples, *nyamu* often translates as 'if' and is used to indicate a very tentative statement. This construction is commonly used in main clauses in *pirntika* 'avoidance speech' (§1.8.3), as befits the vague, circumspect nature of that discourse.

(1558) Ngu=rna karrwa-rna-ngku na ngajik
CAT=1EXC.MIN.S have-IMPF-POT FOC long.time

nyamu=yi=lu=nga pirrkap=ma ma-nku punyu-k=ma.
REL=1EXC.MIN.NS=3AUG.S=DUB make=TOP do-POT good-FACT=TOP
"I'll have it for a long time if they fix it for me." (🔊 VW: FM07_a021: 6:27min)

(1559) **Nyamu**=ngantipa=nga ka-ngku Nangari-lu=rningan.
REL=1EXC.AUG.NS=DUB take-POT SUBSECT-ERG=AGAIN
"If Felicity takes us again." (🔊 VW: FM07_a021: 8:19min)

(1560) **Nyamu**=nga karru week-kari, **nyamu** ya-nku kaput.
REL=DUB stay.POT week-OTHER REL go-POT tomorrow
"He might stay another week, [or] he might go tomorrow."
(McConvell corpus: Meakins et al., 2016, p. 291)

For hypothetical and counterfactual conditionals, an irrealis subjunctive mood clause is used (1561)–(1562). In the main clause *wayi*, the question particle (§10.2.10), is sometimes used as clitic base. As with temporal clauses, *kuya-ngka* 'that's when' may appear in the main clause.

(1561) **Nyamu**=yina=nga ngamayi-lu ngaya-rra
REL=3AUG.NS=DUB mother-ERG excrete-IMP

ngayiny-ja waruju-la=ma
1EXC.MIN.DAT-LOC together-LOC=TOP

kuya-ngka=ma **wayi**=rnayina=nga pa-rra.
thus-LOC=TOP Q=1EXC.MIN.S>3AUG.NS=DUB hit-IMP
"If the mother [cat] had given birth to them while I was around, I would have killed [the kittens]." (McConvell corpus: Meakins et al., 2016, p. 277)

(1562) **Nyamu**=n-ku=rla ma-lu kuya-wurt
REL=2MIN.S-EP=3OBL say-POT thus-TIMES

ngapaku=ma wanku-rra jurlurl.
rain=TOP fall.POT-HORT pour
"You might tell him let the rain pour for so many days." (Source unknown)

Conditional clauses are a special type of clause which have a T(emporal)-relative interpretation, according to Hale (1976, p. 80). Other examples of T-relative clauses which are not conditional clauses are given in (1554), (1555) and (1563)–(1567). Here *nyamu* is translated straightforwardly as 'when'. These clauses do not contain the dubitative clitic *=nga* and are not necessarily in potential mood.

(1563) Kuliyan=ma **nyamu**=n ma-lu kuli-kuli
aggressive=TOP REL=2MIN.S talk-POT argue-REDUP

nyila-rniny=kata=rni ngu=rnangkulu jarrara ma-nku.
that-HITH=IMM=ONLY CAT=1EXC.AUG.S>2MIN.NS follow do-POT
"When you talk aggressively we'll follow you up [with punishment]."
(McConvell 1996 grammar manuscript: Speaking to young people)

(1564) Ngu=rnalu kukij-karra-la,
CAT=1EXC.AUG.S drink-ITER-LOC

nyamu=waa karru jiwily-ing na.
REL=REL be.POT cold-ADJ FOC
"We will drink it when it gets cold." (🔊 VW: FM09_16_1b: 0:29min)

(1565) Ngu=rnalu puntanup ma-na-na, **nyamu=waa**
CAT=1EXC.AUG.S gather do-IMPF-PRS REL=REL

jiwirri=ma karrinyana, muying=ma.
ripe=TOP be.IMPF.PRS black.plum=TOP
"We collect the fruit [from the ground], when the fruit ripens."
(VW: FM09_15_2a: 5:54min)

(1566) **Nyamu**=lu waninyana karu, yapakayi, wal. Ngu=nyunu
REL=3AUG.S fall.IMPF.PRS child small well CAT=RR

tingkirt na ma-na-na kuya julu-ngku=ma.
tie.up FOC do-IMPF-PRS thus umbilical.cord-ERG=TOP
"When children are born, the umbilical cord can wrap itself around [the baby's neck] like this." (VW: FM10_a143: 8:45min)

(1567) Ngu=rnayinangulu kampa-rna-na
CAT=1EXC.AUG.S>3AUG.NS cook-IMPF-PRS

karu, **nyamu**=lu ngajkula karrinyana.
child REL=3AUG.S diarrhoea be.IMPF.PRS
"We 'cook' [treat the kids with medicines] when they have diarrhoea."
(VW: FM07_a085: 0:20min)

The other type of *nyamu* clause is a relative clause (NP-relative in Hale's (1976) terms). Relative clauses are NP modifiers, and serve to "make more determinate or to supply additional information about an argument in the main clause" (Hale, 1976, p. 79). An example is given in (1557). In these examples, *nyamu* occurs after the NP it modifies (1568)–(1571) or it can split the NP, as in (1572) and (1573). The NP it modifies is given in square brackets. In these examples, *nyamu* translates as 'who', 'which' or 'where'.

(1568) [Ngantipany nungkiying] **nyamu**=lu kamparri-jang waninya.
1EXC.AUG.DAT family REL=3AUG.S before-TIME fall.PST
"Our family who have passed away." (VW: FM08_01_3: 1:41min)

(1569) Ngu=lu ya-na-na julujuluj-karra,
CAT=3AUG.S go-IMPF-PRS carry.under.arm.REDUP-ITER

karu=ma, [yala-ny-jawung na kawarla-yawung
child=TOP that-NMLZ-PROP FOC coolamon-PROP

kuya-ny] **nyamu**=rnayinangkulu pirrkap
thus-NMLZ REL=1EXC.AUG.S>3AUG.NS make

ma-na-na yapayapa-wu, murlukurn-ku, julujuluj-ku.
do-IMPF-PRS small-DAT bottle-DAT carry.under.arm-DAT
"[The little girls] walk-around carrying coolamons on their hips which we make for them to carry bottles [as toy babies]." (VW: FM07_a050: 11:55min)

(1570) [Nyawa, kankula, winyji kayi-rni-ngarna]
this up spring north-UP-ASSOC

nyamu jurlurl waninyana ngawa.
REL spill fall.IMPF.PRS water
"There's a spring up north where water spills down from [referring to the spring at Jampawurru]." (VW: FM09_15_2a: 0:47min)

(1571) Ngu=rnalu nya-nga-na tirnung-ku,
CAT=1EXC.AUG.S intake-IMPF-PRS sap-DAT

[karnti-ka] **nyamu=waa** karrinyana.
tree-DAT REL=REL be.IMPF.PRS
"I'm looking for the sap which is on the [bloodwood] tree."
(VW: FM07_01_1b: 0:49min)

(1572) Yatu, ngu=rnalu ma-na-na nyila=ma yatu
white.ochre CAT=1EXC.AUG.S do-IMPF-PRS that=TOP white.ochre

wal, [nyila=ma] **nyamu**=lu kutitij [nyarrulu=ma] karrinya.
well that=TOP REL=3AUG.S stand.REDUP 3AUG=TOP be.PST
"We get the white ochre from where that mob [of Dreaming children] were standing around." (VW: FM10_v30_1a: Karu Dreaming Story: 1:33min)

(1573) [Nungkiying-kulu] **nyamu**=ngantipangulu
family-ERG REL=3AUG.S>1INC.AUG.NS

[ngantipanguny-ju] pinak jayi-nga-ni.
1EXC.AUG.DAT-ERG teach give-IMPF-PST
"Yes, when our old women used to teach us." (VW: FM09_12_5d: 1:02min)

Relative clauses can switch the grammatical relation of the NP between the main clause and the subordinate clause. For example in (1574), the modified NP is the subject of an intransitive clause (S) in the main clause and the subject of a transitive clause (A) in the subordinate clause. Note that the nominal is repeated with ergative marking before *nyamu*. In (1575), the modified NP is the object of a transitive clause (O) in the main clause and the subject of a transitive clause (A) in the subordinate clause.

(1574) Nyila **nyamu** ya-na-na warlaku=ma
that REL go-IMPF-PRS dog=TOP

yalu-ngku=warla ngu=yi paya-rni.
that-ERG=FOC CAT=1EXC.MIN.NS bite-PST
"That dog that's going along is the one that bit me."
(McConvell corpus: Meakins et al., 2016, p. 290)

(1575) Nyila **nyamu**=rna nga-rni wararr ngu=yi
that REL=1EXC.MIN.S eat-PST fat CAT=1EXC.MIN.NS

kampa-rna-na majul-la.
cook-IMPF-PRS stomach-LOC
"That fat that I ate is hurting me in my stomach."
(McConvell corpus: Meakins et al., 2016, p. 393)

Another subtype of relative clause has no verb in the subordinate clause but has a dative NP indicating what/who the head NP belongs to (alienable possession). Possessive specifiers may be rendered just by a dative NP associated with another noun; however particularly when the head is itself in a non-zero case relation in the main clause, the possessive relative clause alternative is often resorted to.

(1576) Kartiya-lu ngu=n kurru karru jaru
non-Indigenous-ERG CAT=2MIN.S hear be.POT story

[ngantipany ngumpit-ku **nyamu**=ngantipa yumi].
1EXC.AUG.DAT Aboriginal-DAT REL=1EXC.AUG.NS law
"You, a *kartiya,* will hear the story of our Aboriginal Law."
(McConvell 1996 grammar manuscript)

McConvell (2006a, p. 114) also observes that *nyamu* clauses in Gurindji can be used as reason clauses. An example of such a function is given in (1577)–(1580).

(1577) Nomo ngarrka ma-nta=yi=wula
NEG remember do-IMP=1EXC.MIN.NS=3UA.S

nyamu=yinpula warlaku-marraj=ma wanyja-ni.
REL=2UA.S>1EXC.MIN.NS dog-COMP=TOP leave-PST
"Don't think you remember me because you left me like a dog."
(◀)) VW: FM10_a155: Ngarlking Karu: 10:12min)

(1578) Nyawa=ma=rna=ngku ngayirrap karrinyani
this=TOP=1EXC.MIN.S=2MIN.NS worry stay.IMPF.PST

nyamu=rlaa ngajik karrinyani.
REL=1INC.AUG.S long.time stay.IMPF.PST
"I was anxious about you because we had stayed together for so long."
(McConvell corpus: Meakins et al., 2016, p. 278)

(1579) **Nyamu**=yi=lu ma-rna-na kanyju-kanyju-k=ma
REL=1EXC.MIN.NS=3AUG.S talk-IMPF-PRS below-REDUP-ALL=TOP

kula=rna punyu kuya-ngka=ma.
NEG=1EXC.MIN.S good thus-LOC=TOP
"I am not happy because they are talking behind my back."
(McConvell 1996 grammar manuscript)

(1580) Ngayu=ma=rna ngurra-mala
1EXC.MIN=TOP=1EXC.MIN.S country-OWN

nyamu=rna=nga ma-nku ngarin=ma.
REL=1EXC.MIN.S=DUB get-POT meat=TOP
"I'm a traditional custodian so I should get meat."
(McConvell 1996 grammar manuscript)

The 'because' meaning of the clitic *=waju/=paju* can be added to an element in the clause (§10.1.6). When used with an NP this suffix has the meaning 'kind of' – local Kriol *tumaj(i)* from English 'too much' has a similar range of functions.

The following example also shows one *nyamu* clause (relative type) embedded in another (reason type). These types of multiple embedding invariably start with the most deeply embedded clause and work up to the main clause. Note here too the COMP+clitics intervening between the coverb *kurrwara* and the inflecting verb *yuwani*.

(1581) Parnkarrang=ma **nyamu**=rna **ngayu=waju**
murderer=TOP REL=1EXC.MIN.S 1EXC.MIN=BECAUSE

kurrwara **nyamu**=yi=nta yuwa-ni nyawa
blame REL=1EXC.MIN.NS=2AUG.S put-PST this

ngu=rna=nyjurra jarrak ma-lu.
CAT=1EXC.MIN.S=2AUG.NS make.speech talk-POT
"Because you have accused me of being the murderer, I want to talk to you people." (McConvell corpus: Meakins et al., 2016, p. 191)

The relativiser *nyamu* also functions much like *that* clauses in English in that it can make statements about states of affairs which may be the complements of verbs of perception and of cognition, as in (1582). Note that this sentence does not mean 'The *kartiya* didn't know the old man who made it rain'.

(1582) Kartiya=ma kula=rla pina karrinya yalu-wu=ma
non-Indigenous=TOP NEG=3OBL know be.PST that-DAT=TOP

marluka-wu=ma **nyamu** ngawa pirrka ma-ni.
old.man-DAT=TOP REL water make do-PST
"The *kartiya* didn't know that the old man made rain [lit. didn't know about that old man, that he made rain]." (McConvell corpus: Meakins et al., 2016, p. 323)

This relativiser is also found in Bilinarra, Ngarinyman and Malngin (Ise, 1998; C. Jones, Schultze-Berndt, Denniss, et al., 2019, p. 53; Meakins & Nordlinger, 2014, pp. 414–417).

9.2.2 *ngaja* ADMONitive

Ngaja was introduced in §7.1.3.11. It was described as expressing admonitive mood in main clauses with the meaning of 'might'. It is possible that its use in main clauses is the result of a historic insubordination process. In this section, we describe its original use in subordinate clauses where it expresses a meaning of 'lest, in case, or else'. In complex clauses of this kind, the main clause indicates an action which is or should be taken to avoid some undesirable event, which is then described by the subordinate clause introduced by *ngaja*. For example, in (1583), pregnant women are instructed not to eat gravid goannas (main clause) in case their baby is born with sores (subordinate clause). In (1584) the main clause describes an action (carrying babies in coolamons flat on their backs) which prevents a potentially negative consequence (back pain).

(1583)

Kula	nga-lu	kampij-jawung=ma	kirrawa=ma,	**ngaja**	janga
NEG	eat-POT	egg-PROP=TOP	goanna=TOP	ADMON	sick

karrinyana	karu=ma	nyila=ma,	ngarturr-jawung-kulu=ma.
be.IMPF.PRS	child=TOP	that=TOP	pregnant-PROP-ERG=TOP

"A pregnant woman shouldn't eat goannas with eggs or else the baby is born with sores." (🔊 VW: FM09_a123: 0:14min)

(1584)

Ngitji	ngu=rnayinangkulu	karrinyani	karu-wu,
care.for	CAT=1EXC.AUG.S>3AUG.NS	be.IMPF.PST	child-DAT

parntawurru-wu	**ngaja**=lu	warrwarrngun	karrinyana.
back-DAT	ADMON=3AUG.S	pain.REDUP	be.IMPF.PRS

"We used to care for the kids' backs or else they have back pain."
(🔊 VW: FM07_a050: 5:07min)

In (1583) and (1584), the subordinate clause is expressed in present tense, which suggests the certainty of a consequence, for example 'or else you will ...'. This certainty is decreased by the use of the dubitative clitic =*nga* in combination with present tense (1585) or potential mood (1586) and (1587), for example 'in case you might ...'. The clitic usually attaches to *ngaja* (1585), but is also found attached to the verb (1586) and (1587).

(1585)

Ngu=rnayinangulu	ma-rna-na	karu=ma,	nomo
CAT=1EXC.AUG.S>3AUG.NS	say-IMPF-PRS	child=TOP	NEG

ma-nta=rla	mungku	warrwarrkuj.	Ngawa-ngka	nyamu
do-IMP=3OBL	red-faced.turtle	pick.up.REDUP	water-LOC	REL

karrinyana	murla-rniny	jeya	bank-kula	im	jidan	wumara-la.
be.IMPF.PRS	this-HITH	there	bank-LOC	3SG	stay	rock-LOC

'No	nomo	ma-nta=rla	nyila.	**Ngaja**=**nga**=rla
NEG	NEG	do-IMP=3OBL	that	ADMON=DUB=3OBL

Kurraj-ju	ngilyipurr	nga-rna-na.'	Nyamu=nta=nga
Rainbow.Spirit-ERG	drown	eat-IMPF-PRS	REL=2AUG.S=DUB

ma-nku=ma.	Kuya	ngu=rnayinangulu	yapayapa	ma-rna-na.
do-POT=TOP	thus	CAT=1EXC.AUG.S>3AUG.NS	small	say-IMPF-PRS

"We tell the kids not to get this kind of turtle which lives under rocks in the water on the side of waterholes. 'No don't get that one or the Rainbow Spirit might drown you if you get it.' That's what we tell the kids."
(🔊 VW: FM10_23_4: 07:34min)

(1586)

Yiparrartu	gigin	Mamurrung	ngu	nyawa=ma.	Murla-nginyi
Emu	again	Dreaming.site	CAT	this=TOP	this-SOURCE

karnti,	nyawa-rra	kula=rlaa	pa-rru	kataj-kataj=ma.
tree	this-PL	NEG=1INC.AUG.S	hit-POT	cut-REDUP=TOP

Ngaja=n	janga	**karru=nga**	na.
ADMON=2MIN.S	sick	be.POT=DUB	FOC

"This [Jampawurru] is an Emu Dreaming place. We can't cut down trees here, in case you get sick." (VW: FM09_13_2d: 2:57min)

(1587)

Ngu=rnayinangulu	wuukarra	karrinyana	ngu=yinangulu
CAT=1EXC.AUG.S>3AUG.NS	scared	be.IMPF.PRS	CAT=3AUG.S>3AUG.NS

kamparri-jang=ma	**ngaja**=yina	ngarlaka	**jiya-wu=nga**
before-TIME=TOP	ADMON=3AUG.NS	head	burn-POT=DUB

wulngarn-tu.
sun-ERG

"In the old days, we used to be worried about [the babies] in case the sun burnt their heads." (VW: FM07_05_1a: 2:56min)

When the time of the event has passed and no negative consequence has occurred, the main clause is expressed in present tense and the subordinate clause in the irrealis mood, as shown in (1588).

(1588)

Ngu=rna	turt	ma-ni	**ngaja**	wanta.
CAT=1EXC.MIN.S	hold	do-PST	ADMON	fall.IMP

"I held him in case he fell [so he didn't]."
(McConvell corpus: Meakins et al., 2016, p. 260)

This form *ngaja* is also used in Bilinarra and Malngin (Ise, 1998, p. 38; Jones, Schultze-Berndt, Denniss, et al., 2019, p. 53; Meakins & Nordlinger, 2014, p. 419). The form in Wanyjirra and Ngardi is *ngarra* (Ennever, 2021; Senge, 2016, p. 487).

9.2.3 *kata* THOught

Kata 'thought' is used to introduce subordinate clauses where the main clause expresses presumed knowledge on the speaker's part which turns out not to be true. It often translates as 'X thought but', 'presumed that' or 'despite the fact that'. It often combines with the dubitative clitic =*nga*, but not always.

(1589)

Kata=yi=n=**nga**	ma-rni	ngajik-ku	ya-nu-wu,
THO=1EXC.MIN.NS=2MIN.S=DUB	say-PST	long.time-DAT	go-INF-DAT

kayi=n	ya-na-na	wart-pa=rnirni	wajija=rni.
follow=2MIN.S	go-IMPF-PRS	return-EP=ONLY.REDUP	quickly=ONLY

"Despite you telling me you would go for a long time, here you are coming back quickly." (McConvell corpus: Meakins et al., 2016, p. 444)

(1590)

Karrinya	nyawa=ma	jingk-abat	na	**kata=nga**	nga-rni	ngilyipurr.
be.PST	this=TOP	think-ATEL	FOC	THO=DUB	eat-PST	drown

"Back at the station he presumed that [Jangala] had drowned."
(🔊 BB: McNair_E2A: 6:53min])

(1591)

Wal	**kata=nga**	jinek-ku=waju	maiti
well	THO=DUB	snake-DAT=BECAUSE	maybe

lungkura	karrinyani	ngu.
blue-tongue.lizard	be.IMPF.PST	CAT

"Well she thought it was a snake but maybe it was a blue-tongue."
(🔊 CN: FM10_29_3b: 5:01min)

It is also common to find *kata=nga* heading a main clause rather than a subordinate clause. In these cases, the speaker is expressing some doubt about the proposition. The relative contribution of *kata* and *=nga* is not clear.

(1592)

Kata=nga	wumara-wu=waju	**kata=nga**.
THO=DUB	money-DAT=BECAUSE	THO=DUB

"Maybe for the purpose of paying us." (🔊 VW: FM09_12_5b: 2:17min)

(1593)

Kata=rna=nyjurra=**nga**	kurany-karra	ma-rna-na,	kuya.
THO=1EXC.MIN.S=2AUG.NS=DUB	lie-ITER	do-IMPF-PRS	thus

"'You mob reckon I'm telling you a lie,' he said."
(🔊 BB: McNair_D1B: 1:53min)

(1594)

Yala-nginyi=ma	**kata=nga**	nyirn	ma-nta.
that-SOURCE=TOP	THO=DUB	forget	do-IMP

"After that incident, Rangiari thought [the spirit] would have forgotten him."
(🔊 PN: McNair_H2B: 0:06min)

This complementiser is not found in the surrounding Ngumpin languages, but a similar form with the same function is found in Warlpiri *kurlangarra*. Sometimes Gurindji speakers code-switch and use this form in Gurindji matrix clauses, as in (1595).

(1595)

Lungkura-la	kanyjurra	i	bin
blue-tongue.lizard-LOC	down	3SG	PST

faind-im	**kurlangarra**	jinek.
find-TR	THO	snake

"She found a bluetongue in the hole, but she thought it was a snake."
(🔈 SO: FM10_29_3a: 4:40min)

9.2.4 *kayi* 'SURPrise'

This complementiser occurs rarely in the corpus. It encodes the basic meaning 'but' but also with an element of surprise.

(1596)

Kata=yin=nga	ma-rni	ngajik-ku	ya-nu-wu,
THO=2MIN.S>1EXC.MIN.NS=DUB	talk-PST	long.time-DAT	go-INF-DAT

kayi=n	ya-na-na	wart-pa=rnirni	wajija=rni.
SURP=2MIN.S	go-IMPF-PRS	return-EP=ONLY.REDUP	quickly=ONLY

"I thought you told me you would go for a long time, but here you are coming back quickly." (McConvell corpus: Meakins et al., 2016, p. 444)

(1597)

Nyawa=ma	kula=yi=lu	punyu-punyu	ka-nga-ni
this=TOP	NEG=1EXC.MIN.NS=3AUG.S	good-REDUP	take-IMPF-PST

nyawa=warla	ngarin=ma,	**kayi**=lu	wurlaj	karrwa-rna-ni.
this=FOC	meat=TOP	SURP=3AUG.S	hide	keep-IMPF-PST

"They never brought me this good meat, they've been keeping it hidden from me." (Appendix: Echidna and Big Shade: Text 1, Line 18)

This complementiser is found in one other Ngumpin language but has a different function. *Kayi* is used in Warlmanpa to encode the meaning of 'while' or 'when' (Browne, 2021).

9.2.5 *kuyangka* 'that's when'

This complementiser is derived from the adverbial demonstrative *kuya* 'thus' and the locative *-ngka*. See §5.1 for more discussion about *kuya*. It combines with *-ngka* to produce the meaning 'that's when' (McConvell, 2006a, p. 114).

(1598)
Yikili	ya-na-na.	**Kuya-ngka**=ma=n	nya-nga-na
far	go-IMPF-PRS	thus-LOC=TOP=2MIN.S	intake-IMPF-PRS

junpurlp	<u>na</u>	ya-na-na	ngu	kuya.
receding.figure	FOC	go-IMPF-PRS	CAT	thus

"He goes a long way away. So when you look he's a receding figure in the distance." (🔊 VW: FM12_a173: 14:08min)

(1599)
Kuya-ngka=ma	ngu=lu	karrinyani	wampal,	kimu.
thus-LOC=TOP	CAT=3AUG.S	be.IMPF.PST	quiet	silent

"That's when they were playing nicely again."
(🔊 VW: LC080305GUR.KALK_02VW.mp3: 1:28min)

The complementiser *kuyangka* also combines with a T-relative clause headed by *nyamu*. It's not entirely clear how to analyse these syntactically since both head subordinate clauses but sequentially they create a 'when X that's when Y' meaning, as in (1600) and (1601).

(1600)
Nyamu=rna	tak	karrinyani	**kuya-ngka**=warla
REL=1EXC.MIN.S	sit	be.IMPF.PST	thus-LOC=FOC

ngu=yi	jayi-nya.
CAT=1EXC.MIN.NS	give-PST

"When I was sitting down that's when he gave it to me."
(McConvell corpus: Meakins et al., 2016, p. 196)

(1601)
Nyuntu	**nyamu**=yi=n	ma-rni	kuli,
2MIN	REL=1EXC.MIN.NS=2MIN.S	talk-PST	argue

kuya-ngka	ngu=rna=ngku	ngarru=ma
thus-LOC	CAT=2MIN.NS=1EXC.MIN.S	talk.rude=TOP

ma-rni	ngayu=ma,	nyununy-jirri-la.
talk-PST	1EXC.MIN=TOP	2MIN.DAT-ALL-LOC

"When you swore at me, that's when I told you off." (🔊 VW: FM10_a152: 1:32min)

9.2.6 *tumaji* beCAUSe

Tumaji, sometimes also pronounced *tumaj*, is an old Kriol borrowing derived from the English 'too much' (Hudson, 1985, p. 181). It is commonly used in Gurindji even in the speech of the oldest speakers which is why it is included in this grammar. It is also found in Bilinarra and Ngardi (Ennever, 2021; Meakins & Nordlinger, 2014, p. 420).

Tumaji introduces subordinate clauses which specify the cause or the reason for the action, state or event described by the main clause. The clause introduced by *tumaji* usually refers to an event which is prior to that of the main clause, or a state which holds up to and during the event described by the main clause (1602)–(1606) and (1608), however the clauses can also be potential descriptions of something that might happen in the future (1607). *Tumaji* is typically translated with the English 'because'.

(1602) Im sacred place nyawa=ma, [**tumaj** Yiparrartu ya-ni ngu].
3SG sacred place this=TOP CAUS Emu go-PST CAT
"It's a sacred place because Emu came here." (🔈 VW: FM09_13_2d: 3:12min)

(1603) Onli ngu=rnalu wart ya-ni kankula na,
only CAT=1EXC.AUG.S return go-PST up FOC

[**tumaji** tupurrung=ngantipa wulngarn-tu tupurrung jiya-rni].
CAUS hot=1EXC.AUG.NS sun-ERG hot burn-PST
"Then we turned back from that area and came back because it was too hot for us." (🔈 VW: FM07_a054: 2:16min)

(1604) Karu-walija,[231] ngawa ngu=lu kukij-karra paya-rni
child-PAUC water CAT=3AUG.S drink-ITER bite-PST

[**tumaji** ngawa=ma ngu=ngantipa jiya-rni].
CAUS water=TOP CAT=1EXC.AUG.NS burn-PST
"The kids, well they drank it up because we were really thirsty."
(🔈 EO: FM10_29_3d: 3:01min)

(1605) Nyawa=rni=ma tampang jiya-rni nyila=ma kajirri=ma,
this=ONLY=TOP die burn-PST that=TOP old.woman=TOP

231 Note that although *karu-walija* 'children' is a transitive subject, it is offset by an intonation break as a dislocated topic which is why it does not receive ergative-marking.

[**tumaji** ngu ngapaku-wu tapu ma-na-ni].
CAUS CAT water-DAT mean do-IMPF-PST
"Just like that the old woman died because she was mean with the water."
(◀) VW: FM10_30_2b: 1:47min)

(1606) Ngu=lu pinarri du karrinya nyarralu=rningan,
CAT=3AUG.S knowledgeable too be.PST 3AUG=AGAIN

[**tumaji** kula=lu ma-rna-na jaru=ma punyu].
CAUS NEG=3AUG.S talk-IMPF-PRS language=TOP good
"They have to learn that one too because they don't speak Gurindji well."
(◀) VW: FM08_11_3: 2:30min)

(1607) Ma-nku ngu=n purrp, [**tumaji** kuya-ny
do-POT CAT=2MIN.S finish CAUS thus-NMLZ

kula=ma week-kula=ma ngu ya-nku].
NEG=TOP week-LOC=TOP CAT go-POT
"You have to do the whole lot because she can't come next week."
(◀) VW: FM07_01_2a: 5:51min)

(1608) Kurrij-karra-la=ma ngu=lu pu-nga-ni
dig-ITER-LOC=TOP CAT=3AUG.S pierce-IMPF-PST

wumara=ma nyampa=ma mayarni-kari, [marntaj na
money=TOP anything=TOP more-OTHER OK FOC

ka-nga-nta=lu **tumaji** pulngayit-nginyi].
take-IMPF-IMP=3AUG.S CAUS floodwater-SOURCE
"We were digging around for money, anything really. We were allowed to take anything [we found] from the floodwaters." (◀) BB: McNair_E2A: 12:53min)

Like other complementisers, *tumaji* is not always the first element in the subordinate clause, with prominent elements of the subordinate clauses appearing before the complementiser. In (1609), the subordinate clause is indicated in square brackets to show the relative position of *tumaji*.

(1609)

Wanyji-kurra=warla=rnalu	ya-ni	kawarla-wu,
which-ALL=FOC=1EXC.AUG.S	go-PST	coolamon-DAT

[kula=rna	nya-ngku	**tumaji**	karrap].
NEG=1EXC.MIN.S	intake-POT	CAUS	look

"Where did we go to get coolamon wood? Because I can't see properly."[232]
(🔈 VW: FM09_a120: 0:18min)

The complementiser *tumaji* also heads a verbless clause (§8.2), as shown in (1610) and (1611) or even simply an NP, as in (1612).

(1610)

[Jarrwa	**tumaji**	Mungamunga]	ngu=rnalu
many	CAUS	Spirit.Women	CAT=1EXC.AUG.S

karru	karu=ma	karla-mpa=rni	kuya.
be.POT	child=TOP	west-PERL=ONLY	thus

"Because there are too many Mungamunga here, we'll stay with the kids right in the west [at Alan Bore]." (🔈 CN: FM10_28_2a: 3:44min)

(1611)

Nyanuny-ju	kaminyjarr-u	ngu=yinangulu	kampa-rni
3MIN.DAT-ERG	grandchild-ERG	CAT=3AUG.S>3AUG.NS	cook-PST

[**tumaji**	ngarlking	ngu=wula	wulawulaj-kaji	kamara-wu=ma].
CAUS	greedy	CAT=3UA.S	hide.REDUP-AGENT	long.yam-DAT=TOP

"Her grandchildren burnt them because they were greedy over the yams and kept them hidden." (🔈 BB: McNair_I1B: 3:16min)

(1612)

Kula=lu=rla	ma-nta	yalu-wu=ma
NEG=3AUG.S=3OBL	get-IMP	that-DAT=TOP

[**tumaji**	nyampayirla-wu	munpa-wu	marntaj].
CAUS	whatsitcalled-DAT	bush.spirit-DAT	OK

"They wouldn't pick it up because it was the malevolent bush spirit's and might have been dangerous." (🔈 BB: McNair_D1C: 6:24min [384667])

This complementiser also behaves like a particle in that it can head a main clause (1613)–(1616), and in this role, often appears in clause-final position (1617) and (1618). It does not host pronominal clitics, as it does in Bilinarra, so also appears more like a particle than complementiser in this respect.

232 We are watching a video of cutting wood for coolamons and she is struggling to see the computer screen well.

(1613)

Tumaji	ngu=rnalu	nyawa	ma-na-na.
CAUS	CAT=1EXC.AUG.S	this	get-IMPF-PRS

"Because we're getting this one." (🔊 TY: FM08_08_4c: 1:18min [78543])

(1614)

Nyawa=ma,	ngu=ngantipa	**tumaj**
this=TOP	CAT=1EXC.AUG.NS	CAUS

pa-ni	purrju-ngku,	wuyurrunkarra=ma.
hit-PST	marchfly-ERG	fishing=TOP

"This is because the march flies would bite us fishing."
(🔊 TD: FM10_a134: 2:27min)

(1615)

Kula=rna=rla	ma-rni	**tumaji**	jarrakap=ma
NEG=1EXC.MIN.S=3OBL	talk-PST	CAUS	talk=TOP

nyawa=ma	ngamanpurru	stori=ma,	Nangari-wu=ma.
this=TOP	conkerberry	story=TOP	SUBSECT-DAT=TOP

"Because I didn't tell that conkerberry story to Nangari before."
(🔊 VW: FM09_16_2: 3:25min)

(1616)

Makurru	**tumaji**	jala=ma.
cold	CAUS	today=TOP

"Because it's a bit cold today." (🔊 VW: FM09_13_2a: 0:49min)

(1617)

Nyila=ma	mirlirti=ma	tirrk,	kula=nga	ya-nku=ma
that=TOP	hook=TOP	tie	NEG=DUB	go-POT=TOP

yilarrp=ma	lawara	ma-nku=nga	nang	warraaj-ju	**tumaj**.
come.off=TOP	nothing	do-POT=DUB	stuck	wax-ERG	CAUS

"This hook [well] tie it on [to the spear-thrower] and it won't fall off because the wax will keep it stuck on." (McConvell corpus: Meakins et al., 2016, p. 214)

(1618)

Ngu=ngayirra	Nangari-lu	ka-nya	ngu=ja
CAT=1EXC.UA.NS	SUBSECT-ERG	bring-PST	CAT=1EXC.UA.S

pinak-pinak	jayi-nga-na,	murlu-wu	na	mangarri-wu
teach-REDUP	give-IMPF-PRS	this-DAT	FOC	veg.food-DAT

yangunungku-wu	kula	pina	**tumaji**.
bush.potato-DAT	NEG	know	CAUS

"Nangari brought us, so we will teach her because she doesn't know about this bush potato." (🔊 VW: FM09_12_6a: 0:27min)

Like *kuyangka, tumaji* can also appear with another subordinate clause headed by *nyamu*. Once again, it is not clear how to analyse this string of subordinate clauses, but it is interesting to note that this sequencing only occurs with the two recently developed complementisers.

(1619) Nyamu=yi=lu ma-nku punyu-k=ma nyila=ma,
REL=1EXC.MIN.NS=3AUG.S do-POT good-FACT=TOP that=TOP

pakipaki=ma, pirrkapirrkap-ku, yunpa-rnu-p-kaji-wu
chisel=TOP make.REDUP-DAT sing-INF-CV-AGENT-DAT

nyampa-waji-wu, **tumaji** wartan=pa=rni hold-im-ap
what-AGENT-DAT CAUS hand-EP=ONLY hold-TR-ATEL

kirlkirlp ngu=rna karrinyana.
hit.together CAT=1EXC.MIN.S be.IMPF.PRS
"If I make a decent chisel for making clapsticks. Because when I go to ceremony, I only use my hands for clapping." (🔊 VW: FM07_a021: 6:58min)

9.3 Non-finite or reduced subordinate clauses

Non-finite or reduced subordinate clauses have either a sole coverb (§7.2) or a non-finite form of the inflecting verb (§7.1.3.6) as their predicate which is then case-marked to indicate (i) temporal information relative to the main clause, and in some cases (ii) which grammatical role the subject of the subordinate clause is co-referential with in the main clause, referred to as switch reference. Example (1621) shows a purposive subordinate clause where the non-finite verb *kamparnu*, coverb *wupkarra* and object nominal *ngarin* are all marked dative to indicate that the action of the main clause has a purpose. In (1621), the coverb *warrkap* 'dance' is marked allative to indicate that the actions denoted by both clauses are simultaneous and the subject of the subordinate clause is the object of the main clause.

(1620) Ma-nta=ngali-ku=rla **nalija-wu**
get-IMP=1INC.MIN.NS-EP=3OBL tea-DAT

kampa-rnu-wu ngarin-ku wupkarra-wu.
cook-INF-DAT meat-DAT cook.on.coals-DAT
"Get us (some wood) to make tea and cook meat." (🔊 VW: FM11_a166: 35:36min)

(1621) Ngu=yi karrap nya-nga-na **warrkap-jirri.**
CAT=1EXC.MIN.NS watch intake-IMPF-PRS dance-ALL
"He is watching me dance." (Unknown source)

These subordinate clauses are reduced in two ways: they provide no TAM information and they delete the subordinate subject under co-reference with a main clause NP argument. Instead, coverbs and non-finite inflecting verbs present in a subordinate clause are inflected with certain nominal case suffixes to provide temporal and subject information. First the case-markers indicate relative tense, i.e. whether the time referred to in the subordinate clause is simultaneous, anterior or subsequent to that of the main clause. The case marker also serves to identify the controller of the subordinate clause, i.e. whether the subject of the subordinate clause is the same as the subject or object of the main clause. See Austin (1981) and Dench and Evans (1988) for discussion of this type of 'complementising case' in Australian languages more generally. Table 49 presents the Gurindji suffix types and their functions.

Table 49: Functions of Gurindji case suffixes in reduced subordinate clauses.

RELATIVE TENSE	SWITCH REFERENCE	CASE SUFFIX
purposive	none	dative
aversive	none	dative+perlative
anterior	none	source
simultaneous	$SUBJ_{SUBORD}=S_{MAIN}$ (also A, O)	locative
simultaneous	$SUBJ_{SUBORD}=A_{MAIN}$	ergative
simultaneous	$SUBJ_{SUBORD}=O_{MAIN}$	allative
simultaneous	$SUBJ_{SUBORD}=DAT_{MAIN}$	locative+dative

9.3.1 Purposive (Dative)

A purposive clause is constructed by adding the dative case marker to the infinitive form of the verb, or to a coverb. Generally dative case marks all of the elements of a subordinate clause, as shown in (1620), however this is not always the case. In (1622), *kayi* 'chase' is not dative-marked despite being a member of the subordinate clause. This is because it is a tight-nexus coverb (see §7.2.2.1.1), closely linked to the inflecting verb *panana* 'hit'. The purposive function is an extension of the dative-case marker's use in main clauses where it marks a nominal to indicate a purpose (§4.3.3.2) and indeed in this function, the dative-marked nominal may also be thought of as an ellipsed subordinate clause, for example (1623) and (1624). Nonetheless, not all dative-marked nominals should be considered ellipsed subordinate clauses and indeed there may be some ambiguity in interpretation, as shown by (1625).

(1622) Ngu=yi ma-rni kayi **pa-nu-wu** **yalu-wu** **yawarta-wu**.
CAT=1EXC.MIN.NS say-PST chase hit-INF-DAT that-DAT horse-DAT
"He told me to chase that horse." (McConvell corpus: Meakins et al., 2016, p. 441)

(1623) **Ngawa-wu** ya-ni.
water-DAT go-PST
"He went for water." (McConvell 1996 grammar manuscript)
[He went in order that [HE GET water]]

(1624) Puul pirrka ma-na-ni **yawu-wu=ma**.
fish.trap make get-IMPF-PST fish-DAT=TOP
"He was making a trap for fish." (McConvell 1996 grammar manuscript)
[He made a fish trap in order that [HE /PEOPLE GET fish WITH IT]]

(1625) Ngu=rna=rla ma-rni **ngawa-wu**.
CAT=1EXC.MIN.S=3OBL talk-PST water-DAT
"I told him about water." (indirect object interpretation) or "I told him [HE SHOULD GET water]." (subordinate clause interpretation) or "I told him [I WILL GET water]." (subordinate clause interpretation)
(McConvell 1996 grammar manuscript)

Purposive clauses do not have a switch reference function. The subject of a subordinate clause is potentially controlled by different grammatical roles in the main clause. In (1626), the subject of the subordinate clause is co-referential with the transitive subject of the main clause (S=A); in (1627), S=S, in (1628) and (1629) S=A, in (1630) A=A, in (1631) and (1632) A=O. Sometimes the cross-referencing of arguments is ambiguous. For example, in (1633), the complex clause could be interpreted as A=IO or A=S.

(1626) **Yirrijkaji-wu** **pirrka-wu=ma** **kirralk-kirralk-karra-wu=ma**
plant.sp-DAT make-DAT=TOP chip.grind-REDUP-ITER-DAT=TOP

yingka-wu=ma **kampa-rnu-wu=ma** nyantu
stone.knife-DAT=TOP cook-INF-DAT=TOP 3MIN

ngu=ngaliny jintaku-lu jayi-nya.
CAT=1INC.MIN.POSS one-ERG give-PST
"[The Snake Dreaming] alone gave us the arts of making pressure-flaking tools for dressing stone and 'cooking' white stone blades."
(McConvell 1996 grammar manuscript)

(1627) Kayi=n ma-rni **ya-nu-wu** marri wanyji=warla=n ya-ni?
chase=2MIN.S say-PST go-INF-DAT BUT which=FOC=2MIN.S go-PST
"You said you were going to go so why didn't you?"
(McConvell corpus: Meakins et al., 2016, p. 231)

(1628) Ngu=yi=n ma-rni **ngarin-ku**
CAT=1EXC.MIN.NS=2MIN.S say-PST meat-DAT

pa-nu-wu, walima=n pa-rru?
hit-INF-DAT Q=2MIN.S hit-POT
"You told me you were going to kill a beast, well are you going to?"
(McConvell corpus: Meakins et al., 2016, p. 381)

(1629) Pinarri karrinyana **kurrurij-ku**
knowledgeable be.IMPF.PRS car-DAT

rarraj-ku ka-nga-nu-wu=ma.
run-DAT take-IMPF-INF-DAT=TOP
"He knows how to drive a car fast."
(McConvell corpus: Meakins et al., 2016, p. 323)

(1630) **Marru-wu pirrka-wu** ngu=lu wanyja-na-na.
house-DAT make-DAT CAT=3AUG.S leave-IMPF-PRS
"They are leaving the building so it can be repaired."
(McConvell 1996 grammar manuscript)

(1631) Jupu ngu=rna=ngku **ka-ngku jala-wu jaartkarra-wu**.
JUST CAT=1EXC.MIN.S=2MIN.NS take-POT today-DAT eat-DAT
"I'll just bring you something to eat today."
(McConvell corpus: Meakins et al., 2016, p. 118)

(1632) Ngayu ngu=rna=rla ma-rni **ka-ngu-wu**.
1EXC.MIN CAT=1EXC.MIN.S=3OBL say-PST take-INF-DAT
"I told him to take me." (McConvell 1996 grammar manuscript)

(1633) Ngu=yi ma-rni **jarrakap-ku (ma-rnu-wu)**
CAT=1EXC.MIN.NS say-PST talk-DAT say-INF-DAT

yalu-wu ngumpit-ku kaput-ku.
that-DAT man-DAT tomorrow-DAT
"He told me [to / he would] speak to that man tomorrow."
(McConvell 1996 grammar manuscript)

Locative-marked and allative marked NPs in subordinate purposive clauses are marked dative following the allative (1634) or locative (1635). These are discussed further in §9.3.4.4 and §9.3.4.5.

(1634) Ngu=rna=ngku ma-rni ka-nga-nu-wu
CAT=1EXC.MIN.S=2MIN.NS say-PST bring-IMPF-INF-DAT

wart-ku lun-ku **murla-ngkurra-wu**.
return-DAT drop-DAT this-ALL-DAT
"I told you to bring it back and drop it here."
(McConvell corpus: Meakins et al., 2016, p. 209)

(1635) Kurla-mpa ngu=lu langkarna-yirri
south-PERL CAT=3AUG.S billabong-ALL

yuwa-ni kaputa-la=ma kaput-ku
put-PST tomorrow-LOC=TOP tomorrow-DAT

yuwa-nu-wu=ma **kurrpu-ngka-wu**=ma.
put-INF-DAT=TOP grave-LOC-DAT=TOP
"They put (the body) south of the billabong intending to bury it / for it to be buried the next day." (McConvell 1996 grammar manuscript)

9.3.2 Aversive (Dative + Edge)

The aversive is a negative purposive used to expresses the notion that something is avoided or feared. The locative is used on nominals in this function, for example *wari-ngka* 'snake!!' (§4.3.4.2), but the aversive is used on coverbs and non-finite verbs to create reduced subordinate clauses. It is only found rarely in the corpus.

In Ngumpin-Yapa languages, aversive case suffixes are sometimes formally independent of other suffixes (Mudburra *-wirri*), sometimes built on the dative case suffix (Gurindji *-kumpal*, Warlpiri *-kujaku*, Warlmanpa *-kuma*) or the locative case suffix (Walmajarri *-Camarra, -karrarla*, Ngardi *-Camarra*). For an overview of the category of apprehension in Ngumpin-Yapa languages, see Browne, Ennever and Osgarby (2021).

The Gurindji aversive is composed of the dative + edge *-ku-mpal* (1636) and *-wu-mpal* (1638) but there are other forms *-kupal* (1637) and *-wupal* (1639) which come about through the process of nasal-cluster dissimilation (§2.3.4). Note that the only other place the edge suffix is found is with directional nominals (§5.2).

(1636) Ngunyju nga-nyja **kurlpak-kumpal.**
tobacco eat-IMP vomit-AVERS
"Eat tobacco to avoid vomiting." (McConvell corpus: Meakins et al., 2016, p. 285)

(1637) Yamak-piya yuwa-rra langa-wu **nyirn-kupal.**
quiet-BIT put-IMP ear-DAT deaf-AVERS
"Make it a bit quieter so people won't go deaf."
(McConvell 1996 grammar manuscript)

(1638) Yangki pa-rra=ngali mangarri-wu
ask hit-IMP=1INC.MIN.NS veg.food-DAT

ya-nu-wumpal kanyjurra-wumpal.[233]
go-INF-AVERS down-AVERS
"Ask him for food for us to avoid (us/you) going down (to settlement)."
(McConvell 1996 grammar manuscript)

As in purposive clauses, the aversive can mark the entire subordinate clause including nominals, as shown in (1638). Also similar to purposive clauses, the aversive can also just attach to a nominal in an ellipsed subordinate clause. For example, in (1639), the use of the aversive after *munpa* expresses the entire action of a malevolent spirit pursuing someone.

(1639) Ya-na-nta manpurr-a=rni **munpa-wupal.**
go-IMPF-IMP shuffle-LOC=ONLY bush.spirit-AVERS
"You should walk with a short stride in case the *munpa* comes after you."
(McConvell 1996 grammar manuscript)

Another similarity to the purposive is the lack of switch reference function. The aversive can indicate that the subject of the subordinate clause is the same as the subject of the main clauses S=A as in (1636), S=S as in (1640) and (1641), S=O as in (1642), S=IO as in (1643) and (1644).

(1640) Karru-rra=yi **jilmung-kupal.**
be.POT-HORT=1EXC.MIN.NS break-AVERS
"Let it stay with me so it doesn't get broken."
(McConvell 1996 grammar manuscript)

233 NCD would be expected here but was not recorded as such. We do not have the original recording to check the example.

(1641) Marntaj jalngak-jalngak-ku **kalu-wumpal**.
OK ride-REDUP-DAT walk-AVERS
"(The horse) is OK to ride a bit to save walking."
(McConvell 1996 grammar manuscript)

(1642) Ngu=rna=ngku karrwa-wu **ya-nu-wumpal**.
CAT=1EXC.MIN.S=2MIN.NS keep-POT go-INF-AVERS
"I'll keep you so you don't go." (McConvell 1996 grammar manuscript)

(1643) Wumara ngu=wuliny jayi-nya nyila=ma
money CAT=3UA.NS give-PST that=TOP

marluka-kujarra-wu=ma **ma-rnu-wumpal**, ngaja=wula ma-lu
old.man-DU-DAT=TOP say-INF-AVERS ADMON=3UA.S say-POT

jaru kuya.
story thus
"He gave those two old men money so they wouldn't talk, in case they were going to talk about it." (McConvell 1996 grammar manuscript)

(1644) Karu-wu=ma ngu=rna=rla mangarri
child-DAT=TOP CAT=1EXC.MIN.S=3OBL food

jayi-nya kunyja **nga-rna-nu-wumpalng.**[234]
give-PST lolly eat-IMPF-INF-AVERS
"I gave the child bread to stop it eating lollies."
(McConvell 1996 grammar manuscript)

9.3.3 Anterior (Source)

The source suffix can be used in reduced subordinate clauses to indicate a previous state, or an event which has already occurred or will have occurred at the time of the main event, as shown in (1645)–(1650) (see also §4.3.8). It has no switch reference function.

234 Note that this form of the aversive also has a nasal. It is not clear how widespread this is, and we do not have audio to check this example.

(1645) Punyu-k ma-nku **janga-nginyi** ngu.
good-FACT do-POT sick-SOURCE CAT
"The honey will make her feel better after being sick."
(🔈 TD: FM07_a028: 12:12min)

(1646) Jirri-ngka ngu=yinangulu yuwa-na-ni
burial.platform-LOC CAT=3AUG.S>3AUG.NS put-IMPF-PST

ngumpit=ma, **tampang-nginyi**=ma.
man=TOP dead-SOURCE=TOP
"They used to put Aboriginal people on tree platforms after they'd died."
(🔈 VW: FM11_a161: 0:38min)

(1647) **Makin-nginyi** ya-na-na ngu parntart.
sleep-SOURCE go-IMPF-PRS CAT stiff
"He walks stiffly after getting up from sleep." (🔈 TD: FM10_a166: 11:20min)

(1648) Nyila **warlarljap-karra-nginyi** ya-na-na,
that roll-ITER-SOURCE go-IMPF-PRS

warlaku. Puka-yawung ngapuk kuya.
dog stinky-PROP smell thus
"After a dog rolls [in a carcass], it gets really stinky."
(🔈 VW: FM12_a179: 9:58min)

(1649) Karrwa=rla jarti-ngka, nyamu=nga ya-nku
hold.IMP=3OBL keep-LOC REL=DUB go-POT

murtamurtap-nginyi, ngumparna-wu nyanuny-ku.
hunt.REDUP-SOURCE husband-DAT 3MIN.DAT-DAT
"Hold it for him to keep after he comes back from hunting. [It's] for her husband." (🔈 VW: FM12_a172: 3:12min)

(1650) Ka-nga-ni nganta nyila=ma wayita=ma **kampa-rnu-nginyi**=ma.
take-IMPF-PST ALLE that=TOP pencil.yam=TOP cook-INF-SOURCE=TOP
"So I think he took the bush yams after they were cooked."
(🔈 VW: FM10_a155: Ngarlking Karu: 2:03min)

Recall from §4.7.18 that *-nginyi* also has a derivational function where it derives nominals from coverbs. In these cases, the source-marked nominal occurs in a verbless clause and is therefore not interpreted as a reduced subordinate clause. However sometimes it is difficult to analyse the function of *-nginyi*. For example, in (1651), the use of *yungkuj-karra-nginyi* 'tree.fall-ITER-SOURCE' could be interpreted as "the fallen bits of wood" or "we take the pieces of wood to the car after chopping the tree down".

(1651) Murrka-murrka ngu=ja ka-nga-na kururij-jirri
drop.off-REDUP CAT=1EXC.UA.S take-IMPF-PRS car-ALL

na, nyila-rra na karnti **yungkuj-karra-nginyi**
FOC that-PL FOC wood tree.fall-ITER-SOURCE

nyamu=ja pa-ni yapayapa.
REL=1EXC.UA.S hit-PST small
"We take the pieces of wood to the car after chopping the tree down." OR
"We take the fallen pieces of wood to the car." (🔈 VW: FM08_a101: 15:09min)

Sometimes *-nginyi* does not mark a coverb, but a nominal in an ellipsed subordinate clause. This is similar to purposive clauses. For example, in (1652) the nominal *ngarlu* 'honey' is marked, but the meaning of the clause has a temporal reference i.e. 'after chopping honey' not a locational reference 'from honey'.

(1652) **Ngarlu-nginyi** na ngu=ngayirra jiya-rna-ni ngawa-wu.
honey-SOURCE FOC CAT=1EXC.UA.NS burn-IMPF-PST water-DAT
"After chopping honey we were thirsty." (🔈 VW: FM09_14_1a: 2:00min)

9.3.4 Simultaneous subordinate clauses

There are a number of case suffixes which indicate simultaneous relative time in complex clauses. They each also have switch reference functions, however the locative in the subordinate clause can more generally cross-reference any grammatical role in the main clause.

9.3.4.1 SUBJ_{subord}=$\mathrm{S/A/O}_{main}$ (Locative)

Locative is the basic marking for non-finite simultaneous clauses. It is the only case-marker which can be used as a same subject marker in simultaneous subordinate clauses (SUBJ_{SUBORD}=S_{MAIN}), however it also overlaps with the functions of the ergative (SUBJ_{SUBORD}=A_{MAIN}, §9.3.4.2) and allative (SUBJ_{SUBORD}=O_{MAIN}, §9.3.4.3).

Firstly, the locative serves to identify the controller of the subordinate clause as the intransitive subject of the main clause (1653) and (1654).

(1653) Juny-pari-la wart, ngu=rnalu
sunset-ADJ-LOC return CAT=1EXC.AUG.S

karrinya	**kampa-rnu-p-kula**	**kirrawa-la**.
be.PST	cook-INF-CV-LOC	goanna-LOC

"When the sun went down [we went] back, sat down cooking a goanna."
(McConvell corpus: Meakins et al., 2016, p. 117)

(1654)

Pulwarr-kuk	jiya-wu	**talwirr-a**=ma.
dry-FACT	burn-POT	hang-LOC=TOP

"It will dry hanging up." (McConvell corpus: Meakins et al., 2016, p. 335)

The locative also cross-references transitive subjects in main clauses (1655) and semi-transitive clauses (1656).

(1655)

Nanaku-lu	pa-ni	ngu	**warnparlk-kula**.
SUBSECT-ERG	hit-PST	CAT	chop.out-LOC

"Nanaku cut [the wood], knocking [the hard bit] out."
(🔊 TD: FM07_a028: 4:46min)

(1656)

Yinka-rna-ni	kurrupartu,	kuya-ngka=ma=yi
plane-IMPF-PST	boomerang	thus-LOC=TOP=1EXC.MIN.NS

ma-rna-ni	jarrakap	**kurrupartu-la**	**yinka-rnu-la**.
say-IMPF-PST	talk	boomerang-LOC	plane-INF-LOC

"He was planing a boomerang and he was talking to me at the same time as he was planing a boomerang." (McConvell corpus: Meakins et al., 2016, p. 446)

Finally, the locative can also be used to cross-reference the object of a main clause which overlaps with the function of the allative, discussed in §9.3.4.3. Examples are given in (1657) and (1658).

(1657)

Ngu=rna	nya-nya	**pirrkapirrkap-kula**.
CAT=1EXC.MIN.S	intake-PST	make.REDUP-LOC

"I saw him making it." (McConvell 1996 grammar manuscript)

(1658)

Ngu=rna=rla	jik	nya-ngku	**pirrkapirrkap-kula**.
CAT=1EXC.MIN.S=3OBL	emerge	intake-POT	make.REDUP-LOC

"I'll go and have a look at him making it."
(McConvell 1996 grammar manuscript)

In some cases, this broad functional distribution makes the interpretation of some complex clauses difficult. In (1659), the absence of an inflecting verb makes the transitivity of 'break' ambiguous between transitive and intransitive 'break', but nearly all plausible contexts give the transitive interpretation here. Similarly, in (1660), it is not clear whether the controller of *-kula* is the subject or object.

(1659) Ngu=rna nya-nya nyila ngumpit **pakirr-a**=ma.
CAT=1EXC.MIN.S intake-PST that man break-LOC=TOP
"I saw that man breaking it." (McConvell corpus: Meakins et al., 2016, p. 300)

(1660) **Walik-kula** ngu=rna=ngku jayi-ngku.
around-LOC CAT=1EXC.MIN.S=2MIN.NS give-POT
"I'll give it to you when I come around." ($SUBJ_{SUBORD}$=A_{MAIN})
"I'll give it to you when you come around." ($SUBJ_{SUBORD}$=O_{MAIN})
(McConvell corpus: Meakins et al., 2016, p. 381)

The variation in the use of locative and allative cases possibly represents a change in progress where the locative case suffix is becoming a general marker of subordination. Under this analysis, the allative marker was originally the DS ($SUBJ_{SUBORD}$=O_{MAIN}) marker and the locative marker, the SS ($SUBJ_{SUBORD}$=S_{MAIN}) marker, which is the pattern found in surrounding languages. However, in Gurindji, the locative case suffix has begun extending its functional domain to mark both DS and SS in reduced subordinate clauses, and in this respect is becoming a general marker of subordination in reduced subordinate clauses. The spread of the locative occurred in three stages: (i) location predicated of an object and (ii) switch-reference in subordinate clauses in Gurindji, and now (iii) inanimate goals in Gurindji Kriol, as shown in Table 50 (Meakins et al., 2020).[235]

Table 50: Functions of locative and allative case-markers in Gurindji and Gurindji Kriol.

	Location in intransitive clauses	Location predicated of event in transitive clauses	Location predicated of object in trans. clauses	Inanimate goal	S=O switch reference in sub. clauses	S=S switch reference in sub. clauses
Gurindji	LOC	LOC	**ALL**	**ALL**	**ALL**	LOC
Gurindji Kriol	LOC	LOC	**LOC**	**LOC**	**LOC**	LOC

There is also some variation in the use of the locative in subordinate clauses which have a dative-marked nominal. In some cases, the locative does not spread to the dative-marked nominal, as in (1661). In other cases, the locative is added, but with the nominaliser in addition, as in (1662). The locative can be important for interpretation.

235 Note that McConvell is not convinced about this explanation.

For example in (1663), the fact that the dative pronoun is not marked locative indicates that it is the indirect object of the main clause and the complex clause cannot be interpreted as "You gave it to me when I got back" (*A_{main}=O_{subord}).

(1661)

Ngu=rna	pura	nya-nga-na	**lungkarrap-kula**
CAT=1EXC.MIN.S	hear	intake-IMPF-PRS	cry-LOC

ngamayi-wu.
mother-DAT

"I hear [the baby] crying for its mother."
(McConvell corpus: Meakins et al., 2016, p. 339)

(1662)

Ngunti	ngu=n	pirrkap	ma-nku	**nyanuny-ja**
light	CAT=2MIN.S	make	do-POT	3MIN.DAT-LOC

karrap-kula,	**Nangari-wu-ny-ja.**
watch-LOC	SUBSECT-DAT-NMLZ-LOC

"You can make the light for Nangari to watch [how you do it]."
(🔊 VW: FM09_17_2a: 1:24min)

(1663)

Ngu=yi=n	jayi-nya	**ngayiny**	wart-ta=ma.
CAT=1EXC.MIN.NS=2MIN.S	give-PST	1EXC.MIN.DAT	return-LOC=TOP

"You gave it to me when you got back." (McConvell 1996 grammar manuscript)

9.3.4.2 $SUBJ_{subord}$=A_{main} (Ergative)

The ergative marks coverbs in non-finite subordinate clauses to indicate that the subject of the subordinate clause is co-referential with the transitive subject of the main clause. The main clause is always transitive, but the subordinate clause can be transitive (1664)–(1667) or intransitive (1668)–(1670). In the case of the transitive subordinate clauses, it is not clear why speakers chose to mark the coverb ergative since the same meaning is achieved if the coverb simply combines unmarked with the inflecting verb in the main clause.

(1664)

Marlarl	yuwa-ni	ngu	**tawirrjip-kulu.**
pelt	throw-PST	CAT	throw.stones-ERG

"He pelted it with stones." (🔊 VW: FM12_a175: 9:21min)

(1665)

Nguyurrp-kulu	yunpa-rna-na	wajarra.
hum-ERG	sing-IMPF-PRS	corroboree

"He's humming the *wajarra* tune." (DD with ECh: Meakins et al., 2016, p. 289)

(1666) **Mirriwantuk-kulu** karrap.
look.into.distance-ERG look
"He looked for it into the distance with his hand to his brow."
(◀ VW: FM10_23_1a: 3:14min – Luma Kurrupartu)

(1667) Ngu=rna kayi pa-ni
CAT=1EXC.MIN.S chase hit-PST

nguran-tu **kawurru-lu** **majul-u.**
longing-ERG feelings-ERG stomach-ERG
"I went after her because of a longing for her."
(McConvell corpus: Meakins et al., 2016, p. 286)

(1668) **Kutij-ju** na warra ka-nga-ni.
stand-ERG FOC watch take-IMPF-PST
"She watched her as she stood." (◀ VW: FM10_23_1b: 6:04min)

(1669) Nyila ngu=ngalang **jalpirri-lu** nya-nga-na.
that CAT=3AUG.S>1INC.AUG.NS squat-ERG intake-IMPF-PRS
"That one is watching us while squatting down."
(McConvell corpus: Meakins et al., 2016, p. 76)

(1670) Kula=ngku yalu-ngku=ma kurru karrinya.
NEG=2MIN.NS that-ERG=TOP hear be.PST

Kart ma-ni ngu=n=nyunu **makin-tu.**
lose.self do-PST CAT=2MIN.S=RR sleep-ERG
"That one can't hear you. You've lost yourself in sleep.
[You're sleeping really soundly]." (◀ VW: FM12_a177: 7:52min)

Warlpiri also uses the ergative in this function, however it shows further applications. The ergative in Warlpiri can attach to other complementiser cases such as the allative to make further connections to the grammatical roles in the main clause (Simpson, 1988). Gurindji only shows case-stacking in reduced subordinate clauses in the locative+dative combination (§9.3.4.4).

9.3.4.3 $\text{SUBJ}_{\text{subord}}$=$\text{O}_{\text{main}}$ (Allative)

The allative case suffix functions in reduced subordinate clauses to indicate that the subject of the simultaneous subordinate clause is the same as the object (1671),

(1672)[236] and (1673)[237] or indirect object of the main clause (1674) and (1675). The subject of the subordinate clause can be a transitive (1671) or intransitive subject (1674) and (1675).

(1671)	Ngu=yi	karrap	nya-nga-na	**warrkap-jirri**.
	CAT=1EXC.MIN.NS	watch	intake-IMPF-PRS	dance-ALL

"He is watching me dance." (McConvell 1996 grammar manuscript)

(1672)	Warlaku-lu	ngalyakap	ma-ni	karu	wartan	**makin-jirri**.
	dog-ERG	lick	do-PST	child	hand	sleep-ALL

"The dog licked the kid's hand while the child slept."
(🔊 VW: FM14_a228: 22:26min)

(1673)	Warlaku-lu	ngalyak	ma-ni	karu-wu	ngaji	**makin-jirri**.
	dog-ERG	lick	do-PST	child-DAT	father	sleep-ALL

"The dog licks the child's father while the child's father is sleeping."
(VW: FM14_a231: 2:08min)

(1674)	Ngu=yi	jayi-nya	**tak-jirri.**
	CAT=1EXC.MIN.NS	give-PST	sit-ALL

"He gave it to me while I was sitting." (McConvell 1996 grammar manuscript)

(1675)	Ngu=rla	pakap-karra	ma-rni	yalu-wu=ma	**muk-jirri**.
	CAT=3OBL	challenge-ITER	talk-PST	that-DAT=TOP	silent-ALL

"He challenged that [man] while he stayed silent."
(McConvell corpus: Meakins et al., 2016, p. 299)

Allative marking in non-finite clauses is related to allative marking on NPs, which are semantically locative, but which are construed as complements of objects (cf. McConvell & Simpson, 2012). Surrounding languages such as Bilinarra, Jaminjung and Warlpiri also use the allative in this function (Austin, 1981, p. 325; Meakins & Nordlinger, 2014, pp. 428–431; Schultze-Berndt, 2000, pp. 112–113; Simpson, 1988). Further east, Jingulu, Warlmanpa and Warumungu also use the allative suffix to mark object-control in reduced subordinate clauses (Austin, 1981, pp. 328–331).

The allative is also commonly used with other oblique functions as controllers. It can cross-reference a comitative (1676), locative (1677), and an affected location, where the subject is transitive (1678) or intransitive (1679).

236 The object here is an inalienable possessor 'the child'.
237 The object here is an alienable possessive phrase 'the child's father'.

(1676) Ngu=rna=rla **Jangala-wunyja** karrinyani
CAT=1EXC.MIN.S=3OBL SUBSECT-COM be.IMPF.PST

kurrupartu-yirri **pirrkap-jirri**.
boomerang-ALL make-ALL
"I was sitting with Jangala while he made a boomerang."
(McConvell corpus: Meakins et al, 2016, p. 450)

(1677) Ngu=rna **yawarta-la** jalngak karrinya **kaya-nu-yirri**.
CAT=1EXC.MIN.S horse-LOC ride be.PST kick-INF-ALL
"I rode on the horse while it was kicking."
(McConvell corpus: Meakins et al., 2016, p. 155)

(1678) Ngu=n-ku=rla jalngak waninya **yawarta-wu** **kaya-nu-yirri**.
CAT=2MIN.S-EP=3OBL mount fall.PST horse-DAT kick-INF-ALL
"I got on the horse while it was kicking."
(McConvell 1996 grammar manuscript)

(1679) **Kalu-ngkurra**=warla ngu=rna=rla jalngak waninya **yawarta-la.**
walk-ALL=FOC CAT=1EXC.MIN.S=3OBL ride fall.PST horse-LOC
"I got on the horse while it was walking."
(McConvell 1996 grammar manuscript)

The use of the allative varies with the locative, as discussed in §9.3.4.1. For example, compare (1679) and (1680) which both cross-reference a locative complement in the main clause. In (1679), the subordinate clause is marked allative, however in (1680), the same thematic structure is expressed with a locative-marked coverb *rarraj* 'run'. Another example is given in (1681) where the subject of the subordinate clause is cross-referencing an indirect object as indicated by the locative-marked coverb *karrap* 'watch'.

(1680) Ngu=rna=rla **kurririj-ja** jalngak waninya **rarraj-ja**=rni.
CAT=1EXC.MIN.S=3OBL car-LOC ride fall.PST run-LOC=ONLY
"I got on the truck while it was moving."
(McConvell corpus: Meakins et al., 2016, p. 348)

(1681) Ngu=**yi** jayi-nya yarti-waji-la **karrap-kula**.
CAT=1EXC.MIN.NS give-PST picture-AGENT-LOC watch-LOC
"He gave it to me while I was watching a movie."
(McConvell 1996 grammar manuscript)

In these examples, the locative case suffix is used in the subordinate clause despite the fact that it is the object of the main clause which is co-referential with the subject of the subordinate clause. Similar variation has been observed for Wanyjirra (Senge, 2008, p. 191) and Bilinarra (Meakins & Nordlinger, 2014, pp. 430–431).

9.3.4.4 SUBJ$_{subord}$=DAT$_{main}$ (Locative+Dative)

The subject of a subordinate clause can be marked with a combination of the locative + dative to indicate that it is controlled by a dative-marked nominal in the main clause. In these cases, there is also a double embedding. The locative indicates subordination and the dative cross-references a dative argument in the main clause. Note that this LOC+DAT case-stacking is distinct from PURPosive because the purposive, although historically LOC+DAT is only syntactically active within the clause and not across clauses, so there is no embedding. In Gurindji, this is the only time you find case-stacking of this kind. On the other hand, Warlpiri shows similar case-stacking within main clauses where the inner case suffix has a relational function and the outer case suffix serves to demonstrate a predicational relationship between the spatial-case marked NP and another clausal argument by agreeing in case (Simpson, 1991).

Examples (1682)–(1685) are of the SUBJ$_{SUBORD}$=IO type. Examples (1686)–(1687) are of the SUBJ$_{SUBORD}$=animate goal type. Example (1688) is of the SUBJ$_{SUBORD}$=alienable possession type. Examples (1689) and (1690) are of the SUBJ$_{SUBORD}$=beneficiary type and (1691) is of the SUBJ$_{SUBORD}$=possessor dissension type.

(1682) **Karrap-kula-wu** ngu=yi jayi-nya **yarti-waji-la-wu**.
watch-LOC-DAT CAT=1EXC.MIN.NS give-PST picture-AGENT-LOC-DAT
"He gave it to me while I was watching a movie."
(McConvell corpus: Meakins et al., 2016, p. 440)

(1683) Warlaku-lu ngu=yi warlakap
dog-ERG CAT=1EXC.MIN.NS search

nya-nya ngayiny **makin-ta-wu=rni**
intake-PST 1EXC.MIN.DAT sleep-LOC-DAT=ONLY
"The dog was looking for me while I slept." (🔈 VW: FM14_a228: 31:27min)

(1684) Kula piyarr ka-ngka=ngantipangulu
NEG tell take-IMP=3AUG.S>1EXC.AUG.NS

pinka-ka-wu=rni **wulaj-ja-wu**.
river-LOC-DAT=ONLY hide-LOC-DAT
"Don't tell on us about hiding by the river."
(McConvell corpus: Meakins et al., 2016, p. 70)

(1685)

Wart-ta-wu	ngu=rna=rla	jayi-ngku.
return-LOC-DAT	CAT=1EXC.MIN.S=3OBL	give-POT

"I'll give it to him when he gets back."
(McConvell 1996 grammar manuscript)

(1686)

Jurlaka=ma	tiwu	ya-ni	ngu=rla
bird=TOP	fly	go-PST	CAT=3OBL

kajirri-wu	**makin-ta-wu**.
old.woman-DAT	sleep-LOC-DAT

"The bird flies to the old woman who is asleep."
(🔊 BW: FM07_a043: 30:30min)

(1687)

Nyanuny-ku	jaju-wu	ngu=rla	ka-nga-na,
3MIN.DAT-DAT	MM-DAT	CAT=3OBL	take-IMPF-PRS

mangarri	punyu,	yarti-ngkurra	**makin-ta-wu**.
cake	good	shade-ALL	sleep-LOC-DAT

"She takes a cake to her grandmother who was sleeping in the shade."
(🔊 VW: FHM146: 1:12min)

(1688)

Ngu=rna=yina	wulyuk	ma-na-na
CAT=1EXC.MIN.S=3AUG.NS	wash	do-IMPF-PRS

makin-ta-wu	Nangari-jpan-ku	kurririj.
sleep-LOC-DAT	SUBSECT-PL.SKIN-DAT	car

"I'm washing the Nangaris' car while they're asleep."
(🔊 VW: FM17_a442: 5:01min)

(1689)

Ngu=rna=yina	kampa-rna-na
CAT=1EXC.MIN.S=3AUG.NS	cook-IMPF-PRS

ngarin	**makin-ta-wu**	karu-walija-wu.
meat	sleep-LOC-DAT	child-PAUC-DAT

"I'm cooking for the kids while they're asleep." (🔊 VW: FM17_a443: 7:51min)

(1690)

Ngu=rna	ma-ni	pujtilip,	kukij-karra-wu,
CAT=1EXC.MIN.S	do-PST	bush.tea.leaf	drink-ITER-DAT

janga-ngka-wu,	tarukap-ku	nyampa-wu,
sick-LOC-DAT	bathe-DAT	what-DAT

karu-wu=purrupurru, jangkakarni-wu.
child-DAT=AND big.REDUP-DAT
"I got some bush tea leaf then to make into a medicine for the kids and adults to drink when they're sick." (🔈 VW: FM09_14_1a: 5:32min)

(1691) Ngu=rna=ngku wulyuk ma-na-na
CAT=1EXC.MIN.S=2MIN.NS wash do-IMPF-PST

nyununy kurrurij **makin-ta-wu.**
2MIN.DAT car sleep-LOC-DAT
"I'm washing your car while you're sleeping." (🔈 VW: FM17_a442: 2:50min)

(1692) Ngu=rna=yina karu-walija warra
CAT=1EXC.MIN.S=3AUG.NS child-PAUC look.after

ka-nga-na **makin-ta-wu** ngamayi-wu=ma.
take-IMPF-PST sleep-LOC-DAT mother-DAT=TOP
"I look after the mother's kids while she sleeps." (🔈 VW: FM17_a443: 3:41min)

When the possessor dissension construction is internal to a benefactive, the benefactive is cross-referenced not the possessor, as shown in (1693). This shows that if there are two datives in the clause, the subject of the subordinate clause needs to refer to the higher-level dative. Note that this is not a problem of the controller being embedded in another NP. Possessors in dissension constructions and alienable possessors may be the controller and they are embedded in a possessor phrase, as shown in (1691) and (1692). This may be a problem of morphology i.e. there is a ban on two overt case-markers controlling switch-reference. The other cases are OK because the accusative and nominative case are zero.

(1693) Ngu=rna=yina=rla kampa-rna-na ngarin
CAT=1EXC.MIN.S=3AUG.NS=3OBL cook-IMPF-PRS meat

karu-walija-wu nyanuny-ku **makin-ta-wu.**
child-PAUC-DAT 3MIN.DAT-DAT sleep-LOC-DAT
"I cooked beef for her children while her children sleep."
(FM elicitation: FM117_a443)

This combination of the locative and dative has also been observed in Wanyjirra (Senge, 2016, p. 139).

9.3.4.5 $SUBJ_{subord}$=DAT_{main} (Locative+Allative)

The subject of a subordinate clause can also be marked with a combination of the locative + allative to indicate that it is controlled by a dative-marked nominal in the main clause. In these cases, the allative marks the clause as subordinate and indicates that the subject of the subordinate clause is the same as the object of the main clause. The additional dative-case marker indicates that it is embedded within a purposive clause. In this respect, the allative is looking across two levels of embedding.

(1694) Ngu=rna=ngku ma-rni ka-nga-nu-wu
CAT=1EXC.MIN.S=2MIN.NS say-PST bring-IMPF-INF-DAT

wart-ku lun-ku **murla-ngkurra-wu**.
return-DAT drop-DAT this-ALL-DAT
"I told you to bring it back and drop it here."
(McConvell corpus: Meakins et al., 2016, p. 209)

10 Unrestricted clitics and particles

In addition to words and affixes, Gurindji also has a number of clitics (§10.1) and particles (§10.2). The pronominal clitics were described in Chapter 6 and a number of clitics which relate only to nominals were discussed in Chapters 4 and 5 and the clitic =*nga* 'dubitative' which relates to verbs was discussed in Chapter 7. This chapter deals with the clitics which attach to different parts of speech and sometimes to the whole clause. They are referred to as unrestricted clitics.

10.1 Unrestricted clitics

Unrestricted clitics are so defined in Gurindji because they follow inflectional morphology. They are considered unrestricted because they have a broad range of hosts. They also have a general lack of allomorphic integration with the stem (with the exception of =*warla*/=*parla* 'FOC' (§10.1.8) and =*waju*/=*paju* 'BECAUSE' (§10.1.7) and =*wayin*/=*payin* 'ETC' (see §4.8.1)).

Gurindji has a number of mostly discourse-related clitics: =*kata* 'IMMediate' (§10.1.1), =*karliny* 'EXPERT' (§10.1.2), =*ma* 'TOPic' (§10.1.3), =*nyiyang*/*nyiyarni* 'PROPERly' (§10.1.4), =*rni* 'ONLY' (§10.1.5), =*rningan* 'AGAIN' (§10.1.6), =*waju*/=*paju* 'BECAUSE' (§10.1.7), =*warla*/=*parla* 'FOCus' (§10.1.8) and =*warluk* 'FIRST' (§10.1.9).

Clitics in Gurindji are positioned after inflectional and derivational morphology, but before the pronominal clitics. The only exception is =*nga* which is found after the pronominal clitics. The order of encliticisation is summarised below:

> STEM – INFLECTION – DERIVATION = [WARLUK] = [MA] = [KATA] = [RNI, RNINGAN] = [WARLA] = [PRONOMINAL CLITIC] = [NGA]

No one example shows the full extent of this template, but a number of examples below show the relative attachment of clitics. Example (1695) has an inflecting verb with =*warluk* 'first' appearing after the inflection and =*rni* 'only' attaching after =*warluk*. In (1696), the stem *nyawa* hosts a sequence of three clitics =*rni* 'only', =*warla* 'focus' and a bound pronoun =*lu* 'they'. Note that the bound pronoun sometimes appears separately attached to the catalyst *ngu*, as shown in (1697). Example (1697) also has the =*ma* clitic attached to the adverbial demonstrative *kuya*. The topic marker =*ma* can also be followed by =*kata* which in turn can have a bound pronoun or =*rni* 'only' attached to it, as in (1700) and (1701). In (1702), the dubitative clitic is shown attached to the bound pronoun.

https://doi.org/10.1515/9783110746884-010

(1695) Ngu=rna=ngku ma-lu=**warluk-pa=rni**.
CAT=1EXC.MIN.S=2MIN.NS talk-POT=FIRST-EP=ONLY
"I want to tell you something first." (🔊 VW: FM10_23_2: Warrija Kirrawa: 6:29min)

(1696) "Nyawa=**rni=warla=lu** ya-ni Rosewood-nganyjuk, kuya-ny.
this=ONLY=FOC=3AUG.S go-PST NAME-GROUP thus-NMLZ
"Those blokes are with Rosewood." (🔊 BR: FM15_52_1e: 8:50min)

(1697) Ngu=rla ma-rni, "Nyawa=**rni=warla** ngu=**n**
CAT=3OBL say-PST this=ONLY=FOC CAT=2MIN.S

nyununy nyawa ya-ni, kuya=**ma**.
2MIN.DAT this go-PST thus=TOP
"Someone said to him, 'That policeman has come for you,' said like that."
(🔊 BR: FM15_52_1b: 0:38min)

(1698) Ngayu=**ma=rna** kula nga-rni jaartkarra=ma.
1EXC.MIN=TOP=1EXC.MIN.S NEG eat-PST eat=TOP
"I never used to eat it [when I was a young girl]." (🔊 VW: FM09_a123: 9:42min)

(1699) Nyila=**ma=kata** karrinyana mintaarraj-jawung kuya-ny.
that=TOP=IMM be.IMPF.PRS waterlily-PROP thus-NMLZ
"That place has water lilies growing right here." (🔊 VW: FM09_a13_2a: 2:24min)

(1700) Yala-ngka=**kata=rnalu** karrinyani, pirrka-pirrka-la=ma.
that-LOC=IMM=1EXC.AUG.S be.IMPF.PST make-REDUP-LOC=TOP
"We used to sit down just there making wooden artefacts."
(🔊 VW: FM09_a120: 2:54min)

(1701) Kuliyan=ma nyamu=n ma-lu kuli-kuli
aggressive=TOP REL=2MIN.S talk-POT argue-REDUP

nyila-rniny=**kata=rni** ngu=rnangkulu jarrara ma-nku.
that-HITH=IMM=ONLY CAT=1EXC.AUG.S>2MIN.NS follow do-POT
"Cheeky people who talk aggressively – we will follow you up right away with punishment." (McConvell 1996 grammar manuscript: Speaking to young people)

(1702) Jala=**ma=rna=nga** karrwa-wu pirrkap-pirrkap-kula na.
now=TOP=1EXC.MIN.S=DUB keep-POT make-REDUP-LOC FOC
"Now I might keep [the wood] to make [the artefacts]."
(🔊 VW: FM08_a101: 2:35min)

10.1.1 =*kata* IMMediate

This suffix mostly appears on demonstratives (1703), but is also found in the corpus on other nominals such as nouns (1704), coverbs (1705) and also on inflecting verbs (1706).

(1703) Nyawa=**kata** nya=lu walu jijal-jawung=ma tal pa-rra.
this=IMM XXX=3AUG.S head rolypoly.grass-PROP=TOP call hit-IMP
"They're calling me grassy-head." (🔈) VW: FM08_a070: 0:41min)

(1704) Kinyuwurra-marraj=**kata** na nyawa-ngku=ma yapayapa
bush.onion-COMP=IMM FOC this-ERG=TOP small

karrwa-rna-na, murlu-ngku=ma karnti-ku=ma nyawa-ngku=ma,
have-IMPF-PRS this-ERG=TOP plant-ERG=TOP this-ERG=TOP

kurlngurrung-tu=ma mayimpa-ku=ma.
water.onion-ERG=TOP spring.sedge-ERG=TOP
"Like the bush onion, this one has small bulbs, this kind of plant, I mean, the water plant." (🔈) VW: FM09_13_2d: 1:19min)

(1705) Walima ngu=rna=ngku jaja, tang-karra=**kata**
Q CAT=1EXC.MIN.S=2MIN.NS MM open.mouth-ITER=IMM

tang-karra nyawa murla jira-wu.
open.mouth-ITER this this fat-DAT
"Guess what I've got for you granny, come quick, open your mouth, open up for this [kangaroo] fat." (🔈) RW: EC97_a006: Jajurlang & Ngawa: 7:25min)

(1706) Pa-na-ni=**kata** punpurru wirlwirlk-karra,
hit-IMPF-PST=IMM all hit.in.grief.REDUP-ITER

turi-yawung-kulu karnti-yawung-kulu.
short.stick-PROP-ERG stick-PROP-ERG
"Then they would immediately hit the backs of their necks with a short piece of wood." (🔈) VW: FM12_a193: 0:06min)

It translates into English as: 'just there' and 'right here' in phrases such as: 'that one just there' or 'this one right here' (1707). In this respect, it has some cross-over with =*rni* when it combines with a locative-marked demonstrative, for example *yala-ngka=rni* 'that-LOC=ONLY, right there' (1710)–(1709). In combination with the adverbial demonstrative, it has the meaning 'just like that' (1711). When it attaches to coverbs (1705) or inflecting verbs (1706), it has the meaning of 'immediately'.

(1707) Nyila=ma=**kata** karrinyana mintaarraj-jawung kuya-ny.
that=TOP=IMM be.IMPF.PRS waterlily-PROP thus-NMLZ
"That place has water lilies growing just there." (🔈) VW: FM09_13_2a: 2:24min)

(1708) Malngak pa-rra mangarli-la=rni nyila=**kata** ngu=yina kuya.
hit.chest hit-IMP chest-LOC=ONLY that=IMM CAT=3AUG.NS thus
"Hit them right there in the chest." (🔈) VW: FM12_a175: 9:20min)

(1709) Kuliyan=ma nyamu=n ma-lu kuli-kuli
aggressive=TOP REL=2MIN.S talk-POT fight-REDUP

nyila-rniny=**kata=rni** ngu=rnangkulu jarrara ma-nku.
that-HITH=IMM=ONLY CAT=1EXC.AUG.S>2MIN.NS follow talk-POT
"Cheeky people who talk aggressively – we will followed you up right away with punishment." (McConvell 1996 grammar manuscript: Speaking to young people)

(1710) Yala-ngka=**kata**=rnalu karrinyani, pirrka-pirrka-la=ma.
that-LOC=IMM=1EXC.AUG.S be.IMPF.PST make-REDUP-LOC=TOP
"We used to sit down right there making wooden artefacts."
(🔈) VW: FM09_a120: 2:54min)

(1711) Or wulngarn-ta ngu=rna kuya=**kata** karrinyana lurlu.
or sun-LOC CAT=1EXC.MIN.S thus=IMM be.IMPF.PRS sit
"Or I sit in the sun, just like this." (🔈) VW: FM12_a177: 3:05min)

(1712) Mangarri=**kata** na wurruja-k-karra jiya-wu.
damper=IMM FOC dry.out-FACT-ITER burn-POT
"The fire will dry the damper out." (🔈) VW: FM09_13_3b: 2:25min)

This clitic is also found in Bilinarra and Mudburra in this function (Meakins & Nordlinger, 2014, pp. 406–407; Osgarby, 2018a, p. 188).

10.1.2 =*karliny* EXPERT

This clitic occurs rarely in the corpus. It has the meaning of 'expert' and derives from a Kija (Jarragan) nominal suffix.

(1713) Jalyirri-lu, Japarta-lu nyanuny ngapuju Japarta,
SUBSECT-ERG SUBSECT-ERG 3MIN.DAT brother.in.law SUBSECT

ngu=lu proper naru=**karliny**, naru=**karliny** ngu=lu.
CAT=3AUG.S very dodge=EXPERT dodge=EXPERT CAT=3AUG.S
"Nor did his brother-in-law, Japarta, who was really fast at dodging."
(🔈 DD: EC98_a013: 10:08min)

10.1.3 =*ma* TOPic

The clitic =*ma* has only one form =*ma* and does not require an epenthetic syllable when being hosted. Gurindji discourse is peppered with this clitic, as shown in (1714), where it attaches to a coverb, inflecting verb and nominals.

(1714) Tirrip-pa=rni kalu=**ma**=lu ya-na-ni=**ma** karu=**ma,**
overnight-EP=ONLY walk=TOP=3AUG.S go-IMPF-PST=TOP child=TOP

marlurluka=**ma,** kajijirri=**ma** jangkakarni=**ma**.
old.man.REDUP=TOP old.woman.REDUP=TOP many.REDUP=TOP
"They were walking all through the night [looking for water] – all of the children, men, women and adults." (🔈 VW: FM10_a155: Ngarlking Karu: 9:19min)

The clitic =*ma* can attach to many different parts of speech including nominals (1714) and (1715), demonstratives (1715) and (1716), free pronouns (1717) and (1718), coverbs (1714) and (1717), and inflecting verbs (1714). When it attaches to nominals in an NP, it can either occur on all members, as shown in (1714), or on any one member. It follows all case and derivational suffixes, as (1714) and (1715) show, but precedes bound pronouns, as in (1717).

(1715) Ngalyakap-kaji=**ma** ngumpit-tu=**ma** murlu-ngku=**ma**
lick-AGENT=TOP man-ERG=TOP this-ERG=TOP

jak wuya-rni mangarri-wu jaartkarra-waji-la.
drop throw-PST food-DAT eat-AGENT-LOC
"The man drops the ice cream on the table." (🔈 BW: FM07_a043 20:45min)

(1716) Wilajkarra-waji[238] nyila=**ma** nyantu-warij karrinyana.
alone-AGENT that=TOP 3MIN-ALONE be.IMPF.PRS
"A *wilajkarrawaji* is someone who is on their own." (🔈 VW: FM12_a183: 05:36min)

(1717) Ngayu=**ma**=rna kula nga-rni jaartkarra=**ma.**
1EXC.MIN=TOP=1EXC.MIN.S NEG eat-PST eat=TOP
"I never used to eat it." (🔈 VW: FM09_a123: 9:42min)

(1718) Mukurl-jayi-lu ngu=ngantipa pinak jayi-nga-ni
aunt-LATE-ERG CAT=1EXC.AUG.NS teach give-IMPF-PST

ngantipa=**ma,** Katarl-u, mukurl-rlang-ku.
1EXC.AUG=TOP NAME-ERG aunt-DYAD-ERG
"Our aunty who has passed away showed us – Katarl."
(🔈 VW: FM09_14_1a: 1:34min)

It has an important, but quite elusive function. McConvell (1980) refers to it as a topic marker. This explains many examples and indeed it cannot co-occur with the focus maker *=warla/=parla*. Nonetheless it does not always seem to act purely as a topic marker. Here we analyse *=ma* as a marker of prominent or contrastive topics.

The function of *=ma* is clearly to mark topics. For example, (1719) is a description of catching crocodiles in the old days. *Warrija* 'crocodile' first appears marked with *=ma* and then later in the topic-marked anaphoric demonstrative, *yaluwu* 'for it' and *nyawa* 'this one'. The use of demonstratives indicates temporal continuity between the clauses and *=ma* links the demonstrative to a previous topical referent.

(1719) Mirlarrang, jik=ma ya-na-ni ngu **warrija=ma.** Jarrwaj
spear emerge=TOP go-IMPF-PST CAT crocodile=TOP spear

ngu=lu pu-nga-ni. **Yalu-wu=ma=lu** taruk
CAT=3AUG.S pierce-IMPF-PST that-DAT=TOP=3AUG.S wade

waninyani nyawa-ngka. **Nyawa=ma** ka-nga-ni mirlarrang=ma.
fall.IMPF.PST this-LOC this=TOP take-IMPF-PST spear=TOP
"A crocodile would emerge then. And they would spear it. Then they would wade in to get it. This [crocodile] would be carrying the spear about [on its back]." (🔈 VW: FM12_a173: 2:32min)

Nonetheless *=ma* can be analysed more specifically to marking prominent topics, i.e. given information which is highlighted discursively. As in the analysis of pronominal clitic placement (§6.2.6.2), we take Choi's (1999) approach to information structure which allows for two different types of topic and focus (Table 51).

Table 51: Information structure categories based on Choi (1999).

	GIVEN INFORMATION	NEW INFORMATION
PROMINENT INFORMATION	prominent topic	prominent focus
NON-PROMINENT INFORMATION	non-prom topic	non-prom focus

A number of structures in Gurindji provide evidence for this analysis. First when the demonstratives *nyila* 'that' or *nyawa* 'this' act as identifiers (see §5.1.4.3), they are always found with =*ma* and translate as "this/that is (about)". In this construction, they set the discourse topic. The demonstrative with topic marker is generally found in first position (1720) and (1721), although occasionally not (1722). First position has been discussed before as the position in the clause which accords prominence to discourse entities. This construction is often used to begin narratives, to describe pictures and is commonly found in sentence elicitation. This construction is discussed in greater detail in §5.1.4.3.

(1720) **Nyawa=ma** ngantipa yapayapa ngu=ngantipa
this=TOP 1EXC.AUG small CAT=1EXC.AUG.NS

ka-nya mukurl-u=ma yala-ny-mawu-la.
take-PST aunt-ERG=TOP that-NMLZ-DWELL-LOC
"This was when we were small when my aunty used to take us as a traditional custodian of the country." (🔈 VW: FM09_14_1a: 3:50min)

(1721) **Nyawa=ma**, Yiparrartu, makin karrinya murla-ngka=ma.
this=TOP Emu sleep be.PST this-LOC=TOP
"This is about the Emu sleeping here." (🔈 BW: FM07_04_1c: 5:38min)

(1722) Kuurrinyji-yawung ngu=rna ma-rna-na
Gurindji-PROP CAT=1EXC.MIN.S talk-IMPF-PRS

nyawa=ma, jaru-yawung.
this=TOP language-PROP
"I am saying this in Gurindji." (🔈 VW: FM07_a050: 9:12min)

The constructions *nyila=ma* and *nyawa=ma* are also used in contrastive topic constructions (McConvell, 1996, pp. 318–320). In (1723), Biddy Wavehill, a Gurindji speaker who works extensively with Felicity, is described as going to another community, and Violet Wadrill contrasts herself as working with Felicity solo on this occasion.

(1723) Jala=ma **Nangala=ma** ya-na-na ngu Barunga-yirri.
today=TOP SUBSECT=TOP go-IMPF-PRS CAT place.name-ALL

Nyawa=ma=ja ngayirra-warij Nangari-wu=ma
this=TOP=1EXC.UA.S 1EXC.UA-ALONE SUBSECT-DAT=TOP

jarrakap ngu=rna=rla ma-rna-na ngayu-warij.
talk CAT=1EXC.MIN.S=3OBL talk-IMPF-PRS 1EXC.MIN-ALONE
"Today Biddy is going to Barunga. So here it's just the two of us, with me on my own talking to Felicity." (🔊 VW: FM09_14_1a: 10:06min)

In addition to setting and contrasting topics, *=ma* combines with demonstratives to mark a shift in topic, for example *yala-nginyi=ma* 'that-SOURCE=TOP' which translates as 'after that' or 'then', as shown in (1724), when the next step in a medicinal procedure is described.

(1724) **Yala-nginyi=ma** ngu=rnayinangulu lurlu yuwa-na-na
that-SOURCE=TOP CAT=1EXC.AUG.S>3AUG.NS sit put-IMPF-PRS

kuya yala-ngarna=**ma** tarlakurru-la=**ma** jungkart-ta=**ma**.
thus that-ASSOC=TOP pit-LOC=TOP smoke-LOC=TOP
"After that we sit them in the hot pit in the smoke."
(🔊 VW: FM07_a085: 1:21min)

Additional evidence for the analysis of *=ma* as a marker of prominent and contrastive topics can be found where free pronouns provide the stem. Free pronouns which occur as the initial constituent of a clause are often suffixed with *=ma* before the bound pronoun complex is attached to them. This construction establishes them as the topic of discourse and highlights the discourse entity. Usually only a bound pronoun is used if the discourse entity is given and consists of non-prominent information. The additional presence of the free pronoun in first position with a topic marker acts to accord prominence to the new topic. An example of a topic reset is seen in (1725). Blanche Bulngari describes the aftermath of the 1924 flood which washed away the original Wave Hill Station (see §1.4.1). She discusses Aboriginal workers finding discarded clothes and putting them on then begins a new topic about how they returned to the station.

(1725) **Nyarrulu** na ngumpit-tu wirr-im-karra na yuwa-ni, nyila-rra=ma
3AUG FOC man-ERG wear-TR-ITER FOC put-PST that-PL=TOP

warrpa=ma. **Ngantipa=ma=rnalu** wart na ya-ni
clothes=TOP 1EXC.AUG=TOP=1EXC.AUG.S return FOC go-PST

kanimparra-nginyi=ma. **Ngu=rnalu** wart ya-ni
downstream-SOURCE=TOP CAT=1EXC.AUG.S return go-PST

murla-ngkurra=ma **ngu=rnalu** nya-nya, lawara na.
this-ALL=TOP CAT=1EXC.AUG.S intake-PST nothing FOC
"Everyone put on the new clothes that they'd picked up. We came back from Rifle Hole then, from downstream. We came to the station and saw that nothing was left." (BB: McNair_E2A: 13:40min)

The other context is in the wrap-up of a story where the speaker establishes their authority as the story-teller. For example, in (1726), Banjo Ryan finishes a story from the old days by stating his authority as a holder of first-hand knowledge. This example can be seen as contrastive where he is setting himself apart from other people who might tell stories about the station days.

(1726) **Ngayu=ma=rna** jangkarni
1EXC.MIN=TOP=1EXC.MIN.S big

boi karrinya, stock-camp-kula waruk.
boy be.PST stock-camp-LOC work
"I was an adult working in the stock camps then."
(BR: FM15_52_1a: 17:51min)

The discourse clitic *=ma* is also often found marking new topics in elicited descriptions such as (1727) where Biddy Wavehill describes a picture of a dog sleeping in front of a shop. She establishes the topic as the dog.

(1727) Kamparra-la karrinyana makin, **nyawa=ma** **warlaku=ma.**
front-LOC be.IMPF.PRS sleep this=TOP dog=TOP
"The dog is sleeping in front [of something]." (BW: FM07_a043: 4:31min)

Despite this analysis, puzzling examples do occur in the corpus which are not easily described as prominent topics. For example occasionally *=ma* attaches to more than one constituent within the one clause, a situation not usually found with topic markers, for example in (1714), (1719) and (1724).

This clitic is very widespread in Ngumpin languages. It is also found in Bilinarra, Ngarinyman, Mudburra, Malngin and Wanyjirra (Ise, 1998, p. 53; Jones, Schultze-Berndt, Denniss, et al., 2019, p. 161; Meakins & Nordlinger, 2014, pp. 391–396; Osgarby, 2018a, pp. 184–185; Senge, 2016, pp. 512–516).

10.1.4 *=nyiyang, =nyiyarni, =nyirrarni* PROPERly

This set of clitics *=nyiyang*, *=nyiyarni* and *=nyirrarni* are discussed together since they have a similar function, although they cannot be considered variants. They are assumption modifiers and suggest that the stem they attach to is counter to the hearer's expectations. With an adjective, coverb or adverb, the suffix indicates 'really' possessing the property described by the stem, implying comparison with other exemplars which are less fully prototypical. Like English 'really', it is also used in a looser sense of 'very', as *tanku-murlung=nyiyang* 'meal-WITHOUT=PROPER; really hungry'. It also attaches to the interjection *yijarni* 'true!' with the meaning 'really'.

(1728) **Kankunungkarra=nyiyarni** pirnti-witi-la piyarti jimpiri-la.
on.top=PROPER side-SITE-LOC near cave-LOC
"Right on top there was a little cave with an opening close to the edge."
(RW: EC98_a012: 11:51min)

(1729) Rarraj ya-ni, marluka, **yijarni=nyiyang** nyawa=ma
run go-PST old.man true=PROPER this=TOP

jawiji, **yijarni=nyiyang,** ya-ni kayirra wumara
MF true=PROPER go-PST north stone

country, na gorge ya-ni wartuwartuj ya-ni.
country FOC gorge go-PST hide.REDUP go-PST
"Tirrknginyi ran off then – this is a true story, it's really true – he went up north, slipping away to the gorge country." (DD: EC98_a013: 5:05min)

When used with nouns, the clitic can have the sense of 'proper' or 'ordinary' similarly related to its meaning of a prototypical instance of something, whether that is an extreme manifestation or not. The opposite of this meaning 'not ordinary', often meaning 'sacred' as opposed to 'profane', can be evoked by negating a noun with this suffix with the negative *kula* or by combining the properly suffix with the *-murlung* privative suffix. It can also just mean 'really' or 'very'.

(1730) Wanku janginyina-murlung **ngapaku=nyiyang**.
fall.POT lightning-PRIV rain=PROPER
"Ordinary rain will fall, with no lightning."
(McConvell corpus: Meakins et al., 2016, p. 268)

(1731) Karlarra karrap, nyila=rni ngunti=ma - kula
west watch that=ONLY light=TOP NEG

ngunti=nyiyang, nyampayirla nyila=ma=yina
light=PROPER whatsitcalled that=TOP=3AUG.NS

ngunti=ma. Nyampayirla nyampayirla nyila=ma=rna?
light=TOP whatsitcalled whatsitcalled that=TOP=1EXC.MIN.S
"Over to the west, there was a light – not a proper light, but that other kind. What do they call it?" (Unknown source)

(1732) Jala=ma **tupurrung=nyirrarni.**
today=TOP hot=PROPER
"It's very hot today." (SM: Hale MS864(1): p. 18)

Malngin and Wanyjirra also has *-nyiyarni* analysed as a derivational suffix, but with a similar meaning (Ise, 1998, p. 31; Senge, 2016, pp. 155–156). It is possibly also a clitic but combinatory evidence with case-marking would be required for such as analysis. Ngardi has *-nyayirni(n)* which is also analysed as derivational because it appears on the inside of case morphology.

10.1.5 =*rni* ONLY

Although the clitic =*rni* has no allomorphs, it remains sensitive to the vowel/consonant/liquid-final stem distinction pervasive in Gurindji morphology. Where a stem is vowel-final, =*rni* is simply attached, as shown in (1733). Where a stem is consonant-final, =*rni* requires the epenthetic syllable *-pa* to attach first, as in (1734). Finally, if the stem is liquid-final, the epenthetic syllable is *-wa*, as demonstrated in (1735). A reduplicated form also exists =*rnirni*, as shown in (1736).

(1733) Kula ngantipa=**rni** kamparri-jang-kulu=ma=yinangulu
NEG 1EXC.AUG=ONLY before-TIME-ERG=TOP=3AUG.S>3AUG.NS

kuya na ka-nga-ni.
thus FOC take-IMPF-PST
"Not only us now, but they used to carry them around in the old days."
(◀)) VW: FM07_02_1c: 1:15min)

(1734) Kawarla pirrkap ma-ni ngu kaput-**pa=rni**
coolamon make do-PST CAT morning-EP=ONLY

ngayiny-ju marluka-lu.
1EXC.MIN.DAT-ERG man-ERG
"My husband made the coolamon early in the morning."
(◀)) BW: FM07_04_1d: 0:33min)

(1735) Juurl-juurl-**wa=rni** ma-nyja=wula=nyunu!
apologise-REDUP-EP=ONLY talk-IMP=3UA.S=RR
"You two just apologise to each other!"
(McNair corpus: Meakins et al., 2016, p. 123)

(1736) Nyamu=lu nya-nga-ni janyja=**rnirni**, nyila ngawa-wu
REL=3AUG.S intake-IMPF-PST dirt=ONLY.REDUP that water-DAT

wal ngu=lu ngarrka ma-na-ni "Yawu jeya," kuya.
well CAT=3AUG.S know get-IMPF-PST fish there thus
"When they saw a small really muddy waterhole, they would know that fish were there." (🔊 VW: FM09_16_2: 5:45min)

The clitic *=rni* can be encliticised to almost all word classes: nominals including nouns (1734), adjective (1737), place names (1738), cardinal directions (1739) and free pronouns (1733), (1740) and (1741), and coverbs (1742). It is never found attached to inflecting verbs (§7.1) or complementisers (§3.8).

(1737) Jama-na-ni ngu=rla jitirnijitirni ngu=rla
grind-IMPF-PST CAT=3OBL half-ground CAT=3OBL

jayi-nga-ni **parntaparntara=rni.**
give-IMPF-PST whole.REDUP=ONLY
"She ground it a bit and gave it to her half-ground, still whole."
(🔊 VW: FM10_23_1b: Yawarlwarl Wanyil: 4:23min)

(1738) Nyawa=ma=lu kamparri-jang-kulu kuya
this=TOP=3AUG.S before-TIME-ERG thus

ma-rna-na, nyamu=rnalu karrinyani
say-IMPF-PRS REL=1EXC.AUG.S be.IMPF.PST

kaa-rni-mpa **Jinparrak-kula=rni**, kuya-rra.
east-UP-PERL Wave.Hill-LOC=ONLY thus-PL
"That's what they used to say in the old days when we were living on the east side right at old Wave Hill station." (🔊 VW: FM09_a123: 10:45min)

(1739) Jarrwa tumaji Mungamunga ngu=rnalu
many CAUS Spirit.Women CAT=1EXC.AUG.S

karru karu=ma **karla-mpa=rni** kuya.
stay.POT child=TOP west-PERL=ONLY thus
"But there are too many *Mungamunga* here so we'll stay with the kids right in the west [at Alan Bore]." (🔈 CN: FM10_28_2a: 3:44min)

(1740) Nyila=ma nya-nga-nku ngu=nta
that=TOP intake-IMPF-POT CAT=2AUG.S

nyurrulu=rni **kirri-walija-lu=rni** karrap.
2AUG=ONLY woman-PAUC-ERG=ONLY look
"[When you take a photo], only you women are allowed to look."
(🔈 VW: FM07_a085: 19:15min)

(1741) Ngu=rna=ngku jama-rru **ngayu=rni**.
CAT=1EXC.MIN.S=2MIN.NS grind-POT 1EXC.MIN=ONLY
"I'll grind it for you, I will." (🔈 VW: FM10_23_1a: Yawarlwarl Wanyil: 2:53min)

(1742) Ngu=wuli **pampaya=rni** na wart na
CAT=3UA.NS shout=ONLY FOC return FOC

ngu=lu ya-ni, **pampaya=rni** ma-rna-ni.
CAT=3AUG.S go-PST shout=ONLY talk-IMPF-PST
"[With her] still shouting at the two of them, back they went, still shouting."
(🔈 DD: EC99_a029: Kinyjirrka-wu Murtap: 28:27min)

As with all clitics, *=rni* follows all case marking, but must precede the focus clitic *=warla/=parla* (§10.1.8), as shown in (1743) and (1744) and any bound pronouns (§6.2), as shown in (1696). It is rarely found in conjunction with topic clitic *=ma* but occurs afterwards, as shown in (1745).

(1743) Ngu=rna karru murla-ngka=**rni=warla** yawarra.
CAT=1EXC.MIN.S stay.POT this-LOC=ONLY=FOC rest
"I'm going to rest right here instead." (🔈 VW: FM12_a179: 10:24min)

(1744) Yala-ngku=**rni=warla** ngu pa-ni bamboo-ku=ma
that-ERG=ONLY=FOC CAT hit-PST didjeridoo-ERG=TOP

pangkily nyila=ma murnungku=ma Gordon Stott=ma.
hit.head that=TOP policeman=TOP NAME=TOP
"He was the one who bashed Gordon Stott over the head with a didjeridoo."
(🔈 BR: FM15_52_1b: 1:37min)

(1745) Ngu=rnayinangulu kampa-rna-na
CAT=1EXC.AUG.S>3AUG.NS cook-IMPF-PRS

karu=**ma=rni**, yapayapa=ma.
child=TOP=ONLY small=TOP
"We treat them, the toddlers that is." (◀)) VW: FM07_a085: 3:34min)

The clitic *=rni* has a number of different functions, often dependent on the category of the word to which it is attached. McConvell (1983, pp. 16–22) discusses in detail the different uses of this clitic in Gurindji. Broadly speaking, *=rni* is an expectation modifying clitic (McConvell, 1983, p. 14). The scope of this clitic seems to be only over the word it attaches to whereas the particle *jupu* (§10.2.1), which has a similar meaning, has scope over an inflecting verb or a whole sentence.

When *=rni* attaches to nominals such as nouns (1734), adjectives (1737), free pronouns (1740), and demonstratives (1746), it expresses the meaning 'only' or 'just'.

(1746) Ngu=ngantipangkulu=rla nganany ma-rna-ni,
CAT=3AUG.S>1EXC.AUG.NS=3OBL warn say-IMPF-PST

"Nomo=rnalu partartaj-nginyi. Nyila=**rni**
NEG=1EXC.AUG.S climb.REDUP-SOURCE that=ONLY

ma-nta=rla kanyjurra-nginyi nomo partaj-nginyi."
get-IMP=3OBL down-SOURCE NEG climb-SOURCE
"They warned us about that saying, 'Don't get them from the tree. Only collect the ones from below, not from the tree.'" (◀)) VW: FM09_15_2a: 9:03min)

In conjunction with the proprietive suffix *-yawung/-jawung* (§4.6.2), the meaning expressed is 'with the same X', as shown in (1747).

(1747) Karrinyani ngu=lu tanku=ma nyawa=ma ka-nga-ni
be.IMPF.PST CAT=3AUG.S food=TOP this=TOP bring-IMPF-PST

Wyndham-nginyi=ma. Murla-ngkurra=ma nyawa=ma=wuliny-pa
place.name-SOURCE=TOP this-ALL=TOP this=TOP=3UA.NS-EP

kujarra-kari-wu=ma. Yala-nginyi=ma ngu=wula
two-OTHER-DAT=TOP that-SOURCE=TOP CAT=3UA.S

ya-na-ni wart kankula, yukuwip-**jawung-pa=rni.**[239]
go-IMPF-PST return up camel-PROP-EP=ONLY
"They lived here and [another Afghan] used to bring stores from Wyndham. Here to the other two [Afghans]. Then [Charlie Palyung and Mayawi] went back [to Inverway with their stores] with the same camels."
(🔈 VW: FM10_22_1a: 4:06min)

(1748) Kaju-pari-k marri, jintapa-kari warrara warrulirli
close-ADJ-FACT BUT another-OTHER throw.spear spear.flying

kankula-la wawu, jintapa-kari warrulirli kankula-la
up-LOC sticking.up another-OTHER spear.flying up-LOC

wawu, nyawa wanta, karna-**yawung-pa=rni**.
sticking.up this fall.IMP spear-PROP-EP=ONLY
"He got closer, sent another one flying and it hit the target sticking in vertically. He threw one at the other one and it got him the same way. He fell here with the same spears sticking in him."
(🔈 RW: EC98_a027: Kujilirli: 7:46min)

When *=rni* is hosted by pronouns, it has the same sense as 'own' in English as in 'my own' or 'myself', as shown in (1749)–(1751).

(1749) Ngu=rna=ngku jama-rru ngayu=**rni.**
CAT=1EXC.MIN.S=2MIN.NS grind-POT 1EXC.MIN=ONLY
"I'll grind it for you myself." (🔈 VW: FM10_23_1a: Yawarlwarl Wanyil: 2:53min)

(1750) Marluka-wu=**rni** ngu=rla ma-rni
old.man-DAT=ONLY CAT=3OBL talk-PST

nyanuny-pa=**rni** kalkalang yarrulan.
3MIN.DAT-EP=ONLY talk.rudely.to young.man
"The young man talked rudely to his own father."
(McConvell corpus: Meakins et al., 2016, p. 131)

238 Note that this use of *=rni* could also mean "only with camels, no donkeys or horses".

(1751) Jartaj ma-ni ngu=rla=nyanta
hit.with.boomerang do-PST CAT=3OBL=3OBL2

nyanuny-ja=**rni** kuya.
3MIN.DAT-LOC=ONLY thus
"He aimed at him all by himself." (🔊 VW: FM12_a172: 02:42min)

On numerals, =*rni* has the meaning of 'each'.

(1752) Jintaku=**rni** ngu=rnalu ka-nga-ni ngayirra.
one=ONLY CAT=1EXC.AUG.S bring-IMPF-PST 1EXC.UA
"We brought one log back each." (🔊 BW: FM09_a119: 12:22min)

When =*rni* attaches to spatial case-marked nominals or demonstratives in adverbial function, it has a meaning of 'precisely', 'exactly', 'directly', 'limited to', 'bang on' or 'right on', as shown in (1753)–(1757).

(1753) Karru-rra=wula murla-ngka=**rni**.
be.POT-HORT=3UA.S this-LOC=ONLY
"Let the two of them stop right here." (McConvell 1996 grammar manuscript)

(1754) Ngu=rnayinangulu ka-nga-ni
CAT=1EXC.AUG.S>3AUG.NS take-IMPF-PST

juluj kawarla-la=**rni**.
carry.under.arm coolamon-LOC=ONLY
"We only used to carry them right in a coolamon."
(🔊 VW: FM07_05_1a: 2:30min)

(1755) Nga-rna-ni ngu kamurra-a=**rni** kamurra-a=**rni**,
eat-IMPF-PST CAT halfway-LOC=ONLY halfway-LOC=ONLY

purrp jaartkarra kuya.
finish eat thus
"The child had eaten it exactly half-way back."
(🔊 VW: FM10_a155: Ngarlking Karu: 4:49min)

(1756) Malngak pa-rra mangarli-la=**rni** nyila=kata ngu=yina kuya.
hit.chest hit-IMP chest-LOC=ONLY that=IMM CAT=3AUG.NS thus
"Hit them bang in the chest." (🔊 VW: FM12_a175: 9:20min)

(1757) Murrkun-kari=ma nyawa=ma karrinya, karnti-ka=**rni**.
three-OTHER=TOP this=TOP be.PST tree-LOC=ONLY
"Another three were right there in the tree." (🔊 VW: FM07_a085: 11:32min)

The sequence of 'stem+LOC+ONLY' has fused to produce many place names in the Victoria River District (McConvell, 2009b). Evidence for the fossilisation of these suffixes is seen in examples such as (1758) where another spatial case suffix is required to express static location at that place or movement to it. In this example, the place name Karungkarni is composed of *karu* 'child' + *-ngka* 'LOC' + *=rni* 'ONLY' to mean 'right at the place of the children' which is indeed a Child Dreaming site and now the name of the local arts centre (Wadrill et al., 2019). It is a hill visible from Kalkaringi.

(1758) Kaa-rni-mpal-a kuya ngu=lu ya-ni kankulu-pal
east-UP-EDGE-LOC thus CAT=3AUG.S go-PST up-EDGE

ngarlaka-yirri yala-ngkurra, **Karungkarni**-yirri.
hill-ALL that-ALL place.name-ALL
"They came and climbed up Karungkarni." (🔊 VW: FM07_01_2a: 3:10min)

In some cases, the stem was originally a nominal such as *Jantura-la=rni* 'bustard-LOC–ONLY' and *Kurturtu-la–rni* 'mother's children-LOC=ONLY'. In other cases, for example Purtpangkarni 'Number 3 Bore on Wave Hill Station', the stem was originally a coverb such as *purtpa-ngka=rni* 'crotch clap-LOC=ONLY'. In these cases, where the stem is transparent, the meaning of the stem is often associated with a Dreaming story about the site. An interesting example is Marlukalarni which is a popular fishing spot where Jesus is said to have visited and his sacred donkeys now come from. The place name is composed of 'old man-LOC=ONLY'. In many cases, the place names are so old that the meaning of the stem is no longer known, for example Mawujalarni 'Sambo Yard'. The meaning of *mawuja* is not clear.[239]

The clitic *=rni* is also used to mean 'all the way' or 'up until' in both a spatial and temporal sense. This meaning is found with noun phrases in the allative case, such as (1759) and (1760), and time expressions, such as (1761).

(1759) Wart, makin-ku=ma=wula ya-na-ni yala-ngkurra=**rni**
return sleep-DAT=TOP=3UA.S go-IMPF-PST that-ALL=ONLY

Palyilarra-yirri=**rni** kayirra-ngkarra.
place.name-ALL=ONLY north-DOWN
"They went right back north to Palyilarra to sleep." (🔊 VW: FM10_30_1a: 4:56min)

239 Note that the word for poison is *mawuya* so *mawuja* could be an older form without lenition j>y. Older forms are often preserved in place names, but this is not conclusive in this case.

(1760) Kalurirrp ngu=wula ya-na-ni, lurrpu, tiwu-ngarna-yirri=**rni.**
walk.around CAT=3UA.S go-IMPF-PST return fly-ASSOC-ALL=ONLY
"Looking around and then returning to the plane to stay inside it."
(🔈 DD: McNair_G1: 2:11min)

(1761) Jiwarn-jiwarn ngu=lu yunpa-rna-na
all.day-REDUP CAT=3AUG.S sing-IMPF-PRS

kaput-ngurlu juny-pa=**rni.**
morning-ABL sunset-EP=ONLY
"They sing all day from morning to night."
(RW with ECh: Meakins et al., 2016, p. 108)

Another context where *=rni* has a temporal meaning of 'until' is when it attaches to factitive-marked nominals, as in (1762).

(1762) Yingi-yingi-murlu karra=lu punyu-**k-pa=rni**=lu
tease-REDUP-PRIV be.IMP=3AUG.S good-FACT-EP=ONLY=3AUG.S

karra yingi-yingi-murlu.
be.IMP tease-REDUP-PRIV
"You mob stop teasing and sit down until you're behaving properly, don't tease him." (🔈 VW: LC080305GUR.KALK_02VW.mp3: 1:34min)

When *=rni* attaches to a coverb, it gives a meaning of intensity which translates as 'all the time' or 'really', as in (1763)–(1765), or 'still', as in (1742) and (1766).

(1763) Tirrip-pa=**rni** kalu=ma=lu ya-na-ni=ma karu=ma,
overnight-EP=ONLY walk=TOP=3AUG.S go-IMPF-PST=TOP child=TOP

marlurluka=ma, kajijirri=ma jangkakarni=ma.
old.man.REDUP=TOP old.woman.REDUP=TOP many.REDUP=TOP
"They were walking all through the night [looking for water] – all of the children, men, women and adults."
(🔈 VW: FM10_a155: Ngarlking Karu: 9:19min)

(1764) Lawarrkap-pa=**rni** wanyja-ni ngu=yina.
dodge-EP=ONLY leave-PST CAT=3AUG.NS
"He continually dodged them." (🔈 VW: FM11_a164: 16:54min)

(1765)

Ngu=rnalu	ma-na-na	kuya	yamak-pa=**rni**.
CAT=1EXC.AUG.S	do-IMPF-PRS	thus	carefully-EP=ONLY

"We are pulling it off very carefully." (🔊 BW: FM08_11_2a: 13:48min)

(1766)

Ngu=rna=rla	kurrurij-ja	jalngak	waninya	rarraj-ja=**rni**.
CAT=1EXC.MIN.S=3OBL	truck-LOC	mount	fall.PST	run-LOC=ONLY

"I got on the truck while it was still moving."
(McConvell corpus: Meakins et al., 2016, p. 348)

There are also some apparently fossilised uses of *=rni* which are not clearly related to any of the above senses, and may be considered idiomatic in this respect, as given in (1767), with examples given in (1771)–(1770).

(1767)

kaput	'(in the) morning'
kaput-pa=rni	'early in the morning'
kujarra	'two'
kujarrap-pa=rni	'a pair' (perhaps < 'only two')
ngajik	'long time'
ngajik-pa=rni	'permanently'
purrp	'finish'
purrp-pa=rni	'the whole lot'

(1768)

Kaput-pa=rni	jujup	ma-na-na.
morning-EP=ONLY	start	do-IMPF-PRS

"He is starting [work] early in the morning."
(McNair corpus: Meakins et al., 2016, p. 111)

(1769)

Ngu=rnawula	pa-na-na	**kujarrap-pa=rni**
CAT=1EXC.UA.S	hit-IMPF-PRS	pair-EP=ONLY

kaa-rni-wariny	karla-rni-wariny.
east-UP-FAR	west-UP-FAR

"We both cut down a pair of trees further up east and west."
(🔊 VW: FM08_a101: 12:56min)

(1770)

Ngajik-pa=rni	<u>na</u>	ngu=wula	Mamungkul	waninya.
long.time-EP=ONLY	FOC	CAT=3UA.S	Dreaming.feature	fall.PST

"Those two became a Dreaming feature for good then." (🔊 VW: FM07_01_2a: 1:19min)

(1771)

Nyamu=lu=waa	**purrp-pa=rni**	waninya=ma	purlka-purlka.
REL=3AUG.S=REL	finish-EP=ONLY	fall.PST=TOP	old.people-REDUP

"Those old people who have all passed away now." (🔊 VW: FM08_11_2c: 1:43min)

A final common construction is the combination of *=rni* 'ONLY' and *=warla* 'FOC' which is found in first position hosted by the demonstratives *nyila* 'that' and *nyawa* 'this'. Often is means "that's all I know" or "that's all I can say".

(1772) Nyila=**rni=warla** ngu=rna
that=ONLY=FOC CAT=1EXC.MIN.S

ma-rna-na jaru=ma nyila na.
talk-IMPF-PRS story=TOP that FOC
"That's the story as I know it." (BR: FM15_52_1a: 7:54min)

(1773) Nyawa=**rni=warla**=lu ya-ni Rosewood-nganyjuk, kuya-ny.
this=ONLY=FOC=3AUG.S go-PST NAME-GROUP thus-NMLZ
"Those blokes are with Rosewood." (BR: FM15_52_1e: 8:50min)

Finally, McConvell (1983, p. 22) describes the reduplicated form of *=rnirni* as an 'emphatic' form. It is used only in the sense of English 'only' and is only found marking nominals simply to add weight to the restriction to a sub-set of the 'expected' set, particularly where this restricted set is explicitly contrasted with its complement. An example was given in (1736).

All of these above uses of *=rni* appear, when translated into English, to be relatively diverse. Nonetheless McConvell (1983, p. 9) suggests that these senses are alike in that they all serve to modify and/or deny pre-supposed expectations. Thus, the speaker makes an assessment of what they think the hearer expects to happen or to have happened. The speaker then uses an 'expectation' modifier to highlight deviation from this expectation. Sense (i) 'only' is the most straight-forward example of this. In this sense, *=rni* is used with the typical pragmatic function of 'only' in many languages, namely to "restrict the scope of an assertion against a presupposition that more would be expected" (Evans, 1995b).

The other three senses can all be seen to also function as 'expectation modifiers'. Thus, sense (ii) 'precisely, exactly' (used with the locative case) denies the pre-supposition that the action or event is to take place, or to be located, in a number of different locations. Sense (iii) 'all the way, until' denies an expectation that the distance is only "partially realised" in the particular case (McConvell, 1983, p. 25); and sense (iv) 'all the time' implies that something is engaged in a state "to the exclusion of all alternatives" (McConvell, 1983, p. 26), therefore it is 'only' in that state during the period involved. This clitic is used with these same senses in Bilinarra and Mudburra (Meakins & Nordlinger, 2014, pp. 381–389; Osgarby, 2018a, pp. 189–190). The equivalent clitic in Wanyjirra and Jaru is *=lu* (Senge, 2016, pp. 506–512; Tsunoda, 1981, p. 210), and in Ngardi is *=mipa* (Ennever, 2021). There is another clitic in Jaru which has similar functions: *=muwa* (Tsunoda, 1981, p. 208).

10.1.6 =*rningan* AGAIN

Like the clitic =*rni*, =*rningan* has no allomorphs, however where a stem is consonant-final, =*rningan* requires the epenthetic syllable -*pa* to attach, as in (1774), and when the stem is liquid-final, the epenthetic -*wa* is used to host the clitic, as shown in (1775).

(1774) Yarrapuru-nginyi ngu=rna wankaj-pa=**rningan**.
recover-SOURCE CAT=1EXC.MIN.S sick-EP=AGAIN
"Having recovered I'm sick again." (RW with ECh: Meakins et al., 2016, p. 439)

(1775) Limpal-wa=**rningan** ngu=rnalu ma-rni.
mens.business-EP=AGAIN CAT=1EXC.AUG.S talk-PST
"We talked about important men's business again."
(◀)) JK: McConvell_A3464_B: 5:14min)

This clitic is used in two senses. It can attach to a coverb or a nominal and has the meaning of the repetition of an activity, or 'too', 'again', 'also', 'as well as' or 'more'.

(1776) Ngu=rna jutu-k-pa=**rningan** yuwa-ni.
CAT=1EXC.MIN.S straight-FACT-EP=AGAIN put-PST
"I got on the right track again."
(McConvell corpus: Meakins et al., 2016, p. 122)

(1777) Nyamu=ngantipa=nga ka-ngku Nangari-lu=**rningan**.
REL=1EXC.AUG.NS=DUB take-POT SUBSECT-ERG=AGAIN
"If Nangari takes us again." (◀)) VW: FM07_a021: 8:19min)

(1778) Ngamayi-lu=ma=ngantipa=wula[241] ka-nya
mother-ERG=TOP=1EXC.AUG.NS=3UA.S take-PST

kuya-ny-ja=**rningan**, juluj-juluj.
thus-NMLZ-LOC=AGAIN carry.under.arm-REDUP
"Our mothers used to carry us in this sort of coolamon too."
(◀)) VW: FM07_02_1c: 1:07min)

The clitic =*rningan* can also attach to inflecting verbs to produce a reading in which the event described by the verb, and therefore the entire clause, is repeated.

240 This bound pronoun sequence is odd for two reasons. Firstly, it does not obey the unit augmented neutralisation rule (§6.2.3.4) and secondly the object pronoun precedes the subject pronoun (§6.2.3.2). We have no explanation for this.

(1779) Karu-ngku wumara=ma jakarr ma-ni=**rningan**.
child-ERG money=TOP cover do-PST=AGAIN
"A child covered up the money again." (McConvell, 1983)

In the speech of many Gurindji people, the Kriol particle *(g)igin* '< again' and *du* '< too' has largely replaced this Gurindji clitic, as shown in (1780)–(1783).

(1780) Yiparrartu **gigin** Mamurung ngu nyawa=ma. Murla-nginyi
Emu again Dreaming.place CAT this=TOP this-SOURCE

karnti, nyawa-rra kula=rlaa pa-rru kataj-kataj=ma.
tree this-PL NEG=1INC.AUG.S hit-POT cut-REDUP=TOP

Ngaja=n janga karrinyana.
ADMON=2MIN.S sick be.IMPF.PRS
"This is an Emu Dreaming place [Jampawurru]. We can't cut down trees here, or you might get sick." (🔊) VW: FM09_13_2d: 2:57min)

(1781) Jilipija=ma, nyila=ma ngu=lu ma-na-ni kuya **gigin**.
seed.husks=TOP that=TOP CAT=3AUG.S do-IMPF-PST thus again
"They'd put the seed husks [in a coolamon] too." (🔊) VW: FM10_a147: 0:54min)

(1782) Maiti ngu=lu yunpa-rna-ni **du** kamparri-jang-kulu=ma.
maybe CAT=3AUG.S sing-IMPF-PST too before-TIME-ERG=TOP
"Maybe they would also sing in the old days [to make the smoke rise]."
(🔊) VW: FM12_a193: 0:30min)

(1783) Ngantipa **du** ngu=rnalu=nga nya-nga-ni
1EXC.AUG too CAT=1EXC.AUG.S=DUB intake-IMPF-PST

tanku-murlung-kula=ma, larrpa-larrpa=ma.
food-PRIV-LOC=TOP before-REDUP=TOP
"Us too, we used to eat it when we were hungry in the old days."
(🔊) VW: FM09_12_6a: 1:41min)

This clitic is also found in Bilinarra (Meakins & Nordlinger, 2014, p. 390). The equivalent form in Ngardi and Jaru is *=rra* (Ennever, 2021; Tsunoda, 1981, p. 209). Mudburra has the clitic *=ja* which attaches to nouns to mean 'too' which matches some of the function of *=rningan* (Osgarby, 2018a, pp. 186–187).

10.1.7 =*waju/paju* BECAUSE

There are few examples of this clitic in the corpus. It attaches to different types of nominals in the small set we have including nouns (1784), interrogatives (1785) and pronouns (1786).

(1784) Kata=nga wumara-wu=**waju** kata=nga.
THO=DUB money-DAT=BECAUSE THO=DUB
"Maybe for the purpose of paying us money."
(🔈 VW: FM09_12_5b: 2:17min)

(1785) Kata=nga nyampa=rla=**waju,** ngarin jaartkarra-waji, water-snake.
THO=DUB something=3OBL= BECAUSE meat eat-AGENT water-snake
"Maybe because it was some sort of edible – a water snake."
(🔈 VW: FM10_23_4: 0:23min)

(1786) Kata=nga nyantu=**waju.**
THO=DUB 3MIN=BECAUSE
"They thought it was because of someone." (🔈 VW: FM10_23_4: 0:32min)

It has a general meaning of 'because'. In the examples where =*waju* combines with *kata=nga* 'though=dubitative', it seems to add to the doubt or uncertainty of the assertion. In other examples, it seems to have the meaning that something is not quite the prototype. For example, in (1787) the speaker is being accused of being a murderer but is claiming otherwise. In (1788) someone is being described as a kind of doctor but does not entirely meet the criteria. In (1789) the function of =*waju* is more prototypically 'because'.

(1787) Parnkarrang=ma nyamu=rna ngayu=**waju**
murderer=TOP REL=1EXC.MIN.S 1EXC.MIN=BECAUSE

kurrwara nyamu=yi=nta yuwa-ni.
blame REL=1EXC.MIN.NS=2AUG.S put-PST
"When you mob blamed me saying falsely that I am the murderer."
(McConvell corpus: Meakins et al., 2016, p. 191)

(1788) Nyila=ma ngu=yinangku=rla ma-na-ni,
that=TOP CAT=3AUG.S>3AUG.NS=3OBL do-IMPF-PST

kurnpirlirn-tu=**waju.**
doctor-ERG=BECAUSE
"He was the only kind of doctor they had in those days."
(🔈 PN: McNair_K2J: 1:00min)

(1789) Yuwa-rra=yi jimarri ngayiny-ju=**waju**
put-IMP=1EXC.MIN.NS friend 1EXC.MIN.DAT-ERG=BECAUSE

yuwa-rra=yi lurrpuwupu ngu=rna jawurruk ya-nku.
put-IMP=1EXC.MIN.NS return.REDUP CAT=1EXC.MIN.S descend go-POT
"Come on mate, put it back for me because I want to come down!"
(🔊) DD: McNair_C2A: 4:04min)

10.1.8 =*warla/parla* FOCus

The focus clitic is one of two clitics which show allomorphy. The variant =*warla* follows a vowel (1790) and =*parla* follows a consonant (1791). An alternative to =*parla* is the use of the epenthetic with =*warla* i.e. -*pa*=*warla* (1792).

(1790) Ngu=wula=rla karrinya kuli=**warla.**
CAT=3UA.S=3OBL be.PST angry=FOC
"The two of them were angry with him because of it."
(🔊) BR: FM15_52_1a: 11:06min)

(1791) Nyila=ma kaarnirra ngu ya-ni,
that=TOP east CAT go-PST

lirlaj=**parla** kaarnirra kaa-rni-yin-jarrk.
swim.along=FOC east east-UP-ABL-CROSS
"He then swam east across the river." (🔊) BR: FM15_52_1b: 1:08min)

(1792) Warrij na wart-**pa=warla**=lu ya-ni parnkarrang
leave FOC return-EP=FOC=3AUG.S go-PST murderer

ngu=lu jangka=warla ka-nya.
CAT=3AUG.S claim.victory=FOC take-PST
"The murderers left and returned [having] claimed the fight."
(🔊) BB: McNair_D1A: 5:31min)

The focus clitic =*warla*/=*parla* can be encliticised to all free-standing parts of speech, including nouns (1793), interrogatives (1794), demonstratives (1795), inflecting verbs (1796), coverbs (1797), and particles (1798) – and indeed all other parts of speech. It encliticises after all case and verbal inflections, must follow the clitic =*rni* 'ONLY', if it is present.

(1793) Jaalij=**parla** ngu=rna=rla ma-ni nguwa=rni.
prawn=FOC CAT=1EXC.MIN.S=3OBL do-PST bait=ONLY
"Then I got a prawn instead for her to only use as bait."
(Appendix: Fishing text: Text 2, Line 22)

(1794) 'Ngantu-ku=**warla** pa-rra nyila ngarin?' Ngu=wuliny
who-DAT=FOC hit-IMP that meat CAT=3UA.NS

ma-rni nyila=ma murnungku=ma Gordon Stott=ma.
talk-PST that=TOP policeman=TOP NAME=TOP
"'Who killed the cattle?' the police officer Gordon Stott asked the two blokes."
(🔊 BR: FM15_52_1a: 9:00min)

(1795) Nyurruluny=**parla** nungkiying?
2AUG.DAT=FOC family
"Is he your family?" (🔊 DD: EC98_a024: Boxer: 24:38min)

(1796) Ngu=lu ya-ni=**warla** kayirra nyawa karu-yawung=ma.
CAT=3AUG.S go-PST=FOC north this child-PROP=TOP
"Then they left and headed north with the boy." (🔊 BR: FM15_52_1a: 13:27min)

(1797) Jirrpu waninya nyiwunyiwun=**parla** ya-nku ngu.
dive fall.PST swim.underwater=FOC go-POT CAT
"He dived in and swam underwater instead." (🔊 BW: FM07_a043: 32:23min)

(1798) Larrpa-nginyi=ma jupu=**warla** ngu=rna
before-SOURCE=TOP JUST=FOC CAT=1EXC.MIN.S

karrwa-wu wapurtkarra.
keep-DAT anyway
"I'll keep that old one for fun anyway."
(RW with ECh: Meakins et al., 2016, p. 372)

The clitic =*warla*/=*parla* has two functions: (i) as a discourse clitic in which it marks the new and prominent information being presented (in the sense of Choi (1999), (ii) as a sequential marker of time 'now, then'. The first use is clearly demonstrated in question-answer pairs. The interrogative nominal is almost always marked with =*warla*, as shown in (1794) and (1799)–(1803).

(1799) Ngu=rna yangki pa-ni, “**Wanyji-ka=warla=n** ya-ni.”
CAT=1EXC.MIN.S ask hit-PST which-LOC=FOC=2MIN.S go-PST
“I asked her, ‘Where did you go?’” (VW: FM11_a168: 7:30min)

(1800) ‘**Wanyji-ka-ngurlu=warla** nyawa ngu=lu ya-na-na,’ kuya.
which-LOC-ABL=FOC this CAT=3AUG.S go-IMPF-PRS thus
“’Where have you mob come from?’ he asked.” (BR: FM15_52_1a: 12:33min)

(1801) ‘**Nyampa-wu=warla** ngu=rla ma-rna-na,’ kuya?
what-DAT=FOC CAT=3OBL talk-IMPF-PRS thus
“’Why does she talk like that to her,’ he asked her.”
(VW: FM11_a168: 26:02min)

(1802) Nyawa marluka wayi, **nyampa-wu-[ny]-ja=warla**?[242]
this old.man TAG what-DAT-[NMLZ]-LOC=FOC
“This old fellow hey, what’s amiss now?” (BR: FM15_52_1a: 16:16min)

(1803) That’s all now ngu=rna=ngku ma-rna-na
that’s all now CAT=1EXC.MIN.S=2MIN.NS talk-IMPF-PRS

nyila=rni=warla piyarrp nyila=ma jaru=ma?
that=ONLY=FOC inform that=TOP story=TOP
“That’s the story. I told you that story now.” (BR: FM15_52_1a: 17:22min)

The focus clitic is also used to emphasise new information in discourse and can be translated as ‘really’.

(1804) Witkarra=**warla** karrinya ‘Nyampa-wu=ja wayi ngu=rna?’
sick=FOC be.PST what-DAT=TOP TAG CAT=1EXC.MIN.S
“He was really sick, ‘What’s wrong with me?’” (BR: FM15_52_1a: 15:33min)

(1805) Nyila na nyampayirla kiliny kula nya-ngku
that FOC whatsitcalled gravid.goanna NEG intake-POT

ngarturr-u=ma lawara ngaja=rla nyila=ma karu=ma
pregnant-ERG=TOP nothing ADMON=3OBL that=TOP child=TOP

nyamu=nga wanku paraj=ma ngaja karrinyana maitbi,
REL=DUB fall.POT find=TOP ADMON be.IMPF.PRS maybe

241 The -*ny* ‘NMLZ’ has been deleted due to the NSD rule.

jangkarni-piya=ma	nyila=ma=nga	karru	wumpulung-karra-waji=ma
big-BIT=TOP	that=TOP=DUB	be.POT	roll.over-ITER-AGENT=TOP

karlapa-yawung=**parla**	wankaj,	kula=lu	nya-ngku.
boil-PROP=FOC	sick	NEG=3AUG.S	intake-POT

"An expectant mother shouldn't eat goannas with eggs in case the child is born with [sores]. When the baby is a bit bigger and can roll over itself – it will still have boils. (🔊) BW: FM09_a122: 2:42min)

Finally, in line with its first function as marking prominent new information, it is used as a contrast marker and often translates as 'instead' in this role, as shown in (1806)–(1809).

(1806)	Lawara	ya-nta=lu,	murlu-wu	waringarri-wu=**warla**.
	nothing	go-IMP=3AUG.S	this-DAT	warrior-DAT=FOC

"No more fighting for us now." (🔊) BR: FM15_52_1e: 5:10min)

(1807)	Yala-ngka=**warla**	ngu=lu	karrinyani	jurlujpurru.
	that-LOC=FOC	CAT=3AUG.S	be.IMPF.PST	new.mothers

"It was there that the new mothers lived [not somewhere else]." (🔊) VW: FM11_a167: 0:35min)

(1808)	Narranyjana-la=**warla**	nyamu=lu	karrinyani	tupa-tupa-la.
	windbreak-LOC=FOC	REL=3AUG.S	be.IMPF.PST	windbreak-REDUP-LOC

"When they lived in windbreaks instead." (🔊) VW: FM11_a167: 0:38min)

(1809)	Karrinya	ngajik	yala-ngka=**warla**	kanyjurra	pinka-ka.
	be.PST	long.time	that-LOC=FOC	down	river-LOC

"They camped there in the riverbed instead." (🔊) VW: FM17_a440: 2:29min)

The other function of *=warla* is as a sequential marker, as shown in (1796) and (1810) and (1811). It is often used to emphasise an action taking place immediately or sequential to another action.

(1810)	Ngu=rla	ya-ni	na	purlp-karra=**warla**.
	CAT=3OBL	go-PST	FOC	sneak.up-ITER=FOC

"He snuck up on him then." (🔊) BR: FM15_52_1e: 6:54min)

(1811) Ngu pa-ni na, marntaj. Ngu=yina led-im-gu=**warla**
CAT hit-PST FOC OK CAT=3AUG.NS let-TR-go=FOC

yuwa-ni ngu=yina ma-ni yilayilarrp
put-PST CAT=3AUG.NS do-PST take.off.REDUP

na ngirlkirri-nginyi wartan-nginyi marntaj.
FOC neck-SOURCE hand-SOURCE OK
"He hit him then, OK. Then he let them go, taking the chains from their necks and wrists, OK." (🔊 BR: FM15_52_1a: 7:09min)

There are many other cases in the data where it is not clear to us the function of the discourse clitics, particularly combinations of *=rni* and *=warla* on single words and in single clauses. Note also that function of this clitic has changed across generations of Gurindji speakers. Younger speakers now split the original functions of *=warla* between this clitic and the old borrowing from the Kriol *na* '< now', which is a particle. We discuss the change in use in the following section (§10.2.5).

This clitic is also found in Bilinarra (Jones, Schultze-Berndt, Denniss, et al., 2019, p. 210; Meakins & Nordlinger, 2014, pp. 397–402). In Mudburra, the equivalent is *=wanya* (Osgarby, 2018a, pp. 190–192).

10.1.9 *=warluk* FIRST

The ending *=warluk* is analysed as a clitic because it is found on the outside of case-marking, as shown in (1812). It is found mostly on nominals, such as nouns (1813), and is particularly common on free pronouns (1814). But it is also found on other parts of speech such as adverbial demonstratives (1812), and inflecting verbs (1815).

(1812) Yala-ngka=warla ngu=lu yuwa-na-ni marntaj
that-LOC=FOC CAT=3AUG.S put-IMPF-PST OK

ngu=lu **kuya-ngku=warluk** yuwa-na-ni.
CAT=3AUG.S thus-ERG=FIRST put-IMPF-PST
"Then they used to put it in the little coolamon and toss out the dirt first like this." (BB: McNair_D2B)

(1813) Ngu=rna pa-na-na kataj-karra na, **parnngirri=warluk**.
CAT=1EXC.MIN.S hit-IMPF-PRS cut-ITER FOC bark=FIRST
"I'm hitting the bark off first." (🔊 VW: FM07_a050: 0:31min)

(1814) Ngu=yi=wula nya-nga-na karrap
CAT=1EXC.MIN.NS=3UA.S intake-IMPF-PRS watch

Nangala-kujarra-lu=ma **ngayu=warluk** pa-ni.
SUBSECT-DU-ERG=TOP 1EXC.MIN=FIRST hit-PST
"Those two Nangalas are watching me cutting first." (🔈 VW: FM07_a027: 3:35min)

(1815) Ngu=rna=ngku **ma-lu=warluk**-pa=rni.
CAT=1EXC.MIN.S=2MIN.NS talk-POT=FIRST-EP=ONLY
"I want to tell you something first."
(🔈 VW: FM10_23_2: Warrija Kirrawa: 6:29min)

This clitic is also found in Bilinarra and Ngarinyman (Jones, Schultze-Berndt, Denniss, et al., 2019, p. 22; Meakins & Nordlinger, 2014, p. 147), but not in Mudburra. Ngarinyman has the forms *=warlu*, *=warluk* and *=warlung*. Wanyjirra uses *=la* (Senge, 2016, pp. 519–523). Warlpiri has the form *-wiyi* which has a similar meaning but can also attach to imperative verbs in Warlpiri to attenuate a command. In Warlmanpa *-wiyi* has a temporal meaning which is an extension of the 'first' meaning, for example *child-wiyi* 'when you were a child first'.

10.2 Particles

Particles are uninflected function words, which can occur anywhere in the clause, but attract pronominal clitics when they are found in first position. Ten particles exist in Gurindji: *jupu* 'JUST' (§10.2.1), *kula* 'NEG' (§10.2.2), *kutikata* 'MAYBE' (§10.2.3), *marri* 'BUT' (§10.2.4), *na* 'FOC' (§10.2.5), *nganta* 'ALLEgedly' (§10.2.6), *palarni* 'BETTER' (§10.2.7), *waku* 'WELL, BUT' (§10.2.8), *walima* 'Q' (10.2.9) and *wayi* 'Q' (§10.2.10).

10.2.1 *jupu* JUST

McConvell (1983, p. 14) classifies *jupu* as an adverb in Gurindji, but it does not receive case-marking (even optionally) so we classify it as a particle here (see §7.3 for a discussion of adverbs). *Jupu* modifies expectations about the whole sentence, the verb or the predicate. In this respect, it contrasts with the clitic *=rni* 'ONLY' which qualifies the part of speech it attaches to, for example nouns (§10.1.5). McConvell (1983, pp. 14–15) describes *jupu* as having four senses: (i) 'just', (ii) 'for nothing', (iii) 'not serious', and (iv) 'just for a while'. We discuss each of these in turn.

Firstly, *jupu* is used in context where it has been anticipated that the action may have been accompanied or followed by another action, but this did not take place. This is the 'just' sense, as shown in (1816) and (1817).

(1816) Jurlak ngu=rna paraj pu-nya nyila=ma
bird CAT=1EXC.MIN.S find pierce-PST that=TOP

jurkak=ma **jupu** ngu=rna parik wanyja-ni.
bird=TOP JUST CAT=1EXC.MIN.S leave.behind leave-PST
"I spotted the bird but I just left it alone." (McConvell, 1983, p. 14)

(1817) Kula=rnalu wumara ma-na-ni lawara.
NEG=1EXC.AUG.S money do-IMPF-PST nothing

Jupu ngu=ngantipa tanku na jayi-nga-ni.
JUST CAT=1EXC.AUG.NS food FOC give-IMPF-PST
"We didn't used to get money. He just used to give us food."
(🔈 VW: FM09_12_5b: 2:52min)

The 'just' meaning can be extended to the denial of possible expectation about there being an additional motive or special reason behind the action (i.e. intent towards an accompanying action). This meaning is often translated into Kriol as 'but nothing', as in (1818) and (1819).

(1818) **Jupu** ngu=ngala kalurirrp ya-ni.
JUST CAT=1INC.AUG.NS walk.around go-PST
"He just visited us." (i.e. just for a social chat without a specific purpose in mind). (McConvell, 1983, p. 14)

(1819) **Jupu** ngu=rna=ngku ka-ngku jala-wu jaartkarra-wu.
JUST CAT=1EXC.MIN.S=2MIN.NS bring-POT today-DAT eat-DAT
"I'll just bring you something to eat today."
(McConvell corpus: Meakins et al., 2016, p. 118)

A further extension of this meaning is a denial of serious intent or expected serious consequences e.g. here 'nothing much' is sometimes used as the Kriol translation. This fits within the stated type of expectation modification of earlier examples: restriction to one action, without further consequential actions which might have been expected. However, it does tend towards a more scalar interpretation, i.e. a slap is lower on a scale than punch, kick etc, as in (1820).

(1820) **Jupu** ngu=rna=ngku nangat yuwa-ni.
JUST CAT=1EXC.MIN.S=2MIN.NS slap put-PST
"I only just slapped you." (not meaning to start a serious fight)
(McConvell, 1983, p. 14)

The final meaning of *jupu* is more distinct and translates as 'just for a while', modifying an expectation that the event or its consequences will continue indefinitely, as in (1821)–(1823). In this meaning, *jupu* often takes the =*warluk* clitic, as shown in (1824). There is also an extension to spatial meaning where 'just for a little while' becomes 'just a bit above/below/near etc', as in (1824).

(1821) **Jupu** warra ka-nga-nku=rla.
JUST care.for take-IMPF-POT=3OBL
"Let's just keep taking care of it for a little while." (McConvell, 1983, p. 14)

(1822) **Jupu** kurnka karra=nga, tuliny ya-nta=nga.
JUST dead be.IMP=DUB get.up go-IMP=DUB
"He would have just been dead for a while and got up."
(but for the action of Dog, in the 'Origin of Death' myth)
(McConvell, 1983, p. 14)

(1823) **Jupu** ngu=rnalu ya-ni.
JUST CAT=1EXC.AUG.S go-PST
"We just went for a little while." (🔈) TD: FM07_021: 4:33min)

(1824) **Jupu**=warluk jayi-ngka=yi.
JUST=FIRST give-IMP=1EXC.MIN.NS
"Just lend it to me for a while." (McConvell, 1983, p. 14)

(1825) Nyila kankuli-yit **jupu** kumpaying=ma.
that up-ABL JUST honeycomb=TOP
"The honeycomb is just above it." (🔈) TD: FM07_a021: 4:04min)

10.2.2 *kula* NEGation

There are two different types of negation in Gurindji, each marked with a different negation marker. Firstly the privative suffix *-murlung* attaches to a noun to negate the presence of an entity, as in (1826)–(1827) and secondly it attaches to a coverb to indicate the cessation of a state (for further examples, see §4.6.3) (1828). It is also used in negative imperatives where an inflecting verb is not present. In these constructions it is found attached to the coverb, as in (1829) (see §7.2.4).

(1826) Ngamayi-lu=ma nyamu=waa karrwa-wu jintapa-kari,
mother-ERG=TOP REL=REL have-POT another-OTHER

wal jajarra na ngu=yinangulu
well child.without.milk FOC CAT=3AUG.S>3AUG.NS

tal pa-na-na, ngapulu-**murlung**=ma.
call hit-IMPF-PRS milk-PRIV=TOP
"When the mother is going to have another baby, well they call them 'jajarra', without milk." (🔊) VW: FM11a_167: 4:00min)

(1827) Namata tanku-**murlung**-kula ngu=yinangulu nyampayirla
no.matter food-PRIV-LOC CAT=3AUG.S>3AUG.NS whatsitcalled

ma-na-ni mumungku ma-na-ni.
do-IMPF-PST restrict do-IMPF-PST
"Even during the times we were hungry, they would stop us from eating it."
(🔊) VW: FM09_a123: 8:01min)

(1828) Jaalap-**murlung**-pa=rni warrij ya-ni.
say.goodbye-PRIV-EP=ONLY leave go-PST
"He went away without saying anything."
(McNair corpus: Meakins et al., 2016, p. 71)

(1829) Kawayiwayi, karu-walija, yilying-**murlu**
come.here.REDUP child-PAUC make.noise-PRIV

muk karra=lu.
quiet be.IMP=3AUG.S
"Come here all you kids. Stop being noisy. Keep quiet now!"
(🔊) DD: EC97_a002: 10:19min)

The negative particle *kula* is used to mark all other types of negation. It has two functions: (i) it can negate the existence of an event/state (clausal scope), and (ii) it can negate the existence of an entity. Firstly, *kula* is used to negate nouns, as shown in (1830)–(1833). The difference between a NP such as *kula tanku* 'not food' versus *tanku-murlung* 'without food' is that *kula* directly negates a noun, whereas *-murlung* indicates the absence of something with respect to another noun.

(1830) Warlupurr ma-na-na ngu, warlayarra-lu=ma nyampa-ku=ma,
stingy do-IMPF-PRS CAT tobacco-ERG=TOP everything-ERG=TOP

kawurn-tu=ma, mangarri, ngarin **kula** jayi-ngu-waji.
ashes-ERG=TOP bread meat NEG give-INF-AGENT

Nyantu-warij=junu nga-lu jaartkarra.
3MIN-ALONE=RR eat-POT eat
"She is stingy about her tobacco, ashes and everything. She's the type of person who won't give bread or meat. She eats on her own."
(🔈) VW: FM11_a164: 13:52min)

(1831) Kurla-rni-mpa, **kula** kajupari nyila=ma kurla-rni-mpa
south-UP-PERL NEG near that=TOP south-UP-PERL

ngarlaka=ma nganayirla=ma Ngangi=ma, Ngangi
hill=TOP whatsitcalled=TOP place.name=TOP place.name

na ngarlaka Number Seventeen-ta kaa-rni-mpa kuya.
FOC hill Number Seventeen-LOC east-UP-PERL thus
"To the south, not close by, in the south and up the hill is Ngangi. Ngangi is that hill to the east of No.17 bore." (🔈) RW: EC98_a027: Kujilirli: 14:14min)

(1832) Marnta-kurra na ngu=rnalu ya-na-ni. **Kula**
place.name-ALL FOC CAT=1EXC.AUG.S go-IMPF-PST NEG

ngantipa=rni ngu=rnalu ya-na-ni, kirri
1EXC.AUG=ONLY CAT=1EXC.AUG.S go-IMPF-PST woman

jarrwa. Melon-ku yalu-wu=rni ngu=lu
many watermelon-DAT that-DAT=ONLY CAT=3AUG.S

ya-na-ni Marnta-ka=ma. Melon=ma
go-IMPF-PST place.name-LOC=TOP watermelon=TOP

karrinyani karil=ma nyampa=ma **kula** yangujpa.
be.IMPF.PST bush.cucumber=TOP something=TOP NEG few
"We used to go to Marnta. It wasn't just us who went but a big group of women. They used to go to Marnta to collect watermelons. There were watermelons and bush cucumbers there – heaps of them!" (🔈) VW: FM09_14_1a: 4:22min)

(1833) Ngiing-kaji-lu ngu=yi paya-rna-na, kaja-ngka,
buzz-AGENT-ERG CAT=1EXC.MIN.NS bite-IMPF-PRS bush-LOC

makin-ta=ma. Parlng-karra ngu=rna pa-na-na
sleep-LOC=TOP slap-ITER CAT=1EXC.MIN.S hit-IMPF-PRS

nyawa=ma ngiing-kaji. **Kula** yapayapa. Billabong-kula parlkij-ja
this=TOP buzz-AGENT NEG small billabong-LOC level-LOC

maitbi ngawa-ngka parlkij-ja. Kuliyan ngiing-kaji=ma
maybe water-LOC level-LOC aggressive buzz-AGENT=TOP

kuya-ny-ja=ma. Rein-nginyi-la=ma.
thus-NMLZ-LOC=TOP rain-SOURCE-LOC=TOP
"Mosquitoes bite me in the bush when I'm sleeping. So I am slapping the mosquitoes. They aren't small ones. At the billabong where you are level with the water. There are aggressive mosquitoes there after it has rained."
(🔊 VW: FM10_a152: 5:34min)

The negation particle *kula* can also combine with indefinites such as *ngana* 'someone', for example *kula ngana* 'no one'.

Secondly, *kula* can be used to negate a whole clause. In this function, it usually appears clause initially and attracts the pronominal clitics.

(1834) **Kula**=lu yuwa-ni kurrku karnti-ka
NEG=3AUG.S put-PST grave tree-LOC

ngu=lu yuwa-ni jirri-ngka.
CAT=3AUG.S put-PST burial.platform-LOC
"They didn't put her in a grave, they put her on a burial platform in a tree."
(🔊 DD: LC071220GURdd.nangala.mp3: 0:29min)

(1835) **Kula**=rnalu wumara ma-na-ni lawara.
NEG=1EXC.AUG.S money do-IMPF-PST nothing

Jupu ngu=ngantipa tanku na jayi-nga-ni.
JUST CAT=1EXC.AUG.NS food FOC give-IMPF-PST
"We didn't used to get money. He just used to give us food."
(🔊 VW: FM09_12_5b: 2:52min)

(1836) Kawilarl ngu nyila=ma, **kula**=ngku kurru karru.
memory.loss CAT that=TOP NEG=2MIN.NS listen be.POT
"This one isn't aware of much. She won't listen to you."
(🔈 VW: FM12_a174: 0:30min)

(1837) Karla-yarra-kijak=ma **kula**=lu pinarri, lawara.
west-SIDE-TERM=TOP NEG=3AUG.S knowledgeable nothing
"As far as the west they are not very knowledgeable."
(🔈 VW: FM08_08_4a: 1:03min)

(1838) Wanyja-ni ngu=wula warrij na ngu=wula
leave-PST CAT=3UA.S leave FOC CAT=3UA.S

ya-ni. **Kula**=wula=rla luyurr karrinya
go-PST NEG=3UA.S=3OBL feel.sorry be.PST

majul=ma yalu-wu=ma karu-wu=ma.
stomach=TOP that-DAT=TOP child-DAT=TOP
"They left him. They didn't feel bad about the kid."
(🔈 VW: FM10_a155: Ngarlking Karu: 5:29min)

Occasionally *kula* does not attract the pronominal clitic when there is a more prominent element. Nonetheless it still has scope over the entire clause, as in (1840).

(1839) Ngayu=ma=rna **kula** nga-ni jaartkarra=ma.
1EXC.MIN=TOP=1EXC.MIN.S NEG eat-PST eat=TOP
"I never used to eat it [when I was a young girl]." (🔈 VW: FM09_a123: 9:42min)

When *kula* combines with potential mood, it sometimes simply negates a potential event, as in (1840), but it also refers to something that has not happened or should not happen, but might (but with negative consequences if it does), as shown in (1841) and (1842).

(1840) **Kula**=rnangkulu **ma-nku** punyu-k.
NEG=1EXC.AUG.S<2MIN.NS do-POT good-FACT
"We can't make you better."
(🔈 VW: FM10_27_1a: Kurraj Story from Halls Creek: 5:55min)

(1841) Jungkuwurru=ma **kula**=lu **nya-ngku**
echidna=TOP NEG=3AUG.S intake-POT

ngarturr-lu=ma lawara.
pregnant-ERG=TOP nothing
"Pregnant women should not eat echidnas, not at all."
(🔊) BW: FM09_a122: 5:04min)

(1842) Nyila-ngku=ma **kula**=ngku wanji **yuwa-rru**.
that-ERG=TOP NEG=2MIN.NS alive put-POT
"That one won't leave you alive."
(🔊) VW: FM10_27_1a: Kurraj Story from Halls Creek: 3:02min)

The strength of *kula* can be softened with the use of the dubitative clitic *=nga* and potential inflecting verb. The combination suggests that something should not happen but might be possible given the right circumstances.

(1843) Nyila=ma mirlirti=ma tirrk, **kula=nga** **ya-nku**=ma
that=TOP hook=TOP tie.up NEG=DUB go-POT=TOP

yilarrp=ma lawara ma-nku=nga nang warraaj-ju tumaj.
take.off=TOP nothing do-POT=DUB stick wax-ERG CAUS
"This hook [well] tie it on [to the spear-thrower] and it shouldn't fall off, because the wax should keep it stuck on."
(McConvell corpus: Meakins et al., 2016, p. 214)

(1844) Ngumpin-walija **kula**=lu **ya-nku=nga**
man-PAUC NEG=3AUG.S go-POT=DUB

puriripuririri-ngkurra=ma ngantipanguny-jirri=ma.
birth.camp-ALL=TOP 1EXC.AUG.DAT-ALL=TOP
"Men shouldn't come to our women's camp [when a woman has just had a baby]." (🔊) VW: FM10_a133: 16:08min)

Many speakers of Gurindji now use the Kriol negative particle *nomo* instead of the Gurindji equivalent *kula*, as shown in (1845) The Kriol *nomo* is fully integrated into the Gurindji clause as demonstrated by the following example where bound pronouns encliticise to *nomo*, as in (1846).

(1845) Ngu=rnalu ma-na-na nyawa=ma kayili-yin-karra-la
CAT=1EXC.AUG.S do-IMPF-PRS this=TOP north-ABL-SIDE-LOC

tirnung=ma. **Nomo** karla-yin-karra. **Nomo** kaarra-yin-karra.
sap=TOP NEG west-ABL-SIDE NEG east-ABL-SIDE

Nomo kurla-yin-karra. Najing kula=rnalu
NEG south-ABL-SIDE nothing NEG=1EXC.AUG.S

ma-na-na. Kuya=rni nyamu=rnalu ma-na-na.
do-IMPF-PRS thus=ONLY REL=1EXC.AUG.S do-IMPF-PRS
"This sap from a bloodwood tree sits on the northside of the tree. We collect it from the northside of the tree. Not the westside. Not the eastside. And not the southside either. We don't collect it [from those sides of the tree]. We only collect it this way." (🔈 TD: FM09_17_2d: 0:30min)

(1846) Ngu=ngantipangkulu=rla nganany ma-rna-ni,
CAT=3AUG.S>1EXC.AUG.NS=3OBL warn say-IMPF-PST

'**Nomo**=rnalu partartaj-nginyi. Nyila=rni
NEG=1EXC.AUG.S climb.REDUP-SOURCE that=ONLY

ma-nta=rla kanyjurra-nginyi **nomo** partaj-nginyi.'
get-IMP=3OBL down-SOURCE NEG climb-SOURCE

'Nyampa-wu[-ny]-ja=rla.' 'Ngaja=rla mila janga karrinyana,'
what-DAT[-NMLZ]-LOC=3OBL ADMON=3OBL eye sick be.IMPF.PRS

kuya. Nganta=yina yumi kuya=ma kamparri-jang. Kuya
thus ALLE=3AUG.NS law thus=TOP before-TIME thus

ngu=ngantipangkulu=rla ma-rna-ni nganany.
CAT=3AUG.S>1EXC.AUG.NS=3OBL talk-IMPF-PST warn
"They warned us about that saying, 'Don't get them from the tree. Only collect the ones from below, not from the tree.' 'Why can't we?' 'In case your eyes become diseased.' That's what the old ladies told us. I think that was their law from the old days. That's how they warned us about it." (🔈 VW: FM09_15_2a: 9:03min)

The negative particle *kula* is also found in Mudburra, Bilinarra, Ngarinyman, Malngin, Wanyjirra. Warlmanpa and Warlpiri (Green et al., 2019, p. 58; Ise, 1998, p. 38; Jones, Schultze-Berndt, Denniss, et al., 2019, p. 52; Laughren, 1982, p. 131; Meakins & Nordlinger, 2014, pp. 410–413; Nash, 2008; Senge, 2016, pp. 490–491).

10.2.3 *kutikata* MAYBE

The particle *kutikata* 'maybe, might be, perhaps' lowers the certainty of a proposition. The particle may be composed of *kuti* + *=kata* 'IMMediate', but it is not known what *kuti* means on its own. This analysis comes from *kuti=rni* 'soon, wait up, hang on'.

(1847) **Kutikata** ngu=rna nya-ngku ngayi=rni
MAYBE CAT=1EXC.MIN.S intake-POT 1EXC.MIN=ONLY

ngayiny-ju mila-ngku.
1EXC.MIN.DAT=ERG eye-ERG
"Maybe I'll go see for myself with my own eyes."
(RW: HM070529GUR.DAGU_01rw: Warrija Kirrawa)

(1848) 'Yaa marntaj karra murla-ngka,' ngu=lu=rla ma-rni
yeah OK stay.IMP this-LOC CAT=3AUG.S=3OBL talk-PST

punyu. Nungkiying, jarrakap ngu=lu=rla ma-rna-ni,
good family talk CAT=3AUG.S=3OBL talk-IMPF-PST

nungkiying ngu=lu=rla ma-rni. Nyininy ngu=yina
family CAT=3AUG.S=3OBL talk-PST Nyininy CAT=3AUG.NS

ma-rna-ni. Nyininy. Ngu=lu pina nyila marlarluka=ma
talk-IMPF-PST Nyininy CAT=3AUG.S know that old.man.REDUP=TOP

yirrap=ma, ngu=lu=rla ngarrka ma-na-ni. Ngu=lu
group=TOP CAT=3AUG.S=3OBL remember do-IMPF-PST CAT=3AUG.S

karrwa-rni, **'Kutikutikata**, nyamu=rnalu ma-nku mangarri.'
hold-PST MAYBE.REDUP REL=1EXC.AUG.S get-POT veg.food
"'Yeah, alright. You can stay here. You're right.' They welcomed him and talked about family they had in common. He was speaking to them in Nyininy, which they knew. Those old people acknowledged him and knew his language. 'Wait on, we'll get some food'." (🔈 DD: EC98_a025: 3:39min)

(1849) Aaa, **kutikata** liwart karra=yi.
oh MAYBE wait stay.IMP=1EXC.MIN.NS
"Oh, hang on. Maybe wait a minute." (🔈 DD: EC97_a004: 4:49min)

These days the Kriol particle *maitbi* 'maybe, might be' is used instead, although it is not an exact match since it does not encode the 'wait' meaning:

(1850) **Maitbi** kaya-ngkurra ngaja=lu taarlak ya-nku.
maybe bad.spirit-ALL ADMON=3AUG.S danger go-POT
"They might be in danger of a bad spirit." (🔈 VW: FM12_a177: 4:52min)

Warlpiri has a particle *marda* which seems to have a similar function (Laughren, 1982, pp. 150–152), Wanyjirra has *nyangka* which also seems to be similar (Senge, 2016, p. 487) and Ngardi has *parda* and *ngarda* in this function (Ennever, 2021). Warlmanpa has *ngarra* (Browne, 2021).

10.2.4 *marri* BUT

The particle *marri* is used to present a contrast or exception to the previous clause. Note that it can host bound pronouns. It is also found in Western Mudburra (Osgarby, 2018a, p. 202). A similar particle *marri(ga)* is found in Bilinarra (Meakins & Nordlinger, 2014, p. 410). Wanyjirra also has *marri* but it is described as a particle meaning 'maybe, might be' (Senge, 2016, p. 494). It could be that it is confused with 'might be' which is used from the local Kriol and sounds similar.

(1851) Lawi-ngurlung=ma **marri**=rnalu=nga ma-nku yawu-wu.
place.name-ABL=TOP BUT=1EXC.AUG.S=DUB do-POT fish-DAT
"From Lawi but then we might get some fish." (🔈 DB: McNair_A1B: 3:59min)

(1852) Nyila=ma ngawa=ma **marri**=warla ya-ni.
that=TOP water=TOP BUT=FOC go-PST
"The water had gone away at last." (🔈 PN: McNair_K1D: 5:23min)

(1853) Wijku-k-pari na ngu=lu
close-FACT-ADJ FOC CAT=3AUG.S

marri tarap na wanta papa.
BUT dive FOC fall.IMP brother
"They are getting close you so you should dive under brother."
(🔈 DD: McNair_F2A: 15:37min)

(1854) Kayi=n ma-rni ya-nu-wu
chase=2MIN.S say-PST go-INF-DAT

marri wanyji=warla=n ya-ni?
BUT which=FOC=2MIN.S go-PST
"You said you were going to go so then why didn't you?"
(McConvell corpus: Meakins et al., 2016, p. 231)

(1855) **Marri** ngamanpurru mirtamirta yuwa-rru=rli.
BUT conkerberry large.round put-POT=1INC.MIN.S
"We'll put the large conkerberry fruit." (🔈 DD: McNair_F2A: 13:22min)

(1856) Ya, ya-nku=rli murtap, nyuntu-ja
yeah go-POT=1INC.MIN.S hunt 2MIN-LOC

marri ngayu=ma na ya-nku ngarlu-wu.
BUT 1EXC.MIN=TOP FOC go-POT honey-DAT
"Yeah, let's go hunting. I'm going to go for honey, what about you?"
(🔈 DD: EC97_a004: 0:33min)

(1857) Wal walik ya-ni ngu yikili=rni **marri** murla-marraj-ngurlu=ma
well turn go-PST CAT far=ONLY BUT this-COMP-ABL=TOP

nyawa-marraj kayi-rni nyamu school jeya kaa-rni
this-COMP north-UP REL school there east-UP

yalu-wu-marraj murla-ngka=ma nyila=ma marluka=ma.
that-DAT-COMP this-LOC=TOP that=TOP old.man=TOP
"Well he turned around keeping north, a little bit of a long way, like from here to the school there up and east, he was that far away that man."
(🔈 RW: EC98_a026: Karukany II: 4:14min)

10.2.5 *na* FOCus

All speakers of Gurindji, old and young now use the Kriol particle *na* in their speech. It is a very common borrowing across north Australia, and is in widespread use in the Victoria River Region (Schultze-Berndt, 2007; Schultze-Berndt et al., 2013). It is derived from the English word *now* and has the same functions in Kriol that *=warla/=parla* has in Gurindji. It has been described as a marker of emphasis (Hudson, 1983, p. 122; Sandefur, 1979, p. 92). It has also been described as a sequential marker (Sandefur & Sandefur, 1982, p. 19). These functions are examined in more detail by Graber (1987).

The particle *na* has two major functions. It acts as a marker of prominent, new information (1858)–(1860), and it acts as a sequential marker (1861).

(1858) Bow Hill-a **na** ngu=rnalu karrinya.
place.name-LOC FOC CAT=1EXC.AUG.S be.PST
"We were at Bow Hill." (🔈 VW: FM10_30_1a: 2:01min)

(1859) Nyila **na** ngu=rna pa-na-na pirrkap
that FOC CAT=1EXC.MIN.S hit-IMPF-PRS make

ngayu=ma jala=ma, ngurra-ngka
1EXC.MIN=TOP today=TOP camp-LOC

ngayiny-ja yarti-ngka, kaarra-yin-karra-la.
1EXC.MIN.DAT-DAT shade-LOC east-ABL-SIDE-LOC
"I'm making that one today, I am, at my camp in the shade on the east side of my house." (🔈 VW: FM07_a050: 2:25min)

(1860) Ngantipa ngu=rnalu nya-nga-na
1EXC.AUG CAT=1EXC.AUG.S intake-IMPF-PRS

ngumayi-jang-kulu **na** kuya, jalayi-lang-kulu.
before-TIME-ERG FOC thus now-TIME-ERG
"We who have been left behind [the older generation] know about this now, and the present generation." (🔈 BW: FM07_01_1a: 4:45min)

(1861) Ngamayi-lu=ma nyamu=waa karrwa-wu jintapa-kari,
mother-ERG=TOP REL=REL have-POT another-OTHER

wal jajarra **na** ngu=yinangulu
well child.without.milk FOC CAT=3AUG.S>3AUG.NS

tal pa-na-na, ngapulu-murlung=ma.
call hit-IMPF-PRS milk-PRIV=TOP
"When the mother is going to have another baby, well they call the first child 'jajarra', without milk." (🔈 VW: FM11a_167: 4:00min)

Among younger Gurindji speakers, *na* has completely taken over the sequential function of =*warla* and is encroaching on its function as a marker of prominent new information. In the speech of younger generations of Gurindji people who speak Gurindji Kriol (see §1.7.3), =*warla* is only retained as a marker of contrast, as in (1862).

(1862) a. Dat mukmuk bin kuli la=im. (Gurindji Kriol)
the owl PST attack OBL=3SG.NS
"The owl attacked (the boy)."

b. Dem bi-ngku kuli la=im dat **warlaku=warla.**
those bee-ERG attack OBL=3SG.NS the dog=FOC
"(And) the bees really went for the dog instead." (Meakins, 2009, p. 82)

In Bilinarra, this particle has become a clitic. Inflected words provide a stem to which the bound pronouns then encliticise.

(1863) Ngawa-ngku=**na**=lu ma-na pantij-pijik nyila=ma. (Bilinarra)
water-ERG=FOC=3AUG.S do-PRS mud-FACT that=TOP
"Then they make the antbed into mud using water."
(Meakins & Nordlinger, 2014, p. 93)

10.2.6 *nganta* ALLEgedly

This particle is frequent in the speech of Gurindji people and is maintained in the mixed language Gurindji Kriol. In fact, it is used liberally by younger Gurindji people. It signals uncertainty in reported information which might be why it is common in the speech of younger people, who are not the authorised knowledge bearers in a society that upholds elders for their wisdom. Even respected elders, such as Violet Wadrill, use *nganta* often when reporting on something that their own elders told them, i.e. hearsay, but for which they do not have first-hand experience themselves, as in (1864). In this respect, *nganta* has the hallmarks of evidentiality, except that Gurindji is not a language which is required to mark this category. The best translation for it is 'allegedly' or 'I think'.

(1864) Ngu=ngantipangkulu=rla nganany ma-rna-ni,
CAT=3AUG.S>1EXC.AUG.NS=3OBL warn say-IMPF-PST

'Nomo=rnalu partartaj-nginyi. Nyila=rni
NEG=1EXC.AUG.S climb.REDUP-SOURCE that=ONLY

ma-nta=rla kanyjurra-nginyi nomo partaj-nginyi.'
get-IMP=3OBL down-SOURCE NEG climb-SOURCE

'Nyampa-wu=ja=rla.' 'Ngaja=rla mila janga karrinyana,'
what-DAT=TOP=3OBL ADMON=3OBL eye sick be.IMPF.PRS

kuya. **Nganta**=yina yumi kuya=ma kamparri-jang. Kuya
thus ALLE=3AUG.NS law thus=TOP before-TIME thus

ngu=ngantipangkulu=rla ma-rna-ni nganany.
CAT=3AUG.S>1EXC.AUG.NS=3OBL talk-IMPF-PST warn
"They warned us about that saying, 'Don't get them from the tree. Only collect the ones from below, not from the tree.' 'Why can't we?' 'In case your eyes become diseased.' That's what the old ladies told us. They say it was their law from the old days. That's how they warned us about it." (🔈 VW: FM09_15_2a: 9:03min)

(1865) Najing ngu=yina tilykurr-tilykurr **nganta**
nothing CAT=3AUG.NS strike-REDUP ALLE

pa-na-ni janginyina-lu=ma.
hit-IMPF-PST lightning-ERG=TOP
"Lightning kept striking like that, I think."
(🔊) VW: FM10_27_1a: Kurraj Story from Halls Creek: 4:57min)

(1866) Jipu-jipu ma-na-ni **nganta** warlu=ma,
extinguish-REDUP do-IMPF-PST ALLE fire=TOP

yalu-ngku=ma mungku-ku=ma.
that-ERG=TOP red-faced.turtle-ERG=TOP
"The turtle kept extinguishing the fire, I think, [but it kept flaring up]."
(🔊) VW: FM10_23_4: 6:17min)

(1867) Jintapa=ma ngu=yi=lu yurrk ma-rna-ni,
another=TOP CAT=1EXC.MIN.NS=3AUG.S tell.story talk-IMPF-PST

karla-ngkarla nyawa, ngu=lu ya-na-ni **nganta**
west-DOWN this CAT=3AUG.S go-IMPF-PST ALLE

nyanawu Seale River murla-ngurlu=rni kaa-rni-yin-karra.
RECOG place.name this-ABL=ONLY east-UP-ABL-SIDE
"Another one they told me about, along the west from here, they went down to that Seale River, on the eastern side of it, I think."
(🔊) RW: EC98_a027: Kujilirli: 18:21min)

This particle is also found in Warlpiri, Warlmanpa and Ngardi with a similar function and ability to host pronominal clitics (Browne, 2021; Ennever, 2021; Laughren, 1982, pp. 137–141). Another form *murra* has a similar function in Warlpiri (Laughren, 1982, p. 158). Warlpiri has other evidential particles such as *kari* which expresses direct evidence of a proposition (Laughren, 1982, pp. 141–144). Gurindji does not have similar particles.

10.2.7 *palarni* BETTER

This particle appears rarely but means 'better'.

(1868) Ngu=ja palki-ny=ma karrwa-wu
CAT=1EXC.UA.S cover-NMLZ=TOP keep-POT

murla-ngka **palarni.**
this-LOC BETTER
"It's much better if we keep the blanket over here."
(RW & DD with ECh: Meakins et al., 2016, p. 301)

10.2.8 *waku* WELL

The particle *waku* is best translated as 'well' or 'but'. It functions to either describe an event that happened despite another event i.e. 'but', as in (1869), or to begin a topic after some background information is given to frame the next part of a story or description, as in (1870).

(1869) Ka-nga-ni ngu nganta Palmer Spring-kulawu **waku**
take-IMPF-PST CAT ALLE place.name-PURP WELL

ngu=rla yala-nginyi=ma wart ya-ni.
CAT=3OBL that-SOURCE=TOP return go-PST
"She maybe took it to Palmer Spring, but [the baby Rainbow Spirit] came back to her." (🔈 VW: FM10_27_1a: Kurraj Story from Halls Creek: 4:20min)

(1870) **Waku** karrwa=warla kaput-ku.
WELL hold.IMP=FOC tomorrow-DAT
"Well we'll save it for tomorrow." (🔈 BW: FM09_a119: 0:59min)

The Kriol particle *wal* which is derived from English is now also used in these functions.

(1871) Nyamu=lu nya-nga-ni janyja=rni=rni, nyila ngawa-wu
REL=3AUG.S intake-IMPF-PST dirt=ONLY=REDUP that water-DAT

wal ngu=lu ngarrka ma-na-ni 'Yawu jeya,' kuya.
well CAT=3AUG.S know do-IMPF-PST fish there thus
"When they saw a small muddy waterhole, they would know that fish were there." (🔈 VW: FM09_16_2: 5:45min)

10.2.9 *walima* Question

This particle has the appearance of an ignorative but, although it acts like an interrogative, it does not have an indefinite counterpart, hence its classification as a particle. It introduces information question phrased as 'did you . . . ', 'how about . . . ' or 'is there any . . . '. This particle has overlapping functions with *wayi*, discussed in §10.2.10, but unlike *wayi*, it cannot act as a tag question. It is generally found in first position, and, like many particles, it can host pronominal clitics in this position. This particle is also found in Wanyjirra and Jaru (Senge, 2016, pp. 491–492; Tsunoda, 1981, pp. 207–208). Some examples are given in (1872)–(1875).

(1872) **Walima**=nta ngapaku-wu=ma?
Q=2AUG.S water-DAT=TOP
"Do any of you want water?"
(McConvell corpus: Meakins et al., 2016, p. 381)

(1873) **Walima** ngu=rna=ngku jaja, tang-karra=kata
Q CAT=1EXC.MIN.S=2MIN.NS MM open.mouth-ITER=IMM

tang-karra nyawa murla jira-wu.
open.mouth-ITER this this fat-DAT
"Guess what I've got for you granny, come quick, open your mouth, open up for this [kangaroo] fat." (🔈 RW: EC97_a006: Jajurlang & Ngawa: 7:25min)

(1874) **Walima**=ja=ngku ya-nku wirti-wirti-wu=ma liwaya=ma?
Q=1EXC.UA.S=2MIN.NS go-POT block-REDUP-DAT=TOP company=TOP
"How about we come with you to back you up?"
(🔈 RW: EC97_a007: Warli: 7:56min)

(1875) **Walima**=ngku ka-nga-na ngayu nyamu=rna=ngku
Q=2MIN.NS take-IMPF-PRS 1EXC.MIN REL=1EXC.MIN.S=2MIN.NS

yujuk pa-na-ni, kirrawa?
send hit-IMPF-PST goanna
"Did you get the goanna meat I sent you?"
(🔈 VW: FM10_a155: Ngarlking Karu: 4:23min)

10.2.10 *wayi* Question

The question particle is related to the question clitic =*wayi* which attaches to interrogatives and is discussed in §5.3.7.1. This particle appears either clause-initially with pronominal clitics attached to produce a polar interrogative clause (1876) and (1877), or it appears clause-finally as a tag question often translated as "isn't it?", demonstrating uncertainly to the proposition expressed by the clause (1877)–(1880).

(1876) **Wayi**=rna yuwa-ni ngawa-ngka kanyjurra japurr?
Q=1EXC.MIN.S put-PST water-LOC down dip
"Did I throw it into the lake?" (◀) VW: FM10_23_1a: Luma Kurrupartu: 1:06min)

(1877) **Wayi**=rlaa wart ya-nku **wayi**?
Q=1INC.AUG.S return go-POT TAG
"Shall we go back?" (◀) VW: FM10_30_1a: Karu Dreaming Story: 1:06min)

(1878) Wanyji-ka=warla jarrakap-kaji nyawa=rni
which-LOC=FOC talk-AGENT this=ONLY

ngu=rna karrwa-rna-na **wayi**?
CAT=1EXC.MIN.S hold-IMPF-PRS TAG
"Where's the minidisc recorder, have I still got it?"
(◀) VW: FM07_01_1d: 1:57min)

(1879) Nyila na ngu=rna ma-nku lawa **wayi**?
that FOC CAT=1EXC.MIN.S get-POT lemon.wood TAG
"I'll go and get lemonwood now, shall I?" (◀) VW: FM07_01_1b: 2:59min)

(1880) On the olden time dei bin pirrkap mangarri, yala-ngka=ma,
in the old days 3PL PST make bread that-LOC=TOP

nyampayirla-la-ma, seed-ta-ma nganta **wayi**?
whatsitcalled-LOC=TOP seed-LOC=TOP ALLE TAG
"In the old days I think they used to make bread out of seeds, didn't they?"
(◀) VW: FM09_13_2a: 4:32min)

Bilinarra, Ngarinyman, Malngin, Wanyjirra and Warlmanpa have this form as well (Browne, 2021; Ise, 1998, p. 38; Jones, Schultze-Berndt, Denniss, et al., 2019, p. 216; Meakins & Nordlinger, 2014, p. 410; Senge, 2016, pp. 491–492). Warlpiri has a related form *mayi* which has the same function. It also has a particle *wayi* but this form is a focus marker (Laughren, 1982, pp. 156–157). Ngardi has *wayi* and *mayi* in an interrogative function but uses only *mayi* uses as the tag question (Ennever, 2021). Mudburra uses a clitic =*nya* as a tag question which appears on the clause final constituent (Osgarby, 2018a, p. 199).

List of suffixes

More information about different word classes and their morphology can be found in the following sections: nominals §4.3–§4.8, demonstratives §5.1.2, free pronouns §6.1.2, inflecting verbs §7.1.3, coverbs §7.2.4.

-a	locative
-ap	coverbaliser
-arra	iterative
-ing	adjectival
-irrik	factitive
-ja	locative
-jang	timealiser
-jarrk	cross river
-jawu	purposive
-jawung	proprietive
-jayi	late
-jirri	allative
-jpan	skin group
-ju	ergative
-k	allative
-k	factitive
-ka	locative
-kawu	purposive
-kaji	agent
-kari	other
-karra	iterative
-karra	riverside
-kayirnikayirni	etcetera
-kijak	terminative
-kik	factitive
-kilang	properly
-kirlirlaj	toy
-kirlikirlaj	toy
-ku	dative
-ku	epenthetic
-ku	ergative
-kuja	comitative
-kuja	lacking
-kujarra	dual
-kuk	factitive
-kula	locative
-kulawu	purposive
-kulu	ergative
-kumpal(ng)	aversive
-kunyja	comitative
-kunyja	lacking
-kupal(ng)	aversive
-kurra	allative
-kurt	times
-kuwang	and someone else
-la	locative
-lang	timealiser
-lawu	purposive
-lu	ergative
-lu	potential
-rlang	dyadic
-rlangkurla	dyadic plural
-mala	owner
-marnany	2nd possessive
-marnanyparra	2nd augmented possessive
-marraj	comparative
-mawu	dweller
-mayin	perlative
-mirntij	season
-mpa	perlative
-mpal	edge
-murlu(ng)	privative
-mungkuj	owner
-na	imperfective
-na	present
-ni	past
-nku	potential
-nta	imperative
-nu	cross river
-nu	infinitive
-nga	imperfective
-ngali	female name ending
-ngaliny	1st inclusive possessive
-nganang	axis
-nganayak	motivative
-nganyju(k)	group
-ngarna	associative
-ngari	female name ending
-ngarri	female name ending
-ngayarri	male name ending
-ngayirrang	1st unit augmented possessive
-ngka	imperative
-ngka	locative
-ngkarla	down

https://doi.org/10.1515/9783110746884-011

-ngkarra	down
-ngkawu	purposive
-ngku	epenthetic
-ngku	ergative
-ngku	potential
-ngkurla	down
-ngkurra	allative
-nginyi(ng)	source
-ngu	epenthetic
-ngu	infinitive
-ngu	2nd possessive
-ngurlu(ng)	ablative
-ngurniny	superlative
-nguwuyarra	2nd augmented possessive
-ny	nominaliser
-nya	past
-nyan	3rd possessive
-nyanparra	2nd possessive
-nyarrarra	etcetera
-nyja	imperative
-rna	imperfective
-rni	past
-rni	up
-rniny	hither
-rntarn	excess
-rntil	belonging
-rnu	infinitive
-p	coverbaliser
-pa	epenthetic
-pa	perlative
-pal	edge
-pari	adjectiviser
-partak	thither
-pijik	factitive
-pirrji	factitive
-piti	site
-piya	bit
-rra	imperative
-rra	locative
-rra	plural
-rrirniny	hither
-rru	potential
-tawu	purposive
-tu	locative
-rtarn	excess
-u	dative
-u	ergative
-wa	epenthetic
-waji	agent
-walija	paucal
-wari	adjectiviser
-warij	alone
-wariny	alone
-wariny	far
-warra	iterative
-warrp	together
-wirrirri	owner
-witi	site
-wu	dative
-wu	potential
-wuja	comitative
-wuja	lacking
-wuk	turn
-wulp	among
-wuluk	apex
-wumpal(ng)	aversive
-wunyja	comitative
-wunyja	lacking
-wupal(ng)	aversive
-wurru	shade
-wurt	times
-yarra	side
-yarri	male name ending
-yawung	proprietive
-yayi	late
-yin	ablative
-yirri	allative
-yit	ablative
-yu	dative
-yukawuk	almost

List of enclitics

More information about the form of pronominal enclitics can be found §6.2.1.1 and §6.2.2.7; and other clitics §8.3.1.

=ja	we (but not you)
=ja	topic
=jangku	we (but not you) do it to you
=junu	reflexive or reciprocal
=karliny	expert
=kata	immediate
=lu	they
=rla	to/or/for him/her/it/them
=rlaa	you and me
=rlaangulu	you and me do it to them
=rlaayinangkulu	you and me do it to them
=rli	we two (not you)
=rliwula	we two and him/her
=ma	topic
=n	you
=njina	you do it to them
=njinangkulu	you mob do it to them
=nkuwula	the two of you, you two
=nngala	you do it to me and you
=nngali	you do it to us (inc. me)
=nngaliwula	you do it to us three
=nngantipa	you do it to them
=nngantipangkulu	you mob do it to us
=nngayirra	you do it to them
=npula	you two
=npuliny	you do it to those two
=nta	you mob
=nga	dubitative
=ngala	us
=ngalangkulu	they do it to us
=ngali	us (you and me)
=ngaliwula	us two and him/her
=ngantipa	us (but not you)
=ngantipangkulu	they do it to us
=ngayirra	the two of us (but not you)
=ngku	you
=ngkulu	they do it to you
=ngkuwula	the two of them do it to you
=nyanta	3OBL2
=nyiyang	properly
=nyiyarni	properly
=nyjurra	you mob, you lot
=nyjurrakulu	they do it to you mob
=nyunu	reflexive or reciprocal
=rna	I
=rnalu	we (but not you)
=rnangala	I do it to you and me
=rnangali	I do it to you and me
=rnangaliwula	I do it for us three (including you)
=rnangantipa	I do it to us (but not you)
=rnangayirra	I do it to us two (but not you)
=rnangku	I do it to you
=rnangkulu	we do it to you
=rnangkuwula	I do it to you two
=rnanyjurra	I do it to you mob
=rnanyjurrakulu	we do it to you mob
=rnawula	we (but not you)
=rnawuliny	I do it to those two
=rnayina	I do it to them
=rnayinangkulu	we do it to them
=rni	only
=rningan	again
=paju	because
=parla	focus
=payin	etcetera
=pirak	correct
=purrupurru	and
=waa	relativiser
=waju	because
=warla	focus
=warluk	first
=wayi	question
=wayin	etcetera
=wula	those two
=wuliny	the two of them
=yi	me
=yilu	they do it to me
=yin	you do it to me
=yina	them
=yinangkulu	they do it to them
=yinpula	you two do it to me
=yinta	you mob do it to me
=yiwula	two of them do it to me

https://doi.org/10.1515/9783110746884-012

Appendices

A.1 Echidna and the big shade

Tommy Ngalngun Japarta, mid 1970s.
Recorded, transcribed and translated by Patrick McConvell.

1. Jungkuwurru jangkarni ngu=yina marluka
   Echidna big CAT=3AUG.NS old.man

   yalu-rra-wu yapayapa-wu=ma.
   that-PL-DAT children-DAT=TOP
   "Echidna was the elder for a group of little ones."

2. Yapayapa yirrap-kari yalu-wu miyat-kari-wu
   children other.group-OTHER that-DAT initiated.man-OTHER-DAT

   Pangarra-wu nyampa-wu yalu-wu ngu=lu=rla
   Corella-DAT what-DAT that-DAT CAT=3AUG.S=3OBL

   ma-rna-ni Pangarra=ma.
   talk-IMPF-PST Corella=TOP
   "There was another group there, Little Corellas, children of other initiated men, Little Corellas and other cockatoos, and they used to tell Echidna."

3. 'Kaput=ma ngu=rnalu ya-na-na warrij,
   tomorrow=TOP CAT=1EXC.AUG.S go-IMPF-PRS away

   purlka=ma nyuntu=ma karrinyanta ngurra-ngka=rni,
   old.person=TOP 2MIN=TOP be.IMPF.IMP camp-LOC=ONLY

   warra ka-ngka=ngantipa.'
   look.after take-IMP=1EXC.AUG.NS
   "'Tomorrow we're going out and you old man can stay at home and look after the camp for us.'"

https://doi.org/10.1515/9783110746884-013

4. ‘Ngurra ngu=rnalu ya-na-ngku ngarin
camp CAT=1EXC.AUG.S go-IMPF-POT game

ngu=rnalu pa-na-ngku, ngu=rnalu
CAT=1EXC.AUG.S hit-IMPF-POT CAT=1EXC.AUG.S

ka-nga-nku murla-ngka-wu=rni ngurra-wu.’
take-IMPF-POT this-LOC-DAT=ONLY camp-DAT
“‘We’re going to go camping out, kill some game and bring back the meat back here for the camp.’”

5. ‘Yuu, marntaj, ya-nta=lu ngarin-ku=ma,
yes all.right go-IMP=3AUG.S game-DAT=TOP

pa-rra=ngalangkulu.’
hit-IMP=3AUG.S>1INC.AUG.NS
“‘Yes, all right,” [said Echidna]. “Go for meat, kill something for us all.’”

6. Palngana, Pirntipirnti, yala-kijak ngu=lu
Flora.Valley Sturt.River that-TERM CAT=3AUG.S

ya-na-ni ngarin-ku.
go-IMPF-PST game-DAT
“They used to go hunting as far as Flora Valley and Sturt River.”

7. Ngu=lu pa-na-ni kirrawa nyampa nyila jangana,
CAT=3AUG.S hit-IMPF-PST goanna what that possum

jarrampayi, luma, ka-nga-ni ngu=lu=rla
big.goanna bluetongue take-IMPF-PST CAT=3AUG.S=3OBL

wart purlka-wu.
return old.person-DAT
“They used to kill goannas and such like, possums, big goannas and bluetongues, and take them back to the old man.”

8. Ka-nga-ni ngu=lu=rla yala-ngkurra, ngu=lu=rla
take-IMPF-PST CAT=3AUG.S=3OBL that-ALL CAT=3AUG.S=3OBL

jayi-nga-ni, ngu tanku nga-rna-ni purlka-ngku=ma.
give-IMPF-PST CAT meal eat-IMPF-PST old.person-ERG=TOP
“They used to bring the meat back to him there and give it to him, and the old man ate his fill.”

9.

Karnti	mana	yala-ngka=warla	walilik	yarti.
tree	tree.base	that-LOC=FOC	around.REDUP	shade

"There was the base of a tree there at the camp and shade all around."

10.

Yarti	jintaku	nyila=ma	yarti=ma,	yarti-ngka=rni
shade	one	that=TOP	shade=TOP	shade-LOC=ONLY

ngumpit=ma	ngu=lu	karrinyani.
person=TOP	CAT=3AUG.S	be.IMPF.PST

"That shade was the one and only shade, and the people lived in the shade"

11.

Nyila=rni=warla	yarti=ma	jintaku=rni	Nangkurru=rni.
that=ONLY=FOC	shade=TOP	one=ONLY	Nongra.Lake=ONLY

"That was the only one shade, Nongra Lake."

12.

Yarrkankuna	ma-rni	'Marluka,	nyawa=warla	ngu=rnangkulu
Cockatoo	talk-PST	old.man	this=FOC	CAT=3AUG.S>2MIN.NS

jiya-na-ni	wurlawurlaj,	kula=ngkulu	jayi-na-ni.'
snatch-IMPF-PST	hide.REDUP	NEG=3AUG.S>2MIN.NS	give-IMPF-PST

"Major Mitchell Cockatoo [gave him some meat and] said, 'We have been secretly keeping this meat from you, old man, they would not give it to you.'"

13.

'Ya-nta=lu	pakarli=ma	miyat=ma	ngarin
go-IMP=3AUG.S	paperbark=TOP	initiated.man=TOP	game

luwa=ngalangkulu.'
spear.IMP=3AUG.S>1INC.AUG.NS

"[Echidna said], 'Go, women and men, spear some game for us.'"

14.

'Ya-nta=ngalangkulu	ngarin-ku.'
go-IMP=3AUG.S>1INC.AUG.NS	game-DAT

"'Go out for meat for us.'"

15.

'Ngayu=ma	murla-ngka=rni	ngurra	ngu=rna=nyjurra
1MIN=TOP	this-LOC=ONLY	camp	CAT=1EXC.MIN.S=2AUG.NS

nyurruluny	karrwa-rna-ngku.'
2AUG.DAT	keep-IMPF-POT

"'I'll look after the camp for you mob.'"

16.

Malany	paya-rni	marluka-lu	Jungkuwurru-lu.
taste	bite-PST	old.man-ERG	Echidna-ERG

"[When they had gone] Old Man Echidna tasted the meat."

17.

Tarlak	ngu=rla	ya-ni.
sweet.taste	CAT=3OBL	go-PST

"He savoured its sweet flavour."

18.

'Nyawa=ma	kula=yi=lu	punyu-punyu	ka-nga-ni
this=TOP	NEG=1EXC.MIN.NS=3AUG.S	good-REDUP	take-IMPF-PST

nyawa=warla	ngarin=ma,	kayi=lu	wurlaj	karrwa-rna-ni.'
this=FOC	meat=TOP	SURP=3AUG.S	hide	keep-IMPF-PST

"'They never brought me this good meat, they've been keeping it hidden from me.'"

19.

'Ngayu=warla	nyatpa=rna=yina	karru?'
1MIN=FOC	how=1EXC.MIN.S=3AUG.NS	be.POT

"'What shall I do to them?'"

20.

'Kula=yi=lu	jayi-nya	ngarin=ma	nyawa=ma=rna
NEG=1EXC.MIN.NS=3AUG.S	give-PST	meat=TOP	this=TOP=1EXC.MIN.S

ma-nku	tip	yarti=ma.'
get-POT	uproot	shade=TOP

"'They didn't give me meat so I'll take away the shade.'"

21.

Yingin-yingin-karra	yuwa-ni	yingin-yingin-karra	kuya-ngku=ma	yuwa-ni.
jerk-REDUP-ITER	put-PST	jerk-REDUP-ITER	thus-ERG=TOP	put-PST

"He jerked the tree around, he jerked like this."

22.

'Ah	marntaj,	yinpi-yinpi=warla	marntaj	kayi.'[243]
ah	OK	loose-REDUP=FOC	OK	SURP

"'Oh good, at last it's loose enough.'"

23.

Tup	ma-ni	ngu.
uproot	do-PST	CAT

"He uprooted it."

243 This use of *kayi* is not clear and might have been 'OK' but we no longer have the audio to check.

24.

Nya-nya	ngu=yina	karrakarrap	'Ah	kula	ngana,
intake-PST	CAT=3AUG.NS	look.REDUP	ah	NEG	anyone

nyawa=ma=rna	ngayu-warij.'
this=TOP=1EXC.MIN.S	1MIN-ALONE

"He looked around for them [the Cockatoos, and said] 'There's nobody around, I'm on my own.'"

25.

Tup	ma-ni	ngu,	jalngak	yuwa-ni	parntawurru-la	nyila	karnti.
uproot	do-PST	CAT	mount	put-PST	back-LOC	that	tree

"He uprooted that tree and put it on his back."

26.

Warrij=ma	ya-ni	kurlarra,	ka-nga-ni	warrij	kurlarra.
leave=TOP	go-PST	south	take-IMPF-PST	leave	south

"He went south, he was carrying it south."

27.

'Nyawa=ma	ngu	yingin-karra=warla	karnti=ma,
this=TOP	CAT	jerk-ITER=FOC	tree=TOP

nyampa=warla=ngala	kurlarra-nganang	kanimparra.'
what=FOC=1INC.AUG.NS	south-AXIS	downstream

"[The Cockatoos said] 'The tree is jerking around, moving south and downstream – what's going on at our place?'"

28.

'Ya-nku=rlaa	ngurra-ngkurra.'
go-POT=1INC.AUG.S	camp-ALL

"'Let's go home.'"

29.

Ya-ni	ngu=lu	ngurra-ngkurra.
go-PST	CAT=3AUG.S	camp-ALL

"They went to the camp."

30.

'Lawara	kanyjal	nyawa=ma	karrinyana	parramparra=warla
nothing	below	this=TOP	be.IMPF.PRS	plain=FOC

karnti-murlung-nginyi	nyanawu-rntil=warla.'
tree-PRIV-SOURCE	RECOG-BEL=FOC

"'There's nothing, down below there's a plain where there used to be that tree.'"

31\.	‘Janga-ngku	purlka-ngku	Jungkuwurru-lu.’
	sick-ERG	old.man-ERG	Echidna-ERG

“‘The sick old Echidna has done it.’”

32\.	‘Wayi=rlaa	nyatpa?’
	Q=1INC.AUG.S	how

“‘What can we do?’”

33\.	‘Ma-nku=rlaa	karna	warlmayi	punyu-punyu-k
	get-POT=1INC.AUG.S	spear	woomera	good-REDUP-FACT
	ma-nku=rlaa.’	Kuya	ngu=lu	ma-rni.
	get-POT=1INC.AUG.S	thus	CAT =3AUG.S	say-PST

“‘Let’s fix up our spears and woomeras,’ they said.”

34\.	‘Ya-nku=rlaa	kurlarra	nyila=ma	ngu=rlaa
	go-POT=1INC.AUG.S	south	that=TOP	CAT=1INC.AUG.S
	wu-ngku	jarrwaj-karra.’	
	pierce-POT	spear-ITER	

“‘Let’s go south and spear him.’”

35\.	Kurlarra	yangkarra=warla	larrmij-jarung	karna	karna	karna	mirlarrang.
	south	follow=FOC	weapons-PROP	spear	spear	spear	spear

“They tracked him south carrying bundles of spears.”

36\.	‘Nyawa	kumpu	ngaya-ni.’
	this	urine	excrete-PST

“‘He urinated here,’ [they said, looking at the track].”

37\.	‘Kurlarra	kurlarra	kurlarra	kurlarra	nyawa	nyawa
	south	south	south	south	this	this
	kurla-rni-mpa-wuk	ka-nga-na-wu.’[244]			
	south-UP-PERL-TURN	take-IMPF-PRS-EXCL			

“‘He’s carrying it south all the way and turning south and uphill.’”

244 This *-wu* has the appearance of a dative but is likely to be an attenuation associated with an exclamative.

38. Rarraj ngu=lu ya-ni talyak=parla ngu=lu wu-nya.
run CAT =3AUG.S go-PST spear=FOC CAT=3AUG.S pierce-PST
"They ran and speared him."

39. Talyak-karra nyila=warla jingki-waji
spear-ITER that=FOC forearm.bone-AGENT

ngu=lu=rla karna=ma wuya-rni.
CAT=3AUG.S=3OBL spear=TOP throw-PST
"They threw spears at him."

40. Kayili kurlila jingki-waji nyawa=ma karna=ma
north south forearm.bone-AGENT this=TOP spear=TOP

nyantu karna murla-ngka=ma karrwa-rni parntawurru-la=ma.
3MIN spear this-LOC=TOP have-PST back-LOC=TOP
"He had spears stuck all over his back."

41. Kirt-kirt waninya karnti=ma.
break-REDUP fall.PST tree=TOP
"The tree fell [from his back] and broke into pieces."

42. 'Nyila=warla yarti=ma ngu=warla waninya kirt-kirt-nginyi
that=FOC shade=TOP CAT=FOC fall.PST break-REDUP-SOURCE

nyamu=ngala ngaliwany=parla larrpa=ma
REL=1INC.AUG.NS 1INC.AUG.DAT=FOC before=TOP

nyila=rni=rni jintaku karrinyani karnti=ma.'
that=ONLY=REDUP one be.IMPF.PST tree=TOP
"'That shade tree which used to be our one and only shade was broken into pieces now.'"

43. Ngu=lu wu-nya jarrwaj-karra=warla kurnka.
CAT=3AUG.S pierce-PST spear-ITER=FOC dead
"They speared him to death."

44.

Yala-nginyi-la=ma	nangkurru=ma	nyila=ma
that-SOURCE-LOC=TOP	pit=TOP	that=TOP

mana-nginyi-la=ma.
tree.base-SOURCE-LOC=TOP
"From then on there was a pit (Nangkurru) where the base of that tree had been."

45.

Kanyjal	nangkurru=warla	pirrka	ma-ni	ngawa-ngku=ma.
below	pit=FOC	make	get-PST	water-ERG=TOP

"At the bottom of it, the water made Nangkurru (Nongra Lake)."

A.2 Fishing

Date and speaker unknown.
Recorded, transcribed and translated by Patrick McConvell.

1.

Kankarra	ngu=rnalu	ya-ni	murla-ngurlung=ma	kankarra.
upstream	CAT =1EXC.AUG.S	go-PST	this-ABL=TOP	upstream

"From here we went upstream."

2.

Lawi-ngka	kanimparra	kuya	kajkuru-yawung-kula,
place.name-LOC	downstream	thus	pandanus-PROP-LOC

yala-ngka	ngu=rnalu=rla	wuya-rni.
that-LOC	CAT=1EXC.AUG.S=3OBL	throw-PST

"We went fishing downstream of Lawi where the pandanus grows."

3.

Kurla-rni-yin-karra	Nawurla,	kayili-yin-karra-la
south-UP-ABL-SIDE	SUBSECT	north-ABL-SIDE-LOC

Namija,	karla-rni-yin-karra	ngayirra.
SUBSECT	west-UP-ABL-SIDE	1EXC.UA

"Nawurla was on the south side, Namija was on the north side, Namija and I were both towards the west side."

4.

Ngu=rnalu=rla	yuwa-ni	wuyurrunkarra.
CAT=1EXC.AUG.S=3OBL	put-PST	fishing

"We cast our lines."

5.

Kartipa=warla	ya-ni,	tarukap	waninya.
non-Indigenous=FOC	go-PST	bathe	fall.PST

"A *kartipa* came and bathed."

6.

'Kartipa	ngu=nkuwula	lirlaj	ya-na-na'	Nawurla	ma-rni.
non-Indigenous	CAT=2UA.NS	swim	go-IMPF-PRS	SUBSECT	talk-PST

"'A *kartipa* is swimming towards you two,' Nawurla said."

7.

Crossing-jirri	ya-ni	lirlaj=ma.
crossing-ALL	go-PST	swim=TOP

"He swam to the crossing."

8. Wart=parla lirlaj ya-ni.
return=FOC swim go-PST
"He swam back."

9. Ngu=yinangkulu nyila=rni karrinyani
CAT=3AUG.S>3AUG.NS that=ONLY be.IMPF.PST

kajirri-kujarra kartipa-walija-wunyja=ma.
woman-DU non-Indigenous-PAUC-COM=TOP
"Two *kartiya* women were with several *kartiya* men there."

10. Kula=wula nyanpula-warij manungka[245]-la karrinyani tarukap.
NEG=3UA.S 3UA-ALONE single.camp-LOC be.IMPF.PST bathe
"The two women were not bathing in a separate women's area by themselves."

11. Nawurla wuukarra ya-ni.
SUBSECT afraid go-PST
"Nawurla was scared and moved away."

12. 'Nawurla, wanyji-ka=warla nyila kartipa?'
SUBSECT which-LOC=FOC that non-Indigenous
"'Nawurla, where's that *kartipa*?'"

13. 'Wart lirlaj ya-ni nyila=rni kanka-yit-karra-nganang
back swim go-PST that=ONLY upstream-ABL-SIDE-AXIS

kani-yin-karra.'
downstream-ABL-SIDE
"'He swam back to the upstream end.'"

14. 'Ya-nku=rliwula kanimparra Lawi-ngkurra palwa-ny-jirri.'
go-POT=1INC.UA.S downstream place.name-ALL flat-NMLZ-ALL
"'Let's go downstream to the Lawi flat rocks.'"

15. Japurrp ngu=rnalu ya-ni palwa-ny-jirri.
wade CAT=1EXC.AUG.S go-PST flat-NMLZ-ALL
"We waded to the flat rocks."

245 Note that this term only refers to a bachelor's camp according to Ronnie Wavehill so perhaps this sentence should be interpreted as "'They didn't bathe by themselves, they swam with the single men / they went in the men's area" (thanks to Erika Charola).

16. Palwa-ny-ja=warla wuyurrunkarra.
flat-NMLZ-LOC=FOC fishing
"[We did some] fishing at the flat rocks."

17. Ngu=rnalu nya-nya mangarri=warluk.
CAT=1EXC.AUG.S intake-PST food=FIRST
"We ate some lunch first."

18. Ngayu=ma yawu=ma ngu=rna
1MIN=TOP fish=TOP CAT=1EXC.MIN.S

kampa-rni wupkarra=warla marntaj.
cook-PST cook.on.coals=FOC OK
"I cooked a fish on the coals."

19. Ngu=yiwula purrp jiya-rni
CAT=3UA.S>1EXC.MIN.NS finish snatch-PST

kamparri-jang=ma ngayiny.
front-TIME=TOP 1EXC.MIN.DAT
"The other two got in before me and finished [the fish]."

20. 'Tanku-murlung=nyiyang ngu=rna.'
replete-PRIV=PROPER CAT=1EXC.MIN.S
"'I'm really hungry.' [I said]"

21. Tanku-murlung ngu=rna karrinya ngarin-murlung ngarin-kuja.
replete-PRIV CAT=1EXC.MIN.S be.PST meat-PRIV meak-LACK
"I was really hungry, without any meat to eat."

22. Jalij=parla ngu=rna=rla ma-ni nguwa=rni.
prawn=FOC CAT=1EXC.MIN.S=3OBL get-PST bait=ONLY
"Then I got a prawn for her to use as bait."

23. Jalij-ja=warla ngu=rla waj yuwa-ni
prawn-LOC=FOC CAT =3OBL throw put-PST

yala-ngurlung palwa-ny-ngurlung Namija-lu=ma.
that-ABL flat-NMLZ-ABL SUBSECT-ERG=TOP
"Namija threw the line from the flat rocks using prawn bait."

24. Kuya-ny-ja ma-ni warlujurlurru.
thus-NMLZ-LOC get-PST short.nose.catfish
"With that kind [of bait], she got a small catfish."

25. Ngu=rna ma-rni kuya, 'Ka-ngku=rna=rla=nga
CAT=1EXC.MIN.S talk-PST thus take-POT=1EXC.MIN.S=3OBL=DUB

Nangari-wu=rna=rla=nga ka-ngku kurlarra.'
SUBSECT-DAT=1EXC.MIN.S=3OBL=DUB take-POT south.
"I said, 'Let me take it south to Nangari.'"

26. Ngu=wula=nga makin.
CAT=3UA.S=DUB sleep
"Those two must have been asleep."

27. Ngu=rna ka-nya wart=parla.
CAT=1EXC.MIN.S take-PST return=FOC
"I took it back."

28. Ngu=rna kampa-rni yawu=ma, wararr marrimarri.
CAT=1EXC.MIN.S cook-PST fish=TOP fat plenty
"I cooked the fish, and it had plenty of fat."

29. Ngu=rnalu ya-ni wart kankuli-yit.
CAT =1EXC.AUG.S go-PST return up-ABL
"We went back from on top [of the rocks]."

30. Jamana=ma ngayu=ma=rna wankaj karrinya.
foot=TOP 1MIN=TOP=1EXC.MIN.S bad be.PST
"My feet got bad."

31. Wumara-lu ngu=yi yuwa-ni
rock-ERG CAT=1EXC.MIN.NS put-PST

jakayaka majarta=warla kalu-wu=ma.
lame crippled=FOC walk-DAT=TOP
"The stones made me lame, too crippled to walk."

A.3 How Kurrajnginyi got his nickname by Pincher Nyurrmiari

June 1979, Wattie Creek 8:40–11:37min.
Transcribed by Norm McNair, Ena Oscar, Sarah Oscar and Felicity Meakins.

1. Karla-mpa ngurra-ngka nyila=ma ngurra=ma Rainbow.
west-PERL country-LOC that=TOP country=TOP Rainbow
"There's an area west of here called Rainbow."

2. (Ngu=lu kartiya-lu=ma ma-rna-na).
CAT=3AUG.S non-Indigenous-ERG=TOP talk-IMPF-PRS
"(That's what *kartiya* call it – [it is on Mistake Creek])."

3. Yala-ngka=warla jarrwa ngumpit ngu=lu ya-na-ni
that-LOC=FOC many man CAT=3AUG.S go-IMPF-PST

kanyjurra ngawa-ngkurra nampang-jirri.
down water-ALL deep.waterhole-ALL
"A lot of men went down to the edge of a deep waterhole."

4. Ngu=lu=rla mararap ma-na-ni.
CAT=3AUG.S=3OBL fish.by.hands do-IMPF-PST
"They were feeling around for [long-neck turtles and fish with their hands]."

5. Ngu=lu yilimpi ma-na-ni.
CAT=3AUG.S feel.around do-IMPF-PST
"They kept feeling around."

6. Mararap ngu=lu=rla wayiwarrang-ku.
fish.by.hands CAT=3AUG.S=3OBL long-neck.turtle-DAT
"They were getting long-neck turtles."

7. Yawu-wu ngu=lu ma-na-ni.
fish-DAT CAT=3AUG.S do-IMPF-PST
"They were also fishing."

8. Wayiwarrang-ku warrija-wu ngu=lu=rla ma-na-ni
long-neck.turtle-DAT crocodile-DAT CAT=3AUG.S=3OBL do-IMPF-PST

mararap ngumpit-tu jarrwa-ngku.
fish.by.hands man-ERG many-ERG
"There were a lot of men hunting around for crocodiles and turtles."

9. Nyila=ma kula=lu Kurraj=ma nya-nga-ni.
that=TOP NEG=3AUG.S Rainbow.Serpent=TOP intake-IMPF-PST
"They didn't see the Kurraj."

10. Nyila=rni karrinyani ngapaku-la=ma.
that=ONLY be.IMPF.PST water-LOC=TOP
"[But] it was living right there in the water."

11. Ngu=lu mararap ma-na-ni pirnti-witi-kari-yirri.
CAT=3AUG.S fish.by.hands do-IMPF-PST side-SITE-OTHER-ALL
"They kept feeling around on the other side [of the waterhole.]"

12. Mayarni ngu=lu ma-na-ni
more CAT=3AUG.S do-IMPF-PST

kayirra-kayirra-k=parla kankula-rra.
north-REDUP-ALL=FOC up-??
"They hunted around some more up on the northern bank of the waterhole."

13. Pirnti-witi-ngurlu=ma nampang-jirri-?piya ngu=lu ma-na-ni.
river.edge-SITE-ABL=TOP waterhole-ALL-?BIT CAT=3AUG.S do-IMPF-PST
"They were reaching into the deep water from the side of riverbank."

14. Nyila=ma nurt ka-nya.
that=TOP press.down take-PST
"[Then] Kurraj grabbed [Japalyi] and pinned him down."

15. Nyawa=ma Kurrajnginyi=ma Japalyi=ma nurt=parla ka-nya.
this=TOP Jimmy=TOP SUBSECT=TOP press.down=FOC take-PST
"It held him underwater [which is how] Japalyi got his nickname, Kurrajnginyi."

16. Yuwa-ni kaninyjal lurlurr kayirra-ngkarra-k.
put-PST under push north-DOWN-ALL
"Kurraj shoved Japalyi down northwards [into an underwater cave]."

17. Jamana=rni=warla karrinyani jik=ma.
feet=ONLY=FOC be.IMPF.PST appear=TOP
"Only his feet were sticking out."

18. Nyila=ma=lu ya-na-na kankula
that=TOP=3AUG.S go-IMPF-PRS up

partartaj yirrap=ma ngumpit.
climb.REDUP another.group=TOP man=TOP
"The rest of men had climbed up on the riverbank by then."

19. Waku jintaku ma-ni wayi-wa=?rli
WELL one do-PST Q-EP=?1INC.MIN.S

ngu=nga Kurraj-ju=rni=warla.
CAT=DUB Rainbow.Serpent-ERG=ONLY=FOC
"So Kurraj only managed to grab one man."

20. 'Kanyjurra nya-ngku=rlaa=rla!'
down intake-POT=1INC.AUG.S=3OBL
"'We should look down there for it!'"

21. Jintaku=ma kurnpirlirn ngumpit kanyjurra wirrwawu
one=TOP sorcerer man down dive

waninyana wurinykurr-jawung=parla karnti-yawung.
fall.IMPF.PRS magic.stick-PROP=FOC stick-PROP
"Then a clever man dived in with a magic stick."[246]

22. Kinang wuya-rna-na ngu=rla nyila=rni jimpiri=rni.
go.after throw-IMPF-PRS CAT=3OBL that=ONLY cave=ONLY
"He went after him [since he knew about] the cave."

23. (Ngu=rla pina nya-nga-na
CAT=3OBL know intake-IMPF-PRS

nyanuny-ku=rni munuwu-wu=rni).
3DAT-DAT=ONLY home-DAT=ONLY
"(He knew it was [Kurraj's] home)."

24. 'Nya nya!'
this this
"'Take this and this!'"

246 It was made from the wood of *kungkarla* 'firestick tree (Clerodendrum floribundum)'

25. Wirinykurr-jawung-kulu=ma turrturrp pu-nga-ni.
magic.stick-PROP-ERG=TOP poke.REDUP pierce-IMPF-PST
"He jabbed him with the stick."

26. Karrinyani ngu ramarra-la Kurraj=ma.
be.IMPF.PST CAT dodge-LOC Rainbow-Serpent=TOP
"He dodged the Kurraj."

27. Warrkuj ma-ni wulu-ngurlu=rni jamana-ngurlu.
pick.up do-PST shin-ABL=ONLY foot-ABL
"[The clever man] grabbed [Jimmy Manngayarri] by the ankle."

28. Tartartap=parla ka-nya kankula ngapaku-ngurlu=ma
drag.REDUP=FOC take-PST up water-ABL=TOP

kankunungkarra-yirri ngumpit-jirri jarrwa-ngkurra.
on.top-ALL man-ALL many-ALL
"He dragged him to the surface [back] to the group of men."

29. Kurnka=warla.
dead=FOC
"[But Japalyi was] unconscious."

30. Nyila=ma ngu=lu=rla talwarrirn yuwa-ni warlu.
that=TOP CAT=3AUG.S=3OBL build.up.fire put-PST fire
"They built up a fire [on all sides of him]."

31. Warlu-ngka=warla warnan karrinya.
fire-LOC=FOC lie.down be.PST
"[Japalyi] was lying by the fire."

32. Nyangurla-kari ngayirrp ma-ni.
sometime-OTHER breathe get-PST
"After a while he got his breath back."

33. Wartan=ma yingirn ma-ni.
hand=TOP move do-PST
"A hand started moving."

34. Waninya lurlu=warla.
fall.PST sit=FOC
"And he sat up."

35.

Ngu=lu	yangki-yangki	pa-ni,	'Nga	ngu=yi	ma-ni
CAT=3AUG.S	ask-REDUP	hit-PST	hey	CAT=1EXC.MIN.NS	do-PST

Kurraj-ju	kanyjurra	nyawa	marntaj.'
Rainbow.Serpent-ERG	down	this	OK

"They asked him about it, 'Kurraj took me underwater but I'm OK,' [he said]."

36.

Yura=warla	nyawa=warla	ngajik-pa=rni.
good=FOC	this=FOC	long.time-EP=ONLY

"And he recovered completely."

A.4 Flood Events at Rifle Hole by Blanche Bulngari

March 1978, Wattie Creek.[247]
Transcribed and translated by Helen McNair, Ena Oscar, Sarah Oscar and Felicity Meakins.

1.

Kitirlwari	ngantipa=ma	Kitirlwari-la	ngu=rnalu
Riflehole	1EXC.AUG=TOP	Riflehole-LOC	CAT=1EXC.AUG.S

karrinyani	jimpiri-la=rni	wayi=ngantipa	pulngayit-tu=ma
be.IMPF.PST	cave-LOC=ONLY	Q=1EXC.AUG.NS	floodwater-ERG=TOP

ka-ngka	nyamu=nga	kaputa-la	ya-nta	nyila	pulngayit
take-IMP	REL=DUB	night-LOC	go-IMP	that	floodwater

ngu=ngantipa=nga	ngilyipurr	nga-nyja.
CAT=1EXC.AUG.NS=DUB	drown	eat-IMP

"We were camping at Rifle Hole in an overhang when the flood came our way. If it had come at night we would have all drowned."

2.

Ngawa-ngka	parlkij-ja	nyawa=kata	wumara=ma	jimpiri=ma
water-LOC	near-LOC	this=IMM	rock=TOP	cave=TOP

ngawa-ngka=ma	nyawa=warla	pinka=ma	ngawa-ngka	parlkij-ja
water-LOC=TOP	this=FOC	river=TOP	water-LOC	near-LOC

wayi=ngantipa	ngilyipurr	nga-nyja	nyamu=waa	kaputa-la=ma.
Q=1EXC.AUG.NS	drown	eat-IMP	REL=REL	night-LOC=TOP

"The overhang was near the water's edge so if the flood had come at night time we would have all drowned."

3.

Ya-nta	kaput-kaput	ya-ni.
go-IMP	morning-REDUP	go-PST

"Instead it came early in the morning."

4.

Ngayiny=ma	ngaji=ma	kankarra	kalurirrp
1EXC.MIN.DAT=TOP	father=TOP	upstream	walk.around

247 This was originally published (but not glossed) as Bulngari, B. (2016). Flood Events at Rifle Hole. In Erika Charola & Felicity Meakins (Eds.), *Yijarni: True Stories from Gurindji Country* (pp. 107–111). Canberra: Aboriginal Studies Press.

yawu-wu	jakap-jakap	ya-ni	kankarra.
fish-DAT	sneak-REDUP	go-PST	upstream

"My father went up the Victoria River to hunt for fish."

5.

Ngu	pat	ma-ni	kuya-ngku=ma	nya-nya	yapawurru
CAT	touch	do-PST	thus-ERG=TOP	intake-PST	small

pulngayit	pat	ma-ni	kuya-ngku	pulngayit-ta.
floodwater	touch	do-PST	thus-ERG	floodwater-LOC

"He touched the water like this and noticed that it was coming up."

6.

'Ngu=rnayina	wart	ya-nku	karu
CAT=1MIN.S>3AUG.NS	return	go-POT	child

ngaja=yina	ngilyipurr	nga-lu.'
ADMON=3AUG.NS	drown	eat-POT

"'I'd better go back to my kids. They might drown.'"

7.

Ngu	wart=parla	ya-ni.
CAT	return=FOC	go-PST

"So he went back."

8.

'Yunany=ma	yuwa-rra=lu	kaa-rni-yin-karra-yirri.'
belongings=TOP	put-POT=3AUG.S	east-UP-ABL-SIDE-ALL

"'Put your blankets and everything up on the eastside of the river,' he said."

9.

'Ngu=rnayinangkulu	ka-ngku	karu	pulngayit
CAT=1EXC.AUG.S>3AUG.NS	take-POT	child	floodwater

jangkarni	ngaja=ngala	wirti	pa-rru.'
big	ADMON=1INC.AUG.NS	block	hit-POT

"'We'd better get the kids up the east bank of the river because it's rising fast and it might cut us off.'"

10.

Ngu=rnalu	ya-ni	yununy=ma=rni
CAT=1EXC.AUG.S	go-PST	belongings=TOP=ONLY

yuwa-ni=warla	marntaj.
put-PST=FOC	OK

"So we went and packed up our things."

11. Ngu=rnalu ya-ni ngu=rnalu ya-ni
CAT=1EXC.AUG.S go-PST CAT=1EXC.AUG.S go-PST

langkarna-la=ma ya-ni kaarra-yarra kuya=ma langkarna-la
billabong-LOC=TOP go-PST east-SIDE thus=TOP billabong-LOC

lawara langkarna-la=ma ya-ni parrngany na lirlarlaj
nothing billabong-LOC=TOP go-PST full FOC swim.REDUP

na ngu=ngantipangkulu ka-nya ngantipa=ma
FOC CAT=3AUG.S>1EXC.AUG.NS take-PST 1EXC.AUG=TOP

yapayapa=ma kaa-rni-yin-karra-yirri wart ngu=lu
children=TOP east-UP-ABL-SIDE-ALL return CAT=3AUG.S

ya-ni yunany na warrkuwarrkuj ngantipa=ma.
go-PST belongings FOC pick.up.REDUP 1EXC.AUG=TOP
"We got out of there then. The water had already risen in the eastern area and the billabong there was already full. They swam the kids over to the other side and then went back to pick up all of our gear."

12. Kankunungkarra-la na palyja-la ngu=lu yuwa-na-ni
on.top-LOC FOC blanket-LOC CAT=3AUG.S put-IMPF-PST

puturn pirrka-pirrka palyja palyja-la marntaj.
shelter make-REDUP blanket blanket-LOC OK
"They were up on the other side of the riverbank and made shelters out of blankets."

13. Ngu=rnalu kalurirrp na ya-ni.
CAT=1EXC.AUG.S walk.around FOC go-PST
"[When they finished making the shelters] we went to look around."

14. Kajirri murrkun yala-ngka=rni ngu=rlaa=yina
old.woman three that-LOC=ONLY CAT=1INC.AUG.S=3AUG.NS

murrkun ngu=rlaa=yina murrkun kajirri
three CAT=1INC.AUG.S=3AUG.NS three old.woman

wanyja-ni parik ngantipa=ma yapayapa
leave-PST leave.behind 1EXC.AUG=TOP children

tumaji	ngu=rnalu	yapayapa	ngantipa=ma.
CAUS	CAT=1EXC.AUG.S	children	1EXC.AUG=TOP

"We left three old ladies there to look after the shelters. We were just little kids then."

15.

Nyila=ma	ya-ni	pulngayit=ma	partaj-pa=rningan	yala-ngkurra=ma
that=TOP	go-PST	floodwater=TOP	climb-EP=AGAIN	that-ALL=TOP

ngantipany-jirri=ma	camp-jirri=ma	munuwu-yirri=ma
1EXC.AUG.DAT-ALL=TOP	camp-ALL=TOP	camp-ALL=TOP

kajikajirri-lu	na	warrkuwarrkuj	ngu=lu	ka-nya
old.woman.REDUP-ERG	FOC	pick.up.REDUP	CAT=3AUG.S	take-PST

kankunungkarra=nyiyang-jirri	na	kankunungkarra=nyiyarni	na
on.top=PROPER-ALL	FOC	on.top=PROPER	FOC

kayi	kankunungkarra-yirri	na.
SURP	on.top-ALL	FOC

"The floodwaters came right up to our camp so the old ladies grabbed everything and took it right to the top of the riverbank. They got everything right to the highest point."

16.

Ngu=rnalu	nya-nya	ngantipa=ma
CAT=1EXC.AUG.S	intake-PST	1EXC.AUG=TOP

karu-walija-lu	kankuli-yit-tu.
child-PAUC-ERG	above-ABL-ERG

"All of us kids were looking down at the floodwater from on top of the bank."

17.

Ngu=rnalu	ngawa	nya-nga-ni	karrap
CAT=1EXC.AUG.S	water	intake-IMPF-PST	see

nyila	pulngayit	watermelon-ku=ma	pumpkin-ku=ma
this	floodwater	watermelon-DAT=TOP	pumpkin-DAT=TOP

any kind case	jangkarni	kuya-ny	box	nyila-rra=ma
any kind case	big	thus-NMLZ	box	that-PL=TOP

kankunungkarra	takurl-takurl	kingin-ta.
on.top	inside-REDUP	flotsam-LOC

"We could see watermelons, pumpkins and large tucker boxes bobbing around in the flotsam."

18. 'Wartayi ngu=nga marru=ma ngilyipurr nga-rni,'
hey CAT=DUB station=TOP flood eat-PST

ngu=rnalu ma-rni.
CAT=1EXC.AUG.S say-PST
"'Hey it might have flooded the station,' we speculated."

19. Nyakayi ka-nga-na yununy=ma kankapa murla=ma ngu=nga
xxx take-IMPF-PRS belongings=TOP upstream this=TOP CAT=DUB

ngilyipurr nga-rni kuya-ny=ma makin-kaji=ma partartaj
drown eat-PST thus-NMLZ=TOP sleep-AGENT=TOP climb.REDUP

kankula karnti-ka coolabah-la yawarta=ma milker=ma
up tree-LOC coolabah-LOC horse=TOP dairy.cow=TOP

camel=ma talwirr-a ngilyipurr-ngilyipurr kankula karnti-ka
camel=TOP hang-LOC drown-REDUP up tree-LOC

partartaj yuwa-na-ni.
climb.REDUP put-IMPF-PST
"The flood was washing everything away – beds were stuck up in the coolibah trees - horses, milking cows and camels too had drowned and were hanging from the trees where the floodwaters put them."

20. Kartipa jintaku ngu=rnalu meet-im ma-ni
non-Indigenous one CAT=1EXC.AUG.S meet-TR do-PST

ngantipa tuwa ya-ni kartipa jintaku.
1EXC.AUG meet go-PST non-Indigenous one

'Jintaku marluka pulngayit-tu ka-nya kurnka.'
one old.man floodwater-ERG take-PST dead
"One *kartiya* came up to meet up. He got close. "One bloke was taken by the flood and killed," he said."

21. "Wayi?" Lungkarra na ngu=lu karrinya lungkarra.
Q cry FOC CAT=3AUG.S be.PST cry
"'Oh no really?' They were all crying then."

22. Lungkarra=parla marntaj ngu=lu karrinyani
cry=FOC OK CAT=3AUG.S be.IMPF.PST

na nganta murla-ngka=ma.
FOC ALLE this-LOC=TOP
"They sobbed until they could cry no more."

23. Nyila marru kankula-ngarna-yin-pa=rni ngu=lu=rla warnparlk
that station up-ASSOC-ABL-EP=ONLY CAT=3AUG.S=3OBL open

ma-ni kankunungkarra-la na Mr Moray kankula partaj
do-PST on.top-LOC FOC NAME up climb

kankunungkarra-yirri walyak ngu=lu warnparlk ma-ni
on.top-ALL inside CAT=3AUG.S open do-PST

kankunungkarra-yirri partaj ya-ni karu-walija karnti-ka
on.top-ALL climb go-PST child-PAUC tree-LOC

partartaj nganta=lu karrinyani kajikajirri
climb.REDUP ALLE=3AUG.S be.IMPF.PST old.woman.REDUP

partartaj marlumarluka partapartaj na karnti-ka.
climb.REDUP old.man.REDUP climb.REDUP FOC tree-LOC
"At the station upstream from Rifle Hole, they had knocked out the windows so they could climb up on the roof of the station houses. The kids climbed trees where they could – and the old ladies and men were all up in trees too."

24. Jintaku Nampijina[248] yalu-wu Wangkirirri[249] ngumparna-wu
one SUBSECT that-DAT NAME husband-DAT

yalu-wu ngumparna nyamu=rla Wangkirirri-wu
that-DAT husband REL=3OBL NAME-DAT

Nangari-wu Jampijina yalu-wu kawurlu Nampijina.
SUBSECT-DAT SUBSECT that-DAT sister SUBSECT
"Well there was one Nampijina, Marie King's sister-in-law. The eldest sister of her promised husband."

248 Marie King's *ngajala* – her husband's big sister.
249 Marie King Nangari.

25. Nyawa=kata=lu karnti-ka partartaj karrinyani
this=IMM=3AUG.S tree-LOC climb.REDUP be.IMPF.PST

karu-walija=purrupurru jangkakarni - marntaj nyantu=ma
child-PAUC=AND big.REDUP OK 3MIN=TOP

kutij karnti-ka karrinyani karnti nyawa=kata
stand tree-LOC be.IMPF.PST tree this=IMM

kutij measure-im yalu-wu pulngayit-ku.
stand measure-TR that-DAT floodwater-DAT
"All of them were right up in the trees, kids and adults – all right well Nampijina was standing next to a tree in the water measuring the water against her height."

26. Nyila Nampijina juwal karrinyani lutup=parla.
that SUBSECT tall be.IMPF.PST short=FOC
"She was a tall woman!"

27. Dat Jangala, marluka, big one karnti,
the SUBSECT old.man big one tree

pakarli im bin paj-im-ap.
river.paperbark 3SG PST get-TR-up
"There was a Jangala who was perched on top of a big paperbark log."

28. Ka-nya ngu Kilkil-nginyi, pulngayit-tu.
take-PST CAT Gordy.Springs-SOURCE floodwater-ERG
"The flood had taken him all the way from Gordy Springs."

29. Murla-ngka na jalngak waninya, jarlaparl=ma ya-na-ni kuya.
this-LOC FOC ride fall.PST on.belly=TOP go-IMPF-PST thus
"He'd clung onto the log by lying down with his legs on either side."

30. Yarrinti-lu na yunpa-rna-ni ngawa=ma, yarrinti-lu
magic.song-ERG FOC sing-IMPF-PST water=TOP magic.song-ERG

yunpa-rna-ni yarrinti-lu yunpa-rna-ni yunpa-rna-ni
sing-IMPF-PST magic.song-ERG sing-IMPF-PST sing-IMPF-PST

ngawa kanimparra pinka=ma.
water downstream river=TOP
"He was singing the water trying to get it to recede."

31. 10 Mile-la na, Kayawurru, karnti=ma=rla nyila=ma
place.name-LOC FOC 10 Mile tree=TOP=3OBL that=TOP

ya-ni kaarnirra-k na pirnti-witi-yirri na.
go-PST east-ALL FOC river.edge-SITE-ALL FOC
"At 10 Mile, the log he was on started going sideways, northwards to the side of the river."

32. Kartarr kartarr kartarr kartarr kartarr karnti-ku pa-na-ni.
shudder shudder shudder shudder shudder tree-ERG hit-IMPF-PST
"Shudder, shudder shudder!" The log hit something.

33. I bin touch-im dat ground dat karnti nyampayirla.
3SG PST touch-TR the ground the tree whatsitcalled
"The log hit the ground!"

34. I bin gaj-im dat karnti garram nyampayirla wirnturru.
3SG PST catch-TR the tree PROP whatsitcalled root
"He reached with a root from the log to hook it up on another tree on the bank."

35. Wirnturru-yawung-pa=rni.
root-PROP-EP=ONLY
"With a root."

36. Kartarr kartarr kartarr kartarr kartarr.
shudder shudder shudder shudder shudder
"Shudder, shudder shudder!"

37. "Aaaa maitbi, maitbi im kalyja nyawa=ma," kuya.
Ah maybe maybe 3SG shallow this=TOP thus
"'Ah maybe it's shallow here!'"

38. Jawurruk waninya 'Aaaa marntaj!'
descend fall.PST ah goodness
"'So he got off the log, 'Oh thank goodness!'"

39. Partaj nganta ya-ni kankunungkarra-yirri clothes-murlung
climb ALLE go-PST on.top-ALL clothes-PRIV

nyampa-murlung lawara.
something-PRIV nothing
"He must have been naked as he climbed up the riverbank."

40. Jalyi na ma-ni jalyi jilmung ma-ni jalyi im bin
leaf FOC do-PST leaf break.off do-PST leaf 3SG PST

put-im kuya nganta ka-nga-ni kankunungkarra-yirri
put-TR thus ALLE take-IMPF-PST on.top-ALL

yuka ma-ni tup-tup.
grass do-PST uproot-REDUP
"He broke off some leaves to cover himself up and gathered some grass for a bed."

41. Makin. Makin yala-ngka=rni karrinya.
sleep sleep that-LOC=ONLY stay.PST
"Then he slept right there, totally exhausted."

42. Karrinya.
stay.PST
"He stayed there."

43. Karrinya, nyawa=ma jingk-abat na kata=nga nga-rni ngilyipurr.
stay.PST this=TOP think-ATEL FOC THO=DUB eat-PST drown
"Back at the station they presumed that Jangala had drowned."

44. Lungkalungkarra na yalu-wu marluka-wu=ma lungkalungkarra.
cry.REDUP FOC that-DAT old.man-DAT=TOP cry.REDUP
"They were crying and crying for him."

45. Ya-ni.
go-PST
"But he had travelled."

46. Nyantu=ma karrinya tirrip.
3MIN=TOP stay.PST overnight
"And Jangala had camped right where he'd landed."

47. Jinta-kurt munuwu tirrip karrinya nyampayirla purrku.
one-TIMES camp overnight stay.PST whatsitcalled tired
"He stayed overnight because he was tired."

48. Tired you know pulngayit-nginyi purrku
tired you know floodwater-SOURCE tired

karrinya ngawa-ngka nyamu ya-na-ni.
be.PST water-LOC REL go-IMPF-PST
"He was tired from clinging onto the log."

49. Karrinya tirrip jinta-kurt nganta
be.PST overnight one-TIMES ALLE

kaput-kaput na warrij ya-ni.
morning-REDUP FOC leave go-PST
"So he camped and then in the morning he started walking back."

50. Lungkalungkarra na murla-ngka=ma.
cry.REDUP FOC this-LOC=TOP
"They were all still crying at the station."

51. Nganta=lu nya-nya kaa-rni-yin jik, nyangurla-kari.
ALLE=3AUG.S intake-PST east-UP-ABL emerge when-OTHER
"But then I think they saw him emerge from the east at last."

52. Somebala ola girl, bin knock-im dat karnti na bushes.
someone all girl PST knock-TR the tree FOC bushes
"The women were all wearing leaves instead of their usual dresses which had been swept away when they climbed the trees to escape."

53. Olabat bin broke-im-bat igin laikajat na.
everyone PST break-TR-ATEL again like.that FOC
"They'd broken off bushy branches to cover themselves up."

54. Dat ola clothes finished.
the all clothes gone
"Their clothes had gone."

55. Dat floodwater bin teik-im.
the floodwater PST take-TR
"The floodwaters had taken them."

56. Pulngayit-tu=rni purrp ka-nya ngu=yina
floodwater-ERG=ONLY gone take-PST CAT=3AUG.NS

nyila-rra=ma warrpa=ma.
that-PL=TOP dress=TOP
"The floodwaters had taken all of their clothes."

57. Majarti-yawung jalyi-yawung na ngu=lu ya-na-ni.
loincloth-PROP leaf-PROP FOC CAT=3AUG.S go-IMPF-PST
"The women were wearing leaves instead of their usual dresses which had fallen off."

58. Kankula partartaj.
up climb.REDUP
"When they climbed the trees to escape."

59. You know Japalyi Lunkurr ngu=rnalu tal pa-na-na
you know SUBSECT NAME CAT=1EXC.AUG.S call hit-IMPF-PRS

Lunkurr jabaroo Six Mile-la ngawa=ma nyila=ma marrimarri
NAME stockman place.name-LOC water=TOP that=TOP fast

kuliyan lirlaj-ku=ma pulngayit nyamu ya-na-ni kuya
aggressive swim-DAT=TOP floodwater REL go-IMPF-PST thus

punu lajalaja pirnti-witi-kijak ngarlaka-kijak karla-nu-nyu
tree on.shoulder river.edge-SITE-TERM hill-TERM west-CROSS-?

yala-ngka nyantu=ma lirlaj=ma ya-ni pulngayit-tu nyamu
that-LOC 3MIN=TOP swim=TOP go-PST floodwater-ERG REL

ka-nya kajkuru yapakaru wingman nyila=ma warrkuj ma-ni
take-PST pandanus small xxx that=TOP pick.up do-PST

kuntu=ma yala-ngka=rni jalngak waninya nyantu marluka nyila
log=TOP that-LOC=ONLY ride fall.PST 3MIN old.man that

Lunkurr nyanuny janka yuwa-ni kuya-rniny nyila=ma lirlaj=ma ya-ni.
NAME 3MIN.DAT woman put-PST thus-HITH that=TOP swim=TOP go-PST
"You know Lunkurr Japalyi from Yarralin. Well we called him "Lunkurr" which means "tree trunk". The floodwater was moving fast but he was a strong swimmer and managed to swim from the west side of the river. He swam strongly and got a hold of a pandanus log which had been swept away by the flood. He grabbed it and climbed up on it, sitting astride. He pulled his wife up on it too. They floated on the log to the other side. So the floodwater didn't take them away. They headed straight to the bank and climbed up the north side. He was an extremely strong swimmer. He climbed right up the bank."

60. Kula pulngayit-tu ka-nya.
NEG floodwater-ERG take-PST
"The floodwaters didn't take him away."

61. Kuya=warla nganta=lu=waa nya-nya nyamu ngawa na
thus=FOC ALLE=3AUG.S=REL intake-PST REL water FOC

waji puna-wu ya-ni najing najing najing.
?rainbow ?tree-?DAT go-PST nothing nothing nothing
"They looked for all of their belongings but they had all been washed away!"

62. Nganta=lu nya-nya=ma anything.
ALLE=3AUG.S intake-PST=TOP anything
"I don't think they could find anything."

63. Yununy-ku=ma nyampa-wu=ma lawara.
belongings-DAT=TOP everything-DAT=TOP nothing
"Belongings, everything, gone!"

64. Garden=ma nyamu=lu pirrka=ma ma-na-ni nyila=ma
garden=TOP REL=3AUG.S make–TOP do-IMPF-PST that=TOP

patawan=rni binij ngawa-ngkawu pirnti-witi-la-ju
strong=ONLY finished water-PURP river.edge-SITE-?LOC-?ERG

karrinya garden=ma ngu ya-ni.
be.PST garden=TOP CAT go-PST
"The garden that they'd made, anything that would normally stand up to a small flood - it all ended up on the riverbank. The garden had gone."

65. Purrp!
gone
"It was all gone!"

66. An kartiya, wagon-jarung kayirra-la
and non-Indigenous wagon-PROP north-LOC

kaa-rni-yin-karra nyila karrinya.
east-UP-ABL-SIDE that be.PST
"The *kartiya* with the wagon who came from the eastside."

67. Old Burt Drew weya im bin teik-im-bat load you know.
old NAME where 3SG PST take-TR-ATEL load you know
"Old Burt Drew[250] who used to cart supplies to the stations."

68. Nyila=ma big wagon=ma nyila=ma jangkarni=ma nganta
that=TOP big wagon=TOP that=TOP big=TOP ALLE

ka-nya close up ngawa-ngka taruk kanyjurra.
take-PST close up water-LOC wade down
"Well his big wagon had been taken close to the river's edge."

69. Kutij kamurra=rni=warla.
stand halfway=ONLY=FOC
"It was perched half in."

70. Nyila yapakaru dray, nyila=ma kutij karrinyani
that small dray that=TOP stand be.IMPF.PST

jintaku-la=rni strong-bala marrimarri nyila=ma.
one-LOC=ONLY strong-ADJ strong that=TOP
"The smaller dray was standing in the middle so it didn't go under. It was a strong dray!"

71. Warlaku kartipa-wu kartipa-lu kujarra-lu Burt Drew
dog non-Indigenous-DAT non-Indigenous-ERG two-ERG NAME

Ted Bracey dat tubala wagon=ma=wuliny na kartiya kujarra.
NAME the 3DU wagon=TOP=3UA.NS FOC non-Indigenous two
"The *kartiya*'s dog – the two called Burt Drew and Ted Bracey[251] who owned the wagon."

72. Waj ngu=wula kankula rope yuwa-ni,
throw CAT=3UA.S up rope throw-PST

ngarramirli-la jangkarni-la.
white.gum-LOC big-LOC
"They threw a rope up a large white river gum."

250 Bert Drew was a donkey teamster who operated in the Victoria River District (Riddett, 1990: 64).
251 This name is not confirmed.

73. Ngu=wula=nyunu pull-im na ma-ni kankula partaj.
CAT=3UA.S=RR pull-TR FOC do-PST up climb
"So they could haul themselves up."

74. Jintara-kari partaj.
one-OTHER climb
"They went one at a time."

75. Partaj-ja na ngu=wula karrinyani,
climb-LOC FOC CAT=3UA.S be.IMPF.PST

yala-ngka na ngarramirli-la kaa-rni-yin.
that-LOC FOC white.river.gum-LOC east-UP-ABL
"The two of them then perched up in the tree."

76. Parraji ngu=wuliny ma-ni yala-ngkurra nyawa=ma ngawa=ma.
xxx CAT=3UA.NS do-PST that-ALL this=TOP water=TOP
"The water covered absolutely everything."

77. Nyampa=n parrkany ya-na-na.
what=2MIN.S XXX go-IMPF-PRS
"??"

78. Nyawa=rni=warla kunturru, ngawa=ma.
this=ONLY=FOC sky water=TOP
"The water was like a wide sky."

79. Pulngayit=ma jawurruk na ya-ni yinparrng na.
floodwater=TOP descend FOC go-PST dry.up FOC
"They looked down at the water and saw that it had gone down."

80. Yinparrng weya im go down na you know yinparrng.
dry.up where 3SG go down FOC you know dry.out
"It had dried out where the waters had gone down."

81. Yinparrng ngawa=ma ya-ni.
dry.out water=TOP go-PST
"The water had receded."

82. Nyampayirla=ma camel=ma nyampa=ma
whatsitcalled=TOP camel=TOP something=TOP

yawarta=ma milker=ma nyampa=ma purrp.
horse=TOP dairy.cow=TOP something=TOP gone
"All the animals, horses, camels and dairy cows had drowned."

83. Ngilyipurr-a nga-rni.
drown-LOC eat-PST
"They drowned."

84. Lirlaj=ma kuya=ma ngilyipurr tarap.
swim=TOP thus=TOP drown sink
"The animals had tried to swim but had been taken under in the end."

85. Nganta=yi=rla ka-nga-ni.
ALLE=1EXC.MIN.NS=3OBL take-IMPF-PST
"It might have taken me too."

86. Kutirni yala Jangala-wu ngu=rla
soon that SUBSECT-DAT CAT=3OBL

yurrk yuwa-rru Pincher-ku.
recount put-POT NAME-DAT
"Wait – [Norm McNair will] talk to my husband Pincher for his version of the story."

87. Im wantu tell-im this mob.
3SG want.to tell-TR this mob
"He wants to tell this mob."

88. Im bin here darran marluka mine.
3SG PST here during old.man 1SG.O
"He was here during the flood."

89. Ngantipa=ma tumaji we bin langa
1EXC.AUG=TOP CAUS 1PL PST LOC

bush, kanimparra Kitirlwari-la.
bush downstream Rifle.Hole-LOC
"Not like us. We were still living in the bush at Rifle Hole."

90. Anything ngunyju tin-ta you know ngunyju tinned tobacco.
anything tobacco tin-LOC you know tobacco tinned tobacco
"All of the tobacco tins, you know the word for 'tobacco'."

91. Nyila=ma jimpiri-la walyak-walyak.
that=TOP hole-LOC inside-REDUP
"They were stuck in the holes left by the flood."

92. Jarlarl-wari-la jarlarl-jarlarl you know where im cracked that
crack-ADJ-LOC crack-REDUP you know where 3SG cracked the

jimpiri, wumara yala-ngka na walyak-walyak.
hole rock that-LOC FOC inside-REDUP
"There were cracks in the mud from the flood which they were inside."

93. Flour=ma mangarri=ma, tinned sugar=ma,
flour=TOP flour=TOP tinned sugar=TOP

kankula partartaj karnti-ka.
up climb.REDUP tree-LOC
"Flour and tins of sugar were up in the trees which had been knocked down by the floodwater."

94. Wirlka-ngku na ngu=lu=rla bush-ngarna-lu na karrinya
axe-ERG FOC CAT=3AUG.S=3OBL bush-ASSOC-ERG FOC be.PST

nyamu=lu kaja-nginyi ya-na-ni kaa-rni-yin yalu-ngku na
REL=3AUG.S bush-SOURCE go-IMPF-PST east-UP-ABL that-ERG FOC

wirlka-ngku kataj-kataj yungkuj karnti=ma.
axe-ERG cut-REDUP fall tree=TOP
"They knocked open the tins with axes."

95. Kankulu-pal-a=rni wet-bala=ma pantij=ma, kanyjal=ma larrwa=rni.
up-EDGE-LOC=ONLY wet-ADJ=TOP wet=TOP under=TOP dry=ONLY
"The sugar and flour in the top of the tin was wet and hard but underneath was still dry."

96. Ngu=lu nya-nga-ni.
CAT=3AUG.S intake-IMPF-PST
"They ate that."

97. Warrayarl=purrupurru - warrayarl sugar
sugar=AND sugar sugar

you know – ngu=lu nya-nga-ni.
you know CAT=3AUG.S intake-IMPF-PST
"They ate the sugar as it was."

98. Kuya-ny=ma clothes=ma, kaninyjal kanimparra
thus-NMLZ=TOP clothes=TOP under downstream

pinka, warrpa=ma.
river dress=TOP
"Clothes and everything had washed away downstream."

99. Money=ma, money you know bank-kula nyamu karrinyani.
money=TOP money you know bank-LOC REL be.IMPF.PST
"Coins were lodged in the mud so everyone found them and dug them up."

100. Kanyjurra-k-pa=rni jipij-jipij yala-ngka=rni
down-ALL-EP=ONLY dig-REDUP that-LOC=ONLY

?janka-ka ?jakap.
woman-LOC sneak
"They dug them up down there."

101. Kurruj-karra-la na ngu=lu paraj pu-nga-ni
dig-ITER-LOC FOC CAT=3AUG.S find pierce-IMPF-PST

kuya-ny too nyila waraj.
thus-NMLZ too that lost
"They were digging and finding stuff."

102. Im-in talk 'Karrwa-rna-ni wartan-ta.'
3SG-PST say have-IMPF-PST hand-LOC
"The *kartiya* said, 'You can have that money.'"

103. Nyila-rra jipij-jipij-ta na kurruj-karra
that-PL dig-REDUP-LOC FOC dig-ITER

na ngu=lu pu-nga-ni.
FOC CAT=3AUG.S pierce-IMPF-PST
"They dug around for everything stuck in the mud."

104. Ngantipa=ma yapayapa=ma nyila=rni
1EXC.AUG=TOP children=TOP that=ONLY

ngu=rnayinangulu karrinyani.
CAT=1EXC.AUG.S>3AUG.NS be.IMPF.PST
"Us little kids were with them then."

105. Kurruj-karra-la=ma ngu=lu pu-nga-ni
dig-ITER-LOC=TOP CAT=3AUG.S pierce-IMPF-PST

wumara=ma nyampa=ma mayarni-kari.
money=TOP anything=TOP more-OTHER
"Everything we found, we were allowed to keep, money and anything in the mud."

106. 'Marntaj ka-nga-nta=lu tumaji pulngayit-nginyi!'
OK take-IMPF-IMP=3AUG.S CAUS floodwater-SOURCE
"'No worries, you can keep anything that's washed up.'"

107. 'Pulngayit-nginyi marntaj ka-nga-nta=lu,' kuya.
floodwater-SOURCE OK take-IMPF-IMP=3AUG.S thus
"'You mob should take anything you want from the flood,' he said."

108. Wirlka=ma nyampa=ma ngu=lu paraj-paraj pu-nga-ni
axe=TOP everything=TOP CAT=3AUG.S find-REDUP pierce-IMPF-PST

kurrij-karra, kiyarri-yawung-kulu=ma.
dig-ITER digging.stick-PROP-ERG=TOP
"They dug up axes and everything with their digging sticks."

109. Ngu=lu warrkuwarrkuj ma-na-ni.
CAT=3AUG.S pick.up.REDUP do-IMPF-PST
"They grabbed everything they could."

110. Mangarri alright.
flour OK
"Flour, OK."

111. Mangarri=ma warrayarl=ma partapartaj karnti-ka.
flour=TOP sugar=TOP climb.REDUP tree-LOC
"There were flour and sugar bags stuck up in the trees."

112. Tealeaf crate-ta.
tealeaf crate-LOC
“And tea in crates.”

113. Kuya-ny-ja partartaj kankula yuwa-ni.
thus-NMLZ-LOC climb.REDUP up put-PST
“[The floodwaters] had deposited this stuff in the trees.”

114. Clothes=ma somebala=ma new-bala new-bala.
clothes=TOP someone=TOP new-NMLZ new-NMLZ
“There were even some new clothes.”

115. Cage-ja jangkarni=warla kuya-ny-ja kankula partartaj.
cage-LOC big=FOC thus-NMLZ-LOC up climb.REDUP
“And some big things stuck in a cage up in the tree.”

116. Warrkuwarrkuj ngumpit-tu na nyarrulu warrkuwarrkuj.
pick.up.REDUP man-ER FOC 3AUG pick.up.REDUP
“The men picked things up too.”

117. Kula=lu ka-nga-ni na wart na.
NEG=3AUG.S take-IMPF-PST FOC return FOC
“They didn’t take it back.”

118. Nyarrulu na ngumpit-tu wear-im-karra na yuwa-ni,
3AUG FOC man-ERG wear-TR-ITER FOC put-PST

nyila-rra=ma na warrwarrkuj=ma.
that-PL=TOP FOC pick.up.REDUP=TOP
“Everyone put on the new clothes they’d picked up.”

119. Ngantipa=ma=rnalu wart ya-ni.
1EXC.AUG=TOP=1EXC.AUG.S return go-PST
“We came back from Rifle Hole then.”

120. Ngu=rnalu wart ya-ni murla-ngkurra=ma
CAT=1EXC.AUG.S return go-PST this-ALL=TOP

ngu=rnalu nya-nya.
CAT=1EXC.AUG.S intake-PST
“We came to the station and saw that nothing was left.”

121.

Lawara	na!
nothing	FOC

"Everything was gone!"

122.

Purrp	take-im-at-karra.
gone	take-TR-out-ITER

"The flood had washed everything away."

123.

Yala-ngkurra	nyawa	na	wagon-ta	nyila
that-ALL	this	FOC	wagon-LOC	this

nyamu=wula	karrinyani	Burt Drew-kuwang.
REL=3UA.S	be.IMPF.PST	NAME-AND

"The two men who brought supplies in the wagon, Bert Drew and his associate."

124.

Yala-ngkurra	nyawa	na	wagon-lu	kaarra-ngkarra-jirri
that-ALL	this	FOC	wagon-ERG	west-DOWN-ALL

lun-karra	na	Jinparrak-jirri	na	ka-nga-ni	ngu=wula
put.down-ITER	FOC	place.name-ALL	FOC	take-IMPF-PST	CAT=3UA.S

iron=ma	kuya-ny=ma	pirrkap-ku=ma	yala-ngka-wu=ma.
iron=TOP	thus-NMLZ=TOP	make-DAT=TOP	that-LOC-DAT=TOP

Ngu=rnalu	karrinya	murla-ngka=rni	yapayapa=ma,
CAT=1EXC.AUG.S	be.PST	this-LOC=ONLY	children=TOP

alright	marru=ma	nyila=ma	ngu=lu	purrp=parla
all.right	house=TOP	that=TOP	CAT=3AUG.S	finish=FOC

pirrka	ma-ni.	Ah	nyila	na	ngu=rnalu	ya-ni,
make	do-PST	ah	that	FOC	CAT=1EXC.AUG.S	go-PST

kaa-rni-mpa	Jinparrak-kulawu	na.
east-UP-PERL	place.name-PURP	FOC

" . . . loaded up everything and took it to Jinparrak – iron and other building materials for new houses. We stayed at the old station for a while until they finished the new houses. Then when they were done we went east to old Wave Hill Station."

125. Ngantipa=ma yapayapa=ma.
1EXC.AUG=TOP children=TOP
"We were still little then."

126. Properly=ma=rnalu karrinya jangkarni-k na
properly=TOP=1EXC.AUG.S be.PST big-FACT FOC

Jinparrak-kula na grow-im-up you know.
place.name-LOC FOC grow-TR-up you know
"Then we all grew up at Jinparrak."

127. Only we bin little-bala yet when i bin drowned dijan house.
only 1PL PST little-ADJ yet when 3SG PST flooded this house
"We were just little girls in the flood."

A.5 The Cook at Catfish by Violet Wadrill

19 June 2014, Kalkaringi, FM14_a203.[252]
Translated by Felicity Meakins, Violet Wadrill and Biddy Wavehill.

1. Yurrkan marluka-yayi ngu=rna ngaji ngayu=ma
NAME old.man-LATE CAT=1EXC.MIN.S father 1EXC.MIN=TOP

tal pa-ni im-in hab-im Japan-ku ngapuju tumaji.
call hit-PST 3SG-PST have-TR NAME-DAT FM CAUS
"There was an old man called Yurrkan who has passed away, well I call him "father". He was married to Marie Japan's father's mother who was called Yuruna."

2. Yeah wal ngu=yilu jaju-ngku na tikarl[253] yuwa-ni
yeah well CAT=3AUG.S>1EXC.MIN.NS MM-ERG FOC tell.story put-PST

kujarrap-pa=rni-lu, xxx ngu=yinangulu ngayirra=ma.
pair-EP=ONLY-ERG xxx CAT=3AUG.S>3AUG.NS 1EXC.UA=TOP
"My two grandfathers told me this story."

3. Nyarruluny-ja=ma nganta waruju-la.
3AUG.DAT-LOC=TOP ALLE together-LOC
"When I was with them."

4. An Punayi-lu nyamu=yina wanyja-ni pakutu ngayiny.
and NAME-ERG REL=3AUG.NS leave-PST cousin 1EXC.MIN.DAT
"And Punayi who left my cousin who was her husband."

5. Nyila-rra na.
that-PL FOC
"That lot now."

6. An ngayiny brother Lajayi-lu wanyja-ni.
and 1EXC.MIN.DAT brother NAME-ERG leave-PST
"And Lajayi left my brother too."

252 This story was originally published as: Wadrill, V. (2016). The cook at catfish. In Erika Charola & Felicity Meakins (Eds.), *Yijarni: True stories from Gurindji country* (pp. 157–159). Canberra: Aboriginal Studies Press.
253 The word *tikarl* is from Mudburra. The Gurindji equivalent is *yurrk*.

7. Nganta=lu ya-na-ni na.
ALLE=3AUG.S go-IMPF-PST FOC
"I think they went away now."

8. Ankaj dat marluka bin kam-ap karra=nga
poor.thing the old.man PST come-up be.IMP=DUB

good reason-ta kanyjuli-yit.
good reason-LOC below-ABL
"Poor bugger, that old man came back from the river with bush tucker but the head stockman told him disparagingly that they had enough meat."

9. Nyanawu jupajupart nyamu karrinyana
RECOG goanna.hole.REDUP REL be.IMPF.PRS

milapirta yu nou kirrawa.
reptile.hatchling you know goanna
"You know the hatchling goannas which you can dig up."

10. Jupart-jupart.
dig-REDUP
"You can dig them up."

11. Karrinyani nyamu=waa long-taim na.
be.IMPF.PST REL=REL long-time FOC
"Up until recently there were plenty around."

12. Jala-jala=ma lawara na.
now-REDUP=TOP nothing FOC
"Not anymore [because of the canetoads]."

13. Nyila na marluka nganta im-in kam na kanyjuli-yit.
that FOC old.man ALLE 3SG-PST come FOC below-ABL
"The old man came up from the river, I believe. He was the camp cook."

14. Nganta ka-nga-ni, wirriji-ngka kuya tai-im-ap.
ALLE take-IMPF-PST hair.belt-LOC thus tie-TR-up
"He had a lot of lizards hanging from his belt."

15. Wirriji-ngka yu nou ka-nya, kirrawa
hair.belt-LOC you know take-PST goanna

mila yapayapa jupart-jupart-nginyi.
eye small dig-REDUP-SOURCE
"He was carrying the lizard hatchlings that he'd just dug up on his belt."

16. Karrinyani nyamu=waa kamparra.
be.IMPF.PST REL=REL before
"That's where you used to find them before canetoads.

17. Alrait im-in kam-ap jik na.
alright 3SG-PST come-up arrive FOC
"Alright he arrived now."

18. 'What you got there marluka,' kuya ngu=rla ma-rni.
what you got there old.man thus CAT=3OBL say-PST
"'What have you got there old man?' he said to him."

19. 'Nyampa=warla=n nyila karrwa-rna-na?'
what=FOC=2MIN.S that have-IMPF-PRS
"'What's that you've got there?'"

20. 'Nyampa=warla=n ka-nga-na nyila?'
what=FOC=2MIN.S take-IMPF-PRS that
"'What are you carrying?'"

21. Nganta shirt-murlung du angkul-jayi=ma, no dadi-yayi.
ALLE shirt-PRIV too uncle-LATE=TOP NEG dad-LATE
"He'd taken his shirt off when he went hunting."

22. 'Nyampa=warla=n ka-nga-na nyawa=ma guana.'
what=FOC=2MIN.S take-IMPF-PRS this=TOP goanna
"'What are you doing with those goannas? said the *kartiya*.'"

23. 'Guana ai garram yapayapa,' kuya, ngu=rla ma-rni.
goanna 1SG PROP small thus CAT=3OBL say-PST
"'I have some small goannas,' he said to him."

24. Bat kula English jaru ngu=rla ma-rni.
but NEG English language CAT=3OBL talk-PST
"But not in English. He spoke in Gurindji to him."

25. Kula=lu pina yet karrinyani English-ku=ma lawara.
NEG=3AUG.S know yet be.IMPF.PST English-DAT=TOP nothing
"They didn't know English in those days."

26. Nyila=ma nganta ma-ni kuya=rna=ngku=rla
that=TOP ALLE do-PST thus=1EXC.MIN.S=2MIN.NS=3OBL

jou-im=ma nganta jayi-nya wartan=purrupurru=warla
show-TR=TOP ALLE give-PST hand=AND=FOC

turt ma-ni kartipa-lu=ma nganta.
hold do-PST non-Indigenous-ERG=TOP ALLE
"The *kartipa* held out his hand to get what he was holding."

27. Ai dunno wijan dat kartiya.
1SG NEG.know who the non-Indigenous
"I don't know who the *kartiya* was."

28. Binij.
finish
"That's it!"

29. Kula=yi=lu yini=warla ma-rni
NEG=1EXC.MIN.NS=3AUG.S name=FOC say-PST

kartipa=ma nyila=ma.
non-Indigenous=TOP that=TOP
"They didn't tell me the name of the *kartipa*."

30. Belt-im im na.
belt-TR 3SG.O FOC
"Then he started belting him."

31. Whip-im im garram dat kirrawa jawurt, dat marluka.
whip-TR 3SG.O PROP the goanna tail the old.man
"He whipped the old man with the goanna tail."

32. Whip-im im ebriweya rungrung nganta.
whip-TR 3SG.O everywhere swell.up ALLE
"He whipped him all over so his skin started swelling up. [The tail was really rough]."

33. Kanyjal foot-ngurlu=ma kankula ngarlaka-kijak an wartan-kujarra.
down foot-ABL=TOP up head-TERM and arm-DU
“From down on his feet right up to his head and on his arms.”

34. Cruel-baga broba nyila=ma kartiya=ma.
cruel-ADJ very that=TOP non-Indigenous=TOP
“That *kartiya* was really cruel.”

35. Wartayi wartayi-la na pa-ni nganta lingi-ngku.
goodness goodness-LOC FOC hit-PST ALLE persist-ERG
“Bloody hell he just kept hitting him I believe.”

36. ‘Ya-na-nta=yi=lu=rla boy,’ kuya.
go-IMPF-IMP=1EXC.MIN.NS=3AUG.S=3OBL boy thus
“‘You boys should come and help me,’ he cried out.”

37. ‘Ya-na-nta=yi=lu=rla nyawa
go-IMPF-IMP=1EXC.MIN.NS=3AUG.S=3OBL this

pa-na-nta=yi=lu kartik,’ kuya.
hit-IMPF-IMP=1EXC.MIN.NS=3AUG.S intervene thus
“‘You mob should come and stop him,’ he called out.”

38. ‘Ngu=yi luwa-na-na kungukungulu-k na.’
CAT=1EXC.MIN.NS strike-IMPF-PRS blood.REDUP-FACT FOC
“‘He’s whipping me to the point that I’m bleeding.’”

39. ‘Ngu=yi kungukungulu-k pa-ni.’
CAT=1EXC.MIN.NS blood.REDUP-FACT hit-PST
“‘He’s made me bleed.’”

40. ‘Kartik pa-na-nta=yi=lu=rla
intervene hit-IMPF-IMP=1EXC.MIN.NS=3AUG.S=3OBL

na wuukarra=ma=lu.’
FOC scared=TOP=3AUG.S
“‘They should stop him hitting me but they’re too scared.’”

41. Lawara nganta=lu nya-nga-ni
nothing ALLE=3AUG.S intake-IMPF-PST

yangyang-bala-lu tumaji karrap.
young.REDUP-NMLZ-ERG CAUS watch
"I think the young ones there were just watching and not doing anything."

42. Ngu=lu nya-nga-ni karrap nganta ankankaj.
CAT=3AUG.S intake-IMPF-PST watch ALLE poor.thing.REDUP
"They just watched on poor buggers."

43. Pa-ni nganta binij kanyjurra yeah.
hit-PST ALLE finish down yeah
"He fell down from being hit."

44. Waninya nganta janyja-ka.
fall.PST ALLE ground-LOC
"He just fell to the ground."

45. 'Ka-ngka=lu' nganta, kuya.
take-LOC=3AUG.S ALLE thus
"'You fellas can take him now.' said the *kartiya*."

46. Ngurra-ngkurra na nganta=lu ka-nya.
camp-ALL FOC ALLE=3AUG.S take-PST
"They took him back to camp, as I understand it."

47. Kula=rnayinangulu help-im ma-na-ni nganta pipul=ma.
NEG=1EXC.AUG.S>3AUG.NS help-TR do-IMPF-PST ALLE people=TOP
"The young ones wouldn't help other people back then, I think."

48. Yangyang-bala-lu nyamu=yina=nga kartiya-lu
young.REDUP-NMLZ-ERG REL=3AUG.NS=DUB non-Indigenous-ERG

pa-na-ni belt-im na, lawara.
hit-IMPF-PST beat-TR FOC nothing
"When the *kartiya* was beating them."

49. Ngu=lu wuukarra du nyarrulu=ma karrinyani.
CAT=3AUG.S frightened too 3AUG=TOP be.IMPF.PST
"They were just too frightened."

50. Kuya.
thus
"That's how it was."
. . .

51. Ngayiny hasben du im luk-in-at nganta karrap.
1EXC.MIN.DAT husband too 3SG look-CONT-at ALLE see
"I understand my husband saw it happen too."

52. Nyantu na im-in tal mi dat stori.
3MIN FOC 3SG-PST tell 1SG.O the story
"It was him who told me the story."

53. Nyawa marluka-yayi im wartayi-wartayi-la
this old.man-LATE 3SG call.out-REDUP-LOC

weya im-in kil-im im.
where 3SG-PST hit-TR 3SG.O
"The old man was crying out when he flogged him."

54. Nyarrulu=ma wuukarra yangyang-bala tumaji.
3AUG=TOP afraid young.REDUP-NMLZ CAUS
"All of the young ones didn't do anything because they were afraid."

55. Ngu=lu=rla kartipa-wu=ma wuukarra karrinya.
CAT=3AUG.S=3OBL non-Indigenous-DAT=TOP afraid be.PST
"They were afraid of the *kartipa*."

56. Nyamu=yina nganta jing-in-at-karra ma-rni
REL=3AUG.NS ALLE call-CONT-out-ITER talk-PST

marluka=ma yala=ma yipurrk.
old.man=TOP that=TOP in.vain
"When the old man was calling out to them. It was all in vain."

57. 'Ya-na-nta=yi=lu=rla hey kartik
go-IMPF-IMP=1EXC.MIN.NS=3AUG.S=3OBL hey intervene

pa-rra=yi=lu=rla nyawa,' kuya.
hit-IMP=1EXC.MIN.NS=3AUG.S=3OBL this thus
"'You mob should come and stop him from hitting me,' he said."

58. Lawara <u>holot</u> <u>bin</u> wuukarra.
nothing whole.lot PST scared
"But they didn't do anything because they were scared."

59. Marntaj.
OK
"That's all."

A.6 When they took my little brothers away by Biddy Wavehill Yamawurr

19 June 2014, Kalkaringi, FM14_a205.[254]
Translated by Felicity Meakins, Biddy Wavehill and Violet Wadrill.

1.

Yuu,	ngu=rna=ngku	yurrk	kuya	nyila
yes	CAT=1EXC.MIN.S=2MIN.NS	tell.story	thus	that

na	ngayiny	papa-kujarra	pilyingpilying.
FOC	1EXC.MIN.DAT	brother-DU	*pilyingpilying*

"Yes, I'm going to tell you about my two *pilyingpilying* brothers."[255]

2.

Ngu=wuliny	ka-nya	jaju-ngku=ma	ngayiny-ju=ma
CAT=3UA.NS	take-PST	MM-ERG=TOP	1EXC.MIN.DAT-ERG=TOP

Kayi-rni-rra-k	mangarri-wu	kitchen-jirri	kurla-yin-ngarna.
north-UP-LOC-ALL	veg.food-DAT	kitchen-ALL	south-ABL-ASSOC

"My grandmother Lizzie Brian Nyalpngarri took the two of them up north from the southern part of the Blacks Camp to the kitchen for some food."

3.

Aaaa	kula=rla	pina	karrinya	yalu-wu=ma	kurrurij-ku=ma
ahh	NEG=3OBL	know	be.PST	that-DAT=TOP	car-DAT=TOP

jangkarni-wu=ma=yina	ma-na-ni,	pilyingpilying=ma	warrkuwarrkuj
big-DAT=TOP=3AUG.NS	do-IMPF-PST	*pilyingpilying*=TOP	pick.up.REDUP

kurlarra	Lajaman-ta,	an	Wave Hill-la	Jinparrak-kula.
south	place.name-LOC	and	place.name-LOC	Wave.Hill-LOC

"She didn't know that the car had come up from Lajamanu to get the *pilyingpilying* kids at Hooker Creek Welfare Settlement and old Wave Hill Station."

---

254 This story was originally published (unglossed) as: Wavehill, B. (2016). How they took my little brothers away. In Erika Charola & Felicity Meakins (Eds.), *Yijarni: True Stories from Gurindji Country* (pp. 133–134). Canberra: Aboriginal Studies Press.

255 Jim Ryan and Ted Henry.

4. Aaaa karla-rni-yin karla-rni-yin nyila=ma
ahh west-UP-ABL west-UP-ABL that=TOP

jangkarni=ma kurrurij=ma, xxx langa im.
big=TOP car=TOP xxx LOC 3SG
"The large car was coming from the yards in the west along the old Lajamanu road."

5. Kata=nga nyampa-wu jarrakap-ku ngayiny-ku=ma
THO=DUB something-DAT talk-DAT 1EXC.MIN.DAT-DAT=TOP

jaju-wu=ma ngu=wuliny na kartiya=ma
MM-DAT=TOP CAT=3UA.NS FOC non-Indigenous=TOP

jawurruk nyila=ma welfare=ma.
descend that=TOP welfare=TOP
"She thought they wanted to say something to her when he got out of the car."

6. Ngana=warla wayi, yangki pa-rra ngayiny brother im nou,
who=FOC TAG ask hit-IMP 1EXC.MIN.DAT brother 3SG know

nyila=ma kartiya-nginyi-la=ma larrpa-nginyi-la=ma
that=TOP non-Indigenous-SOURCE-LOC=TOP long.ago-SOURCE-LOC=TOP

ma-na-ni warrkuwarrkuj pilyingpilying=ma.
do-IMPF-PST pick.up.REDUP *pilyingpilying*=TOP
"What's the names of those *kartiya* who took away the *pilyingpilying* kids – well ask my brother Ronnie."[256]

7. Ma-ni ngu warrkuj.
do-PST CAT pick.up
"They picked them up."

8. Alrait, kutij ngu=wula karrinya
alright stand CAT=3UA.S be.PST

ngayiny-ku=ma jaju-wu=ma.
1EXC.MIN.DAT-DAT=TOP MM-DAT=TOP
"Alright, the two little boys were standing with my grandmother."

256 Ted Evans and Creed Lovegrove.

9. Ngu=wuliny grab-im ma-ni.
CAT=3UA.NS grab-TR do-PST
"One of the welfare officers grabbed the two of them."

10. Naja kartiya-kari bin jarrakap langa im.
another non-Indigenous-OTHER PST talk LOC 3SG.O
"Another *kartiya* talked to her."

11. Ngu=wuliny grab-im ma-ni kankula ngu=wuliny partaj
CAT=3UA.NS grab-TR do-PST up CAT=3UA.NS climb

yuwa-ni ngayiny=ma papa-kujarra=ma.
put-PST 1EXC.MIN.DAT=TOP brother-DU=TOP
"The other one grabbed my two brothers and shoved them into the car."

12. Nyantu=ma, 'Nyampa-wu=warla yu garra teik-im?'
3MIN=TOP what-DAT=FOC you got.to take-TR
"She said, 'Why are you taking my two grandsons?'"

13. Kartiya-kari bin wapurr im laik yu nou jarrakap.
non-Indigenous-OTHER PST distract 3SG.O like you know talk
"The other welfare officer was distracting her by talking to her."

14. Kankula partaj karra na wanyji-ka-wu karra=nga murla-wu.
up climb be.IMP FOC which-LOC-DAT be.IMP=DUB this-DAT
"She thought they were just climbing in to go for a ride around the community."

15. Kanyjurra bij-im-bat-ku karrinya-rra
down fish-TR-ATEL-DAT be.PST-HORT

murla-ngkurra-wu kuya-wu yu nou.
this-ALL-DAT thus-DAT you know
"Or had gone fishing down at the river you know."

16. Nyantu=ma ngayiny jaju bin rekin kuya.
3MIN=TOP 1EXC.MIN.DAT MM PST think thus
"That's what my grandmother thought."

17. Aaa jarrakap=pula=rla ma-rni alrait, 'You right?'
Ahh talk=3UA.S=3OBL say-PST alright you alright
"The two of them said to her, 'That's OK then?'"

18. 'OK.'
OK
"'OK,' she said." [not realising what was happening]

19. 'Wal yu kan gon for lunch na,' ngayiny-ku=ma
well you can go for lunch now 1EXC.MIN.DAT-DAT=TOP

jaju-wu=ma ngu=rla ma-rni tumaji ngu waruk
MM-DAT=TOP CAT=3OBL say-PST CAUS CAT work

ma-ni laundry-la ngayiny=ma jaju=ma.
do-PST laundry-LOC 1EXC.MIN.DAT=TOP MM=TOP
"'Well you can go for lunch now,' he said to my grandmother because she worked in the laundry."

20. Warrij ya-ni kayirra.
leave go-PST north
"She went back north." [because she didn't really know what was happening.]

21. Kayi-rni-rra wal ngayiny ngamayi bin kam-at
north-UP-LOC well 1EXC.MIN.DAT mother PST come-out

langa im na im-in wok-in la turnaran.
LOC 3SG FOC 3SG-PST work-CONT LOC churn
"In the north my mother come out of the dairy where she worked churning butter."

22. Yang pipul-lu ngu=yina ma-rni marntaj laik
young people-ERG CAT=3AUG.NS say-PST OK like

ngayiny mother=purrupurru 'Kartiya kamparra=rni
1EXC.MIN.DAT mother=AND non-Indigenous front=ONLY

welfare pilyingpilying away from you-mob,' kuya yu nou.
welfare *pilyingpilying* away from you-GROUP kuya you know
"Young people told my mother and the others, 'Welfare just came and took the *pilyingpilying* children away you know.'"
. . .

23. 'Wanyji-ka=warla?'
which-LOC=FOC
"'Where are they?'"

24. 'Nyampa-wu=wuliny   nyawa   karu-walija   partapartaj
what-DAT=3UA.NS   this   chid-PAUC   climb.REDUP

yuwa-ni   kurrurij-ja   jangkarni-la   yard-jawung-kula.'
put-PST   car-LOC   big-LOC   yard-PROP-LOC
"'Why did they take the kids and put them in the back of the welfare car with wooden slates.'"

25. 'Nyila=ma=yina   ka-nga-ni   na   mami,   kanimparra
that=TOP=3AUG.NS   take-IMPF-PST   FOC   mum   downstream

kula=rlaa=yina   wart   ma-nku.'
NEG=1INC.AUG.S=3AUG.NS   return   get-POT
"'They've taken them away mum, we won't be able to get them back.'"

26. Ngu=rnayinangkulu   tumaji   kartiya   karu
CAT=1EXC.AUG.S>3AUG.NS   CAUS   non-Indigenous   child

ka-nya   kartiya   wantu   teik-it-awei   na.
take-PST   non-Indigenous   want.to   take-TR-away   FOC
"Those kids of ours are gone because the *kartiya* want to take them."

27. Ngu=yinangkulu   ka-ngku   pilyingpilying=ma   lurtju-kari-yirri.
CAT=3AUG.S>3AUG.NS   take-POT   *pilyingpilying*=TOP   island-OTHER-ALL
"They going to take the *pilyingpilying* children to an island."

28. "Ngayiny   kartiya   bin   tok-in   la   mi,   bikos
1EXC.MIN.DAT   non-Indigenous   PST   talk-PST   LOC   1SG.O   CAUS

ngayiny   mother   bin   work-in   la   turnaran.
1EXC.MIN.DAT   mother   PST   work-CONT   LOC   churn
"The *kartiya* had talked to my grandmother because my mother was working in the dairy."

29. Kuya,   ngu=rla   ma-rni.
thus   CAT=3OBL   talk-PST
"That's why he spoke to her."

30. Start   im   lungkarra   na.
start   3SG   cry   FOC
"She started crying then."

31. 'Nyampa-wu=warla-nku=rla ma-rni.'
what-DAT=FOC-EP=3OBL say-PST
"'Why did you tell them about them?'"

32. 'Kurla-yin-ta ma-ni kamparra=rni nyamu=rna=wuliny=nga
south-ABL-LOC do-PST front=ONLY REL=1EXC.MIN.S=3UA.NS=DUB

ka-ngka wartuj.'
take-IMP hide
"'What's wrong with you two first time, I would have taken them out bush and hidden them.'"
. . .

33. Lungkarrap na kuya-ngka=ma.
cry FOC thus-LOC=TOP
"That's when my grandmother just cried and cried totally distraught."

34. Marntaj, nyila=rni=warla jarrakap.
OK that=ONLY=FOC talk
"That's all for that story."

A.7 Gordon Stott (The Deeds of an Early Policeman) by Banjo Ryan

15 April 2015, Kalkaringi, FM15_52_1a.
Translated by Felicity Meakins and Ronnie Wavehill.

1.

Dat	murnungku	im-in	kam-ap	kaarra-yin.
the	policeman	3SG-PST	come-up	east-ABL

"A policeman called Gordon Stott travelled from Timber Creek."

2.

Im-in	kam-ap	la	Waterloo	an	ngu=lu	yangki
3SG-PST	come-up	LOC	place.name	and	CAT=3AUG.S	ask

ma-rni	nyila	ngumpin	Japalyi,	ngumpit-tu	jambala-lu
say-PST	that	man	SUBSECT	man-ERG	someone-ERG

Waterloo-ngarna-lu,	'Nyampa-wu=warla=npula	ya-ni?'
place.name-ASSOC-ERG	what-DAT=FOC=2UA.S	go-PST

"He arrived at Waterloo Station and the Aboriginal workers asked his policeboy Kurnmali, 'Why are the two of you here?'"

3.

Ngu=wula	ya-ni	'Ngu=rliyarra	ya-ni
CAT=3UA.S	go-PST	CAT=1INC.MIN.S	go-PST

murlu-wu,	raiful-u	ngu	sign-im	yuwa-rru	raiful.'
this-DAT	rifle-DAT	CAT	sign-TR	put-POT	rifle

"The two of them came up, 'We came to register a rifle.'"

4.

'Ngu	paper-la	yuwa-rru	raiful,'	kuya.
CAT	paper-LOC	put-POT	rifle	thus

"'He's got to sign for the rifle,' said Kurnmali."

5.

Kula=yina	jutu-k	ma-rni.
NEG=3AUG.NS	straight-FACT	talk-PST

"But he wasn't telling them the truth."

6.

Ngu	ya-ni	nyila=ma	yala-ntirl-u	ngumpit-ku	stock-camp-kulawu.
CAT	go-PST	that=TOP	that-BEL-DAT	man-DAT	stock-camp-PURP

"The policeman had really come for those stockmen."

7.

Yalu-ngku	ngumpit-tu	ngu=lu	pa-ni	ngarin	jamwei.
that-ERG	man-ERG	CAT=3AUG.S	hit-PST	game	somewhere

"Some Aboriginal men had speared a killer somewhere."

8. An ngu=yinangkulu piyarrp na
and CAT=3AUG.S>3AUG.NS report FOC

ka-nya nyila=ma Waterloo boi=ma.
take-PST that=TOP place.name boy=TOP
"And some other people reported that the Aboriginal workers at Waterloo had done it."

9. Alrait ngu=lu tirrip karrinya na.
alright CAT=3AUG.S overnight stay.PST FOC
"OK, so then the policeman and tracker camped overnight."

10. Ngu=lu ask-im kaputa-la=ma abta supper
CAT=3AUG.S ask-TR evening-LOC=TOP after supper

ngu=lu yangki ma-rni nyila=ma Japalyi=ma.
CAT=3AUG.S ask say-PST that=TOP SUBSECT=TOP
"The Waterloo mob questioned Japalyi in the evening after supper."

11. 'Nyampa=warla eni jaru ngu=npula ka-nya wal im-in nyampa.'
what=FOC any news CAT=2UA.S take-PST well 3SG-PST something
"'Have you two brought any news from the north.'"

12. 'Lawara nyawa=ma ngu=rliyarra ya-ni murlu-wu=rni=warla
nothing this=TOP CAT=1INC.MIN.S go-PST this-DAT=ONLY=FOC

turlk-kaji-wu, sign-im-bat-ku yuwa-rru paper-la,' kuya.
shoot-AGENT-DAT sign-TR-ATEL-DAT put-POT paper-LOC thus
"'No we just came to register the station manager's rifle,' he said."

13. Ngu=yina ma-rni kurany-karra.
CAT=3AUG.NS talk-PST lie-ITER
"But he was lying to them."

14. Kurany-karra ngu=yina ma-rni.
lie-ITER CAT=3AUG.NS talk-PST
"He wasn't telling the truth."

15. Ngu=rla ma-rni nyila=ma murnungku=ma yalu-wu=rni
CAT=3OBL talk-PST that=TOP policeman=TOP that-DAT=ONLY

head-stockman-ku=rni kartipa-wu ngu=rla ma-rni.
head-stockman-DAT=ONLY non-Indigenous-DAT CAT=3OBL talk-PST
"In the meantime, Gordon Stott was talking to the head stockman who was a *kartipa* called Don McLaughlin."

16. Ngu=rla ma-rni kuya yala=ma kartiya=ma
CAT=3OBL talk-PST thus that=TOP non-Indigenous=TOP

ma-nyja=yina yalu-wu=ma ngumpit-ku=ma.
talk-IMP=3AUG.NS that-DAT=TOP man-DAT=TOP
"McLaughlin told him to talk to the Aboriginal stockmen."

17. Ngu=yina xxx yini-yini ma-rni
CAT=3AUG.NS xxx name-REDUP say-PST

ngumpit=ma na nyila=ma marntaj.
man=TOP FOC that=TOP OK
"He told him the names of the Aboriginal stockmen."

18. An kaput-kaput=ma ngu tirrip=ma karrinya
and morning-REDUP=TOP CAT overnight–TOP be.PST

ngu=lu bridle ma-ni after breakfast=ma.
CAT=3AUG.S bridle get-PST after breakfast=TOP
"Early in the morning after breakfast, McLaughlin grabbed a bridle."

19. Ngu=yina ya-ni cut-across nyawa=ma stockman=ma.
CAT=3AUG.NS go-PST cut-across this=TOP stockman=TOP
"And intercepted the stockmen."

20. Ngu=yina ma-rni stockman=ma 'Nyuntu
CAT=3AUG.NS say-PST stockman=TOP 2MIN

nyuntu an nyawa an nyila nyawa.'
2MIN and this and that this
"[He picked out some stockmen] saying to them, 'You, you, and this one and that one and this one too.'"

21. 'Nyurrulu ya-nta=lu=rla murnungku-ku ngu=nyjurra ma-lu.'
2AUG go-IMP=3AUG.S=3OBL policeman-DAT CAT=2AUG.NS talk-POT
"'You mob go with the policeman," said McLaughlin, "The policeman wants to talk to you.'"

22. 'Nyatpa=nyjurra ma-lu murnungku-wu?'
how=2AUG.NS talk-POT policeman-DAT
"'I don't know what the policeman wants with you mob.'"

23. 'Im garram jaru la yubala jeya,' kuya, ngu=yina ma-rni=ma.
3SG got news LOC 2PL there thus CAT=3AUG.NS say-PST=TOP
"'He's got some news for you mob,' he said to them."

24. Ngu=lu ya-na-ni na ngumpit=ma, ya-ni
CAT=3AUG.S go-IMPF-PST FOC man=TOP go-PST

kurlpap one-line ngu=lu waninya.
heap.up one-line CAT=3AUG.S fall.PST
"The men walked over to the policeman and formed a line."

25. 'Kartiya-la kuya na one-line,' ngu=yina
non-Indigenous-LOC thus FOC one-line CAT=3AUG.NS

ma-rni nyila Japalyi=ma Kurnmali=ma.
say-PST that SUBSECT=TOP NAME=TOP
"'Form one line next to the policeman,' Kurnmali told them."

26. 'Kuya na karra=lu=rla.'
thus FOC be.IMP=3AUG.S=3OBL
"'You mob [stand near] him like that.'"

27. 'Yuu ngu=nyjurra ma-lu.'
yeah CAT=2AUG.NS say-POT
"'Yeah, he's got something to say to you,' said Japalyi."

28. 'Nyatpa=nyjurra ma-lu, kuya.'
how=2AUG.NS talk-POT thus
"'He's wants to talk to you mob,' he said."

29. Bat ngu=rla ma-rni yalu-wu=ma nyanuny-ku=ma
but CAT=3OBL say-POT that-DAT=TOP 3MIN.DAT-DAT=TOP

police-boy-yu=ma Japalyi-yu=ma, 'Nyila wananga
police-boy-DAT=TOP SUBSECT-DAT=TOP that bag

ma-nta, murla-ngkawu ka-ngka=yin.'
get-IMP this-PURP take-IMP=2MIN.S>1EXC.MIN.NS

nyila wananga garra long chain darran.
that bag got long chain that
"But instead Gordon Stott said to Kurnmali, 'Get that bag and bring it to me.' There was a long chain in the bag."

30. Im-in bring-im-ap na.
3SG-PST bring-TR-up FOC
"He brought the bag to him."

31. Ngu wanyja-ni jeya kanyjurra.
CAT leave-PST there down
"And left on the ground there."

32. Ngu ka-nya ngu wanyja-ni.
CAT take-PST CAT leave-PST
"He brought it and left it."

33. Ngu wirr ma-ni kuya-ngku murnungku-lu=ma
CAT open do-PST thus-ERG policeman-ERG=TOP

yalu-ngku=ma marntaj ngu ma-ni.
that-ERG=TOP OK CAT do-PST
"The policeman opened up the bag and then started pulling the chain out."

34. Ngu=wula ma-ni kujarrap-kulu murnungku-lu
CAT=3UA.S do-PST pair-ERG policeman-ERG

an yalu-ngku Japalyi-lu.
and that-ERG SUBSECT-ERG
"The pair of them got the chain out – both Gordon Stott and Kurnmali."

35. Ngu=yinangkulu yuwa-ni ngirlkirri-la na.
CAT=3AUG.S>3AUG.NS put-PST neck-LOC FOC
"Then they chained the stockmen together by the neck."

36. Ngirlkirri-la ngirlkirri-la ola-wei nyawa=ma ngumpit-ku=ma,
neck-LOC neck-LOC all-way this=TOP man-ERG=TOP

kutitij-ja=ma one-line-ta=ma.
stand.REDUP-LOC=TOP one-line-LOC=TOP
"They were all standing there in a line with a chain around their neck."

37. Alrait an wartan-ta ngu=yinangkulu
alright and hand-LOC CAT=3AUG.S>3AUG.NS

yuwa-ni police-boy-lu an murnungku-lu.
put-PST police-boy-ERG and policeman-ERG
"And the policeman and the tracker also chained their hands together."

38. Ngu=yinangkulu yuwa-ni marntaj.
CAT=3AUG.S>3AUG.NS put-PST OK
"They chained them together."

39. Rait ngu=rla, ngu=rla jarrakap na ma-rni
alright CAT=3OBL CAT=3OBL talk FOC talk-PST

ngu=rla ma-rni, manka-ka=rni ngu=rla ma-rni,
CAT=3OBL talk-PST ear-LOC=ONLY CAT=3OBL talk-PST

nyila=ma murnungku=ma yalu-wu=ma Japalyi-wu=ma.
that=TOP policeman=TOP that-DAT=TOP SUBSECT-DAT=TOP
"Then policeman spoke in Kurnmali's ear so the others couldn't hear."

40. 'Yu gu kanyjurra na, kataj-karra-ku=ma karnti short-short-bala.'
you go down FOC cut-ITER-DAT=TOP stick short-REDUP-NMLZ
"'You go down to the river to cut some short sticks.'"

41. 'Kataj-karra-ku=ma, marntaj ngu=rna=yina
cut-ITER-DAT=TOP OK CAT=1EXC.MIN.S=3AUG.NS

jarrakap=parla ma-lu na.'
talk=FOC talk-POT FOC
"'Cut some sticks, I want to talk to the others on my own.'"

42. 'An nyuntu=ma=yi=nta[257] kanyjurra kataj-karra
and 2MIN=TOP=1EXC.MIN.NS=2AUG.S down cut-ITER

na pa-rra, karnti short-short-bala,' kuya.
FOC hit-IMP stick short-REDUP-NMLZ thus
"'You go down there and cut some sticks for me,' he said."

257 This was later corrected to =*n* '2MIN.S'.

43. 'Lututu=ma karnti=ma, kuya=ma,' 'Yuu.'
short.REDUP=TOP stick=TOP thus=TOP OK
"'Some short sticks,' he said, 'OK,' Kurnmali replied."

44. Ngu ka-nya na nyila=ma karnti=ma kanyjuli-yit.
CAT bring-PST FOC that=TOP stick=TOP down-ABL
"So he brought some sticks from the river."

45. Warnkurr ka-nya ngu wijkik kiya-rni kanyjurra-k kuya.
carry.on.shoulder bring-PST CAT throw put-PST down-ALL thus
"He carried the sticks across his shoulder and threw them on the ground at Gordon Stott's feet."

46. Yalu-ngku murnungku-lu ma-ni kuya-ngka wirr-wirr
that-ERG policeman-ERG do-PST thus-LOC break.up-REDUP

na nyila=ma karnti=ma yapayapa=ma marntaj.
FOC that=TOP stick=TOP small=TOP OK
"The policeman distributed the sticks among the chained-up stockmen."

47. Jangkakarni karnti jarlart-baga.
big.REDUP stick thick-NMLZ
"Some of the sticks were really thick."

48. Ngu=yina ma-rni 'Nyawa nyununy nyawa nyununy,
CAT=3AUG.NS say-PST this 2MIN.DAT this 2MIN.DAT

nyawa nyununy nyawa nyununy, nyawa nyununy
this 2MIN.DAT this 2MIN.DAT this 2MIN.DAT

nyawa nyununy', ngu=yina ma-rni.
this 2MIN.DAT CAT=3AUG.NS say-PST
"'This one is yours, this is yours, yours, yours and yours,' he said to them as he handed them out."

49. An ngu=rla ma-rni police-boy-wu=ma 'Nyawa=ma
and CAT=3OBL say-PST police-boy-DAT=TOP this=TOP

nyununy,' kuya, police-boy-wu=ma.
2MIN.DAT thus police-boy-DAT=TOP
"Finally he said to Kurnmalu, 'And this one is yours.'"

50.

Ngu	luwa-wu	yalu-ngku=ma=nyjurra
CAT	strike-POT	that-LOC=TOP=2AUG.NS

ngumayila	last-ta	ngumpit,	kuya.
behind	last-LOC	man	thus

"He planned for him to hit the last man in the line."

51.

Murtuyarri	ngu	pa-na-ni.
NAME	CAT	hit-IMPF-PST

"He would be hitting Mick Tailer Murtuyarri Janama."

52.

'Alrait,	ngu=rna=nyjurra	ma-lu,	redi-bala
alright	CAT=1EXC.MIN.S=2AUG.NS	talk-POT	ready-NMLZ

na	punyu-k-pa=rni	karra=lu.'
FOC	good-FACT-EP=ONLY	be.IMP=3AUG.S

"'All right – I'm going to give you some instructions when you're ready.'"

53.

Kutitij-ju	ngu=lu	punyu-k	na
stand.REDUP-ERG	CAT=3AUG.S	good-FACT	FOC

karrinya	kutitij	karnti-yawung	na	purrp.
be.PST	stand.REDUP	stick-PROP	FOC	finish

"They all stood there ready with the sticks."

54.

'Raito,	nyuntu=ma,	marntaj	na	pa-rra=lu=nyunu
alright	2MIN=TOP	OK	FOC	hit-IMP=3AUG.S=RR

murlu-ngku=ma	ngu=nyjurra	nyurrulu	murla-ngka=rni
this-ERG=TOP	CAT=2AUG.NS	2AUG	this-LOC=ONLY

led-im-gu=ma	yuwa-rru,'	kuya.
let-TR-go=TOP	put-POT	thus

"'OK – you mob hit each other with these sticks and then I'll let out of the chains.'"

55.

'Ngu=rna=nyjurra	purr[258]	yuwa-rru	murla-ngka=rni.'
CAT=1EXC.MIN.S=2AUG.NS	release	put-POT	this-LOC=ONLY

"'I'll let you go straight afterwards.'"

258 This is a Malngin word. The Gurindji is *jarlak*.

56. 'Pa-rra=lu=nyunu.'
hit-IMP=3AUG.S=RR
"'Right, start hitting each other now.'"

57. Nyawa na ngu=lu=nyunu pa-ni.
this FOC CAT=3AUG.S=RR hit-PST
"So they started hitting each other."

58. Ngu=lu=nyunu pa-ni na.
CAT=3AUG.S=RR hit-PST FOC
"They bashed each other then."

59. Wan-bala ngumpit, marluka, im-in, murla-ngka ngu karrinya
one-NMLZ man old.man 3SG-PST this-LOC CAT be.PST

kanyju-pal langa Daguragu, marluka Kamanyjingarna=ma.
down-EDGE LOC place.name old.man NAME=TOP
"One of those fellows – he was called Yirrkalkari or Kamanyjingarna Janama and he used to live at Daguragu."[259]

60. An im-in hab-im nyanuny mali nyawa=ma ngumayila=ma.
and 3SG-PST have-TR 3MIN.DAT *mali* this=TOP behind =TOP
"His *mali* was standing behind him – (he was called Waterloo Bob Jikirr Jungurra)."[260]

61. Mali-ngku=rni ngu pa-ni nyila=ma marluka=ma
mali-ERG=ONLY CAT hit-PST that=TOP old.man=TOP

Kamanyjingarna=ma.
NAME=TOP
"Kamanyjingarna's *mali* started hitting him."

62. An ngu=rla ma-rni Kamanyjingarna=ma kuya, 'Yamak=parla
and CAT=3OBL talk-PST NAME=TOP thus gently=FOC

pa-rra=yi=lu ngayiny-ju=waju mali-ngku' kuya.
hit-IMP=1EXC.MIN.NS=3AUG.S 1EXC.MIN.DAT-ERG=BECAUSE *mali*-ERG thus
"And Kamanyjingarna pleaded with him, 'Please hit me gently – you're my *mali* – you're not supposed to touch me.'"

259 Waterloo Bob Jikirr Jungurra was made to hit Yirrkalkari.

63.

Ngu=rla	ma-rni.
CAT=3OBL	say-PST

"That's what he said to him."

64.

'Ngayiny-ju=waju	mali	pa-rra=yi=lu
1EXC.MIN.DAT-ERG=BECAUSE	*mali*	hit-IMP=1EXC.MIN.NS=3AUG.S

yamak	kula	parra=yi=lu,'	kuya.
gently	NEG	hit-IMP=1EXC.MIN.NS=3AUG.S	thus

"'You're my *mali*, please don't hit me hard.'"

65.

An	ngu=rla	ma-rni	murnungku=ma,
and	CAT=3OBL	say-PST	policeman=TOP

murnungku-lu	im	nou	jaru=ma.
policeman-ERG	3SG	know	language=TOP

"The policeman understood what he was saying and said to him."

66.

Ngu=rla	ma-rni	murnungku=ma	nyila=ma
CAT=3OBL	say-PST	policeman=TOP	that=TOP

'Gu-an	pa-rra	nyila=ma.'
go-on	hit-IMP	that=TOP

"The policeman said to him, 'Go on – hit that one.'"

67.

'Pa-rra!'
hit-IMP

"'Hit him.'"

68.

'Nyila=ma=ngku	ma-rna-na	nganta=wayi
that=TOP=2MIN.NS	say-IMPF-PRS	ALLE=Q

wankaj	pa-rra=yi,'	kuya.
bad	hit-IMP=1EXC.MIN.NS	thus

"'It doesn't matter what he's saying to you, just hit him.'"

69.

Ngu	pa-ni	na,	marntaj.
CAT	hit-PST	FOC	OK

"He hit him then, OK."

70.

Ngu=yina	led-im-gu=warla	yuwa-ni	ngu=yina	ma-ni
CAT=3AUG.NS	let-TR-go=FOC	put-PST	CAT=3AUG.NS	do-PST

yilayilarrp	na	ngirlkirri-nginyi	wartan-nginyi	marntaj.
take.off.REDUP	FOC	neck-SOURCE	hand-SOURCE	OK

"Then he took the chains from their necks and wrists."

71.

Ngu=lu	nyawa=ma	wankaj	na	karrinya	luwa-nu-nginyi.
CAT=3AUG.S	this=TOP	bad	FOC	be.PST	strike-INF-SOURCE

"They were all battered from the beating."

72.

Nyila=ma	najan=ma	Japalyi-lu=ma	pa-ni	nyila=ma	Murtuyarri=ma.
that=TOP	NEG=TOP	SUBSECT-ERG=TOP	hit-PST	that=TOP	NAME=TOP

"One Japalyi (not the police boy) had beaten Murtuyarri."

73.

Najing	pangkily-pangkily	pa-ni	ngu	kuya-rniny=ma	binij.
nothing	hit.head-REDUP	hit-PST	CAT	thus-HITH=TOP	finish

"He had hit him again and again over the head."

74.

An	Jampin	ngu	pa-ni.
and	SUBSECT	CAT	hit-PST

"And he beat Jampin too – George Wangararra Jampin from Newrie Station."

75.

Wan-bala	Jampin,	yala-ny-mawu=rni	marluka
one-NMLZ	SUBSECT	that-NMLZ-DWELL=ONLY	old.man

kayirra-mpa.
north-PERL

"That Jampin was a traditional custodian of the area north of Waterloo."

76.

Im	nyila=ma	Jampin=ma	blanganta	Kildurk.
3SG	that=TOP	SUBSECT=TOP	LOC	place.name

"Jampin was a traditional custodian of Kildurk."

77.

Ngu	nyila	na	pa-ni	jurtakik-karra	Japalyi-lu=ma	marntaj.
CAT	that	FOC	hit-PST	hit.back.neck-ITER	SUBSECT-ERG=TOP	OK

"Japalyi had bashed him on the back of the neck."

78.

Nyila=rni=warla	ngu=rna	ma-rna-na	jaru=ma	nyila	na.
that=ONLY=FOC	CAT=1EXC.MIN.S	talk-IMPF-PRS	story=TOP	that	FOC

"That's the story."

79. Nyila=rni=warla ngu=rna=ngku piyarrp yuwa-ni.
that=ONLY=FOC CAT=1EXC.MIN.S=2MIN.NS report put-PST
"I told you that story now."

80. Marntaj=warla wayi?
OK=FOC TAG
"It's over, OK?"

A.8 Bill Crow and Jim Crow by Dandy Danbayarri

1999, Kalkaringi.[260]
Recorded and transcribed by Erika Charola.
Translated by Felicity Meakins.

1. Ngu=rna=ngku jawiji yurrk yuwa-ni,
CAT=1EXC.MIN.S=2MIN.NS MF tell.story put-PST

nyamu=rna karrinyani yapakaru ngayu.
REL=1EXC.MIN.S be.IMPF.PST small 1EXC.MIN
"Before I was telling you a story, granddaughter, from when I was a little kid,"

2. Mirntiwirri-la nyamu=yi karrwa-rna-ni ngaji-ngku.
place.name-LOC REL=1EXC.MIN.NS have-IMPF-PST father-ERG
"When my father was looking after me at Mirntiwirri."

3. Nyamu=yi wiit jayi-nya wakwak.
REL=1EXC.MIN.NS show give-PST crow
"When he showed me some crows"

4. Nyamu=yi wiit jayi-nya wakwak murrkun.
REL=1EXC.MIN.NS show give-PST crow three
"When he pointed out three crows to me."

5. 'Ngu=rna ya-ni partaj.
CAT=1EXC.MIN.S go-PST climb
"I climbed [a tree]."

6. 'Partaj ya-nta kankula=rni!'
climb go-IMP up=ONLY
"'Climb further up!' [he said]."

7. Ngu=rna ya-ni kankula, kankula
CAT=1EXC.MIN.S go-PST up up
"I climbed higher and higher . . ."

warrkuj ngu=rna=wuli ma-ni murrkun.
pick.up CAT=1EXC.MIN.S=3UA.NS get-PST three
". . . and grabbed three of them."

260 Note that we have made the connection with the Jim Crow laws that that enforced racial segregation in the southern United States but we think this is pure coincidence.

8. Ngu=rna ka-nya kanyjurra, jawurruk,
CAT=1EXC.MIN.S take-PST down descend
"Then I brought them down."

9. 'Nyawa ka-ngka ngurra-ngkurra. Jayi-ngka=rla majka ja
this take-IMP camp-ALL give-IMP=3OBL try there

mangarri!'
bread
"'Take them home and try giving them some bread,' [he said]."

10. '<u>Little bit</u> kutirni, kutirni.'
little bit wait wait
"'Just a little bit, hang on, wait.'"

11. 'Ngurra-ngkurra ka-ngka!'
camp-ALL take-IMP
"'Take them home!'"

12. Ngu=rna=yina ka-nya ngurra-ngkurra.
CAT=1EXC.MIN.S=3AUG.NS take-PST camp-ALL
"So I took them home."

13. Ngamayi <u>na</u> ngu=yi ma-rni 'Wayi,
mother FOC CAT=1EXC.MIN.NS say-PST Q

wanyji-ka=warla=n ma-ni nyila wakwak?'
which-LOC=FOC=2MIN.S do-PST that crow
"Mum said to me, 'Hey where did you get those crows?'"

14. Nyanawu nyamu=yi ma-rni ngayiny ngaji <u>intit</u>?
RECOG REL=1EXC.MIN.NS say-PST 1EXC.MIN.DAT father TAG
"You know the ones which my father talked about, remember?"

15. 'Ngu=rna karrwa-wu jangkarni-k nyawa=ma wakwak
CAT=1EXC.MIN.NS have-POT big-FACT this=TOP crow

ngayiny, wajawajarra-wu.'
1EXC.MIN.DAT play.around.REDUP-DAT
"'I'm going to grow up these crows of mine to play with.'"

16. 'Nyampa=warla=n jayi-ngku mangarri, tanku?'
what=3OBL=2MIN.S give-POT bread food
"'What are you going to feed them?' [she asked]."

17. 'Mangarri ngu=rna jayi-ngku, ngarin.'
bread CAT=1EXC.MIN.S give-POT meat
"'I'll give them some bread and meat.' [I replied]."

18. 'Ngu=lu nga-rna-na ngarin, intit?'
CAT=3AUG.S eat-IMPF-PRS meat TAG
"'They eat meat, don't they?'"

19. 'Ngu=rna=yina nya-nga-na, ngayu=ma.'
CAT=1EXC.MIN.S=3AUG.NS intake-IMPF-PRS 1EXC.MIN=TOP
"'I watch them.'"

20. 'Wakwak ngu=lu nga-rna-na ngarin.'
crow CAT=3AUG.S eat-IMPF-PRS meat
"'Crows eat meat.'"

21. 'Ngu=lu nga-rna-na mangarri.'
CAT=3AUG.S eat-IMPF-PRS bread
"'They also eat bread.'"

22. 'Ngu=rna jayi-ngku majka.'
CAT=1EXC.MIN.S give-POT try
"'I'll try giving them some.'"

23. Ngu=rna jayi-nya; ngu=lu nga-rna-ni.
CAT=1EXC.MIN.S give-PST CAT=3AUG.S eat-IMPF-PST
"I gave them some and they ate it."

24. Ngu=lu nga-rna-ni jaartkarra ngarina.
CAT=3AUG.S eat-IMPF-PST eat meat
"They ate the meat."

25. Nyarrulu=ma ngarlking nyila=ma yapakayi=ma!
3AUG=TOP greedy that=TOP small=TOP
"Those little ones were greedy!"

26. Ngarlking, ngu=lu nya-nga-ni.
greedy CAT=3AUG.S intake-IMPF-PST
"They ate greedily."

27. Jintaku=ma tampang karrinya.
one=TOP dead be.PST
"[But] one of them died."

28. Ngu=rna=rla luyurr ma-ni.
CAT=1EXC.MIN.S=3OBL feel.sad do-PST
"I grieved for it."

29. 'Ngama, tampang,' ngu=rna=rla ma-rni
mum dead CAT=1EXC.MIN.S=3OBL say-PST

ngayiny-ku ngamanti-wu.
1EXC.MIN.DAT-DAT mother-DAT
"'Mum, it's died!' I said to my mother."

30. 'Well ka-ngka jipij-ku.'
well take-IMP bury-DAT
"'Well take it and bury it,' [she replied]"

31. Ngu=rna ka-nya karrawarra pinka-kurra
CAT=1EXC.MIN.S take-PST east river-ALL

ngu=rna=rla kurrij-karra pu-nya janyja.
CAT=1EXC.MIN.S=3OBL dig-ITER pierce-PST ground
"I took it east to the river and I dug a hole in the ground."

32. Ngu=rna=rla jakarr ma-ni, ngu=rna jakarr.
CAT=1EXC.MIN.S=3OBL bury do-PST CAT=1EXC.MIN.S bury
"[Then] I buried it."

33. Ngu=rna=rla luyurr ma-ni.
CAT=1EXC.MIN.S=3OBL feel.sad do-PST
"I felt really sad about it."

34. Karrawarra ngu=rna yuwa-ni.
east CAT=1EXC.MIN.S put-PST
"I laid it to rest in the east."

35. Kujarra na ngu=rna=wuli karrwa-rna-ni.
two FOC CAT=1EXC.MIN.S=3UA.NS have-IMPF-PST
"Then I had two to raise."

36. Yapakayi-wu, yapakayi-wu, jangkarni-k; maiti murrkun week.
small-DAT small-DAT big-FACT maybe three week
"Within three weeks, they'd gone from little birds to big ones."

37. Jangkarni na ngu=wula karrinya, pinkirr-jawung na.
big FOC CAT=3UA.S be.PST feather-PROP FOC
"The two of them were big now with feathers."

38. Ngu=rna=wuli jayi-nga-ni tanku=ma,
CAT=1EXC.MIN.S=3UA.NS give-IMPF-PST food=TOP

mangarri=ma ngu=wula pina;
bread=TOP CAT=3UA.S know
"I would give them food and they came to know bread."

39. Ngu=wula pina, ngu=wula pina.
CAT=3UA.S know CAT=3UA.S know
"They knew, they did."

40. Ngu=lu nga-rna-ni, ngu=rna=yina ka-nga-ni
CAT=3AUG.S eat-IMPF-PST CAT=1EXC.MIN.S=3AUG.NS take-IMPF-PST

mangarri, ngu=rna=wuliny ka-nga-ni mangarri.
bread CAT=1EXC.MIN.S=3UA.NS take-IMPF-PST bread
"They would eat it up, I would give them bread, I mean I would give the two of them bread."

41. Ngu=rna=wuliny ma-rna-ni, 'Ngayu=ma
CAT=1EXC.MIN.S=3UA.NS say-IMPF-PST 1EXC.MIN=TOP

wajawajarra, kurrurij-kirlirlaj ngu=rna ya-ni kurlarra.'
play.around.REDUP car-TOY CAT=1EXC.MIN.S go-PST south
"I would say to them, 'I'm going south to play toy cars.'"

42. Kaarra-yarra kurrurij-kirlirlaj ngu=rna ya-na-ni wart.
east-SIDE car-TOY CAT=1EXC.MIN.S go-IMPF-PST return
"I would play toy cars on the eastside and then I would return."

43. Ngu=rna=yina ma-rna-ni ngayiny
CAT=1EXC.MIN.S=3AUG.NS say-IMPF-PST 1EXC.MIN.DAT

ngamayi-wu, 'Wanyji-ka=wula wakwak nyila?'
mother-DAT which-LOC=3UA.S crow that

'Mirntiwirri-la yarti-ngka!'
place.name-LOC shade-LOC
"I would say to my mothers, 'Where are those two crows'. 'In the shade at Mirntiwirri!' [they would reply]"

44. 'Ngu=rna=wuliny jayi-ngku tanku na!'
CAT=1EXC.MIN.S=3UA.NS give-POT food FOC
"'I have to feed them now!'"

45. 'Yuu!'
"'Yeah!'"

46. Ngu=rna=wuliny ma-rna-ni jaru=ma,
CAT=1EXC.MIN.S=3UA.NS say-IMPF-PST language=TOP

kula English.
NEG English
"I would speak to the two of them in language, not English."

47. 'Wak wak wak wak,' kurru na wakwak-kulu=ma.
squawk squawk squawk squawk listen FOC crow-ERG=TOP
"'Squawk, squawk, squawk, squawk,' the crows would hear."

48. Kankuli-yit, kankuli-yit tiwu.
up-ABL up-ABL fly
"[When they were] flying above."

49. 'Wak,' kuya ngu=rna=wuliny ma-rni.
squawk thus CAT=1EXC.MIN.S=3UA.NS say-PST
"'Squawk!' I called to them."

50. Kankuli-yit, parr ngayiny-ja.
up-ABL land 1EXC.MIN.DAT-LOC
"[Then] they'd land next to me."

51. Tubala warungkarr kalu=ma.
3DU alone walk=TOP
"They walked around by themselves."

52. Ngu=rna=wuliny jayi-nga-ni kirt
CAT=1EXC.MIN.S=3UA.NS give-IMPF-PST break.off

jayi-nga-ni ngarin=ma.
give-IMPF-PST meat=TOP
"I'd share out bits of meat."

53. Ngu=rna=wuliny jayi-nga-ni kirt ngarina,
CAT=1EXC.MIN.S=3UA.NS give-IMPF-PST break.off meat

ngu=wula nga-rna-ni.
CAT=3UA.S eat-IMPF-PST
"I'd break off bits and give it to them and they'd eat it."

54. Warlaku=ma=yina ngu=lu pina
dog=TOP=3AUG.NS CAT=3AUG.S know

karrinya=lu wakwak=ma warlaku=ma ngantipany=ma.
be.PST=3AUG.S crow=TOP dog=TOP 1EXC.AUG.DAT=TOP
"Our dogs got to know them."

55. Ngu=yi=wula ngayiny=ma na.
CAT=1EXC.MIN.NS=3UA.S 1EXC.MIN.DAT=TOP FOC
"The two of them were mine."

56. Ngu=wula, nyila=ma wakwak ngu=wula karrinyani.
CAT=3UA.S that=TOP crow CAT=3UA.S be.IMPF.PST
"The two of those crows stayed."

57. Well ngu=wula ma-ni ngarlaka na.
well CAT=3UA.S get-PST head FOC
"Well they started learning then."

58. Ngarlaka ngu=lu, kula=lu kula=lu ya-na-ni
head CAT=3AUG.S NEG=3AUG.S NEG=3AUG.S go-IMPF-PST

jurlak-kari=ma wakwak=ma nothing.
bird-OTHER=TOP crow=TOP nothing
"They didn't go and mix with other birds, not even crows."

59. Wajilan alright, wajilan, pulukura ngu=lu ya-ni;
galah alright galah whistling.kite CAT=3AUG.S go-PST
"There were plenty of galahs and whistling kites flying around."

60. Kula=yina ya-na-ni nyila=ma=wula wakwak=ma nothing.
NEG=3AUG.NS go-IMPF-PST that=TOP=3UA.S crow=TOP nothing
"But those two crows wouldn't go near them."

61. Ngantipany-ngarna nyila=ma.
1EXC.AUG.DAT-ASSOC that=TOP
"Those two were ours."

62. Ngurra=ma ngu=wula nyila=rni, kankula-piya.
camp=TOP CAT=3UA.S that=ONLY up-BIT
"They had their camp where we slept, higher up."

63. Ngu=wula karrinyani yarti-ngka ngurra=ma.
CAT=3UA.S be.IMPF.PST shade-LOC camp=TOP
"They would camp in the shade."

64. Ngu=wula ma-rna-ni.
CAT=3UA.S say-IMPF-PST
"They would talk there."

65. Wakwak punyu ngu=wula=ma kuya.
crow good CAT=3UA.S=TOP thus
"Those two crows were happy like that there."

66. Nyila=ma nyamu=rna=wuliny tanjarri-k ma-ni
that=TOP REL=1EXC.MIN.S=3UA.NS raise-FACT do-PST

wakwak=ma...
crow=TOP
"When I raised those crows..."

67. ...ngu=rna=wuli yini yuwa-ni.
CAT=1EXC.MIN.S=3UA.NS name put-PST
"I gave them names."

68. Ngu=rna=wuli ma-rni ngayiny-ku
CAT=1EXC.MIN.S=3UA.NS say-PST 1EXC.MIN.DAT-DAT

ngaji-wu,
father-DAT
"I talked about them to my father,"

69. 'Ngu=rna=wuli yuwa-rru yini na.'
CAT=1EXC.MIN.S=3UA.NS put-POT name FOC
"'I want to name them now.'"

70. 'Ngu=rna=wuli yuwa-rra yini. Nyampa=wula-ka
CAT=1EXC.MIN.S=3UA.NS put-POT name what=3UA.S-LOC

yini=ma?'
name=TOP
"'I want to give them names. What should I name them?'"

71. 'Wakwak-pa=rni wayi? 'Aa,' ngu=yi ma-rni
crow-EP=ONLY TAG aah CAT=1EXC.MIN.NS say-PST

ngayiny ngaji=ma.
1EXC.MIN.DAT father=TOP
"'They're only crows, aren't they?' 'Ah,' I said to my father."

72. 'Aaa yuwa-rra=wuli . . . Bill Crow and Jim Crow, wayi?'
aah put-IMP=3UA.NS NAME and NAME TAG
"'Ah well you could name them . . . Bill Crow and Jim Crow.'"

73. 'Yeah, that's good' ngu=rna=wuli ma-rni, 'Marntaj,
yeah that's good CAT=1EXC.MIN.S=3UA.NS say-PST OK.

marntaj.'
OK
"'Yeah that's good,'" I said to them, "OK OK.'"

74. 'Bill Crow nyawa, Jim Crow nyawa,' ngu=rna=wuliny
NAME this NAME this CAT=1EXC.MIN.S=3UA.NS

ma-rni.
say-PST
"'Bill Crow is this one, Jim Crow is this one,' I said to those two."

75. Ngu=rna=wuli ma-rni 'Aaa, alright, nyamu=wula
CAT=1EXC.MIN.S=3UA.NS say-PST aah alright REL=3UA.S

ya-na-ni, nyamu=wula karrinyani yarti-ngka=ma, wanyarri-la
go-IMPF-PST REL=3UA.S be.IMPF.PST shade-LOC=TOP bauhinia-LOC

karrawarra ngayiny=ma,
east 1EXC.MIN.DAT=TOP
"I said to them, 'Ah, when the two of them would go and stay in the shade of the bauhinia in the east with me.'"

76. Nyamu=rna=wuliny ma-rna-ni ngayiny-ku,
REL=1EXC.MIN.S=3UA.NS say-IMPF-PST 1EXC.MIN.DAT-DAT

wajarra.
play.around
"Like what I was saying about them before, when I used to go and play."

77. 'Bill Crow, come on, Jim Crow come on ai got-im ngarina.'
NAME come on NAME come one 1SG have-TR meat
"'Bill Crow come on, Jim Crow come on, I've got some meat.'"

78. Tiwu kankuli-yit ngu=yi=wula ya-na-ni
fly up-ABL CAT=1EXC.MIN.NS=3UA.S go-IMPF-PST

wakwak=ma nyila=ma kujarra=ma.
crow=TOP that=TOP two=TOP
"The two crows would fly to me from above."

79. Ngu=yi=wula ya-na-ni 'Come on!'
CAT=1EXC.MIN.NS=3UA.S go-IMPF-PST come on
"The two of them would come to me, 'Come on!'"

80. 'Jim Crow nyawa ngu ngarin nyununy.'
NAME this CAT meat 2MIN.DAT
"'Jim Crow – this is your meat.'"

81. 'Bill Crow nyawa ngu=ngku nyununy ngarin.
NAME this CAT=2MIN.NS 2MIN.DAT meat

Nga-nyja=wula na, tanku,' kuya
eat-IMP=3UA.S FOC food thus

ngu=rna=wuliny ma-rna-ni.
CAT=1EXC.MIN.S=3UA.NS say-IMPF-PST
"'Bill Crow – this is your meat. Eat up your tucker,' I would say to them."

82. Pinarri ngu=wula karrinya nyila=ma wakwak=ma
clever CAT=3UA.S be.PST that=TOP crow=TOP

ngayiny=ma.
1EXC.MIN.DAT=TOP
"Those two crows of mine understood."

83. Ngu=rna=wuliny pinarri-k ma-ni, ngu=wula.
CAT=1EXC.MIN.S=3UA.NS clever-FACT do-PST CAT=3UA.S
"I trained them up."

84. Ngu=wula yini=ma Bill Crow, Jim Crow;
CAT=3UA.S name=TOP NAME NAME

ankaankaj wakwak=ma. Marntaj.
poor.thing.REDUP crow=TOP OK
"They were called Bill Crow and Jim Crow, what lovely crows they were. That's the story."

85. Kula=lu karrinyana murla-ngka jala-jala=ma,
NEG=3AUG.S be.IMPF.PRS this-LOC today-REDUP=TOP
"They don't hang around here these days."

86. Wanyji-ka=warla=lu, Jangala?
which-LOC=FOC=3AUG.S SUBSECT

Wanyji-ka=warla=lu wakwak murla-rra?
which-LOC=FOC=3AUG.S crow this-PL
"Where are they Ronnie? Where are these crows?"

87. (laughs) Kata=nga rubbish-dump-kula.
THO=DUB rubbish-dump-LOC
"Maybe at the rubbish dump!"

A.9 Yangkarrp by Ronnie Wavehill

1999, Kalkaringi.
Recorded and transcribed by Erika Charola.
Translated by Felicity Meakins.

1.

Yuu,	ngu=rna=nga	ma-lu	nyawa=ma	yurrk	ngayiny
yeah	CAT=1EXC.MIN.S=DUB	talk-POT	this=TOP	tell.story	1EXC.MIN.DAT

ngaji,	ngayirra	parnara-rlang.
father	1EXC.UA	trirel.kin-DYAD

"Right well I might tell a story from my dad, us two, father and son."

2.

Ngu=yi	ka-nya	ngayiny-ju	ngaji-ngku
CAT=1EXC.MIN.NS	take-PST	1EXC.MIN.DAT-ERG	father-ERG

yangkarrp.
hunt

"My father took me hunting for kangaroos."

3.

Warrkuj	ma-ni	mirlarrang=ma=nyunu,	murrkunpurru
pick.up	do-PST	spear=TOP=RR	three

mirlarrang=ma;	ngu=ja	ya-ni	ngarlaka-ngarlaka	country
spear=TOP	CAT=1EXC.UA.S	go-PST	hill-REDUP	country

warik.
around

"He grabbed his three spears; and we headed out around the hill country."

4.

Paraj	pu-nya	ngu	langa=rni	jik-	pamarr-ngarna=ma	'Hey
find	pierce-PST	CAT	ear=ONLY	arrive	rock-ASSOC=TOP	hey

nyila	na	nyila	na	kutirni,	kutirni	karra	Jangala
that	FOC	that	FOC	wait	wait	stay.IMP	SUBSECT

murla-ngka=rni	karra.'
this-LOC=ONLY	stay.IMP

"He spotted just the ears sticking up – a rock wallaby, "That one, there, wait now, wait here Jangala," [my father said to me].

5.

Pamarr-ngarna	nyila,	karrinyani	ngu,	'Murla-ngka=rni
rock-ASSOC	that	be.IMPF.PST	CAT	this-LOC=ONLY

karra=yi	kutirni	nyuntu=ma.'
stay.IMP=1EXC.MIN.NS	wait	2MIN=TOP

"That rock wallaby was there, "'You wait right here for me.'"

6.

Ngu=yi	wanyja-ni	parik	kujarra	mirlarrang.
CAT=1EXC.MIN.NS	leave-PST	leave	two	spear

"He left me and two spears."

7.

Jintaku-yawung	mirlarrang-jawung	ngu=rla	walik	ya-na-ni
one-PROP	spear-PROP	CAT=3OBL	around	go-IMPF-PST

kuya,	karrap	nya-nga-ni	mayawun=ma	kuya.
thus	look	intake-IMPF-PST	wind=TOP	thus

"He was walknig around it with one spear like this, looking at the wind like this."

8.

Mayawun=ma	kaa-rni-yin-nganang.
wind=TOP	east-UP-ABL-AXIS

"The wind was coming across from up in the east to the west."

9.

'Ngu=rna=rla	ya-na-na	kayi-rni-yin-nganang-nginyi,
CAT=1EXC.MIN.S=3OBL	go-IMPF-PRS	north-UP-ABL-AXIS-SOURCE

kuya	walik	kayi-rni-yin-nganang-nginyi.	Kayi-rni-yin-nganang
thus	around	north-UP-ABL-AXIS-SOURCE	north-UP-ABL-AXIS

walik.'	Kayi-rni-nganang,	wuntu	ngu=rla	kayi
around	north-UP-AXIS	behind	CAT=3OBL	chase

pa-na-na	wuntu-ka	wuntu-ka=rni	ngamanpurru-la-
hit-IMPF-PRS	behind-LOC	behind-LOC=ONLY	conkerberry-LOC

ngamanpurru	nyila	mangarri.
conkerberry	that	veg.food

"'I'm going to go around for it from up along the north-side. Walk north to south.' He was chasing after it [hidden] behind a fruiting conkerberry bush."

10. Nyawa na ngamanpurru-la wuntu, wuntu-ka=rni
this FOC conkerberry-LOC behind behind-LOC=ONLY

ngumayila yapart=parla, yapart ya-nu jintaku-yawung
behind sneak.up=FOC sneak.up go-INF one-PROP

mirlarrang-jawung.
spear-PROP
"He snuck up behind it from behind a conkerberry bush, sneaking up with a spear."

11. Yapart aa murla-ngurlu na, nyila=ma wirnangpurru;
sneak.up aah this-ABL FOC that=TOP kangaroo

wapurt karrinyu; jukul karrinyani ngu.
unaware be.INF lie.down be.IMPF.PST CAT
"He snuck up from here. The kangaroo was unaware [of his presence] and was lying down."

12. Yarram.
hook.up.spear
"He hooked up a spear."

13. Jalk ma-ni nyila=ma mirlarrang=ma jalk=parla,
hook.up.spear do-PST that=TOP spear=TOP hook.up.spear=FOC

kutirni, punyu-punyu-k ngu=nyunu yuwa-ni
wait good-REDUP-FACT CAT=RR put-PST

ngayiny-ju=ma ngaji-ngku=ma.
1EXC.MIN.DAT-ERG=TOP father-ERG=TOP
"He hooked up a spear and waiting. My father made himself ready."

14. Ngayu=ma karrap, jutu-jutu-k na karrap
1EXC.MIN=TOP watch straight-REDUP-FACT FOC watch

nya-nga-ni.
intake-IMPF-PST
"I was watching with a direct sight of events."

15. Yarram na.
hook.up.spear FOC
"He hooked it up."

16. Warrulirli nyila=ma, warrulirli=ma, kurrp pu-nya
spear.flying that=TOP spear.flying=TOP stab pierce-PST

ngu yala-ngka=rni.
CAT that-LOC=ONLY
"The spear flew and speared it right there."

17. Tipart=ma waninya na mirlarrang-jawung.
hop=TOP fall.PST FOC spear-PROP
"It hopped and fell with the spear."

18. Finish!
dead/done
"Dead!"

19. Lanti-ka=rni pingkily wu-nya.
hip-LOC=ONLY cripple pierce-PST
"[The spear] had crippled its hip."

20. Ngayu=ma rarraj nyila na kil-im im tampang
1EXC.MIN=TOP run that FOC hit-TR 3SG kill

jurtakik nyila=ma ngu=ja ka-nya lajap,
hit.back.neck that=TOP CAT=1EXC.UA.S bring-PST carry.on.shoulder

'Aa murla-ngka na kampa=wuli Jangala kuya, turturl,' kuya.
aah this-LOC FOC cook.IMP=3UA.NS SUBSECT thus roast thus
"I ran and finished it off by hitting it in the back of the neck. Then we took it on our shoulders, 'Ah you two roast it here,' he said."

21. Warawurnku warawurnku=ma nyila=ma wirnangpurru=ma.
male.kangaroo male.kangaroo=TOP that=TOP kangaroo=TOP

Yang-wan, nyampayirla.
young-ADJ whatsitcalled
"It was a male kangaroo. A young one, what's it called."

22. Minawurt.
male.hill.kangaroo
"A male hill kangaroo."

23. Jarrwaj pu-nya ngu.
spear pierce-PST CAT
"He'd speared it."

24. Ngu=ja kampa-rni, purlk pa-ni ngu jarluyurr-jarluyurr.
CAT=1EXC.UA.S cook-PST gut hit-PST CAT break.legs-REDUP
"We cooked the guts and broke its hind legs."

25. Wumpu-wumpu ngu=ja ma-ni marntaj.
singe.fur-REDUP CAT=1EXC.UA.S do-PST OK
"We singed the fur then, OK."

26. Turturl ngu=ja kampa-rni,
roast CAT=1EXC.UA.S cook-PST

ngayiny-ju ngaji-ngku=ma nyila=ma turturl;
1EXC.MIN.DAT-ERG father-ERG=TOP that=TOP roast

wurraj ma-ni ngu turturl-nginyi=ma,
uncover do-PST CAT roast-REDUP-SOURCE=TOP

jarlujarluyurr pa-ni ngu.
break.legs.REDUP hit-PST CAT
"My father and I roasted it and uncovered it after it was cooked. He broke the legs."

27. Marntaj na kankuli na ngurra-ngkurra mami-wu
OK FOC up FOC camp-ALL mum-DAT

wart ngamayi-wu kuya. Xxx. Tanku-murlung ngu=lu
return mother-DAT thus xxx food-PRIV CAT=3AUG.S

papa-walija, kapuku-walija=ma.
brother-PAUC sister-PAUC=TOP
"OK we returned home to mum. My brothers and sisters were hungry."

<About 45 sec of transcript missing here>

28.

Wirnangpurru=ma	nyila=ma	jaartkarra	nga-rni=warla,
kangaroo=TOP	that=TOP	eat	eat-PST=FOC

ngayiny-ju	ngamayi-lu	ngaji-ngku=ma	marntaj.
1EXC.MIN.DAT-ERG	mother-ERG	father-ERG=TOP	OK

"My mother and father ate some kangaroo then OK."

29.

Tanku;	kula=rnalu	karrinya	ngayiny-ju
food	NEG=1EXC.AUG.S	be.PST	1EXC.MIN.DAT-ERG

ngaji-ngku=ma	xxx	tanku-murlung.
father-ERG=TOP	xxx	food-PRIV

"My father and all of us weren't hungry then!"

30.

Murlarrik	ngayiny=ma	ngaji=ma.
good.hunter	1EXC.MIN.DAT=TOP	father=TOP

"My father was a good hunter."

31.

Karna	jintaku	ngu	pamarr-ngarna	nyamu	ya-na-ni	japap
spear	one	CAT	rock-ASSOC	REL	go-IMPF-PST	hunt

kula	ya-na-ni	japap	kula	yarrp-jawung,	nyamu
NEG	go-IMPF-PST	hunt	NEG	miss.target-PROP	REL

ya-na-ni	wumaj-wumaj	mayawun	wumaj	nyamu	ya-na-ni
go-IMPF-PST	wind-REDUP	wind	wind	REL	go-IMPF-PST

kula	yarrp-jawung.
NEG	miss.target-PROP

"It was a one shot rock wallaby. He never missed when he went hunting. He hunted according to the wind so he would never miss."

32.

Marntaj.
OK

"That's the story."

References

Amberber, Mengistu., Baker, Brett., & Harvey, Mark. (Eds.). (2010). *Complex predicates: Cross-linguistic perspectives on event structure*. Cambridge: Cambridge University Press.

Anderson, Stephen. (2005). *Aspects of the Theory of Clitics*. Oxford: Oxford University Press.

Austin, Peter. (1981). Switch-reference in Australia. *Language, 57*(2), 309–333.

Austin, Peter. (1982). Transitivity and cognate objects in Australian languages. In Paul Hopper & Sarah Thompson (Eds.), *Studies in Transitivity* (pp. 37–47). California: Academic Press.

Austin, Peter. (1995). Double case marking in Kanyara and Mantharta languages. In Frans Plank (Ed.), *Agreement by suffixaufnahme* (pp. 363–379). Oxford: Oxford University Press.

Austin, Peter. (2001). Word order in a free word order language: The case of Jiwarli. In Jane Simpson, David Nash, Mary Laughren, Peter Austin, & Barry Alpher (Eds.), *Forty years on: Ken Hale and Australian languages* (pp. 205–323). Canberra: Pacific Linguistics.

Austin, Peter & Bresnan, Joan. (1996). Non-configurationality in Australian Aboriginal languages. *Natural language and linguistic theory, 14*, 215–268.

Baker, Brett. (2014). Word structure in Australian languages. In H. Koch & R. Nordlinger (Eds.), *The Languages and Linguistics of Australia: A Comprehensive Guide* (pp. 139–214). Berlin: Mouton de Gruyter.

Baker, Mark. (1996). *The Polysynthesis Parameter*. Oxford: Oxford University Press.

Berndt, Catherine. (1950). *Women's Changing Ceremonies in Northern Australia*. France: Librairie Scientifique Herrman et co.

Berndt, Catherine., & Berndt, Ronald. (1948). Pastoral stations in the Northern Territory and native welfare. *Aborigines Protector, 2*(4), 13–16.

Berndt, Ronald. (1974). *Australian Aboriginal Religion*. Leiden: Brill.

Berndt, Ronald., & Berndt, Catherine. (1948). *A Northern Territory Problem: Aboriginal Labour in a Pastoral Area*. Sydney.

Berndt, Ronald., & Berndt, Catherine. (1987). *End of an Era: Aboriginal Labour in the Northern Territory*. Canberra: AIAS.

Bittner, Maria., & Hale, Kenneth. (1995). Remarks on definiteness in Warlpiri. In Emmon Bach, Eloise Jelinek, Angelika Kratzer, & Barbara Partee (Eds.), *Quantification in Natural Languages* (pp. 81–105). Dordrecht, Holland: Kluwer.

Blake, Barry. (1983). Structure and word order in Kalkatungu: The anatomy of a flat language. *Australian Journal of Linguistics, 3*, 143–175.

Blake, Barry. (1987). *Australian Aboriginal Grammar*. Kent: Croom Helm.

Blythe, Joe. (2009). *Doing referring in Murrinh-Patha conversation*. University of Sydney, Sydney.

Blythe, Joe. (2018). Genesis of the trinity: the convergent evolution of trirelational kinterms. In Patrick McConvell, Patrick Kelly, & Sebastian Lacrampe (Eds.), *Skin, Kin and Clan: The Dynamics of Social Categories in Indigenous Australia* (pp. 431–471). Canberra: ANU ePress.

Blythe, Joe., Mardigan, Kinngirri Carmelita, Perdjert, Mawurt Ernest, & Stoakes, Hywel. (2016). Pointing out directions in Murrinhpatha. *Open Linguistics, 2*(1), 132–159.

Bobaljik, Jonathan., & Wurmbrand, Susi. (2002). Notes on agreement in Itelmen. *Linguistic Discovery, 1*(1).

Bowern, Claire., & Atkinson, Quentin. (2012). Computational phylogenetics and the internal structure of Pama-Nyungan. *Language, 88*, 817–845.

Bresnan, Joan. (1982). Control and complemetation. *Linguistic Inquiry, 13*(3), 343–434.

Bromham, Lindell., Hua, Xia., Algy, Cassandra., & Meakins, Felicity. (2020). Indigenous language endangerment: A multidimensional analysis of risk factors. *Journal of Language Evolution, 5*(1), 75–91. doi:10.1093/jole/lzaa002

https://doi.org/10.1515/9783110746884-014

Browne, Mitchell. (2021). *A Grammatical Description of Warlmanpa: A Ngumpin-Yapa Language Spoken around Tennant Creek (Northern Territory).* (PhD). University of Queensland, Brisbane.
Browne, Mitchell., Ennever, Thomas., & Osgarby, David. (2021). Apprehension as a grammatical category in Ngumpin-Yapa languages (Australia). In Eva Schultze-Berndt, Marine Vuillermet & Martina Faller (Eds.), *Apprehensional Constructions in a Cross-Linguistic Perspective*. Berlin: Language Sciences Press.
Bulngari, Blanche. (2016). Flood events at Rifle Hole. In Erika Charola & Felicity Meakins (Eds.), *Yijarni: True Stories from Gurindji Country* (pp. 107–111). Canberra: Aboriginal Studies Press.
Bybee, Joan., & Dahl, Östen. (1989). The creation of tense and aspect systems in the languages of the world. *Studies in Language, 13*, 51–103.
Capell, Arthur. (1940). The classification of languages in north and north-west Australia (Continued). *Oceania, 10*(4), 404–433.
Capell, Arthur. (1965). *A new approach to Australian linguistics (Handbook of Australian languages, part 1)*. Sydney: University of Sydney.
Capell, Arthur. (1979). Classification of verbs in Australian languages. In Stephen Wurm (Ed.), *Australian Linguistic Studies* (pp. 229–322). Canberra: Pacific Linguistics.
Casagrande, Joseph. B. (1948). Comanche baby language. *International Journal of American Linguistics, 14*(1), 11–14.
Cataldi, Lee. (2011, 2011). *Ngardi Dictionary*. Unpublished manuscript.
Chappell, Hillary., & McGregor, William. (1995). Prolegomena to a theory of inalienability. In Hillary Chappell & William McGregor (Eds.), *The grammar of inalienability: A typological perspective on body part terms and the part-whole relation* (pp. 3–30). Berlin: Mouton de Gruyter.
Charola, Erika., & Meakins, Felicity. (2016a). European and further accounts of the early murders. In Erika Charola & Felicity Meakins (Eds.), *Yijarni: True Stories from Gurindji Country* (pp. 80–83). Canberra: Aboriginal Studies Press.
Charola, Erika., & Meakins, Felicity. (Eds.). (2016b). *Mayarni-kari Yurrk: More Stories from Gurindji Country*. Batchelor, Australia: Batchelor Press.
Charola, Erika., & Meakins, Felicity. (Eds.). (2016c). *Yijarni: True Stories from Gurindji Country*. Canberra: Aboriginal Studies Press.
Chew, John. J. (1969). The structure of Japanese Baby Talk. *Journal-Newsletter of the Association of Teachers of Japanese, 6*, 4–17.
Choi, Hye-Won. (1999). *Optimizing structure in context: Scrambling and information structure*. Stanford CA: CSLI Publications.
CLC. (1994). *The Land is always alive: The story of the Central Land Council*. Alice Springs: CLC.
Comrie, Bernard. (1981). *Language Universals and Linguistic Typology: Syntax and Morphology*. Oxford: Blackwell.
Cook, Anthony. (1988). Participle sentences in Wakiman. In Peter Austin (Ed.), *Complex Sentence Constructions in Australian Languages* (pp. 69–75). Amsterdam: Benjamins.
Cowen, Anna. (2017). *My Vice-Regal Life: Diaries 1978 to 1982*. Melbourne: Melbourne University Press.
Croft, Brenda., Toussaint, Sandy., Meakins, Felicity., & McConvell, Patrick. (2019). For the children...": Aboriginal Australia, cultural access, and archival obligation. In Linda Barwick, Jennifer Green, & Petronelle Vaarzon-Morel (Eds.), *Archival Returns: Central Australia and Beyond* (pp. 173–191). Honolulu: University of Hawai'i Press.
Cruttenden, Alan. (1994). Phonetic and prosodic aspects of Baby Talk. In Clare Gallaway & Brian J. Richards (Eds.), *Input and Interaction in Language acquisition* (pp. 135–152). Cambridge: Cambridge University Press.
Cysouw, Michael. (2006). *Towards a typology of pronominal cliticization*. Paper presented at the ALT V Conference, Cagliari, Italy.

Daguragu-Community-Council. (2000). *Mumkurla-nginyi-ma Parrngalinyparla (From Darkness into Light, Gurindji Freedom Banners: A Celebration of the Determination and Vision of the People of Daguragu and Kalkaringi.* Kalkaringi.

Dalrymple, Mary., & Nikolaeva, Irina. (2011). *Objects and Information Structure.* Cambridge: Cambridge University Press.

Danbayarri, Dandy. (2016a). Picking up after the flood and finding Jinparrak. In Erika Charola & Felicity Meakins (Eds.), *Yijarni: True stories from Gurindji country* (pp. 116–123). Canberra: Aboriginal Studies Press.

Danbayarri, Dandy. (2016b). Waringarri (War parties). In Erika Charola & Felicity Meakins (Eds.), *Yijarni: True Stories from Gurindji Country* (pp. 7–11). Canberra: Aboriginal Studies Press.

Dench, Alan. (1995). *Martuthunira: A Language of the Pilbara region of Western Australia.* Canberra: Pacific Linguistics.

Dench, Alan., & Evans, Nicholas. (1988). Multiple case-marking in Australian languages. *Australian Journal of Linguistics, 8*, 1–48.

Diessel, Holger. (1999). *Demonstratives: Form, Function and Grammaticalization.* Amsterdam: John Benjamins.

Dik, Simon. (1997). *The Theory of Functional Grammar. Part 1: The Structure of the Clause.* Berlin: Mouton de Gruyter.

Dixon, R. M. W. (1979). Ergativity. *Language, 55*(1), 59–138.

Dixon, R. M. W. (1980). *The Languages of Australia.* Cambridge: Cambridge University Press.

Dixon, R. M. W. (2001). The Australian linguistic area. In A. Y. Aikhenvald & R. M. W. Dixon (Eds.), *Areal Diffusion and Genetic inheritance. Problems in Comparative Linguistics* (pp. 64–104). Oxford: Oxford University Press.

Dixon, R. M. W. (2002). *Australian Languages: Their Nature and Development.* Cambridge: Cambridge University Press.

Dodson, Patrick. (2000). Lingiari: Until the chains are broken. In M. Grattan (Ed.), *Reconciliation* (pp. 264–274). Melbourne: Black Inc.

Donald, Violet. (1998). We're not coming back. In Alexis Wright (Ed.), *Take Power like this Old Man Here: An Anthology Celebrating 20 yrs of Land Rights in Central Australia.* Alice Springs: IAD Press.

Donaldson, Tamsin. (1980). *Ngiyambaa: The Language of the Wangaaybuwan.* Cambridge: Cambridge University Press.

Doolan, J. K. (1977). Walk-off (and later return) of various Aboriginal groups from cattle stations: Victoria River District, Northern Territory. In R. M. Berndt (Ed.), *Aborigines and Change: Australia in the 70s* (pp. 106–113). Canberra: AIATSIS.

Du Bois, John. (1987). The discourse basis of ergativity. *Language, 63*(4), 805–855.

Dunn, Vivien., Meakins, Felicity., & Algy, Cassandra. (2021). Acquisition or shift: Interpreting variation in Gurindji children's expression of spatial relations. In Enoch Aboh & Cécile Vigouroux (Eds.), *Variation Rolls the Dice.* Amsterdam: John Benjamins.

Ennever, Thomas. (2021). *A Grammar of Ngardi, a Language of northern Australia.* Berlin: Mouton de Gruyter.

Ennever, Thomas., Meakins, Felicity., & Round, Erich. (2017). A replicable acoustic measure of lenition and the nature of variability in Gurindji stops. *Laboratory Phonology, 8*(1), 1–32. doi:https://doi.org/10.5334/labphon.18

Evans, Nicholas. (1995a). *A Grammar of Kayardild: With Historical-Comparative Notes on Tangkic.* Berlin: Mouton de Gruyter.

Evans, Nicholas. (1995b). A-quantifiers and scope in Mayali. In Emmon Bach, Eloise Jelinek, Angelika Kratzer, & Barbara Hall Partee (Eds.), *Quantification in Natural Language* (pp. 207–270). Dordrecht, Holland: Kluwer.

Evans, Nicholas. (2007). Insubordination and its uses. In Irina Nikolaeva (Ed.), *Finiteness: Theoretical and Empirical Foundations* (pp. 366–431). Oxford: Oxford University Press.
Evans, Nicholas, & Wilkins, David. (1998). The knowing ear: An Australian test of universal claims about the semantic structure of sensory verbs and their extension into the domain of cognition. *Arbeitspapiere von Institut für Sprachwissenschaft Universität zu Köln (Neue Folge), 32*, 1–63.
Everett, Caleb. (2009). A reconsideration of the motivations for preferred argument structure. *Studies in Language, 33*(1), 1–24.
Ferguson, Charles. A. (1964). Baby talk in six languages. *American Anthropologist,* 66, 103–114.
Ferguson, Charles. A. (1977). Baby talk as a simplified register. In C. E. Snow & C. A. Ferguson (Eds.), *Talking to children: Language input and acquisition* (pp. 209–235). Cambridge: Cambridge University Press.
Foley, William. (1992). *The Yimas Language of New Guinea*. Stanford: Stanford University Press.
Frith, Nancy. (1998). We went on strike. In Alexis Wright (Ed.), *Take Power like this Old Man Here: An Anthology Celebrating 20 yrs of Land Rights in Central Australia*. Alice Springs: IAD Press.
Gaby, Alice. (2021). Reflexives and reciprocals. In Claire Bowern (Ed.), *Oxford handbook of Australian languages*. Oxford: Oxford University Press.
Garde, Murray. (2013). *Culture, Interaction and Person Reference in an Australian Language*. Amsterdam: John Benjamins.
Genetti, Carol, & Crain, L. D. (2003). Beyond preferred argument structure: Sentences, pronouns and given referents in Nepali. In John Du Bois, Lorraine Kumpf & William Ashby (Eds.), *Preferred Argument Structure: Grammar as Architecture for Function*. Amsterdam: John Benjamins.
Goddard, Cliff. (1982). Case systems and case marking in Australian languages: A new interpretation. *Australian Journal of Linguistics, 2*, 167–196.
Graber, Paul. (1987). The Kriol particle 'na'. *SIL Working Papers in Language and Linguistics, 21*, 1–21.
Green, Jennifer, Algy, Cassandra, & Meakins, Felicity. (2017). *Takataka: Gurindji Sign Language Posters*. Batchelor, Australia: Batchelor Press.
Green, Jennifer., Bauer, Annastacia., Gaby, Alice., & Ellis, Elizabeth. M. (2018). Pointing to the body: kin signs in Australian Indigenous sign languages. *Gesture, 17*(1), 1–36.
Green, Jennifer., Meakins, Felicity., & Algy, Cassandra. (forthcoming). Alternate for some and primary for others: Sign language in a Gurindji community in northern Australia.
Green, Rebecca., Green, Jennifer., Hamilton-Hollaway, Amanda., Meakins, Felicity., Osgarby, David., & Pensalfini, Robert. (2019). *Mudburra to English Dictionary*. Canberra: Aboriginal Studies Press.
Griffen-Foley, Bridget., & Scalmer, Sean. (Eds.). (2017). *Public Opinion, Campaign Politics & Media Audiences: New Australian Perspectives*. Melbourne: Melbourne University Press.
Grimes, Joseph. E. (1955). Style in Huichol structure. *Language, 31*, 31–35.
Haig, Geoff, & Schnell, Stefan (2016). The discourse basis of ergativity revisited. *Language, 92*(3), 1–14.
Hale, Kenneth. (1973). Person marking in Walbri. In Stephen Anderson & Paul Kiparsky (Eds.), *A Festschrift for Morris Halle* (pp. 308–344). New York: Holt, Rinehart and Winston.
Hale, Kenneth. (1976). The adjoined relative clause in Australia. In R. M. W. Dixon (Ed.), *Grammatical Categories in Australian Languages* (pp. 78–105). Canberra: AIAS.
Hale, Kenneth. (1982). Some essential features of Warlpiri verbal clauses. In Steven Swartz (Ed.), *Papers in Memory of Lother Jagst: Work paper of SIL-AAB* (pp. 217–315). Darwin: SIL.
Hale, Kenneth. (1983). Warlpiri and the grammar of non-configurational languages. *Natural Language and Linguistic Theory, 1*(1), 5–47.
Hale, Kenneth. (1992). Basic word order in two "free word order" languages. In Doris Payne (Ed.), *Pragmatics of Word Order Flexibility.* (pp. 63–82). Amsterdam: John Benjamins.

Halliday, Michael. (1967). Notes on transitivity and theme in English. Part 1 and 2. *Journal of Linguistics, 3*, 37–81, 199–244.
Halpern, Aaron., & Zwicky, Arnold. (Eds.). (1996). *Approaching Second: Second Position Clitics and Related Phenomena*. Stanford: CSLI.
Hansen, Ken. (1974). *Pintupi Kinship*. Alice Springs: IAD Press.
Hardy, Frank. (1968). *The Unlucky Australians*. Melbourne: Nelson.
Haspelmath, Martin. (1996). Word-class-changing inflection and morphological theory. In Geert. Booij & Jaap van Marle (Eds.), *Yearbook of Morphology 1995* (pp. 43–66). Dordrecht, Holland: Kluwer.
Haviland, John. (1998). Guugu Yimithirr cardinal directions. *Ethos, 26*(1), 25–47.
Heath, Jeffrey. (1976). Topic E: Simple and compound verbs: Conjugation by auxiliaries in Australian verbal systems. North-east Arnhem Land. In R. M. W. Dixon (Ed.), *Grammatical Categories in Australian Languages* (pp. 735–740). Canberra: AIAS.
Heath, Jeffrey. (1984). *A Functional Grammar of Nunggubuyu*. Canberra: AIAS.
Heath, Jeffrey. (1986). Syntactic and lexical aspects of non-configurationality in Nunggubuyu (Australia). *Natural Language and Linguistic Theory, 4*, 375–408.
Hector, Ivy., Kalabidi, George., Banjo, Spider., Dodd, Topsy., Wavehill, Ronnie., Danbayarri, Dandy., Wadrill, Violet., Puntiyarri, Bernard., Malyik, Ida Bernard., Wavehill, Biddy., Morris, Helen., Campbell, Lauren., Meakins, Felicity., Wightman, Glenn. (2012). *Bilinarra, Gurindji and Malngin Plants and Animals*. Darwin: Northern Territory Department of Land Resource Management.
Heine, Berndt. (1997). *Possession: Cognitive Sources, Forces, and Grammaticalization*. Cambridge, U.K. ; New York, NY, USA: Cambridge University Press.
Hoddinott, William., & Kofod, Frances. (1988). *The Ngankikurungkurr Language (Daly River Area, Northern Territory)*. Canberra: Pacific Linguistics.
Hokari, Minoru. (2000). From Wattie Creek to Wattie Creek: An oral historical approach to the Gurindji walk-off. *Aboriginal History, 24*, 98–116.
Hokari, Minoru. (2002). Reading oral histories from the pastoral frontier: A critical revision. *Journal of Australian Studies: New Talents, Jumping the Queue, 72*, 21–28.
Hokari, Minoru. (2011). *Gurindji Journey: A Japanese Historian in the Outback*: UNSW Press.
Hudson, Joyce. (1977). Some common features in Fitzroy Valley Kriol.
Hudson, Joyce. (1978). *The Core of Walmatjari grammar*. Canberra: AIAS.
Hudson, Joyce. (1983). Transitivity and aspect in the Kriol verb. *Papers in Pidgin and Creole Linguistics (Pacific Linguistics A-65) 3*: 161–75.
Hudson, Joyce. (1985). *Grammatical and Semantic Aspects of Fitzroy Valley Kriol*. Darwin: SIL.
Hudson, Joyce., & Richards, Eirlys. (1978). *The Walmatjari: An Introduction to the Language and Culture*. Darwin: Work Papers of SIL-AAB, B:1.
Ise, Magumi. (1998). *Grammatical Sketch of Malngin Language.* (MA thesis). University of Hokkaido,
Jelinek, Eloise. (1984). Empty categories, case and configurationality. *Natural Language and Linguistic Theory, 2*, 39–76.
Jones, Alex. (1978). Form and meaning in an Australian language. *Language and Speech, 21*(3), 264–278.
Jones, Caroline., & Meakins, Felicity. (2013a). The phonological forms and perceived functions of janyarrp, the Gurindji 'baby talk' register. *Lingua, 134*, 170–193.
Jones, Caroline., & Meakins, Felicity. (2013b). Variation in voice onset time in stops in Gurindji Kriol: picture naming and conversational speech. *Australian Journal of Linguistics, 33*(2), 194–217.
Jones, Caroline., Meakins, Felicity., & Muawiyath, Shujau. (2012). Learning vowel categories from maternal speech in Gurindji Kriol. *Language Learning, 62*(4), 997–1260.
Jones, Caroline., Schultze-Berndt, Eva., Denniss, Jessica., & Meakins, Felicity. (2019). *Ngarinyman to English Dictionary*. Canberra: Aboriginal Studies Press.

Kendon, Adam. (1988). *Sign Languages of Aboriginal Australia: Cultural, Semiotic and Communicative Perspectives.* Cambridge: Cambridge University Press.

Kijngayarri, L. Johnny. (1986 (1974)). The Wave Hill strike (P. McConvell, Trans.). In Luis Hercus & Peter Sutton (Eds.), *This is What Happened: Historical Narratives by Aborigines* (pp. 305–311). Canberra: AIAS Press.

Kofod, Frances. (1996). *Verb Stems in Jarragan Languages of the East Kimberley.* Paper presented at the Australian Linguistics Society conference, Canberra.

Kroeger, Paul. (2005). *Analyzing Grammar: An Introduction*. Cambridge: Cambridge University Press.

Lambrecht, Knut. (1994). *Information Structure and Sentence Form: Topic, Focus, and the Mental Representations of Discourse Referents.* Cambridge: Cambridge University Press.

Laughren, Mary. (1978). Directional terminology in Warlpiri. *Working Papers in Language and Linguistics, 8*, 1–16.

Laughren, Mary. (1982). A preliminary description of propositional particles in Warlpiri. In Steven Swartz (Ed.), *Papers in Warlpiri Grammar in Memory of Lothar Jagst* (pp. 129–163). Berrimah, N.T.: SIL-AAB.

Laughren, Mary. (1984). Warlpiri Baby talk. *Australian Journal of Linguistics, 4*, 73–88.

Laughren, Mary. (1989). The configurationality parameter and Warlpiri. In Laszlo Maracz & Pieter Muysken (Eds.), *Configurationality: The Typology of Asymmetries* (pp. 319–353). Dordrecht, Holland: Foris Publications.

Laughren, Mary. (1992). Secondary predication as a diagnostic of underlying structure in Pama-Nyungan languages. In Iggy Rocca (Ed.), *Thematic Structure* (pp. 199–246). Berlin: Mouton de Gruyter.

Laughren, Mary. (2002). Syntactic constraints in a 'free word order' language. In Mengistu Amberger & Peter Collins (Eds.), *Language Universals and Variation* (pp. 83–130). Westport CT: Praeger.

Laughren, Mary. (2010). Warlpiri verbs of change and causation: The thematic core. In Mengistu Amberber, Brett Baker, & Mark Harvey (Eds.), *Complex Predicates: Cross-Linguistic Perspectives on Event Structure* (pp. 167–236). Cambridge: Cambridge University Press.

Laughren, Mary. (2011). *Reconstructing First and Second Singular Pronouns across Northern Pama-Nyungan Languages*. Paper presented at the TELC Meeting at Charles Darwin University, Darwin.

Laughren, Mary., & Hoogenraad, Robert. (1996). *A Learner's Guide to Warlpiri. Tape Course for Beginners. Wangkamirlipa Warlpirilki. Based on a Tape Course Prepared by Kenneth Hale & Robin Japanangka Granites*. Alice Springs: IAD Press.

Laughren, Mary., & McConvell, Patrick. (1999). *Down Under in Central Australia*. Paper presented at the American Anthropological Association Meeting, Chicago.

Lauridsen, Jan. (1990). *Women's Jarata of North Central Australia.*

Laves, Gerhardt. (1929–31). *'Anyumarla' Fieldnotes*. AIATSIS. Canberra. Retrieved from www.anu.edu.au/linguistics/nash/aust/laves/Anjumarla.html

Legate, Julie. (2002). *Warlpiri: Theoretical Implications.* (PhD thesis). Massachusetts Institute of Technology, Boston.

Levinson, Steven. (1997). Language and cognition: The cognitive consequences of spatial description in Guugu Yimithirr. *Journal of Linguistic Anthropology, 7*, 98–131.

Levinson, Steven. (2003). *Space in Language and Cognition: Explorations in Cognitive Diversity*. Cambridge: Cambridge University Press.

Levinson, Steven., & Wilkins, David. (2006a). Background to the study of the language of space. In Steven Levinson & David Wilkins (Eds.), *Grammars of Space: Explorations in Cognitive Diversity* (pp. 1–23). Cambridge: Cambridge University Press.

Levinson, Steven., & Wilkins, David. (2006b). Patterns in the data: Towards a semantic typology of spatial description. In Steven Levinson & David Wilkins (Eds.), *Grammars of Space: Explorations in Cognitive Diversity* (pp. 512–575). Cambridge: Cambridge University Press.
Lewis, Darrell. (1993). *In the Western Wilds : A Survey of Historic Sites in the Western Victoria River District*. Retrieved from Darwin:
Lewis, Darrell. (1997). *A Shared History: Aborigines and White Australians in the Victoria River District Northern Territory*. Darwin: Create-a-Card.
Lewis, Darrell. (2002). *Slower than the Eye can See: Environmental Change in Northern Australia's Cattle Lands*. Darwin: Tropical Savannas CRC.
Lewis, Darrell. (2012). *A Wild History: Life and Death on the Victoria River Frontier*. Melbourne: Monash University.
Libert, Alan. (1988). Going from the allative to a theory of multiple case marking. *McGill Working Papers in Linguistics, 5*(1), 93–129.
Lichtenberk, Frank. (2000). Inclusory Pronominals. *Oceanic Linguistics, 39*(1), 1–32.
Lingiari, Vincent. (1986 (1975)). Vincent Lingiari's Speech (P. McConvell, Trans.). In Luis Hercus & Peter Sutton (Eds.), *This is What Happened: Historical Narratives by Aborigines* (Vol. AIAS Press, pp. 313–315). Canberra.
Long, Jeremy. (1996). Frank Hardy and the 1966 Wave Hill walk-off. *Northern Perspective, 19*(2), 1–9.
Lyons, John. (1968). *Introduction to Theoretical Linguistics*. Cambridge: Cambridge University Press.
Makin, Jock. (2002 [1970]). *The Big Run: The Story of Victoria River Downs Station*. Adelaide: J. B. Books.
Manngayarri, Jimmy. (2016a). Bow Hills Police Station: Police and trackers. In Erika Charola & Felicity Meakins (Eds.), *Yijarni: True Stories from Gurindji Country* (pp. 198–199). Canberra: Aboriginal Studies Press.
Manngayarri, Jimmy. (2016b). Murders on Limbunya Station. In Erika Charola & Felicity Meakins (Eds.), *Yijarni: True Stories from Gurindji Country* (pp. 58–65). Canberra: Aboriginal Studies Press.
Mathews, R. H. (1900). The Wombya Organization of the Australian Aborigines. *American Anthropologist 2*, 494–501.
Mathews, R. H. (1901). Ethnological Notes on the Aboriginal Tribes of the Northern Territory. *Queensland Geographical Journal (Proceedings of the Royal Geographical Society of Australasia), 16*, 69–90.
McConvell, Patrick. (1976). *The Aborigines of the Northern Tanami Area*. Darwin.
McConvell, Patrick. (1980). Hierarchical variation in pronominal clitic attachment in the Eastern Ngumpin languages. In Bruce Rigsby & Peter Sutton (Eds.), *Papers in Australian Linguistics No. 13* (pp. 31–117). Canberra: Pacific Linguistics.
McConvell, Patrick. (1982a). Neutralisation and degrees of respect in Gurindji. In Jeffrey Heath, Francesca Merlan, & Alan Rumsey (Eds.), *Languages of Kinship in Aboriginal Australia* (pp. 86–106). Sydney: University of Sydney.
McConvell, Patrick. (1982b). Supporting the two-way school. In J. Bell (Ed.), *Language Planning for Australia Aboriginal Languages* (pp. 60–76). Alice Springs: IAD Press.
McConvell, Patrick. (1983). *"Only" and related concepts in Gurindji*. Batchelor, Australia.
McConvell, Patrick. (1985a). Domains and codeswitching among bilingual Aborigines. In Michael Clyne (Ed.), *Australia, Meeting Place of Languages* (Vol. C-92, pp. 95–125). Canberra: Pacific Linguistics.
McConvell, Patrick. (1985b). The Origin of subsections in Northern Australia. *Oceania. 56*, 1–33.
McConvell, Patrick. (1988a). Mix-im-up: Aboriginal codeswitching old and new. In Monica Heller (Ed.), *Codeswitching: Anthropological and sociolinguistic perspectives* (pp. 97–124). Berlin: Mouton de Gruyter.

McConvell, Patrick. (1988b). Nasal cluster dissimilation and constraints on phonological variables in Gurindji and related languages. *Aboriginal Linguistics, 1*, 135–165.
McConvell, Patrick. (1991). Understanding language shift: A step towards language maintenance. In Susanne Romaine (Ed.), *Language in Australia* (pp. 143–155). Melbourne: Cambridge University Press.
McConvell, Patrick. (1993). Malngin and Nyininy Claim to Mistake Creek. Alice Springs: Central Land Council.
McConvell, Patrick. (1996). The functions of split-wackernagel clitic systems: Pronominal clitics in the Ngumpin languages. In Aaron Halpern & Arnold Zwicky (Eds.), *Approaching Second: Second Position Clitics and Related Phenomena* (pp. 299–332). Stanford CA: CSLI Publications.
McConvell, Patrick. (1998). 'Born is nothing': Roots, family trees and other attachments to land in the Victoria River District and the Kimberleys. *Aboriginal History, 22*, 180–202.
McConvell, Patrick. (2001). Looking for the two-way street. *Cultural Survival Quarterly, Summer*, 18–21.
McConvell, Patrick. (2002a). Changing places: European and Aboriginal styles. In Luis Hercus, Flavia Hodges, & Jane Simpson (Eds.), *Land is a Map: Placenames of Indigenous Origin in Australia* (pp. 51–61). Canberra: Pandanus Books.
McConvell, Patrick. (2002b). Linguistic stratigraphy and Native Title: the case of ethnonyms. In John Henderson & David Nash (Eds.), *Language in Native Title* (pp. 259–290). Canberra: Aboriginal Studies Press.
McConvell, Patrick. (2006a). Grammaticalization of demonstratives as subordinate complementizers in Ngumpin-Yapa. *Australian Journal of Linguistics, 26*(1), 107–137.
McConvell, Patrick. (2006b). Shibbolethnonyms, Ex-Exonyms And Eco-Ethnonyms In Aboriginal Australia : The Pragmatics Of Onymization And Archaism. *ONOMA, 41*, 185–214.
McConvell, Patrick. (2008). Language mixing and language shift in indigenous Australia. In Jane Simpson & Gillian Wigglesworth (Eds.), *Children's Language and Multilingualism: Indigenous Language Use at Home and School* (pp. 205–227). New York: Continuum.
McConvell, Patrick. (2009a). Loanwords in Gurindji, a Pama-Nyungan language of Australia. In Martin Haspelmath & Uri Tadmor (Eds.), *Loanwords in the World's Languages: A Comparative Handbook* (pp. 790–822). Berlin: Mouton de Gruyter.
McConvell, Patrick. (2009b). Where the spear sticks up: The variety of locatives in placenames in the Victoria River District, Northern Territory. In Harold Koch & Luis Hercus (Eds.), *Aboriginal Place Names: Naming and Re-Naming the Australian Landscape* (pp. 359–402). Canberra: ANU Research School of Pacific Studies.
McConvell, Patrick. (2010). Language contact and Indigenous languages in Australia. In Raymond Hickey (Ed.), *Handbook of Language Contact* (pp. 770–794). Oxford: Blackwell.
McConvell, Patrick. (2012). Mood Swings: Imperative attracts pronominal clitics in Southern European and Ngumpin languages (Australian). In Rachel Hendery & Jennifer Hendriks (Eds.), *Grammatical Change: Theory and Description* (pp. 123–156). Canberra: Pacific Linguistics.
McConvell, Patrick. (2016). Kinship loanwords in Indigenous Australia, before and after colonization. In Felicity Meakins & Carmel O'Shannessy (Eds.), *Loss and Renewal: Australian Languages since Colonisation* (pp. 89–112). Berlin: Mouton de Gruyter.
McConvell, Patrick., & Hagen, Rod. (1981). *A Traditional Land Claim by the Gurindji to Daguragu Station*. Alice Springs: Central Land Council.
McConvell, Patrick., & Laughren, Mary. (2004). Ngumpin-Yapa languages. In Harold Koch & Claire Bowern (Eds.), *Australian Languages: Reconstruction and Subgrouping*. (pp. 151–177). Amsterdam: Benjamins.
McConvell, Patrick., & Meakins, Felicity. (2005). Gurindji Kriol: A mixed language emerges from code-switching. *Australian Journal of Linguistics, 25*(1), 9–30.

McConvell, Patrick., & Schultze-Berndt, Eva. (2001). *Complex Verb Convergence and Bilingual Interaction in the Victoria River District, Australia*. Paper presented at the Workshop on language contact and areal convergence, Leipzig (Germany).

McConvell, Patrick., & Simpson, Jane. (2012). Fictive motion down under: The locative-allative case alternation in some Australian Indigenous languages. In Diana Santos, Krister Lindén & Wanjiku Ng'ang'a (Eds.), *Shall We Play the Festschrift Game? Essays on the Occasion of Lauri Carlson's 60th Birthday* (pp. 159–180). Berlin: Springer.

McGregor, William. (1990). *A Functional Grammar of Gooniyandi*. Amsterdam: John Benjamins.

McGregor, William. (1994). *Warrwa*. München: Lincom Europa.

McGregor, William. (1996). *Nyulnyul*. München: Lincom Europa.

McGregor, William. (2002). *Verb classification in Australian Languages*. Berlin: Mouton de Gruyter.

McGregor, William. (2006). Prolegomenon to a Warrwa grammar of space. In Steven Levinson & David Wilkins (Eds.), *Grammars of Space: Explorations in Cognitive Diversity* (pp. 115–156). Cambridge: Cambridge University Press.

McGregor, William. (Ed.) (2010). *The Expression of Possession*. Berlin: Mouton de Gruyter.

Meakins, Felicity. (2008). Unravelling languages: Multilingualism and language contact in Kalkaringi. In Jane Simpson & Gillian Wigglesworth (Eds.), *Children's Language and Multilingualism: Indigenous Language Use at Home and School* (pp. 247–264). New York: Continuum.

Meakins, Felicity. (2009). The case of the shifty ergative marker: A pragmatic shift in the ergative marker in one Australian mixed language. In Johanna Barðdal & Shobhana Chelliah (Eds.), *The Role of Semantics and Pragmatics in the Development of Case*. (pp. 59–91). Amsterdam: John Benjamins.

Meakins, Felicity. (2010a). The development of asymmetrical serial verb constructions in an Australian mixed language. *Linguistic Typology, 14*(1), 1–38.

Meakins, Felicity. (2010b). The importance of understanding language ecologies for revitalisation In John Hobson, Kevin Lowe, Susan Poetsch, & Michael Walsh (Eds.), *Re-awakening Languages:Theory and Practice in the Revitalisation of Australia's Indigenous Languages* (pp. 225–239). Sydney: Sydney University Press.

Meakins, Felicity. (2011a). Borrowing contextual inflection: Evidence from northern Australia. *Morphology, 21*(1), 57–87.

Meakins, Felicity. (2011b). *Case marking in Contact: The Development and Function of Case Morphology in Gurindji Kriol*. Amsterdam: John Benjamins.

Meakins, Felicity. (2011c). Spaced out: Inter-generational changes in the expression of spatial relations by Gurindji people. *Australian Journal of Linguistics, 31*(1), 43–77.

Meakins, Felicity. (2012). Which Mix? – Code-switching or a mixed language – Gurindji Kriol. *Journal of Pidgin and Creole languages, 27*(1), 105–140.

Meakins, Felicity. (2013). *Bilinarra to English Dictionary*. Batchelor, Australia: Batchelor Press.

Meakins, Felicity. (2014). Nominals as adjuncts or arguments: Further evidence from language mixing. In Robert Pensalfini, Myfany Turpin, & Diana Guilleman (Eds.), *Language Description Informed by Theory* (pp. 283–315). Amsterdam: John Benjamins.

Meakins, Felicity. (2015a). From absolutely optional to only nominally ergative: The life cycle of the Gurindji Kriol ergative suffix. In Francesco Gardani, Peter Arkadiev, & Nino Amiridze (Eds.), *Borrowed Morphology* (pp. 189–218). Berlin: Mouton de Gruyter.

Meakins, Felicity. (2015b). Not obligatory: Bound pronoun variation in Gurindji and Bilinarra. *Asia-Pacific Language Variation, 1*(2), 128–161.

Meakins, Felicity. (2016a). Background to the removal of children. In Erika Charola & Felicity Meakins (Eds.), *Yijarni: True Stories from Gurindji Country* (pp. 135–136). Canberra: Aboriginal Studies Press.

Meakins, Felicity. (2016b). No fixed address: The grammaticalisation of the Gurindji locative as a progressive suffix. In Felicity Meakins & Carmel O'Shannessy (Eds.), *Loss and Renewal: Australian Languages Since Colonisation* (pp. 367–396). Berlin: Mouton de Gruyter.

Meakins, Felicity., & Algy, Cassandra. (2016). Deadly reckoning: Changes in Gurindji children's knowledge of cardinals. *Australian Journal of Linguistics, 36*(4), 479–501.

Meakins, Felicity., Disbray, Samantha, & Simpson, Jane. (2020). Which MATter matters in PATtern borrowing? The direction of case merger. *Morphology*. 30(4), 373–393. doi:10.1007/s11525-020-09357-3

Meakins, Felicity., Ennever, Thomas., Osgarby, David., Browne, Mitchell., & Hamilton-Hollaway, Amanda. (2021). Ngumpin-Yapa languages. In Claire Bowern (Ed.), *Handbook of Australian languages*. Oxford: Oxford University Press.

Meakins, Felicity., Green, Jennifer., & Turpin, Myfany (2018). *Understanding Linguistic Fieldwork*. London: Routledge.

Meakins, Felicity., Hua, Xia., Algy, Cassandra., & Bromham, Lindell. (2019). The birth of a new language does not favour simplification. *Language, 95*(2), 294–332.

Meakins, Felicity., Jones, Caroline., & Algy, Cassandra. (2016). Bilingualism, language shift and the corresponding expansion of spatial cognitive systems. *Language Sciences, 54*, 1–13.

Meakins, Felicity., McConvell, Patrick., Charola, Erika., McNair, Norm., McNair, Helen., & Campbell, Lauren. (2013). *Gurindji to English Dictionary*. Batchelor, Australia: Batchelor Press.

Meakins, Felicity., & Nordlinger, Rachel. (2014). *A Grammar of Bilinarra: An Australian Aboriginal Language of the Northern Territory*. Berlin: Mouton de Gruyter.

Meakins, Felicity., & Nordlinger, Rachel. (2017). Possessor dissension: Agreement mismatch in Ngumpin-Yapa possessive constructions. *Linguistic Typology, 21*(1), 143–176.

Meakins, Felicity., & O'Shannessy, Carmel. (2010). Ordering arguments about: Word order and discourse motivations in the development and use of the ergative marker in two Australian mixed languages. *Lingua, 120*(7), 1693–1713.

Meakins, Felicity., & O'Shannessy, Carmel. (2012). Typological constraints on verb integration in two Australian mixed languages. *Journal of Language Contact, 5*(2), 216–246.

Meakins, Felicity., & O'Shannessy, Carmel. (Eds.). (2016). *Loss and Renewal: Australian Languages since Colonisation*. Berlin: Mouton de Gruyter.

Meakins, Felicity., & Wilmoth, Sasha. (2020). Overabundance resulting from language contact: Complex cell-mates in Gurindji Kriol. In Peter Arkadiev & Francesco Gardani (Eds.), *The Complexities of Morphology* (pp. 81–104). Oxford: Oxford University Press.

Meggitt, Mervyn. (1955). Notes on the Malngin and Gurindji Aborigines of Limbunya, N.W. Northern Territory. *Mankind, 5*(2), 45–50.

Meggitt, Mervyn. (1962). *Desert People*. London: Angus and Robertson.

Merlan, Francesca. (1994). *A Grammar of Wardaman. A Language of the Northern Territory of Australia*. Berlin: Mouton.

Mulligan, Martin. (1999). Reading storied landscapes. *Arena Magazine, 39*, 39–42.

Munro, Jennifer. (2000). Kriol on the move: A case of language spread and shift in Northern Australia. In Jeff Siegel (Ed.), *Processes of Language Contact: Studies from Australia and the South Pacific* (pp. 245–270). Saint-Laurent (Quebec): Fides.

Mushin, Ilana. (1995). Epistemes in Australian Languages. *Australian Journal of Linguistics, 15*, 1–31.

Mushin, Ilana. (2006). Motivations for second position: Evidence from North-Central Australia. *Linguistic Typology, 10*, 287–326.

Mushin, Ilana., & Simpson, Jane. (2008). Free to bound to free? Interactions between pragmatics and syntax in the development of the Australian pronominal systems. *Language, 84*, 566–596.

Nash, David. (1981). *Preliminary Vocabulary of the Warlmanpa Language*. Canberra.

Nash, David. (1982). Warlpiri verb roots and preverbs. In Steven Swartz (Ed.), *Papers in Warlpiri Grammar: In Memory of Lothar Jagst* (pp. 165–216). Darwin: SIL.
Nash, David. (1986). *Topics in Warlpiri Grammar*. New York: Garland.
Nash, David. (1992). An Australian kinship affix *-rti. *Australian Journal of Linguistics, 12*(1), 123–144.
Nash, David. (1996). Pronominal clitic variation in the Yapa languages. In William McGregor (Ed.), *Studies in Kimberley Languages in Honour of Howard Coate* (pp. 117–138). München: Lincom Europa.
Nash, David. (2008). Warlpiri verb roots in comparative perspective. In Claire Bowern, Bethwyn Evans, & Luisa Miceli (Eds.), *Morphology and Language History: In Honour of Harold Koch* (pp. 221–234). Amsterdam: John Benjamins.
Nichols, Johanna (1992). *Linguistic Diversity in Space and Time*. Chicago: University of Chicago Press.
Nikolaeva, Irina. (1999). Object agreement, grammatical relations, and information structure. *Studies in Language, 23*(2), 331–376.
Nikolaeva, Irina. (2001). Secondary topic as a relation in information structure. *Linguistics, 39*(1), 1–49.
Nikolaeva, Irina., Bárány, András., & Bond, Oliver. (2019). Introduction. In András. Bárány, Oliver Bond, & Irina Nikolaeva (Eds.), *Prominent Internal Possessors* (pp. 1–38). Oxford: Oxford University Press.
Nordlinger, Rachel. (1998a). *Constructive Case: Evidence from Australian Languages*. Stanford CA: CSLI Publications.
Nordlinger, Rachel. (1998b). *A Grammar of Wambaya, Northern Territory (Australia)*. Canberra: Pacific Linguistics.
Nordlinger, Rachel. (2006). Spearing the emu drinking: Subordination and the adjoined relative clause in Wambaya. *Australian Journal of Linguistics, 26*(1), 5–29.
Nordlinger, Rachel. (2010). Complex predicates in Wambaya: Detaching predicate composition from syntactic structure. In Mengistu Amberber, Brett Baker, & Mark Harvey (Eds.), *Complex Predicates: Cross-Linguistic Perspectives on Event Structure* (pp. 237–258). Cambridge: Cambridge University Press.
Nyurrmiari, Pincher. (2016). When the floodwaters came to the station. In Erika Charola & Felicity Meakins (Eds.), *Mayarni-kari Yurrk: More Stories from Gurindji Country* (pp. 16–18). Batchelor, Australia: Batchelor Press.
O'Shannessy, Carmel. (2011). Young children's social meaning making in a new mixed language. In Ute Eickelkamp (Ed.), *Growing up in Central Australia: New Anthropological Studies of Aboriginal Childhood and Adolescence* (pp. 131–155). New York: Berghahn Books.
O'Grady, Geoffrey., & Mooney, K. (1973). Nyangumarta kinship terminology. *Oceania, 2*, 296–333.
Osgarby, David. (2018). *Verbal Morphology and Syntax of Mudburra: an Australian Aboriginal Language of the Northern Territory.* (MPhil). University of Queensland, Brisbane.
Pajusalu, Karl. (2001). Baby talk as a sophisticated register: A phonological analysis of South Estonian. *Psychology of Language and Communication*, 5(2), 81–92.
Pascoe, Bruce. (2014). *Dark Emu*. Broome, Western Australia: Megabala Books.
Payne, Doris, & Barshi, Immanuel. (Eds.). (1999). *External Possession*. Amsterdam: John Benjamins.
Pensalfini, Robert. (2002). Vowel harmony in Jingulu. *Lingua, 112*(7), 561–586.
Pensalfini, Robert. (2003). *A Grammar of Jingulu: An Aboriginal Language of the Northern Territory*. Canberra: Pacific Linguistics.
Pensalfini, Robert. (2004). Towards a typology of configurationality. *Natural Language and Linguistic Theory, 22*, 359–408.

Pensalfini, Robert. (2021). Vowel harmony in Australia. In Harry van der Hulst & Nancy Ritter (Eds.), *Oxford Handbook of Vowel Harmony*.

Peterson, Nicholas., McConvell, Patrick., Wild, Stephen., & Hagen, Rod. (1978). *A Claim to the Traditional Land by the Warlpiri and Kartangururru*. Alice Springs: Central Land Council.

Radcliffe-Brown, Alfred. R. (1930–31). *The Social Organization of Australian Tribes* (Vol. 1). London: Macmillan & Company.

Rangiari, Mick. (1997). Talking history. In G. Yunupingu (Ed.), *Our Land is our Life*. Brisbane: UQ Press.

Rangiari, Mick. (1998). They been get rich by the Gurindji people. In Alexis Wright (Ed.), *Power like this Old Man Here: An Anthology Celebrating 20 yrs of Land Rights in Central Australia*. Alice Springs: IAD Press.

Reid, Nicholas. (1990). *Ngan'gityemerri. A Language of the Daly River Region, Northern Territory of Australia.* (PhD). Australian National University, Canberra.

Richards, Eirlys. (1979). The Walmatjarri noun phrase. In Christine Kilham (Ed.), *Four Grammatical Sketches: From Phrase to Paragraph* (Vol. Series A Volume 3, pp. 93–125). Darwin: SIL.

Richards, Eirlys., & Hudson, Joyce. (1990). *Walmajarri – English Dictionary with English Finder List*. Berrimah, N.T: Summer Institute of Linguistics.

Riddett, Lyn. A. (1990). *Kine, Kin and Country: The Victoria River District of the Northern Territory, 1911–1966*. Darwin: Australian National University: North Australian Research Unit.

Riddett, Lyn. A. (1997). The strike that became a land rights movement: A southern 'do-gooder' reflects in Wattie Creek 1966–74. *Labour History, 72*, 50–64.

Rose, Deborah. B. (1991). *Hidden Histories: Black Stories from Victoria River Downs, Humbert River and Wavehill Stations*. Canberra: Aboriginal Studies Press.

Rose, Deborah. B. (2000). *Dingo Makes Us Human: Life and Land in an Australian Aboriginal Culture*. Cambridge: Cambridge University Press.

Round, Erich. (2021). Phonotactics in Australian Languages. In Claire Bowern (Ed.), *Oxford Handbook of Australian languages*.

Rumsey, Alan. (2000). Bunuba. In R. M. W. Dixon & B. Blake (Eds.), *Handbook of Australian Languages Vol V* (pp. 35–152). Oxford: Oxford University Press.

Ryan, Banjo. (2016a). Gordon Stott: The deeds of an early policeman. In Erika Charola & Felicity Meakins (Eds.), *Yijarni: True Stories from Gurindji Country* (pp. 216–227). Canberra: Aboriginal Studies Press.

Ryan, Banjo. (2016b). Payback on Bony Bream Jangari. In Erika Charola & Felicity Meakins (Eds.), *Mayarni-kari Yurrk: More Stories from Gurindji Country* (pp. 124–127). Batchelor, Australia: Batchelor Press.

Ryan, Maurie. (2016). I was taken. In Erika Charola & Felicity Meakins (Eds.), *Yijarni: True Stories from Gurindji Country* (pp. 129–132). Canberra: Aboriginal Studies Press.

Sandefur, John. (1979). *An Australian Creole in the Northern Territory: A Description of Ngukurr Bamyili Dialects (Part 1)*. Darwin: SIL.

Sandefur, John., & Sandefur, Joy. (1982). *An Introduction to Conversational Kriol*. Darwin: SIL.

Schultze-Berndt, Eva. (2000). *Simple and Complex Verbs in Jaminjung: A Study of Event Categorisation in an Australian Language* (Vol. 14). Wageningan: Ponsen and Looijen.

Schultze-Berndt, Eva. (2001). Ideophone-like characteristics of uninflected predicates in Jaminjung (Australia). In F. K. E. Voeltz & C. Killian-Hatz (Eds.), *Ideophones* (pp. 355–373). Amsterdam: John Benjamins.

Schultze-Berndt, Eva. (2003). Preverbs as an open word class in Northern Australian languages: Synchronic and diachronic correlates. *Yearbook of Morphology, 2003*, 145–177.

Schultze-Berndt, Eva. (2006a). Secondary predicates in Australian languages. In M. Everaert & H. van Riemsdijk (Eds.), *The Blackwell Companion to Syntax* (Vol. IV, pp. 180–208). Oxford: Blackwell.

Schultze-Berndt, Eva. (2006b). Sketch of a Jaminjung grammar of space. In Steven Levinson & David Wilkins (Eds.), *Grammars of Space: Explorations in Cognitive Diversity* (pp. 63–114). Cambridge: Cambridge University Press.

Schultze-Berndt, Eva. (2007). Recent grammatical borrowing into an Australian Aboriginal language: The case of Jaminjung and Kriol. In Yaron Matras & Jeanette Sakel (Eds.), *Grammatical Borrowing in Cross-linguistic Perspective* (pp. 363–386). Berlin: Mouton de Gruyter.

Schultze-Berndt, Eva. (2012). Pluractional posing as progressive: A construction between lexical and grammatical aspect. *Australian Journal of Linguistics, 32*(1), 7–39.

Schultze-Berndt, Eva., Meakins, Felicity., & Angelo, Denise. (2013). Kriol. In Susanne Michaelis, Philippe. Maurer, Martin Haspelmath, & Magnus Huber (Eds.), *The Survey of Pidgin and Creole Languages, Vol I* (pp. 241–251). Oxford: Oxford University Press.

Senge, C. (2016). *A Grammar of Wanyjirra, A Language of Northern Australia.* Australian National University, Canberra.

Shankara Bhat, D. N. (1967). Lexical suppletion in baby talk. *Anthropological Linguistics, 9*, 33–36.

Silverstein, Michael. (1976). Hierarchy of features and ergativity. In R. M. W. Dixon (Ed.), *Grammatical Categories in Australian Languages* (pp. 112–171). New Jersey: Humanities.

Simpson, Jane. (1988). Case and complementiser suffixes in Warlpiri. In Peter. Austin (Ed.), *Complex Sentence Constructions in Australian Languages* (pp. 205–218). Amsterdam: John Benjamins.

Simpson, Jane. (1991). *Warlpiri Morpho-syntax: A Lexicalist Approach*. Dordrecht, Holland: Kluwer.

Simpson, Jane. (2005). Depictives in English and Warlpiri. In Nicholas Himmelmann & Eva Schultze-Berndt (Eds.), *Secondary Predication and Adverbial Modification: The Typology of Depictives.* (pp. 69–106). Oxford: Oxford University Press.

Simpson, Jane. (2007). Expressing pragmatic constraints on word order in Warlpiri. In Annie. Zaenen, Jane Simpson, Chris Manning, & Jane Grimshaw (Eds.), *Architectures, Rules, and Preferences: Variations on Themes by Joan W. Bresnan* (pp. 403–427). Stanford CA: CSLI Publications.

Simpson, Jane., & Mushin, Ilana. (2008). Clause-initial position in four Australian languages. In Ilana Mushin & Brett Baker (Eds.), *Discourse and Grammar in Australian Languages* (pp. 25–58). Amsterdam: Benjamins.

Simpson, Jane., & Withcott, Margaret. (1986). Pronominal Clitic Clusters and Templates. In H. Borer (Ed.), *The Syntax of Pronominal Clitics. Syntax and Semantics* (Vol. 19, pp. 149–174). New York: Academic Press.

Singer, Ruth. (2001). The Inclusory construction in Australian languages. *Melbourne Papers in Linguistics and Applied Linguistics, 1*(2), 81–96.

Stanner, William. (1934). *Fieldnotes taken at Wave Hill.* AIATSIS. Canberra.

Stanner, William. (1935 [1979]). *Report on Field Work in North Central and North Australia 1934–35.* Canberra.

Stanton, Juliet. (2019). Constraints on contrast motivate nasal cluster dissimilation. *Phonology, 36*(4), 655–694. doi:10.1017/S0952675719000332

Stewart, Jesse., Meakins, Felicity., Algy, Cassandra., Ennever, Thomas., & Joshua, Angelina. (2020). Fickle Fricatives: Fricative and Stop Perception in Gurindji, Gurindji Kriol, Roper Kriol, and Standard Australian English. *Journal of the Acoustical Society of America, 147*(4).

Stewart, Jesse., Meakins, Felicity., Algy, Cassandra., & Joshua, Angelina. (2018). The development of phonological stratification: Evidence from stop voicing perception in Gurindji Kriol and Roper Kriol. *Journal of Language Contact, 11*(1), 71–112. doi:10.1163/19552629-01101003

Street, Charles. (1987). *An Introduction to the Language and Culture of the Murrinh-Patha*. Darwin: SIL.

Swartz, Steven. (1988). Pragmatic structure and word order in Warlpiri. In Peter Austin (Ed.), *Papers in Australian Linguistics No.17* (pp. 151–166). Canberra: Pacific Linguistics.

Swartz, Steven. (1991). *Constraints on Zero Anaphora and Word Order in Warlpiri Narrative Text.* Darwin: SIL.

Swartz, Steven. (2012). *Warlpiri to English Dictionary*. Darwin: AuSIL.

Tabain, Maria., & Beare, Richard. (2018). An ultrasound study of coronal places of articulation in Central Arrernte: Apicals, laminals and rhotics. *Journal of Phonetics, 66*, 63–81. doi:10.1016/j.wocn.2017.09.006

Tabain, Maria., Butcher, Andy., Breen, Gavan., & Beare, Richard. (2020). A formant study of the alveolar versus retroflex contrast in three Central Australian languages: Stop, nasal, and lateral manners of articulation. *Journal of the Acoustical Society of America, 147 2745–2765.* doi:10.1121/10.0001012

Terry, Michael. (1925). *Expedition Logbook Darwin to Broome. (AA* 333/5/5).

Terry, Michael. (1926). A surgical operation as performed by the Boonarra tribe of Northern Australia, and a short vocabulary of the languages of some North Australian tribes. *Man, 129*, 193–194.

Terry, Michael. (1927). *Through a Land of Promise: With Guns, Car and Camera in the Heart of Northern Australia*. London: Herbert Jenkins.

Tindale, Norman. (1952–54). *18th Expedition under Auspices of Board for Anthropological Research University of Adelaide and University of California at Los Angeles 1952–1954*. South Australia Museum. Adelaide.

Tindale, Norman. (1974). *Aboriginal Tribes of Australia*. Canberra: ANU Press.

Tsunoda, Tasaku. (1981). *The Djaru Language of Kimberley, Western Australia*. Canberra: Pacific Linguistics.

Tsunoda, Tasaku. (2007). Reciprocal-reflexive constructions in Djaru. In V. P. Nedjalkov, E. S. Geniushene, & Z. Guentcheva (Eds.), *Reciprocal Constructions* (pp. 859–884). Amsterdam: John Benjamins.

Turpin, Myfany., Demuth, Katherine., & Campbell, April. N. (2012). *Phonological Aspects of Arandic Baby Talk*. Paper presented at the 11th Annual Australian Languages Workshop, Stradbroke Island, Australia.

Turpin, Myfany., & Meakins, Felicity. (2019). *Songs from the Stations: Wajarra as sung by Ronnie Wavehill Wirrpa, Dandy Danbayarri, Topsy Dodd Ngarnjal*. Sydney: Sydney University Press.

van den Bos, Jackie., Meakins, Felicity., & Algy, Cassandra. (2017). Searching for "Agent Zero": The origins of a relative case. *Language Ecology, 1*(1), 4–24.

Wadrill, Violet. (2016a). They took the kids away. In Erika Charola & Felicity Meakins (Eds.), *Yijarni: True Stories from Gurindji Country* (pp. 127–128). Canberra: Aboriginal Studies Press.

Wadrill, Violet. (2016b). Weekends and station knock-off time. In Erika Charola & Felicity Meakins (Eds.), *Yijarni: True Stories from Gurindji Country* (pp. 169–172). Canberra: Aboriginal Studies Press.

Wadrill, Violet., Wavehill, Biddy., Dodd, Topsy., & Meakins, Felicity. (2019). *Karu: Growing Up Gurindji*. Melbourne: Spinifex Press.

Wadrill, Violet., Wavehill, Biddy., & Meakins, Felicity. (2015). *Kawarla: How to Make a Coolamon*. Batchelor, Australia: Batchelor Press.

Ward, Charlie. (2016). *A Handful of Sand*. Melbourne: Monash University Press.

Wavehill, Biddy. (2016a). How they took my little brothers away. In Erika Charola & Felicity Meakins (Eds.), *Yijarni: True Stories from Gurindji Country* (pp. 133–134). Canberra: Aboriginal Studies Press.

Wavehill, Biddy. (2016b). When my granny died at Number 7 Bore. In Erika Charola & Felicity Meakins (Eds.), *Yijarni: True Stories from Gurindji Country* (pp. 160–162). Canberra: Aboriginal Studies Press.

Wavehill, Ronnie. (2016a). Early massacres. In Erika Charola & Felicity Meakins (Eds.), *Yijarni: True Stories from Gurindji Country* (pp. 32–53). Canberra: Aboriginal Studies Press.

Wavehill, Ronnie. (2016b). How Gurindji were brought to work on Wave Hill Station. In Erika Charola & Felicity Meakins (Eds.), *Yijarni: True Stories from Gurindji Country* (pp. 84–97). Canberra: Aboriginal Studies Press.

Wavehill, Ronnie. (2019). Ronnie Wavehill's account of learning wajarra. In Myfany Turpin & Felicity Meakins (Eds.), *Songs from the Stations: Wajarra as Sung by Ronnie Wavehill Wirrpnga, Topsy Dodd Ngarnjal and Dandy Danbayarri at Kalkaringi* (pp. 35–51). Sydney: Sydney University Press.

Wilkins, David. (2003). Why pointing with the index finger is not a universal (in sociocultural and semiotic terms). In Seppo Kita (Ed.), *Pointing: Where Language, Culture and Cognition Meet.* Mahwah, N.J.: L. ErlbaumAssociates.

Wilkins, David. (2006). Towards an Arrernte grammar of space. In Steven Levinson & David Wilkins (Eds.), *Grammars of Space: Explorations in Cognitive Diversity* (pp. 24–62). Cambridge: Cambridge University Press.

Index of names

https://doi.org/10.1515/9783110746884-015

Index of subjects

https://doi.org/10.1515/9783110746884-016

www.ingramcontent.com/pod-product-compliance
Lightning Source LLC
Chambersburg PA
CBHW080116020526
44112CB00037B/2750

* 9 7 8 3 1 1 1 2 7 5 9 4 9 *